INTIMATE RELATIONSHIPS, MARRIAGES, AND FAMILIES

INTIMATE RELATIONSHIPS, MARRIAGES, AND FAMILIES

F. PHILIP RICE

University of Maine

Mayfield Publishing Company
Mountain View, California
London ▪ Toronto

Library of Congress Cataloging-in Publication Data

Rice, F. Philip.
    Intimate relationships, marriages, and families/F. Philip Rice.
        p.   cm.
    Includes bibliographical references.
    ISBN 0-87484-864-4
    1. Family life education—United States.   I. Title.
    HQ10.5.U6R53 1990   89-39461
    306.85--dc20   CIP

Manufactured in the United States of America

10 9 8 7 6 5 4 3 2 1

Mayfield Publishing Company
1240 Villa Street
Mountain View, California 94041

Sponsoring editor, Franklin C. Graham; managing editor, Linda Toy; manuscript editor, Joan Pendleton; text designer, Anna George; cover designer, Jeanne M. Schreiber; cover art, Guy Magallanes; illustrators, Joan Carol and Judith Ogus; photo researcher, Monica Suder and Associates. The text was set in 10/12 Palatino by Jonathan Peck Typographers and printed on 50# Mead Pub Matte by Ringier America.

Text and photo credits appear on a continuation of the copyright page, p. 690.

BRIEF CONTENTS

CONTENTS

PART I

SOCIAL AND PSYCHOLOGICAL PERSPECTIVES 1

CHAPTER 14
MANAGING MATERIAL RESOURCES 347

CHAPTER 15
COMPANIONSHIP IN AND OUTSIDE THE FAMILY 373

CHAPTER 16
POWER AND DECISION MAKING 394

CHAPTER 20
PARENTING 507

PREFACE

The need for intimacy seems to be a universal quality of human beings. Almost all adult men and women will seek to marry or form a permanent, stable relationship with another person. Most married couples will want to have children and raise a family. In contrast to the 1960s and early 1970s, the question today is not whether marriage and family will survive. Rather, most people want to know in what forms intimate relationships, marriages, and families will survive and how each individual can find fulfillment within them. This book has been written to help students understand how intimate relationships are formed, maintained, and sometimes fail. Throughout, the focus is on diversity and individual choice, on our capacity to grow and change.

GROWTH, CHANGE, AND CHOICE

Three major themes of this book are growth, change, and choice. Each of us has a tremendous capacity to grow and to change, but to grow and change in the ways that are best for us, we need to know what choices we have and what the consequences of those choices may be. It is here that the information provided by the social and behavioral sciences can help. For instance, we know more about the biology of sex and reproduction than ever before, and such knowledge can contribute immeasurably to a successful marriage.

As we grow in knowledge we may also grow in other ways, especially in objectivity and tolerance for others. The more we study intimate relationships, marriages, and family patterns, the more we see that no one way can be considered the "right way" or the ideal for everyone. We also can grow by examining and clarifying our personal attitudes and values directly. We can grow in our ability to love, to express warmth and affection, to show empathy with others. And we can develop social skills and seek friendships that fulfill us and enrich our lives. We can learn to resolve interpersonal conflicts. Throughout this book we focus on these various dimensions of growth.

One of the questions most frequently asked of a therapist or counselor is: Do you believe people ever really change? The conclusion of experts and researchers is that we do change. And, while we can't expect to change others, and probably shouldn't try, we can change ourselves. We can change if we want to, and sometimes we have to if we are to grow in ways that are healthy for us. Obviously, such change is more likely to be fruitful if it is the result of informed choice based on sound knowledge.

This book gives particular attention to changes that occur over the life cycle. Life is not static, and neither are intimate relationships. People change, situations change, relationships change. The love we may feel today may not be exactly the same as the love we feel ten years from now. However, there is also continuity to life; what happens now greatly influences tomorrow. And there is similarity as well as diversity in the ways humans develop and cope with events. To show students how others have responded to change and how those responses have affected the quality of their intimate relationships is an important aim of this book.

Life involves many choices. Shall I marry or remain single? What should I look for in a mate? What are my priorities in life? Do I want marriage, a career, or both? Do I want children? If I cannot have children of my own, is adoption a desirable choice? How do I raise a child? If I find myself in a troubled marriage, do I choose to divorce or to try to save the marriage? How does one choose a marriage counselor? If divorced, will I choose to marry again? What should my relationship be with my parents, and what is the best way to help them if they cannot help themselves? One purpose of this book is to stimulate and equip readers to find their own individual answers to such questions as these and make wise choices in the light of realistic expectations.

ORGANIZATION AND CONTENT

Part I, Social and Psychological Perspectives, places our study in social and historical context (Chapter 1); examines the many ways in which differences of class, race, ethnicity, and family background influence our individual values, needs, and wants and our intimate relationships and family life (Chapters 2 and 3); and explores the qualities essential to healthy intimate relationships and marital success (Chapter 4).

Part II (Chapters 5–10) focuses on the nature of intimate relationships, exploring such questions as these: What are attraction and love? Are there different kinds of love? What does it mean to remain single or to seek a marriage partner? How does one find a partner, and know if the partnership is really what one wants? What is the sexual basis of relationships? How do people express their sexual and intimate needs? How should we regard and manage the transition to marriage or perhaps nonmarital cohabitation?

Marriage brings with it a new set of demands for growth and change. Part III considers first what is known about marriage and family relationships over the life cycle (Chapter 11). The remaining chapters (12–17) explore sex and gender roles, work and the family, the management of material resources, companionship within and outside the family, power and decision making, and communication and conflict.

In Part IV, the presentation shifts from an emphasis on couples to a focus on the family as a unit. Chapters 18 and 19 discuss the decisions involved in parenthood and family planning and follow the birth process from conception through pregnancy and preparations by the family as a whole for a new member. A separate chapter (20) on parenting is followed by a chapter on extended family relationships, a subject of increasing interest to students of the family.

Most families experience periods of crisis. Part V explores families under stress, with an emphasis on how to recognize and manage crises and how to seek help. Chapters 23 and 24 discuss divorce and the special challenges of remarriage and stepparenting.

SPECIAL FEATURES

Several features distinguish *Intimate Relationships, Marriages, and Families* from other textbooks:

As students become aware of the remarkable range of individual and cultural differences in human relationships, they gain not only in tolerance for others but also in control over their own lives; yet few textbooks devote much attention to such diversity. This book emphasizes diversity from the outset, and especially in Chapter 2, but also throughout all of the chapters—in discussions and examples and in the sequences of full-color illustrations.

Though concrete and thoroughly practical in its aims, the book gives students a sound theoretical framework for the information it offers them. The major theories identified and discussed include structural-functional, conflict, symbolic interaction, and social exchange theory. Numerous other minor theories are introduced where they are most appropriate. These include theories of mate selection (Chapter 8), of attraction and love (Chapter 7), of power in relationships (Chapter 16), of sex role learning (Chapter 12), of parenting (Chapter 20), and of marital and family therapy (Chapter 22).

New information is most meaningful to students when it is placed within the context of the personal narrative, the case study, the carefully chosen excerpt from a client interview. This book offers students the benefit of many real experiences drawn from the notes of counselors and therapists, including the author. While details have been altered to protect the anonymity of clients, the described experiences are no less real and meaningful.

Another feature of this textbook is the three types of special-focus "boxes" that appear throughout all the chapters: *Perspective, Classroom Forum,* and *Assessment.* A *Perspective* box highlights an especially interesting research finding, opinion, issue, or viewpoint related to the subject under discussion. *Classroom Forums* offer case studies with discussion questions; they are intended to stimulate active analysis and class debate. *Assessment* boxes often include personal inventories and invite students to discover and consider their own opinions and values.

ANCILLARY MATERIALS

Available with this book is a complete package of supplemental materials.

The Instructor's Manual, by F. Philip Rice and Jeanne Kohl of the University of Washington, includes learning objectives for each chapter; lecture outlines; teaching strategies; individual and classroom activities; and a list of key journals. A set of 58 transparency masters that augment, not merely reproduce, material in the textbook is available to instructors upon request. The Instructor's Manual also includes, in printed form, the complete Test Item File.

The Test Item File consists of over 1200 items, including, for every chapter, true/false, multiple choice, fill-in, short-answer, and essay questions. It is available not only in the Instructor's Manual but also on computer disk in the powerful, easy-to-use Brownstone test generation system. Available for IBM-compatible and Apple computers, Brownstone allows the instructor to select, edit, and add questions, randomize them, keep a record of their use, and print tests (with an answer key) for individual classes. Brownstone also includes a convenient "gradebook" that makes it easy for the instructor to keep detailed performance records for individual students and for the entire class; maintain student averages; graph each student's progress; and set the desired grade distribution, maximum score, and weight for every test.

The *Study Guide to Accompany Intimate Relationships, Marriages, and Families,* by Jeanne Kohl, helps students to master and retain the concepts in each chapter of the textbook, prepare for examinations, assess their own personal attitudes and beliefs, and (through exercises) apply their knowledge to real-life situations.

Each chapter of the *Study Guide* has three parts. The first part contains learning objectives, a chapter summary, and a practice test. These components are designed to facilitate student mastery of the content. The types of questions in the Test Item File are also in the practice test.

The second part, the Personal Involvement Assessment, gives students the opportunity to examine in depth one of the important issues discussed or referred to in the textbook chapter and to apply the knowledge gained from the chapter to their own behavior, their own life (for example, their views on stereotypes, their awareness of the consequences of AIDS on their lives, how they would react to a spouse's having extramarital affairs).

The final part of each chapter, Knowledge in Action, serves to highlight key research studies on a specific topic from the textbook. Following a recapitulation of the topic, the section contains a project or projects in which students are asked to apply what they have learned to "real-life" situations involving others. Examples of such projects are content analyses of sex roles found in the media, interviews with single parents and married couples about child-care arrangements, and surveys of youth attitudes about alcohol or marijuana use.

ACKNOWLEDGMENTS

The author would like to thank the following professors who have reviewed and offered guidance and suggestions during the writing process: Jeanne H. Ballantine, Wright State University; Bruce L. Campbell, California State University at Los Angeles; Eugene W. Jacobs, Presbyterian College; Jeanne Kohl, reviewer and preparer of Student Guide and Testbank, University of Washington; Sherrill Richarz, Washington State University; Jay D. Schvaneveldt, Utah State University; Barbara H. Settles, University of Delaware; Benjamin Silliman, Louisiana Technical University; W. Fred Stultz, California Polytechnic State University.

The author also thanks the staff of Mayfield Publishing who have been so helpful: Franklin C. Graham, sponsoring editor; Linda Toy, managing editor; Gwen Larson, director of production; Joan Pendleton, copy editor; and Pamela Trainer, permissions editor. A special thanks also to Irma Rice for her proofreading and suggestions.

To
Irma Ann Rice
with deepest love

INTIMATE RELATIONSHIPS,
MARRIAGES,
AND FAMILIES

The need for intimacy seems to be a universal quality of human beings. Many contemporary theories emphasize the role of intimate relationships in fulfilling personal needs for emotional security and companionship.

For most couples, the wedding ceremony remains both a sacred rite and a legal recognition of their new status. The couple publicly acknowledges their complete willingness to be married.

Few people would disagree that the quality of a marriage is strongly related to personal happiness and satisfaction with life. Newlywed couples face unique adjustments. How much they desire each other's companionship is perhaps the most critical factor in determining the success of their marriage. Companionship means sharing enjoyable activities, being best friends, and spending leisure time together.

How does love grow and sustain an intimate relationship? The *wheel theory* of love's development, according to Ira Reiss in Chapter 7, maintains that love grows through successive stages of rapport, self-revelation, mutual dependence and, finally, need fulfillment.

Pairing and mate selection culminate in marriage for the vast majority of couples. Marriage may be as dramatic as the mass wedding or as private as the expression of permanent commitment between two individuals. Today, many people seem more accepting of differences in age, race, socioeconomic status, religion, and sexual orientation.

Traditional views of intimate relationships, marriages, and families emphasize such ideals as the formal religious wedding ceremony, the large family with the father as head of the household, and couples enjoying leisure time together.

Changing social realities affect intimate relationships. Single, divorced fathers increasingly take on the responsibilities of raising their dependent children; many couples choose to remain childless or have only one child; and more women now contribute to and participate in the family's financial security.

Whatever the forces are in society that promote continuity or change in intimate relationships, some new realities cannot be ignored or avoided. Marriage without children is becoming an accepted, even desireable, lifestyle for many, regardless of age or economic status. The number of unmarried teenage parents is reaching critical proportions and threatens to overwhelm public assistance agencies.

PART I
SOCIAL AND PSYCHOLOGICAL PERSPECTIVES

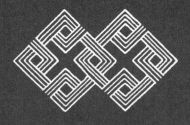

1

INTIMATE RELATIONSHIPS, MARRIAGES, AND FAMILIES IN THE TWENTIETH CENTURY

KEY TERMS

voluntarily childless family
single-parent family
nuclear family
family of orientation
family of procreation
extended family
blended or reconstituted family
stepfamily
binuclear family
polygamous family

polygynous family
polyandrynous family
patriarchal family
matriarchal family
multilateral family
group marriage
communal family
homosexual family
cohabiting family

structural-functional view of the family
instrumental role of the family
expressive role of the family
patrilineal
patrilocal
matrilineal
matrilocal
bilateral descent
neolocal
cohort

Families as we know them today are different from those of previous generations. They are different in structure and composition, size, and function. The reasons why people marry and marital expectations have changed. Changes have also occurred in the ways families are governed, in who supports families, and in sexual behavior. An analysis of marriage rates and ages, birthrates, the percentages of working mothers, divorce and remarriage rates, the numbers of reconstituted families, and rates of unwed pregnancy and parenthood reveal some significant trends.

We are going to examine some of these changes and trends and their effects on the society and the individual. In addition, an important consideration for each of us is: How have these changes affected me?

WHAT IS A FAMILY?

Some Definitions

The U.S. Bureau of the Census defines a family as "any two or more related people living in one household." By this definition, the family may consist of two persons who are not necessarily of different genders: two brothers, two female cousins, a mother and daughter, and other combinations. They may also be of opposite genders: a husband and wife, a father and daughter, a brother and sister, and others. If the family does consist of a husband and wife, they may or may not have children. The common characteristics included in this definition are twofold: (1) the individuals must be related by blood or law, and (2) they must live together in one household. Thus, according to the Census Bureau, if adult children move out of their parents' household and establish families of their own, they are no longer considered a part of their parents' family.

Other definitions have been proposed. Winch (1971) defined the family as "a set of persons related to each other by blood, marriage, or adoption and whose basic societal function is replacement." But this definition seems to limit family functions to child rearing. Burgess and Locke (1953) defined the family "as a group of persons united by ties of marriage, blood, or adoption; constituting a single household; interacting and communicating with each other in their respective social roles (husband and wife, mother and father, son and daughter, brother and sister); and creating and maintaining a common culture." This definition would eliminate those cohabiting, though not legally related or married. It seems to assume also that individuals in a family must conform to some sort of prescribed social roles.

None of these definitions seems to cover all types of family situations: group marriage, communal living, nonmarried cohabiting couples, homosexual couples, single-parent households, and childless couples. A more comprehensive and less stereotyped definition is used in this book: "A family is any group of persons united by the ties of marriage, blood, or adoption, or any sexually expressive relationship, in which (1) the people are committed to one another in an intimate, interpersonal relationship, (2) the members see their identity as importantly attached to the group, and (3) the group has an identity of its own." (Chilman, 1978; Lamanna and Riedmann, 1985, p. 19).

This definition has a number of advantages. It includes a variety of family structures: the traditional married couple with or without children, single-parent families, families consisting of blood relatives (such as two widowed sisters, a grandparent and grandchildren, a multigenerational extended family, and others). But it also includes persons not related by marriage, blood, or adoption who have a sexually expressive relationship: an unmarried cohabiting couple, a homosexual couple, a group marriage, a communal family. Because this definition insists that the persons are committed, in an intimate, interpersonal relationship, it would eliminate cohabiting couples who live together for practical reasons, without commitment, or those who have only a casual relationship, even though they may have sex together. The members must see their identity as importantly attached to the group, and the group must have an identity of its own. The definition doesn't say that people have to be together continuously, so it can include commuting couples, or family members away at college or in the armed services for a period of time.

Family Forms

We can categorize families according to their structural arrangement and composition, the persons in them, and their relationship to one another.

A **voluntarily childless family** is a couple who decides not to have children.

A **single-parent family** consists of a parent (who may or may not have been married) and one or more children (McLanahan, Wedemeyer, and Adelberg, 1981).

A **nuclear family** consists of a father, mother, and their children. This type of family as a proportion of all families has been declining in recent years (White and Tsui, 1986).

A **family of orientation** is the family into which you are born and in which you are raised. The family consists of your parents and siblings.

A **family of procreation** is the family you establish when you have children of your own.

The **extended family** consists of you, a possible mate, any children you might have, and other relatives who might live with you in your household.

The **blended or reconstituted family** is formed when a widowed or divorced person, with or without children, remarries another person who may or may not have been married before and who may or may not have children (Dowling, 1983). If either the remarried husband or wife has children from the former marriage, a **stepfamily** is formed.

A **binuclear family** is an original family divided into two by divorce. It consists of two nuclear families, the maternal nuclear family headed by the mother, and the paternal family headed by the father. The families include whatever children have been in the original family and may be headed by a single parent or two parents if former spouses remarry (Ahrons and Rodgers, 1987).

A **polygamous family** is a single family unit based on the marriage of one person to two or more mates. If the man has more than one wife, a **polygynous family** is formed. If a woman has more than one husband, a **polyandrynous family** is formed. Polyandry is rare, but polygyny is widely practiced in African and Asian countries. Both are illegal in the United States.

A **patriarchal family** is one in which the father is head of the household with authority over other members of the family.

Families exist in a variety of forms, but the nuclear family is still very much in evidence. It may be that its most enduring function is the care and guidance of children.

A **matriarchal family** is one in which the mother is head of the household with authority over other members of the family.

A **multilateral family** has been defined as "three or more partners, each of whom considers himself/herself to be married (or committed in a functionally analogous way) to more than one of the other partners" (Constantine and Constantine, 1973). The three or more individuals may represent any distribution by sex as long as they share in a community of sexual and personal intimacy. A **group marriage**, according to the Constantines, is "a marriage of at least four people, two female and two male, in which each partner is married to all partners of the opposite sex" (Constantine and Constantine, 1973).

A **communal family** consists of a group of people who live together, sharing various aspects of their lives. Some communal groups call themselves "families" and would fit the definition adopted here. Others are not "families" in the strict sense of the word, but just groups of people living together with wide variations in type and structure.

A **homosexual family** consists of members of the same sex, living together, sharing sexual expression and commitment.

A **cohabiting family** consists of two people of the opposite sex living together, sharing sexual expression, who are committed to their relationship without formal legal marriage.

When talking about the family, then, we need to specify which type we are referring to. With such a wide variety of family forms, we can no longer assume that the word **family** is synonymous with nuclear family.

FAMILY STRUCTURE AND FUNCTION

Structural-Functional Theory

A **structural-functional view of the family** looks at the family as a social institution in terms of the needs of society. What does society need for its survival? How is the family organized and what functions does it serve in meeting society's needs? When talking about the family, structural-function-alists usually refer to the nuclear family. From this point of view, the family is considered successful to the extent that it fulfills societal expectations and needs.

Family functions have been described in numerous ways. Murdock (1949) was typical of sociological thought a generation ago in insisting that the nuclear family was universal and that it always had four functions: *providing a common residence, economic cooperation, reproduction,* and *sexuality.*

Providing a Common Residence

Since Murdock's time, sociologists have been finding exceptions to his views of the family. In commuter marriages, the husband and wife maintain separate residences for much of the time, seeing one another only on weekends or occasionally during the month. If family members do not share a common residence all the time, however, this does not necessarily make them less of a family.

Economic Cooperation

Economic cooperation is a broad term that can include a wide range of activities from cooking to household maintenance and income production. It includes the production, allocation, distribution, and management of resources. Resources may be money, material goods, food, drink, services, skills, care, time, and space.

Historically, the family was almost a self-sufficient economic unit. The traditional rural family produced much of its own food, housing, and clothing. Family members cooperated in this production and depended on one another for providing goods and services.

During and after the industrial revolution, many families moved off the family farm and depended more on those outside the family for the production of goods and services. As families became consumers rather than producers, earning an income became even more necessary. Partly because of increasing demands for income, wives as well as husbands were enlisted in the task of providing a living. Thus, husbands and wives become mutually dependent in fulfilling this task.

The economic functions of the family are still important, but the nuclear family has never been able to assume all functions. Some needs have been met by other groups. Insurance companies provide health insurance, unemployment insurance, and life insurance. Industries and the Social Security Administration provide pensions for the retired or disabled.

Reproduction

Although the reproductive function of the family has always been important, nonmarital reproduction is now common as well. Births to unmarried women now constitute one out of four of all live births (U.S. Bureau of the Census, 1989). Advances in reproductive technology — artificial insemination, for example — have made it possible for fertilization to take place without sexual contact between a man and woman at all.

Sexual Functions

Murdock's concept of sexuality was synonymous with heterosexual relationships within the family. Obviously, sexual expression may take place between two people outside a family unit. Sexual relationships may involve homosexuals, and some homosexual couples have been able to legally adopt children.

Nurture and Socialization of Children

Taking exception to Murdock's view of the family, sociologists have described other functions. Reiss (1980) insists that the only universal function of the family (nuclear, extended, or otherwise) is the nurturance and socialization of children. According to this view, parents do not have to be biologically related to one another or even to their children (the children may be adopted), but society insists that socialization is the responsibility of the family group (Moss and Abramowitz, 1982). Whether parents are single, separated, divorced, married, or remarried, they are expected to be responsible for their children's physical, emotional, social, intellectual, and moral needs. The family is not the only care-giving or socialization unit. Schools, churches, and social groups such as Cub Scouts, Brownies, Girl and Boy Scouts, YMCA and YWCA members, and others participate in the socialization process (Hoge, Petrillo, and Smith, 1982). But society delegates the family primary responsibility in guiding this process. Failure to do so constitutes legal grounds for child neglect or abuse.

ASSESSMENT
My Socialization

Think about your childhood and the way you were reared. In what kind of family situation were you brought up? Who was most influential in your own socialization? Was it your family? Do you agree or disagree with the way you were brought up? What were the effects on you?

CLASSROOM FORUM
Should We Stay Together?

9

INTIMATE
RELATIONSHIPS,
MARRIAGES, AND
FAMILIES IN THE
TWENTIETH CENTURY

Mary B. describes her marriage. "Bob and I have been married for eight years. We have two children, ages two and five. Our marriage was fine until our first child was born, and then we began to drift apart. Now we don't have any warm, loving feelings for one another. There's no romance left and little companionship. He does his thing, and I do mine. We pretty much go our separate ways. We have sex together maybe once a month.

"Bob is a nice guy and good provider. He's hard working and spends at least 60 hours a week on his job. He earns an excellent salary and does all the heavy chores around the house and yard on weekends. I work part time and could work full time if I wanted. But even full time, I'd earn half as much as Bob; and I would have trouble supporting myself, even with his help with the support of the children.

"I always wanted a loving marriage with a lot of companionship and togetherness. I feel families should do things together, but we don't. Bob doesn't seem to have the time. Ours has become a marriage of convenience. I don't know whether to stay married to him so I can keep the life-style I'm used to, even though I don't have any companionship, or to leave him, live on less, and look for someone else" (Author's counseling notes).

QUESTIONS

If you were Mary or Bob, what would you do?

2. What are some things the couple might do before making any decisions?

3. Should the fact that Mary and Bob have children be a factor in deciding whether to stay married or not?

4. Is it wrong or right, according to your views, to stay in a loveless relationship for financial reasons?

5. Is there any way that Mary and Bob can find love again with one another?

6. Can this marriage be saved? How? What would have to be done?

CHANGES IN FAMILY PHILOSOPHY AND EMPHASIS

From Institution to Companionship

One of the most important changes in the family has been a shift in emphasis. Structural-functional views emphasized the role of the family as an institution whose function was to meet the needs of society. (This is the **instrumental role** of the family.) Modern views of the family tend to emphasize its role in fulfilling personal needs for emotional security and companionship (the **expressive role** of the family). In an industrial society where the majority of people live in large urban centers, neighbors remain strangers and it becomes harder for people to find friendship, companionship, and emotional support. Affectional needs may not be met; the individual feels isolated and alone even though surrounded by millions of people. In such an impersonal society, it becomes more important to find intimacy, a sense of belonging, and emotional security in the family itself. Neubeck (1979) suggests that there is a universal longing to be attached, to relate, to belong, to be needed, to care. Most humans have a need for a "profoundly reaffirming experience of genuine intimacy"

(Kennedy, 1972). Erikson (1959) suggests that the achievement of intimacy is one of the major goals of life. In a highly impersonal society, where emotional isolation is frequent, developing a close relationship with others is vital to one's identity and security (Rice, 1983).

There has been some shift, therefore, in emphasis in family functions. Traditionally, people were married for economic security, to provide goods and services for one another, to attain social status, to reproduce and to raise children. Today, people marry for love, companionship, and the satisfaction of emotional needs (Mace, 1972b).

Necessary as this shift in emphasis has been, it has also placed more burden upon the family itself. When people establish a family for love, companionship, and emotional security, but don't find fulfillment, they become disappointed, frustrated, and full of feelings of failure. The higher their personal expectations, the greater the possibilities of failure. Sometimes expectations are charged with romantic fantasy to the point where fulfillment becomes impossible. This is one reason for the high rate of divorce. Rather than "stay together for the sake of the family," couples often separate if their personal needs and expectations are not met.

From Patriarchy to Democracy

Throughout most of our history, the American family was patriarchal. The father was considered head of the household with authority over and responsibilities for other members of the family. He was the supreme authority in decision making and matters of dispute. He was entitled to the deference and respect of other family members who were expected to be submissive and obedient to him.

As head of the household, he owned the property, which was passed **patrilineally** to the next generation (through the male line). The wife and children were expected to reside with the husband and with or near the husband's family according to his choice. (The term is **patrilocal residence**. The corresponding terms that refer to female descent and residence are **matrilineal** and **matrilocal**).

One of the characteristics of the traditional patriarchal family was a clear-cut distinction between the husband's and wife's roles in the family. The husband, the breadwinner in the family, was usually responsible for clearly defined chores that were considered "men's work." Clearing and plowing land, growing and hunting food, gathering and cutting firewood, building construction, and repairs were among his responsibilities. Duties on a farm were divided into women's work and men's work, but the woman was also expected to share part of the farm work if it was allocated to her. Thus, milking cows, tending a vegetable garden, and selling eggs might be considered "woman's work," along with housecleaning, cooking, sewing and mending, child care, and other responsibilities.

The traditional patriarchal family is often portrayed in idealized form so that people long for the "good old days" and "life with father" as it used to be. But cracks often developed in the patriarchal structure. The father who was a tyrant was a difficult and unpleasant taskmaster, feared and respected but not necessarily loved by his wife and children. "Life with father" was

"Life with Father" as pictured here was once considered the ideal American family. The father was traditionally the head of the household with authority over all the family members.

often a life of toil and obedience, regardless of personal desires and feelings. Sons waited impatiently to inherit family wealth or property and for the time when they could marry and achieve a man's status. A daughter might hope that marriage would fulfill her dreams, but she sometimes experienced friction in living in close proximity to her husband's family. Husband-wife relationships lasted because there was no other choice and no way out, but there may have been little emotional closeness and companionship between them. Sex was considered "a man's pleasure and a woman's duty" and involved an endless succession of pregnancies.

Not all patriarchal families were unhappy or unsuccessful. The structures were stable, sustained by law and social custom as well as the lack of economic and social opportunities. Nevertheless, the changes that led to today's family involved a decline of the patriarchy and the advent of the democratic family in which women were treated more as equals and given more voice in family governance.

This change was brought on by several causes. *First,* the rise of the feminist movement brought some economic power and freedom to women. The first feminist movement in the United States was launched at Seneca Falls, New York, in 1848 when the first women's rights convention was held. The convention said that "men *and* women are created equal . . . endowed . . . with certain inalienable rights." Starting with almost no political leverage, no money, and with conventional morality against them, the suffragists won the

Married Women's Property Act in the latter half of the nineteenth century and won the enactment of the *Nineteenth Amendment to the Constitution* in 1920, which gave women the right to vote. The Married Women's Property Act recognized the right of women to hold property and borrow money. As some economic power gradually shifted to women, they gained more power and authority in family governance as well. Property could now be passed on through **bilateral descent** (through both the father and the mother).

Second, increasing educational opportunities for women and the gradual increase in the percentages of married women working outside the home encouraged the adoption of more egalitarian sex roles in the family (Knox, 1980). As wives became more involved in earning income, more husbands were asked to bear equal responsibility for homemaking and child care. While a sharing of responsibilities was the developing ideal, it was not always followed in practice. Even when working, many wives continued to do most of the housework (Blumstein and Schwartz, 1983). The general trend, however, is toward a more equal voice in decision making and a more equitable and flexible distribution of family responsibilities. (See Chapter 12 for a detailed discussion.) In democratic, egalitarian, dual-career families, residence is often determined by choosing a place where both the husband and the wife can find jobs. Thus, residence has become **neolocal,** where the couple resides in a new location of their choice rather than with either family.

Third, the demand for equality of sexual expression resulted from the recognition of the sexual capabilities of women. With such recognition, marriages developed based upon the mutual exchange of love and affection. Development of efficient contraceptives also freed women from unwanted childbearing and enabled them to develop a personal life of their own and a social life with their husband.

Fourth, the child study movement after World War II resulted in the development of the child-centered family, where the emphasis shifted from what children could do to serve the family to what the family could contribute to the total development of the child. The rights and needs of children as important members of the family were emphasized.

ASSESSMENT
Patterns of Power in My Family of Origin

Was your family of origin patriarchal, matriarchal, or democratic? What roles did your father and mother play in decision making? Who had what power over what? Do you agree or disagree with the way your parents (or parent substitutes) shared responsibilities? What are your views of men's roles and women's roles in the family?

The net result of these and other changes has been the development of a democratic family ideal that emphasizes egalitarian rights and responsibilities in a group concerned about the welfare of all. Fulfillment of these ideals has not always kept pace with idealism, but family philosophies, forms, and functions continue to change as new needs arise.

MARRIAGE AND PARENTHOOD

13

INTIMATE
RELATIONSHIPS,
MARRIAGES, AND
FAMILIES IN THE
TWENTIETH CENTURY

Marriage Rates

The marriage rate is measured as the number of persons who marry during the preceding 12 months per 1,000 population. The rate reached a peak of 12.2 per 1,000 population during the year 1945, the last year of World War II. (The rate always increases during war time.) The rate then declined very rapidly after the war, reaching a low point of 8.9 per 1,000 in 1960. The rate stayed low until 1965 when it began to climb again as the war boom babies reached marital age. The rate varied at a fairly high level and then began to fall again in 1984 after most of the war boom babies had already married. The dip in the rate between 1975 and 1977 was due to an economic recession. (See Figure 1.1.) Thus, the rate depends on economic and political conditions as well as on the percentages of persons of marriageable age in the population (U.S. Bureau of the Census, 1989).

Age at Marriage

One of the most important trends in the changing family has been the increase in the median age at first marriage. The median age at first marriage in 1987

FIGURE 1.1 Marriage Rate per 1,000 Population.

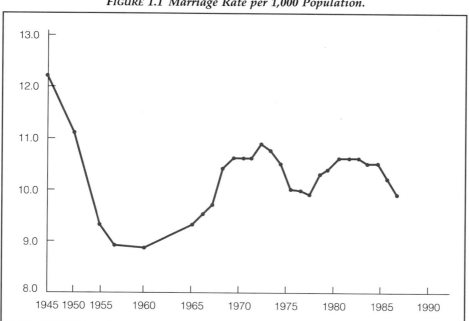

Source: U.S Bureau of the Census. (1989). *Statistical abstract of the United States, 1989* (109th ed.). Washington, DC: U.S. Government Printing Office, p. 61.

was 25.8 years for men and 23.6 years for women. This rate for women was higher than any previously recorded level. The rate for men was nearing the level recorded in 1890, 26.1 years. At the beginning of the twentieth century, the median age at first marriage started a decline that ended in the mid-1950s, reaching a low of 22.5 years for men and 20.1 years for women. Since that time, the estimated median age has been rising, with especially rapid increases during the past 10 years. Furthermore, the gap in median age of marriage for men and women has narrowed substantially. The four-year difference in 1890 has narrowed to about a two-year difference in 1987 (U.S. Bureau of the Census, 1989). Figure 1.2 shows the trend. This trend is significant because those who wait until they are in their middle or late twenties to marry have a greater chance of marital success than do those who marry earlier (Rice, 1983).

The delay of marriage also has resulted in a marked increase in unmarried young adults in the population. More than one-third of the men and one-fourth of the women in the country still have not married before 30 years of age (U.S. Bureau of the Census, 1989). See Chapter 5 for a complete discussion.

FIGURE 1.2 *Median Age at First Marriage, by Sex: 1890 to 1987.*

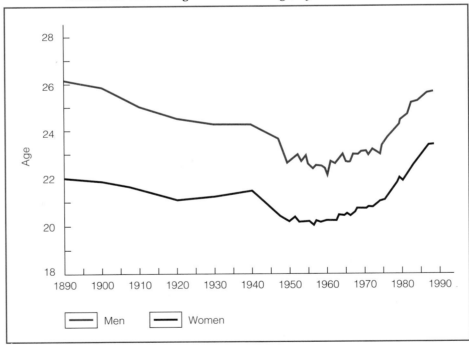

Source: U.S. Bureau of the Census (1986). Marital status and living arrangements, March 1985. *Current Population Reports*, ser. p-20, no. 411, p. 2. Washington, DC: U.S. Government Printing Office; and U.S. Bureau of the Census. (1987). Households, families, marital status, and living arrangements, March 1987. *Current Population Reports*, ser. P-20, no. 417, p. 4. Washington, DC: U.S. Government Printing Office.

ASSESSMENT
Ideal Age for Marriage

To singles: In your opinion, what is the ideal age of marriage for men? For women? Explain the reasons for your answer.

To marrieds: How old were you and your spouse when you were first married? According to how you feel about it now, were you too old, too young, or at the right age to marry? Explain.

Birthrates and Family Size

The birthrate in the United States climbed very rapidly after 1945 (the last year of World War II) and stayed high for the next 20 years. This **cohort,** known as the war boom babies, was larger than any that had been born since the years before the 1910s and 1920s. Declining birthrates since 1965 have resulted in smaller families. The average number of persons per family was 3.7 in 1965 and 3.16 in 1990. Figure 1.3 shows the average population per family from 1950 to 1990.

As you can see in Figure 1.4, 52 percent of white families in 1987 had no children of their own under 18 years of age at home. An additional 21 percent of white families had only one child of their own at home who was under 18

FIGURE 1.3 *Average Population per Family: 1950 to 1990, and Birthrates per 1,000 Population.*

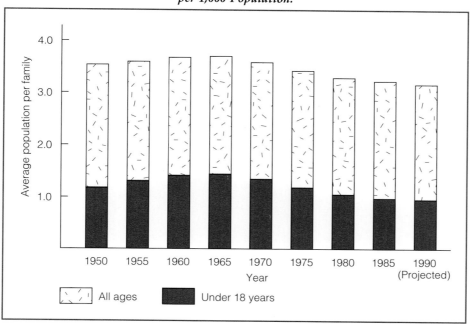

Source: U.S. Bureau of the Census. (1987). Households, families, marital status, and living arrangements, March 1987. *Current Population Reports,* ser. p-20, no. 417. Washington, DC: U.S. Government Printing Office.

years of age. Both black families and families of Spanish origin had greater numbers of children.

These figures seem almost incredible. Seventy-three percent of white families had only one or no children under 18 at home. Among black families, the figure was 66 percent.

These figures reflect the fact that American women of all races are having fewer children. At the beginning of the twentieth century, the average married woman had five children (Westoff and Parke, 1972). Today, the average number of total births to ever-married women age 15–55 has declined to 1.9.

The decline in family size can be attributed to several developments. Until the twentieth century women were expected "to be fruitful and multiply." Large families were considered a blessing and an economic asset: more hands were available to work the family farm. Furthermore, reliable birth control methods were largely unavailable. Congress enacted the "Comstock Law" in 1873, which imposed heavy fines and 10 years in prison for sending information on contraceptives through the mail. Twenty-four states passed additional statutes that banned the advertising, publication, and distribution of information on contraceptives. Another 14 states made it illegal for anyone, including physicians, to provide information about contraception.

As families moved from farms to the city, having many children became a financial burden. It became economically expedient for women to have fewer children (Margolis, 1984). Women began to go to work in factories and offices and could not take care of large families. At the same time, more efficient means of contraception became available, and couples were more willing to use them. Federal and state laws prohibiting dispensing contraceptive information and methods were gradually repealed. When married women began a massive movement into the world of work, the birthrate decreased even

FIGURE 1.4 Percent Distribution of Families, by Number of Own Children Under 18 Years Old: 1987.

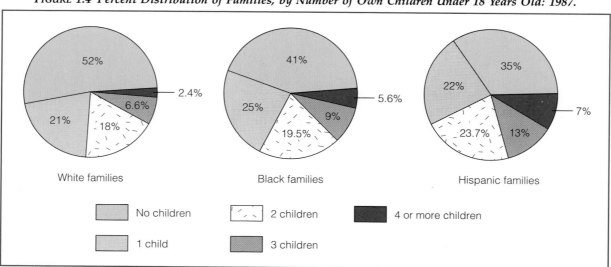

White families

Black families

Hispanic families

| No children | 2 children | 4 or more children |
| 1 child | 3 children | |

Adapted from U.S. Bureau of the Census. (1989). *Statistical abstract of the United States, 1989.* (109th ed.). Washington, DC: U.S. Government Printing Office, 50.

more (Margolis, 1984). Ecological, economic, and demographic concerns relating to world population added to the pressure to keep the birthrate down. Together, these factors resulted in smaller families.

Working Mothers

Another important change in family living has been the large influx of married women into the work force. Up until the early 1970s, married women with no children under age 18 had higher labor force participation rates than did those with children. This long-standing pattern began to change during the 1970s and has now reversed. In 1990, married women whose youngest children are aged 6–17 will have the largest labor force participation rates (76 percent) (Figure 1.5). Sixty-one percent of married women with the youngest child under age 6 also will be employed. This will represent a larger percentage than that of married women without children (U.S. Bureau of the Census, 1989).

Mothers are entering the working force for reasons both economic and noneconomic. The major reason is financial need. Many families can't make

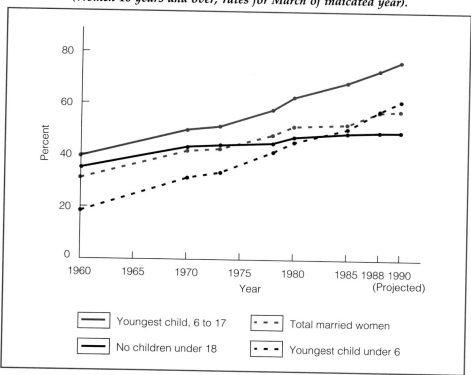

FIGURE 1.5 Labor Force Participation Rates of Married Women, by Presence and Age of Children (Women 16 years and over; rates for March of indicated year).

Source: U.S. Bureau of the Census. (1986). Women in the American economy, by C. M. Taeuber and V. Valdisera. Current Population Reports, ser. p-23, no. 146, p. 7, Washington, DC: U.S. Government Printing Office, and U.S. Bureau of the Census (1989). Statistical abstract of the United States, 1989. Washington, D.C: U.S. Government Printing Office, p. 386.

it financially without the mother's working. Employment opportunities for women have also increased. Factors such as inflation, periodic recessions, and unemployment among husbands have also pressured married women to join the labor force.

Noneconomic reasons for employment are also important. Large numbers of women want to work for purposes of personal fulfillment. For many, this is the primary motive.

These trends have added to women's burdens. Most working wives try to satisfy the usual demands for housework and family care in addition to their work in the labor force. Research indicates that the wife's employment has only a minimal effect on the husband's household responsibilities. Women's satisfaction is greatly enhanced when husbands are willing to assume a fair share of the total responsibilities.

Increased employment for mothers has also intensified the demand for child care. Only one-fourth of employed mothers arrange child care in their own home, which means that someone, usually the mother, must stop at a babysitter's home or group care center on the way to and from work (U.S. Bureau of the Census, 1986c).

PERSPECTIVE
Women in the Labor Force

Following are some facts related to working women.

The labor force participation rate of women over 44 years old was 56.7 percent in 1988.

One out of five families with children is maintained by a woman.

Sixty-five percent of all children under 18 had a mother in the labor force in 1988.

Fifty-seven percent of all married women with children under the age of six were in the labor force in 1988, compared with only 12 percent in 1950.

Fifty-two percent of women with babies under one year old were in the labor force in 1988 as were 59 percent of mothers with toddlers under age three.

Twenty-three percent of the children of mothers who work full time are cared for in their own home.

From U.S. Bureau of the Census. (1989). *Statistical abstract of the United States, 1989.* Washington, DC: U.S. Government Printing Office, pp. 370, 386.

ASSESSMENT
Effects of Mother Working

Was your mother (or mother substitute) working outside the home when you were growing up? When? For how long? Part time or full time? How did she feel about it? What were some possible effects on you?

One of the most far-reaching changes during the 1970s and 1980s has been the increase in the number of families that consist of a single parent maintaining a household with one or more children. The high rates of separation and divorce, plus the increased number of out-of-wedlock births, have resulted in the large increase in this family type (Norton and Glick, 1986). In 1985, one out of every four families with children under 18 years old was a one-parent family, up from 1 in 10 in 1970. The number of one-parent families more than doubled during the years spanning 1970 to 1987 (from 3.8 million to 9.2 million). This increase occurred at a time when two-parent families actually declined by 5 percent. The decline in the number of two-parent families can be traced in large part to the falling birthrate after the baby boom (U.S. Bureau of the Census, 1986a).

In addition to the household maintained by a lone parent (usually a mother) with one or more children under 18 at home, there are three other types of one-parent families (Norton and Glick, 1986).

1. *One-parent families with only adult children over 18 years old present.*
2. *Related subfamilies.* A typical example would be a young mother and her young child living in the house of the mother's parents.
3. *Unrelated subfamilies.* This is a home maintained by a person to whom the one parent and his/her children (all under 18) are not related. Most of the parents in this group are older, divorced mothers. Some are cohabiting with an adult to whom they are not married.

All together then, there were 14 million one-parent families and subfamilies in the United States in 1985. Eighty-eight percent of one-parent families in 1987 were mother-child families. The older the age of the parent (and the children), the more likely the father will maintain a one-parent family with his children. Boys are more likely than girls to be living with their father. However, mother-child families are disproportionately concentrated among blacks. Fifty-five percent of all black children under 18 are currently living with a lone mother, as compared with 18 percent of all white children under 18. Figure 1.6 shows the percentages (U.S. Bureau of the Census, 1986a and 1989).

Statistics for a particular year fail to show the true extent of one-parent families (Hofferth, 1985). Cross-sectional studies show only the percentages of one-parent families during the year of the survey, not the total number that have ever been one-parent families. So although 27 percent of children under 18 years old in 1987 were living with only one parent, projections show that nearly 60 percent of all children born in 1986 may be expected to spend a large part of a year or longer in a one-parent family before reaching the age of 18 (Norton and Glick, 1986). Bumpass (1984) estimates that the majority of children whose parents' marriages are disrupted and who remain with the mother will spend at least five years in a mother-child family and that many may experience at least two periods of living in a one-parent family during childhood. From the point of view of the mothers involved, 37 percent of

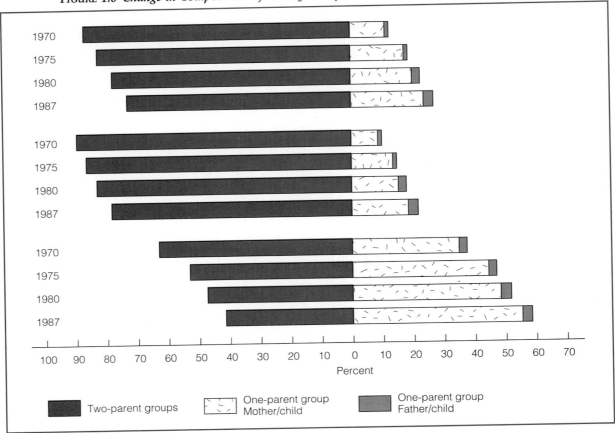

FIGURE 1.6 *Change in Composition of Family Groups with Children, by Race: 1970 to 1987.*

Two-parent groups

One-parent group
Mother/child

One-parent group
Father/child

Source: U.S. Bureau of the Census. (1986). Household and family characteristics, March 1985. *Current Population Reports,* ser. p-20, no. 411, p. 10. Washington, DC: U.S. Government Printing Office. U.S. Bureau of the Census (1989). *Statistical Abstract of the United States, 1989.* Washington, D.C.: U.S. Government Printing Office, p. 50.

women who were in their late twenties in 1984 could expect sooner or later to maintain a one-parent family involving children under 18 (Norton and Glick, 1986). The effects on the mothers and on the children are discussed in detail in Chapters 20 and 23.

DIVORCE AND REMARRIAGE

Divorce Rates

Divorce rates increased steadily from 1958 until 1979. After 1979, they leveled off and even declined. (See Figure 1.7.) Whether rates will continue to decline remains to be seen. As they now stand, the high rates mean that a large number of marriages end in divorce. A survey in 1985 showed that nearly

FIGURE 1.7 *Number of Divorces and Divorce Rate: United States, 1940 to 1987.*

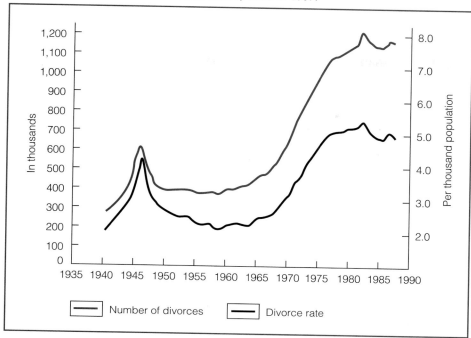

Source: U.S. Bureau of the Census. (1979). Divorce, child custody, and child support. *Current Population Reports,* ser. p-23, no. 84, p. 2. Washington, DC: U.S. Government Printing Office; U.S. Department of Health and Human Services. (1980). Births, marriages, divorces, and deaths for May 1980. *Monthly Vital Statistics Report,* (PHS) 30–1120, vol. 29, no. 5, p. 1. Washington, DC: U.S. Department of Health and Human Services. (1987). Births, marriages, divorces, and deaths for November 1986. *Monthly Vital Statistics Report, 35,* February 20, 1987. Hyattsville, MD: National Center for Health Statistics.

one-third of ever-married women aged 35 to 39 had ended a first marriage in divorce by the survey date and that a projected figure of 56 percent would eventually end a first marriage in divorce (Norton and Moorman, 1987). The proportion for this age group is greater than that for women 10 years younger or older. Figure 1.8 shows the differences.

The cohort 35 to 39 years old in 1985 is a unique group for a number of reasons. They represent the vanguard of the post–World War II baby boom. They were of draft age during the war in Vietnam. Technical advances in fertility control and the rising employment of women have also been associated with the divorce behavior of the early baby boomers (Cherlin, 1981). The rising divorce rates of the 1970s and the stable rates of the first half of the 1980s reflect a combination of period and cohort influences. The oldest members of the baby boom generation were at peak divorcing age in the 1970s, which was also a time of rapid institutional changes in many other spheres. In the 1980s, the early baby boomers had aged just beyond the highest divorce years, while society itself was adjusting to several new behavioral standards created during the previous decade. These are the most plausible theoretical explanations for recent divorce trends (Norton and Moorman, 1987).

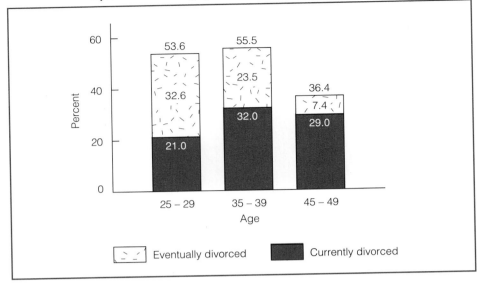

FIGURE 1.8 *Percentage Currently (1985) and Eventually Divorced After First Marriage for Ever-Married Women, by Age.*

From Norton, A. J., and Moorman, J. E. (1987). Current trends in marriage and divorce among American women. *Journal of Marriage and the Family, 49,* 3–14. Copyright (1987) by the National Council on Family Relations, 1910 West County B, Suite 147, St. Paul, Minnesota 55113. Reprinted by permission.

ASSESSMENT
You and Divorce

Did your parents divorce while you were growing up? If so, how old were you? How did you feel about it? What effect do you think it had on you?

Remarriage Trends

The majority of people who divorce eventually remarry. Recent analysis of remarriage has indicated that about three out of four divorced women and about four out of five divorced men will ultimately remarry (Furstenberg and Spanier, 1984; Glick, 1984). Remarriage happens fairly quickly too. The median number of years between divorce and remarriage is 3.9 years for men and 3.1 years for women (U.S. Bureau of the Census, 1989). However, the proportion who remarry appears to be declining. Redivorce of remarried persons also shows signs of decline, so that the future incidence of redivorce may be quite similar to the incidence of first divorce. Overall, divorce, remarriage, and redivorce may have peaked in the late 1970s and will probably recede to some new normative level (Norton and Moorman, 1987). However, the incidence of divorce in the United States remains among the highest in the world. The net effect of a high rate of divorce and remarriage is an increase in reconstituted or blended families.

Overall, about 25 percent of American families are blended or reconstituted families, in which a parent remarries and brings children from a previous marriage into the new family unit. If they have children by each other, the blended family may consist of children from her previous marriage, children from his previous marriage, and children born to them since they remarried.

Family relationships in a blended family can become quite complicated, because each parent is faced with the challenge of forming new relationships with stepchildren, with the children of the new marriage, and perhaps with the spouse's ex-spouse. The children have the challenge of adjusting to stepparents and to stepsiblings, as well as maintaining relationships with natural parents both inside and outside their new family unit. If both their natural parents remarry, the children involved are faced with adjusting to both a stepfather and stepmother plus any stepsiblings that are brought into their newly reconstituted families. Also, both parents and children may have to form new relationships with other relatives on all sides of the families. It becomes obvious that many new adjustments are required. See Chapter 24 for a detailed discussion of remarriage and stepparenting.

ASSESSMENT
The Stepparent Family

If your parents divorced, did either of them remarry? Did you live a part of your life with a stepparent? Stepsibling? How did you get along? Were there any special problems that upset you a great deal? What has been the effect on you now?

SEXUAL BEHAVIOR

Premarital Sexual Behavior

For a number of years, researchers indicated that the real revolution in sexual attitudes and behavior had occurred in the 1920s and had remained fairly constant since that time. In the late 1960s and early 1970s, however, researchers began to notice significant changes in attitudes and behavior (Bell and Coughey, 1980). Studies indicated a rapid rise in the percentage of youths engaging in heavy petting and premarital sexual intercourse. Figure 1.9 compares the findings in 1980 with those in 1965, 1970, and 1975 (Robinson and Jedlicka, 1982). The student sample consisted of undergraduates attending a large, southern state university (the University of Georgia). The students were representative of the university population in terms of class standing, major fields of study, and fraternity and sorority membership. It is obvious that standards for both men and women became more liberal over the 15-year period and that the changes for females were particularly large. As light petting and medium petting decreased, the percentage engaging in heavy petting and premarital sexual intercourse increased substantially.

Furthermore, permarital sexual intercourse began to occur at younger ages. Zelnick and Kantner (1980) conducted the most complete national study of premarital sexual behavior of adolescent females 15–19 years of age. No

FIGURE 1.9 *Percentage of College Students Petting
and Having Premarital Sexual Intercourse, 1965, 1970, 1975, and 1980.*

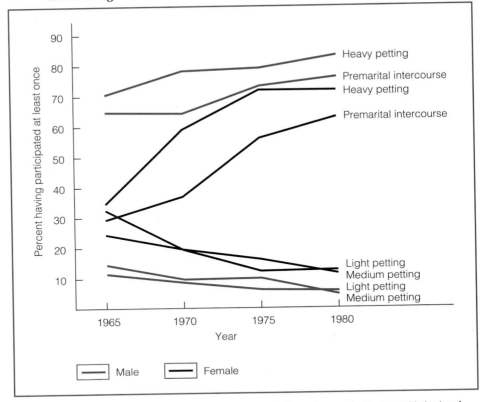

Adapted from Robinson, I. E., and Jedlicka, D. (1982). Change in sexual attitudes and behavior of
college students from 1965 to 1980: A research note. *Journal of Marriage and the Family, 44*, 238.

nationwide study of premarital sexual behavior of adolescents has been conducted since theirs. However, the study is significant because surveys were
conducted in 1971 and repeated in 1976 and 1979. A trend toward an increase
in premarital sexual intercourse during this period was evident. The proportion of U.S. teenage women residing in metropolitan areas who had premarital
sexual intercourse rose from 30 percent in 1971 to 50 percent in 1979. It is
evident that premarital sexual activity increased with age also. In 1979, 23
percent of 15-year-old girls had had premarital sexual intercourse. That percentage increased to 69 percent by age 19. The average age at which they first
had intercourse was 16.2 years (Zelnik and Shah, 1983).

With more than one-third of 16-year-old females and about two-thirds of
19-year-old females having premarital coitus, the rate of contraceptive use
becomes important (Zabin, 1981). What percentage of these young people
are using some form of protection against pregnancy and sexually transmitted
diseases? Results from the 1979 Zelnik and Kantner (1980) study show that
only 39 percent of 15- to 19-year-old unmarried girls *sometimes* used contraception; overall only 34 percent of these teenage girls *always* used some
method of contraception whenever they had intercourse; and 27 percent *never*
used contraceptives.

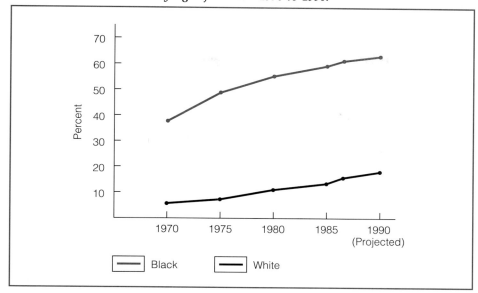

FIGURE 1.10 *Births to Unmarried Women,*
by Age of Mother: 1970 to 1990.

Adapted from U.S. Bureau of the Census. (1989). *Statistical abstract of the United States, 1989* (109th ed.). Washington, DC: U.S. Government Printing Office, 66.

Unmarried Pregnancy and Parenthood

The marked increase in premaritial sexual activity accompanied by an inefficient use of contraceptives has also resulted in an increase in unmarried parenthood. The birthrate per 1,000 unmarried white women of all ages (those never-married, widowed, and divorced) has increased, while the rate per 1,000 unmarried black women has decreased. However, the number of births to unmarried women as a percent of all births has increased for both whites and blacks (U.S. Bureau of the Census, 1989). The total number of live births to unmarried women of all races increased from 224,000 in 1960 to 879,000 in 1986. Figure 1.10 shows these trends, which result in increasing numbers of children being brought up without the benefit of two parents in their home.

The rapid rise in unwed pregnancy among teenage mothers has been particularly tragic. The number of out-of-wedlock pregnancies to women 15–19 years of age was estimated at 1,101,588 during 1986. Of this number, 121,128 were miscarriages or still births, 469,409 (43 percent) were induced abortions, leaving 511,050 babies born alive. About 230,050 expectant mothers married hastily before their babies were born, leaving 281,100 babies born out of wedlock (U.S. Bureau of the Census, 1989). About 70 percent of firstborn children among teenage women are conceived out of wedlock (O'Connell and Rogers, 1984).

Over 90 percent of unwed mothers decide to keep their babies (Alan Guttmacher Institute, 1981). Some let their parents or their relatives adopt their babies, but the remainder want to raise their children themselves, assisted by whatever family or other help they can get.

From most points of view, unmarried motherhood of a young teenage girl is a tragedy (Kellam et al., 1982). The single mother who decides to keep her baby may become entangled in a self-destructive cycle consisting of failure to finish school, repeated pregnancies, failure to establish a stable family life, and dependence on others for support. If she marries, the chances of her remaining married are only about one in five. Because few manage to complete their education, they are unable to get a good job to support themselves and their family and are likely to require welfare assistance for years (Dillard and Pol, 1982).

SUMMARY

1. A family is any group of persons united by the ties of marriage, blood, or adoption, or any sexually expressive relationship, in which (1) the people are committed to one another in an intimate, interpersonal relationship, (2) the members see their identity as importantly attached to the group, and (3) the group has an identity of its own.

2. The wide variety of family forms are determined by their structural arrangement, the persons in them, and their relationship to one another. Families differ in life goals and philosophies, family governance, sex roles, husband-wife relationships, sexual values and behavior, child-rearing patterns, economic circumstances, and other ways.

3. A structural-functional view of the family portrays the family as a social institution in terms of the needs of society. Murdock said that the nuclear family has four functions: providing a common residence, economic cooperation, reproduction, and sexuality. Other sociologists have found numerous exceptions to Murdock's views. Reiss insists that the only universal function of the family is the nurturance and socialization of children.

4. Modern views of the family emphasize its role in fulfilling personal needs for emotional security and companionship.

5. Although, historically, the American family was patriarchal, there has been a gradual shift to a more democratic power structure.

6. The marriage rate has stabilized since 1986.

7. The median age at first marriage is increasing for both men and women, resulting in an increase in unmarried young adults in the population.

8. Declining birthrates since 1955 have resulted in smaller families.

9. The percentage of married women in the work force has been increasing steadily. At the present time, greater percentages of women with either preschool or grade-school children are working outside the home than are women without children.

10. The number of one-parent families, especially mother-child families, has risen considerably.

11. Divorce rates increased steadily from 1958 until 1979, at which time they leveled off and even declined. Altogether, 54 percent of women aged 25–29 in 1985, 56 percent of women aged 35–39 in 1985, and 36 percent of women aged 45–49 in 1985 will eventually divorce.

12. Three out of four divorced women and four out of five divorced men will eventually remarry, although the percent who remarry appears to be declining. However, the relatively high rates of divorce and remarriage have resulted in a large number of reconstituted or blended families.

13. Premarital sexual intercourse occurs among increasing percentages of adolescents and begins at younger ages.

14. Unmarried teenagers are also inefficient users of contraceptives. The result has been an increase in unmarried parenthood. Altogether, over one-quarter million babies in the United States are born out of wedlock each year. About 90 percent of unwed mothers decide to keep their babies. The results are often tragic, with the single mother becoming entangled in a self-destructive cycle of failure to finish school, repeated pregnancies, failure to establish a stable family life, and dependence on others for support.

SUGGESTED READINGS

Albein, M., and Cavallo, D. (eds.). (1981). *Family Life in America, 1620–2000*. St. James, NY: Revisionary Press. Twenty-four articles on the history of the family.

Allan, G. (1985). *Family Life*. New York: Basil Blackwell. Changes in modern family living.

Caplow, T., Bahr, H. M., Chadwick, B.A., Hill, R., and Williamson, M. H. (1982). *Middletown Families: Fifty Years of Change and Continuity*. Minneapolis: University of Minnesota Press. A replication of Robert and Helen Lynd's classic research in Muncie, Indiana.

Gittins, D. (1985). *The Family in Question: Changing Households and Familiar Ideologies*. London: Macmillan. A feminist view of the family.

Gordon, M. (1983). *The American Family in Social-historical Perspective* (3rd ed.). New York: St. Martin's Press. Articles dealing with issues of family structure and function.

Masnick, G., and Bane, M. J. (1980). *The Nation's Families: 1960–1990*. Boston: Auburn House.

U.S. Bureau of the Census. (1986). Marital status and living arrangements, March 1985. *Current Population Reports*, ser. p-20, no. 410. Washington, DC: U.S. Government Printing Office. Detailed information on the marital status and living arrangements of the noninstitutional population of the United States.

2

CLASS, RACIAL, AND ETHNIC DIFFERENCES IN FAMILIES

KEY TERMS

low socioeconomic status
underclass
barrios
familism
compadres
machismo

Families differ in many ways. Although the nuclear family still exists successfully, single parent families are becoming more and more common. Many families may consist of several generations living together, or generations may be separated from each other when grown children leave the nest.

Families differ according to socioeconomic status and racial and ethnic groupings as well as in family structure, household composition, life goals and philosophies, family governance, sex roles, husband-wife relationships, sexual values and behavior, child-rearing patterns, and economic circumstances. This chapter examines a wide range of family patterns and analyzes some of the implications and effects of these differences.

VERY LOW SOCIOECONOMIC STATUS FAMILIES

The term **low socioeconomic status** refers to two important aspects of living condition: low social class, which includes cultural deprivation, and low income. Social class and income influence all aspects of family life: the values accepted, the goals sought, the jobs held, the age at which one marries, the selection of a mate, and the way children are socialized. Not all families from any one socioeconomic status are identical, so there is some blending of characteristics between classes. In this section, we emphasize some general characteristics that we are more likely to find in only the very low socioeconomic status families. Individual families, especially of a higher socioeconomic status, may not fit these general descriptions at all.

Stress, Insecurity, Powerlessness

With limited education and income, these families of very low socioeconomic status are at the mercy of life's unpredictable events: loss of work, injury, legal problems, illness, school difficulties, and others. Family members strive for security because they never feel certain about their lives (Rank, 1987). Coping is especially difficult for mothers with very low income who have to care for themselves and their children. Many are never able to free themselves from their situation (Dill et al., 1980).

Early Marriage and Family Instability

Youths from these families strive to escape parental authority and to gain adult status by leaving home at a young age. Sexual relationships begin at an early age, resulting in a high rate of illegitimacy (Gabriel and McAnarney, 1983). Another result is hasty and early marriage (often because of unwanted pregnancy), followed by early parenthood. Very low socioeconomic status families tend to be unstable, with high rates of separation and divorce (Booth and Edwards, 1985). Divorce, in turn, creates additional poverty for the woman who is usually left with children to support and with few resources with which to do it (Slesinger, 1980). Large numbers of these mothers work, leaving their children under the care of relatives, friends, or whomever they can afford.

Sex Roles

In very low socioeconomic families, the husband strives to be head of the household and the final authority in the family. This is sometimes difficult, especially when his employment is tenuous. The wife usually performs chores that are traditionally considered her responsibility and often is employed outside the home as well. She may have learned to exchange sex for favors, but has little emotional satisfaction herself if she was reared with negative attitudes about sex or her husband is selfish and unfeeling (Leslie and Korman, 1985). Locksley (1982) found that wives with the lowest education were the most likely to be upset with their sexual relationship in marriage.

Husband-wife companionship in the very low socioeconomic status family is minimal (Rainwater, 1966). Wives socialize with other neighborhood women and relatives, husbands with their male buddies at the local bar or sports arena. They don't spend much leisure time together (Locksley, 1982). There may also be little husband-wife communication. The spouses seldom confide in one another or seek each other's advice. Lopata's (1971) study of housewives found that working-class wives considered themselves lucky if

The ideal for American families has often been described as a house in the suburbs with two cars in the garage. But for many, the reality remains one of low income and cultural deprivation. The effects of such factors as stress and insecurity on the children of low income families can have long term consequences.

their husbands brought home their paychecks, were good to them, and did not use physical violence. Considerable tension and hostility may exist between the sexes, especially if the husband tends to be chauvinistic and sexist in his views of women.

Child-Rearing Patterns

Child-rearing patterns of very low socioeconomic status families tend to emphasize imperatives, absolutes, obedience, and physical punishment that is often harsh, impulsive, and inconsistent. There is concern for obedience, showing respect for parents, conformity to externally imposed standards, and staying out of trouble. Parents tend to be concerned with overt behavior rather than personality growth and the development of creativity, curiosity, independence, or self-direction (Gecas and Nye, 1974). Greater family control is exercised over daughters than sons, which is one reason why adolescent girls use marriage as an escape from home.

Families tend to be large, and there is little time to pay attention to older children. The youngest babies require the mother's care. Emancipation from family comes early and is often psychologically premature. Youths are often not ready to take their place in the adult world, and many turn to peers to replace family ties (DiCindio, Floyd, Wilcox, and McSeveney, 1983).

Dropout rates from school are high among youth of low socioeconomic status (Rice, 1987). Although parents usually want their children to have more education that they did, they also pressure their adolescents to get a job to help support the family; and this pressure may contribute to adolescents dropping out of school after they reach the minimum legal age. Furthermore, lower socioeconomic status youths feel the prejudices of middle-class society, and so experience isolation from the mainstream of school activities. If they are doing poorly academically, they can't wait to quit school entirely. Of course, doing so perpetuates the cycle of poverty and cultural deprivaton.

CLASSROOM FORUM
Stereotypes of the Poor

Following are some common stereotypes of low socioeconomic people:

The poor are that way because they are lazy and don't want to work.

She's having another baby so that she can collect more welfare money.

Most of the women on welfare are very promiscuous. I think they're oversexed.

Most of them neglect their children. They don't seem to care what happens to them. They don't take care of them properly.

The poor kids I have seen are all dumb. They do terrible in school.

The kids are out in all kinds of weather, but they are healthy as animals. They never get sick.

They don't know how to handle the money they do have. They spend it foolishly on things they don't need.

She uses her food stamps to buy all kinds of fancy food. I can't afford to buy the things she buys.

QUESTIONS

To what extent, if any, are these stereotypes true? Discuss the ideas presented here and what you think about them.

RACIAL AND ETHNIC VARIATIONS

Four Groups

Not only class differences but also racial and ethnic background affect family living. Our discussion focuses on four groups: blacks, Mexican Americans as representative of Spanish Americans, Chinese Americans as representative of Asian Americans, and American Indians as our only native American group.

Demographics

Figure 2.1 shows the population of selected racial and ethnic groups in the United States. As you can see, 30.3 million blacks constitute the largest racial minority group. They represent a little over 12 percent of the total U.S. population. Hispanics, or Spanish-speaking persons, are the second largest group and include about 19.9 million persons. Three-fifths, or about 12.1 million, are Mexican Americans. Asian Americans number 3.7 million persons; a little over 860,000 are Chinese. Native Americans number 1.5 million persons. Each group has some distinctive features. Some of these distinctive characteristics, especially as related to family living, will be discussed here (U.S. Bureau of the Census).

BLACK FAMILIES

In 1965, Daniel Patrick Moynihan (1965), assistant secretary of labor under President Johnson, issued the famous report on *The Negro Family: The Case for National Action*. He reported that the black community was a "tangle of pathology" and that at the heart of this was the deterioration of the black family. The major problem was the large number of young blacks growing up in mother-centered families without the helpful influence of two parents. Moynihan argued that this situation was the major reason why blacks were making only limited gains. Moynihan also traced the high percentage of mother-centered families back to the days when slave owners sold slaves as individuals, not as families.

This report raised a storm of protest, primarily because it was erroneous. Gutman (1976) examined 1865–66 census data in Virginia and found that slavery had not destroyed the black family. Three-fourths of the households contained either a father or husband. The archetypal matrilocal family hardly existed among southern blacks. Steckel (1980) examined the records of fifty-one plantations from eight southern states and found no evidence that slave marriages were ripped apart or were unstable. Gutman (1976) also examined 13,924 black households in the central Harlem area of New York City in 1925

FIGURE 2.1 *Size of Selected Minority Groups in the United States, 1988.*

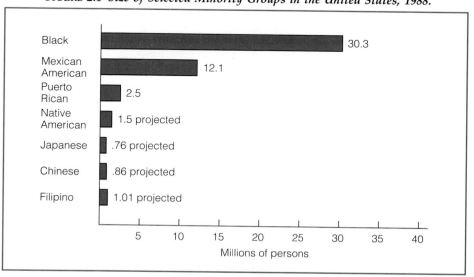

Adapted from U.S. Bureau of the Census. (1989). *Statistical Abstract of the United States, 1989.* Washington, DC: U.S. Government Printing Office, 39. U.S. Bureau of the Census (1988). The Hispanic Population in the United States, March 1988. *Current Population Reports*, ser. P-20, no. 431. Washington, DC: U.S. Government Printing Office.

In spite of recent concern over the rise of one-parent families among blacks, as well as whites, studies show that blacks believe strongly in the institution of family.

and found that 85 percent of the households were headed by both parents. Even at the time of the Moynihan report itself, three-fourths of black families were headed by a husband and wife (Staples, 1985).

Increase in One-Parent Families

Moynihan was clearly wrong in his statistics and analysis of causes. But since his report, there has been a dramatic increase in one-parent families among blacks, as well as among whites (Staples and Mirande, 1980). In 1970, one-third of black children under 18 were living in one-parent families, most with their mother. In 1987, 55 percent were living in a one-parent family with their mother. Why the increase?

The primary reason has been the rapid rise in births to unmarried women. In 1990, births to unmarried black women will be 63 percent of all live births in this racial group (U.S. Bureau of the Census, 1989). This is attributed largely to high rates of unprotected intercourse among teenagers, resulting in out-of-wedlock pregnancies. Furthermore, black females are far less likely to marry or have an abortion if they become pregnant than are comparable white women (Zelnick and Kantner, 1974). Another reason for the rise of one-parent black families is the high divorce rate (Norton and Moorman, 1987). Two out of three black marriages will eventually dissolve, and these women are less likely to remarry than are their white counterparts.

This modern breakup of the black family has not been because of any deficiency in ideology in relation to the family. Blacks believe strongly in the institution of the family. Gary and associates (1983) found that the greatest source of life satisfaction among middle-class black subjects was family life. Zollar and Williams (1987) found that married black persons, regardless of gender, tend to be happier than unmarried black persons. There are, however, significant differences according to income level. Family life satisfaction is highly correlated with income level; the higher the income, the greater the marital satisfaction (Ball and Robbins, 1986a).

Motherhood and child rearing are also among the most important values in black society. The role of mother is regarded as more important than any other role, including that of wife. Blacks also have strong kinship bonds, and a strong work achievement and religious orientation (Staples, 1985). Why, then, do blacks — who place such an emphasis on the traditonal nuclear family — find a majority of their members living in single-parent households?

Reality and Sex-Role Fulfillment

Both black men and women are unable to fulfill prescribed family roles because of situations beyond their control. There is first of all a shortage of black males of marriageable age. There are a million and a half fewer black men than women over age 14 (U.S. Bureau of the Census, 1989). Among those still unmarried, large numbers of men are underemployed, can't find jobs, or have dropped out of the labor force.

One-third of young black males in the inner city have serious drug problems (Staples, 1982). Although the percentages are small, more black men than women marry outside their race. Thus, the major reason for the increase in black female-headed households is the lack of desirable men with whom to form monogamous marriages (Joe and Yu, 1984).

The problem is especially acute for college-educated black women. More black women are obtaining undergraduate and advanced degrees than are black men (National Center for Education Statistics, 1983). And the gap is widening. Not wanting to marry men with less education than they themselves have, almost one-third of college-educated black women remain unmarried past the age of thirty (Staples, 1981).

Blacks tend to feel that the male's primary role is that of provider. Yet, it is the role he finds hardest to fulfill. He is the last to be hired, the first to be fired. Even if he is working, he earns on the average only about 55 percent of the income of whites (U.S. Bureau of the Census, 1989). It is hard for him to feel good about himself or be happy in marriage when he knows he is not fulfilling expectations, no matter how hard he tries (Ball and Robbins, 1986b).

Class Differences Among Black Families

Many variations among black families stem from class differences (Billingsley, 1968). Willie (1981) described the levels of black families in three different class categories: *affluent or middle class, working class,* and *poor.* Middle-class families consisted mainly of nuclear households with one or two children.

The parents were sometimes college graduates, and there was a strong emphasis on the work ethic and education as a means of getting ahead.

Working-class families were often broken, with the male absent. Families were often large, consisting of four or more children living with relatives; often non-related lodgers were living in as well. The families lived just above the poverty level. All members worked, including older children, when they could find employment. Parents' aspirations for their children did not exceed their own by very much.

Poor families adapted to poverty through "necessary, clever, or sometimes foolish arrangements" (Willie, 1981, p. 55), ranging from extended family households to taking in boarders and foster children. There was a great deal of distrust between men and women and fierce loyalty between mothers, kin, and children. Parents often held themselves up to their children as examples of what not to do (marry too soon or have children too soon).

Some researchers refer to a low-low lower class group, called the **underclass,** or nonworking poor. Adults are school dropouts, have few saleable skills, work only periodically, and exist largely on support from relatives and public welfare. In a study of 5,000 poor families, Duncan (1984) found that a large minority move in and out of poverty. Relatively few people remain on welfare for long periods of time or pass the habit of welfare dependency to their children. The small segment of the black poor that is underclass is a small minority of the black population.

PERSPECTIVE
Black Family Strengths

Many of the problems that beset the black family are due to racial discrimination and the economic conditions under which many live. Black families show a number of positive characteristics that have enabled them to function and survive in a hostile social environment (Gary et al., 1986). These characteristics are:

Strong kinship bonds. Extended families are common (Ball, 1983), and family members rely on one another for care, strength, and mutual support (Ball, 1983; McAdoo, 1982; Taylor, 1985, 1986).

A favorable attitude toward the elderly. At all socioeconomic levels, blacks have a more favorable attitude toward the elderly than do whites (Register, 1981).

Adaptable roles. Husband-wife relationships in most middle-class black families are egalitarian, with black husbands sharing significantly in the performance of household tasks (Hill, 1971). Roles of all family members are flexible. An uncle or grandfather can assume the vacated position of a father or an absent mother.

Strong achievement orientation. The median number of years of schooling completed is nearly equal to that for whites (U.S. Bureau of the Census, 1989). Moreover, most blacks are highly motivated to get ahead and have pride in their own accomplishments and those of black people generally.

Strong religious orientation. Religion has been a source of solace for downtrodden people, but also a vehicle for rebellion and social advancement.

A love of children. This is true not only for children in nuclear families, but also for all children, including those born out of wedlock.

Mexican Americans constitute the second largest minority group in the United States. About 87 percent reside in Arizona, California, Colorado, New Mexico, and Texas, with the vast majority in California and Texas. The majority now live in urban areas in residential ghettos called **barrios**.

Familism

Familism among Mexican Americans means that they emphasize the needs of the family above those of the individual. Individuals may stay home from school or work to care for a sick person or visit an aunt who is bedridden. Individuals find their identity and sense of belonging in family groups. There is pride in the family and usually a close emotional bond among members. Families are large; extended families are common. Mexican Americans are taught to bring elderly relatives into their homes if they are not able to care for themselves (Markides, Hoppe, Martin, and Timbers, 1983). However, trigenerational households have never been the norm for Mexican Americans, except in times of stress. Rather, Mexican extended families are groups of independent nuclear households forming social organizational units that might be called "kin-integrated." Family group structures might include first cousins, aunts and uncles, as well as grandparents, parents, brothers, and

The majority of Mexican American families live in urban areas. Most live in intact families and will experience less divorce than either whites or blacks.

sisters. Members of these groups offer aid as needed, provide resources, and help raise children (Sena-Rivera and Moore, 1979).

Traditional families also include **compadres** (godparents) as part of the extended family network. Compadres are the godparents of a child's baptism and will readily help in time of need. Those families that do not have relatives or compadres on whom to rely must turn to public welfare, thus publicly acknowledging their humiliation (Horowitz, 1983).

Divorce and Birthrates

The majority (75 percent) of Mexican Americans live in intact families. Nineteen percent of the families consist of a female householder with no spouse present. Six percent are male householders with no spouse present. Divorce rates are far lower among Mexican Americans than among blacks or Puerto Ricans, and slightly lower than among whites (U.S. Bureau of the Census, 1989). There is a higher proportion of single and a lower proportion of widowed or divorced persons among Mexican Americans than in the general population (Staples and Mirande, 1980). Mexican American families are younger and, because of the high fertility rate, tend to average one more child per family than Anglo-Americans do (Staples and Mirande, 1980). Births to unmarried Mexican American mothers are higher than among whites, but lower than among blacks, Native Americans, or Puerto Ricans. Figure 2.2 shows the comparisons among ethnic groups.

Power and Decision Making

Historically, Mexican American families have been considered patriarchal (male-dominated). In order to prove his **machismo** (masculinity), the male was expected to be dominant over his wife and children. He could have extramarital affairs to further prove his machismo but could not flaunt them, for that would demonstrate lack of respect for his wife. The sexual purity of

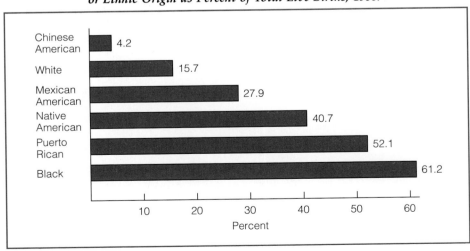

*FIGURE 2.6 Births to Unmarried Women by Race
or Ethnic Origin as Percent of Total Live Births, 1986.*

Adapted from U.S. Bureau of the Census. (1989). *Statistical abstract of the United States, 1989* (109th ed.). Washington, DC: U.S. Government Printing Office, 64.

women — the faithfulness of his wife and the virginity of an unmarried woman — were symbolized by the Virgin Mary. The honor of a man was besmirched if a wife was not faithful or a daughter was not a virgin at marriage. Girls were taught to be modest and were not supposed to learn about sexual relations by either conversation or experience. Males learned about sex from other males and from experience with "bad" girls (Horowitz, 1983).

The most recent views of Mexican American families now emphasize that male dominance is still a persistent feature, but that the fathers usually exercise their authority in a just, dignified, and fair manner, showing honor and respect for other family members. The Mexican American family has been characterized as warm and nurturing with cooperation among family members and with egalitarianism the dominant pattern of decision making (Cromwell and Cromwell, 1978; Hawkes and Taylor, 1975). Ybarra (1977) found that role relations ranged from patriarchal to completely egalitarian and the most prevalent pattern was one in which the husband and wife shared in decisions.

The most important role of women still is in the home, primarily as mothers. In the past, working outside the home was frowned upon. Today, it has become a necessity in female-headed households. The husband-wife bond is based on procreation and expression of love, but little on companionship. Most socializing occurs in single-sex groups since the expanded family network fulfills companionship needs.

Child Rearing and Education

Recent research indicates that parent-child relationships may be warm and nurturing and that fathers are playful and companionable to their children (Burrows, 1980). However, children's ties with their mother are still primary and lifelong; they seldom become distant with age.

Mexican American children are still poorly educated. Table 2.1 shows the comparisons with whites and blacks (U.S. Bureau of the Census, 1989). The low level of education has several causes. There is often a language problem if parents do not speak English at home (Mendelberg, 1984). Teachers may be poorly trained, may not speak Spanish, or may be prejudiced against Mexican American children. Schools are more often poorly funded and educational programs are inferior (Casas and Ponterotto, 1984). Many parents don't value formal education or give their children the support they need for academic success. Under these circumstances, it is not surprising that scholastic performance is poor.

TABLE 2.1 *Percentage of People Age 25 or Older
with Designated Years of Schooling, by Race and Ethnic Origin, 1987.*

Number of Years of Schooling	White	Black	Mexican
Elementary: 0–8	12.0	18.4	40.6
Four years of high school or more	76.9	63.5	44.9
Four years or more of college	20.5	10.7	5.8

From U.S. Bureau of the Census. (1989). *Statistical Abstract of the United States, 1989* (109th ed.). Washington, DC: U.S. Government Printing Office, 38.

In comparison to the general population of the United States, the Chinese American population includes greater percentages of the college educated and college graduates; its unemployment rate is also lower, and it includes greater percentages with incomes of $25,000 or more per year (U.S. Bureau of the Census, 1989). These figures result partly from the Chinese American emphasis on education and industriousness and reflects the characteristics of those who have immigrated to the United States.

Immigration

A minority of modern Chinese Americans are descendants of the Chinese who immigrated to the United States during the period of open immigration from 1820 to 1882. After 1882, a series of exclusion acts were passed that restricted Asian immigration. As a result, for a number of years, more Chinese left than entered the United States. Not until 1965 was the national origin quota system that discriminated against Asians abolished. Today each country is given an equal quota of 20,000 immigrants per year (McLeod, 1986). Chinese now immigrate according to these quotas on a first-come, first-served basis (Sih and Allen, 1976).

Traditionally, Chinese males entered the United States without their wives and children. Custom required that a man marry before he left China and that his wife remain in the house of her husband's parents. The man's duty was to send money to his patiently waiting family and to return home eventually. Frequently, years passed before he returned. Many hoped to earn enough to bring their families to the United States. But under the Immigration Act of 1882, no Chinese women were permitted to enter except for a minority from exempt classes plus wives of U.S. citizens. This restriction continued until 1943. As a result, Chinese men who remained in the U.S. were faced with a life without intimate family relations. Many joined together in clans and secret societies that provided a sense of family solidarity. Some engaged in gambling, opium smoking, and prostitution and were stereotyped by white Americans as lowly, immoral, and dangerous. In 1930, there were four Chinese males to every Chinese female in the United States. Today the gender ratio is almost equal (Lyman, 1977).

Family and Children

Well-educated Chinese American immigrants have lower rates of divorce, mental illness, and public assistance — and higher family income — than does the general U.S. population (McLeod, 1986). In comparison to other minorities, Chinese Americans have more conservative sexual values, a lower fertility rate, fewer out-of-wedlock births, and more conservative attitudes toward the role of women (Monahan, 1977; Braun and Chao, 1978). Most

*Part of the material in this section is from the author's book *The Adolescent: Development, Relationships, and Culture,* 5th edition, 1987. Used by permission of the publisher Allyn and Bacon.

Chinese American families enjoy a higher standard of living than most minority groups and include greater percentages of college educated members.

Chinese Americans have a strong sense of family ties. They have a high sense of duty to family, feel responsible for relatives, and express self-blame when a young person fails to live up to expectations. A child who misbehaves brings shame to the family name (Lott, 1976).

Philosophies and methods of child rearing depend on the degree of acculturation. Traditional approaches use authoritarian methods: a strict interpretation of good and bad behavior, the limitation of social interaction, firm discipline involving physical punishment, little verbal communication other than commands or scoldings, the expectation of obedience and conformity, and the absence of overt parental praise (Young, 1972).

Americanized Chinese parents use different approaches. The parents are nurturing and expose their children to more varied experiences than do other immigrant families. They use more verbal praise, talk and joke more with their children, and give them more freedom and choice in decision making (Young, 1972). Chinese mothers play a significant role in decision making and discipline in the family. They consider teaching to be an important part of their maternal role and give regular formal instruction to children at home (Stewart and Stewart, 1975).

Chinese children are taught that everyone has to work for the welfare of the family. They are given a great deal of responsibility and are assigned specific chores. Adolescents are responsible for supervising young children and for work around the house or in the family business. (Sih and Allen, 1976).

Chinese Americans have always stressed the importance of education and hard work as the means of getting ahead. Parents who are shopkeepers or farmers urge their children to go to college to be professionals. The emphasis is on the technical professions such as engineering, pharmacy, and dentistry. Rand Corporation's Kevin McCarthy says, "They are the most highly skilled of any immigrant group our country has ever had" (McLeod, 1986, p. 50). More than one-third of today's Asian immigrants have a college degree, almost double the rate among white Americans. So great is the drive for educational accomplishment that Asian Americans now outscore all other groups on college-entrance math exams and are disproportionately represented at top universities such as Harvard, Princeton, University of California at Berkeley, Brown, MIT, and California Institute of Technology. Such academic and occupational success has earned Asian Americans the title of "model minority" (McLeod, 1986).

Prejudices

Racial prejudices are still important limiting factors in the lives of Chinese Americans. Although some employers like to hire Chinese persons because they are hard working and dependable, the employers sometimes pay them below standard wages. In seeking more desirable employment, many Chinese feel they do not have an equal chance with Anglo-Americans. A successful engineer may still be labeled a "Chinese engineer," whereas one hardly hears reference to a German or Swedish engineer. Frequent reminders of their racial origin make some Chinese Americans feel that they are not fully accepted as Americans (Sih and Allen, 1976). "In the past we had the coolie who slaved," said Jim Tso, president of the Organization of Chinese Americans of Northern Virginia. "Today we have the high-tech coolie" (McLeod, 1986, 51).

Housing

Nowhere is racial discrimination more evident than in segregated housing. Large numbers of Chinese are forced to live in the Chinatowns of San Francisco, New York, or Boston. The social conditions in which some live are appalling. Whole families live in rundown, overcrowded, cramped, rat- and roach-infested tenements owned by absentee landlords who charge high rents and have no interest in doing repairs.

Health

Partly because of superstitions, the more traditional Chinese are reluctant to seek health care; they have strong taboos against hospitals. As a result, the incidence of tuberculosis and many other diseases is higher among Chinese than among Anglos. Local clinics, partly staffed by Chinese-speaking personnel, help to overcome reluctance to obtain care (Huang and Grachow, n.d.).

The complexities of acculturation have produced many identity conflicts in Chinese Americans, especially among young Chinese women. They seek equal opportunities and reject the traditional image of Asian women as docile, submissive dolls or exotic sex objects. They want equality of social and economic status but do not want to abandon their cultural heritage, and they resent being seen as "too Americanized" (Sih and Allen, 1976). Many second-generation Chinese are ashamed of their heritage; but by the third generation, they make determined efforts to recapture and preserve their heritage (Rice, 1987, pp. 65–69).

NATIVE AMERICAN FAMILIES

Population, Distribution, and Relocation

At the present time, the Bureau of Indian Affairs (BIA) defines Native Americans as those with one-fourth or more Indian blood. The latest census figures (1988) indicate that 1,500,000 persons identify themselves as Native Americans (U.S. Bureau of the Census, 1989). Of the total population, 45 percent live in the West and Southwest: Arizona, New Mexico, California, and Oklahoma. Arizona and Oklahoma represent two extremes in tribal representation. Arizona has the largest number; and the largest single tribe, the Navaho, lives on the largest reservation in the United States, most of which lies within Arizona. Oklahoma, in contrast, has the largest number of tribes, about 60 (U.S. Department of the Interior, 1965). This land was once Indian Territory, to which Native Americans from all over the country were moved when their tribal lands were coveted by whites. Because the Oklahoma Indians were newcomers, living on land next to their white neighbors (who had also recently immigrated), most lived among the general population, although there are some remote reservations in the state. In states such as New Mexico and the Dakotas, the majority of the population is still confined to original reservations. In other states, such as North Carolina, California, and New York, the majority either resisted movement to reservations or now live on land where government control has terminated (Rice, 1987).

Since the beginning of World War II, there has been a rapid migration of Native Americans to urban areas (Red Horse, Lewis, Feit, and Decker, 1979). The government encouraged migration and offered assistance through a relocation program that sought to promote rapid integration into American life. But this relocation program created many problems. Native Americans in cities are not integrated but are an alienated, invisible minority group. In their study of 120 urban Native American families, Miller (1975) and her Native American researchers discovered that (1) one-third were female-headed, (2) 27 percent were receiving public welfare, (3) the average number of children was three and (4) only one-third had an adequate income. A follow-up study revealed that 40 percent had returned to the reservation (Miller, 1980). Some returned because of dislike for the city; others went back because they could not cope with its demands.

The federal relocation program and its effects on Native Americans highlight one of the major problems of contemporary Indians: the cultural conflict between the way of life on reservations and the way of life in urban America.

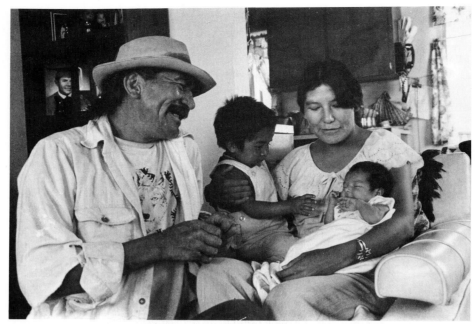

Will these Native American children grow up in urban areas where individualism and competition is emphasized? Or, will they experience the more traditional values of tribal identity and cooperation some leaders believe is so important to their culture's future?

Vital Statistics

Native Americans have the highest birthrate, the highest death rate, and the shortest life expectancy of any other group in the United States (Hill and Spector, 1974). They are afflicted with all major diseases to a much greater degree than other Americans. They suffer more from hunger and malnutrition than does any other group in the United States. Accidents, cirrhosis of the liver (attributable to poor nutrition and excessive drinking), and homicide are nearly triple the national rate. Suicide is the leading cause of death among Indian youths 15 to 19 years old, with a rate five times the national average (National Institute of Mental Health, 1973). The rate varies tremendously from tribe to tribe, however (Dizmang et al., 1974; Shore, 1975). Native Americans have a lower standard of living than do any other minority group in the United States, with unemployment high and income low. Approximately 24 percent of the families live below the poverty level (U.S. Bureau of the Census, 1989). Unemployment on some reservations runs as high as 80 to 90 percent. In most communities, the pattern is one of bare subsistence, with the result that some of the worst slums in the United States are on Indian reservations.

Education

The record of education is one of broken promises, inadequate resources, the poorest teachers, and — worst — attempts to use education to destroy the Indians' culture and way of life in order to make them into white people.

Altogether, over two-thirds of the children not in public schools attend boarding schools, living away from their homes and families (Farris and Farris, 1976). Life at boarding schools is regimented. Estranged from family, regimented by an alien culture, and unable to talk to teachers (who do not know Indian dialects), many Native American students perform poorly at school.

In addition, the BIA operates a number of day schools located on or near the reservations. In these schools physical facilities are notoriously inadequate; texts and supplies are scarce and outdated; and little money is available to hire competent staff. The schools conduct all classes in English, yet some of the children speak little or no English. The dropout rate is very high.

At the secondary level the school curriculum is the standard white one. A report on education in Indian schools in Alaska said that "education which gives the Indian, Eskimo, and Aleut knowledge of — and therefore pride in — their historic and cultural heritage is nonexistent" (Henninger and Esposito, 1971).

The Indian Education Act of 1972 (known as Title IV) resulted in some improvements. A study of boarding schools revealed that more than half the teachers had taken one or more courses related to tribes, cultures, and history. Several schools had started courses in Native American history, tribal governments, and Native American art and craftwork. In addition, many tribes are trying to gain control over their schools, with school boards made up of tribal appointees (Chavers, 1975).

Many problems remain. Some tribes want to keep the boarding schools open so that they have a place to send problem students. One hopeful sign is the rise in the number of young people going to college. Today, one in four Native American youth has had some college education. Nationwide, increasing numbers have acquired advanced degrees (U.S. Bureau of the Census, 1989).

Family Life

There is no such institution as an American Indian family. Tribal identity is primary, and family structure and values differ from tribe to tribe. Despite the attempt to impose Western family models on them, various family forms still exist among the different tribal groups (Unger, 1977). Some families are matrilineal, with descent through the mother's line (Keshna, 1980). For many Native Americans, the extended family is the basic unit for carrying out family functions, despite the absence of extended kin in the same household. Children may be raised by relatives residing in different, noncontiguous households. The existence of multiple households sharing family functions is quite common. Redhorse et al. (1979) discovered one community where 92 percent of the elderly population resided in independent households, but maintained close functional contact with their children, grandchildren, and great-grandchildren. They fulfilled traditional family roles on a daily basis.

Children

Most Native Americans view children as assets to the family. Children are taught that family and tribe are of the utmost importance. Grandmothers are very important, and the aged in general are looked up to for wisdom and counsel. The aged play the important role of storyteller, relating traditions, beliefs, and customs (Backup, 1979). Children are taught to be independent (there are no rigid schedules for eating and sleeping) and to be patient and unassuming. They are taught not to show emotions but to maintain a rather severe reserve. The ability to endure pain, hardship, hunger, and frustration without external discomfort is emphasized, as are bravery and courage.

Cultural Conflict

Native Americans are making a determined effort to retain and to teach their cultural values to their young people. Religion has always been important, but many practices were banned when the federal government conducted its sixty-year (1870–1930) program of enforced enculturation ("The Denial of Indian Civil and Religious Rights," 1975). Puberty rights for girls and boys were banned during the year, but allowed between July 1 and July 4. Native Americans have made an effort to retain native garb, dances, and crafts and to resist the white man's ways.

Most important, their values are at variance with modern American culture. The Native American is present-oriented, concerned with decisons about the present, not the future; they are not concerned with time. White people are future-oriented, concerned about time and planning ahead. Native Americans see human life as being in harmony with nature; whites seek conquest over nature. Native American life is group-oriented and emphasizes cooperation; white people emphasize individualism and competition, which is one reason Native Americans do not easily succeed and assume positions of leadership in white society.

As a result of conflicting cultures, Native Americans today are faced with a dilemma: whether to accommodate themselves to the white world and learn to compete in it or to retain traditional customs and values and live apart from the white world. An ideal solution would be for both Native Americans and whites to appreciate and understand the values of their culture and the importance of preserving a rich heritage. The individual who is proud of being a Native American, as many are, and who is respected by white society, can contribute richly to a Western world that prides itself on being the world's melting pot.

ASSESSMENT
My Family in Comparison

How does your family of origin compare to the families described in this section? Compare your family with low socioeconomic families in relation to stress in your family, age of marriage, family instability, sex roles, child-rearing practices, and educational levels. Compare your family with black families in relation to family composition, ideology, sex roles, and class differences. Compare your family to Mexican American families in relation to familism, fertility, family governance, child rearing, and education. Compare your family with Chinese American families in relation to child-rearing practices, education, housing, health, and women's roles. Compare your family to Native American families in relation to schools and education, family life, and conflict with the culture in which you live.

1. Low socioeconomic status refers to low social class, including cultural deprivation, and low income. Such families are characterized by much stress, insecurity, and powerlessness. Youths from these families tend to marry young and have children early. Men and women from these families tend to be traditional in their views of sex roles in the family. Child-rearing patterns may emphasize imperatives, absolutes, obedience, and physical punishment to make children behave, with little thought to personality development. Educational levels of the children are low, thus perpetuating the cycle of poverty and deprivation.

2. Black Americans are the largest racial minority in the United States. There has been a marked increase in the number and percentage of one-parent black families. The acute shortage of marriageable black men leaves large numbers of black women, especially the educated ones, without husbands. There are considerable differences among black families, depending upon class. Black families show a number of strengths: strong kinship bonds, a favorable attitude toward the elderly, adaptable roles, strong achievement orientation, strong religious orientation, and a love of children.

3. Familism (putting the needs of the family above those of the individual) is common among Mexican Americans. Extended family networks are common and sometimes include *compadres* (godparents). Divorce rates are lower among Mexican Americans than among blacks or Puerto Ricans. There is also a higher proportion of singles and lower porportion of widowed or divorced persons than in the general population. A high fertility rate results in large families. Historically, the Mexican American family was patriarchal, with the dominant male trying to prove his *machismo* (manhood). The most recent views suggest male dominance, but the male exercises his authority in a fair manner; fathers are warm, nurturing, and playful in relation to their children. The most important role of the woman is in the home. Educational levels of Mexican American children lag behind those of much of the population.

4. The Chinese American population has a greater percentage of college graduates, a lower rate of unemployment, and a greater percentage of families with incomes over $25,000 per year than does the general population. Well-educated Chinese Americans have lower rates of divorce, mental illness, and public assistance, and have more conservative sexual values, a lower fertility rate, less illegitimacy, and more conservative attitudes toward women than is true in the general population. They have a high sense of duty to family. Methods of child rearing tend to be traditional, although the more Americanized parents are more nurturing and use more positive approaches to development of their children. Racial discrimination against Chinese is evident in housing. Health care is often poor. Chinese women seek equality but don't want to abandon their culture.

5. Forty-five percent of Native Americans live in the West and Southwest. Some live on reservations, others among the general population. Large numbers have migrated to urban areas where they have encountered many problems. They have the highest birthrate, the highest death rate, and the shortest life expectancy; suffer more hunger and malnutrition; and have a lower standard of living than any other minority group in the U.S. High-quality education is lacking, although some improvements

have been made. Various family forms exist depending upon the tribe. Some families are matrilineal, and extended families are common. Children are often raised by relatives even if they don't live together in the parents' household. The aged are important leaders of the people. Native Americans are making a determined effort to retain their culture, but have been in conflict with the white man who seeks to enculturate them.

SUGGESTED READINGS

Gary, L., Beatty, L., Berry, G., and Price, M. (1983). *Stable Black Families.* Final report. Institute for Urban Affairs and Research. Washington, DC: Howard University. A factual report.

Horowitz, R. (1983). *Honor and the American Dream.* New Brunswick, NJ: Rutgers University Press. Mexican American families.

Komarovsky, M. (1967). *Blue-collar Marriage.* New York: Vintage Books. Study of 58 working-class families.

McAdoo, H. P. (ed.). (1981). *Black Families.* Beverly Hills, CA: Sage. Twenty articles on a variety of issues and differences in black families.

Rubin, L. B. (1976). *World of Pain: Life in the Working-class Family.* New York: Basic Books. Comparison of 50 working-class families with 25 professional middle-class families.

Sih, P.K.T., and Allen, L. B. (1976). *The Chinese in America.* New York: St. John's University Press. Background and situation.

Staples, R. (1981). *The World of Black Singles: Changing Patterns in Male-Female Relations.* Westport, CT: Greenwood Press. College-educated single black Americans.

Staples, R., and Mirande, A. (1980). Racial and cultural variations among American families: A decennial review of the literature on minority families. *Journal of Marriage and the Family, 42,* 887–903. Research findings on the black family, Chicano family, and Asian American families.

Willie, C. U. (1981). *A New Look at Black Families* (2nd ed.). Bayside, NY: General Hall. Eighteen case studies of contemporary black families from different income levels.

3

FAMILY BACKGROUNDS AND HOW THEY INFLUENCE US

KEY TERMS

generational transmission
reciprocal parent-child interaction
observational modeling
sex role
misogynist

The marital relationship neither exists nor evolves in isolation. It has a family in back of it and one in front of it (Klagsburn, 1985). Every marriage is influenced by the family backgrounds the partners bring to the relationship. Each couple, in turn, influences the family relationships their children will establish after them.

The first purpose of this chapter is to examine a representative variety of family relationships to illustrate possible effects of these on the family relationships of the next generation. The second purpose of this chapter is to stimulate and facilitate the examination of our own family backgrounds to see how they have influenced us.

WHY EXAMINE FAMILY BACKGROUND?

Understanding the Socializing Influence of the Family

The family is the chief socializing influence on children. This means that the family is the principal transmitter of knowledge, values, attitudes, roles, and habits that one generation passes on to the next. Through word and example the family shapes children's personality and instills modes of thought and ways of acting that become habitual. Peterson and Rollins (1987) refer to this process as **generational transmission**.

This learning takes place partly through formal instruction that parents provide their children and partly by the efforts of parents to control children through rewards and punishments. Learning also takes place through **reciprocal parent-child interaction** as each influences and modifies the behavior of the other in an intense social process (Stryker, 1980). Learning also occurs through **observational modeling**, as children observe, imitate, and model the behavior that they find around them (Bandura, 1976). It is not only what parents say that is important, but it is also what children actually perceive parents to believe and do that most influences them.

Every marriage is influenced by the family backgrounds the partners bring to the relationship. Will these children be influenced by their grandparents? How much of what the parents learned as children will be passed on to the young?

Because children observe, imitate, and model the behavior of their parents, parents have the opportunity to exert both positive and negative influence over their children.

Determining Differential Effects

Not all children are influenced to the same degree by their families. For one thing, the degree of influence that parents exert depends partly on the frequency, duration, intensity, and priority of social contacts with their children. Parents who are emotionally close to their children, in loving relationships, for long periods of time, exert more influence than do those not so close who relate to their children less frequently. For another thing, family influence may be either modified or reinforced by influences outside the family: the school, church, other social organizations, peer groups, or the mass media. Here again, the extent of influence depends partly upon the duration and intensity of the exposure.

Another important factor in determining the influence of the family is the difference in individual children (Chess, 1984). Not all children react in the same way to the same family environment due to differences in temperament, cognitive perception, developmental characteristics, and maturational levels. Because A happens does not mean that B will inevitably result. When children are brought up in an unhappy, conflicting family, it is more difficult for them to establish happy marriages themselves (Fine and Hovestadt, 1984). However, some do. A person's marital fate is not cast in concrete, resisting all efforts to change it. Divorce also seems to run in families; those whose parents are divorced are most likely to get divorced themselves (Glenn and Shelton, 1983). Children from divorced homes more easily accept divorce for themselves when their marriages break down (Greenberg and Nay, 1982). However, many of the children do establish stable marriages themselves.

Not all children are influenced by their families to the same degree, and not all react the same way to the same environment. However, whatever it is, background has an effect. The first task in developing self-understanding is for us to determine what effects our families have had on us and to evaluate these and the dynamics of their development.

What we have learned in our family of origin may be either helpful or detrimental to subsequent group living. Thus, a family may instill qualities of truth or deceit, of kindness or cruelty, of cooperation or self-centeredness, or of tolerance or obstinancy (Elliot, 1986). In relation to marriage and family living itself, the family may teach flexible or rigid sex roles. It may exemplify and teach democratic or authoritarian power patterns. It may teach rational communication skills or habits of destructive conflict. The family may teach children how to express love and affection or how to withhold it. The family may teach responsibility or irresponsibility, that sex is healthy and pleasurable or dirty and painful. The family helps children develop positive self-images and self-esteem or negative images. The family may teach the value of work and the wise management of money, or how to avoid work and mismanage money. The family may teach children what a happy marriage can be like, or the extent to which marriage can be a miserable experience (Gadpaille, 1982); Ganong, Coleman, and Brown, 1981). By examining family background we can determine the extent and directions of influence of our family of origin.

Assuming Personal Responsibility

Another task for us is to begin to choose for ourselves the goals and directions we want to take and to assume responsibility for our own selves. We can't continue to blame our parents for our problems if these problems are ever to be solved (Caplan, 1986). Nor can we assume that everything will be all right just because we grew up in a happy home.

When grown children enter into intimate relationships themselves, they bring with them the background of experiences from their own families. There is a tendency for them to feel that the way they were brought up is the right way (which they try to duplicate in their own families) or the wrong way (which they try to avoid). By examining family background, we can develop insight into our own attitudes, feelings, and habits; how these might cause us to respond; and whether we need to change any of these.

One couple in their middle fifties went to a marriage counselor after the wife announced she wanted to divorce her husband. The wife's chief complaint was her husband's authoritarian dominance over the family. The wife explained: "Everything has to be done his way. He never considers my wishes. Several years ago I wanted to remodel the kitchen. It was going to cost five thousand dollars, but I was going to pay for it out of my own salary. He said he didn't want the kitchen remodeled and that was that. Our relationship has always been like that. I never do anything I want to do. So I decided I couldn't stand it any longer. I'm leaving him."

In subsequent counseling sessions, the family backgrounds of the couple were explored. The husband pointed out that his father was a dictator in his family. "I really got so I couldn't stand my father," the husband explained.

"And you're just like him," the wife remarked.

It was difficult for the husband to accept this observation at first, but by talking about his experiences with his dad compared to his present role as a father, he was able to determine that he needed to change himself.

He did, and the marriage survived. (Author's counseling notes)

Making Peace with the Past

Examining family background also enables us to "make peace with our past." For example, if we are afraid of marriage because our parents were unhappily married, examining background experiences helps us to face these anxieties honestly and to rid ourselves of them so that we can dare to marry. Similarly, men who become hostile toward women because of unhappy experiences with their own parents may have difficulty relating to a wife in a positive, warm way. They tend to take out the anger they felt toward their mothers on their wives (Forward, 1986). Facing the past squarely, talking about it, and releasing the anger will often help them to change their feelings and actions.

In this chapter, we look at a variety of family patterns and situations and discuss some of the possible effects of these on individuals. The family situations selected represent only a small fraction of the infinite varieties that exist in real life.

FAMILY CLOSENESS: ATTITUDES TOWARD INTIMACY

The Need for Affection

A common complaint of men and women in intimate relationships is that their partners are not affectionate enough (Kaplan, 1979). By affection, they don't always mean sexual intercourse. They mean touching, holding, hugging, cuddling, kissing, and caressing (Grusky, Bonacich, and Perjiot, 1984). Ann Landers (1985) asked women readers to reply to the question, "Would you be content to be held close and treated tenderly and forget about the act?" Seventy-two percent of 100,000 respondents answered "yes" to the question. This survey revealed that these women wanted to feel cared about, to receive tender and loving embraces more than intercourse with an inexpressive male. Other women have expressed the same complaint: "I am so hungry for him to touch, hug, or hold me. He will not, or cannot touch — not in the bedroom or anywhere else" (Renshaw, 1984, p. 63). Husbands, too, complain of the need for physical expression of affection. One husband complained because he and his wife slept at either end of a king-sized bed with her poodle between. He remarked, "I'm so jealous of the attention, loving, stroking, and petting she gives it . . . I want to touch her, but she will not let me" (Renshaw, 1984, p. 64).

Children's need of physical contact with parents, for "contact comfort," has been well documented (Harlow, 1958). The desire for physical closeness seems to be inborn. It is one way that children feel secure and develop positive self-esteem (Barber and Thomas, 1986). By being loved, children see themselves as both lovable and able to love. By being stroked, carried, cuddled, and loved, the child learns to stroke, caress, cuddle, and love others. Receiving parental love is important in learning how to express affection.

Families vary considerably in the way they express love. Leo Buscaglia (1984), a popular lecturer on love, recalls the physical expressiveness of his large Italian family:

> Everybody hugs everybody all the time. On holidays, everyone gets together, and it takes 45 minutes just to say hello, and 45 minutes to say goodbye. Babies, parents, dogs — everybody's got to be loved! (p. 116)

Undemonstrative Families

Children who grow up in undemonstrative families often have difficulty expressing affection as adults. Males especially have difficulty because they generally receive less affection while growing up than do females (Grusky et al., 1984). They are often brought up to feel that it is "sissy" or "unmanly" to express tender emotions. They are embarrassed if a girlfriend or wife tries to kiss them in public. Women complain that such men show little tenderness or gentleness even in lovemaking. One woman comments:

> All the sex I had with men, they were always on top, bouncing up and down. I always wished a little bit of kissing or even tight holding would go on during it, but the men seemed to be off in their own world (Hite, 1981, p. 346).

Sometimes, the people who grow up in an undemonstrative family have been so starved for affection that they try to make up for this lack when they get married. They expect their spouse to fulfill all those needs that were not met while they were growing up. Their need for affection seems almost insatiable. They want to be with their mate all the time, to be assured and reassured that they are loved. Sometimes, they become so dependent that their love is stifling and smothering. The more they demand affection, the more their partner tries to push them away. When this happens, they end up blaming their mates for not loving them.

The importance of affection in enduring relationships is well established, and it does not always mean sexual intercourse. It can also mean touching, holding, hugging, and caressing.

While the need for affection is inborn, learning ways of expressing it is not. We can learn to express affection, but it takes conscious effort and considerable motivation if we didn't learn to do so when growing up. Sometimes therapy is needed to help us unlock, accept, and express our feelings.

FAMILY ATTITUDES TOWARD SEX

Positive Attitudes and Teachings

Attitudes about sex and sexual expression are also developed partly at home from the time children are young. Some parents are very matter-of-fact about the body and nudity. They don't get upset if preschool children see them nude or walk in on them while they are in the shower or going to the bathroom. Young children have no embarrassment at exposing their bodies or at seeing their siblings naked. Their interest in how other people look is a naive innocence, motivated by curiosity. Their interest soon turns to boredom when their curiosity is satisfied. Gradually, as they get older, they usually want some privacy.

Similarly, parents who exhibit matter-of-fact attitudes toward bodily functions are helping their children develop accepting feelings toward these things. We know, for example, that parents who prepare their daughters for menstruation in a positive way (Ruble and Brooks-Gunn, 1982), or their sons for nocturnal emissions, minimize any negative emotional reactions that otherwise might accompany these. Similarly, parents who try to give positive instruction about human reproduction, masturbation, and sexual response and expression are helping their children accept their sexuality in a positive way as part of their lives.

Negative Attitudes and Teachings

At the opposite extreme are parents who try to repress any interest, thoughts, or feelings about human sexuality. They never allow anyone in the family to see anyone else nude (not even the baby). Toileting always takes place behind closed doors. Dressing and undressing are strictly private, with the sexes separated. Children are brought up to feel that touching the genitals, or playing with them, is wrong or dirty. A baby boy innocently holds his penis; his father slaps his hand and shouts, "Don't do that, it's dirty." A baby girl scratches her itchy vagina. Her mother pulls her hand away and warns, "Nice girls don't do that" (F. P. Rice, 1978a). Normal childhood curiosity about the facts of human reproduction is denied and repressed. The children wouldn't dare ask any questions about sexual arousal, response, and expression.

Possible Effects on Sexual Behavior

Many parents who initiate sexual discussions with their children, especially with adolescents, do so primarily to try to prevent early sexual activity and pregnancy (Fox, 1980). Data from several research studies indicate that these effects are only minimally successful (Furstenberg, Herceg-Baron, Shea, and Webb, 1984; Newcomer and Udry, 1984, 1985). One national survey of 15-

and 16-year-olds did reveal that daughters of traditional parents who had communicated with them about sex were less likely to have had intercourse than were those whose parents had not talked to them (Moore, Peterson, and Furstenberg, 1986). However, family communication about sex had little influence on discouraging early sexual activity of sons.

There is ample clinical evidence to show that repressive sex education can have a detrimental effect on mature sexual functioning (Kaplan, 1979). In trying to prevent their children from being sexually promiscuous or especially in trying to prevent their daughters from "getting into trouble," some parents unwittingly make it harder for their children to achieve mature and loving sexual adjustments (Darling and Hicks, 1982). One teenage girl remarked:

> Every time I go out the door my mother says to me, "Now don't get into trouble, don't let anything bad happen to you." After several weeks of this I asked her: "Exactly what do you mean, Mother?" and she replied: "I mean don't let any boy touch you." (Author's counseling notes)

Without realizing it, in trying to "keep her daughter out of trouble," the mother was also making it harder for her to relate to any man in a warm, loving way. Another mother told her daughter over and over again, "All men are lechers and filthy-minded. All they are interested in is one thing." As a result of this mother's teaching, this daughter never dated throughout high school; she dressed in "granny dresses," wore gold-rimmed glasses, braided her hair, wore shawls and "hippie style" beads and clothes. Only when she went away to college was she able to get out from under her mother's influence and begin to date.

The effects of negative, repressive sex education vary from person to person. Fortunately, many persons, given time, and sometimes therapeutic assistance, are able to overcome the effects of quite repressive upbringing. The

Knowledge and attitudes about sex are developed from the time children are young. When and in what setting should children learn about sex and sexual expressions?

important question is: Was I brought up with positive or negative attitudes about sex and how has this influenced me?

SEX ROLE SOCIALIZATION IN THE FAMILY

Sex role refers to a person's outward expression of maleness or femaleness in a social setting. Traits and behavior thought to be appropriate for a male are considered masculine. Those that are thought to be appropriate for a female are considered feminine. However, sex roles vary according to cultural expectations and are developed partly by environmental influences, the most important of which is the family. Children learn expected sex roles through identifying with parents and modeling their behavior (Klein and Shulman, 1981).

Sex role learning in the family can be divided into three categories:

Children develop masculine or feminine personality traits. Children are taught how men and women are supposed to look and act; they also learn the attitudes, values, and behavior considered appropriate for their gender. Of course, roles are highly variable, depending upon societal teachings and expectations.

Children learn masculine or feminine sex roles and responsibilities in marriage and family living. This includes decision-making roles, the division of household responsibilities, parental responsibilities, and others.

Children learn vocational roles of men and women in our culture.

This child is learning that doing laundry is a family job, not a "mommy" role. What children are taught about common household tasks has a lot to do with their adult attitudes.

The extent to which identification and modeling take place depends upon the amount of time parents spend with their child and the intimacy and intensity of the contact. It also depends upon the relative influence that parents exert (Acock, Barker, and Bengston, 1982). High-status parents exert more influence than do low-status parents (Tomeh, 1978). Mothers employed outside the home have more prestige and so exert more influence on their children than do nonworking mothers. The parent with more education is able to exert more influence (Lueptow, 1980; Smith and Self, 1980). Of course, the gender concepts the child learns depend upon the patterns of role models exemplified. A girl who closely identifies with a masculine mother becomes only weakly identified with a typically feminine personality. One brought up by a mother who is a professional career woman will have a less stereotyped concept of femininity than will one whose mother is primarily a homemaker. Similarly, a boy brought up by a father who represents very traditional ideas of masculinity and of the role of the husband and father in the family will likely develop quite different concepts than will a boy brought up by an egalitarian parent.

Expectations

Sex role expectations are in a state of flux, with many persons advocating a more egalitarian sharing of income earning, household chores, and child rearing (Cook, 1985). In actual practice, role performance has not kept up with ideology. Large numbers of people still hold tenaciously to traditional concepts of the roles husband and wife play in the family (Caplow et al., 1982). See Chapter 12 for a more detailed discussion.

Individual Evaluation

The important question for each person to answer is: What did I learn from my family? What role am I expected to play in my marriage as a male or female spouse or parent? The real problem in marriage arises when the role enactments of husbands and wives, and fathers and mothers, are different from role expectations of others.

VARIATIONS IN FAMILY VALUES AND WORK HABITS

Workaholic Families

Patterns of work and industry may also be developed in one's family of origin. One husband described his family situation.

> When I was growing up, all I ever did was work — from the time I was eight years old. My parents had a corner grocery store. I was expected to come right home from school and help my parents in the store. I never had time to play, or have fun like other kids. When I was in high school, I never could join any

clubs or participate in activities. I had to work. The store was open seven days a week from eight o'clock in the morning until nine at night. That's where I spent my childhood when I wasn't in school. (Author's counseling notes)

This husband had never learned how to play. When his wife wanted him to take time off to enjoy social activities and have fun, he felt very guilty doing it. He could never relax and enjoy himself. His wife felt isolated and alone because she and her husband never had any companionship. The wife complained, "He gives everything to his job: all of his time and energy. By the time he works eighty hours a week he's exhausted. He has nothing left to give me" (Author's counseling notes).

Laid-Back Families

At the opposite extreme are those families where work is avoided as much as possible, where major effort is invested only in finding ways and means of getting out of doing things. Family members work just enough to get by, or they work long enough to become eligible for unemployment and then quit working until their benefits are exhausted.

Family Values

The work habits that people develop are related to family goals and values. Some people are never happy unless they reach a high level of material prosperity and own many things. They want to live in a large house, to have fine clothes and luxury cars, and to take expensive vacations. They are used to a certain standard of living in their family of origin and seek to duplicate this life-style in their own marriage. They are willing to work to achieve what they want. Other people want similar things but have never learned to

---

PERSPECTIVE
Different Values

Research indicates that having an adequate income is helpful to marital satisfaction, but that marital satisfaction is not always the greatest when income is the highest. Many spouses want love more than a lot of money. In relation to income, what is important is whether the husband and wife agree that the level they have achieved is satisfactory (Jorgensen, 1979). The real problem arises when a husband and wife each have different values in relation to their standard of living and work ethic. If both the husband and wife are workaholics, they may not have much time for leisure activities and a social life; but if they're happy with one another, there is no real problem. If their life goals and life-styles are similar, they can both be content with the level at which they are living. If they both lack ambition, have very inadequate work habits, and agree on just laying back and enjoying life without too much effort or without many material possessions, at least they're compatible. A problem may arise when they have been brought up with different values systems.

Orientation toward work and life-style are most influenced by the way we are brought up. It's helpful to explore our family background and philosophies in trying to evaluate compatibility.

develop work habits and assume the responsibilities necessary to fulfill their expectations. Other people have more modest goals, which they're willing to work just hard enough to achieve. They are quite content with a modest life-style and income.

Parental Role Models

The role models parents provide are crucial in establishing life goals and work patterns in their children. Children whose parents have high expectations and standards of work performance tend to adopt these standards themselves (Bandura, 1976). One man commented, "My father and mother both went to college and held good jobs when we were growing up. They always assumed that we would go to college too, and make something of ourselves. And we all did. They also taught us how to do physical labor around the house." In contrast to this family, some parents present lenient standards of performance, whether on a job or at home. They place less value on working hard, doing a good job, and getting ahead in life.

COMMUNICATIVE, NONCOMMUNICATIVE, AND CONFLICTING FAMILIES

Effective communication is one of the most important requirements in intimate relationships (Montgomery, 1981). Couples who are close usually have good verbal and nonverbal communication, talk enough and listen carefully, discuss important issues, understand one another, show sensitivity to one another's feelings, say positive things to one another, and keep open the channels of communication (Snyder, 1979). Chapter 17 discusses communication in more detail.

The patterns of communication that exist in a family also influence communication patterns that the children establish in families of their own. These communication patterns may be divided into six basic categories.

Open, Honest, Tactful Communication

Family members are able to reveal what they think and how they really feel, but in a tactful, sensitive manner. They voice their concerns and worries and talk about important issues. They each can talk about themselves, their lives, and know that others will listen and understand.

Superficial Communication

In these families, the members talk a lot, but never about anything important. They avoid disclosing themselves and discussing "gut" issues. Because of denial, fear, or distrust, they haven't learned to share their concerns. They are taught to be independent, to be strong, and to handle their own problems themselves. As a result, their family conversations avoid discussing feelings and problems. When someone asks: "How is everything?" the answer is usually "just fine," even though it may not be true. As a result, no one really knows or understands what the others are thinking and feeling.

One-Sided Communication

In this situation, one person does all the talking while the others listen. A wife may do all the talking and not give her husband a chance to express his opinions. He either sits passively or tries to withdraw so he won't have to hear it. A man's ideal of talking to his wife or children may be to give them lectures, to talk to them rather than with them. He wants to tell them something, but he doesn't really want to discuss anything. If others try to talk, they are criticized for interrupting or talking back, and so they have learned to be quiet. When children marry and establish their own families, they often repeat their passive roles in family interaction or model their behavior after their talkative parent and dominate the conversation in their own families.

False Communication

In this pattern, family members have learned to lie to keep out of trouble. If they were punished or ridiculed when they told the truth, they have learned to make up stories or to tell others what they thought they wanted to hear. Sometimes they said just the opposite of what they really felt to give false impressions.

Avoidance of Communication

In this pattern, family members have learned not to talk about sensitive issues because it leads to quarreling or a fight. They hate arguments and so avoid touchy, controversial subjects. They squelch their own ideas and feelings for the sake of family harmony. They try to escape from problems, to deny them, and hope they will go away. They are taught to inhibit honest feelings and to keep everything in. It's very difficult to resolve any issues, because they are never discussed (Jorgensen and Gaudy, 1980).

Noncommunication

Some people in families are nonverbal people. Some haven't learned how to talk or to express themselves, so they seldom discuss anything. Sometimes they are basically shy or afraid others won't like them or accept them, or will criticize them and think they are stupid. As a result, they keep quiet.

Here again, the important question is: What patterns of communication existed in my family while growing up and how has this affected me?

PERSPECTIVE
Self-Disclosure

Successful communication in intimate relationships depends partly on the willingness to reveal one's self voluntarily, to risk private information and feelings in order to build companionship, affective exchange, understanding, and acceptance. However, self-disclosure needs to be mutual and positive, reflecting deep acceptance and commitment to the relationship (Galvin and Brommel, 1986).

Littlejohn (1983) has summarized the findings of research on self-disclosure as follows:

1. Disclosure increases with increased relational intimacy.
2. Disclosure increases when rewarded.
3. Disclosure increases with the need to reduce uncertainty in a relationship.
4. Disclosure tends to be reciprocal.
5. Women tend to be higher disclosers than men.
6. Women disclose more with individuals they like, whereas men disclose more with people they trust.
7. Disclosure is regulated by norms of appropriateness.
8. Attraction is related to positive disclosure but not to negative disclosure.
9. Positive disclosure is more likely in nonintimate or moderately intimate relationships.
10. Negative disclosure occurs with greater frequency in highly intimate settings than in less intimate ones.
11. Satisfaction and disclosure have a curvilinear relationship; that is, relational satisfaction is greatest at moderate levels of disclosure.

THE CONTROLLING, ABUSIVE FAMILY

Men Who Control and Abuse Women

Men who have learned to hate women are called **misogynists**. The term comes from the Greek words *miso*, meaning to hate, and *gyny*, meaning woman. Misogynists are hostile, aggressive, contemptuous, and cruel in their relationships with women. They usually show their hatred through (1) their efforts to control women and (2) abuse of them. The misogynist seeks total control of a woman's life: what she does, how she behaves, and how she thinks and feels. His control is established through fear, humiliation, and physical and psychological abuse (Burns, 1983). Physical abuse includes violence and bodily harm. Psychological abuse includes yelling, threatening harm, verbal attacks, name calling, and constant criticism. If the misogynist is confronted with what he does, he often denies that it is happening, or he blames the woman. He seeks to exercise his control in the bedroom by criticizing his partner's lovemaking, by satisfying his own needs and denying hers, by sexual brutality, or through constant demands for sex. He seeks to gain financial control by withholding money, or even by controlling what she earns as well. He seeks control over her social life by choosing her friends, and limiting her social activities and contacts with her family. He is jealous of his own children and may abuse them as well as attack their mother (Forward, 1986).

What about the women who are abused? What are they like, and why do they allow themselves to be mistreated? The abused woman is confused about herself and her partner. Sometimes her partner is nice to her and says he loves her and needs her; at other times he is abusive. He tries to make her feel that the reason he gets violent and abusive is because she makes him angry, because she does something wrong. She comes to feel that he's doing it to try to make her a better person. She doesn't want to be hurt (she's not a masochist), so she searches for the right way to behave so her partner will be consistently loving. She feels that he's good and she's bad. She doesn't confront him or question his behavior. Her security depends upon his approval, so she is compliant and renounces her own wishes. She gives up her freedom if he demands she quit her job or give up her activities, interests, and friends. Every part of her life is affected by his control. Her self-confidence and self-esteem continue to drop because he makes her feel that she is a bad person and everything is her fault. She doesn't leave him because she hopes things will change, because she feels if she just tries harder everything will be all right, because she's afraid she'll lose his love, and because she's fearful of what he might do to her (Forward, 1986).

How Men Learn to Hate Women

In most cases, men learn to hate women because of their relationship with their own parents while growing up (Bernard and Bernard, 1983). Often the boy's father is a misogynist himself. The father's philosophy is, "Somebody has to be in charge in our family, and it is I." The father believes that his way is the only way. He has contempt for women, whom he sees as helpless and treacherous and not to be trusted. For him, the way to control women is to abuse them.

Sometimes the father is abusive toward his son as well as toward his mother. If the frightened boy seeks protection from his mother and she is passive, he gets no reassurance from her. The abused mother has abdicated her rights and power and can't protect her children from their father. She becomes like a helpless child; and instead of trying to meet her son's needs, she turns to him to meet hers, to give her comfort, protection, and care, and to make her happy. She makes her son feel that it is his responsibility to look after her, instead of the other way around.

Sometimes the parental roles are reversed. The mother becomes the controlling, abusive parent, and the father is passive. The mother terrorizes her son. Severe punishment makes him helpless, inadequate, and afraid. The more cruel she is toward him, the more the son is bound to her in his search for love and approval. Other mothers control through smothering, overindulgence, and overprotection. They dominate every aspect of their son's life, and make him feel inadequate and helpless. The mother prevents him from developing control over his own life, so that the boy doesn't learn how to make decisions or to deal with disappointments.

Most men who hate women learned to do so from their fathers. Will this woman endure abuse from a man who has contempt for women, or will she seek help? Can or should this marriage be saved?

The cold, rejecting mother is just the opposite. She withholds love and approval and frustrates his needs so much that he cannot cope. If he tries to express normal needs, she may punish him for "acting like a baby," so he gets the message that to have needs is unacceptable. As a result, he tries to defend himself against any feelings of vulnerability. He denies all warm feelings and at the same time denies his partner's needs.

Whether the father is the misogynist and the mother is passive — or the mother is smothering or cold, cruel, and rejecting and the father is passive — the son suffers because his needs are not met. He feels vulnerable because he has no parent to protect him from the wrath of the other. He is filled with rage and humiliated by the treatment he receives. He grows up an angry person.

When he enters into a relationship with a partner or marries, he may transfer the feelings he has toward his mother to his female partner. These feelings include fear that he can't depend upon her any more than he could his mother. He is afraid of dependency, afraid of abandonment, afraid of being alone, and afraid he can't cope. As a result, he tries to gain control over his partner, to destroy her self-confidence, so she can never leave him and he will be safe. He is caught in a bind between his need to feel loved, to be taken care of and to feel safe, and his fear of her. He is afraid that if he loves a woman, she will have the power to hurt him, to smother him, to leave him; and thus his goal is to make her less powerful so that she will become dependent on him. If he makes her weak, he loses his fear of abandonment (Forward, 1986).

CLASSROOM FORUM
The Cruel Husband and the Passive Wife

Sam and Barbara had been married for 12 years. They had two daughters and one son — five, seven, and nine years old. Barbara was a warm, maternal woman, very easygoing and passive, with low self-esteem, and with a desire to please her husband and "be a good wife," though, according to Sam, she was not.

Sam was cruel to the extreme. He was cold, rejecting, critical, and abusive. While he had never actually hit her, he was verbally abusive. Barbara was slightly plump. Sam would call her a pig in front of everyone they met. He would call her on the phone and say, "Oink, Oink. You pig."

In talking about Barbara, Sam said that as far as he was concerned, she was a "nonperson." "She's an it, a thing. For me she's just like a stick of furniture."

Sam had been in the army in Vietnam. After his tour of duty, he enrolled for another hitch, because he liked it over there. He was sorry when the war was over. Sam described his experiences: "I can rape, I can murder, I can pillage. It doesn't bother me a bit. It's really exciting."

Barbara couldn't understand why Sam was so mean to her. "I try to be a good wife. What am I doing wrong?" (Author's counseling notes)

DISCUSSION

1. Why does Sam want to stay married even though he is cruel to his wife?
2. Why does Barbara put up with Sam's abuse?
3. If you were counseling Sam and Barbara, what would you want to accomplish in the counseling process?
4. What sort of help does Sam need? Barbara need?

Women Who Hate Men

A girl's relationships with her own parents also has a profound influence on how she feels about men. Contempt, hatred, or distrust of men develop in several ways. If a girl's father is a misogynist and is controlling and abusive to her or her mother, she may grow up with an intense dislike for her father and transfer these same feelings to all men, including her partner. In other instances, the father may be cold and rejecting so that the daughter can never depend on him to fulfill her own needs for love and affection. Or, if a girl's mother hates men and takes out her hostility and contempt for men on her husband, the daughter may model her own behavior after her mother and develop contempt for her father because he is weak and doesn't stand up to his wife. The daughter dislikes him because he doesn't defend her from her mother's attacks. The daughter grows to feel that men are weak and useless, and she loses all respect and warm feelings for them because of her relationship with her father.

Sexually Abused Daughters

Sometimes girls are sexually abused by their father, an older brother, an uncle, grandfather, or stepfather. The effects of the abuse will depend upon who is abusive, in what manner, and for how long (Kilpatrick, 1987). Some sex play involving mutual consent between brothers and sisters who are close in age is not uncommon. When an experience is exploitative, when an older sibling blackmails, bribes, or forces the other to comply, the effects may be quite negative.

> Diane, a woman of 23, was molested by two older brothers from the time she was 6 until age 13. The molestation included intercourse with her older brother. When her brother told her father that she had her clothes off, the father beat her. When she told her uncle at age 14, he began where her brother left off. Intercourse with him continued until she was 17. Diane has been hospitalized in psychiatric wards five times since age 17. Her psychiatrist describes her as "devoid of all meaningful social relationships . . . helpless, empty, quite depleted, suicidal . . . depressed." (Siegall, 1977)

Much of the research on incest has focused on father-daughter relationships. The father is often a dependent, shy, socially incompetent man. His sexual relationship with his own wife is usually unsatisfactory. In such situations, he turns to his daughter for affection and sex. If the mother chooses not to believe her daughter's accounts, or if the mother knows and encourages or does nothing about the situation, the girl becomes even more embittered (Herman and Hirschman, 1977; Meiselman, 1978).

Long-term effects of forceful, hurtful, exploitative relationships can be severe (Kilpatrick, 1986). The girl may carry a burden of guilt, shame, bitterness, anger, and lowered self-esteem for years. It becomes hard to trust any man or to let men touch her (Tsai and Wagner, 1978).

ASSESSMENT
What About My Family?

We have talked about two different kinds of combinations of parents: one where the father is a misogynist and the mother passive, and the other where the mother is cold, cruel, and rejecting and the father passive. Did either combination exist in your family, and how has this affected you and your attitudes toward men and women?

Did you suffer any sexual abuse while growing up? If so, how have you been affected?

THE ALCOHOLIC FAMILY

In recent years, a number of books have been written for adult children of alcoholics. (See Ackerman, 1983; Gravitz and Bowden, 1985; Seixas and Youcha, 1985; Woititz, 1983). These books describe some of the possible effects of growing up in an alcoholic family and how the negative influences can be overcome.

Some Characteristics of Adult Children of Alcoholics

Woititz (1983) discusses 13 common characteristics of adult children of alcoholics (p. 4). The reader is cautioned that while these are frequent character-

There may be negative effects on children who grow up in alcoholic families. Children of alcoholics can only guess at what is normal, and they may grow up believing that consumption of alcohol is normal and necessary.

istics of adult children of alcoholics, not every child is affected to the same extent and in exactly the same way. Each person who has been raised in an alcoholic family needs to evaluate the effect on him or her personally.

Adult children of alcoholics can only guess at what normal behavior is. They have no experience by which thay can judge what a normal home life is like. Their family situation was always tense and upset. They never knew when they walked in the door whether a parent would be passed out on the floor, would be drunk and start a fight, or would be warm and loving; in fact they never knew whether the alcoholic parent would come home at all. Life was never predictable, resulting in anxiety and insecurity.

When children of alcoholic parents get married themselves, they have no positive frame of reference to guide them in establishing harmonious relationships. What is a good wife supposed to be and do? What is a good husband supposed to be and do? What is a good marriage? They don't know. Never knowing whether their marriage is normal or not, they tend to live in anxiety and fear that they will fail. If they follow the example set by their parents, they duplicate some of the same turmoil under which they grew up.

They may have difficulty following a project through. They tend to be procrastinators. In this regard, they have become like their alcoholic parent, who made a lot of promises but never followed through.

They often lie when it would be just as easy to tell the truth. Denial that a problem exists is the great defense of the alcoholic. Denial, covering up, and lying are also the way the alcoholic's family avoids reality, unpleasantness, and having to face the problem. Children become part of the masquerade and deception to keep others from knowing. They also learn to lie to stay out of trouble.

When these same children get married, their well-developed habit of lying is not conducive to establishing an honest, trusting relationship.

They tend to judge themselves without mercy. When they were growing up, they were never good enough and were always criticized. As a result, they grew up with negative self-images. Some become perfectionists, constantly striving to meet impossible standards. Others quit trying to please. They are so immobilized with fear that they are afraid to try anything, and so they operate well below the levels of which they are capable.

They may have difficulty having fun. Childhood was never fun; they never learned to laugh and play, to relax and enjoy life. There were too many problems. As adults, they still cannot let themselves go and have difficulty participating in social and recreational activities.

They take themselves very seriously. This characteristic is linked to not having fun. Life is a trauma. Spontaneity has been squashed. Pressure to be adult has kept the child repressed: life is serious business.

They often have difficulty with intimate relationships. As children, they felt loved one day and rejected the next. Woititz (1983) refers to this as a push-pull experience. "I want you — go away." As a result, they grow up with a terrible need to feel close, but are afraid of it. Some become so dependent that they make their partner feel smothered. Others make certain not to let their partner get emotionally close to them.

They constantly seek approval and affection. Their negative feelings about themselves motivate them to seek repeated affirmation of their worth. Even if they get it, however, they may feel that the person giving it is not very discerning, and so they reject the approval they so desperately need.

They feel they are different from other people, so they have difficulty with social relationships. They isolated themselves socially while they were growing up; consequently, they have not developed the social skills needed to feel comfortable with others. When they do socialize, they may pick inappropriate role models. One man explained what he did when he was a teenager:

> All the people I hung out with were worse than I was. I picked out all the teenage alcoholics, the guys that drank codeine cough syrup, women who could not have close sexual relationships with men. I was very frustrated as an adolescent. I picked out the fat ones. I would not dare to date a good-looking woman. I still have very few friends. (Woititz, 1983, p. 47)

They are either extremely responsible or extremely irresponsible. Because their parents were so critical, the children did more and more to try to please them. As adults, they either continue to do the same thing, or they have quit trying and accomplish little of what they are supposed to do. When married, these same adults may constantly strive to please their spouse and can't say no to their children, or they rebel and refuse to do what is ordinarily required.

They are sometimes extremely loyal even though the loyalty is undeserved. This loyalty stems from insecurity and fear. Finding a friend or establishing a relationship is so difficult that when they find someone to be their lover or spouse, they hang on even if they are treated poorly. They are fearful that if the relationship dissolves they will never find another one. They don't know what a good relationship is supposed to be, and so they stay with what they have. Their poor self-images and lack of self-esteem results in their accepting considerable abuse: "I know John hits me, but I deserve it. I get him mad. I'll have to try harder."

They may be impulsive. Children of alcoholics could never predict an outcome of any given behavior; there was never any consistency at home. As adults, they don't know how to plan, because they don't know what the results will be. They tend to lock themselves into courses of action without considering alternatives and consequences. When things don't work out, they spend a lot of energy trying to straighten out the mess. Their impulsiveness results in confusion, loss of control and self-esteem. They don't intend to hurt anyone. The impulsiveness is not deliberate, but it is behavior over which they have no control.

This impulsiveness shows up in many ways. They get married without really knowing the person. They quit one job before getting another one. They make foolish investments. They want immediate gratification because as children they never got what they asked for at the time they wanted it.

They overreact to changes over which they have no control. As children, they never had control; as adults they often try to be controlling, but are rigid. The effort comes from fear that if a change is made, they will lose control.

These are all possible results of being brought up in an alcoholic family. Let's apply these findings to ourselves. Was I brought up in an alcoholic family? If so, what has been the effect on me? Do I manifest any of the 13 characteristics outlined? Have I been able to overcome the negative effects?

Children with negative feelings about themselves have an extraordinary need for approval and affection as an affirmation of their worth.

ASSESSMENT
My Family Background and Its Influence on Me

Describe the family in which you grew up and how your family has influenced you in the following areas:

Your attitudes and feelings about men and women

Your attitudes and feelings about whether you want to marry

Your attitudes and feelings about the qualities you want in an ideal mate

Your attitudes and feelings about the things that are most important in marital success

Your attitudes and feelings about sex

Your attitudes and feelings about using contraceptives

Your attitudes and feelings about husband-wife roles in marriage

Your attitudes and feelings about vocational roles after marriage

Your attitudes and feelings about decision-making roles in marriage

Your attitudes and feelings about whether you want children

Your attitudes and feelings about the characteristics of the ideal father

Your attitudes and feelings about the characteristics of the ideal mother

Your attitudes and feelings about the best ways to bring up children

Your attitudes and feelings about divorce

Your attitudes and feelings about remarriage

Your attitudes and feelings about going to a marriage counselor in times of difficulty

Your habits and skill in interpersonal communication

Your habits and skill in money management

Your habits and skill in social situations

Your habits and skill as a housekeeper

Your habits and skill in child care

SUMMARY

1. The family is the chief socializing influence on children. Examining our own family background helps us understand how our own family has affected us. This is necessary if we are to develop self-understanding, assume responsibility for our own behavior, and make peace with our past.

2. People are born with a need for affection. Some adults have a greater need for affectional expression than others. Husbands or wives sometimes complain that their spouse is not affectionate enough. Expressing affection is behavior that is learned in the family.

3. The family is also instrumental in instilling either positive or negative attitudes about sex, which influence sexual behavior during adolescence and adulthood.

4. The family also has an influence on sex-role socialization. This socialization includes: (1) the development of masculine or feminine personality traits, (2) teaching masculine or feminine sex roles and responsibilities in marriage, and (3) vocational roles of men and women.

5. The role models parents exhibit are crucial in establishing the life goals and work patterns that adults take into their own marriages.

6. Communication patterns are also influenced by one's family of origin. Types of patterns include: open, honest, tactful communication, superficial communication, one-sided communication, false communication, avoidance of communication, and noncommunication.

7. Men who learn to hate women are called misogynists. They express their hatred through control and abuse of women. Women who are abused have little self-confidence or self-esteem. They do everything to get their husbands to love them, because they are afraid of losing their husbands and because they fear what their husbands might do to them.

8. Women may learn to hate men by being brought up in a family where the father is a misogynist and the mother passive, or the mother is a man hater and the father passive. Sexual abuse of daughters is also an important cause of women hating men.

9. Children are affected by alcoholism in their family of origin. Not all children are affected to the same degree in exactly the same way. This chapter discusses thirteen common characteristics of adult children of alcoholics. These characteristics make it more difficult for the adult children of alcoholics to establish successful marriages and happy family relationships themselves.

SUGGESTED READINGS

Buscaglia, L. (1982). *Living, Loving, and Learning.* New York: Fawcett Columbine. The importance of love.

Calderone, M., and Ramey, J. (1982). *Talking With Your Child About Sex.* New York: Random House. A guide for parents.

David, D. S., and Brannon, R. (Eds.). (1976). *The Forty-nine Percent Majority: The Male Sex Role.* Reading, MA: Addison-Wesley. A fascinating analysis of male sex roles in our society.

Forward, S. (1986). *Men Who Hate Women. The Women Who Love Them.* New York: Bantam. Causes, results, help.

Freeman, J. (1984). *Women: A Feminist Perspective* (3rd ed.). Palo Alto, CA: Mayfield. A classic reader dealing with feminism.

Galvin, K. M., and Brommel, B. J. (1986). *Family Communication. Cohesion and Change* (2nd ed.). Glenview, IL: Scott, Foresman. Improving family communication.

Rubin, L. (1983). *Intimate Strangers — Men and Women Together.* New York: Harper. Intimacy and communication between men and women.

Straus, M. A., Gelles, R. J., and Steinmetz, S. K. (1980). *Behind Closed Doors: Violence in the American Family.* New York: Doubleday. Written by the foremost researchers on family violence.

Woititz, J. G. (1983). *Adult Children of Alcoholics.* Pompano Beach, FL: Health Communications. Effects of alcoholism on children and how they may be helped.

4

QUALITIES OF SUCCESSFUL MARRIAGES

KEY TERMS

selfism

affective sensitivity

resonates

noncontingent reinforcement

unconditional positive regard

This book is about relationships: marriage relationships, family relationships, and intimate relationships between unmarried persons. We want to end Part I of this book on a positive note by discussing how we can get along with other people, how we can live together in a harmonious, fulfilling way. Living together is an art, requiring important qualities of character, a high degree of motivation, and finely tuned personal and social skills.

The focus in this chapter is on the marriage relationship itself. However, most of the principles discussed here may be applied to all intimate relationships and to interpersonal relationships in the larger family unit.

CRITERIA FOR EVALUATING MARITAL SUCCESS

Durability

What constitutes a successful marriage? One measure that has been used is durability. The marriage that lasts is considered more successful than one that is broken (Todd, 1982). In many cases, marital stability and marital quality do go together. However, some marriages last a lifetime and are filled with hatred, conflict, and frustration (Bohannon, 1984). I know one husband and wife who are together but haven't spoken to one another, except through the children, for 20 years. For many of us, marriage success includes more important criteria than the number of years a couple stay together, regardless of other aspects of the relationship.

Approximation of Ideals

Another way of evaluating marital success is the extent to which it approximates a couple's ideals or fulfills their expectations. Each couple has its own concepts of an ideal relationship. When asked the question, "What is your concept of a good marriage?" one student replied:

> A good marriage is one in which two people love one another, get along well together, in which they think alike on important issues, share common goals and interests, enjoy each other's company and have fun together, in which they are really good friends, are able to talk to one another to work out problems together.

The answer is fairly typical of student replies. Other students may add to the list. A good marriage is:

One that allows you to be yourself and to be completely honest with one another.

Fifty-fifty, where partners share everything.

One that allows you freedom to do your own thing and to grow.

One where your partner is your best friend

Other students add characteristics that are important to them. Marital success, according to this viewpoint, is determined by the extent to which idealistic expectations are actually fulfilled.

One problem with this viewpoint is that some people have very unrealistic expectations in the first place. The standards by which they judge their marriage are impossible to achieve. Expectations need to be realistic, not just romantic fantasy.

Fulfillment of Needs

Another criterion of marital success is whether the marriage makes a sufficient contribution to individual needs (Ammons and Stinnet, 1980). Human needs may be grouped into categories:

Psychological needs — for love, affection, approval, and self-fulfillment

Social needs — for friendship, companionship, and new experiences

Sexual needs — both physical and psychic needs for sexual fulfillment

Material needs — "room and board" needs and physical maintenance and services

From this point of view, the successful marriage is one that makes an acceptable contribution to psychological, social, sexual, and material need fulfillment. This view assumes that partners are aware of one another's needs and willing and partly able to fulfill them (Tiggle, Peters, Kelley, and Vincent, 1982).

Note the emphasis here on partial fulfillment. Marriage can never meet every need. Some needs will always have to be met apart from the marriage itself. One's job, friendships, hobbies, and recreational pursuits all contribute to need fulfillment. However, a successful marriage makes an acceptable

The number of years a couple stays together is not the most important indicator of marital success. Such qualities as empathy, respect, companionship, and affection are but a few of the characteristics of a successful marriage.

contribution; and any marriage that doesn't, has failed in the eyes of most couples.

Two cautions need to be added. *One*, it is helpful if need fulfillment is mutual (Fowler, 1982). In relationships where one person does all the giving and the other the receiving, the giver often becomes drained, exhausted, and unable to continue. *Two*, mutual need fulfillment is most possible if needs are within the limits of realistic expectations. A highly dependent, possessive person, for example, may demand so much love and approval that no one could possibly fulfill those needs. In this case, the marriage might not succeed, not because of the unwillingness of the giving person to fulfill needs, but because of the insatiable, unreasonable demands of the other partner.

Satisfaction

Much of the research on marriage success measures marital satisfaction: the extent to which couples are content and fulfilled in their relationship (Roach, Frazier, and Bowden, 1981; Spanier and Lewis, 1980). *According to this view, marital success is defined as the extent to which both partners in the relationship are satisfied that it has fulfilled reasonable expectations and mutual needs.* Marital satisfaction is a comprehensive concept and the one accepted here as the criterion for marital success. This definition recognizes that there are individual differences in expectations and need requirements so that what satisfies one couple might not satisfy another. It is important, however, that *both* partners be satisfied. Sometimes one partner is very content with a relationship at the same time the other is ready to file for divorce.

Obviously, there are degrees of success. Few marriages live up to *all* expectations and fulfill *all* needs all the time. Furthermore, successful couples strive for improvement. Their marriages are in the process of becoming, and few ever feel they have completely arrived. However, if they are satisfied with the progress they have made, they judge their effort as successful. More will be said about growth and fulfillment in Chapter 11.

TWELVE CHARACTERISTICS OF SUCCESSFUL MARRIAGES

Numerous research studies have delineated the qualities of successful marriage. In their research, Spanier and Lewis (1980) list 87 probable factors that are related to marital quality. Some of these are background factors. Some outline qualities in the relationship, while others emphasize personality characteristics. Some couples would emphasize particular criteria more than others. Additional factors may exist that research has not yet delineated.

In our discussion here, family background factors that influence marital success have been omitted. Some of these were discussed in Chapter 3. Such factors as age, race, and length of acquaintance have also been omitted, because they are discussed in appropriate chapters. Here we are concerned with a mixture of personality characteristics of the partners and characteristics of the relationship itself. Together they constitute qualities important to marital success.

The latest studies show a remarkable consistency. They reveal that successful marriages exhibit many similar qualities. Twelve of these qualities are described in this chapter.

Table 4.1 shows a comparison of four representative studies. The twelve characteristics of successful marriages are listed in the left-hand column. The findings of each study are summarized in the other vertical columns under the authors of each study. Study 1 by Bell, Daly, and Gonzalez (1987) described the strategies married couples use to maintain the quality of their bonds. Data were obtained from two groups. The first group (130 females and 32 males) consisted of 144 married people and 18 individuals cohabiting with their romantic partner. The second group comprised 109 married females (median age 33.9 years) in graduate courses at an eastern U.S. university. Ninety-five of these women were in their first marriage; 12 had been married once before; two were in their fourth marriage. Participants completed measures of marital quality and evaluated the frequency and importance of each strategy used.

Study 2 by Lauer and Lauer (1985) was a survey of 351 couples with enduring marriages. The study summarized the factors that kept the couples together. Three hundred of the couples said they were happily married, 19 said they were unhappily married but staying together for a variety of reasons, such as "for the sake of the children." Among the remaining 32 couples, only one partner said he or she was unhappy in the marriage.

Study 3 by Curran (1983) reported on the responses of 500 professionals who work with families to questions designed to determine the qualities of "healthy" families.

Study 4 by Stinnett and DeFrain (1985) reported on a survey of 1,000 families across the United States in a Family Strength Research Project. Some South American families were questioned also.

Four characteristics of successful marriages were mentioned in all four studies: *communication, admiration and respect, companionship,* and *spirituality.* Three characteristics of successful marriages were delineated by three of the studies: *commitment, affection,* and *ability to deal with stress and crises.* Three characteristics of successful marriages were described in two of the studies: *responsibility, unselfishness,* and *empathy and sensitivity.* Two characteristics of successful marriages were each described in only one of the studies: *honesty, trust, and fidelity,* and *adaptability and flexibility.*

Commitment

Successful marriage requires a high degree of motivation: the desire to make the marriage work and a willingness to expend personal time and effort to accomplish it. Some couples encounter serious problems in their relationship, so much so that one wonders how their marriage will ever succeed. But through extraordinary motivation and determination, they overcome their obstacles, solve their problems, and emerge with a satisfactory relationship. Other couples give up after very little effort; some of these really didn't want to be married in the first place, so they never really tried.

Marital success is more attainable if the commitment is mutual. One person can't build a relationship or save a marriage, no matter how much he or she tries. In their research with 301 married persons, Sabatelli and Cecil-Pigo (1985) found that when both partners were participating equally in a relationship and when there was maximum interdependence, they were also most committed. People aren't going to put forth their best effort if their partner is not equally involved.

TABLE 4.1 *Characteristics of Successful Marriages: Summary of Findings From Four Studies*

Marital Quality	STUDY			
	Bell et al.	Lauer and Lauer	Curran	Stinnett and DeFrain
Commitment		Marriage is long-term commitment; enduring marriage important; want marriage to succeed	Commitment to family	Commitment to family is most important. Invests time/energy in family
Honesty, Trust, Fidelity	Honest, truthful, sincere			
Responsibility	Dependable in carrying out responsibilities		Share responsibility	
Adaptability, Flexibility, Tolerance				Adaptable, flexible, enables people to bend, change, adjust
Unselfishness	Altruism, assists partner in whatever possible. Gives nice things to partner		Help each other	
Communication	Listens, self-discloses, polite conversation	Confides in spouse, discuss calmly, stimulating exchange of ideas	All listen, respond, respect other's feelings, thinking, avoid turn-offs and put-downs	Good communication technique. Spend time talking, listening, fight fairly
Empathy, Sensitivity	Warm, caring, sensitive			Compassion for others
Admiration, Respect	Builds partner's self-esteem. Supports partner in endeavors	Likes spouse as a person, spouse interesting, proud of spouse's accomplishments	Respect individual differences, privacy, property, institutions of society, admire, support each other	Express appreciation of one another, make one another feel good
Affection	Physical and verbal affection	Agree on expressing affection, sex		Mutual affection, caring
Companionship	Share enjoyable social activities, closeness	Spouse best friend, laugh together, share hobbies, interests	Play together, quality time together	Desire to spend time together
Ability to deal with crises, stress	Cheerful optimist		Expect problems to be normal part of life, develop problem-solving skills	Able to weather storms of life
Spirituality, Values	Share spiritual activities, similar beliefs, values	Marriage is sacred; agree on goals, values, philosophy of life	Strong, shared values manifested in religious behavior. Sense of right and wrong, help others	Strong value system, high degree of religious orientation, religious involvement

Adapted from:
   Bell, R. A., Daly, J. A., and Gonzalez, H. C. (1987). Affinity-maintenance in marriage and its relationship to women's marital satisfaction. *Journal of Marriage and the Family, 49,* 445–454.
   Lauer, J., and Lauer, R. (1985). Marriages made to last. *Psychology Today, 19,* 22–26.
   Curran, D. (1983). *Traits of a healthy family.* New York: Ballantine.
   Stinnett, N., and DeFrain, J. (1985). *Secrets of strong families.* Boston: Little, Brown.

One of the important questions is: To whom and to what is the commitment? The commitment is really threefold:

1. *The commitment is of the self, to the self* — to grow, to change, to be a marriageable person. Some people who come for marriage counseling want their partner to change, but they are unwilling to change themselves or to assume any personal responsibility for making things better. None of us can really change other people if they don't want to change, but we can change ourselves if we need to. It's not easy, but it can be done.

2. *The commitment of the partners is also to one another.* When people say "I do" in a marriage ceremony, they make a personal promise or pledge to one another: to love, honor, cherish, and be faithful under all circumstances of life. Their commitment is a highly personal one (Quinn, 1982).

3. *The commitment is also to the relationship, to the marriage and the family.* The Maces (1980) define commitment as a willingness to grow. They write: "There must be a commitment on the part of the couple to ongoing growth in their relationship . . . there is a tremendous potential for loving, for caring, for warmth, for understanding, for support, for affirmation; yet, in so many marriages of today it never gets developed." Also, when children are involved, the commitment goes beyond the couple relationship to include the whole family unit.

Another question that arises is whether the commitment to the marriage and the family or to one's partner is more important. Mae West described marriage as an institution but asked, "Who wants to live in an institution?" Indeed, who does, unless it serves the needs of those in it? Some people are able to work out troubled relationships because marriage is sacred and they want to preserve the family unit. In so doing, they may find individual and couple fulfillment. For other people, however, commitment to "save the marriage" comes at great cost to themselves, and they end up hating one another. When the family unit is harmful to members, including the children, it has become dysfunctional. In such cases, the family unit may be kept legally intact, but it is broken in spirit.

Another dilemma that arises is the question of commitment versus personal autonomy and freedom (Eidelson, 1983). How can one give oneself in a relationship and to it and still maintain personal individualism and a high level of independence? Achieving a reasonable balance between the two is not easy. If people give up too much of themselves for the sake of the relationship, they lose their identity and self-worth. Sometimes their partner loses respect for them because they have lost respect for themselves. However, if they give little of themselves, make no concessions or sacrifices at all in order to maintain their independence and freedom, they remain separated individuals. Successful couples have mastered the art of losing themselves in their relationship without losing their sense of self in the process (Ammons and Stinnett, 1980). This requires a well-developed identity and high self-esteem. Figure 4.1 pictures different types of relationships. In **A** two people each maintain their individual identities, but little effort is made to achieve oneness as a married couple. In **B** two people lose their separate identities which become swallowed up in the relationship. In **C** there is sufficient commitment to form a union, but enough separateness for them each to maintain their sense of self.

Commitment is also enhanced if it is made with an assumption of permanence, which is the ideal according to our religious cultural values. One

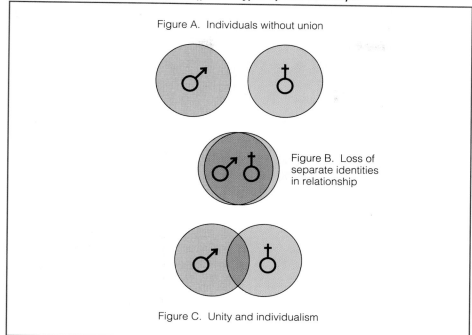

Figure A. Individuals without union

Figure B. Loss of separate identities in relationship

Figure C. Unity and individualism

survey of over 5,000 students in four universities revealed that 92 percent viewed marriage as a commitment for life (Martin and Martin, 1984). Certainly, couples are more highly motivated to work out marital problems if they expect their relationship will last forever.

No matter how great the commitment, not all marriages succeed. Reasons may be complex. (See Part V, Families Under Stress.) Some of these reasons are beyond the control of the partners. There may be severe personality problems that originated long before they met one another, as we discussed in Chapter 3. The partners may be very fine, capable, dedicated people, but completely incompatible; Chapter 8 discusses this issue. Unforeseen circumstances may create an unsolvable crisis for the relationship, as we see in Chapter 22. Whatever the cause, wisdom sometimes requires knowing when to try or when to quit; Chapter 23 discusses divorce.

Honesty, Trust, Fidelity

According to the research of Bell and colleagues (1987), the old-fashioned virtues of honesty, trust, and fidelity are important ingredients even in contemporary successful marriages. Sincerity, truthfulness, faithfulness, and trust are the cement that bind people together. Partners know they can accept each other's word, believe in one another, depend on one another to keep promises, and be faithful to commitments that are made. One young wife comments:

> I never have to worry about my husband. When he tells me something I know it's true. He's a very sincere, up-front person. I know just where I stand with

Several research studies have focused on the meaning and importance of trust in relationships (Larzelere and Huston, 1980; Rotter, 1980).

Meaning. Trust is the degree of confidence people feel when they think about their relationship. Trust means they feel a person is predictably dependable, that they can count on that individual in times of need. Trust is generalized expectancy that the promise, the word, the written or verbal statement of another person can be relied upon (Larzelere and Huston, 1980).

Characteristics of trusters. People who trust others are more dependable themselves and more likely to be trustworthy. Conversely, those who score low on trust are less trustworthy and actually more likely to lie and cheat themselves. People who feel other people cannot be trusted also feel they can lie and cheat themselves because others are doing it; they see it as a necessary defensive reaction. Furthermore, if they are dishonest themselves, they project their faults unto others.

High trusters are more likable than others and are rated happier, more ethical, more attractive to the opposite sex, and more desirable as a close friend. Psychologists rate them as better adjusted than low trusters. High trusters tend to base their code of ethics on conventional morality.

High trusters are not more gullible or less intelligent than low trusters. When they have evidence that others are deceiving them, they are not more trusting than are low trusters (Rotter, 1980).

Broken trust. Once trust has been violated, it becomes doubly difficult to reestablish. Even if a partner promises to change and begins to work at rebuilding the trust, doubt remains because to be fooled again would hurt too much. Any error becomes evidence that the new effort is merely a sham and that nothing has changed. This cycle of doubt and distrust can be changed, but requires considerable motivation and care if a solid relationship is to be rebuilt.

him all the time. He always keeps his word. If he promises the kids something, he never disappoints them. He travels a lot, but I trust him completely. I know he's faithful to me. He isn't the kind of man to sneak around. If two people can't believe in one another, or depend on one another, they don't have much of a relationship in my opinion. (Student comments)

When two people first start going together, one of the things each seeks to discover is if the other is honest and sincere. If the man tells a woman she is beautiful and he loves her, does he really mean it, or is he "handing her a line" to gain approval or perhaps to win sexual favors? She begins to judge the future potential of the relationship partly to the degree she feels he is honest and sincere. The more she feels she can trust him, the more comfortable she is in the relationship and the less vulnerable she feels (Larzelere and Huston, 1980). If the man is not honest and sincere, the woman begins to feel insecure and has doubts about his future intentions. In marriage itself, once one person begins to doubt the honesty, sincerity, and faithfulness of the other, the more insecure and vulnerable he or she feels. The whole future of the relationship seems in doubt.

Responsibility

Successful marriage depends upon the mutual assumption, sharing, and division of responsibility in the family. Typical complaints brought to marriage counselors include the following:

Mutual agreement on what needs to be done in the household and by whom directly contributes to a successful marriage.

My partner is completely irresponsible.

My husband never does anything around the house. I do everything: inside and outside work both.

My wife is irresponsible in handling money.

My husband doesn't like to work. He'd rather be out with friends partying and having a good time.

My wife doesn't take enough responsibility for cleaning the house. She knows that eventually if she doesn't do it, that I'll get it done.

My husband doesn't show any interest in taking care of the children. He feels that because he brings home a paycheck that it is the end of his responsibilities. He leaves everything else to me.

I have to make all the decisions and plans for our social life. I wish my husband would assume some of this responsibility. (Author's counseling notes)

In marriages where couples report a high degree of satisfaction, two conditions exist in relation to the division of responsibility. *One,* the partners feel there is a fairly equal division of labor. In situations where one partner is working 100 hours a week and the other works little, the working spouse rightfully resents the uneven distribution of responsibility.

Ed worked hard all his life building up a cleaning business. He was very successful and decided to retire at age 60. He spends his time playing golf at the country club and playing cards at the Elks club. Since the family needs the money and the business needs attention, his wife Edith spends her days managing the company. She resents deeply the fact that she is still working and her husband isn't. (Author's counseling notes)

Numerous studies reveal conflict in families because of an inequitable division of household and child-care responsibilities. Generally, husbands spend only a few hours doing housework, even if their wives are employed full-time (Nichols and Metzen, 1982). The husband's contribution remains basically unchanged regardless of the wife's employment status (Condron and Bode, 1982). In reviewing the research on household task performance, Scanzoni and Fox (1980) found little evidence of egalitarianism in marriage when it comes to housework. This lack of equity is a major source of dissatisfaction for many wives.

Two, marriage is more successful if sex role performance matches sex role expectations (McNamara and Bahr, 1980). Many couples have set ideas about who should perform what responsibilities. Thus, if a husband expects his wife to perform traditional feminine roles in the family — caring for children, taking care of the home, attending to his needs — but she's more interested in pursuing her career, conflict develops. If the wife expects the husband to be the primary breadwinner and an all-around handyman around the house, and he doesn't live up to her expectations, she may become very dissatisfied with the relationship.

Adaptability, Flexibility, Tolerance

Couples whose marriages are successful are usually adaptable and flexible (Fisher, Gibbin, and Hoopes, 1982; Wilcoxon, 1985). They recognize that people differ in the way they think and in their attitudes, values, habits, and ways of doing things. They recognize that their own preferences are not necessarily the only way, so they accept individual and group differences. They don't need to insist that everyone they live with be a carbon copy of themselves.

They recognize also that life is not static, that situations and circumstances change as we go through various stages of the life cycle. They are able to accept change as the norm for living, and are willing to adjust to varying circumstances (de Turck and Miller, 1986). They are willing to grow with the relationship as time passes (Anderson, 1986).

Adaptability and flexibility require a high degree of emotional maturity. People have to be secure enough to let go of thoughts and old habits that are no longer functional. But to let go requires some confidence that the new will work as well. Such people are not threatened by change. In fact, they welcome new challenges because it gives them a chance to grow and develop. Marcus (1983) writes:

> One person's capacity to adapt to another requires a degree of security . . . Instead of feeling threatened by flexibility, they . . . feel proud of their capacity to be flexible. Because marriage requires a series of adaptations, it is of itself a stimulus toward achieving mature adult status. (p. 120)

The most difficult persons for marriage therapists to deal with are perfectionists who have only one rigid standard by which they judge everyone. Perfectionists have no tolerance for imperfection. They have impossibly high standards for themselves and others and are completely rigid in the way they think. Since they feel they are right and other ideas are wrong, they insist that the changes that are made in a relationship have to be made by someone else. As one husband said, "When my wife and I discuss anything, I'm right 99 percent of the time, and she's wrong" (Author's counseling notes). How can problems be worked out with a person who is so arrogant and rigid in his thinking? It becomes very difficult (Barrow and Moore, 1983).

Because they fear appearing foolish and inadequate and are afraid that their thoughts and feelings will not be acceptable to others, they inhibit self-disclosure and are unable to communicate effectively. This further deprives them of the warmth and unconditional acceptance they crave but which they cannot earn through accomplishment. Marital closeness becomes difficult, because they never let other people really know them (Burns, 1980).

CLASSROOM FORUM
My Husband Is Too Rigid

Mrs. L. was having difficulty with her husband, whom she described as "too rigid." She described him as a man in his early twenties, an engineer. The couple had one daughter. The husband was very "set in his ways" with definite ideas about everything. He tried to tell his wife how she should dress, how to get ahead in her job, how and what to cook, how to clean the house, and how to raise their daughter. He insisted on instructing her in everything so that she would "do things right." One of the things he insisted on was that the wife cook just the right amount of food so none would go to waste. If she cooked two potatoes and he felt like eating only one, he yelled at her for wasting food; but he wouldn't eat leftovers. He might want two potatoes the next time. She never knew. He took a class in first aid and learned that it was a safety hazard to leave things on the stairs. Sometimes his wife would leave a newly purchased package of toilet paper or a laundry basket of clothes at the foot of the stairs (not on them) to be taken up the next time she went upstairs. He became very agitated whenever this happened and insisted "he did not want to be married to anyone who put things on the stairs."

Whenever Mrs. L. tried to confront her husband with his actions, he became very defensive, tried to change the subject, or had an explanation for his behavior. No matter how his wife explained her feelings, he either refused to listen, or he ended up telling her why she was wrong. (Author's counseling notes)

DISCUSSION

1. What might be some of the reasons Mr. L was so rigid?

2. Will Mr. L. ever change? Can you think of any reason or circumstance that might motivate him to change?

3. How might Mrs. L. deal with the situation?

4. What do you think of the idea of Mrs. L. giving in to her husband for the sake of family harmony? What might be the effect on him? On her? On their daughter?

5. Have you ever known anyone as rigid as Mr. L? Describe.

Unselfishness

Ours is an age of individualism where some try to find happiness through gratification and narcissistic "**selfism**" (Neubeck, 1979). Selfism in marriage lessens each partner's responsibility for the success of the relationship. Social exchange theory emphasizes that people seek relationships where the cost-benefit ratio is satisfactory and fair. From this perspective, decreased investment on the part of one spouse decreases the likelihood that the other mate will receive the rewards deemed desirable to continue the relationship. The result is marital instability, since associations are continued only if each partner feels he or she is receiving what is deserved and expected (Ammons and Stinnett, 1980).

It is not surprising, therefore, that the most successful marriages are based on a spirit of mutual helpfulness, where each partner unselfishly attends to the needs of the other as well as his or her own (Bell, Daly, and Gonzalez, 1987). One wife explained:

> My husband is the most generous, giving man I have ever known. He will give you the shirt off his back. Every day he does so many little things for me. When we go out, he always makes sure that I'm having a good time. He insists on bringing my coffee while I'm in bed in the morning. He helps me around the house all the time. He never seems to think about himself. He's too busy thinking about the rest of us. (Author's counseling notes)

It is not evident in the quotation, but the wife was just as giving and unselfish as the husband. She and her husband had a wonderful marriage, primarily because the unselfishness was reciprocal. The wife had come in for counseling because she was concerned about a friend who was having marital problems.

Paradoxically, the people who are most self-centered and self-serving least often feel as fulfilled or as happy as those who seek to meet the needs of others. Psychologist Bernard Rimland at the Institute for Child Behavior Research in San Diego asked 216 college students to write the names of up to ten persons whom they knew best and after each name to write either H for happy or N for unhappy. Then they were asked to go down the list again and write either S for selfish or U for unselfish. Only 78 people whom the students rated as selfish were also happy, while 827 whom the students rated

Can this couple talk about anything? Are they able to share their feelings? Does either one hold back from the other? Answers to such questions about communication in a relationship can tell a lot about how long the relationship is likely to last.

as happy were also rated unselfish. By definition, selfish people are devoted to bringing themselves happiness. Judged by others, however, they seem to succeed less often than people who work at bringing happiness to others (Cox, 1982).

Communication

According to numerous studies, good communication is one of the most important requirements in a successful marriage (Curran, 1983; Fisher, Giblin, and Hoopes, 1982; Wachowiak and Bragg, 1980). Couples who are able to communicate effectively report:

We can talk about everything.

We are able to talk about our problems and to work them out.

We're able to share our feelings.

Talking helps us to understand one another and keeps us close (Honeycutt, 1986).

We each try to listen when the other is talking.

We don't believe in holding things in.

We talk about things and it clears the air (Student comments).

When marriages are troubled, it is often because of poor communication (Wilcoxon, 1985). Poor communication results in increasing anger, tension, and frustration at the difficulty in getting others to listen and to understand (Allen and Thompson, 1984). One wife comments:

I try to talk to him, but he doesn't seem to care. Finally, I get so upset that I scream and holler at him and start to cry. He just walks away and says to me, "I'm not going to talk to you if you holler at me." There's no way to get through to him (Author's counseling notes)

Effective communication involves sending and listening skills, the ability to exchange ideas, facts, feelings, attitudes, and beliefs so that a message from the sender is accurately heard and interpreted by the receiver and vice versa (Fisher, Giblin, and Hoopes, 1982). However, not all communication is helpful to relationships. Communication can be either productive or destructive to a relationship (Brandt, 1982). Saying critical, hurtful things in a cold, unfeeling way may worsen a relationship. One member of a couple who openly shares negative feelings the other can't handle may increase tension and alienation. Thus, politeness, tact, and consideration are required if communication is to be productive. The issue is so important that Chapter 17 is devoted entirely to a detailed discussion of communication.

Empathy and Sensitivity

Empathy means the ability to identify with the feelings, thought, and attitudes of another person (Wampler and Powell, 1982). It is the vicarious sharing of the experiences of another person. Kagan and Schneider (1987) use the term **affective sensitivity** to others. According to Kagan and Schneider, empathy develops in five steps:

Phase 1: *Perception.* Developing empathy begins with contact and interaction during which people perceive the thoughts, feelings, memories, anticipation, and aspirations of another, and the emotional tones associated with them.

Phase 2: *Experiencing*. The observer **resonates** or experiences the emotions of the other (Barrett-Lennard, 1981).

Phase 3: *Awareness*. Awareness is the process of acknowledging to oneself that one has perceived and resonated the emotions of another. In current usage, this is the process of recognizing the "vibes" of another.

Phase 4: *Labeling*. Awareness is acknowledged verbally; the observer speaks of having sensitivity to what another has communicated.

Phase 5: *Stating*. Empathy requires a person to communicate in language or by some other deliberate means that he or she has perceived another person's message. Communication may be nonverbal, such as touching. The purpose of this final phase is to let the other person know that one understands.

According to the research, empathy is an important ingredient in successful marriage (Bell, Daly, and Gonzalez, 1987; Ammons and Stinnet, 1980).

Admiration, Respect

One of the most important human needs is for acceptance and appreciation. The most successful marriages are those in which these needs are partly fulfilled in the relationship (Cousins and Vincent, 1983). Two people who like one another, who admire and support one another in their respective endeavors, who are proud of each other's achievements, who openly express appreciation of one another, and who build one another's self-esteem, are fulfilling their emotional needs and building a satisfying relationship (Bell, Daly, and Gonzalez, 1987; Lauer and Lauer, 1985). Respect in marriage encompasses respect for individual differences and respect for the other person as an important human being (Curran, 1983).

Partners who are able to meet these needs are usually emotionally secure people themselves. They don't have to criticize one another, or put one another down to build themselves up (Madden and Janoff-Bulman, 1981). They like sharing appreciation and giving compliments. Their approval is not conditional, requiring the partner to do certain things before they can approve. Their approval is what psychologists call **noncontingent reinforcement**. It is **unconditional positive regard**. They don't try to change their spouse, but are able to accept their partner as he or she is. If they have any complaints, they voice them in private, not when entertaining company. They are not threatened by a competent, achieving spouse and so avoid destructive competition. They like themselves and one another and show their approval in word and deed.

Affection

One important expectation of most married partners is they will meet one another's need for love and affection. This need varies from couple to couple, depending upon the way they are socialized. Some people have a higher need for emotional intimacy and affection than others. But most expect their needs to be met in their marriage.

Several related factors are important. Lauer and Lauer (1985) emphasized the importance of spouses agreeing on how to show affection and how often. Some people want a lot of physical contact: hugging, kissing, cuddling, touching, caressing. Others are satisfied with an occasional kiss. Some people are very uninhibited in sexual expression and desire playful sex (Crosby, 1985). Others are more restrained. There are differences in the desired frequency of intercourse. In successful marriages, couples are able to work out such differences (Ammons and Stinnett, 1980).

In their research, Bell and colleagues (1987) found that both *physical* and *verbal affection* were important to successful marriages. As one wife expressed it, "I know he loves me, but I want him to tell me." Words that express warmth, appreciation, endearment, and approval, that soothe dejected spirits, that caress damaged egos, may be as needed as the rhythmic pulses of orgasm.

Interestingly, even though fulfillment of affectional and sexual needs is important to marital success, strong feelings of romantic love are not a requirement (Todd, 1982). Romantic love is one of the most important factors in emotional attraction and in motivating couples to want to be together. And it is not dysfunctional in marital success as long as it is based on reality (Lee and Stone, 1980). It is dysfunctional if it is blind fantasy (Buehler and Wells, 1981). In successful marriages, love may continue to grow, but it changes over the years, with fewer components of superromanticism and more and deeper bonds of attachment and affection. Emotional bonding and affective expression are important ingredients in marital success (Anderson, 1986; Kinston, Loader, and Miller, 1987).

These two people obviously like one another and feel comfortable expressing their affection. Is this what psychologists mean by unconditional positive regard?

One important motive for marriage is companionship. Successful married couples spend sufficient time together, quality time. They enjoy each other's company, share common interests and activities, and enjoy a lot of laughs together. They are interested in one another's hobbies and leisure-time preferences. Furthermore, the partners try to be interesting companions to one another. They consider their spouse their best friend.

It is usually not necessary for partners to do everything together or to have all their interests in common. Most people want some separateness in their togetherness; they want to be able to do some things with their own friends. But it is helpful to have enough interests and friends in common. Problems arise when partners continue to seek most of their social life with friends they knew before marriage rather than spend time together. Some couples drift apart simply because they seldom see one another. Curran (1983) goes so far as to state, "Lack of time may be the most pervasive enemy the healthy family has."

People also differ on how close a companion they want their spouse to be. When one wants close companionship and the other doesn't, the differences become a source of tension and conflict. Mace and Mace (1974) likened the marriage relationship to the dilemma of two porcupines settling down to sleep on a cold night. If the porcupines get too close, their quills prick one another. If they move too far apart, they can't benefit from one another's body heat. So the porcupines shift back and forth, first together, then apart, until they arrive at a position in which they can achieve the maximum amount of warmth with a minimum amount of hurt.

Successful married couples share common interests and activities; they enjoy each other's company.

All couples, both those who achieve marital success and those who do not, experience problems and stress in and outside their relationship. One of the factors that distinguishes the two groups is that couples who have successful marriages are able to solve their problems and manage stress in a creative fashion. Stinnett and DeFrain (1985) found that successful couples are "able to weather the storms of life." Successful couples expect problems as a normal part of life and develop problem-solving skills so they can cope (Curran, 1983). They often interpret crises as a growth experience in a valued, positive direction. They feel they have grown from struggling and coping through the crisis (Caplan, 1981). In one study of strong families, 77 percent felt that something good had developed as a result of coping with the crisis (Stinnett, Knorr, DeFrain, and Rowe, 1981). One of the characteristics of strong families is that family members turn to one another for strength and assistance. This enhances family unity, cohesiveness, and commitment (McCubbin, Joy, Cauble, Comeau, Patterson, and Needle, 1980).

Successful couples also have a greater frustration tolerance than do unsuccessful couples. In this sense, they are more emotionally mature and stable. They have learned healthy, constructive ways of dealing with anger, rather than taking it out on other family members (Hardy, Orzek, and Heistad, 1984).

Spirituality, Values

Another factor that contributes to successful marriage is shared spirituality and values (Hatch, James, and Schumm, 1986). Successful couples share spiritual activities; they have a high degree of religious orientation and similar beliefs and values that are manifested in religious behavior. They have a

Successful couples commonly share spiritual activities and similar beliefs. Studies on marital adjustment found such shared values consistent regardless of how liberal or conservative the couple's beliefs.

strong value system and have similar goals and philosophy of life. They try to live up to their own high ideals. They have a strong sense of right and wrong and a desire to help other people.

Filsinger and Wilson (1984) conducted a study of marital adjustment of 208 marital dyads selected from a cross section of both fundamental and liberal Protestant churches in a large Southwestern metropolitian area. Marital adjustment was measured by the *Dyadic Adjustment Scale* (Spanier, 1976). Religiosity was measured by the *DeJong-Faulkner-Warner* (1976) *Religiosity Scale*, which is based on a multidimensional conceptualization of religiosity consisting of religious belief, religious ritual, religious experience, religious knowledge, and the social consequences of religion. The researchers found that religiosity was the most consistent and strongest predictor of marital adjustment. This finding is in agreement with other studies that show religiosity is correlated with *marital adjustment* (Hansen, 1981), with *marital satisfaction* (Bell, Daly, and Gonzalez, 1987), with *marital success* (Curran, 1983; Stinnett, and DeFrain, 1985), and with *marital stability* (Glenn and Supancic, 1984; Lauer and Lauer, 1985).

ASSESSMENT
Which Qualities Do We Possess?

On the following scales, evaluate first yourself and then your partner on the extent to which you and he or she possess these characteristics that are considered important in successful marriage. Then have your partner evaluate himself/herself and you also. Draw a circle around each of the numbers that applies.

1 — Very much
2 — Much
3 — Some
4 — Little
5 — Very little

CHARACTERISTIC	YOUR NAME:	YOUR PARTNER'S NAME:
Commitment	1 2 3 4 5	1 2 3 4 5
Honesty, Trust, Fidelity	1 2 3 4 5	1 2 3 4 5
Responsibility	1 2 3 4 5	1 2 3 4 5
Adaptability, Flexibility	1 2 3 4 5	1 2 3 4 5
Unselfishness	1 2 3 4 5	1 2 3 4 5
Communication	1 2 3 4 5	1 2 3 4 5
Empathy, Sensitivity	1 2 3 4 5	1 2 3 4 5
Admiration, Respect	1 2 3 4 5	1 2 3 4 5
Affection	1 2 3 4 5	1 2 3 4 5
Companionship	1 2 3 4 5	1 2 3 4 5
Ability to deal with crises, stress	1 2 3 4 5	1 2 3 4 5
Spirituality, Values	1 2 3 4 5	1 2 3 4 5
Total Scores (By Vertical Column)	_ _ _ _ _	_ _ _ _ _
Grand Total (All Columns)	_____	_____
Ranking (Grand Total ÷ 12)	_____	_____

1. Successful marriage has been defined as the extent to which it is durable, approximates ideals, fulfills mutual needs, and is satisfying.

2. The definition accepted here is: Marital success is the extent to which both partners in a relationship are satisfied that it has fulfilled reasonable expectations and mutual needs.

3. Twelve characteristics of successful marriage are commitment, honesty, fidelity and trust, responsibility, adaptability and flexibility, unselfishness, communication, empathy and sensitivity, admiration and respect, affection, companionship, ability to deal with crises and stress, and spirituality and values.

SUGGESTED READINGS

Beaver, D. (1983). *Beyond the Marriage Fantasy*. San Francisco: Harper and Row. How to achieve marital intimacy.

Curran, D. (1983). *Traits of a Healthy Family*. New York: Ballantine. Five hundred professionals who work with families summarize the qualities of healthy families.

Mace, D. (1983). *Toward Family Wellness*. Beverly Hills, CA: Sage. Characteristics of healthy families and how to create them.

O'Brien, P. (1977). *Staying Together: Marriages That Work*. New York: Random House. A description of six marriages.

Stinnet, N., and DeFrain, J. (1985). *Secrets of Strong Families*. Boston: Little, Brown. Report of survey of 1,000 families across the United States.

PART II

INTIMATE RELATIONSHIPS: GROWTH, CHOICES, AND CHANGE

5

BEING SINGLE

KEY TERMS

pushes and pulls
voluntary temporary singles
voluntary stable (permanent)
    singles
involuntary temporary singles
involuntary stable (permanent)
    singles

One of the choices that adults face is whether to get married. Less choice was offered in previous generations, when it was just assumed that everyone who could would get married. Those who didn't marry faced social disapproval. Few women wanted to become "spinsters" or "old maids"; men didn't mind being young bachelors but didn't want to be "mama's boys," living without the companionship of a woman. Today, the number of never-married adults has increased dramatically, reflecting changing social conditions and attitudes.

In this chapter we examine the facts regarding single persons and the reasons for the increase in numbers. We examine why some people remain single and some advantages and disadvantages of being single. We discuss the life-styles and living arrangements of singles as well as such factors as social life and leisure time, loneliness and friendships, sexual behavior, and employment and income. Finally, we examine the situations of older, never-married adults. An assessment instrument is provided at the end of the chapter to assist in answering the question: What do I think of singlehood?

MARITAL STATUS OF THE POPULATION

Overall Figures

Figure 5.1 illustrates the marital status of the U.S. population, 18 years of age and older, in 1987. Overall, 62.9 percent were married, 21.8 percent were single (never-married), with the remaining 15.3 percent evenly split between widowed (7.5 percent) and divorced (7.8 percent). Obviously, the great majority of adults were married, and an additional number had been married at one time. Nevertheless, a little over one in five adults had never been married, but these were primarily in the youngest age groups.

FIGURE 5.1 *Marital Status of the Population,*
18 Years Old and Over, 1987.

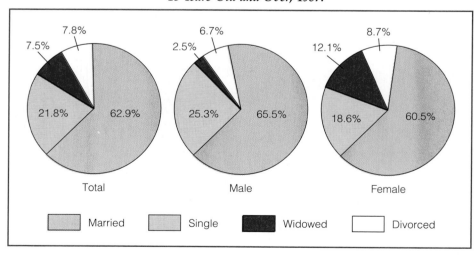

Adapted from U.S. Bureau of the Census. (1989). *Statistical abstract of the United States, 1989* (109th ed.). Washington, DC: U.S. Government Printing Office, 42.

When these figures are examined according to race, we find some surprising results. Only 47.7 percent of blacks 18 years of age or older were married. Over one-third (34.2 percent) had never been married. The percentage of those widowed (8.3 percent) or divorced (9.8 percent) was only a little greater than for whites. The statistics for Americans of Spanish origin showed that about one in four was single compared to one in five for whites. About the same percentage of both groups was married, and slightly fewer Hispanics than whites were widowed or divorced. Marriage was actually more popular among white Americans than among those of other groups.

The reasons for lower percentages of married blacks are several. There are fewer black men than women of marriageable age (Spanier and Glick, 1980). A disproportionately high percentage of low-income blacks cannot afford to marry (Staples, 1981). The number of college-educated black women exceeds the number of college-educated black men; as a result, many of these women are not able to find mates that satisfy their expectations. The sharpest discrepancy between the races shows up when we examine the tendency of those with less than a high school degree to remain unmarried. Today, 23 percent of black men, aged 25–44, with less than a high school degree have never married, compared to a figure of 7 percent among their white counterparts (Cherlin, 1981). This represents the response of the poorest, most disadvantaged blacks to the social and economic situations they face in our cities. Unemployment among blacks is far higher than among whites. It may be that government assistance programs such as Aid to Families with Dependent Children (AFDC) encourage the existence of single-parent families and reduce incentives to be married. Many black women find they can depend more on welfare assistance than they can on uneducated husbands who have difficulty in finding employment; nevertheless, most prefer not to remain on welfare. The close family ties in the extended black family also give support to the unmarried black woman.

TABLE 5.1 *Marital Status of U.S. Population, 18 Years and Older, 1987, by Race or Ethnic Origin.*

Marital Status	PERCENT DISTRIBUTION		
	All Races	Black	Spanish Origin
Single	21.8	34.2	26.1
Married	62.9	47.7	62.0
Widowed	7.5	8.3	4.3
Divorced	7.8	9.8	7.7
Total	100.0	100.0	100.0

Adapted from: U.S. Bureau of the Census. (1989). *Statistical abstract of the United States, 1989* (109th ed.). Washington, DC: U.S. Government Printing Office, 42, 43.

There are various categories of single persons. Stein (1981) has developed a typology of single persons based on whether their status is voluntary or involuntary. Table 5.2 shows four major categories of singles according to Stein.

TABLE 5.2 Typology of Singles

	Voluntary	Involuntary
Temporary	Never-marrieds and previously marrieds who are not opposed to the idea of marriage but are not currently seeking mates	Those who have actively been seeking mates but have not found them
Stable (Permanent)	All those (never-marrieds and former-marrieds) who choose to be single	Never-marrieds and former-marrieds who wanted to marry, who have not found a mate, and who have more or less accepted being single

Adapted from Stein, P. (1981). *Single life: Unmarried adults in social context.* New York: St. Martin's Press. Used by permission of Haworth Press.

Voluntary Singles

Voluntary temporary singles is a category that includes young persons who have never been married and are not currently looking, who are postponing marriage even though they are not opposed to the idea of marriage. It includes cohabitors who will eventually marry each other or someone else. It includes recently divorced or widowed persons who need time to be single, though they may eventually want to marry again. It also includes older never-marrieds who are not actively looking, but who would marry if the right person came along.

Voluntary stable (permanent) singles is a category that includes never-marrieds of all ages who have no intention of marrying, cohabitors who never intend to have a ceremonial marriage, and formerly married persons who never want to marry again. It also includes those who have taken religious vows not to marry.

Involuntary Singles

Included in **involuntary temporary singles** are young adults who have never been married but are actively seeking a mate, and divorced or widowed persons who want to remarry soon.

The category **involuntary stable (permanent) singles** includes never-married persons or widowed or divorced persons who wanted to marry or remarry and who have not found a mate; they have become reconciled to their single state. It also includes physically or mentally impaired persons.

PERSPECTIVE
Singles — Myths and Realities

Singles have often been described with stereotypical images, usually negative, that often lead to misunderstanding and discrimination against them (Etaugh and Malstrom, 1981). In their studies of singles, Cargan and Melko (1982) examine these stereotypes to discover which ones are myths and which ones approach reality. A summary of their findings is presented here.

Myth	Fact
Singles (especially men) are too attached to parents, so don't get married.	There is little difference between marrieds and singles in their perceptions of relations with parents.
Singles are rich.	On the whole, marrieds are better off financially.
Singles are happier.	On several measurements, singles are less happy than marrieds.
Singles are increasing in numbers.	This is true in the U.S. if we are considering numbers, but the percentage of singles has declined since World War II.
There is something wrong with singles.	This is a destructive and elusive myth. There is nothing wrong with being single.

Realities	Explanation
Singles are deviant.	Yes, but only because they are not following the norm, not because they are abnormal.
Singles have more free time.	Yes, they have more time to devote to activities of their own choosing.
Singles have more fun.	They are more involved in a variety of social activities than are marrieds, but don't necessarily have more fun.
Singles are swingers.	Singles have more variety of sexual partners; married people have more frequent sex.
Singles are lonely.	Sometimes, especially divorced persons.
Life for singles is changing for the better.	Yes, single life seems to be more rewarding and less frustrating than it used to be, although the alternative of marriage does not appear to have become less attractive.

Adapted from Cargan, L., and Melko, M. (1982). *Singles: Myths and Realities.* Beverly Hills, CA: Sage, 193–213.

MARITAL DELAY*

Trends

In fact, most singles are only temporarily unmarried, since by age 45–54 only 5.9 percent of males and 4.5 percent of females have never married. (See Figure 5.2.) However, the trend is for adults to get married at older ages than they used to, as Figure 5.3 shows (U.S. Bureau of the Census, 1987b).

---

*Parts of this and subsequent sections are based in part on material from the author's book *Adult Development and Aging.* (1986). Used by permission of the publisher Allyn and Bacon.

FIGURE 5.2 Never-Married Persons as Percent of Total Population, 18 Years Old and Older by Age and Sex: 1987.

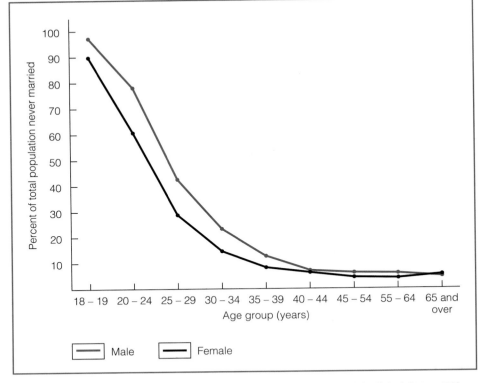

Adapted from U.S. Bureau of the Census. (1989). *Statistical abstract of the United States, 1989* (109th ed.). Washington, DC: U.S. Government Printing Office, 43.

Reasons for Delay

The reasons for delay in marriage are social, economic, and personal. One particular reason is the *changing attitude toward single life* (Thornton and Freedman, 1982). Existing prejudices against single persons, especially against unmarried women, are declining. It is no longer unacceptable for a woman in her thirties to be unmarried, especially if she has a flourishing career, an active social life, and an outgoing personality. However, both family and friends continue to expect that ultimately she will marry. The attitudinal change accepts her decision not to marry young, but not necessarily the idea of remaining single permanently.

The *lengthening of the period of education and economic dependency* has greatly influenced the delay of marriage. One study of women in their twenties showed that those who had career aspirations married later in life than did those who planned to be housewives (Cherlin, 1980). Lower socioeconomic status individuals, with lower educational and vocational aspirations, are more likely to marry at earlier ages.

The *sexual revolution* has also influenced the age at first marriage. An increasing acceptance of premarital sexual intercourse has made sexual expression

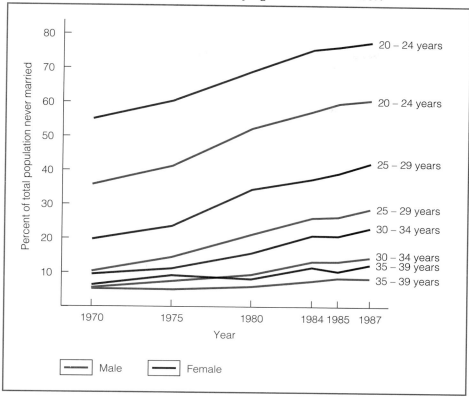

FIGURE 5.3 *Never-Married Persons as Percent of Total Population 18 Years Old and Over, by Age and Sex: 1970–1987.*

Adapted from U.S. Bureau of the Census. (1989). *Statistical abstract of the United States, 1989* (109th ed.). Washington, DC: U.S. Government Printing Office, 43.

possible at young ages without necessitating marriage. An increase in the acceptance of nonmarital cohabitation also provides some benefits of marriage without the commitment — for example, companionship, sex, shared housing, living expenses, and physical services.

The *women's movement* has also influenced views of marriage. Women are encouraged to seek their own identity, apart from marital identity, and to find career fulfillment and economic self-sufficiency. Feminists are not opposed to marriage, but women are encouraged to explore opportunities in addition to family fulfillment. At the least, this attitude has led to marital postponement as women search out and explore other options.

WHY SOME PEOPLE REMAIN SINGLE

Deliberate Choice

Some of the small minority who never marry have deliberately chosen to stay single. A survey of 3,000 single men and women from 36 states revealed that one-third of single men and one-fifth of single women were so by choice

(Simenauer and Carroll, 1982). Members of some religious orders take vows of chastity. Some people perceive marriage as incompatible with their careers. A minority of singles are homosexual in their sexual orientation.

Fear

Fear of marriage is a powerful deterrent. Some of these who are afraid were brought up in unhappy homes where their parents fought all the time. Others have been disappointed in love and are afraid to try again. Some were married before and failed; they prefer not to remarry. Lutwak (1985) did a study of fear and intimacy among college women and found that, for some, emotional involvement was a risk that was not worth taking. These women were so terrified of possible dependency that they could not conceive of healthy mutuality and interdependence. They were fearful of possible pain, vulnerability, and — most important — the possible loss of self. Many had a profound sense of insecurity about the consequences of caring. Many thought that marriage was a deception, a farce, a trap.

Lack of Opportunity

At the other extreme are people who would prefer to marry but never have the chance. Included are people with marked physical or mental handicaps that preclude marriage. Also included are women who are caught in the marriage squeeze; that is, who have difficulty finding eligible male partners. Until 1940, the male population in this country exceeded the female population. Since then, adult women have outnumbered men. The older the age group, the greater the discrepancy in numbers.

Singles often value having time for themselves. The distinction between being alone and being lonely, however, is an important one.

One common stereotype portrays people who do not marry as having personality problems. Some are regarded as immature, unwilling to assume responsibility, neurotic, or emotionally fixated on a parent; others are deemed socially inadequate or fixated on a lost love. Certain stereotypes focus on economics: people are too poor to marry or are unwilling to share their wealth (Cargan and Melko, 1982). These stereotypes imply that marriage is a desired state and that the single person has not attained it because he or she is unfit, incomplete, or abnormal. Although common in years past, this view is oversimplified; and at the least, it applies to only a small percentage of singles.

Circumstances

For many people, remaining unmarried permanently is not necessarily a matter of deliberate choice but rather a result of such circumstances as family situations, geography, social isolation, or financial condition.

> Mary lived with her widowed father, who was very possessive and protective of her. He made her feel she had an obligation to take care of him. Her father was also very critical of every young man she dated or brought home. According to her father, no one was ever good enough for her. She had several chances to marry but was always dissuaded by her father. She vowed that she would marry after her father died, but the years slipped by. Her father lived until his mid-eighties. By this time, Mary was in her sixties and had remained single. (Author's counseling notes)

A comparison of the life histories of 20 never-married men over the age of 35 with the experiences of 20 men who first married after the age of 35 showed that bachelorhood is primarily a situational rather than a psychological condition (Darling, 1976). All bachelors had been insulated against the usual pressures to marry early, but those who eventually married had experienced changes in their social situations, including shifts in reference groups, changes in their familial relationships (for example, a parent died), and greater exposure to social pressures to marry.

Timing was a crucial factor. Many bachelors married at turning points in their careers: at times of promotion, career changes, or geographical moves. Some married after times of stress, when they felt vulnerable and received the support of significant others, particularly the women they eventually married. Darling concluded that any social state, whether singlehood or marriage, develops as the end point of a series of "situational contingencies, turning points, and commitments" (Darling, 1976, p. 3).

Parents

One stereotypical view of singles says that their failure to marry is due to immaturity. A man is considered still tied to his mother's apron strings; a woman living at home is still dependent on parents. Actually, many single men and women are anxious to leave home. They want their independence, the freedom to do as they please without having to answer to parents. Most singles who strain for independence are embarrassed or ashamed of living at home. Their friends make them feel they have not really grown up.

One question that arises is whether a significant percentage of never-marrieds remain single because of unresolved conflicts or problems with parents. The research evidence is somewhat contradictory. Spreitzer and Riley (1974) found that among men and women who never married, very poor relations with mothers were far more characteristic than good or even poor relations. Men who never married were twice as likely to report very poor relations with fathers as men who did marry.

A different relationship existed between girls who never married and their fathers. Twice the percentage of never-married women had good relations with their fathers as had poor relations. Except for the relationships between girls and fathers, Spreitzer and Riley's findings do not support the apron-strings image. The majority of findings indicate singles may have been discouraged by unpleasant family situations. Apparently they were deterred from marriage not by family bonds, but by the lack of them.

According to Cargan and Melko (1982), married people were more likely than single people to have warm, stable current relations with parents. Single people were more likely to report cool relations and arguments with parents.

Pushes and Pulls

The decision to remain single or to marry involves complex factors. Stein (1978) described the negative and positive influences on this decision as **pushes and pulls**. Pushes are negative factors in a situation. For the single person, pushes are influences to marry; for the married, they are influences to leave the situation. Pulls are positive attractions. The single person is pulled to remain so; the married person is pulled to remain married. Table 5.3 shows the pushes and pulls (Stein, 1978, p. 4).

The strength of these pushes and pulls is affected by a number of variables, including age, stage of the life cycle, sexual identification, extent of involvement with parents and family, availability of friends and peers, and perception of choice. For some people, dating patterns, parental pressures, and an acceptance of the cultural script leads to early involvement and marriage. Those who postpone marriage find greater pulls toward satisfying careers, colleagues at work, and developing friendships, all of which are possible outside marriage (Stein, 1978).

ADVANTAGES AND DISADVANTAGES OF BEING SINGLE

Advantages

People find both advantages and disadvantages in being single. Advantages include:

1. *Greater opportunities for self-development and personal growth and fulfillment.* If singles want to take a course, go on to graduate school, or travel, they are freer to do so than are married people. As one mother of three said, "I don't even have time to sit down and read a book."

2. *Opportunities to meet different people and to develop and enjoy different friendships.* Singles are free to pursue friendships with either men or women, according to their own preferences.

TABLE 5.3 Pushes and Pulls Toward Marriage or Singlehood

TOWARD MARRIAGE

Pushes (negatives in present situations)	Pulls (attractions in potential situations)
Socialization	Approval of parents
Pressure from parents	Desire for children and own family
Desire to leave home	Example of peers
Fear of independence	Romanticization of marriage
Loneliness	Physical attraction
No knowledge or perception of alternatives	Love, emotional attachment
Job availability, wage structure, and promotions	Security, social status, social prestige
Social policies favoring the married and the responses of social institutions	Legitimation of sexual experiences

TOWARD SINGLEHOOD

Pushes (to leave permanent relationships)	Pulls (to remain single or return to singlehood)
Lack of friends, isolation, loneliness	Career opportunities and development
Restricted availability of new experiences	Availability of sexual experiences
Suffocating one-to-one relationship, feeling trapped	Exciting lifestyle, variety of experiences, freedom to change
Obstacles to self-development	Psychological and social autonomy, self-sufficiency
Boredom, unhappiness, and anger	
Role playing and conformity to expectations	Support structures: sustaining friendships, women's and men's groups, political groups, therapeutic groups, collegial groups
Poor communication with mate	
Sexual frustration	

From Stein, P. J. (1978). The lifestyles and life chances of the never-married. *Marriage and Family Review, 1* (July/August), 4. Copyright © 1978 The Haworth Press, Inc., New York.

3. *Economic independence and self-sufficiency.* As one woman said, "I don't have to depend on a husband for money. I earn it myself and I can spend it as I want."

4. *More and better sexual experience.* Singles are free to seek experiences with more than one partner.

5. *Freedom* to control one's own life, to do what one wants without answering to a spouse; more psychological and social autonomy.

6. *More opportunities for career change, development, and expansion.* Singles are not locked in by family responsibilities and so can be more mobile and flexible in the climb up the career ladder.

Not all of these advantages can be applied to all singles. For example, not all singles have opportunities to meet different people. Not all are economically well off, nor are all free of family responsibilities. Nevertheless, some singles would list some of these or even all of these items as advantages for them.

Disadvantages

Those who are not in favor of remaining single describe a number of disadvantages:

1. *Loneliness and lack of companionship.* This is one of the most pressing problems of singles.
2. *Economic hardship,* especially for single women. Single women earn less than single or married men and, without access to a husband's income, have a lower standard of living than do married men or women. Also, employers tend to feel that unmarried persons are less stable than are those who are married, so top positions are more often given to married persons, especially to men.
3. *Feeling out of place in many social gatherings because social life is organized around married couples.* In addition, singles may not be invited to some social events.
4. *Sexual frustration* for some persons.
5. *Not having children, or lack of a family* in which to bring up children.
6. *Prejudices against single persons in our society and social disapproval of their lifestyle* (Etaugh and Malstrom, 1981). This creates problems for singles if society considers them a threat to the established social order or to other people's marriages. Much pressure is put upon them to get married.

Health and Well-Being

In general, single people are less healthy than married persons and have a shorter life expectancy (Verbrugge, 1979a). However, whether being single is relatively unhealthy or whether healthier people marry more often is not known. The divorced, separated, or widowed have the poorest health, perhaps because the less fit more often get divorced or separated from their spouses. Or it may reflect the painful experiences they have faced. In addition, this group may be somewhat older than the total group of married persons.

There are some gender differences in health and well-being. Never-married men particularly have poorer physical and mental health than do married men (Bernard, 1982). Some studies show that never-married women fare as well or better than married women on a number of mental health, physical health, and life satisfaction indexes (Veroff, Kulka, and Douvan, 1981). This is particularly true for those who choose to be single. However, the latest studies by Cargan and Melko (1982) do not support the notion that "marriage is bad for women." The authors advise against "trying to develop a score sheet to establish, between the sexes, who has the best of marriage and the best of singlehood" (p. 65).

Many variables in addition to marital status determine life satisfaction and physical and mental well-being. Gigy (1980) found few differences in the morale or happiness of never-married versus married women. Baruch, Barnett, and Rivers (1983) studied the effects of marital status and employment

CLASSROOM FORUM
The Ten Pillars of Happiness

Social psychologist Jonathan Freedman (1978) examined what makes people happy. He quizzed both single and married men and women. The results are given in the following Table.

The Ten Pillars of Happiness

Rank	Single Men	Single Women	Married Men	Married Women
1.	Friends and social life	Friends and social life	Personal growth	Being in love
2.	Job or primary activity	Being in love	Being in love	Marriage
3.	Being in love	Job or primary activity	Marriage	Partner's happiness
4.	Recognition; success	Recognition; success	Job or primary activity	Sex life
5.	Sex life	Personal growth	Partner's happiness	Recognition; success
6.	Personal growth	Sex life	Sex life	Personal growth
7.	Finances	Health	Recognition; success	Job or primary activity
8.	House or apartment	Body and attractiveness	Friends and social life	Friends and social life
9.	Body and attractiveness	Finances	Being a parent	Health
10.	Health	House or apartment	Finances	Being a parent

From Freedman, J. (1978). *Happy People: What happiness is, who has it, and why.* New York: Harcourt Brace Jovanovich. Used by permission.

DISCUSSION

1. After looking at the above table, what factors do you believe are most important to your personal happiness? Explain.

2. Can people be happy without being married? What are your views, and why do you feel this way?

on never-married versus married women. They found that women who showed the highest level of well-being were those who were married, had children, and a high-prestige job. But it was a high-prestige job rather than a husband that was the best predictor of well-being for these women. Being single alone was not associated with diminished well-being, but being single and in a low-level job was.

In addition to employment status, dozens of other variables influence well-being. We cannot, therefore, intelligently compare married persons with single people on the basis of marital status alone without controlling for these many other variables. Researchers have been too anxious to try to discover the advantages of marriage or singlehood, and many unwarranted conclusions have been drawn (Johnston and Eklund, 1984).

One survey of male and female readers of *Psychology Today* showed that the happiest women were those who were married and employed outside the home (Shaver and Freedman, 1976). They were happier than single women and had fewer psychological problems than did women who stayed home. These and other findings indicate that modern women want the best of all possible worlds — marriage, career, and children — and are happiest if they succeed at all three.

LIFE-STYLES OF SINGLES

Research on life-styles of singles reveals a variety of patterns. An in-depth study of never-married college-educated men and women over age 36 described six life-style patterns (Schwartz, 1976):

Professional. These persons organized their lives around work and identified with their occupational roles. Most of their time and energy was spent on their careers.

Social. These persons had extensive social lives and many personal relationships. Friends and social activities were given priority over work. They were deeply involved in hobbies, organizations, and family activities.

Individualistic. These persons focused their attention on self-growth. They enjoyed freedom, privacy, living alone, and not having to answer to anyone. They enjoyed hobbies, reading, and other solitary pursuits, along with classes on self-improvement.

Activist. The lives of these persons were centered on community and political causes. Work was important, but much time was devoted to trying to create a better world.

Passive. These were loners who spent much free time alone, in solitary pursuits such as shopping or attending movies. They had negative outlooks on life and showed little initiative in using their lives creatively.

Supportive. These persons spent their time in service to others. The few persons in this category were mostly women who were very satisfied with their lives.

It is obvious that not all single adults fit into the same life-style. There is as great a variation among members of this group as among other segments of the population, and so it is misleading to try to describe singles as a homogeneous group.

LIVING ARRANGEMENTS

Singles' Communities

In the stereotyped fantasy, groups of singles occupy apartments or condominiums that cater especially to their needs. A case in point is Carl Sandburg Village in Chicago, transformed from a skid-row neighborhood with rundown

Singles' communities can offer a variety of recreational facilities, restaurants, bars, and other built-in amenities for their residents. For many people, this kind of life style may contribute to a feeling of satisfaction with single life.

apartments, greasy spoon taverns, and transient hotels, into nine high-rise buildings surrounded by townhouses and renovated apartments. Nearly three-quarters of the residents 18 and older are unmarried. Occupants enjoy an indoor swimming pool, gymnasiums, restaurants, and other built-in amenities. Rents have skyrocketed, but people who cannot afford the leases often get roommates, increasing the number of unwed couples living together ("The Ways 'Singles' Are Changing U.S.," 1977).

One of the most popular singles areas on the West Coast is Marina del Rey, adjacent to Los Angeles, where 9,500 apartment dwellers live on 400 acres of Pacific waterfront. Singles outnumber marrieds by almost two to one. Residents live amidst office buildings, restaurants, and bars and enjoy swimming pools; tennis and handball courts; a facial salon; and limousine, bodyguard, and charter-jet services. They also have the largest man-made pleasure harbor in the world, which moors 6,000 sailboats, yachts, and cruisers ("The Ways . . . ," 1977).

Many people criticize the life-style epitomized by Marina del Rey as rootless and superficial. The aging baby boom generation of post–World War II is beginning to look for a more stable life-style, oriented more toward family and career. In many communities, singles are settling easily and quickly into traditional family neighborhoods.

Singles' living areas have had their problems. As singles flooded into new and restored apartments in the Yorkville section of Manhattan, cases of venereal disease increased dramatically, as did the number of prostitutes and burglaries. Skyrocketing rents and taxes drove out many older people.

110

INTIMATE
RELATIONSHIPS:
GROWTH, CHOICES, AND
CHANGE

Shared Living Spaces

Although large numbers of unmarrieds live in singles' areas or apartments, more live with the general population. The majority occupy individual apartments, usually with roommates. The usual pattern is to share apartments and living expenses with one or more persons who provide emotional support and companionship.

Living with Parents

The percentage of young adults (18 to 29 years of age) who lived with parents reached a high in 1940, near the end of the economic depression. The percentages declined to a low point in 1960, near the end of the baby boom, and have risen modestly since then (Glick and Lin, 1986). The increase has occurred because of marriage postponement and high rates of college enrollment, unemployment, divorce and separation, and birth to unmarried mothers. Table 5.4 shows the percentages of young adult men and women of different ages and races living at home with parents. Note that greater percentages of men than women of all ages lived at home with parents.

Table 5.5 shows the marital status of young adults who lived at home with parents or other relatives. Once married, separated, or divorced, greater percentages of women than men lived at home with parents or other relatives. Also, married, separated, or divorced women with one or more children were more likely to live at home with parents or relatives than were those who did not have any children (Glick and Lin, 1986). This often creates problems for both the parent and relatives and the young adults who come to live with them.

Living Alone

Table 5.6 shows the percent distribution, by age group, of singles living alone (U.S. Bureau of the Census, 1989). However, this table includes divorced, separated, or widowed people, as well as the never-married. As illustrated, greater numbers and percentage of males than females in the 15–24 and 25–44 age group live alone. With each succeeding age group (45–64 and 65 and over), the relative numbers and percentages of females living alone increase rapidly. This is due to the greater numbers of older females in the population.

SOCIAL LIFE AND LEISURE TIME

Singles Versus Marrieds

Is it true that singles have more leisure time and more fun than marrieds? It is easy for married persons to envy their apartment-dwelling single friends. But singles who work all week still have to clean their living quarters, make beds, cook, and do laundry. They go bicycling or to an art gallery; but if they

TABLE 5.4 *Young Adults Living with Their Parents,*
by Age, United States, 1987.

	PERCENT IN EACH CATEGORY	
	18–24 Years of Age	25–34 Years of Age
Total	54.3	11.1
Men	61.3	14.5
Women	47.5	7.7

Source: U.S. Bureau of the Census. (1989). *Statistical abstract of the United States, 1989.* Washington, DC: U.S. Government Printing Office, 49.

TABLE 5.5 *Marital Status of Young Adults,*
18–29 Years, Living with Parents or Other Relatives

	PERCENT IN EACH CATEGORY			
	Never Married	Married	Separated	Divorced
Men	94	3	1	2
Women	89	5	3	3

Source: U.S. Bureau of the Census. (1984). Summary, detailed population characteristics. *1980 Census of the United States,* 1-D1-A, U.S. Washington, DC: U.S. Government Printing Office.

TABLE 5.6 *Persons Living Alone, by Age and Sex, 1987*

Age Group	NUMBERS OF PERSONS (1,000)			PERCENT DISTRIBUTION		
	Both Sexes	Male	Female	Both Sexes	Male	Female
15–24	1,324	750	573	6.4	3.6	2.8
25–44	6,218	3,713	2,514	30.2	18	12.2
45–64	4,939	1,845	3,095	24.0	9	15.0
65 & over	8,112	1,614	6,498	39.4	7.8	31.5
All ages	20,602	7,922	12,680	100.0	38.5	62.5

Adapted from U.S. Bureau of the Census. (1989). *Statistical abstract of the United States, 1989* (109th ed.). Washington, DC: U.S. Government Printing Office.

want company, they have to call friends and probably encounter some rejections before plans are completed.

In spite of this, singles do have more time for optional activities. They can make more choices and devote more time to leisure activities if they choose.

Marrieds are more likely to have houses and children requiring time and attention (Cargan and Melko, 1982).

Types of Social Activities

According to Cargan and Melko (1982), visiting friends was the preferred social activity of never-marrieds, followed (in declining order of preference) by going to movies, restaurants, nightclubs, and theaters; visiting relatives; or going to social clubs. Couples married once preferred going to restaurants or visiting relatives. The entertainment preference of never-marrieds was more a preference of youth. Both never-marrieds and marrieds spent a lot of time watching television. Never-marrieds spent more time on hobbies.

Fun and Happiness

Despite the fact that singles spent more time on social activities, a greater percentage of marrieds than never-marrieds said they got a lot of fun out of life and that they were happy (Cargan and Melko, 1982). Marrieds may derive happiness and fun in different ways. Gardening or taking the children on a picnic can be fun. When asked what was most important to their happiness, marrieds mentioned health first, then marriage, children, love, religion, and friends in that order. Only the category of friends was more important to singles than to marrieds. Surprisingly, success and money were not listed as important to happiness in either group (Cargan and Melko, 1982).

Singles' Bars

Studies of singles' bars reveal that they function as social centers, as places to meet potential dates or sexual partners and to enjoy a casual evening with acquaintances and friends. But most popular bars are noisy and crowded and arranged to discourage sitting or prolonged conversation. Starr and Carns (1972), who studied Chicago's singles' community, found that most singles did not establish dating relationships in bars. Most dates resulted from work contacts or from friends introducing friends.

LONELINESS AND FRIENDSHIPS

Contradictory Views

The greatest need of single people is to develop interpersonal relationships, networks of friendships that provide emotional fulfillment, companionship, and intimacy (Verbrugge, 1979b). Single people value freedom and varied activities, but they also place a high value on enduring, close friendships.

The picture we have of singles is contradictory. They may go out more, but marrieds say they have more fun and are happier. Most singles have friends, but they are perceived as being lonely, having to initiate social relationships, and having no permanent, sharing relationship.

There is a difference between being alone and being lonely (Shaver and Rubenstein, 1980). Many never-marrieds do not perceive themselves as especially lonely. Two-thirds of them still live at home or with roommates of either sex (Cargan and Melko, 1982). Most have many friends with whom they spend considerable time. Loneliness is partly a psychological state, independent of whether a person is in the company of someone else (Meer, 1985a). Married people who are estranged from their mate may be quite lonely, even though they still live together. Many people enjoy being by themselves. A frequent complaint of busy housewives is that they never have an opportunity to be alone.

Loneliness is not related to doing things with someone, but rather to having someone to turn to, to call or touch when the need is there. We are lonely when we feel there is nobody upon whom we can rely, especially in conditions of stress or threat.

The Importance of Companionship

When Cargan and Melko (1982) asked both marrieds and singles to describe the greatest advantage of being married, most replied in terms of shared feelings: "Companionship and someone to share decisions with," "companionship," "love and companionship," "the opportunity to converse with someone every day," "being able to share your life with someone you love," "togetherness is very important to me," "love is caring and having children and sharing things, and doing things together." The concept that turned up most frequently was companionship.

A minority of singles feel the lack of sharing with someone. A physician (now married) commented:

> Med school for me was the loneliest period of my life. I lived alone, studied alone, and was alone most of the time. I didn't really have any friends or anyone with whom to socialize. I think I married Chris soon after I met her because I was so terribly lonely. At last, I had someone to talk to and to do things with. (Author's counseling notes)

One woman remarked, "I'm not lonely every day, only when I have something to share, or want to do something with someone. The rest of the time I'm perfectly content."

Males Versus Females

Loneliness is a problem for a significant minority of never-marrieds (Cargan, 1981). Some evidence suggests that among single young adults, male-male friendships are less intimate and spontaneous than are female-female friendships. Single males are more isolated and have fewer intimate relationships than do single females (Tognoli, 1980). Although men sometimes exceed women in the number of voluntary associations in which they hold memberships, they spend less time in group activities and their participation is less stable. The norms of competition and fear of homosexuality have hindered the development of male friendships. Yet, males as well as females need close, caring friendships that develop into a sense of mutuality and constitute a major source of social support (Stein, 1978).

SEXUAL BEHAVIOR

According to a 1983 national survey of unmarried women, 82 percent of women aged 20–29 had had sexual intercourse (Tanfer and Horn, 1985). Hunt's (1974) survey of a national sample revealed that 97 percent of men had sexual intercourse by 25 years of age. The most sexually active singles are those who are divorced. Hunt (1974) found that of divorced persons under age 55, all of the men and 90 percent of the women were sexually active. Cargan and Melko (1982) reported that over half of divorced persons said they had intercourse twice a week or more. Only one-third of never-marrieds had intercourse twice a week or more (Cargan and Melko, 1982).

To what extent are single persons promiscuous; that is, to what extent do they have a variety of sexual partners? Hunt (1974) reported that during 1973 the median number of sexual partners for single men in the survey who were under age 25 was two; for single men between 25 and 34, it was four. The corresponding figures for women were two and three. Hunt concluded that the patterns of unmarried sex still seemed to be operating largely "within the framework of long-held cultural values of intimacy and love" (Hunt, 1974, p. 154). Cargan and Melko (1982) found the same thing. Among never-marrieds, 63 percent had three or fewer partners during their lifetime. Women were less promiscuous than men. Cargan and Melko (1982) found that 81 percent of never-married women had three or fewer partners. A minority of both men and women were more promiscuous. Fifteen percent of never-marrieds and 31 percent of divorced persons had had more than 10 partners during their lifetime (Cargan and Melko, 1982).

A study of 400 subjects in the Dayton, Ohio, area included never-married, first-married, divorced, and remarried individuals (Cargan, 1981). About 63 percent of never-marrieds claimed they had 3 or fewer sexual partners in their sexual history and 15 percent said they had had 11 or more partners. In contrast, 31 percent of the divorced reported they had had 11 or more partners. Cargan concluded that only a minority of singles fit the "swinger" stereotype and they were more likely to be divorced than never-married. He also found that both never-married and divorced persons were far less likely to be satisfied with their sex life than were married persons (Cargan, 1981).

EMPLOYMENT AND INCOME

One stereotype is that never-marrieds are richer than marrieds. They have no spouses or children to support; they do not require expensive homes; and they can live more cheaply than marrieds.

Actually, marrieds are financially better off than never-marrieds. The median income of married male householders (wife present) in 1987 was $34,782; for single male householders it was $21,493. The median income of married female householders in 1987 was $34,847; for single female householders it was $15,759. Figure 5.4 shows the comparison (U.S. Bureau of the

FIGURE 5.4 Median Income, by Household Type and Marital Status: 1989.

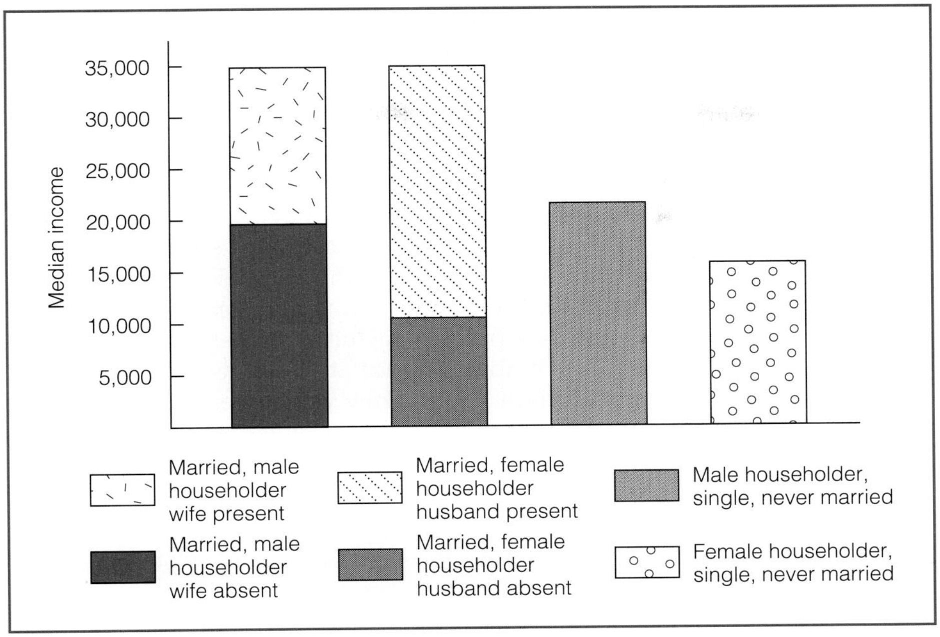

Adapted from U.S. Bureau of the Census. (1989). *Statistical abstract of the United States, 1989* (109th ed.). Washington, DC: U.S. Government Printing Office, 441.

Census, 1989). According to these figures, greater percentages of married householders are in high-income brackets than are never-married householders.

There are a number of reasons for these differences. Slightly more than half of all married women are employed outside the home, contributing substantially to the total household income. The combined incomes of two wage earners is likely to be greater than the income of one wage earner.

Another reason is that employers are prejudiced in favor of married persons. There are only certain kinds of jobs for which employers would prefer a single person. Employers assume that married people are more stable, will stay on the job longer, and are more qualified for promotions than single people. Married people do receive higher wages and more promotions than single persons. It is assumed that married couples will become an integral part of the community and fit into the corporate structure; single people are sometimes considered outsiders, occupying their own worlds apart from the corporate family.

A third reason for the income discrepancies is that singles constitute a younger, less experienced age group and so earn less money. However, when age differences are considered, singles still earn less than married people.

A fourth reason is a practical one. Married people, especially those with families, have to earn more money because their needs are greater, and they are more highly motivated to earn higher incomes. Despite the many exceptions to this principle, it is generally true. Many marrieds are forced to work more than one job to provide sufficient incomes for their families.

Finally, the discrepancies reflect deep-seated prejudices against women. Overall, the average female with education, experience, and position comparable to that of a male is paid only about 62 percent as much for the same work (Rice, 1987). As shown in Figure 5.4, the never-married female householder earns a median income of $15,759 per year compared to $21,493 per year for the never-married male householder. This clearly reflects the disadvantage under which women work.

THE OLDER, NEVER-MARRIED ADULT

The major differences between older adults who have never married and younger ones is that most younger singles consider their status temporary, whereas older singles are often well-adjusted to their situation. Older singles may not be interested in dating, but they usually have some social life and a variety of things to do with a few friends. A study of older singles between 60 and 94 found that they saw nothing special about being married: it was "just another way of life" (Gubrium, 1976). They valued being independent, were relatively isolated (but not lonely), and were generally satisfied with

Many older singles value their independence, rarely feel isolated, and are generally happy with their lives.

their activities. They did not have to face widowhood or divorce and tended to accept and take for granted their life-style. They were unique persons, not misfits, who had adjusted to life differently from most.

The following comments from a 71-year old male are typical:

> I have been single all my life (seventy-one years). I am living alone now and have a beautiful, well-furnished, two-and-a-half-room apartment. I work at home and keep the apartment clean. I don't think I would like to live together presently. I'd rather not be married, even though I have plenty of opportunities. (Hite, 1982, p. 266)

It's hard to find fault with this man's point of view or life-style. The important thing is that he is happy and satisfied.

In contrast to the situation of this man, other single adults who have never married are not completely happy with their situation. Keith (1986) found that a sizeable minority of unmarried aged felt isolated from neighbors, friends, and relatives. Men were more likely to be isolated from family than were women. Divorced and never-married men and women were more isolated from family than were those who were widowed. Both never-married men and women, however, compensated for their isolation from relatives by maintaining more ties with friends.

Overall, however, the happiness of these older adults was very dependent on satisfaction with their level of living and with their level of activity rather than just on the extent of social contacts. Adequate financial resources permitted mobility and reciprocation in the development and maintenance of friendships. Also, if persons were satisfied with their level of activity even though they might be isolated from family or friends, they tended to express greater happiness.

ASSESSMENT
What Do I Think of Singlehood?

1. List as many advantages of being single as you can.
2. List the disadvantages of being single.
3. Which are greater, the advantages or disadvantages? Explain.
4. *To never-marrieds*
   Do you want to remain single permanently? Why? Why not?
   Ideally, are there any particular years of your adult life when you would rather be single than married? During which years? Why? Are there any particular years of your adult life when you would rather be married than single? During which years? Why? Are your preferences possible to achieve? That is, is it realistic to expect you can be single for a period of your adult life and married for another period?
5. *To marrieds*
   Are you glad or sorry you married? Explain.
   If you had it to do over again, would you make any changes? What? Why?
   Do you ever wish you were single again? Explain.
6. *To divorced*
   Are you satisfied with your present marital situation?
   Would you prefer remaining single or remarrying? Why?
7. *To widowed*
   Are you satisfied with your present marital situation? Would you prefer remarrying, or staying as you are? Why?

1. Overall, the great majority of people in the United States marry. Fewer blacks than whites marry.

2. Adult singles may be divided into four groups: voluntary temporary singles, voluntary permanent singles, involuntary temporary singles, and involuntary permanent singles.

3. Singles are often described with stereotypical images, usually negative, that often lead to misunderstanding and discrimination against them.

4. Actually, most adults who are single delay marriage rather than remain permanently single. By age 45–54, only 5.9 percent of men and 4.5 percent of women have never married.

5. Some people remain single because of deliberate choice, fear of marriage, lack of opportunity, personality problems, circumstances, or parents.

6. The negative and positive influences on the decision to marry or to remain single have been described as pushes and pulls.

7. There are both advantages and disadvantages to being single. Overall, single people are less healthy physically or mentally than married people and have a shorter life expectancy. The divorced, separated, and widowed have the poorest health. There are also many gender differences. Never-married men have poorer physical and mental health than do married men. Never-married women may fare as well or better than married women on a number of mental health, physical health, and life satisfaction indexes. However, married women who have children and satisfying high-prestige jobs usually rate very high on measures of happiness and well-being.

8. There are wide variations in the life-styles of singles. Some singles live in predominantly singles' communities; others share living spaces with friends, live with parents, or live alone.

9. Singles spend more time than marrieds on social acitivities of their own choosing, but marrieds report they have more fun.

10. One of the greatest needs of single persons is to develop fulfilling friendships. Loneliness is often a problem, although it is not necessarily synonymous with being alone. Single men more often join organizations than do single women, but have more difficulty than women in establishing intimate relationships.

11. Most single adults have had sexual intercourse, but are not promiscuous, confining their sexual experiences to only a few partners during their lifetime. Divorced persons are likely to have had more partners than never-marrieds. However, both never-marrieds and divorced persons are less likely to be satisfied with their sex life than are married persons.

12. Marrieds are usually better off financially than are single persons.

13. Many older singles are well-adjusted to their situation. Others are not completely happy, especially if they feel isolated from neighbors, friends, and relatives. Adequate financial resources and an acceptable level of activity are important to satisfaction.

Barkas, J. L. (1980). *Single in America: A Candid Look at the Rewards and Drawbacks of Living Single*. New York: Atheneum, 1980. Based upon 200 interviews.

Cargan, L., and Melko, M. (1982). *Singles: Myths and Realities*. Beverly Hills, CA: Sage. A study of singles in Dayton, Ohio.

Lopate, P. (1981). *Bachelorhood: Tales of the Metropolis*. Boston: Little, Brown. A funny and shrewd observation of bachelor life.

Shahan, L. (1981). *Living Alone and Liking It: A Complete Guide to Living on Your Own*. New York: Warner. A best-seller.

Simenauer, J., and Carroll, D. (1982). *Singles: The New Americans*. New York: Simon and Schuster.

Simenauer, J., and Carroll, D. (1984). *Singles and Sex: A New Study*. New York: Simon and Schuster.

Staples, R. (1981). *The World of Black Singles: Changing Patterns of Male-Female Relationships*. Westport, CT: Greenfield. Detailed discussion.

Stein, P. (Ed.). (1981). *Single Life: Unmarried Adults in Social Context*. New York: St. Martin's Press. Good articles.

6

DATING, GOING TOGETHER, AND COURTSHIP

KEY TERMS

bundling
dating
steady dating
date rape
imaging
extradyadic sexual activity

In 18th century America, if a man desired the company of a woman, he had to meet her family, be formally introduced, and obtain permission to court her.

Dating as a means of heterosexual social interaction is very rare in most of the world. It is virtually unknown in China and India, which together hold over half the world's population. It is still rare in most areas of Africa, South America, and in some countries around the Mediterranean: Greece, Spain, Sicily, and Portugal. It is forbidden in Egypt, Saudia Arabia, Iran, Libya, and other Muslim countries (Saxton, 1986).

Dating is widely practiced in most of Western Europe and is most common in the United States, Great Britain, Canada, Australia, and New Zealand. In these countries, it is now recognized as *the* method by which young people get to know one another, learn to get along heterosocially, and select mates by mutual choice.

THE DATING SYSTEM

Courtship in Early America

Dating is a relatively recent phenomenon; it did not become firmly established until the years after World War I (Mead, 1959). In the 1700s and 1800s, casual meetings at unsupervised social affairs were condemned, and "pickups" were unknown. Parents carefully supervised the activities of their children, especially of their daughters. Young women were not left alone to meet young

PERSPECTIVE
Bundling

Bundling was a fascinating courtship system that existed in colonial America. It allowed couples to talk and visit while keeping warm on a cold night. If a young man wanted to court a woman, he might have to walk a long distance on a snowy winter evening to see her. The family usually prepared for bed shortly after supper; and if the young man were asked to leave, he had very little time to visit the woman whom he had walked miles to see. Since fuel and candles were scarce, it would be wasteful to burn them exclusively for the couple while they stayed up and visited. The couple was allowed to climb onto a bundling bed and get under the covers with only outer garments removed. There they would talk late into the night. Some beds had a "bundling board" that was placed between the two people. In other instances, the woman got into a sack that was sealed at the neck. Rigid sex codes forbade any sexual contact, so the custom didn't seem to encourage sexual experimentation. Doten (1938) quotes a poem that reflects the attitudes of country folk toward the practice.

> Nature's request is, give me rest
>   Our bodies seek repose;
> Night is the time, and 'tis no crime
>   To bundle in our clothes.
>
> Since in a bed, a man and maid
>   May bundle and be chaste;
> It doth no good to burn up wood
>   It is a needless waste.
>
> Let coat and shift be turned adrift,
>   And breeches take their flight,
> An honest man and virgin can
>   Lie quiet all the night. (p.26)

The practice gradually diminished as transportation improved so that a young man could return home the same evening. As fuel became more plentiful, courting was moved from the bedroom to the parlor. With the advent of the automobile, it moved to the seat of the car.

From Doten, D. (1938). *The art of bundling.* New York: Farrar. Used by permission of Henry Holt and Company.

men casually and indiscriminately. If a man desired the company of a woman, he had to meet her family, be formally introduced, and obtain permission to court her as well as gain her permission to be courted before they could go out. Even after a couple had been formally introduced, they were often chaperoned (especially upper-class women) or attended social functions only in the company of friends or relatives. Although parents had no legal control over their children's choice of partner, they exerted considerable influence, and even veto power, over whom a son or daughter might be seeing or considering for marriage. Parents were concerned about the social standing and prestige, economic status, education, and family background of possible suitors. Parents also sought to control the courtship process itself. If a young man wanted to marry a woman, he had to ask her father's permission for her hand in marriage.

At this time, marriage in Europe was typically arranged by parents, with little emphasis on romantic attraction. Arranged marriages sought to merge the wealth, property, and good name of the families to insure economic well-being and the perpetuation of family status and prestige. Only a few American marriages were parentally arranged. These were limited to the most aristocratic families, who sought to expand their financial empires through marriage. American courtship was controlled more by the participants, who exercised autonomy and freedom (Reiss, 1980).

Emergence of Dating

By the late nineteenth and early twentieth century, chaperonage and close supervision of courtship had declined. A new pattern of **dating** emerged whereby young people themselves arranged a time and place to meet so they could get to know one another better and participate in activities together. The primary purpose was to have fun and enjoy one another's company. Parents might seek to maintain some control of dating partners, but generally the system allowed a high level of freedom from parental supervision.

In the years following World War I, the dating system was still comparatively stylized and formal. The man was expected to take the initiative in asking the woman for a date. Generally, he was expected to plan the activities, pay all the expenses, and exercise his masculine prerogatives as the leader. Gradually, over the years, the pattern became less structured and more informal, with greater equality between the sexes in initiating and planning dates. Today couples frequently just "get together" to do things or to "go out," without going through a specific ritual. "Going together" has replaced the formal patterns of courtship of previous generations.

The emergence of dating was due to numerous factors. The most important was *the rise of the industrial revolution*. Thousands of families moved from farms to crowded cities where young people had increased opportunities for social contact. Lower-class women were employed in the mills and factories where they met male workers. Some girls from farm families took up residence in boarding houses away from home and so were separated from parental supervision. The invention of the telephone enabled youths to contact one another from considerable distances.

At the same time, the late 1800s saw *the rise of free, public high schools*, where large numbers of physically mature youths were brought together for coeducational schooling (the private academies had segregated the sexes). This encouraged heterosexual activities that allowed youths to band together for emotional support, companionship, status, and various activities, including dating.

Increased affluence and leisure time enabled youths to devote more time to their own pursuits and to social life. Having a date became a pleasant way of spending an evening. During and after World War I, middle-class women began to work in offices and stores and attained greater economic and personal freedom. For the first time, they were allowed to wear less restrictive clothing and to engage in strenuous sports. (They participated in the Olympic Games for the first time in 1920.) This new freedom allowed them to engage in many of these activities with men.

The invention and use of the automobile increased mobility and provided transportation to roadhouses, nightclubs, parties, dances, theaters, and restaurants. Youths could go to a variety of places on dates or simply park and neck or "spoon." The automobile became a bundling bed on wheels.

The 1920s represented an early *surge of the feminine equality movement*. The women's movement encouraged women's rights politically, socially, and sexually and made it possible for young women to participate on a more equal basis with young men in the total life of the community. Liberated women with their bobbed hair and flapper dresses were now free to take a ride in their boyfriend's jalopy and to engage in a little petting on the sly without being under the watchful eye of chaperones. As a result, dating emerged as an important part of the life of American youths, replacing the previous system of formalized courtship.

The Rating-Dating Complex

During the 1930s, Willard Waller (1937) observed dating behavior on the campus of Pennsylvania State University and published a paper entitled "The Rating-and-Dating Complex." The report caused quite a stir because it described dating as a superficial, exploitative relationship rather than as a means of finding and selecting a future marriage partner. Men outnumbered women six to one on the campus, which resulted in much competition for dates. The fraternity system was flourishing. Men and women were rated according to their desirability as a date. Class A men belonged to one of the better fraternities, were prominent in prestigious activities, had plenty of money and access to an automobile, were good conversationalists (had a good line), were good dancers, were well dressed, and were considered a popular date by others. Men who did not rate in Class A were placed in a lower class: B, C, and D. Women with high ratings wore good clothes, had a smooth line and the ability to dance well, and were considered popular. Coeds tried to give the impression of being more sought after even if they did not belong to Class A. Young women often allowed themselves to be paged several times in the dorm when the telephone rang for them. They were never supposed to make themselves available for last-minute dates. They avoided being seen too often with the same young man so as not to discourage others. They tried to have many partners at dances. Above all, Class A women dated only Class A men, and so forth.

The system emphasized physical stimulation. Pretending to be in love was an important part of the game. Each person wanted to feel more involved than he or she was.

Other research has substantiated part of Waller's description of campus life of the 1920s and 1930s, especially the role that fraternities and sororities played in creating social activities. According to Fass (1977) the University of Wisconsin was reported to have hosted 30 college dances and 80 fraternity and sorority dances each month in 1925. However, other observers looked at campus life in the 1930s and reported that a cooling of intensity of the rating game was already in evidence (Gordon, 1981). Certainly, the economic depression altered undergraduate culture. College enrollments dipped; Greek letter societies declined and were less able to maintain the dominant role on campuses. World War II completed the transformation. Automobiles and partying declined for the duration.

Today, there are still some prestige dimensions to cross-sex socializing, but the rating and dating complex has virtually disappeared. Pluralistic dating has given way to exclusive dating, but not necessarily to choosing-a-mate oriented relationships.

Dating and Courtship in the 1940s to 1960s

The most important dating pattern to develop just prior to World War II was that of **steady dating**. This pattern developed as an outgrowth of both heterosexual contacts at younger ages and the practice of group and random dating that developed in junior high school and the early years of high school. Steady dating was an intermediate form between casual dating and engagement, since it involved a transition between the noncommitment of casual dating and the very high commitment of engagement. Such an intermediate stage was necessary for individuals who were allowed personal responsibility for the selection of their own mate.

One of the best descriptions of the dating and courtship system of the 1950s was given by LeMasters (1957) in his book, *Modern Courtship and Marriage*. The six stages LeMaster identified are shown in Table 6.1. These stages represented an orderly progression from the first date in the junior high school years until marriage in the late teens or early twenties. An adolescent girl usually had her first crush in junior high school; boys reached this stage one or two years later. At each stage, the relationship was excessively romantic, with other considerations subordinated to the fact that the two were madly in love. Also, each successive stage involved a progressively deeper commitment. Each stage also implied an appropriate degree of sexual intimacy. The more commitment, the greater the intimacy that was allowed. This led one young man to remark:

> I often had the uncomfortable feeling that the California coed dispensed passion by some sort of rule book. It had all been decided beforehand: the first date, so many kisses, the second date, lips apart, tongue enters, fifth date, three buttons, next time, one zipper . . . (Greene, 1964, p. 131)

TABLE 6.1 *Stages in Dating and Courtship in the 1950s*

Ages or Grades	Stage
7th, 8th grades	Group dating
9th, 10th grades	Random dating between "steadies"
11th, 12th grades	Steady dating
College years (earlier for women, later for men	Pinning
College years, or post–high school years	Engagement
Ages 19 to 21 for women, 20 to 24 for men	Marriage

Adapted from LeMasters, E. E. (1957). *Modern courtship and marriage.* New York: Macmillan. Copyright © 1957 by Macmillan. Used with permission.

"Steadies" frequently broke up and realigned themselves with others, but broken engagements were serious matters.

There was sense and logic to the system except when youths moved too rapidly from the earliest stages to marriage. Speeding up the courtship process was more common among lower socioeconomic status youths than among the middle class — resulting in an increasing number of marriages at younger ages — until the trend began to be reversed in the early 1960s (Rice, 1983).

Dating and Courtship Today

Dating and courtship have undergone many changes since they emerged as a social phenomenon. One major change is that *dating begins at younger ages*. The median age at which youths begin dating has decreased by almost three years since World War I, from 16 to 13 years. This change is primarily because of peer pressure to date earlier (Hennessee, 1983). Bell and Coughey (1980) report that the average age at first going steady was 17 in 1958 and 15.9 in 1978.

Another major change is in the *increased opportunities for informal heterosexual contacts*. High schools and colleges that used to be exclusively for men or women are now coeducational. Many college dormitories have become coed. Academic programs that used to attract only one sex or the other now enroll both men and women. Men and women share apartments. Some fraternities are now coeducational. These changes represent a drastic departure from the days when college men and women ate and slept on different parts of the campus. With such segregation, it was more difficult to get together, often requiring a formal phone call to arrange a meeting or a date. Today, group or paired social activities develop as a natural result of daily informal contacts in residences, classrooms, and social centers.

Another major change is in *the lack of any set pattern of progression of intimacy and commitment from initial meeting to marriage*. Previously, couples followed a fairly consistent pattern: casual dating, steadily dating, going steady, an understanding (engaged to be engaged), engagement, and marriage. Today patterns vary. Some couples follow closely the traditional pattern already described. Other couples decide to date one another exclusively and, after a period of time, decide to live together before getting married. There may be no formal engagement, but marriage develops out of the cohabitation experience. In other words, not all couples become formally engaged and follow the traditional pattern. Patterns of dating and courtship vary among different couples.

Dating today is also much less formal than in previous generations. It is not necessary for the man to make a formal request in order to arrange a date. This sometimes happens, but a date may be arranged by mutual consent as a result of conversation about the evening activities. Also, more and more women are taking the initiative in arranging a get-together. Dress is certainly more casual, and the activities are often less formal or more casually planned. Many times, a social evening can not really be called a date. The couples just go out together for an informal evening.

One of the most significant changes in dating patterns is in the reasons for dating. These changes are discussed in detail in the following section.

Dating fulfills a number of important functions in the lives of today's youths.

Dating is recreation. One of the reasons couples go out is simply to relax, enjoy themselves, and have fun. It is a form of entertainment and thereby an end in itself.

Dating is for companionship, friendships, and personal intimacy. Many youths indicate an intense desire to develop close, intimate relationships through the dating experience. One study found that those couples who were able to share their most important thoughts and feelings in an egalitarian relationship were those most likely to be compatible and in love (Rubin et al., 1980).

Dating is a means of socialization. Dating helps the individual learn social skills, gain confidence and poise, and begin to master the arts of conversation, cooperation, and consideration for others.

Dating is a means of personality development. One way individuals have of finding their own personal identity is in relationship to other persons. Since individuals mature as persons primarily through successful experiences with others and since an adequate self-concept is partly a result of successful human associations, an important part of all individuals' personality development is that they have successful dating experiences. One of the reasons that students go steady is precisely because such associations give them security and feelings of individual worth.

Dating provides an opportunity for trying out sex roles (Davis, 1978). Sex roles must be worked out in actual situations with the opposite-sex partner. Many women today find that they cannot accept a traditionally passive role; dating helps them to discover this and to learn what kind of a role they find fulfilling in a close relationship.

Dating is a means of fulfilling the need for love and affection. No matter how many casual friends students have, they fulfill their deepest emotional needs for love and affection in close relationships with individuals. This need for affection is one of the major motives for dating.

Dating provides an opportunity for sexual experimentation and satisfaction. Dating has become more sex-oriented, with increasing percentages of students engaging in sexual intercourse (Robinson and Jedlicka, 1982).

Dating is a means of mate sorting and selection. Dating is the method in our culture of sorting out compatible pairs. The process is one of filtering out, gradually narrowing the field of eligibles from a pool of several to a specific few and eventually to one individual. Whether dating results in the selection of the most compatible pairs will depend on the total experience. Not all dating patterns result in wise mate selection, especially if dating partners are chosen on the basis of superficial traits (Cote and Koval, 1983).

Dating is a means of preparation for marriage. Not only can dating result in the sorting of compatible pairs, but it can also become a means of socialization for marriage itself. Through dating, couples develop a better understanding of the behavior and attitudes of the opposite sex; each partner learns how to get along with another person and how to discuss and solve problems. The longer the dating period before marriage, the more dating fulfills this function of "anticipatory socialization" for marriage (Lloyd and Cote, 1984).

Of all of the reasons for dating just discussed, which ones seem uppermost as actual motivations of modern students? An important study of male students at Harvard University showed that students were most interested in dating as a form of companionship and as a means of finding sexual intimacy (Vreeland, 1972):

> For today's student, the most important dating motive is *finding a friend who is female*. The most essential characteristic in a good date is her ability to make conversation, and the primary dating activity is sitting around the room talking. At the same time, the sexual component of dating should not be ignored. Sex was one of the most important dating activities. (p.68)

DATING PARTNERS VERSUS MARRIAGE PARTNERS

In spite of its benefits, not all dating is helpful in mate selection or marital preparation. It can be counterproductive if it emphasizes personal qualities that are not always important in marriage. In a survey of 1,135 college students, they were asked to name three qualities they considered to be most important in a date, and then to name three qualities considered most important in a spouse. Table 6.2 shows the results. The most important characteristics in a date were *extrinsic characteristics*: being physically attractive, having a sense of humor, being fun, and being a good conversationalist. The most important characteristics in a spouse were *intrinsic qualities*: being loving and affectionate, honest, ambitious, and loyal. This pattern was true for both males and females. These findings suggest that youths tend to look for somewhat different qualities in a spouse than in a date, a fact that may hinder the selection of a compatible marriage partner. In another study, this at the College of San Mateo in California, 350 randomly selected males and 350 randomly selected females were asked to write down the three qualities most valued in a date and the three qualities most valued in a spouse (Saxton, 1977). For both men and women, *looks* and *personality* in a date ranked first and second in importance. In addition to the qualities desired in a date, both men and women mentioned *love*, *being compatible*, and *being understanding* as important

TABLE 6.2 *Rank Order of Desirable Qualities
in a Date and in a Spouse for 1,135 College Students*

Most Important Qualities of a Date	Most Important Qualities of a Spouse
1. Physical attractiveness	1. Loving and affectionate
2. Congenial personality	2. Honest
3. Sense of humor	3. Congenial personality
4. Intelligent	4. Respectful
5. Manners/being considerate	5. Intelligent
6. Sincere, genuine	6. Mature/responsible
7. Compatible interests	7. Ambitious
8. Conversational ability	8. Loyal and trustworthy
9. Fun to be with	9. Physical attractiveness

From Jorgensen, S. R. (1986). *Marriage and the family.* New York: Macmillan, 260. Copyright © 1986 by Stephen R. Jorgensen. Used with permission.

qualities in a spouse. Women also desired a husband who was *loyal and faithful* and *responsible*. The point is, if dating is the primary means of mate sorting, but different qualities are desired in dates than are expected in marriage, how can suitable mates be discovered through the dating experience? It becomes more difficult.

FINDING AND MEETING DATES

Where and How They Meet

One of the major problems of those who want to date is where and how to meet prospective partners. Knox and Wilson (1981) surveyed a random sample of 334 students at East Carolina University to find out how they met, where they went, and what they did on dates. About a third of the students met their current dating partner "through a friend." The next most frequently mentioned way of meeting was "at a party." A lesser number met "at work" or "in a class." Those not meeting in these ways checked "other," which included "I grew up with him/her" and "we met on the school newspaper" (p. 256). Table 6.3 summarizes the information.

College Bars

Strouse (1987) studied two samples of college-age individuals to determine the reasons why they frequented college bars. The first sample comprised 637 students in a University of Michigan class in *Human Sexuality*. Over half (51 percent) of these students indicated that they went to bars "to socialize with friends." Seven percent of these students (11.7 percent of men and 3.4 percent of women) said they went to a bar to meet a sexual partner. Thirty-five percent said they would prefer going to a bar if they wanted to meet opposite-sex persons. The second sample comprised 260 patrons of three bars in a town in the north central United States. The majority (57 percent) of these persons indicated that the main reason for going to bars was to see friends, meet people, and to socialize. Fourteen percent of the men and

TABLE 6.3 How 334 University Students Met
Their Dating Partner

Ways of Meeting	Percent Female N = 227	Percent Male N = 107
Through a friend	33	32
Party	22	13
At work	12	5
Class	6	9
Other	27	41

From Knox, D., and Wilson, K. (1981). Dating behaviors of university students. *Family Relations, 30,* 255–258. Copyright © 1981 by the National Council on Family Relations. Reprinted by permission.

PERSPECTIVE
The College Mixer

Schwartz and Lever (1985) describe a college mixer at Yale University. Even with coeducation at Yale, there are many more men than women attending, so various groups sponsor dances to which they invite women from nearby schools. Vassar, Smith, and Mount Holyoke are about 80 miles distant. The typical mixer at Yale starts around 8:30 P.M. The men take positions in the hall before the women arrive. Since the women will not be there throughout the week, both men and women are under time pressure to get to know each other better before the women have to leave. People must quickly evaluate each other and attempt to make contact with those they have decided they like. Some are mutually attracted, but many more get rebuffed or end up with someone they do not really care for. All night long people are being approved or discarded on the basis of one characteristic that is hard, or at least painful, to discount — their appearance.

There is little chance to talk since the music is deafening. Therefore, there is no opportunity to evaluate a person on the basis of ideas, philosophy of life, world views, or things in common. Only one criterion for evaluation exists. When rejection is obvious and even recurrent within the same four-hour period, it makes inroads on one's self-image. Students reported feelings of "ugliness," "fatness," "clumsiness," and so forth during and after the mixer.

None of the women interviewed, and only one of the men, claimed personally to like mixers. They referred to mixers as "body exchanges" and "meat markets." The women reacted most strongly against the mixer system. A junior transfer described her feelings:

> I generally think mixers are grotesque. There you are a piece of meat lined up along a wall in this herd of ugly females. You try to stand casually as guys walk back and forth and you know you're on display. You just want to crawl up the wall. Then you're asked to dance by these really gross creatures. I'm so revolted by the whole thing . . .

Throughout the evening men and women are conscious of being constantly evaluated, desired, or disregarded. But they don't leave the mixer even though they feel uncomfortable there. The women are captive until their buses leave at midnight; the men stay because the mixer is the place to secure names for the year's dating events.

For the majority, however, it is clear that the effects of the mixer are seen as personally destructive. Repeated failures can cause people to doubt their attractiveness to the opposite sex. A junior transfer reflected back on her three years in the mixer system:

> I always ended up with someone I was very unhappy with. I used to wonder why I attracted that type. Very few people ever found anyone decent. Most people came back from those things feeling negatively about the experience and feeling negatively about themselves. (p. 223)

From Schwartz, Pepper and Lever, Janet (January 1976). Fear and loathing at a college mixer. *Urban Life*, 4, no. 4, 413–431. Copyright © 1976 by Sage Publications. Reprinted by permission.

18 percent of the women went to bars to find a partner for sexual intercourse. Overall, the data suggested that these individuals went to bars to escape boredom and loneliness, to relax and have fun, to socialize with friends, and to meet a heterosexual partner.

Opening Lines

Psychologist Chris Kleinke asked several hundred students at colleges in California and Massachusetts to suggest opening lines that they might use

Modern dating couples enjoy a variety of informal activities together.

to meet women in general situations, at beaches, supermarkets, and bars. Kleinke divided approaches into three groups: "direct," "innocuous," or "cute/flippant." Men and women both claimed to prefer direct and innocuous approaches to cute/flippant ones. The top-rated openers were:

In general situations: "I feel a little embarrassed, but I'd like to meet you." (direct)

At the beach: "The water is beautiful today, isn't it?" (innocuous)

At a supermarket: "Can you help me decide here? I'm a terrible shopper." (direct)

At a bar: "What do you think of the band?" (innocuous)

The least-favored of the cute/flippant openers were:

In general situations: "Is that really your hair?" "Your place or mine?" "You remind me of a woman I used to date."

At the beach: "Let me see your strap marks."

At a supermarket: "Do you really eat that junk?"

At a bar: "Bet I can outdrink you" (Rice, 1981b).

Self-Advertising

Newspapers and magazines across the country carry personal advertisements from people who are seeking a partner. Some of these sources contain information that allows interested parties to contact the advertiser directly. The following are actual ads:

LUMINOUS, LITHE, LUSCIOUSLY BEAUTIFUL, tantalizingly bright, relaxed 31 SJW [single, Jewish, white] seeks charismatic, handsome, athletic man who, like herself, feels deeply, laughs easily, is tender, warm, strong, sparkling, and playful. Is there a sincere, successful man out there who is in love with his work and looking for an endearing relationship? PO Box 0000, Cambridge, MA 02238.

SOFT SPOKEN, SWM [single, white, male], 6'0", 30, intelligent, professional, stockbroker seeks single, self-confident, attractive female for dating, perhaps more. PO Box 0000, Boston, MA 02114.

Some magazines function as go-betweens in which partners can contact each other only through the publisher of the magazine. An interested reader writes letters in response to one or more advertisements. Each letter is sealed and identified by number. They are then mailed to the publisher, who, for a fee, addresses and forwards each letter (Jedlicka, 1980).

Bolig, Stein, and McKenry (1984) analyzed the self-advertisements from a magazine for singles. Paradoxically, they found that the men who placed profiles in the magazines were not looking for the women who placed profiles, and vice-versa. There were insufficient numbers of older men for the females and an insufficient number of younger women for the males. Physical attractiveness was emphasized more than any other factor, which puts older and less attractive singles at a disadvantage. The women attempted to emphasize education, career, intelligence, and personality traits in themselves, but the men were more interested only in personality and attractiveness. This underscores the difficulty of the older, more-educated, career-oriented woman in finding a suitable partner, and of the younger, less-educated man in finding an attractive woman his own age or younger.

Dating Services

A wide variety of dating services charge a fee to bring people together. Many of the services are open to the general public. One example is *Together*, which operates nationwide. Some organizations serve specialized groups. The *Jewish Dating Service* matches Jewish singles, and *Chocolate Singles* matches blacks. *Preferred Singles* brings together those who are overweight. *Execumatch* charges a fee of $100,000 to find a marriage partner for the wealthy.

Videocassettes

The latest method of finding a partner is to have a videotape made of yourself and to put it on file with a company specializing in the service. This company then sends you videotapes of other people. *Great Resources* in New York charges $350 for a six-month membership. One woman reports she received 40 invitations and sent out nine in the six months she was a member (Kellogg, 1982).

Computer-Matched Services

Some organizations sell computer-matched information to members. Individuals are asked to complete a questionnaire so that information is fed into a

Dating services seek to sort out compatible pairs and bring them together.

computer, which sorts out the information to match those with similar profiles. One organization in Maine called *Matchmaker Dating Service of Maine* has over 6,200 members. It seeks the closest matches possible of characteristics like geographical area, age, height, build, education, and over 200 other traits. The service costs $35 for a lifetime registration and $25 per match on a pay-as-you-go basis.

Home computers may also bring people together. *Computer Information Services* of Columbus, Ohio, allows individuals to use any of its 36 channels to "talk" with other members. Subscribers send written information back and forth on their computers and decide if they want to meet one another.

PARENTS AND DATING

Since our system of courtship emphasizes individual freedom, the question arises as to how much influence parents have in the dating process. In the study of 334 university students by Knox and Wilson (1981), women were significantly more likely than men to report that their parents tried to influence their choice of dates. Sixty percent of the women compared to 40 percent of the men said parental influence was involved. Daughters also were more likely than sons to say that parents interfered with dating relationships. However, daughters were also more likely than sons to say it was important to them that they dated the kinds of people their parents would approve of. Thirty percent of men versus 10 percent of women said they didn't care what their parents thought.

In a study of parental reactions to dating of 159 college sophomores and juniors, Leslie, Huston, and Johnson (1986) reported that young adults also tried to influence their parents' thinking about their dating relationship. Eighty-five percent of respondents said they tried to influence their mothers; 77 percent had tried to influence their fathers.

Also, the more committed the young adults were in their dating behavior, the more likely they were to inform parents and to try to influence their opinion of it. Parents, in turn, were likely to support relationships in which their offspring were more highly involved. This means parents gave most support to engaged offspring, medium support to those going steady, and the least support to those involved in casual dating.

CLASSROOM FORUM
Parents Want To Choose Dates

Barbara is a senior in high school. She met a young man, Bill, whom she found attractive. Bill is a professional horse trainer who trains animals to participate in horse shows. He and Barbara met at a horse show and went riding together afterwards. They seemed to get along well from the moment they met, so they decided to start going out together.

Barbara told her parents about Bill, but they didn't seem pleased. They felt he was too old for her. (He is five years her senior.) She invited him to the house to meet her parents, but they objected to her seeing him even more. "How can you want to date a man who works in a barn? He's not our kind of people" was her mother's reaction. Barbara's parents didn't tell her she couldn't see Bill, but they made it very clear they didn't think he was right for her.

DISCUSSION

1. Should parents try to influence their children's choice of dates? Why? Why not? Are parents always wrong?

2. What role should parents play in date selection?

3. Should Barbara try to understand her parents' point of view? What would you do if you were she?

4. If parents are convinced that a son's or daughter's choice of a dating partner is all wrong for them, what might the parents do? Explain.

5. Have you ever been in a situation similar to Barbara's where your parents objected? Describe the situation. What did you do? What did your parents do? What was the outcome? On the basis of your experience, what would you advise other young people to do?

GENDER ROLES IN DATING

Changing Roles

Male-female roles in the dating process are changing rapidly. Traditionally, males controlled initiation, planning, and paying for the date. This arrangement encouraged an unspoken agreement where females were expected to reciprocate for benefits received by allowing expressions of affection and sexual intimacies (Sprecher, 1985).

With advent of the feminist movement, women became aware of the inequalities between the sexes and suspicious of the power distribution in heterosexual relationships. They have sought to equalize control within the dating situation by initiating and paying for dates, thereby altering both male sexual expectations and female sexual obligations on dates. In a study of 400 college women, Korman and Leslie (1982) found that approximately 55 percent of their sample reported that they helped pay the expenses of dates at least some of the time. Korman (1983a) compared the initiation and expense-sharing behavior on dates of feminists and nonfeminists. The subjects were 258 unmarried, undergraduate women attending classes at a large, Southeastern university. Feminists and nonfeminists were grouped according to summated scale scores on the FEM Scale. In comparison to nonfeminists, feminists were more likely to initiate dates and to share the financial obligations of women-initiated dates. However, their motives were to achieve more egalitarian relationships and not necessarily to reduce sexual obligations. While both feminists and nonfeminists believed that men who paid for dates were more likely to expect sexual favors, both groups said they were unlikely to engage in unwanted sexual activity.

Reactions

Not everyone is pleased with the present trend. One woman remarked:

> Whatever happened to chivalry? Nowadays the guys *expect* the woman to share expenses. I'd still like to think the man wants to ask me out and is willing to pay for the privilege. I think men today are really spoiled. (Author's counseling notes)

Allgeier (1981) has provided evidence that men are more positive in their attitudes toward women initiating and paying for dates than are women themselves. One male student remarked:

> I don't know why I should have to blow my whole paycheck to take a girl to an expensive restaurant to impress her. She ought to be willing to pay a fair share. That way, we can afford to go to such places more often. (Student comments)

In one study of 106 male undergraduates at Texas A&M University, the men said it was perfectly all right for the women to ask them directly for a date. Almost all said they would accept the invitation if they liked the woman (Goodman, 1982). However, the men surveyed also said that intercourse against the woman's wishes was significantly more justifiable under the following conditions: when the woman initiated the date, when the couple went to the man's apartment rather than to a religious function or a movie, and when the man paid for everything.

For this reason, some women hesitate to initiate dates. They don't want the man to think it is an invitation to sexual activity. Another author suggests that women who ask men for dates stand a better chance of not being labeled "sexually active" and not having this invitation misinterpreted if they emphasize their intelligence. For example, they might mention their high score on a biology exam. By emphasizing their intelligence, the women can lower their chances that a man will think they were interested only in sex (Meer, 1985c).

Dating Anxiety

Dating is usually an important part of the social life of young people. Yet many haven't learned the social skills and developed the self-confidence to succeed. A survey of 3,800 undergraduates at the University of Arizona found that a third (37 percent of men, and 25 percent of women) were "somewhat" or "very anxious" about dating. Half the students in a University of Indiana survey rated dating situations "difficult." Nearly a third of Iowa students said they feared meeting new people (Timnick, 1982).

Dating anxiety is handicapping. It is often associated with depression and academic failure; and it can lead to an avoidance of the opposite sex and failure to progress to more intimate relationships and marriage. Some students may be accelerated in their intellectual development, but retarded socially. The problem often goes back to their elementary school years, or before, when they had no friends at all. Such children may grow up in social isolation. Sometimes a family is geographically isolated so that potential friends are not available, or the children have to come home from school each day to do chores and never get a chance to socialize. Children whose families move a lot may never have a chance to establish close friendships. Some children never succeed in moving from homosocial to heterosocial friendships because of shyness or overprotective or fearful parents. Whatever the reasons, lack of social opportunities while growing up make learning dating skills difficult.

Common Problems

A study of 227 women and 107 men in a random sample of students at East Carolina University sought to identify dating problems (Knox and Wilson, 1983). Table 6.4 shows the problems experienced by the women. The most frequent problems expressed by the women were unwanted pressure to engage in sexual behavior, deciding where to go and what to do on dates, communication, sexual misunderstandings, and money. An example of sexual misunderstandings was a man's thinking a woman was leading him on when the woman didn't really want to have intercourse and didn't mean to suggest she did.

The problems most frequently mentioned by the men (Table 6.5) were communication, deciding where to go and what to do on dates, shyness, money, and honesty/openness. By honesty/openness the men meant how much to tell about themselves and how soon and getting their partner to reciprocate. Some of these problems will be discussed in more detail in succeeding sections.

Dates That Fail

What are the factors that result in dates failing? Failure here is defined as neither party's enjoying the event or the company of the other person, or only one of the two having a good time. A study of 517 university students revealed that dating failures could be divided into three categories: circumstantial factors, behavioral factors, and personal factors (Albrecht, 1972).

TABLE 6.4 *Dating Problems Experienced*
by 227 University Women

Problem	Percentage
Unwanted pressure to engage in sexual behavior	23
Places to go	22
Communication with date	20
Sexual misunderstandings	13
Money	9

Adapted from Knox, D., and Wilson, K. (1983). Dating problems of university students. *College Student Journal, 17*, 225–228.

TABLE 6.5 *Dating Problems Experienced*
by 107 University Men

Problem	Percentage
Communication with date	35
Place to date	23
Shyness	20
Money	17
Honesty/openness	8

Adapted from Knox, D., and Wilson, K. (1983). Dating problems of university students. *College Student Journals, 17*, 225–228.

Circumstantial factors accounted for fewer than 10 percent of the problems and included such things as weather, not being able to get tickets, car trouble, illness, exams the next day, or appearance of a former fiancé. A number of the failures were blind dates, and a fraternity party was the setting of most of the blind-date failures. In these situations, the brothers had put pressure on the man to date.

Behavioral factors caused 80 percent of the problems and included such things as drinking too much (more often the man); sexual exploitation; not being able to dance; neglecting partner; talking too little, too much, or too often about self; being too agreeable or too disagreeable; being intolerant or sarcastic; smoking too much; being late for dates (men more often than women); having no plans for the date; not getting along on double dates; or another fellow taking the girl away.

Personal factors caused a little over 10 percent of the difficulties and included such things as the man or woman not being attractive, the woman being too tall, the man being too short, either not being dressed right, being too old or having been married, having social class differences, the woman wanting a status date and the man not measuring up, having nothing in common, the partner's not being a student, or the date lasting too long. In some cases the date was prolonged by such things as weekend beach parties, which caused a strain on the couple who felt "stuck" with one another. Many of those who had accepted blind dates resolved not to do so again (Albrecht, 1972).

With the advent of AIDS, thoughtful couples have become acutely aware of their responsibility in the prevention of sexually transmitted diseases (STDs). How can couples be sure they won't spread diseases or contract them from a partner? If individuals are concerned that they might have been exposed themselves, they can seek medical help in being tested. They may be carriers of the AIDS virus without having the disease or any symptoms of it, yet they can pass it on to others. (See Chapter 9, where AIDS is discussed). They also may be carriers of other STDs of which they are unaware. (Gonorrhea, for example, may not show symptoms in women.) The individual's responsibility is to be certain that he or she is free of disease. Anyone who is not needs to refrain from all sexual activity or make certain that he or she is not exposing another to the disease.

The only really safe sex is either no sex or sex with a mutually faithful monogamous partner who is disease-free. While not 100 percent reliable, a high degree of safety can be assured by use of condoms plus spermicidal jellies, creams, or foams. (See Chapter 9 for a complete discussion of sexually transmitted diseases and Chapter 18 for a discussion of various birth control methods.)

SEXUAL AGGRESSION

Unwanted Sexual Pressure

Unwanted pressure to engage in sexual activities was the most frequently mentioned problem in the survey at East Carolina University (Knox and Wilson, 1983). Some of the women complained that the men wanted to move toward a sexual relationship too quickly. "How quickly he can get his hand in my blouse and up my skirt is what every guy I date seems to have in the front of his brain," one student remarked. Some of the women felt a conflict between not wanting too much sex too soon, but still needing to express enough interest so that dates would ask them out again. The problem was getting the men to slow down sexual advances without hurting their feelings. How to say "no" was sometimes difficult. "You have to be serious when you tell a guy to stop or he'll keep right on," one student commented.

Date Rape

Date rape refers to rape that occurs on a voluntary, prearranged date or after a woman meets a man on a social occasion and voluntarily goes with him. This type of sexual aggression is very common. In a survey of 282 university women, 20 percent said that men tried to forcibly fondle their breasts, 31 percent reported that men tried to forcibly fondle their genitals, and 24 percent reported men tried to have coitus. A third of the coital attempts were successful (Kanin and Parcell, 1977). Over half of the coital attempts were initiated without foreplay, so these women certainly weren't leading the men on. One student writes:

Charlie and I went parking after the movie. He asked me to get in the back seat with him, which I did, because I trusted him and felt safe with him. We necked

Many instances of date rape go unreported. Although the reasons many women are reluctant to report sexual aggression are not fully understood, the availability of help is increasing.

and petted awhile, and then he became violent. He ripped off my panties, pinned me down on the seat, and forced himself on me. I couldn't do anything about it yet he had the nerve to ask me afterward if I enjoyed it. (From a student paper)

Women are told frequently: "Don't go out with a man whom you don't know. If you do, you're taking a big chance." This is probably sound advice, but one of the purposes of dating is to get to know other people. And no matter how well you know an individual, problems can arise. Date rapes occur in relationships where two people have gone together for a long period of time. As familiarity grows, the sexually aggressive male may become more insistent and try to coerce his partner into sexual activity that she finds objectionable.

This may reflect lack of communication and lack of understanding in the man-woman relationship. Some men are brought up to believe that when a woman says "no" she really means "yes," and it's up to the man to do what he feels she really wants to do anyhow. This reflects the same myth that exists in relation to other types of rape — the myth that women want to be forced. It also reflects the social learning in our culture: that men are supposed to be the sexual aggressors and overcome the reluctance and hesitancy of women. Of course, some men rape their dates out of anger, hostility, and contempt, as an expression of negative feelings, certainly not as an act of caring. Many such men engage repeatedly in acts of sexual aggression with a series of partners (Heilbrun and Loftus, 1986).

Many date rapes are never reported. Women might not think of such incidences as rape; they feel ashamed and don't want anyone to know; they hesitate to report someone they know; they may feel partially responsible.

140

INTIMATE
RELATIONSHIPS:
GROWTH, CHOICES AND
CHANGE

DATING VIOLENCE

Increasing Violence

Domestic violence, especially wife abuse, has received increased attention in the media as a growing problem. Straus, Gelles, and Steinmetz (1980) surveyed a representative sample of 2,143 American households and found that one in six would be the setting for violence between husband and wife. But the problems often begin during courtship. Abusers and abused exhibit patterns of violence during courtship that are similar to those seen in marriage (Roscoe and Benaske, 1985). Makepeace (1981) reported on courtship violence among 202 college students. He found incidences of violence in this population that were comparable to those reported for married couples. Furthermore, courtship violence appears to be a training ground for marital violence (Flynn, 1987). Male aggressors using violence against a premarital partner are more likely to continue being violent in marriage. And women who experience violence in a premarital relationship and stay in the relationship are more likely to remain in the abusive marriage than are those who left a premaritally violent relationship or never experienced it at all (Flynn, 1987).

Acceptance of courtship and marital violence are related to attitudes toward them. Some groups of people consider it acceptable for a man to be abusive toward a woman (Bernard, Bernard, and Bernard, 1985). In two studies, both high school (Henton et al., 1983) and college students (Cate et al., 1982) who had been involved in an abusive relationship held less negative attitudes toward premarital violence that did students who had never experienced abuse. Those in abusive relationships may enter marriage with a predisposition to view marital abuse more favorably than will those in nonabusive premarital pairings (Henton et al., 1983).

Studies show that both males and females are abusers and abused, but females suffer higher levels of violence (being struck with an object or beaten up), while males sustain lower levels of violence (thrown objects, pushing, slapping, kicking, biting, punching). Females are more often injured physically (sometimes severely) and more often suffer emotional trauma from the experience than do males (Makepeace, 1986). Table 6.6 shows the motives for use of violence by gender.

TABLE 6.6 Motives for Use of Violence by Gender

Motive	Males (%) (N = 127)	Females (%) (N = 264)
Self-defense	18.1	35.6
To harm	2.4	8.3
To retaliate	16.5	18.9
To intimidate	21.3	6.8
To "get" something	3.9	2.3
Uncontrollable anger	28.3	24.2
Other	10.3	13.7

Columns sum to greater than 100% because many respondents reported multiple motives.
From Makepeace, J. M. (1986). Gender differences in courtship violence victimization. *Family Relations, 35*, 383–388. Copyright © 1986 by the National Council on Family Relations. Reprinted by permission.

A number of factors are related to courtship violence. Social learning theory emphasizes that *aggression is learned* in interaction with intimate personal groups. Those who grow up in families where parental interactions involve aggressive or violent acts learn these behavior patterns and later imitate them in their adult relationship (Gwartney-Gibbs, Stockard, and Bohmer, 1987). A large number of studies support this *positive relationship between aggression in the family of origin and aggression sustained or inflicted in courtship* (Bernard, and Bernard, 1983; Laner and Thompson, 1982).

Social factors also relate to courtship violence. Makepeace (1987) surveyed 2,338 students in seven colleges and found that both offenders and victims in courtship violence exhibited relatively problematic social profiles. The following were of special significance:

Race. Violence was highest among those of what Makepeace classified as "other races" (mainly Native American and Arabic) and lowest among Asians. Violence was higher among both blacks and Hispanics than among white Americans.

Religion. The largest percentage of female victims were those with no religion or who were infrequent church attenders. However, male offenders reported more church attendance than did nonoffenders.

Socioeconomic status. Violence was highest in families with both very low and very high incomes who lived in urban areas. Violence was lowest among those with medium incomes from rural areas.

Family background. Rates were highest among those who were reared in one-parent families, who were less close to their parents, or who had experienced harsh discipline.

Academic achievement. Students who received the poorest grades (Ds or Fs) or who had been suspended or expelled from school were those most likely to exhibit courtship violence.

Work record. Those most likely to exhibit courtship violence were those who had experienced multiple firings from jobs. This was the single condition most related to courtship violence.

Alcohol. Courtship violence was more common among those who drank "somewhat more than most" and for whom alcohol "sometimes" interfered with school or work, than among those who admitted drinking "much more than most" or for whom alcohol "often" interfered. This may reflect denial of violence on the part of those who said they drank the most, or denial of drinking by those who said they drank less, or the depressant effects of high levels of ingestion.

Dating. Courtship violence was associated with both early dating and poor dating success.

Life-events stress. Courtship violence was also related to exposure to life-events stress.

Courtship violence is also related to the *level of emotional commitment* in the relationship. Makepeace (1981) noted that 45 percent of the dating relationships that had experienced violence remained intact, and 29 percent reported that the relationship had become more deeply involved. Both Cote et al. (1982) and Henton et al. (1983) found that between one-fourth and one-third of both the abusers and abused interpreted the violence as love. For others, violence was viewed as a destructive force in the relationship.

When it happens, violence seems to progress as the relationship becomes more serious. Relationships defined as serious and meaningful show higher rates of abuse than do those defined as casual, although violence occurs even at the casual dating level. Overall, however, the studies suggest that greater commitment provides an opportunity for a greater risk of violence (Billingham, 1987).

OTHER PROBLEMS

Personality Faults

Some dating problems may be attributable to *basic personality faults or to immaturity*. An individual may be a very emotionally insecure or unstable person. One female writes, "How can I help curb my boyfriend's temper?" A male writes, "I get my feelings hurt very easily and don't know how to act at such times." One University of Maine man complains:

> My girlfriend is so jealous of me that if I even talk to another girl she gets mad. She discovered another girl was assigned a seat next to me in class and accused me of arranging the whole thing, when actually I don't even know that girl and could care less. She gets mad when I even want to go out with the fellows occasionally; she says she can't stand it when we are not together. She's always mothering me like a mother hen.

A sophomore writes: "What do you do about an ex-boyfriend who still feels possessive and protective and won't leave you alone no matter what you say?" Of course, most persons are capable of some jealousy, but when jealousy turns to extreme possessiveness, it become very hard to live with over a period of time (Rice, 1979a).

Friends

Disagreement over friends is a common occurrence. Frequently, a woman or man dislikes the friends the other goes around with. At other times, one or the other is expected to spend all of his or her time with the other's friends. One University of Maine woman writes:

> When I started going with Jim, I liked him a lot until I met his friends. What a bunch of queers! They're really weird. All they do is sit around and get stoned on grass, listen to records, and think of excuses for goofing off. I try to tell Jim that they aren't a good influence on him, but he accuses me of being a snob. I'm about ready to call off the whole deal!

It is to the advantage of a couple to have some friends that both enjoy (Rice, 1979a).

The problem of *communication* was mentioned by both the men and women in the East Carolina University study (Knox and Wilson, 1983). One man complained:

> I never know what to say. If I ask her a lot of questions, she tells me I'm interrogating her. If I don't ask her quesitons, she says I'm not interested. If I talk a lot and tell her stories, she thinks I don't care what she has to say. If I don't talk much, she says I'm boring, so what am I supposed to do?

Some students become anxious and nervous when the conversation starts to drag. One senior commented: "After a while you run out of small talk about weather and your classes. When the dialogue dies, it's awful." "I just can't stand the embarrassing silences" was the way another student expressed it. As daters get to know one another better, they begin to feel more comfortable and less self-conscious, so conversation comes more easily.

Both college men and women look for *honesty and openness* in a relationship. Part of the problem is caused by the fact that both the man and woman strive to be on their best behavior. This involves a certain amount of pretense or playacting, called **imaging**, to present oneself in the best possible manner.

A study of self-disclosure in college-student dating couples revealed that strikingly high proportions of both men and women reported that they had disclosed their thoughts and feelings "fully" to their partners in almost all areas. However, women revealed more than men in several specific areas, including their greatest fears. Couples with egalitarian sex-role attitudes disclosed more than those with traditional sex-role attitudes. Self-disclosure was strongly related to respondents' reported love for their partners. The highest degree of self-revelation was found in couples who had been dating for the longest time. The median length of time of going together for high self-disclosure was eight months (Rubin, Hill, Peplau, and Dunkel-Schetter, 1980).

Extradyadic Relationships

One of the considerations in dating is *whether to have sexual relationships outside the dating dyad*. Certainly, there is ample evidence to show that both men and women most desire and experience sexual intercourse within a caring relationship (Kallen and Stephenson, 1982; Sherwin and Corbett, 1985). The more involvement, the more men and women both desire and experience intercourse (McCabe, 1987).

The real question, however, is to what extent in committed dating relationships do couples engage in **extradyadic sexual activities**, and with what effect? Hansen (1987) asked 215 college students who had ever been in a committed dating relationship to respond to the following question: "While in a committed dating relationship, have you ever engaged in the following with someone other than your dating partner?" Erotic kissing, petting, and sexual intercourse were listed. Table 6.7 shows the results. As you can see, 35 percent of the men and 12 percent of the women had had sexual intercourse with someone else while involved in a committed dating relationship. A little over 40 percent of the men and women were certain or fairly sure their dating

TABLE 6.7 Percent of Men and Women Saying
They Had Engaged In Various Types of Extradyadic Behavior

	PERCENT ANSWERING IN THE AFFIRMATIVE	
Type of Behavior	Men	Women
Erotic kissing	65.2	39.5
Petting	46.7	18.5
Intercourse	35.2	11.9

From Hansen, G. L. (1987). Extradyadic relations during courtship. *The Journal of Sex Research, 23,* 382–390.

partner knew about it. About 40 percent of both the men and women felt their own extradyadic relations had hurt their dating relationships. But when their partner had had extradyadic relations, over 70 percent of both the men and women felt it had hurt their dating relationship. Apparently, the students were more accepting of their own extradyadic sexual relations than they were of their partners'.

Getting Too Serious

Another of the dating problems students face is the situation of *one person's getting more serious than the other person desires*. A University of Maine woman writes:

> I am not ready for and have no immediate intentions of getting married — for the next five to ten years anyway. Through my dates I have made some very close personal male friends. But for the past three years the situations have ended abruptly because each time the man decided the relationship was more serious than I wanted. How can I keep my enjoyable and good contacts without leading them on?

Sometimes, of course, the woman gets more serious than her partner does. In either case, keeping the relationship on a friendship basis without hurting the other person can become a problem. One man complained, "No matter what we're talking about, Kathy always gets around to hinting about marriage, but I'm not ready to settle down. I have two more years of college and then grad school ahead of me."

Sometimes couples make a *premature commitment*; then they have second thoughts and want to discontinue the relationship. One man writes:

> My current girlfriend is very serious about getting married, but I'm not at all sure about the relationship now. How do I explain this to her (a very sensitive person), especially after I expressed a sincere desire to marry her at one time?

Sometimes both people begin to realize that something is wrong in the relationship, but each is afraid to tell the other. In most instances, each partner needs to express the doubts, inquire about the other person's feelings, and discuss viewpoints tactfully but openly. Most problems can be dealt with only by honest and sensitive communication (Rice, 1979a).

Breaking up a relationship can become a very painful experience, especially if the breakup is unilateral, with one person wanting to end the affair and the other not. Contrary to popular belief, however, women more often break off relationships than do men. A study of 231 couples from four colleges in the Boston area showed that men tended to fall in love more readily than women, that the women tended to fall out of love more readily, and the men tended to cling to their love longer than the women (Rubin, Peplau, and Hill, 1981). Men were also more likely to report that they felt depressed, lonely, unhappy, and less free than were the women who had broken up. Apparently, the

ASSESSMENT
Dating Partners Versus Marital Partners

PART I.   FOR EVERYONE

List the qualities you feel are most important in a dating partner.

List the qualities you feel are most important in a marital partner.

Which qualities desired in a dating partner are similar to those desired in a marital partner?

Which qualities desired in a dating partner are different from those desired in a marital partner?

PART II.   FOR SINGLES

On the basis of Part I, to what extent does your present dating partner fulfill your expectations of an ideal dating partner?

List the qualities he or she possesses that you have mentioned are important in a dating partner.

List the qualities he or she does not possess that you have mentioned are important in a dating partner.

On the basis of Part I, to what extent does your present dating partner fulfill your expectations of a marital partner?

List the qualities he or she possesses that you have mentioned are important in a marital partner.

List the qualities he or she does not possess that you have mentioned are important in a marital partner.

PART III.   FOR MARRIEDS

On the basis of Part I, to what extent did your present spouse fulfill your expectations of an ideal dating partner before you were married?

What qualities did he or she possess that you liked in a dating partner?

What qualities did he or she not possess that you would have liked in a dating partner?

On the basis of Part I, to what extent does your present spouse fulfill your expectations of a marital partner?

What qualities does he or she possess that you like in a marital partner?

What qualities does he or she not possess that you would like in a marital partner?

Were you aware of these things before you got married?

What could you have done to become more aware of these things before you married?

women took a practical approach to the situation. They could not allow themselves to fall in love too quickly, nor could they afford to stay in a relationship with the wrong person. After carefully evaluating their partner's strengths and weaknesses and comparing them to other potential partners, they had to decide whether to continue the relationship.

SUMMARY

1. Dating, such as we know it, is rare in most of the world. It did not become firmly established in the United States until the years after World War I. In colonial America, casual meetings were condemned. If a young man desired to court a woman, he had to meet her family, be formally introduced, and obtain permission to court her.

2. By the late nineteenth and early twentieth centuries, chaperonage and close supervision of courtship had declined. Young people themselves arranged their own get-togethers, and the man was expected to take the leadership role in dating.

3. Dating emerged because of a number of reasons: the industrial revolution; the rise of free, public high schools; increased affluence and leisure time; the invention of the automobile; and the rise of the women's equality movement.

4. Walter described the "rating-and-dating complex" that existed on university campuses during the 1930s. The most important dating pattern to develop prior to World War II was steady dating. LeMasters described six stages of dating and courtship that existed in the 1950s.

5. Dating patterns today are different from those of previous generations in the following ways: dating begins at younger ages; there are increased opportunities for informal contacts; there isn't any set pattern of progression; and dating is much less formal now than in previous generations.

6. Dating fulfills a number of important functions: recreation; companionship, friendship, and personal intimacy; socialization; personality development; opportunity to try out sex roles; the need for love and affection; the opportunity for sex; mate sorting and selection; and preparation for marriage.

7. Dating does not serve adequately its function of sorting out marital partners if the qualities desired in dating partners are different from those preferred in marital partners.

8. Youths meet prospective dates through a friend, at parties, work, in a class, or through other means. Bars, college mixers, self-advertising, and dating services also are utilized to bring people together.

9. Parents influence their daughters' choice of dating partners more than their sons', but youths also try to influence parental opinions of their dates.

10. Gender roles in dating are in the process of change, with females more frequently involved in asking for dates and planning and paying for dates. Not all men and women are pleased with the present trend.

11. Large numbers of youths have dating anxiety. Some common problems in dating are unwanted pressure to engage in sexual behavior, where to go and what to do on dates, communication, sexual misunderstandings, and money.

12. The greatest percentage of dates that fail do so because of problem behavior of one or both of the dating partners. Other causes of dating failure are circumstantial and personal factors.

13. The primary dating problem of females is unwanted pressure to engage in sexual activities too quickly in a relationship. Date rape is involuntary sexual intercourse forced on one by a dating partner. Many date rapes are never reported.

14. Dating violence may also occur and be carried over into the marriage relationship. A number of factors correlate positively or negatively with dating violence: violence in one's family of origin, race, religion, socioeconomic status, family background, academic achievement, work record, use of alcohol, life-events stress, and level of emotional commitment in the relationship.

15. Some dating problems may be attributed to basic personality faults or to immaturity. Couples may also have problems with friends, communication, extradyadic relationships, getting too serious, or breaking up a relationship.

SUGGESTED READINGS

Hendrick, C., and Hendrick, S. (1983). *Liking, Loving, and Relating*. Monterey, CA: Brooks/Cole.

Kelley, H. H., et al. (1983). *Close Relationships*. New York: W. H. Freeman.

Rubin, S. (1983). *Intimate Strangers: Men and Women Together*. New York: Harper and Row.

7

ATTRACTION AND LOVE

CHAPTER OUTLINE

KEY TERMS

romantic love
narcissistic love
limerence
passionate love
companionate love
conscious love
dopamine
norepinephrine
serotonin
endorphins
erotic love
dependent love
D-love
B-love
friendship love
altruistic love
consummate love
eros
ludus
storge
mania
pragma
agape

In this chapter we are concerned with two major subjects: attraction and love. First, what attracts us to others and what qualities do men and women find attractive in one another? And second, what is love, how do you know if you're in love, and how important is it in interpersonal relationships? Can love be a reliable guide in mate selection?

These are some of the questions that have fascinated social scientists. We now have some of the answers — not all of them to be sure — but enough to shed considerable light on the subject of interpersonal attraction and love and their role in relationships.

ATTRACTION

Physical Attractiveness

The most important element in attraction — at least in initial encounters — is physical attractiveness. We are attracted positively to those who are pretty, pleasing to look at, have good builds and well-proportioned bodies, and other physical characteristics that appeal to our aesthetic sensibilities. Study after study finds physical appearance to be one of the chief ingredients in early attraction (Adams, 1980; Reis, Nezlek, and Wheeler, 1980; Shea and Adams, 1984). However, beauty is partly in the eyes of the beholder. Clients will tell their counselors, "My wife is gorgeous" or "My husband is really handsome." When the spouse shows up for the counseling session, it's not unusual to be looking at a very plain-looking, sometimes even homely person. Judgment in such matters tends to be highly subjective.

The standards of beauty by which Miss America contestants are judged have changed over the years.

Standards of attractiveness are culturally conditioned. In our culture, slender women are considered more attractive than obese ones (Bozzi, 1985). Tall men are considered more attractive than short ones (Feingold, 1982). Youthful men and women are considered more attractive than the elderly (Wernick and Manaster, 1984). In contrast, in some cultures, obesity is synonymous with physical beauty.

Furthermore, in our own culture, standards of beauty change over the years. The mean bust-waist-hip measurements of Miss America contest winners in the 1920s were 32-25-35, with no winner having a larger bust than hips. In the 1940s, the mean measurements were 35-24-35, with nearly half the winners having a larger bust than hips. Hollywood had introduced the "sweater girl" Lana Turner and buxom Jane Russell. Since 1950, the norm has been bust-hip symmetry, with equal bust-hip measurements and the ideal measurement usually 35 or a "perfect 36" and a 23- or 24-inch waist. Figure 7.1 shows these trends as well as the increase in ideal height and a gradual decline in ideal weight. Miss Americas have become taller and slenderer.

During the 1950s, *Playboy* magazine featured its "Playmate of the Month" as ever-larger-breasted women. This was a period of "mammary madness," with Hollywood and the fashion industry promoting large, cleaved bustlines, tiny cinch waists, and wiggly-hipped walks (Mazur, 1986). Since that time,

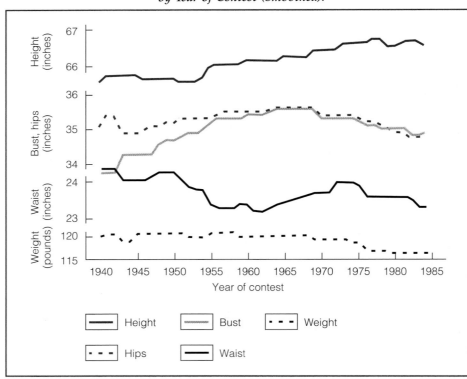

FIGURE *7.1 Body Measurements of Miss America Contestants by Year of Contest (Smoothed).*

From Mazur, A. (1986). U.S. trends in feminine beauty and overadaptation. *The Journal of Sex Research, 22,* 281–303.

Playmates have become increasingly linear, taller, leaner, and nearly hipless, with many still appearing large-breasted in proportion to body size (Katch et al., 1980). According to a 1983 reader's survey of 65,000 men and 15,000 women who mailed in published questionnaires, nearly as many men reported a woman's sexiest feature to be her "ass" (63 percent) as her breasts

---

PERSPECTIVE
What Physical Features Are Noticed First?

The Roper organization asked people, "When you first meet someone, which one or two things about physical appearance do you tend to notice first?" The figure shows the results (Opinion Roundup, 1983, 34). When meeting women, men noticed figure and build first, face second, how the woman was dressed third, and the woman's smile fourth. When meeting men, women noticed how the man was dressed first, the man's eyes second, and his figure and build third; his face and smile tied for fourth place. This survey revealed that body build and figure were more important than face, and that clothes and a pleasant smile were extremely important as well. However, there were men and women who said they noticed hands or teeth first, which shows there are some variations in standards of attractiveness.

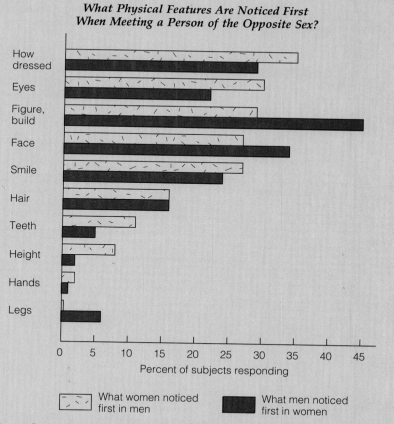

What Physical Features Are Noticed First When Meeting a Person of the Opposite Sex?

Percent of subjects responding

What women noticed first in men

What men noticed first in women

Source: Survey by the Roper Organization (Roper Report 83–5), April 23–30, 1983. *Public Opinion* (August/September 1983), 34. Reprinted with permission of the American Enterprise Institute for Public Policy Research.

(67 percent); and only 28 percent of men (and 26 percent of women readers) thought breast size was important to a woman's sexiness (*Playboy readers' sex survey: Part I*, 1983). Unfortunately, these standards of attractiveness have not always made life easier for the average person. Researchers at Arizona State University reported that after viewing nudes from *Playboy, Playgirl*, and *Penthouse*, undergraduate men and women rated their mates less attractive sexually and said they felt less love from them (*Pinups and letdowns*, 1983).

Personality and Social Factors

Factors other than physical appearance attract people to one another. A study of 30 men and 30 women who were married (not to each other) for two to eight years measured factors that the subjects found most attractive in their spouse (Whitehouse, 1981). The subjects were asked what attracted them to their spouse on first meeting, what attracted them after a few months, and what attracted them at the time of the interview. The factors were divided into five categories: *extroversion, agreeableness, conscientiousness, emotional stability*, and *culture*. Various traits under each category are shown in Table 7.1. Upon initial meeting, the most important factor was extroversion: being talkative, frank, open, adventurous, and social. However, the importance of these traits declined with the years, while characteristics listed under agreeableness became much more important. The traits under conscientiousness also became slightly more important. Figure 7.2 shows the trends.

TABLE 7.1 *Factors That Married Persons Found Attractive in Their Spouses*

Category	Traits
Extroversion	Talkative
	Frank, open
	Adventurous
	Sociable
Agreeableness	Good-natured
	Not jealous
	Mild, gentle
	Cooperative
Conscientiousness	Fussy, tidy
	Responsible
	Scrupulous
	Persistent
Emotional Stability	Poised
	Not nervous
	Calm
	Composed
	Not hypochondriacal
Culture	Artistic
	Sensitive
	Intellectual
	Polished, refined
	Imaginative

From Norton, W. T. (1963). Toward an adequate taxonomy of personal attributes: replicated factor structure in peer nomination personality ratings. *Journal of Abnormal and Social Psychology*, 66, 577.

Other studies have confirmed that *personality traits and the way people act are significant factors in whether others find them attractive or not.* People who are generally warm, kind, gregarious, intelligent, interesting, poised, confident, or humorous, or who exhibit generally admired qualities, are more attractive than those who are rude, insecure, clumsy, insensitive, unstable, or irresponsible, or who manifest other negative traits. Orlofsky (1982) found that conformity to the cultural standards of approved femininity or masculinity was a powerful component of attractiveness.

Unconscious Influences

Sometimes people are not aware of why they find another person attractive. Unconscious factors are often at work. If, for example, we experienced love and security with our opposite-sex parent while we were growing up, we may seek to duplicate the relationship and so are attracted to a dating partner or spouse who reminds us of that parent. Or we are attracted to those who meet our needs and who make us feel good about ourselves. Some people are attracted to those who are helpless, alone, handicapped, or dependent; taking care of someone else makes them feel needed, important, wanted. Other people are attracted to their ego ideal, to someone who has all the qualities they wish they had. A smile, a glance, or a mannerism may trigger a positive response because of conditioning that took place years before. Other factors in attraction are included in the discussion of love that follows.

FIGURE 7.2 Factors in Attraction.

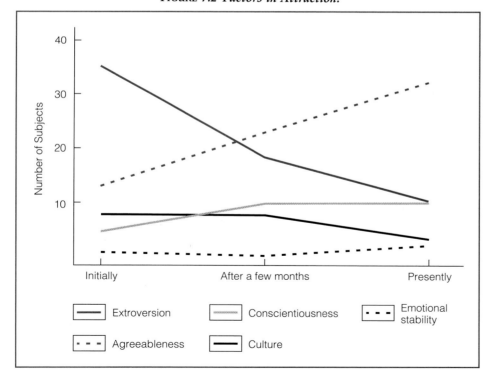

From Norton, W. T. (1963). Toward an adequate taxonomy of personal attributes: replicated factor structure in peer nomination personality ratings. *Journal of Abnormal and Social Psychology*, 66, 577.

Each person defines love according to his or her background and experiences (Lasswell and Lobsenz, 1980). One person may describe love in terms of emotions and strong feelings. Another may describe it as a biological attraction. Another may emphasize that love is a way of acting toward others and a way of treating them. Someone else may emphasize love as liking and friendship. Another may say it is primarily care or concern for another. Still another person may say that there is no such thing as love; that it is just a myth or a delusion (Seeman, 1983).

In fact, there are many different definitions of love. Although, in a sense, love is what each person thinks it is, this subjective view is not always helpful. It leads to misunderstandings between two people who say they love one another, but who have entirely different concepts of what they mean.

When we talk about love, therefore, we need to know what kind of love we are talking about. *The point of view reflected here is that love is not a single concept, but has different dimensions.* Let's start with a five-dimensional view of love: romantic love, erotic love, dependent love, friendship love, and altruistic love.

ROMANTIC LOVE

Characteristics and Effects

Romantic love has been described as a profoundly tender or passionate affection for a person of the opposite sex (Stein, 1973). Its chief characteristic is *strong emotion*, marked by intensity of feelings. A glance, a smile, a brushing of the hand of one's beloved may arouse strong feelings of warmth and affection (Branden, 1980). Individuals report that they "became alive again" and started "to really feel for the first time in years." If the love is mutual and fulfilling, there is a great sense of joy, ecstasy, exhilaration, and well-being (Critelli, 1977).

Because of these feelings, there is a *desire to be together* so that one can continue to enjoy the pleasure of love. When apart, lovers almost become possessed by thoughts of one another. It is common also for romantic love to result in *physiological changes and manifestations*: palpitations of the heart, a quickening pulse, breathlessness, trembling, a tightness in the chest, or halting speech. Loss of love can cause physical upset so that the person can't eat or sleep. The literary portrayal of unrequited or lost love is one of a debilitated and unhappy person.

There is also a strong feeling of *sexual attraction* in romantic love and the desire for physical contact. In such a state of passion, it is probably inevitable that romantic love is accompanied by much *idealization and adoration*. Romantic love exalts feminine beauty and virtue and manly strength, virility, and chivalry. One's love becomes the incarnation of all of those physical traits and qualities of character that are one's ideal of womanhood or manhood. Theo-

---

*Some of the material in these sections on love is taken from the author's book *Human Sexuality*, 1989, and is used by permission of the publisher Wm. C. Brown Co.

dore Reik (1944, 1957) theorized that when individuals fall in love they do so with persons who manifest the characteristics of their ego ideal. They project these characteristics onto the other person with whom they identify (Kemper and Bologh, 1980). This type of love is **narcissistic**, since it is really love of self, as represented in the other person.

But romantic love can also result in much *altruism and unselfishness*. It results in feelings of generosity and in wanting to shower the other person with gifts. The sense of devotion and willingness to serve and to sacrifice is often astounding. Along with this desire to give up much for the sake of love comes a renewed *feeling of self-confidence* that one is beautiful and capable and that one can do the impossible.

These feelings have been substantiated in the research of Tennov (1979). She found that when the passion was strong, the relationship eclipsed all else. The lovers were in a wildly emotional state, seesawing between bliss and jealousy. They were obsessed with thoughts of their loved one. When their loved one responded, they were walking on air; when there was no response, they were depressed. Tennov labeled these feelings **limerence** and found that people could be this passionately involved with only one person at a time. For a while at least, the feelings are completely out of rational control, and the ups and downs of feelings can interfere with work, study, sleep, and peace of mind.

Changes Over Time

For all persons, *love changes over a period of time*. Romantic love becomes more rational and less wildly romantic. Once two people marry, romantic love continues to grow if it is nourished. A study of couples married on the average of five years showed that one-third of the wives felt their husbands were more romantic now than when first married. Two-thirds also said they now loved their husbands more and felt their husbands now loved them more. Ninety percent of the wives felt no decrease in love by either their husbands or themselves (Bell, 1971). It is evident, however, that the couples' ideas of love changed over the years, with fewer components of superromanticism and more components of friendship, trust, cooperation, dependability, and acceptance.

In helping to clarify the meaning of love, Walster and Walster (1978) separate love into two types: **passionate love** and **companionate love**. They define passionate love as "a wildly emotional state associated with tender sexual feelings, elation and pain, anxiety and relief" and companionate love as "a more low-keyed emotion, with feelings of friendly affection and deep attachment." They state that passionate love fades over time and is replaced by companionate love. However, a study of 240 women 50 to 82 years of age showed that for those who were able to report an ongoing intimate relationship, with either a spouse or spouse equivalent (106 of the sample), passionate love remained a significant component of their lives (Traupman, Eckels, and Hatfield, 1982). Admittedly this was a biased sample. The women were highly educated, had above-average incomes, were physically active and in good health, and only those with intimate relationships responded; but the study does show that it is possible to maintain exciting emotion and passionate feelings in a relationship over many years.

A Sound Basis for Marriage?

The crucial question regarding romantic love is this: Is it a sound basis for marriage? (Lee and Stone, 1980). There is no question that romanticism plays a significant role in attraction and whether couples marry. *Romanticism brings individuals into serious male-female associations* that may eventually lead to marriage. In this sense, romantic love is very functional.

However, *if romantic love is taken as the only criterion for marriage, it can become very dysfunctional* (Buehler and Wells, 1981). People can fall romantically in love with those who are completely unsuitable prospective mates and who will make their lives miserable. Feelings alone are not an accurate indication of suitability or marriageability. People "fall in love" with imprisoned rapists, psychotics, drug addicts, alcoholics, wife abusers, child molesters, psychopathic liars — completely emotionally immature, insecure, unstable, irresponsible, hostile individuals. But if they marry in spite of these faults, they are certainly minimizing their chances of being married happily. Perhaps they have emotional reasons for selecting problem people: a poor self-image, a desire to punish themselves, to hurt parents, to be needed by someone; but these are neurotic, not rational, reasons for marriage.

Even the idealism of romantic love itself is not dysfunctional if it approaches reality. What is dysfunctional is the inability of some individuals to separate the idealized from the realistic in real-life relationships (Mukhopodhyay, 1979). Strong et al. (1981) call rational love **conscious love**. They write, "When we love someone consciously, we are aware of who that person really is. We do not relate to their image, but to their reality" (p.201). Romantic love becomes dysfunctional if it blinds us to reality.

Love and Personality

Some efforts have been made to discover significant correlations between personality factors and romanticism. Are romantic persons less emotionally mature than those who are not so romantic? Not necessarily. Overall, romantic love is a normal experience of normal people, not just something that maladjusted and immature people fall into as an escape from life.

Love and Arousal

Several of the most interesting research studies on romantic love show its association with intense emotional stimulation (Jacobs, Walster, and Berscheid, 1971). Schachter and Singer (1962) have a two-component theory of human emotional response. They say that for a person to experience true emotion two factors must coexist: (1) the individual must be physiologically aroused, and (2) the arousal must be interpreted as a particular emotion. Berscheid and Walster (1974) have applied Schachter and Singer's theory to romantic love. They suggest that it does not really matter how one produces an agitated state in an individual. Stimuli that usually produce sexual arousal, gratitude, anxiety, guilt, loneliness, hatred, jealousy or confusion may all increase one's physiological arousal, and thus increase the intensity of emotional experience. As long as one attributes the agitated state to passion, passionate love exists.

One study of college males found that men who were physically stimulated by a two-minute jog and then shown videotapes of a neatly groomed, well-dressed college woman rated her more attractive and higher on personality attributes than did men who were less aroused. Conversely, those shown tapes of a poorly groomed woman found her significantly less desirable and attractive than did men who had not been aroused by jogging (Bridgewater, 1982b).

Emotional arousal, even from a frightening source, facilitates attraction. Perhaps this is why lovers who meet under dangerous conditions or with the threat of discovery experience greater excitement and passion than under more secure conditions. Perhaps this is why the forbidden or secret love is the more intense love.

The *fear breeds passion principle* was also documented in research in Vancouver, British Columbia. Dutton and Aron (1974) conducted their experiment on two footbridges that crossed the Capilano River. One bridge was a narrow, shaky walkway that swayed in the wind, 230 feet above the stream. The other was a solid structure only 10 feet above the water. Near the end of each bridge, an attractive female experimenter approached men who were crossing and asked if they would take part in an experiment on "the effects of exposure to scenic attractions on creative expression." They were asked to write down their associations to a picture she showed them. The men on the narrow suspension bridge were more sexually aroused than were the men on the low, solid bridge. This fact was inferred from the amount of sexual imagery in their associations. The men on the suspension bridge also were more likely to call the researcher afterward "to get more information about the study."

Not just negative emotions but positive ones as well influence romantic love. Sexual arousal produces intense physiological changes in the body, which facilitate attraction. Men label as most attractive the photographs of seminude women that arouse them sexually. If there is no arousal, the pictures are rejected as less attractive.

There have been recent efforts to try to show the precise relationship between specific changes in the autonomic nervous system to various types of emotions (Ekman, Levenson, and Friesen, 1983). Liebowitz (1983) says that the excitement and arousal of romantic love are a result of increased levels of **dopamine** and **norepinephrine** in the bloodstream. These neurotransmitters are activated by visual cues (by observing an attractive nude, for example) and they then bathe the pleasure center of the brain in a sea of chemical messages. Liebowitz also feels that romantic love stimulates the secretion of a separate chemical called **serotonin**, which can produce a psychedelic high. Companionate love, however, results in the brain producing narcotic-like substances called **endorphins** that give a sense of tranquility.

These studies emphasize the importance of emotional excitement as an important component of attraction and of romantic love. *The more positive excitement a relationship generates, the more likely the participants are to report that they are in love.* However, since intense emotional arousal and excitement cannot be sustained, love that is to endure over the years of marriage must include components other than just emotional excitement.

Erotic love is sensual love. This type of love is aroused when one is attracted sexually to another person. It is the biological, sensual component of love relationships. One of the questions that arises is: What is the relationship between love and sex?

Love and Sex Identical

According to Freud (1953), love and sex are really one and the same thing. Freud defined love as "aim inhibited sex," as a yearning for a "love object" — for another person who could meet one's sexual needs. Love, to Freud, was narcissistic in that it was measured by the extent to which the love object could satisfy one's sexual aim.

Freud emphasized two important elements of the sexual aim of adults. One element is *physical and sensual*. In men, this aim consists of the desire to produce sexual products, accompanied by physical pleasure: in other words, the desire for ejaculation and orgasm. In women, the desire is for physical satisfaction and the release of sexual tension (orgasm) but without the discharge of physical products.

The second element of the sexual aim in adults is *psychical*; it is the affectionate component. It is the desire for emotional satisfaction as well as for physical release. Freud emphasized that a normal sexual life is assured when there is a convergence of the affectionate component and the sensual component, both being directed toward the sexual object and sexual aim. The desire for true affection and for the release of sexual tension are the needs that motivate the individual to seek a love object. Freud (1953) also felt that once an appropriate love object was found, this diminished sexual strivings. In turn, diminished yearnings resulted in seeking only one love object at a time.

Separation of Love and Sex

While Freud emphasized that love and sex are the same thing, *other writers would say that love and sex are two separate entities*, that they are not identical, and that a definite distinction must be made between them. Theodor Reik (1944; 1957) said that love and sex are different in origin and nature. Sex, according to Reik, is a biological function whose aim is the release of physical tension. Love stems from psychic needs and seeks affection and emotional satisfaction.

There are those today who feel that romantic love arises when sexual expression is denied (Wilkinson, 1978). This "sexual blockage" theory emphasizes that romantic love is most felt toward those who play "hard to get." Once sexual involvement begins, romantic love declines.

A much more common manifestation of the separation of love and sex today is to emphasize *recreational sex*. This is sex for its own sake, because it is pleasurable and fun, without the necessity of love and commitment. As one student remarked, "What's wrong with just enjoying one another's bodies? Do people have to be in love to do that?" Obviously, many do not, as evidenced by the fact that sex is a popular form of adult play.

Is physical attraction more than skin deep? Freud defined love as "a yearning for a 'love object.'" It's possible that for some, this male's appearance satisfies Freud's definition of a love object.

Sex As an Expression of Love

Many couples can't separate sex from all other aspects of their relationship, at least in the long term. One woman summed up her feelings:

> I like sex a lot. But it can only supplement a warm, affectionate, mutually respecting, full personhood relationship. *It* can't be a relationship. It can't prove love. It can't prove anything. I have found sex with people I don't really like, or who I'm not certain will really like me, or with people I don't feel I know well, to be very shallow and uncomfortable and physically unsatisfying. I don't believe you have to be "in love" and married "till death do us part." But mind and body are one organism and all tied up together, and it isn't even physically fun unless the people involved really like each other. (Hite, 1981, 48)

In modern Western society, there has been considerable fusion between love and sex (Weis, Slosnerick, Cote, and Sollie, 1986). Lowen (1972) points out that love increases the pleasure of sex and that erotic pleasure is reduced when love is at a minimum. Many adults would disagree completely with Lowen's point of view. To them, it simply is not true. However, other writers emphasize that sex is important as a confirmation of the love relationship. It says to the other person, "I love you." In this view, sex can be both a physical and emotional expression of deep feeling. Whichever view the individual holds, *many people want sex with affection, not without it, and insist that love and sex should go together.*

One of the components of a durable love is dependency. **Dependent love** develops when one's needs are fulfilled by another person. In its simplest form it works like this: "I have important needs. You fulfill those needs; therefore, I love you." This is the type of love the dependent child feels for the mother who feeds, clothes, and cares for him or her: "You give me my bottle, you keep me warm, you hold me, cuddle me, and talk to me. That's why I love you."

But it is also the kind of love that develops when the intense psychological needs of adults, which have been denied in the past, are now fulfilled by a lover. The reliable, hard-working man may be captivated by an alert woman who recognizes his potential to be a playful and reckless lover.

Maslow's Theory of Love As Need

Abraham Maslow (1970) is one of the chief exponents of love as dependency and need fulfillment. According to him, human needs may be arranged in a hierarchy, ascending from physiological to psychological. The levels of need go from the bottom up as shown in Figure 7.3.

Maslow referred to the first four levels of need as *D-needs* or *Deficiency-needs* and to the last three levels as *B-needs* or *Being-needs*. He emphasized that the needs at each level must be met before a person can move up the ladder to the next level. An individual develops *"Deficiency-love"* for a person who provides *"D-needs."* *"Being-love"* develops for the person who fulfills *"B-needs."*

FIGURE 7.3 Maslow's Hierarchy of Needs.

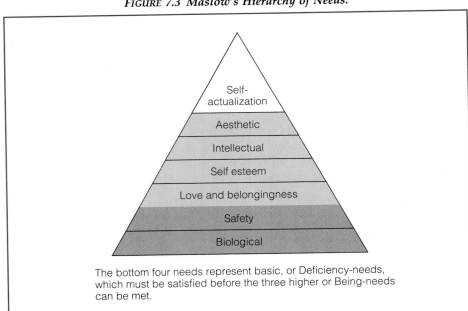

The bottom four needs represent basic, or Deficiency-needs, which must be satisfied before the three higher or Being-needs can be met.

From Maslow, A. (1970). *Motivation and personality* (2nd ed.). New York: Harper and Row, 1970.

Maslow emphasized that in marriage, **D-love** refers to all forms of self-centered love in which two people love one another because the needs of each are met by the other. It is a sort of bookkeeping arrangement, with the man meeting certain needs of the woman as she meets certain needs of his and vice-versa. Since the focus of attention is upon the aggrandizement of self and personal needs, D-love may be fragmented. A wife may enjoy her husband as a sexual partner, because he meets her biological and emotional needs, but dislike him in some other ways because of his sense of values.

This cannot happen in **B-love** because it is love for the very being and uniqueness of the other person. The sexual impulse is anchored in the deep love of the qualities of one's mate. With this type of love, neither person feels insecure and threatened, because each feels accepted and comfortable in the other's presence. The love is not conditioned by the extent the other fills one's needs. It is not possessive, nor is it motivated by any desire to fulfill some personal need or some selfish aim. It is unconditional and offers the kind of relationship in which each person can develop the best that is in him or her as a self-actualizing person.

It is important that need fulfillment be mutual and that mates strive to meet one another's D-needs (Schaefer and Olson, 1981). This assumes the needs are reasonable and capable of fulfillment. However, the difficulty comes when an individual's D-needs have not been met while growing up, so that he or she becomes possessive, domineering, and overly dependent, manipulating the other person only for self-satisfaction. In such a situation, self-actualization and B-love are impossible. There is no room for growth, freedom, fulfillment, and actualization, since the partner is only being exploited and used. If, however, D-needs have been met as one is growing up, the individual is free from striving for their fulfillment and can thus show an active concern for the life and growth of the one loved.

Maslow recognizes that there is some mixture of D-love and B-love in every relationship, but he cannot help but extol the virtues of B-love (Maslow, 1962). Obviously, the more B-love predominates in relationships, the more self-actualization is possible for the persons who are offered such love (see Figure 7.4, Relationship C.)

Reiss's Wheel Theory of Love

The sociologist Reiss (1960) focused his attention on the *process* by which dependent love develops between two people. He called this process the *wheel theory* of love's development. This theory emphasized falling in love as the development of an interpersonal relationship, which Reiss divided into four processes: (1) *rapport*, (2) *self-revelation*, (3) *mutual dependency*, and (4) *need fulfillment*.

Developing *rapport* is the first stage in love's development. It allows a person to feel relaxed in the company of another and therefore to reveal more about himself or herself than he or she otherwise would. The second process in the love cycle then takes place: the process of *self-revelation*. The person may tell much of his or her hopes, desires, fears, and ambitions, although the cultural background of each person helps to determine what is revealed.

Through self-revelation a third process takes place: the development of *mutual dependency*, or of interdependent habit systems. In this process, one

FIGURE 7.4 *Degrees of Mixture of D-Love and B-Love in Relationships.*

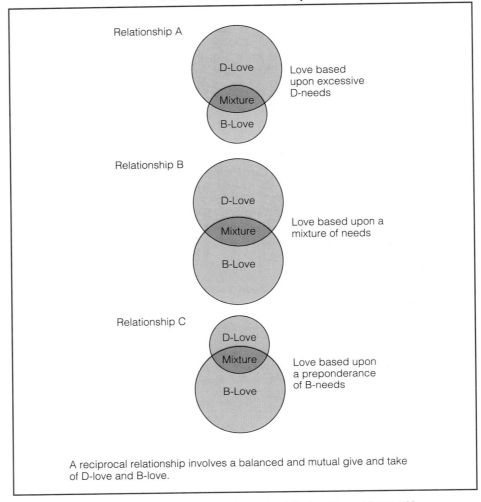

Relationship A

D-Love

Mixture

B-Love

Love based upon excessive D-needs

Relationship B

D-Love

Mixture

B-Love

Love based upon a mixture of needs

Relationship C

D-Love

Mixture

B-Love

Love based upon a preponderance of B-needs

A reciprocal relationship involves a balanced and mutual give and take of D-love and B-love.

From Rice, F. P. (1979). *Marriage and parenthood*. Boston: Allyn and Bacon, 106.

person grows to need the other for fulfillment: as an audience for one's jokes, as a confidante for one's fears and wishes, or as a partner for sexual needs. In so doing, the individual becomes dependent on the dating partner to help fulfill needs that cannot be fulfilled alone.

This leads to the fourth and final process in love's development: *need fulfillment*. Thus, the partner satisfies one's need for love, for someone in whom to confide, for understanding, for help and support, or for other personality needs. To the extent that these needs are fulfilled, one finds a love relationship developing.

Reiss also made a graphic presentation of his wheel, shown in Figure 7.5. As can be seen, love develops through an increase in rapport, which increases self-revelation, which increases mutual dependency, which increases need fulfillment. But the process can also be reversed, with the wheel going in the opposite direction. If one person frustrates the need of the other for appreciation, the sense of dependency may be decreased; and an argument may develop that would affect the communication process and weaken the rapport

FIGURE 7.5 *The Wheel Theory of Love.*

163

ATTRACTION AND LOVE

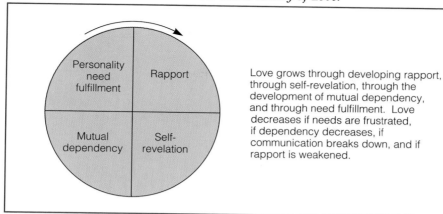

Love grows through developing rapport, through self-revelation, through the development of mutual dependency, and through need fulfillment. Love decreases if needs are frustrated, if dependency decreases, if communication breaks down, and if rapport is weakened.

From Reiss, I. L. (1971). Toward a sociology of the heterosexual love relationship. *Marriage and Family Living, 22,* May, 139–145. Used by permission of Holt, Rinehart, and Winston.

between them. All of these in turn affect the maintenance of the love relationship. "Thus, the processes flow into one another in one direction to develop love and can flow the other way to weaken a love relationship" (Reiss, 1960, p. 94).

Different persons go through this process at different speeds. In an ultra-romantic relationship, one person may feel rapport, reveal himself or herself, become dependent, and feel fulfilled in a very short span of time. In the case of someone "madly in love" with another the person has never met, the entire process may be fantasized. In the case of erotic love, only the sexual aspects

CLASSROOM FORUM
I Feel Smothered

"My husband says that if I really loved him, I would want to be together with him all the time. He didn't want me to go to work (we don't have any children), but I did anyhow. He calls me several times during the day to talk to me. I'd like to go to lunch with the girls once in a while, but he insists on having lunch with me every day. When we're home, he follows me around the house. I can't even go to the bathroom without his following me. If I don't feel like sex, he feels hurt, starts to pout, and starts drinking beer. Sometimes he'll drink the whole weekend because I turned him down (I do so very seldom, however).

"I'm beginning to feel smothered. Am I wrong in wanting a little time to myself?"

In a talk with the husband, it was revealed that he felt very rejected and unloved by his mother when he was growing up. She was never home for him. Unconsciously, he expected his wife to make up for all the love that he never received as a child. His demands were unreasonable; and the more he expected, the more she would come to resent him and push him away. (Author's counseling notes)

QUESTIONS

1. What do you think this wife should do? Should she ignore her husband's demands? Should she try to give him all the love possible? Should she give in to his insatiable demands? What might be some consequences of each of these courses of action?

2. What would be best for the husband? Is he right in expecting so much attention from his wife? What would help him the most?

Research shows that lovers whose involvement includes friendship maintain more enduring relationships.

of the relationship may be emphasized through all four stages. In contrast, a deep, mature love may involve a number of turns of the wheel (as well as a large number of rapport, revelation, dependency, and fulfillment factors), emphasizing the need to know one another in a number of circumstances.

FRIENDSHIP LOVE

Another important element of love is **friendship love**, what Walster and Walster (1978) call companionate love (Hatfield, 1982). This implies a type of love between those with *common concerns*. This type of love may exist between those who are good companions because of *similar interests*; it may arise out of *respect for the personality or character of another* (Rubin, 1973). Research has shown that the most comprehensive and profound relationships are between two lovers whose involvement includes a friendship type of love. While romance may exist without friendship, love becomes more complete and enduring with it (Rosenbaum, 1979).

Loving and Liking

There is some evidence to show that *loving* and *liking* are separate phenomena and may be measured separately (Davis, 1985; Rubin, 1970). But this research defines love only in romantic terms. Other research emphasizes that as love matures over the years it contains more and more elements of friendship (Cimbalo, Faling, and Mousan, 1976; Driscoll, Davis, and Lipetz, 1972). This means couples grow to like one another. In fact, liking has been called the key to loving (Fowler, 1983). Liking in a relationship brings relaxation in the presence of the beloved; it is a stimulus for two people to want to be with one another. It is friendship in the simplest, most direct terms.

Saxton writes, "The companionship component of love, although the least dramatic, is probably the most commonly and frequently experienced (and thus, in a sense, the most important) aspect of . . . love, despite mass media emphasis on romance and sexuality" (Saxton, 1972, p. 35).

Friendship love is certainly more relaxed and less tense than romantic love. It is less possessive, less emotional, and affords more security without anxiety and upset. In such a secure environment, couples can be free to live, work, and to go about their lives because of their friendship

ALTRUISTIC LOVE

Altruistic love is unselfish concern for the well-being of another. It is the investment of one's psychic energies and abilities in caring for another individual and in seeking what is best for the other person. By nurturing someone else and doing all one can to make the other person happy, the individual finds meaning and satisfaction in his or her own life.

Erich Fromm's View of Altruistic Love

One of the chief exponents of altruistic love is Erich Fromm (1956). To Fromm, love is an activity, not a passive affection; it is a "standing in" not a "falling for." In the most general way, the active character of love can be described by stating that love is primarily giving, not receiving (Lester, 1979). To Fromm, giving is not "giving up" something, being deprived of, sacrificing. It is giving of oneself: of that which is alive in one, of one's joy, interest, understanding, knowledge, humor, even sadness. Thus, in giving of one's life, the other person is enriched.

In addition to the element of giving, Fromm emphasizes four basic components of love. These are *care, responsibility, respect,* and *knowledge.* Fromm uses the illustration of a woman who says she loves flowers, but forgets to water them. It would be difficult to believe she really loves her flowers. "Love is the active concern for the life and growth of that which we love" (Fromm, 1956, p. 22). Where concern is lacking, there is no love. Care and concern also imply *responsibility,* not as a duty imposed from the outside, but as a voluntary act in which one responds to the needs (primarily psychic) of the other person. Love also depends upon *respect,* which is not fear and awe but awareness of the unique individuality of the other and concern that the other person should grow and unfold as he or she is. Respect is possible only where freedom and independence are granted. It is the opposite of domination. And finally, love also requires *knowledge* of the other person, in order to see his or her reality, and overcome any irrationally distorted picture.

Need of Mutuality

The love that Fromm describes is an unselfish, caring, giving love. But *ideally, this type of love, like dependent love, should be mutual.* If it is not, it can become very lopsided with one person doing all the giving and the other the receiving.

The five elements of love described here are all important in the most complete love. Western culture emphasizes *romantic love* as the basis for mate selection. Because it is so highly regarded, it cannot be ignored. When based upon reality, romantic love is not dysfunctional as a basis for marriage.

Erotic love is an important part of love. Certainly, sexual attraction is an important beginning, and sexual satisfaction strengthens the bond between two people. If there is repeated frustration, love can be replaced by anger and hostility. Ordinarily, therefore, love and sex are interdependent. A loving relationship becomes a firm foundation for a happy sexual life. A fulfilling sexual relationship reinforces the total love of the couple for one another.

Dependent love is valuable as a basis for a strong relationship when it involves mutual dependency. Integration in the relationship takes place to the extent that each person meets the needs of the other. Unless people need one another and fulfill one another's needs, why have a relationship? The difficulty arises when the needs of one person are excessive, so that neurotic, possessive dependency becomes the basis for the relationship. Most persons need to receive as well as give if they are to remain emotionally healthy. Those who enjoy giving without receiving become either martyrs or masochists.

Friendship love, based upon companionship, is an enduring bond between two people who like one another and enjoy one another's company. It can endure over many years. For most people, friendship alone is not enough for marriage, but it is an important ingredient in loving relationships.

Altruistic love adds genuine concern and care to the total relationship. Behavior, rather than feeling, is the active means by which the individual shows care. Like dependency, giving and receiving must be mutual. Altruistic love allows the person expressing it to gain satisfaction through caring for another. It allows the receiving person to be cared for and loved for his or her own sake.

Research on the Components of Love

The latest research studies reinforce the idea that the most complete love has a number of components. Sternberg (1986) asked subjects to describe their relationships with lovers, parents, siblings, and friends. Analysis of the results revealed three components of close relationships: *intimacy*, *passion*, and *commitment* to maintain the relationship. Sternberg felt that an ideal, which he called **consummate love**, results from a combination of all three components (Trotter, 1986).

Davis (1985) found that love relationships included three categories: *passion*, *caring*, and *friendship*. Each of these, in turn, could be described by a cluster of characteristics. The passion cluster included fascination with one another, a desire for exclusiveness, and sexual desire. The caring cluster included giving the utmost of oneself, being a champion and advocate of the other's interests, and making sure that the partner succeeds. The friendship cluster involved enjoyment, acceptance, trust, respect, mutual assistance, confiding in one another, understanding, and spontaneity. This study reveals that love is not a simple concept.

Canadian sociologist John Alan Lee (1973, 1974, 1976) analyzed 4,000 published accounts of love — from classical Greece to the present — and compared them with empirical studies of contemporary love experience. He identified three different "styles of loving" or meanings of love. Those three were:

Eros — romantic, sexual, sensual love, characterized by love at first sight and definite physiological reactions.

Ludus — a playful, challenging, nonpossessive kind of love. Love is a game to be played for excitement and pleasure.

Storge — a companionate, comfortable, affectionate, best-friends type of intimate love that is slow to develop. Sexual intimacy comes late in the development.

In addition to these primary types, Lee identified three other styles which are combinations of others.

Mania — a combination of eros and ludus that is a possessive, jealous, stressful love, alternating between irrational joy and anxiety, depression, and pain. Feelings are beyond rational control. This love rarely ends happily.

Pragma — a logical, sensible, rational, practical love in which the individual evaluates a partner's good and bad points to determine suitability.

Agape — unselfish, altruistic love involving caring and sensitivity to the partner's needs.

Subsequent research by Reedy (1977) emphasizes the need for balance between the loving styles. Each of the six types contributes something of value to the relationship. A vital, alive marriage, for example, needs romance and sexual attraction (eros), but those who overlook important practical considerations (pragma) are irresponsible. Some mania is exciting, but too much possessiveness and jealousy becomes smothering. *The most complete love includes some of all six types.* Reedy (1977) showed also that those who were among the happily married tended to have the same loving style.

ASSESSMENT
Your Love Profile

Lasswell and Lasswell (1987) analyzed the research of Lee, especially the statements about the meaning of love, and grouped these into six clusters according to Lee's typology, eliminating those statements that showed no statistical significance. The six clusters of statements became six scales: *storge*, *agape*, *mania*, *pragma*, *ludus*, and *eros*. From the acronym for these scales, the combined scores were called "The SAMPLE Profile." You can use this profile to evaluate your love and perhaps compare it with the profile of your lover, to understand your love better.

INSTRUCTIONS FOR RESPONDING TO SAMPLE SCALES

Each of the following questions is to be answered "true" or "false." Answer the questions in consecutive order, and *do not skip or omit any of them*. Some may seem ambiguous or out of your experience, and you may need to let your pencil choose your answer for no special reason. Remember that the test is a research instrument and that the profile was validated by the testing of thousands of men and women. It may help you to answer the questions if you think of your ideal or most memorable love relationship rather than your current one. Finally, complete the questionnaire independently of your classmates or your partner. There are no "correct" or "incorrect" answers to the items. Mark your responses on the answer sheet below or on a facsimile of it.

Answer True or False

		T	F
1.	I believe that "love at first sight" is possible.	☐	☐
2.	I did not realize that I was in love until I actually had been for some time.	☐	☐
3.	When things aren't going right with us, my stomach gets upset.	☐	☐
4.	From a practical point of view, I must consider what a person is going to become in life before I commit myself to loving him/her.	☐	☐
5.	You cannot have love unless you have first had *caring* for a while.	☐	☐
6.	It's always a good idea to keep your lover a little uncertain about how committed you are to him/her.	☐	☐
7.	The first time we kissed or rubbed cheeks, I felt a definite genital response (lubrication, erection).	☐	☐
8.	I still have good friendships with almost everyone with whom I have ever been involved in a love relationship.	☐	☐
9.	It makes good sense to plan your life carefully before you choose a lover.	☐	☐
10.	When my love affairs break up, I get so depressed that I have even thought of suicide.	☐	☐
11.	Sometimes I get so excited about being in love that I can't sleep.	☐	☐
12.	I try to use my own strength to help my lover through difficult times, even when he/she is behaving foolishly.	☐	☐
13.	I would rather suffer myself than let my lover suffer.	☐	☐
14.	Part of the fun of being in love is testing one's skill at keeping it going and getting what one wants from it at the same time.	☐	☐
15.	As far as my lovers go, what they don't know won't hurt them.	☐	☐
16.	It is best to love someone with a similar background.	☐	☐
17.	We kissed each other soon after we met because we both wanted to.	☐	☐
18.	When my lover doesn't pay attention to me, I feel sick all over.	☐	☐
19.	I cannot be happy unless I place my lover's happiness before my own.	☐	☐
20.	Usually the first thing that attracts my attention to a person is his/her pleasing physical appearance.	☐	☐
21.	The best kind of love grows out of a long friendship.	☐	☐
22.	When I am in love, I have trouble concentrating on anything else.	☐	☐
23.	At the first touch of his/her hand, I knew that love was a real possibility.	☐	☐

T   F

24. When I break up with someone, I go out of my way to see that he/she is OK. ☐ ☐

25. I cannot relax if I suspect that he/she is with someone else. ☐ ☐

26. I have at least once had to plan carefully to keep two of my lovers from finding out about each other. ☐ ☐

27. I can get over love affairs pretty easily and quickly. ☐ ☐

28. A main consideration in choosing a lover is how he/she reflects on my family. ☐ ☐

29. The best part of love is living together, building a home together, and rearing children together. ☐ ☐

30. I am usually willing to sacrifice my own wishes to let my lover achieve his/hers. ☐ ☐

31. A main consideration in choosing a partner is whether or not he/she will be a good parent. ☐ ☐

32. Kissing, cuddling, and sex shouldn't be rushed into; they will happen naturally when one's intimacy has grown enough. ☐ ☐

33. I enjoy flirting with attractive people. ☐ ☐

34. My lover would get upset if he/she knew some of the things I've done with other people. ☐ ☐

35. Before I ever fell in love, I had a pretty clear physical picture of what my true love would be like. ☐ ☐

36. If my lover had a baby by someone else, I would want to raise it, love it, and care for it as if it were my own. ☐ ☐

37. It is hard to say exactly when we fell in love. ☐ ☐

38. I couldn't truly love anyone I would not be willing to marry. ☐ ☐

39. Even though I don't want to be jealous, I can't help it when he/she pays attention to someone else. ☐ ☐

40. I would rather break up with my lover than to stand in his/her way. ☐ ☐

41. I like the idea of my lover and myself having the same kinds of clothes, hats, plants, bicycles, cars, etc. ☐ ☐

42. I wouldn't date anyone that I wouldn't want to fall in love with. ☐ ☐

43. At least once when I thought a love affair was all over, I saw him/her again and knew I couldn't realistically see that person again without loving him/her. ☐ ☐

44. Whatever I own is my lover's to use as he/she chooses. ☐ ☐

45. If my lover ignores me for a while, I sometimes do really stupid things to try to get his/her attention back. ☐ ☐

46. It's fun to see whether I can get someone to go out with me even if I don't want to get involved with that person. ☐ ☐

47. A main consideration in choosing a mate is how he/she reflects on my career. ☐ ☐

48. When my lover doesn't see me or call for a while, I assume he/she has a good reason. ☐ ☐

49. Before getting very involved with anyone, I try to figure out how compatible his/her hereditary background is with mine in case we ever have children. ☐ ☐

50. The best love relationships are the ones that last the longest. ☐ ☐

Tally

1. Circle the item number of each T (true) response on the scales to the right. Write the number of true responses per column in the space provided.

S	A	M	P	L	E
2	12	3	4	6	1
5	13	10	9	14	7
8	19	11	16	15	17
21	24	18	28	26	20
29	30	22	31	27	23
32	36	25	38	33	35
37	40	39	42	34	41
50	44	43	47	46	
	48	45	49		

Total circled true in each column

Sample Profile

2. Now fill in the histogram below by shading in each column up to the number of circles counted in the corresponding column in item 1, above.

3. The percentile reading on the right of the profile shows the proportion of the population that has less of the indicated trait than you have.

S = Storge = "Best friends"
A = Agape = "Unselfish"
M = Mania = "Possessive"
P = Pragma = "Logical"
L = Ludus = "Game-playing"
E = Eros = "Romantic"

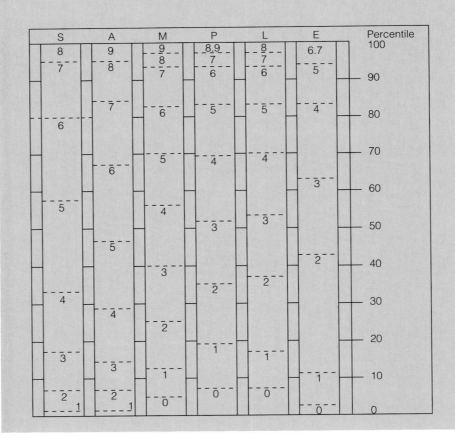

EVALUATING YOUR RESPONSE

You will have some "true" answers in several or, probably, all of the scales. Usually, however, two or three scales will have more "true" answers than others. If you have high percentiles in several or all scales, it does not necessarily mean you are a better lover — nor does scoring low in several or all of them mean that your love is in scarce supply. Instead, this is more likely to be a reflection of your test-taking attitude. Some people agree with a statement if it is true only once in a while, but others never answer "true" unless the situation always or almost always exists. The latter person is inclined to be analytical and cautious. Your relative lower and higher percentiles are more significant than your absolute scores.

The percentile numbers at the right side of the sample profile indicate the percentage of respondents whose profiles have been studied who had lower scores than yours. After the first few hundred profiles had been recorded, these percentages became quite precise, and they have shown no tendency to change in subsequent studies.

We have never seen anyone who had "true" responses in only one column and none in the others. In other words, there are probably no "pure" types. Instead, most people define love as some kind of combination of several or all of the six definitions. There is an enormous number of possible combinations.

Your SAMPLE profile shows graphically how your scores on each of the scales blend into your own distinctinve definition of love. There is no good or bad combination of scores for a person. Nor is one definition of love more or less mature than another.

Most people automatically assume that their own definitions of love are correct or at least "normal," although they may understand that others disagree with the meaning they give it. Social psychologist Daryl Berm has termed such unchallenged beliefs *zero-order* ones. He points out that it is unlikely that a fish recognizes that it is wet since it has known nothing else. If you have never been challenged before by the fact that there are as many definitions of love as there are people, you may want to defend the idea that yours is "real love" and someone else's is only infatuation or immature love. However, each person's definition of love is probably as correct to him or her as yours is to you. It is easy to see why, with such zero-order beliefs, partners with quite different styles of loving may have considerable difficulty in communicating their caring to each other.

It is important to understand that people do not always *behave* in accordance with their definitions of love, even though they believe that people who are in love *ought* to behave that way (just as persons sometimes tell lies even though they believe firmly that people ought not to lie). Most persons, although their *feelings* tend to overpower their intellectual definitions of whether they are in love, still expect others who are in love to behave according to those intellectual definitions! Such inconsistencies are not uncommon, and most people are able to rationalize their violations of their own rules.

From Lasswell, M., and Lasswell, T. (1987). Marriage and the family (2nd ed.). Belmont, CA: Wadsworth. Reprinted by permission.

SUMMARY

1. The most important element in initial attraction is physical attractiveness. Standards of attractiveness are culturally conditioned and change over the years.

2. Personality and social factors are also important in attraction. Personality traits and actions are significant factors in whether others find individuals attractive or not.

3. Sometimes because of previous conditioning, unconscious factors influence a person's evaluation of the attractiveness of others.

4. Love is not a single concept but has different dimensions. The five dimensions discussed here are romantic (emotional) love, erotic (sensual) love, dependent (need) love, friendship (companionship) love, and altruistic (unselfish) love.

5. Researchers have revealed various components of love. Sternberg revealed three components — intimacy, passion, and commitment — which he called together consummate love. Davis included three categories of love: passion, caring, and friendship.

6. Lee outlined six styles of loving: storge (best-friends love), agape (unselfish love), mania (passionate love), pragma (logical love, ludus (game-playing love), and eros (romantic love). A balance between these loving styles is necessary in any relationship. A person's styles of loving may be measured by a love profile questionnaire called "The SAMPLE Profile." The word SAMPLE is an acronym using the first letter of each of the names of the love style.

SUGGESTED READINGS

Adams, G. R., and Crossman, S. (1978). *Physical Attractiveness: A Cultural Imperative.* Roslyn Heights, NY: Libra. The emphasis on attractiveness in our culture.

Fromm, E. (1956). *The Art of Loving.* New York: Harper. A classic on the subject.

Lasswell, M., and Lobsenz, N. (1980). *Styles of Loving.* Garden City, NY: Doubleday. Measuring your love profile according to Lee's styles.

Lee, J. (1976). *The Colors of Love.* Englewood Cliffs, NJ: Prentice-Hall. Six styles of loving explained.

Liebowitz, M. R. (1983). *The Chemistry of Love.* Boston: Little, Brown. Physiological factors in love.

Rubin, Z. (1973). *Liking and Loving.* New York: Holt, Rinehart and Winston. A classic exploration of love and friendship.

Tennov, D. (1979). *Love and Limerence: The Experience of Being in Love.* New York: Stein and Day. Emphasizes romantic love.

Walster, E., and Walster, G. W. (1978). *A New Look at Love.* Reading, MA: Addison-Wesley. Overview of research.

8

PAIRING AND MATE SELECTION

CHAPTER OUTLINE

KEY TERMS

parent image theory
ideal mate theory
birth order theory
complementary needs theory
instrumental needs theory
genderic congruency
exchange theory
equity theory
stimulus-value-role theory
propinquity
homogamy
endogamy
heterogamy
exogamy
consanguinity
compatibility
filtering process
hypergamous union
hypogamous union

Selecting a mate is one of the most important decisions we make during our lifetime. Marrying the right person can result in much personal happiness and fulfillment. Marrying the wrong person may result in much misery. In our country, this important decision is left up to the individual (Lee and Stone, 1980), yet, it is often made lightly, with too little thought given to important considerations in mate selection. We are concerned here with theories of mate selection and their applicability to real life. What factors influence mate selection? How important is family background? What are the possibilities for intermarriage between those of different socioeconomic classes, races, and religions? What personality traits are important for successful marriage? How important is consensus of attitudes and values? How do you know if you are compatible? Is it necessary to have similar role concepts and personal habits?

This chapter shares the wisdom of years of study by researchers of the mate selection process. For those of you not married, perhaps the chapter will help you choose your mate wisely.

THEORIES OF MATE SELECTION

Theories of mate selection attempt to explain the process and dynamics by which mates are selected. Some theories have proven to have more validity than others, and no one theory tells the whole story; but together they provide some explanation of what happens.

The major theories that have been proposed can be divided into four groups as follows:

- Psychodynamic theories
- Needs theories
- Exchange theories
- Developmental process theories

PSYCHODYNAMIC THEORIES

Parent Image Theory

Psychodynamic theories emphasize the influence of experiences of earlier years upon mate selection (Klimek, 1979). One of these theories is the **parent image theory**. It is based upon Freud's psychoanalytic concepts of the *Oedipus complex* and *Electra complex* and states that a man is likely to marry someone resembling his mother and that a woman will likely marry someone resembling her father. Jedlicka (1984) tested this theory and found that the resemblance between a man's wife and his mother and between a woman's husband and her father occurred more frequently than expected by chance. In general, the data supported the theory of indirect parental influence on mate choice.

Ideal Mate Theory

The **ideal mate theory** states that people form a fantasy of what an ideal mate should be like, based partly upon early childhood experiences. Schwartz and

The ideal mate theory states that people form fantasies of what a mate should be like, but sometimes such fantasy images are not realistic.

Schwartz (1980) write:

> Somewhere we "remember" how it felt to have another human being take care of us. We take this memory with us as we mature. Ultimately, it becomes our model, our expectation of a loving relationship. (p. 4)

Carl Jung argued that every man carries within his genes an "archetype form" of a special female image. When the "right" woman (who fits the archetype) comes along, the man becomes instantly aware that he has found his mate (Evans, 1964).

There is little doubt that many people form fantasies of an ideal mate. The problem occurs when these fantasies are unrealistic and their mate never fulfills them. If they pressure their mate to do so, rather than accept him or her as is, the marriage becomes troubled.

Birth Order Theory

An interesting variation of psychodynamic theory is the **birth order theory.** This theory emphasizes the influence of birth order on personality and behavior patterns (Toman, 1969). An only child, for example, has never had to compete in intimate relationships, is used to getting his or her own way, and has an exaggerated sense of importance; an only child, then, would be happiest with a mate who continues to fulfill this expectation. An oldest brother in a family of sons has learned to be aggressive and in control and so would be happiest with a subservient woman. A youngest daughter in a family of female children may be awkward and shy around males and would be most compatible with an oldest brother of sisters, provided he was nurturant and capable. The conclusion of the theory is that people have better chances of happiness in relationships when the partners they choose allow them to enact roles they learned in their families of origin. They would presumably be attracted to such persons more often than chance would dictate. Forer (1976), who has done extensive research on birth order, emphasizes that birth order influences personality and behavior patterns and so has implications for marriage:

> In marriage, consider yourself and your partner as unique people, partly molded and trained in special ways of relating to others by the accident of your birth position. (p. 286)

Other research shows that size of family has more influence on personality than does ordinal (birth order) position (Hayes, 1981).

NEEDS THEORIES

Complementary Needs Theories

Complementary needs theory, which was originated by Robert Winch (1958), says that people tend to select mates whose needs are opposite but complementary to their own. According to this theory, a *nurturant* person who likes to care for others would seek out a *succorant* mate who liked to be cared for. A *dominant* person would select a *submissive* person. Winch (1967) added a third aspect of complementariness: *achievement-vicariousness*. The person who has a need to achieve tends to select a person whose need is to find recognition through vicarious attainment of a spouse.

Winch said that mate selection is largely homogamous (the tendency to select a person like oneself) with respect to social factors such as age, race, religion, social class, education, location of previous residence, and previous marital status. However, these variables only define the field of eligibles. The individual selects from the eligibles by seeking out a person who gives the greatest promise of providing maximum need gratification. This is the person whose needs are complementary to one's own.

Since Winch's formulation, subsequent research has provided either no support or only partial support for this theory (Murstein, 1980). In fact, similarity of need may be more functional in mate selection than complementarity (Rice, 1983).

Instrumental Needs Theory

An **instrumental needs theory** was proposed by Centers (1975), who said that people seek relationships with those who provide maximum gratification and minimum punification for their needs. Centers' theory departs from Winch's in stating that some needs are more important than others. Thus, the needs

During the second stage of stimulus-value-role theory of mate selection, people explore one another's interests, values, philosophies of life, religious beliefs, political views, and attitudes.

for *sex* and *affiliation* are more important than the needs for *nurturance* and *abasement* (to feel inferior, humble). Furthermore, Centers said that some needs are more important to one sex than the other and that those needs most typical of men should be most correlated with the needs most typical of women. He called this principle the principle of **genderic congruency**. Centers (1975) writes:

> Male dominance has *high* attractiveness value for females, but female dominance has *less* attractiveness value for males. Again *female nurturance* has high attractiveness for males, but *male nurturance* has less attractiveness for females. (p. 75)

In this case, when the male was dominant and the female nurturant, the couple would be most attracted to one another.

Centers listed a total of 239 hypotheses, many of which were insignificant and have not been proven. However, he did find support for some of his major hypotheses. Couples correlated significantly if the man's need for *sex* was combined with the woman's need for *affiliation*. When the most masculine need (*dominance*) was correlated with the most feminine need (*affiliation*), the highest cross-need correlation resulted. Also, the correlation for couples for *achievement* was significantly higher if the man was low in *abasement* (inferiority feelings) than if he suffered from inferiority. In other words, he could more easily accept an assertive, successful woman if he had a good self-image.

Centers' theory reeks of sexism. Women fulfill their identity by finding a male with stronger drives than their own. The female is "submissive, dependent, affectionate" (Centers, 1975, p. 690). Nevertheless, some of his predictions are valid. People do seek out persons who will fulfill their needs, and couples are happiest when need fulfillment is mutual, even though their needs vary. Centers' theory, however, does represent an advancement over the monolithic complementary needs theory of Winch (Murstein, 1980).

EXCHANGE THEORIES

Exchange theory holds that the basis for a continuing relationship between two partners is that each believes he or she will get as much or more from the relationship as it will cost. Since each person is trying to maximize chances for a rewarding marriage, the partners wind up being equal in their abilities to reward one another. Those who feel they have the most to offer look for someone who has the most to offer them, and so an equal exchange takes place (Scanzoni, 1979). At other times, however, those who are motivated primarily to maximize their own interest may exploit others, which is not conducive to a loving relationship. This is one reason why exchange theory has been rejected as the primary determinant of marriage commitment (Murstein, Cerreto, and McDonald, 1977).

Equity Theory

Equity theory is an improvement over exchange theory (Walster, Walster, and Traupman, 1978). It insists on fairness, on the principle that it is most fair to get benefits from a relationship in proportion to what is given. The exchanged benefits might not be the same. People desire different things, but they are attracted by a deal that is fair to them. Some people are attracted to others not primarily for what they can get, but for what they can give to a relationship. Judging equity, then, is an individual matter.

Stimulus-Value-Role (SVR) Theory

One of the most influential mate-selection theories has been the **stimulus-value-role theory (SVR)** as outlined by Murstein (1970). His theory combines elements of exchange theory with elements of filter theory into a three-stage process of mate selection (Figure 8.1). The first stage is *stimulus* — each person's being drawn to another primarily because of physical, mental, social, or reputational attraction. It is important that each person feel attraction to the other.

If both persons are attracted during the first stage, they pass on to the second or *value* stage, during which they explore one another's interests and values. They may explore philosophies of life, religious beliefs, political views, attitudes toward sex, attitudes and values relating to marriage and family living, and other factors. If they talk about these and discover they have similar value orientations, deeper feelings are more likely to develop.

They then enter the *role* stage during which they explore behavior patterns, temperament, emotional stability and security, sex-role concepts, sexual behavior and expressions, ability to handle responsibility, and vocational roles, among other things. The goal is to see if the partners are similar enough to build a comfortable partnership. Successful passage through these three

FIGURE 8.1 *Stimulus-Value-Role (SVR)*
Theory of Mate Selection.

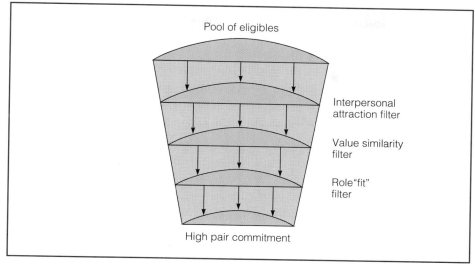

Pool of eligibles

Interpersonal
attraction filter

Value similarity
filter

Role"fit"
filter

High pair commitment

Adapted from Murstein, B. I. (1970). Stimulus-value-role theory: A theory of marital choice. *Journal of Marriage and the Family, 32,* 465–507.

stages may lead to some degree of permanence in the relationship (Murstein, 1980). Murstein has suggested that the motivation to marry is a significant variable influencing movement from one stage to another (Figure 8.1).

In all, 39 hypotheses were tested by Murstein (1976), and he claimed some support for 33, with 6 being unsubstantiated, sometimes despite strong trends. Subsequent research by Leigh, Holman, and Burr (1984) showed only partial support for Murstein's theory, especially the sequence of stages. The theory must be interpreted cautiously because of the difficulties in identifying when couples are in a particular stage.

DEVELOPMENTAL PROCESS THEORIES

Developmental process theories describe mate selection as a process of filtering and weeding out ineligibles and incompatible persons until one person is selected.

Propinquity

One of the factors in mate sorting is **propinquity** (Davis-Brown, Salamon, and Surra, 1987). That is, geographic nearness is a major factor influencing mate selection. Those who have close contact where they live, at work, in school, in church, or in other places are more likely to develop relationships leading to marriage than are those who do not have such contact. Davis-Brown and colleagues (1987) emphasize that *institutional propinquity* is as important as *residential propinquity*. In other words, people meet in places of business, consolidated schools, integrated social organizations, and churches.

Another factor in mate selection is *attraction*. People are drawn to those whom they find attractive. This includes physical attraction and attraction because of specific personality traits. Since this subject has been discussed in detail in Chapter 7, more will not be added here.

Homogamy, Endogamy, Heterogamy, and Exogamy

Another factor in mate sorting is **homogamy**, the tendency to choose individuals similar to oneself. Another factor is **endogamy**, the practice of marrying within one's own group, according to age, race, ethnicity, education, socioeconomic class, or religion. The opposite of homogamy is **heterogamy**, which means to be attracted to those and marry someone different from oneself. While there may be some heterogamy of factors in actual mate selection, such as age, education, or religion, the overall tendency is toward homogamous unions. Furthermore, homogamous marriages tend to be more compatible than heterogamous marriages. There are exceptions, and this subject will be explored in detail in later sections of this chapter.

Exogamy means marrying across social lines, outside one's own social group. There are strong pressures to marry within our own group, but there are also pressures to prevent endogamous marriages that are too close. Incestuous marriages involving **consanguinity** are forbidden, for example. In general, endogamous marriages are more compatible than exogamous ones, although there may be significant exceptions to this generality.

Compatibility

Another important concept is that of **compatibility**, which refers to the capability of living together in harmony. Compatibility may be evaluated according to temperament, attitudes and values, needs, role conceptions and enactment, and habit systems. In the process of mate selection, couples strive to sort out those with whom they are compatible in these various ways.

The Filtering Process

Figure 8.2 shows a schematic representation of the **filtering process**. The figure is based on numerous theories and research studies. Rather than relying on any one narrow view, the diagram represents a composite of various theories to show the process in detail. For more information on specific theories see Bolton (1961), Kerckhoff and Davis (1962), Klimek (1979), Lewis, 1972, 1973), Murstein (1970), Nofz (1984), Whipple and Whittle (1976).

Beginning at the top of the figure, we begin the process of filtering with a very wide field of eligibles. This total group goes through a series of filters, each of which eliminates ineligibles, so that the numbers are reduced before passing to the next filter. Before making a final decision, two people may go through a final trial period, either through cohabitation or formal engagement or both. If they survive this filtering process, the final filter is the decision to marry.

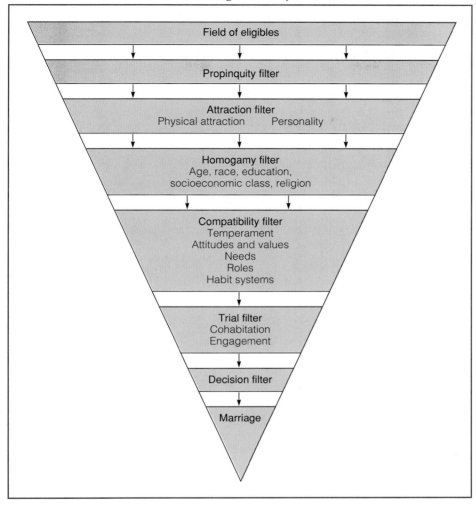

The order is approximate. Obviously, partners are selected according to propinquity first, and physical attraction plays a significant role very early in the relationship, followed by attraction because of other personality traits. Gradually, couples begin to sort out homogamous mates according to sociocultural factors: age, race, education, socioeconomic class, and religion. As the relationship develops, they find out if they are compatible according to temperament, attitudes and values, needs, role concepts, and habit systems. Some couples place more emphasis on some factors than on others (Cote and Koval, 1983). Some may explore compatibility without regard for homogamy. Others are more interested in selecting someone with the same socioeconomic background. Generally speaking, both homogamous factors and compatibility factors are important. A testing of the relationship provides further evidence of whether the choice is a wise one or not.

As you can see, at its best, mate selection is a complex process by which people sort out a variety of social, psychological, and personal factors until the final choice is made. Unfortunately, some people are not this thorough.

CLASSROOM FORUM
Letting Your Parents Select Your Mate

David and Vera Mace (1960) interviewed a group of women in India and found that the women preferred having their parents find and select their mate. Following is an excerpt from the interview.

"Wouldn't you like to be free to choose your own marriage partners, like the young people do in the West?"

"Oh, no!" several voices replied in chorus.

Taken aback, we searched their faces.

"Why not?"

"For one thing," said one of them, "doesn't it put the girl in a very humiliating position?"

"Humiliating? In what way?"

"Well, doesn't it mean that she has to try to look pretty, and call attention to herself, and attract a boy, to be sure she'll get married?"

"Well, perhaps so."

"And if she doesn't want to do that, or if she feels it's undignified, wouldn't that mean she mightn't get a husband?"

"Yes, that's possible."

"So a girl who is shy and doesn't push herself forward might not be able to get married. Does that happen?"

"Sometimes it does."

"Well, surely that's humiliating. It makes getting married a sort of competition in which the girls are fighting each other for the boys. And it encourages a girl to pretend she's better than she really is. She can't relax and be herself. She has to make a good impression to get a boy, and then she has to go on making a good impression to get him to marry her."

Before we could think of an answer to this unexpected line of argument, another girl broke in.

"In our system, you see," she explained, "girls don't have to worry at all. We know we'll get married. When we are old enough, our parents will find a suitable boy, and everything will be arranged. We don't have to go into competition with each other."

They move from physical attraction to marriage without going through the intervening filters. Or outside factors, such as *pregnancy*, pressure them into a marriage that is unwise. The remainder of this chapter will be devoted to a discussion of various factors that might be considered in mate selection.

FAMILY BACKGROUND FACTORS IN MATE SELECTION

Family Influences

Family background influences everything that people are, want to become, or do. A detailed discussion of family background and its influences may be found in Chapter 3. But we need to look at it from the point of view of mate selection. How people are brought up influences their views of marriage, how they want to bring up their children, and their sex-role preferences. It influences their personalities, traits, attitudes, values, and feelings. There is probably no area of living that is unrelated to family background.

"Besides," said a third girl, "how would we be able to judge the character of a boy we met and got friendly with? We are young and inexperienced. Our parents are older and wiser, and they aren't as easily deceived as we would be. I'd far rather have my parents choose for me. It's so important that the man I marry should be the right one. I could so easily make a mistake if I had to find him for myself."

Another girl had her hand stretched out eagerly.

"But *does* the girl really have any choice in the West?" she said. "From what I've read, it seems that the boy does all the choosing. All the girl can do is to say yes or no. She can't go up to a boy and say 'I like you. Will you marry me?' can she?"

We admitted that this was not usually done.

"So," she went on eagerly, "when you talk about men and women being equal in the West, it isn't true. When our parents are looking for a husband for us, they don't have to wait until some boy takes it into his head to ask for us. They just find out what families are looking for wives for their sons, and see whether one of the boys would be suitable. Then, if his family agrees that it would be a good match, they arrange it together."

From Mace, D., and Mace, V. (1960). *Marriage East and West*. Garden City, NJ: Doubleday, 144–146.

QUESTIONS

1. What do you think of the system of mate selection in India? What are some advantages? Disadvantages?

2. If your parents were selecting a mate for you, what factors would they emphasize? How would these be similar to or different from those you would believe important?

3. How could our system of mate selection be improved? What needs to be done to make it work well?

4. Could people be taught how to select a mate? Explain.

Knowing the Family

For these reasons, *it is helpful in mate selection to investigate the family background of persons who seem likely marital choices.* There is a saying, "I'm not marrying his or her family." But that is not completely true. We marry a son or daughter, but that person is a product of his or her family experiences. When we marry someone, we marry everything the family has been able to impart to the individual child. Knowing something about the family helps us to know the person who grew up in that family. Marrying someone without knowing his or her family is like stumbling down a winding pathway with one eye shut and the other one partially closed.

Healthy and Unhealthy Families

When both spouses are exposed to healthy family of origin experiences, they more often achieve greater marital satisfaction than do spouses who have not been exposed to such

Marriage brings together two families, not just two individuals. Knowing something about a marriage partner's family experiences can be important to successful marital adjustment.

experiences (Wilcoxon and Hovestadt, 1983). If we discover things about a person's background that are troublesome or that bother us, we can discuss those things to find out how our partner feels or has been affected. Problems that are discovered may be thought of as caution signals influencing us to slow down while they are examined. Important issues that are unresolved may require professional premarital counseling to see if they can be worked out. If not, they may be reasons to discontinue the relationship.

Socioeconomic Class

The possibilities of marital satisfaction are also greater if people marry within their own socioeconomic class (Haller, 1981). Interclass unions do take place, but Pearlin (1975) found that partners experienced more stress in their heterogamous unions. Moreover, the spouses who married down were more stressed than the one marrying up, but only if status-striving was important. If the spouses from the higher class were very class conscious, they became very aware of the lower background of their spouse, and so the relationship with their spouse was less affectionate, less emotionally supportive, and subject to less consensus.

Education and Intelligence

There is a tendency for couples to enter into homogamous marriages with respect to education. Figure 8.3 shows the percentages of females with some college

FIGURE 8.3 *Percentages of College-Educated Females Who Were Married to Men with Various Degrees of Education: March 1977.*

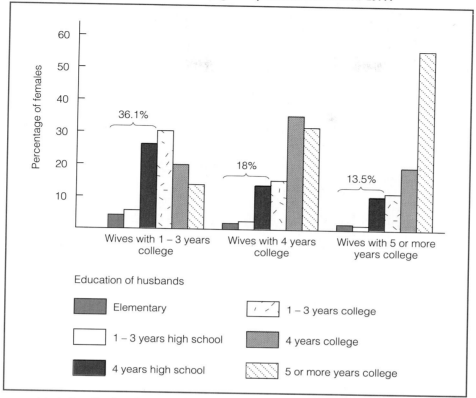

Adapted from Rawlings, S. (1978). Perspectives on American husbands and wives. *Current Population Reports*, ser.p-23, no. 77, p. 13. Washington, DC: U.S. Government Printing Office.

education who married men with similar or different levels of education (Rawlings, 1978). These figures indicate that females with four years of college either married men who were also four-year college graduates or those who had more education than they did. Of those females who had four years of college, only 18 percent married men with an elementary or high school education. Most women would feel that they didn't have enough in common when there was a wide discrepancy in education.

The tendency toward *educational homogamy* among males applies most to those with a high school education. Figure 8.4 shows that slightly more than half of males with some elementary education were married to women with more education than they themselves had. It also shows that among husbands with four years of college, a majority married women with less education than they had (Rawlings, 1978).

What about the compatibility of marriages that are mixed with respect to education? As a general principle, *educationally homogamous marriages tend to be slightly more compatible than educationally heterogamous marriages* (Jaco and Shephard, 1975). If there is a marked difference in education, it is better if the wife marries upward. The **hypergamous unions** (wife marries upward) have lower divorce rates than **hypogamous unions** (wife marries downward). Many men feel threatened by a woman who is more educated than they themselves are. It is a threat to their male ego. The opposite situation also

FIGURE 8.4 *Percentages of Educated Males Who Were Married to Women With Various Degrees of Education: March 1977.*

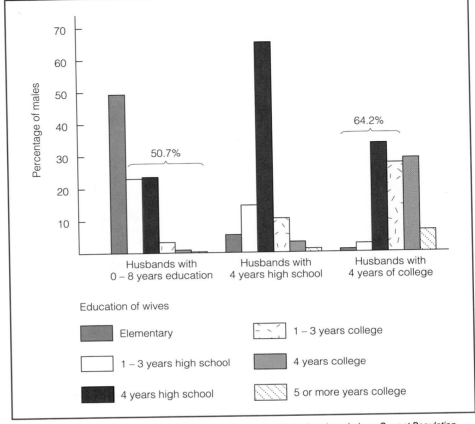

Adapted from Rawlings, S. (1978). Perspectives on American husbands and wives. *Current Population Reports*, ser. p-23, no. 77, p. 13. Washington, DC: U.S. Government Printing Office.

occurs, however; a husband may look down on a wife whom he feels is not as educated as he.

Obviously, however, educational attainment is not the only important factor. People who lack the advantages of a formal education but who are quite intelligent may be very happily married to those who are well educated. Education and brilliance are not necessarily synonymous. When couples are matched according to intelligence levels, their marriages tend to be more compatible than when couples differ in intelligence levels (Rice, 1983).

INTERRACIAL MARRIAGES

Incidence

Marriages tend to be homogamous with respect to race. The 799,000 interracial couples in the United States in 1987 represented only 1.5 percent of all married couples. Figure 8.5 shows that 22 percent of interracial couples were black-white marriages. Sixty-eight percent of black-white couples had a black hus-

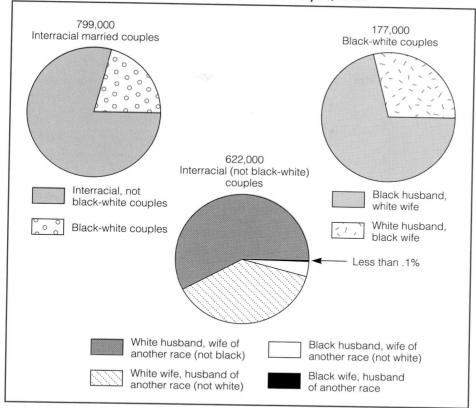

FIGURE 8.5 Interracial Married Couples, 1987.

Statistics from U.S. Bureau of the Census. (1989). *Statistical abstract of the United States, 1989.* Washington, DC: U.S. Government Printing Office, 44.

band and a white wife. The great majority of non–black-white interracial marriages involve white husbands marrying Asian wives. Intermarriage between blacks and Asians is uncommon.

The rate of interracial marriages is increasing rapidly. Between 1970 and 1987, the number of interracial marriages grew by 155 percent at the same time that the total number of marriages increased by only 17 percent (U.S. Bureau of the Census, 1989). This trend results from changes in attitudes and declining social barriers between different groups.

While the rate of interracial marriages is generally low, even though increasing, the rates vary tremendously in different locales and among different groups. Studies in 1980 of rates of intermarriage between Asians and non-Asians (primarily Caucasians) in Los Angeles County showed that the rate was 50 percent for Japanese, 30 percent for Chinese, and 19 percent for Koreans (Kitano, Yeung, Chai, and Hatanaka, 1984). The high rate for the Japanese represents a third generation growing up with existing but lessening community and family controls.

Comparable studies of Asian-Caucasian marriages in Hawaii show overall that 25 percent of adult Caucasians were married to non-Caucasian spouses, a rate far higher than on the mainland (Labov and Jacobs, 1986). This reflects lower prejudices against such unions and a general blending of various racial and ethnic groups.

Friends and parents often disapprove of an interracial marriage, creating conflict and hard feelings. In spite of this, the majority of interracial marriages are intact after ten years.

Marital Stability

Generally speaking, *divorce rates for interracial couples are higher than for same-race marriages.* This is true even in Hawaii, where prejudices against such unions are less than in some other places (Schwertfeger, 1982). However, there are no nationwide, up-to-date figures available. Heer (1974) found that after ten years of marriage, racially homogamous marriages were more successful than black-white marriages. The proportion of marriages still intact were:

Both partners white	90 percent
Both partners black	78 percent
Black husband, white wife	63 percent
White husband, black wife	47 percent

Special Problems

Interracial couples face some special problems. Friends and parents often disapprove, creating conflict and hard feelings. The couple may be deprived of social support networks. Husband-wife differences in family background also make it harder for couples to be compatible. Lena Horne, the famous black singer, said of the divorce to her white husband, "We had a good life together, and I loved him, but he didn't know what it meant to be black." Prejudices extend to the children, who may not be accepted by others. Their unhappiness can affect the stability of the interracial couple. The fact is that large numbers of interracial marriages do succeed, but with great difficulty sometimes. Vitousek (1979) found in Hawaii that Caucasian males showed the *lowest* divorce rates when they married Chinese women.

Declining social barriers between individuals of different ethnic and cultural backgrounds reflect a general decline in prejudice against intergroup marriage.

INTERFAITH MARRIAGES

Trends

One of the factors that is sometimes considered in choosing a mate is religious preference. There may be strong religious and family pressures to marry within one's own faith, based on the assumption that religiously homogamous marriages are more stable, with less likelihood of dilution of religious principles, and greater possibility that the children will grow up with strong religious convictions and well-defined moral standards. The more orthodox and conservative the religious group, the greater the pressures exerted to marry within the faith.

However, some significant trends may be noted. There has been a substantial decline in influence toward religious endogamy. This decline has occurred among Protestants and Catholics alike, and to a lesser extent among Jews. Influence has waned the most among younger members (Glenn, 1984). The result has been an increase in interfaith marriages. Table 8.1 shows the percentages of homogamous and heterogamous marriages of Protestants, Catholics, and Jews in the United States in 1957 and 1973–1978 (Glenn, 1982). The 1973–1978 data are based on six yearly General Social Surveys. As can be seen, outmarriage increased about three percentage points for Protestants, six points for Catholics, and eight points for Jews.

TABLE 8.1 *Homogamous and Heterogamous Marriages of Protestants, Catholics, and Jews in the United States, 1957 and 1973–1978**

	1957	1973-1978	*(N)*
Percentage of married Protestants			
Married to Protestants	95.5	92.6	
Married to Catholics and Jews	4.5	7.4	
	100.0	100.0	(3,846)
Percentage of married Catholics			
Married to Catholics	87.9	82.0	
Married to Protestants and Jews	12.1	18.0	
	100.0	100.0	(1,451)
Percentage of married Jews			
Married to Jews	96.3	88.2	
Married to Protestants and Catholics	3.7	11.8	
	100.0	100.0	(136)
Percentage of Protestants, Catholics, and Jews			
Married to persons of the same religion	93.6	89.7	
Married to persons of a different religion	6.4	10.3	
	100.0	100.0	(5,433)

*Persons married to persons who were not Protestant, Catholic, or Jewish are excluded from the base for the percentages.
From Glenn, N. D. (1982). Interreligious marriage in the United States: Patterns and recent trends. *Journal of Marriage and the Family, 44,* 555–566. Copyright © 1982 by the National Council on Family Relations. Reprinted by permission.

Several explanations need to be made. The percentages of interfaith marriage among Protestants would be much greater, except that a great deal of religious switching takes place for the express purpose of achieving religious homogamy. The rate of interfaith marriages among Catholics has been the highest among the three religious groups and remains so because of Catholics' unwillingness to switch their faith for the sake of religious homogamy. The rate of interfaith marriages among Jews is in between that of Protestants and Catholics and remains high because of unwillingness to change religion.

Effect on Children

One of the things that devout persons worry about is the religious effect on children of interfaith marriage. The fear is that children of interfaith marriages, in comparison to children of homogamous marriages, are subjected to less intense and less consistent religious socialization and therefore are likely to be weakly religious. However, Petersen (1986) found that *offspring of Catholic-Protestant marriages did not consistently score lower on general religiosity measures than did offspring of homogamous marriages.* In general, conservative Protestants score higher on religiosity measures than Catholics, who in turn score higher than liberal Protestants. Parental influences depend upon their religiosity, irrespective of whether they enter into a religiously heterogamous marriage or not.

Catholics wonder about the effect on adults themselves if they marry Protestants. It depends. Petersen (1986) found that Catholics married to liberal Protestants attended Mass and received communion much more often than Catholics married to conservative Protestants. Liberal Protestants were more tolerant and supportive of their spouses' attempts to practice Catholicism than were conservatives.

Effect on Marriage

Another important question is the effect of interfaith marriage on marital happiness and stability. Most studies in the past have shown a moderate negative effect of religious heterogamy on marital stability (Bumpass and Sweet, 1972) and a lower level of marital happiness in religiously heterogamous marriages (Alton, McIntosh, and Wright, 1976).

Often, however, these studies have not sorted out the different variables nor controlled for age, socioeconomic level, and other factors. For example, rates of interfaith marriages are higher among persons of low socioeconomic status and among the very young. But divorce rates are higher among these two groups. If divorce rates are higher, which is responsible: the interfaith marriage, the socioeconomic level, or the age? Through statistical manipulations and regression analysis, Glenn (1982) has determined the following:

> *Persons in marriages in which one or both spouses had no religion had, on the whole, a lower level of reported marital happiness than persons in either homogamous or heterogamous marriages in which both spouses identified with one of the major religious categories.* (p. 562)
> *The estimated heterogamy effect for females is positive and nonsignificant, but the one for males is negative and significant.* (p. 563) [italics added]

This means that a religious difference between spouses resulted in the husbands' being more likely to evaluate the marriage negatively than did husbands in religiously homogamous marriages. Religious heterogamy produced no negative effects on the wives' evaluation of their marriages.

PERSONALITY FACTORS

One of the most important considerations in mate selection is for us to choose someone with the personal qualities that we admire and that are important to marital success. What qualities might be included?

Desirable Traits

A group of 100 men and women in an undergraduate psychology class were asked: What characteristics would you desire in a marriage partner? Men and women showed remarkable consistency in their choices (Author's class notes).

Both men and women mentioned *physical characteristics*. The women wanted a husband who was good looking and sexy. The men mentioned wanting a wife who was good looking and had a nice figure. Women also mentioned the importance of cleanliness and hygiene.

Moral qualities were very important. Men and women wanted partners who were trustworthy, loyal, honest, truthful, generous, unselfish, caring, moral, and religious.

Emotional characteristics included being gentle, sensitive, empathetic, flexible, and accepting, and having self-esteem and self-confidence. Being assertive (but not aggressive) was also considered important.

Intellectual characteristics mentioned included being intelligent and knowledgeable.

Social characteristics included being outgoing, having a good sense of humor, being fun-loving, romantic, and a good lover. The women also wanted a man who had good manners.

Family and vocational role concepts and performance were considered important. The women wanted a husband who was a hard worker, ambitious, and a family man. Other women, however, wanted a man who was adventuresome, exciting, and nontraditional. Some of the men wanted a wife who would perform traditional sex roles. Others preferred a woman who was "full of surprises."

Many of the traits in this list have beeen substantiated by research and were discussed in Chapter 4, Qualities of Successful Marriages. See that chapter for references and a more detailed discussion.

Compatible Traits

Not only are specific personality traits important, but *the combination of traits in couples also influences adjustment.* Two people may be very fine people, but so different that it is hard for them to be compatible. Are those with homogamous traits more compatible than those with heterogamous traits? Yes, according to some research findings (Farley and Davis, 1980). One study showed that happily married couples were significantly similar to one another in such traits as general activity (drive, energy, enthusiasm), restraint (self-control, serious-mindedness, deliberateness), friendliness and personal relations. Unhappily married couples were statistically dissimilar in emotional stability and in objectivity. The dissimilarity in objectivity indicated that the mating of a hypersensitive and suspicious individual with a "thick-skinned," coldly objective individual caused trouble in marital relations (Pickford, Signoria, and Rempel, 1966).

A study of the relationship of personality patterns of marital partners to emotional disorder indicated that when both marital partners were similar in personality patterns, they had far lower incidences of emotional disorders (Boxer, 1970). These findings suggest that divergent personality patterns can be highly destructive emotionally. A case in point is that of a dependent, submissive husband married to an aggressive, dominating woman. If the husband can't accept his dependency needs, the relationship usually develops emotional conflict, and the husband-wife interaction is harmful to them both (Heer, 1974).

Another research study indicated that couples whose marriages were stable had substantially greater numbers of correlations of personality traits between the husband and wife than did couples whose marriages were unstable (Cattell and Nesselroad, 1967). Other research found that the adjustment of married couples — as well as dating couples — was greater when they possessed the same degree of mental health (Murstein, 1980). Other findings suggest that individuals tend to choose partners whose levels of self-esteem and self-acceptance are similar to their own. Another research study using a computer analysis of couples who had married versus couples who had not married indicated that the married couples showed significant homogamy of personality factors such as pessimism-optimism, feelings of adequacy, carefreeness-seriousness, concrete-abstract thinking, emotional stability, submissiveness-dominance, tough-mindedness versus tender-mindedness, trusting versus suspicious nature, confidence versus apprehension, undisciplined versus controlled behavior, or relaxed versus tense nature (Sindberg, Roberts, and McClain, 1972).

The available research studies are not extensive enough to match large numbers of personality traits to show their influence on compatibility; but on the basis of available evidence, *those with homogamous personalities are more likely to marry one another than are those with dissimilar personalities, and — once married — there is some tendency for homogamous traits to contribute to compatibility and stability in marriage* (Murstein, 1980; Rice, 1983).

Age Differentials

Another consideration in selecting a mate is the age differential between the husband and wife. Overall, the median age differential between husbands and wives in first marriage is about two years (U.S. Bureau of the Census, 1989). Only 8 percent of all married couples have an age difference larger than 10 years (Vera, Berardo, and Berardo, 1985). Marriages tend to be age homog-

Age difference between husbands and wives is more common in remarriages than in first marriages. What factors should be considered when contemplating marriage to someone who is much older (or much younger) than oneself?

amous. Age differentials are more common in remarriages and also more common among lower-class groups (Atkinson and Glass, 1985).

What are the effects of age differentiation on marital quality? When allowances were made for variables of gender, age, race, and socioeconomic status, *Vera, Berardo, and Berardo (1985) found no significant differences in marital quality among couples from various age-dissimilar categories.* We do know, however, that those who marry when they are in their teens are more likely to divorce than are those marrying in their twenties (Booth and Edwards, 1985). Frequently there is a disparity in age between the husband and the wife. The younger the wife, the greater the age disparity between her and her husband. However, the higher divorce rates are due to the very young age at marriage rather than to age discrepancy itself.

There may be considerations other than marital quality when thinking marrying someone much older or younger. For example, a young wife married to an older man is likely to be widowed at an early age; while the older man is likely to live longer if married to a younger wife (Foster, Klinger-Vartabedian, and Wispe, 1984). However, the wife may like the security an older husband offers in the meantime. There are a variety of factors to consider.

PERSPECTIVE
Danger Signals

What are some of the signs that the person selected is potentially a problem person? Here is a list of danger signals. If any of the following exist, exercise caution before you commit yourself to marriage. Encourage your partner to do something about the problems, getting professional help if needed. If your partner is not cooperative in getting help or trying to make changes, remember you can't change someone yourself. If you try, chances are the problem will get worse. People have to want to change themselves. And marriage doesn't solve anything, it usually makes things worse. Danger signals exist when your partner:

Has a substance abuse problem: either alcohol or other drugs.

Shows evidence of severe personality faults: mental illness as diagnosed by a professional; excessive jealousy and possessiveness; deep-seated insecurity as evident in excessive fears and anxiety; unstable temperament; very rigid, inflexible, or compulsive thinking and behavior; a cold, insensitive personality; extreme criticism of you and others; and negativism toward life in general.

Has important character flaws: lies; is dishonest, unfaithful, distrustful, immoral, abusive, arrogant, and condescending.

Has continuous and serious health problems that are life-threatening and would make happy marriage difficult.

Has serious problems relating to his or her family. Investigation is needed to discover whether these are primarily the family's fault or the individual's, or both. People who are not able to get along with their own family, or whose family of origin is troubled, have more difficulty in creating harmonious family relationships themselves.

Can't get along with other people, lacks social skills, or is a loner with no friends.

Has an unstable job history, can't hold a job, and is irresponsible in job and task performance.

Marital compatibility is enhanced if couples develop a high degree of consensus and similar attitudes and values about things that are important to them (Lasswell, 1982). Two people can never agree on everything, but ordinarily the greater the consensus the easier it is to adjust to one another in marriage. People who share common ideas, attitudes or values, usually feel more comfortable with one another. There is less friction and stress in adjusting to one another (Nahemow, 1983).

One of the things that research shows, however, is that consensus develops slowly in a relationship. A dating couple may not even get around to talking about important values until after they have gone together for some time. The more intimate dating couples become, the more likely they are to express agreement in a number of important areas. There may be two reasons for this: (1) being together may create greater understanding and agreement, and (2) those who disagree too much may not have progressed to the next stage of intimacy. Whichever reason is more valid, value consensus of a couple is related to satisfaction and to progress toward permanence in a relationship (Booth and Welch, 1978).

From this point of view, compatibility may be described partly as the extent of agreement or disagreement between the husband and wife. The assessment questionnaire that follows may be used to evaluate the consensus between you and your partner.

ASSESSMENT
Our Degree of Consensus

On each of the following items, draw a circle around the number that represents your degree of consensus. Add up your scores and divide by 12. This will give you your average (mean) score. The lower the score, the greater your consensus with your partner.

Then have your partner answer the questionnaire. Add up his or her score and divide by 12. To what extent does your partner feel you have developed consensus?

Note particularly those items that you have marked or that your partner has marked where consensus is low. These areas need more discussion.

1 — Very much in agreement
2 — Somewhat in agreement
3 — Partly agree, partly disagree
4 — Somewhat in disagreement
5 — Very much in disagreement

1 2 3 4 5   *Employment*. Type, place, hours of employment, career goals.

1 2 3 4 5   *Residence*. Geographical area, specific community, character of neighborhood, type of housing preferred.

1 2 3 4 5   *Money matters*. Amount needed, how earned, how managed.

1 2 3 4 5   *Parents, families*. Relationships with parents and in-laws.

1 2 3 4 5   *Social life*. Extent, type, leisure-time activities.

1 2 3 4 5   *Friends*. Selection, relationships with men and women friends.

1 2 3 4 5   *Religion*. Ideas, beliefs, personal faith, church affiliation, participation in religious activities.

(continued)

196

INTIMATE
RELATIONSHIPS:
GROWTH, CHOICES AND
CHANGE

ASSESSMENT (continued)

1 2 3 4 5	*Values, philosophy of life*. Individual ethics, morals, life goals, what the individual wants out of life.
1 2 3 4 5	*Sex, demonstration of affection*. Type, amount, frequency.
1 2 3 4 5	*Matters of conventionality*. Manners, mores, living habits (i.e., table manners, dress, drinking, smoking, attitudes toward drug use or abuse, cleanliness, etc.).
1 2 3 4 5	*Children*. Number wanted, disciplining, caring for and educating them.
1 2 3 4 5	*Roles*. Of man and woman in and outside the home.

SEX ROLES AND PERSONAL HABITS

Compatible Role Concepts

Another measure of compatibility in marriage is to examine male and female role expectations (Araji, 1977). Every man has certain concepts of the kind of roles he would perform and certain expectations of what roles a wife should perform. Every woman has certain concepts of roles she would perform as a wife and certain expectations of what roles a husband should perform. What the two people expect and what they find, however, may be different. The following examples illustrate instances where role expectations were never realized in marriage:

> *A young husband*: "I always wanted a wife who was interested in a home and family. My wife doesn't like housework, hates to cook, and doesn't even want children."
>
> *A new bride*: "In my family, my father always used to help my mother. My husband never lifts a finger to help me."

In each of these examples, either the husband or wife is dissatisfied with the role that the other is assuming in the family. Role concepts may be said to be compatible if the husband's and wife's role expectations are in agreement with the roles their mate is willing to perform.

In evaluating a relationship, we might ask: What am I willing to do, and what do I expect my spouse to do in each of the following areas:

Money — earning the income, paying the bills.

Housework, home maintenance — cooking, doing dishes, doing laundry, mopping the floor, vacuuming, dusting, cleaning bathrooms, keeping the home picked up and neat, yard work, lawn, painting, carpentry, home repairs.

Children — care such as bathing, dressing, feeding, overall supervison, staying home when a child is sick, driving children to activities and friends' houses. Also included are discipline, socialization, religious education, sex education, companionship, leisure-time activities.

Social life — planning and arranging social, recreational activities; contacts with families.

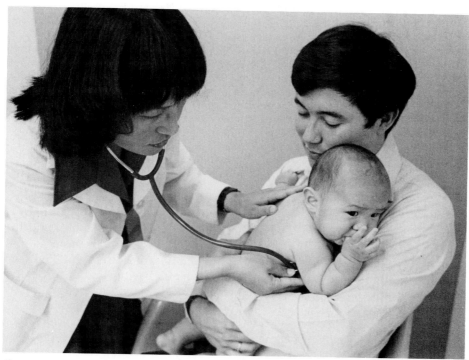

One measure of compatibility in marriage is to examine male and female role expectations and the degree to which these are being fulfilled in the relationship. Many partners are in agreement that the male can be a nurturing parent and the woman can have a satisfying professional career.

Leigh, Holman, and Burr (1984) found that individuals who had been dating their partner for a year were no more likely to have role compatibility than when they first started dating. This indicates that role compatibility in dating was not very important for continuing the relationship. However, it becomes very important after marriage. Couples often assume their spouse will enact the roles they expect, only to find out afterward they have very different ideas and expectations. Role expectations should be discussed before marriage.

Compatible Habit Systems

The newspaper columns "Ann Landers" and "Dear Abby" are filled with letters from husbands and wives complaining about the annoying habits of their mates. Their spouses have terrible table manners, are careless about personal cleanliness, smoke or drink too much, crack their knuckles, snore too loudly, go to bed too late, won't get up in the morning, leave dirty dishes scattered all over the house, never replace the cap on the toothpaste, or have other habits their partners find irritating. The writers have either tried to get their mates to change or tried to learn to accept the habit, often without success. Over the years, some of the habits become serious obstacles to marital harmony. Most problems that are annoying before marriage become even more intensified in the closer and more continuous shared life of marriage. Most problems can be worked out if people are caring, flexible, and willing to assume responsibility for changing themselves (Rice, 1983).

There are a number of reasons why people make the wrong choice of mate. One reason is *they don't really get to know the other person.* They may be in too much of a hurry and may not give themselves enough time for the relationship to develop. Lansky (1983) writes of a young man who asked a girl to marry him after the first date. Getting to know another person usually takes several years of being together under varying circumstances. Even then, the knowledge is incomplete. Sometimes the type of activities a couple share together are not conducive to developing rapport and communication. The couple may participate in a whirl of social activities, depend upon paid entertainment, or spend all their time with other people. The activities are fun, but the relationship remains superficial.

Some people make the wrong choice of mate because they live in a fantasy world. Their concept of marriage has been gleaned from romantic movies and the media. Marriage, to them, is an escape from their own humdrum existence. Their parents may have a troubled marriage, but they are sure it won't happen to them. They completely overlook the faults of their partner and the problems in their relationship. Love will conquer all, and they will live happily ever after. Their views of marriage and their relationship are completely unrealistic.

Other people choose the wrong mate because they look for the wrong qualities in a person. They emphasize physical characteristics and attractiveness without regard for important personal qualities. They don't stop to think about whether their partner is a nice person. They are also looking for the wrong things in their relationship, perhaps for excitement instead of stability. They are thrilled with new relationships that are emotionally arousing, forgetting that the high level of emotions will subside and that they need other things to sustain the relationship.

Some people make the wrong choice because they confuse sex with love. They enjoy one another sexually and have intercouse whenever they are together. Their relationship focuses primarily on sexual passion, and so they assume they are much in love. But as explained in Chapter 7, theirs is an incomplete love. Other components such as friendship and care are needed to sustain the relationship over a period of time. As one man remarked, "After they are married, what are they going to do the other 23 hours of the day?" (Author's counseling notes)

A common reason for marrying the wrong person is a poor self-image and lack of self-esteem (Jedlicka, 1980). Such people can't believe that anyone desirable would really love them and accept them, so they settle for less than they might. They court rejection and unhappiness because they believe they are unworthy of support, love, and nurturance (Abramson, 1983).

Some people succumb to pressures to marry. One pressure is from their *biological time clock.* One woman remarked:

> I'm thirty-two years old and I want to have children. I'm marrying Charlie, because I'm afraid I might not find someone else in time. I don't really love him, but I can't wait any longer. (Author's counseling notes)

Other people develop a *"now or never" attitude.* They are afraid if they don't get married to this person, they may never get another opportunity.

Another pressure is that of *pregnancy.* The number one reason for marrying while still in school is pregnancy. Yet, the prognosis of success for the marriage, particularly if the partners are in their teens, is poor. Most such marriages don't work out (Kellam, Adams, Brown, and Ensminger, 1982; O'Connell and Rogers, 1984). Other pressure to marry comes from *parents*. Parents want their son to marry "that girl down the block" (Leslie, Huston, and Johnson, 1986). Couples are cohabiting, and so parents pressure them to marry. Davis-Brown, Salamon, and Surra (1987) suggest that parental intervention in the process of choosing a mate is more often indirect than direct. Instead of actively expressing approval or disapproval, parents try to arrange conditions so their children will meet and marry suitable partners.

Other pressure to marry comes from *friends*. When two people have gone together for some time, friends begin to ask: "When are you two going to get married?"

There are also unconscious, neurotic needs that people try to fulfill by marrying. One student remarked: "I always seem to be attracted to the wrong type of man. They're neurotic, immature, on drugs, can't hold a job, or are possessive and helpless." In this case, the woman had an unconscious need to mother the man she went with. It made her important to feel he needed her. In other situations, people feel uncomfortable with successful, desirable people, so they marry someone they can feel superior to as a means of building their own ego. Others also go to the extreme, but as a boost to their ego.

> Andy was 35, a college graduate, working as a civil engineer. He met a blond stripper at a local lounge and fell in love with her. She was a very beautiful woman with a fantastic figure, a very flashy dresser. Wherever she went, men stared at her. Andy was so desirous of having her as his girl, he gave up his wife — who was a very plain woman — and his two children and married the stripper. A year later, they were divorced. (Author's counseling notes)

Neurotic persons may be drawn together to enable them to play roles in each other's "games" and transactions. Role combinations include mother-son, sadist-masochist, pursuer-pursued, beater-battered, rescuer-victim (Hoyt, 1986).

> Ralph was 6'4" tall, very muscular, and athletic, and filled with hostility and anger. He married a girl 4'10" tall who was physically disabled, whom he physically abused, and whom he blamed for all his troubles. (Author's counseling notes)

These unconscious feelings and needs may be very powerful motives to marry a particular person.

SUMMARY

1. Selecting a mate is one of the most important decisions we make during our lifetime.

2. Various theories have been developed to explain the process: psychodynamic theories, needs theories, exchange theories, and developmental process theories.

3. Family background factors are important influences in the lives of people and so need to be investigated when a person is choosing a mate. Marriage tends to be homogamous with respect to socioeconomic class, education, and intelligence.

4. Marriages tend to be homogamous with respect to race. Divorce rates are higher in interracial marriage than in those homogamous with respect to race.

5. Persons in marriages where neither spouse has any formal religious affiliation report a lower level of marital happiness than do persons in either homogamous or heterogamous marriage in which both spouses identify with a major religion. The estimated religious heterogamy effect for females is positive and insignificant, but the one for males is negative and significant.

6. One of the most important considerations in mate selection is for us to choose someone with those personal qualities that we admire and that are important to marital success.

7. Persons with homogamous personality traits are usually more compatible than those with heterogamous traits.

8. Age differentials are not a significant factor in marital quality but very young age is.

9. Marital compatibility is enhanced if couples develop a high degree of consensus and similar attitudes and values about things that are important to them.

10. Another measure of compatibility in marriage is to examine male and female role expectations to see if they match possible fulfillment.

11. It is helpful if two people have compatible personal habits.

12. People make the wrong choice of mate for a number of reasons: they don't get to know the other person; they live in a fantasy world; they look for the wrong qualities in a person; they confuse sex with love; they have a poor self-image and self-esteem; they succumb to pressures to marry; or they have unconscious, neurotic needs that they are trying to fulfill by marrying.

13. Danger signals in the choice of a mate include: a substance abuse problem, severe personality faults, important character flaws, continuous and serious health problems, serious problems relating to family, inability to get along with other people, lack of social skills, being a loner, or having an unstable job history.

SUGGESTED READINGS

Carson, R. (1978). *The National Love, Sex, and Marriage Test*. Garden City, NY: Doubleday, Dolphin. Self-tests on love, fighting, sex, feelings, roles, and trust, based on an NBC televised test.

Johnson, R. A. (1980). *Religious Assortative Mating in the United States*. New York: Academic Press. Difficult discussion of interfaith mate selection and marriage.

Loudin, A. (1981). *The Hoax of Romance*. Englewood Cliffs, NJ: Prentice-Hall. The need for making choices based on other than romantic feelings alone.

Rubin, L. B. (1983). *Intimate Strangers: Men and Women Together*. New York: Harper and Row. The different needs of men and women.

Tseng, W., McDermott, J. F., Jr., and Maretzske, T. W. (Eds.). (1977). *Adjustment in Intercultural Marriage*. Honolulu: University Press of Hawaii. Nine essays on intermarriage in Hawaii.

9

THE SEXUAL BASIS OF RELATIONSHIPS

KEY TERMS

excitement phase
plateau phase
orgasm phase
resolution phase
vasocongestion
erection
myotonia
lubrication
sex flush
orgasm
vaginal orgasm
clitoral orgasm
desire stage

erogenous zones
digital foreplay
pheromones
nocturnal emissions
wet dreams
sexual dysfunction
premature ejaculation
erectile dysfunction
primary erectile dysfunction
secondary erectile dysfunction
ejaculatory inhibition
inhibited sexual desire
general sexual dysfunction
orgasm dysfunction

dyspareunia
vaginismus
conjoint therapy
sexually transmitted diseases
AIDS
herpes
hepatitis
genital warts
chlamydial infections
gonorrhea
syphilis
pubic lice
scabies

Sexual expression is an important component of the total man-woman relationship.* As such, it affects the whole relationship and is, in turn, affected by all other aspects of that relationship. It also involves interdependent physical and emotional stimuli and responses. One's emotions and feelings affect physical responses, and physical conditions and responses affect feelings. Most sexual adjustments, therefore, require an understanding of both physical and emotional aspects of sexual response.

Specifically, we are concerned here with the process of sexual stimulation and response, with the sources of sexual arousal, and with how the body responds during the process. We are concerned with basic principles of lovemaking and how to make sexual relationships meaningful and satisfying. We are also concerned here with some of the most common problems of sexual dysfunction: what they are, what causes them, and how they might be overcome through help and treatment. And, finally, we are concerned with understanding and avoiding sexually transmitted diseases.

SEX AND HAPPY MARRIAGE

What is the relationship between sex and a happy marriage? Can one be happily married without a satisfying sex life? We must not forget that what is satisfying to one couple may not be at all acceptable to another. Human beings differ in their sexual appetites, in the manner and means by which they want to enjoy sex, and in their sexual habits and aims. There are couples who want intercourse every day or several times a day. Other couples would find this frequency unacceptable. If both the husband and the wife are satisfied

Human beings differ in their sexual appetites, but most people agree that some form of sexual expression is an important component of a happy marriage.

*Some of the material in this chapter is taken from the author's book *Human Sexuality* and is used by permission of the publisher William C. Brown Co. Copyright © 1989.

with their sex life, it can contribute in a positive way to their overall marital happiness; but if the couple disagrees, or if one or both are frustrated or unhappy with their sexual relationship, it can significantly reduce or even destroy marital satisfaction.

One study showed that 60 percent of the wives who rated their marriages as very happy reached orgasm 90 to 100 percent of the time in coitus. Thirty-eight percent of the wives who rated their marriages as very unhappy never or rarely reached orgasm (only 1 to 9 percent of the time) in coitus (Gebhard, 1966). These findings suggest a positive correlation between marital happiness and sexual orgasm. They tend to be found together. However, the same study also showed that 4 percent of the wives who rated their marriage as very happy never had orgasm, and that 38 percent of the wives who rated their marriages as very unhappy practically always had orgasm. It is clear *that orgasm response did not ensure that wives would have a happy marriage, nor did happy marriages always result in orgasms. Nevertheless, it was harder for wives to be happily married without orgasm, and it was harder to have an orgasm without a happy marriage.*

HUMAN SEXUAL RESPONSE

Stages

In order to gain a better understanding of the total process of sexual response, it is helpful to have a clear understanding of the actual physiological changes that take place in the body during sexual stimulation. According to the research of Masters and Johnson (1966), the stages of sexual response may be divided into four phases: the excitement phase, the plateau phase, the orgasmic phase, and the resolution phase (Figure 9.1). The **excitement phase**

FIGURE *9.1 Human Sexual Response Cycles.*

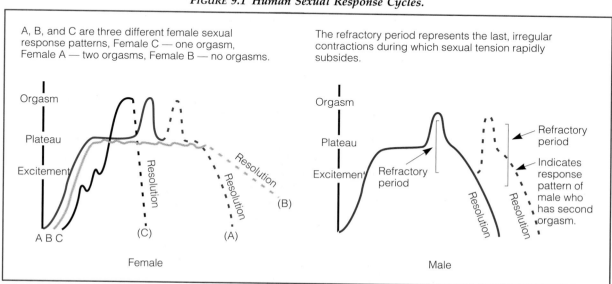

From Masters, W. H., and Johnson, V. E. (1966). *Human sexual response*. Boston: Little, Brown. Used by permission of Masters and Johnson Institute.

extends from the beginnings of sexual stimulation until the individual reaches a high degree of sexual excitation. The duration of this phase may be prolonged or shortened depending upon the intensity of the stimulation and individual reactions to it. Cessation of stimulation, or the presence of objectionable psychological factors, may even abort the process. If sexual stimulation is continued, sexual tensions are intensified; and the individual reaches the second or **plateau phase** of the sexual cycle, from which he or she may move to orgasm. If sexual stimuli are withdrawn, the individual will not achieve orgasm, and sexual tension will gradually subside.

The **orgasm phase** is limited to those few seconds during which sexual tension is at its maximum and then suddenly released. However, there is usually great variation in the intensity and duration of orgasm from time to time as well as differences among persons. After orgasm, the person enters the last or **resolution phase** of the sexual cycle, during which sexual tension subsides as the individual moves back through the plateau and the excitement phases to return to the unstimulated state.

Physiological Responses

As sexual excitement increases, both men and women show similar physical responses.

VASOCONGESTION AND ERECTION The man's penis (Krane and Siroky, 1981), the woman's clitoris, the nipples of the female breast (and often a man's nipples), and the woman's labia become engorged with blood, which causes swelling, enlargement, and erection (Figure 9.2).

One of the most important changes in the female is in the vagina (Figure 9.3). The outer one-third becomes engorged with blood, reducing the opening, with the outer muscles contracting around the penis. At the same time, the vaginal length increases and the inner portion balloons out, increasing considerably in width. Women who use diaphragms for contraception have to be certain they are fitted quite tightly; otherwise the ballooning of the inner vagina under sexual excitement loosens the diaphragm, allowing sperm to pass around the edges or the diaphragm itself to become dislodged.

Another change in the female is in the clitoris. As excitement increases during the plateau phase, the erect clitoris begins to withdraw into the hood, showing a 50 percent total reduction in length by the end of that phase (Figure 9.4). It returns to its normal position in 5–10 seconds, and orgasmic contractions stop during the resolution phase.

The important change in the penis is erection and increase in width and length (Figure 9.5). It is not uncommon for an erection to come and go several times if the excitement phase is prolonged. Erections are also affected by fear, anxiety, changes in temperature, loud noises, changes in lighting, or other distraction. The testes also enlarge by at least 50 percent due to engorgement with blood during sexual excitement.

MYOTONIA Myotonia is muscular tension of both voluntary and involuntary muscles. As excitement increases, there is a tensing and flexing of the muscles of the arms, legs, abdomen, face, neck, pelvis, buttocks, hands, and feet. Muscular tension may result in facial grimaces, flaring of the nostrils, strain around the mouth. The cords of the neck become rigid, the back arches, long

FIGURE 9.2 *Breast Changes During the Female Sexual Response Cycle.*

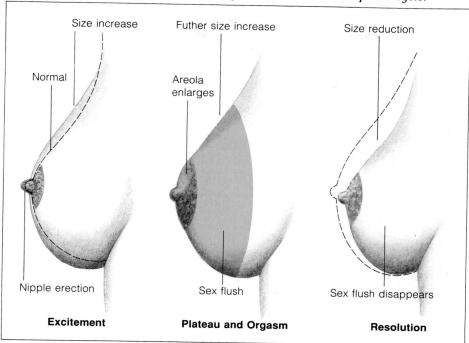

Size increase

Normal

Nipple erection

Excitement

Futher size increase

Areola
enlarges

Sex flush

Plateau and Orgasm

Size reduction

Sex flush disappears

Resolution

From Masters, W. H., Johnson, V. E., and Kolodny, R. C. (1985). *Human sexuality* (2e), Boston: Little, Brown. Used by permission of Masters and Johnson Institute.

muscles of the thighs become tense. The muscles of the buttocks become voluntarily contracted. There is a semispastic contraction of the hand and feet muscles.

LUBRICATION   Within 10–30 seconds after sexual stimulation begins, sweating and self-lubrication of the inner walls of the vagina begin. The presence of this lubricant is one indication of sexual response (Keye, 1983). The male emits two or three drops of preejaculatory fluid, which has been secreted from the Cowper's glands. This too can function as a lubricant during coitus, although the secretion does not appear until the plateau phase of response.

Increase in heart and pulse rate, blood pressure, respiration, and perspiration. The heart, pulse, and respiratory rates may more than double; the blood pressure may increase anywhere from 20 to 80 percent. About a third of men and women evidence perspiration during the resolution phase.

SEX FLUSH   There is a noticeable reddening of the skin of the body, usually in the form of a red, splotchy rash, gradually spreading over more and more of the body as excitement increases. About three out of four orgasmic women and one out of four orgasmic men show this reaction.

ORGASM   During orgasm, there may be severe involuntary muscular contractions throughout the body, gradually subsiding during the resolution phase. These contractions during orgasm are especially strong in the vagina, uterus, and pelvic region of the female and in the penis, vas deferens, seminal

FIGURE 9.3 Internal Changes During the Female Sexual Response Cycle.

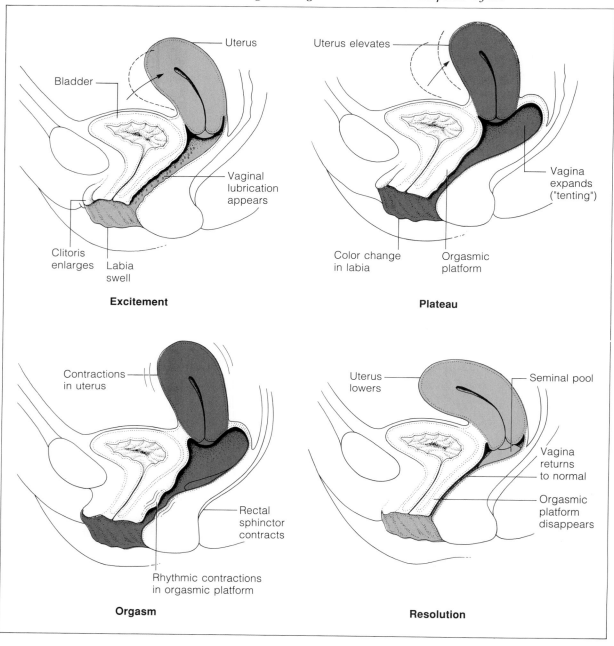

vesicles, and prostate gland of the male. The female may experience 5–12 contractions with gradual lengthening of intervals between and with decreasing density. Under sexual excitement, the uterus increases in size by 50 percent and pushes outward during the contraction of orgasm, expelling any fluids that may be inside (Fisher, 1973). If orgasm occurs during the menstrual period, increased flow may result for a brief period of time. In the male,

FIGURE 9.4 *The Clitoris and Labia During the Female Sexual Response Cycle.*

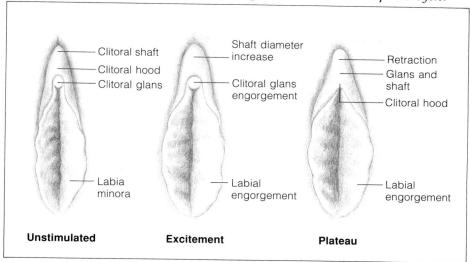

Clitoral shaft
Clitoral hood
Clitoral glans
Labia minora

Unstimulated

Shaft diameter increase
Clitoral glans engorgement
Labial engorgement

Excitement

Retraction
Glans and shaft
Clitoral hood
Labial engorgement

Plateau

From Masters, W. H., Johnson, V. E., and Kolodny, R. C. (1985). *Human sexuality* (2e), Boston: Little, Brown. Used by permission of Masters and Johnson Institute.

contractions of the prostate, vas deferens, seminal vesicles, and penis produce ejaculation.

Summary of Response Patterns

Two observations should be made about these phases of sexual response. *One, the responses of the male and female are very similar, even though the actual sexual organs are different.* Both male and female show vasocongestion of the sex organs when stimulated, and both have erectile tissue that enlarges and becomes firm. Both show evidence of sex flush — the reddening of the skin of the body. Both show myotonia — muscular tension. Both show an increase in heart rate, blood pressure, and respiration. Both evidence lubrication. Both experience orgasm (Wiest, 1977), and both perspire during the resolution phase.

Two, the physiological response to stimulation are similar regardless of the method of stimulation, whether manually by personal masturbation, by mutual foreplay, or by intercourse (Clark, 1970). The only real difference is in the degree of excitation. The important point that Masters and Johnson and others have made is that there is no physical difference between the so-called **vaginal orgasm** (one achieved by stimulation of the vagina) and the **clitoral orgasm** (one achieved by stimulation of the clitoris) (Lydon, 1974). Of the two organs, however, the clitoris — not the vagina — is by far the most sexually sensitive organ of a woman's anatomy. In fact, the nerve endings in the vagina lie deep beneath the surface, so that often no feeling occurs until sexual excitement is already well advanced. *The important point is that female sexual arousal comes far easier by clitoral than by vaginal stimulation.* This knowledge can be used in foreplay to achieve a high level of arousal prior to coitus itself. It must be recognized, however, that intensity of orgasm can vary with any method of stimulation.

FIGURE 9.5 Changes During the Male Sexual Response Cycle.

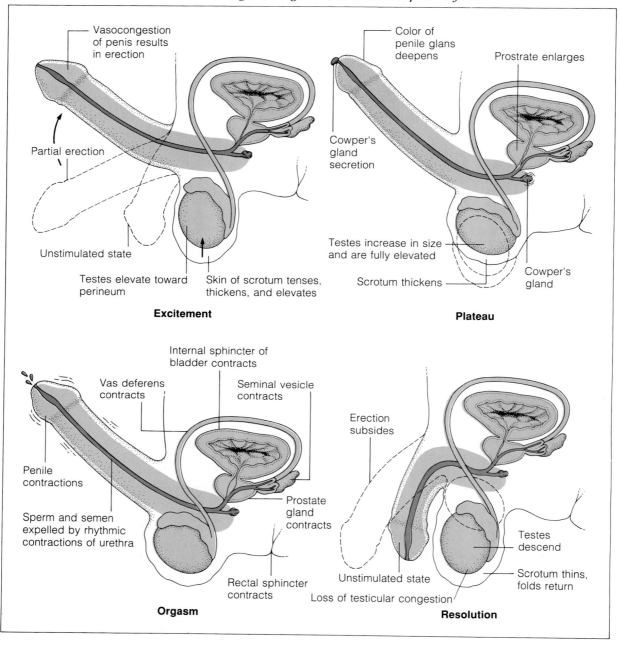

Vasocongestion of penis results in erection

Partial erection

Unstimulated state

Testes elevate toward perineum

Skin of scrotum tenses, thickens, and elevates

Excitement

Color of penile glans deepens

Prostrate enlarges

Cowper's gland secretion

Testes increase in size and are fully elevated

Scrotum thickens

Cowper's gland

Plateau

Internal sphincter of bladder contracts

Vas deferens contracts

Seminal vesicle contracts

Penile contractions

Sperm and semen expelled by rhythmic contractions of urethra

Prostate gland contracts

Rectal sphincter contracts

Orgasm

Erection subsides

Unstimulated state

Loss of testicular congestion

Testes descend

Scrotum thins, folds return

Resolution

From Byer, C. O., Shainberg, L. W., and Jones, K. L. (1988). *Dimensions of human sexuality* (2e). Dubuque, IA: Wm. C. Brown. Used by permission.

Multiple Orgasms

One important male-female difference was "discovered" by Masters and Johnson (1966) even though Kinsey et al. (1953) and others had mentioned it years before. It was that *some females are capable of rapid return to orgasm after an orgasmic experience.* Furthermore, these females are capable of maintaining an orgasmic experience for a relatively long period of time. In other words, *some females are capable of multiple and more prolonged orgasms*, whereas the average male may have difficulty in achieving more than one, unless some time has elapsed in between. Figure 9.1 shows individual differences in response patterns (Masters and Johnson, 1966).

Hartman and Fithian (1984) have been able to teach men to experience multiple, nonejaculatory orgasms by withholding ejaculation until the final orgasm in the series. This is accomplished by tightening the pubococcygeus (PC) and pelvic muscles at the time orgasm is approaching. (If the man tightens his muscles as he does in holding back urine, this contracts the PC muscles.) By tightening the PC muscles, ejaculation is prevented but orgasm continues just the same. This makes it possible to continue stimulation to produce additional orgasms without ejaculation. The process of resolution does not occur until after the final orgasm with ejaculation (Robbins and Jensen, 1978).

There are great individual variations in female responses. Some women desire multiple orgasms to be satisfied, while others seem satisfied with one.

Three-Stage Model

Psychiatrist and sex therapist Helen Kaplan (1979) has developed a three-stage model of the sexual response cycle: *desire*, *excitement*, and *orgasm*. Kaplan's **desire stage** is unique since it does not involve the genitals, but consists of attitudes, ideas, feelings, and stimuli that motivate a person to want sexual expression. The excitement phase is a stage of sexual arousal characterized primarily by vasocongestion. The orgasm phase is described primarily by muscular contractions.

SOURCES OF SEXUAL AROUSAL

Tactile Stimulation

One of the primary means of sexual arousal is through touch, or tactile stimulation of those parts of the body that are sexually sensitive. These sexually sensitive areas are called **erogenous zones**. The erogenous zones in women are the clitoris (particularly the glans), mons, labia minora and the vestibule the labia encloses, the vaginal opening, the outer one-third of the vaginal barrel, the anus, and the perineum (the area between the vagina and the anus). The breasts also, and especially the nipples, are sensitive to touch, as are the tongue and lips.

The most sexually sensitive areas of men are the penis (Figure 9.6), especially the glans and corona (particularly the underneath area — the frenulum), the scrotum, the anus, and the tongue and lips. The nipples of some men are also sexually sensitive. Some men and women find other areas to be sexually responsive.

Tactile stimulation usually begins with body contact: cuddling, hugging, kissing, rubbing, or stroking. Most couples find that this type of tactile contact is deeply satisfying. It encourages relaxation, feelings of security, warmth and affection, as well as being sexually arousing.

The fingers are the most common instrument of stimulation. **Digital foreplay**, as it is called, involves using one or more fingers and sometimes the

FIGURE 9.6 Parts of the Penis.

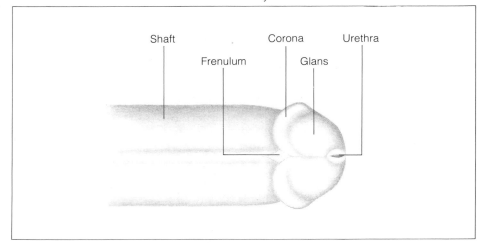

whole hand in massaging, caressing, rubbing, or vibrating sensitive body parts. Usually, a light touch, especially in the beginning, is more arousing that a heavy application of pressure. The pressure and speed of movement are increased as excitement grows. The mouth, especially the lips and tongue, are also used to kiss, lick, nibble, or suck body parts. Oral-genital stimulation is a preferred method of stimulation for many couples. This not only is arousing to the recipient, but also to the person doing it.

Oral-Genital Stimulation

A study of 100,000 women by *Redbook* magazine revealed that 9 out of 10 women had experienced oral-genital sex, both giving and receiving it (Levin and Levin, 1975a). In another study, 9 in 10 husbands said they enjoyed giving oral sex to their wives (Petersen et al., 1983). Seven out of ten of the wives in this same study reported that they enjoyed giving oral sex to their husbands. In both of these studies, however, the population represented a more sexually liberal and experienced group that is found in the general population. What the figures would be for a truly representative sample is unknown.

The stimulation of the clitoris, labia, or vaginal opening with the mouth (using the lips and tongue) is called **cunnilingus**. The word comes from the Latin and means "one who licks the vulva." The technique involves kissing, licking, nibbling, or sucking the shaft and tip of the clitoris, the labia minora, or thrusting the tongue in and out of the vaginal opening. Stimulation usually begins with gentle tongue movements and evolves to more rapid, more intense licking or sucking, or even to nibbling. The warm, moist, pliable tongue on the clitoris feels very good to most women (Kahn, 1983). However, some women complain that the tongue is too rough and desire gentler pressure or stimulation with the lips. Others say cunnilingus encourages vaginal or urinary tract infections.

Most men enjoy cunnilingus (Petersen et al., 1983). It turns them on, and they enjoy giving pleasure to their partner. Many women also like cunnilin-

Kissing is an important means of sexual expression and arousal, but it also encourages relaxation and feelings of security, warmth, and affection.

gus. For some it implies a special kind of acceptance. Other women emphasize the erotic sensation. One woman comments: "A tongue offers gentleness and precision and wetness and is the perfect organ for contact. And, besides, it produces sensational orgasms!" (Hite, 1981, p. 361). Some, however, are embarrassed and self-conscious about it.

Fellatio involves the stimulation of the male genitals, especially the penis, with the mouth, lips, and tongue. The word comes from the Latin *fellare*, meaning "to suck." It may mean licking various parts of the penis or the scrotum, or sucking the penis, especially the glans. The frenulum, which is the underneath tissue joining the end of the penis with the shaft, is especially sensitive. Some women enjoy stimulating only the outside or end of the penis; others are able to put a portion of the penile shaft into their mouth without gagging (actually the base of the shaft does not have much feeling). Fellatio may involve simultaneous digital caressing of the scrotum, perineum, or anus.

Most men thoroughly enjoy fellatio or are taught that they should. The warm, moist, muscular mouth and darting tongue, applying various pressures and rhythms, are versatile instruments of stimulation. But part of the pleasure is psychological. There is an aura about fellatio. Men are taught that it is the ultimate sexual expression, that the woman who does it really loves them and accepts them and their body.

However, one theme of pornographic movies is forcing the woman (or man) to perform fellatio. Thus, it implies sexual submission, which gives the male a sense of power. For this reason, some women refuse to perform fellatio, especially on the male who tries to demand compliance. Other women associate it with something that prostitutes do. Some women, however, find it stimulates them as well as their partner (Petersen et al., 1983), and they enjoy the feel of the penis in their mouth. Like the men, most insist the genitals be kept clean.

Basically, there are two types of vibrators: the plastic, battery-operated, penis-shaped ones, and the larger, electric-motor-driven vibrators that are either hand-held or strapped to the back of the hand. These come with a variety of attachments, and some have variable speeds. The battery-operated devices do not vibrate intensely enough for many persons, so the larger, plug-in types are preferred.

The vibrator provides controllable pressure and intense stimulation, which — when applied to the clitoral area — enables women to reach orgasm easily and quickly. For this reason, vibrators are quite useful in helping the inorgasmic woman to achieve climax. Once she has experienced orgasm through this means, she can be more easily taught how to achieve climax through additional means of stimulation.

The vibrator is a convenient, effective mechanical means of achieving orgasm quickly. It can be used to induce multiple orgasm in some women; it can also be used in foreplay or in self-stimulation.

However, there are some disadvantages. If a woman repeatedly uses the vibrator to achieve instant orgasm, she does not have much opportunity to appreciate the various stages of sexual response, and her overall pleasure is diminished. Or, applied with too much pressure and too fast, the vibrator can have a numbing effect. There is the possibility the woman may become too dependent on it, actually using it as a substitute for her partner, thus missing out on the emotional benefits of a close, warm encounter. Some men grow to resent the vibrator that becomes a substitute for them. A common practice is for the man or woman to use the vibrator during foreplay to stimulate her almost to orgasm just prior to coitus itself (Rice, 1989).

Some men are turned off by fellatio, either because the woman doesn't do it right ("She doesn't use enough pressure"), because of fear of ejaculating in the woman's mouth ("most women don't like it"), or because they feel it's degrading the woman.

Like most types of sexual expression, oral-genital arousal requires the consent and cooperation of both persons. If two people disagree, they need to talk about their feelings and try to reach some sort of consensus. Certainly, trying to force oral sex on one's partner is coercion and an attempt at domination and is deeply resented. However, if encouraging and seductive approaches are made, it may be that the reticent partner will gradually accept the idea. Some persons who have initial misgivings or fears are able to overcome their inhibitions and learn to enjoy this method of arousal. However, for many couples the success or failure of their sexual relationship does not revolve around whether they have oral-genital contact or not. In one study, heterosexual men who gave or received oral sex reported that they were happier with their sex lives than did those who did not participate in oral sex, but the same did not hold true for heterosexual women (Blumstein and Schwartz, 1973).

Visual Stimulation

Traditionally, men and women have been considered different in the way they respond to visual sexual stimuli. Kinsey and others (1948, 1953) observed that men were aroused by erotic writing and pictures, and by talking about sex, looking at women with shapely figures, going to burlesque shows,

Do men and women respond to visual sexual stimuli, such as looking at the physical features of the "sex object?" What social cues do men and women respond to?

observing sexual activities of humans or animals, or looking at nude photographs. Women were thought to be less aroused by these sources than by reading love stories or seeing romantic movies. Men were considered *erotic* and women *romantic*. One of the first comparative studies was by Sigusch (1970), who found that when women were exposed to erotic photographs, they tended to verbally judge them to be less arousing that did men, but showed almost the same degree of sexual-physiological reactions and activation of sexual behavior as men. Apparently, both men and women were responding to social cues. Those cues said that women were not supposed to be stimulated by the pictures, so they reported less arousal when, in fact, they actually were aroused (Henson, Rubin, and Henson, 1979; Kelley, 1985; Przbyla and Byrne, 1984). Men were socialized to accept the fact that they were aroused, which is what they reported. Apparently, *there is not as much difference between the sexes in regard to sources of stimulation as was once thought*; and, when it does exist, it may have its foundation in the socialization process (Fisher and Byrne, 1978).

Couples need to be aware of the importance of visual stimuli in sexual arousal. Most men thoroughly enjoy seeing their partner dress or undress, or they love to see her wear provocative, sexy lingerie, or do a sexy dance. Most women thoroughly enjoy looking at, playing with, and caressing the male body — in full view. Lovemaking and arousal are enhanced if people can see what they are doing and can watch their partner respond to erotic caresses.

Sound as well as sight can also be sexually stimulating. An important way that couples use sound in sexual stimulation is through words. Loving, soothing, adoring, flattering words may have a more romantic effect than much preliminary caressing. One wife remarked: "If he'd only tell me he loves me, he could get me in the mood in a hurry. He never talks to me and certainly doesn't whisper 'sweet nothings' in my ear" (Author's counseling notes).

Of course, sound can be a turn-off as well as a turn-on. A sudden, loud noise, the voices of children in an adjacent bedroom, or the telephone ringing can dampen sexual ardor.

Verbal Stimulation

The printed word can also be an important source of sexual arousal, which is why millions of dollars worth of erotic literature are sold each year. One woman commented; "I can get more aroused by reading a sexy novel than by any other way." A man admitted; "I like to read dirty books before I masturbate. It really puts me in the mood" (Author's counseling notes). Steinman et al. (1981) found that both men and women became aroused by listening to tape recordings of erotic stories. Heiman (1980) found that women were aroused by listening to such tapes, but sometimes were not consciously aware of their own arousal.

Olfactory Stimulation (Through Smell)

To what extent do odors play a role in sexual excitation? Certainly, there is no research evidence that menstrual or genital odors are sources of sexual arousal in humans (Rogel, 1978). Most humans find such odors repulsive, not attractive. We do know, however, that women give off body odors called **pheromones**. Two of these substances, copulins and androstenol have received a good deal of attention. Morris and Udry (1978) had women rub perfumes on their chest each night before bedtime. They used four different perfumes, a different one each night, only one of which contained copulins. Questionnaires filled out each morning by their partners revealed that none of the perfumes appeared to affect either desire or sexual activity. Similarly, tests with androstenol indicated that the substance had no effect on humans (Black and Biron, 1982).

Odors can be turn-offs or turn-ons. A cleanly washed body is a natural turn-on, whereas a dirty, smelly one is a turn-off, at least for most people in our culture. People can keep clean without having to wear a particular scent in order to be sexually attractive. It is unpleasant to be near someone with bad breath or offensive body odor. *There is no research evidence that any particular smells are attractants for humans* (White, 1981).

Mental Stimulation: Fantasies

Fantasy plays a very big role in sexual stimulation (Stock and Geer, 1982); and fantasizing during intercourse facilitates sexual arousal (Sue, 1979). During lovemaking, some people find their thoughts wandering to other things

Andy, a male student of 19 came to the school counselor because he was worried that he masturbated. "Sometimes I do it every day," he explained. Upon questioning, Andy seemed happy and well-adjusted in other ways. He was doing well in college. He had a few close friends; although he was rather shy around girls, he had had a few dates.

1. If you were Andy's counselor, what would you try to accomplish, and what would you say to him?

2. One of the things that Andy said was that he was afraid he was gay because he masturbated. What would you say to Andy about that?

3. Is masturbation harmful? Explain.

4. A lot of ills have been attributed to masturbation: mental illness, idiocy, warts, bodily weakness, epilepsy, acne, weight loss, and early death. Are these things true? Explain.

5. What are some of the things that you were taught about masturbation when you were growing up?

6. What is likely to be the effect on sex adjustment in marriage of masturbating before marriage?

or they have trouble concentrating on love play. Therapists urge couples who are having difficulty responding to conjure up the most sexually arousing images they can think of (Lentz and Zeiss, 1984). Couples are encouraged to concentrate on these as an aid to sexual arousal. Nevertheless, persons who have low sexual desire and arousal problems often have difficulty fantasizing (Nutter and Condron, 1983).

Mental Stimulation: Nocturnal Dreams

Some fantasies occur as dreams. These can be similar in content to daydream fantasies except that they may end in orgasm because inhibitions are lowered during sleep. Kinsey et al. (1953) found that almost all men and the majority of women had nocturnal dreams with sexual content, and that 83 percent of males and 37 percent of females had erotic dreams leading to orgasm. **Nocturnal emissions** or **wet dreams** are most common among adolescent males who do not have other sexual outlets. Dreams to orgasm are common among adolescent females. However, both men and women of any age may experience nocturnal dreams accompanied by orgasm (Abel et al., 1979). Wells (1983) reported that one-third of his sample of college women had experienced nocturnal orgasm.

LOVEMAKING PRINCIPLES

Sexual Initiative

Traditionally, men were the sexual aggressors and women were the recipients. But men often complain that their partner never takes the initiative. One husband complained; "I can remember only once in 15 years of marriage

Both men and women need to feel free to initiate sex.

when my wife initiated sex." But his wife replied; "How can I? He's after me morning, noon, and night. Before I ever have a chance, he's all over me." (Author's counseling notes). *The important thing is that both the man and woman feel free to initiate sex, to be sexually assertive and active during sex itself.*

Communication

Once sex it initiated, *it is helpful if couples communicate their sexual preferences.* James (1983) writes:

> Men are generally pleased with women who let them know what they want and how they want it. With this kind of information the man can perceive her sexual interest as flattering and provocative. (p. 250)

The man can also derive pleasure from knowing that he is satisfying the sexual needs of his partner. A few males resent suggestions, they like to believe they are great lovers and don't need instruction. Actually, this may be a sign of immaturity and insecurity.

Time Factors

Time plays an important role in sexual arousal. Both men and women show variations in desire over a period of time. But some of the woman's variations in sexual drive relate to her monthly cycle. Overall, some women report an increase in sexual thoughts and feelings just before and during menstruation. Others report increased sexual desire and activity at the time of ovulation (Friedman et al., 1980; Matteo and Rissman, 1984). Others report no differences at different stages of the menstrual cycle (Morrell, Dixen, Carter, and Davidson, 1984). Of course, *many factors affect desire: general health, the degree of marital harmony, events that happen in and outside the family, even current events. Whatever is upsetting may influence sexual drive and desire.*

Men are affected by these events as well as women. A man who is in temporary ill health, who is tired and exhausted, or who is upset by his relationship with his wife or children, by events at work or in the world may evidence a temporary decrease in sexual drive. However, there is no male counterpart to female fluctuations during different time of the menstrual cycle (Knoepfler, 1983). Male sexual drive is affected by the testosterone level. Fatigue may lower that level, and in most men the testosterone level is highest in the morning and lowest at night; as a result, many men show greater interest in intercourse in the morning than at night. Emotional factors may play a role in influencing sexual desire in both men and women.

When couples have intercourse, they need to give themselves an uninterrupted period of time to make love. Feeling pressured to hurry up interferes with relaxed response. Love play can be a leisurely time in which couples have a chance to pleasure one another and to respond. One of the biggest complaints of women is that men are in too much of a hurry (Denny, Field, and Quadagno, 1984). One woman comments; "I like long arousals, but it usually doesn't last as long as I need because he is rushing me to move along toward orgasm" (Hite 1981, p. 145). Kinsey et al. (1953) found that through coitus alone the average female took 10–20 minutes to have orgasm, whereas the average male had orgasm in four minutes. However, with proper stimulation and sufficient love play, females could have an orgasm in just under four minutes and males in two to four. *The problem is not that women require a longer period to have orgasm. The problem is that they are sometimes not stimulated in the right way so that they can be sufficiently aroused before intercourse takes place.*

Ordinarily, an important goal would be to see that the woman is aroused first and even has orgasm before the man to ensure that his erection is sustained long enough for coitus. If he should have his orgasm first, her stimulation could be continued manually or orally. Certainly, it is not necessary to have simultaneous orgasm to have good sex.

Coitus can become so lengthy, however, that it becomes uncomfortable. After a period of time, lubrication ceases, the vaginal tissues become dry, and thrusting becomes painful. Using lubricants and decreasing the time of coital thrusting both help. If either partner has trouble having orgasm, lengthy foreplay and then brief coitus is one answer.

Physical Setting

Physical surroundings play a role in enhancing or retarding lovemaking. Some couples can make love freely in their own bedroom, but are inhibited in someone else's house. One couple stayed in the husband's mother's house for the first year of marriage, and the husband was not able to have orgasm the entire year. Obviously he had been negatively conditioned sexually from the time he was small (Author's counseling notes). Some couples find it exciting to go to a motel, make love in the automobile, or retreat into the woods. While the bare ground, covered with stones and insects, may not be too comfortable, the change of locale may be enough to stimulate intense excitement. Sex need never become boring if couples introduce variety and change from time to time. Certainly, assuring privacy helps couples to be uninhibited. Locked doors add assurance that the children can't walk in unexpectedly.

Being Uninhibited

One of the uncertainties in the beginning is how uninhibited to be, but *couples can learn to let themselves go completely, to be as completely uninhibited as possible, consistent with their mutual feelings and desires.* They can also avoid deliberately shocking or doing things that disgust the other. Their lovemaking can lead them to do things that are acceptable to them both. In most cases, the longer they have been sharing sexual expression, the more uninhibited they become. The important thing is to feel free to experiment with a variety of activities.

Learning to Relax

Sometimes people are tense, and have trouble relaxing and getting in the mood. Several things can help. One is to take a hot, *leisurely bath* until tension is gone. Once the couple has relaxed, love play can be initiated in the bathtub or shower or jacuzzi, or immediately upon leaving it. A complete *body massage* also enhances relaxation, helps each partner to become sensitized to erotic caresses and to learn to freely give and experience sexual pleasure.

Being Willing To Try and To Learn

One of the most important requirements for satisfaction is the willingness to try and to learn. Sometimes after a few failures or unsatisfying attempts at intercourse and climax, couples feel they have failed. Such is not true. It is not uncommon for intercourse to be frustrating in the first days or weeks. Various problems can occur. The man has orgasm too fast; the woman doesn't have orgasm at all; intercourse is painful; the man loses his erection because he ejaculates prematurely; he can't even get an erection; or the woman can't have an orgasm through intercourse but only by manual or oral stimulation. Sometimes the couple doesn't really try to work out differences. They just avoid each other. Or they continue mutual masturbation because they are used to it, can have orgasm more easily that way, and don't have to worry about contraceptives. Since a mutually satisfying sex life can be an enriching relationship, it is important for both the man and woman to be motivated to work things out. If they can't succeed by themselves, they might read all they can and get qualified help if needed.

Frequency of Intercourse

One question often asked is how frequently couples have intercourse and what is the relationship between frequency and sexual satisfaction? It is always dangerous to play the numbers game, because whatever figures are mentioned are going to be disappointing to someone. But as a starter, what do other couples do? Realizing that all persons are individuals and that they should not try to do what everyone else does, let's look at some figures on the frequency of intercourse. One study of married men showed that frequency varied from person to person (Pearlman, 1972). In general, younger husbands had intercourse more often than older ones, and most men showed some decline in frequency with advancing age. For example, according to Pearlman, three out of four married men in their twenties had intercourse two to four times per week. Among married men in their fifties, 31 percent still had intercourse that often. Seven percent of married men in their sixties and 4 percent in their seventies were still having intercourse two to four times per week.

What were the percentages of married men who had intercourse at least once a week or more often? Ninety-three percent of those in their twenties, 82 percent of those in their thirties, 70 percent of those in their forties, 49 percent of those in their fifties, 26 percent of those in their sixties, and 11 percent of those in their seventies had intercourse once a week or more often.

It is evident that the frequency with which married men had sexual relations declined only slowly with age. Only a little over half of all married men 70 to 79 years of age were completely sexually inactive (Pearlman, 1971).

One cannot assume that all couples who have intercourse with above-average frequency have better sexual lives and that couples who have relations with below-average frequency have worse ones. The number of times per week or month is not in and of itself the only measure of sexual satisfaction. Overall, however, those who have frequent intercourse are more likely to report satisfaction with their sexual lives than are those who have infrequent intercourse (Levin and Levin, 1975a).

An equally important factor in satisfaction is frequency of orgasm. In a *Redbook* magazine survey, 8 out of 10 women who were orgasmic all or most of the time reported satisfaction with marital sex, but only half of those who were only sometimes orgasmic reported satisfaction. It is significant, though, that over one-fourth of those who were never orgasmic also rated their sexual lives as satisfying. Apparently, these nonorgasmic women found pleasure in intercourse other than through orgasm (Levin and Levin, 1975a, 1975b).

If we combine frequency of intercourse and frequency of orgasm, these two factors taken together become one of the most important criteria of sexual satisfaction. The frequency with which couples make love and experience orgasm is directly related to the probability of their reporting a high degree of satisfaction with sex.

Another important consideration is how couples feel about the frequency with which they are participating. One report of female college graduates whose median age was 26.2 years and who had been married a median period of 4.2 years revealed that 69 percent felt that their frequency of intercourse was about right, 6 percent said it was too frequent, and 25 percent said it was too infrequent (Bell, 1972).

In cases of marked differences in sexual appetite, overlooking the problem is no solution. To do so is to create tension in the marriage or relationship. If couples are not able to work things out themselves, they may need outside help from a sex therapist.

Part A of the inventory is to enable those of you who are sexually active to assess your general sexual satisfaction. Part B is to enable you to assess your sexual satisfaction with your partner. Evaluate your replies according to the following scales by circling the appropriate number:

1 — Strongly agree
2 — Mostly agree
3 — Mildly agree
4 — Neutral, neither agree or disagree
5 — Mildly disagree
6 — Mostly disagree
7 — Strongly disagree

PART A.   GENERAL SEXUAL SATISFACTION

1 2 3 4 5 6 7   I feel that nothing is lacking in my sex life.

1 2 3 4 5 6 7   I am satisfied that my physical needs are completely met during lovemaking.

1 2 3 4 5 6 7   Generally, I am satisfied with my sex life.

1 2 3 4 5 6 7   I am satisfied with the amount of time my partner(s) and I spend together immediately after intercourse.

1 2 3 4 5 6 7   I am satisfied with the amount of time that my partner(s) and I spend together when we make love.

1 2 3 4 5 6 7   I am satisfied with the amount of foreplay involved in my lovemaking.

1 2 3 4 5 6 7   I am satisfied with the spontaneity of my lovemaking.

1 2 3 4 5 6 7   I am satisfied with the frequency with which I have sexual intercourse.

1 2 3 4 5 6 7   I am satisfied with the quality of time my partner(s) and I spend together immediately after intercourse.

1 2 3 4 5 6 7   I am satisfied with my capacity for enjoying sex.

1 2 3 4 5 6 7   I am satisfied with the importance my partner(s) place(s) on lovemaking in the relationship.

1 2 3 4 5 6 7   I am satisfied with my ability to make my physical needs known to my partner.

1 2 3 4 5 6 7   I am satisfied with the times of day and night when my partner(s) and I usually make love.

1 2 3 4 5 6 7   I am satisfied with the frequency with which I have orgasms.

Add up the total scores for the 14 items and divide by 14. *The lower your score, the more strongly you agree with the items, and the greater your sexual satisfaction.*

PART B.   SATISFACTION WITH PARTNER

1 2 3 4 5 6 7   I wish my partner(s) were more loving and caring when we make love.

1 2 3 4 5 6 7   I wish my partner(s) were more romantic when we make love.

1 2 3 4 5 6 7   I wish my partner(s) were more affectionate during foreplay.

1 2 3 4 5 6 7   I wish my partner(s) would make me feel more attractive.

1 2 3 4 5 6 7   I wish my partner(s) were a better lover(s).

1 2 3 4 5 6 7   I wish my partner(s) were more sensitive to my physical needs when we make love.

1 2 3 4 5 6 7   I wish my partner(s) could communicate more openly about what he/she wants in our sexual encounters.

1 2 3 4 5 6 7   I wish my partner(s) were more patient when we make love.

1 2 3 4 5 6 7   I wish I were less inhibited when I make love.

1 2 3 4 5 6 7   I wish my partner(s) initiated sex more often.

Add up the total score for the 10 items and divide by 10. *Note that on this part, the higher your score, the more strongly you disagree with the items, and the greater your sexual satisfaction.*

Adapted from Pinney, E. M., Gerrard, M., and Denney, N. W. (1987). The Pinney Sexual Satisfaction Inventory. *The Journal of Sex Research, 23*, 233–251.

SEXUAL DYSFUNCTION

Under most circumstances the body functions quite smoothly, reacting in predictable ways to certain sexual stimuli. Sometimes, however, the sex organs do not respond. When the penis is rubbed, it remains flaccid. The nipples may not become enlarged and erect when the breasts are stimulated. After copulating for a long period of time, a couple may never reach a climax. Obviously, something has gone wrong if a particular stimuli does not produce the expected response. Any malfunction of the human sexual response system is termed **sexual dysfunction**, because a person has not reacted as would normally be expected. In this section both male and female dysfunctions are addressed.

Male Sexual Dysfunction

Male sexual dysfunctions include premature ejaculation, erectile dysfunction, ejaculatory inhibition, and inhibited sexual desire.

    Premature ejaculation *has been defined as a condition wherein a man is unable to exert voluntary control over his ejaculatory reflex, with the result that once he is sexually aroused, he reaches orgasm very quickly* (Kaplan, 1974). According to Masters and Johnson (1970), a male who is unable to delay ejaculation long enough to place his penis within the vagina and thrust long enough for the woman to have an orgasm 50 percent of the time is a premature ejaculator. This definition assumes that the woman can ordinarily have an orgasm; when she does not, it is because of the rapidity of the man's ejaculation.

    A man's ability to control ejaculation helps a couple attain sexual satisfaction. The couple needs to be able to engage in sexual play and in intercourse until both partners are sufficiently aroused for orgasm to take place. If the man climaxes, and his penis becomes flaccid before the woman is aroused sufficiently, the couple may have to rely on other means of stimulation to bring her to orgasm. Premature ejaculation curtails the woman's sensuous enjoyment, even if she has an orgasm afterward. The couple's pleasure and lovemaking are heightened if the man can prolong the period of intense excitement prior to orgasm. At best, prematurity restricts the couple's sexuality. If the couple becomes anxious and worried about their sex life or angry and rejecting to the point of avoiding one another, premature ejaculatory dysfunction can reduce the harmony of the relationship. The fact that premature ejaculation is one of the easiest of male sexual dysfunctions to treat is an encouraging aspect (Masters and Johnson, 1970).

If a male is unable to produce an erection so that coital connection can take place or maintain one long enough to complete the sexual act, he has **erectile dysfunction**. Actually, the situation occurs in most men at some time or another, but is temporary in nature.

Sometimes a man has never been able to achieve and/or maintain sufficient erection to accomplish intromission. If this condition has always existed, it is known as **primary erectile dysfunction**. Some men develop **secondary erectile dysfunction**. In this case, erection has been sufficient for successful intercourse some of the time only; however, episodes of erectile failure occur one or many times. Fortunately, the condition is treatable in the great majority of cases.

A minority of males suffer from **ejaculatory inhibition**. They are able to become sexually aroused, have a firm erection and normal intercourse, but are unable to reach a climax. As a result, intercourse becomes frustrating. Even though a man desires an orgasm and is stimulated enough to trigger a climax, he cannot come.

The severity of ejaculatory inhibition varies considerably. At one extreme is the male who has never experienced an orgasm, although a person with this condition is rarely encountered in clinical practice. At the other end of the spectrum is the man who occasionally finds himself unable to ejaculate. Mild forms of the disorder may be highly prevalent, as attested to by the increasing number of patients applying for treatment.

There is little reference in the literature to the fact that men can experience **inhibited sexual desire**, *or almost nonexistent sexual drive*. Low sexual drive in women is discussed at length, but men are assumed to have ample drive, persistent desire for intercourse, and healthy sexual appetites. A few men do not fit this stereotype, however, because they seldom have any interest in sexual expression. Although in the minority, these cases are not at all unusual. A man who has inhibited sexual desire may create a great deal of misery for a partner who desires regular sexual expression.

Female Sexual Dysfunction

Female sexual dysfunctions include general sexual dysfunction, orgasm dysfunction, painful intercourse (dyspareunia), and vaginismus.

Women who experience **general sexual dysfunction** *lack desire for or lack pleasure in sexual relations*. Some may have little or minimal interest in sexual activity. If they participate, they derive no erotic pleasure from the experience. On the physiological level, women with general sexual dysfunction have limited vaginal lubrication and vasocongestion. On a psychological level, they often

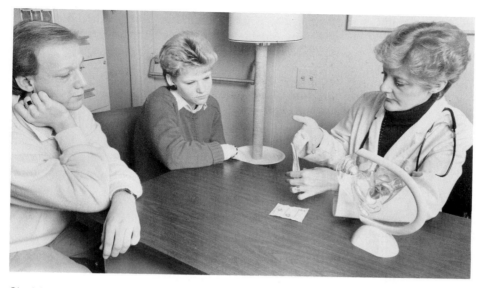

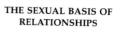

Obtaining and using efficient and acceptable forms of contraception can minimize the fear of pregnancy. The fear of pregnancy can inhibit sexual desire and increase sexual frustrations between couples.

are averse to sex, consider it a frightening or disgusting ordeal, and try to avoid sexual contact. The dysfunction may be situational; that is, a woman may be unresponsive in a particular situation or with a certain person but not on other occasions or with another man. Degrees of sexual interest and responsiveness vary. Complete and permanent lack of sexual interest is rare.

A woman may manifest general sexual dysfunction in ways other than by refusing to have intercourse most of the time. For example, a woman may want intercourse with her partner because she desires to please him, although she does not derive satisfaction from the experience. For such a woman, sex is like brushing the teeth or combing the hair: something that has to be done.

In some instances, a woman may be responsive in the beginning of a relationship but becomes unresponsive later on. Intercourse may have ceased to offer her pleasure, or other problems may have occurred in the relationship to make her unresponsive sexually (Henker, 1984). General sexual dysfunction may be primary, because the woman has never derived erotic satisfaction with any partner in any situation. This condition is rare. Secondary general sexual dysfunction is characterized by the woman who has responded to some extent on at least one occasion, but is unresponsive, or becomes so, on other occasions.

Some women are able to become sexually aroused, but are unable to reach a climax. This condition, referred to as **orgasm dysfunction**, is one of the most common in women. Only a minority have never had an orgasm (primary orgasm dysfunction). Women with secondary orgasm dysfunction can reach a climax under certain circumstances or with a particular person, but not in other situations or with another person. Some women are able to have an orgasm through masturbation, oral-genital stimulation, or other stimulative techniques, such as with the use of a vibrator, but not through coitus. Some may have an occasional "random" orgasm, but are otherwise nonorgasmic. Others may have difficulty in reaching a climax under all circumstances.

Another common female difficulty is **dyspareunia** *or painful intercourse* (Semmens and Tsai, 1984). The pain may be severe or slight, the degree depending on its origin and the woman's condition. Although dyspareunia is not unusual, it is not "natural." Except for intercourse in the early days of consummation or soon after childbirth, it should not be a painful experience. Persistent pain is a symptom of an underlying problem that usually requires medical attention.

Vaginismus, which is rather rare, refers to an involuntary contraction and spasm of the vaginal muscles. This spasm becomes apparent not only when intercourse is attempted but also when a physician gives a pelvic examination. As soon as the physician approaches such a patient with a vaginal speculum, the muscles of her vagina go into spasm, making speculum insertion impossible or extremely painful. The woman also may have trouble inserting a tampon. Even if vaginismus exists in a mild form, sexual intercourse may be very unpleasant.

Causes of Sexual Dysfunction

In general, physical or emotional disorders (or both) cause sexual dysfunctions in men and women (LoPiccolo, 1985). From a purely physical point of view, sex involves many of the organs of the body in addition to the penis and vagina. Thus, the whole body is involved in sexual expression. Sexual expression also involves one's feelings and emotions. In fact, the emotional component of sex can have a definite effect upon physical response. Feelings of love and affection can stimulate sexual response and pleasure. Worry, fear, or disgust may completely inhibit sexual feelings. Negative feelings or emotional upset may block the body's normal sexual response systems. Therefore, how people feel about themselves, their bodies, their sex organs, their partners, or the sex act itself influences their sexual function. Negative feelings in relation to any emotional conditioning may inhibit sexual expression.

Because our physical and emotional makeup influence our sexual expression, an examination of the causes of sexual dysfunction is a complicated matter. For purposes of clarity, these causes may be grouped into six categories.

1. *Ignorance, or lack of knowledge and understanding*, regarding sexual anatomy, sexual response, and lovemaking techniques may be reasons why couples have problems. Humans are not born with an understanding of male and female differences or with the knowledge of how to make love.

2. *Environmental and situational circumstances* can prevent couples from achieving satisfactory sexual function.

3. *Inadequate stimulation*, consisting of improper techniques, inappropriate ways, or insufficient time given to lovemaking, can cause sexual dysfunctions.

4. *Psychological blocks* that include negative attitudes toward sex, the human body, the sex organs, masculinity or femininity, or oneself may inhibit sexual response. Fear and anxiety are psychological blocks. Fear of pregnancy, hurt, rejection, or failure are common causes of difficulties, as are feelings of guilt, embarrassment, or disgust. Emotional illness can also cause sexual dysfunction.

5. *Negative feelings toward one's partner or disturbance in the relationship* can precipitate sexual dysfunction. People respond best to those whom they love, admire, and trust. Contrary feelings can influence their ability to respond sexually. The quality and emotional tone of a couple's relationship influence sexual function.

6. *Physical abnormalities, illnesses, surgery, or drugs* can cause sexual difficulties.

Getting Help

Sexual difficulties, left untreated, can wreck a marriage. This is even more tragic because most of the difficulties might have been cleared up by obtaining help.

Basically there are four types of help: (1) *medical,* for physical problems, (2) *psychotherapy* when counseling is needed for emotional problems and hangups, (3) *marriage counseling* that deals with the total marital relationship, and (4) *sex therapy* that emphasizes sensate-focus or symptom-focus approaches that concentrate on the immediate sexual problem. Sex therapy assigns couples sexual tasks that enable the couples to learn how to caress or "pleasure" one another in a nondemanding way until they are able to respond to one another.

Whatever type of help is needed, and it sometimes involves a combination of one or more of these approaches, most therapists agree that **conjoint therapy,** involving both the husband and wife, is desirable since sexual functioning necessarily affects them both. Couples who are having problems need to decide to get help together.

SEXUALLY TRANSMITTED DISEASES

Categories

Sexually transmitted diseases may be arranged into three categories according to their cause:

1. *Those caused by viruses:* **AIDS, herpes, hepatitis B,** and **genital warts.**
2. *Those caused by bacteria:* **chlamydial infections, gonorrhea,** and **syphilis.**
3. *Those caused by parasites:* **pubic lice** and **scabies.**

Of the diseases listed, only AIDs and herpes are incurable. Any of the STDs caused by viruses or bacteria can be serious if left undetected and untreated.

AIDS

AIDS is of special concern today not only because it is incurable, but also because it is always fatal once a person really contracts it. A blood test measures the presence of AIDS virus antibodies in the bloodstream. A person who tests positive for

PERSPECTIVE
Protecting Oneself from AIDS Infection

Individuals can do a number of things to protect themselves from the AIDS virus.

1. Maintain a mutually faithful, monogamous relationship.
2. If you do not know your partner, get as much of a sexual history as possible. If you have any doubts at all, insist that both you and your partner have an anti-body test before engaging in sex.
3. If you do not know with absolute certainty that you and your partner are free of the AIDS virus, use high-quality, latex condoms (the virus passes through lamb-skin condoms) during oral, vaginal, or anal intercourse and protective shields over the female genitalia to prevent transmission during cunnilingus (Conant et al., 1986). Use of spermicides also keeps the virus from multiplying.
4. Do not assume that just because you are heterosexual that you can't get AIDS. "Straights" as well as gays and bisexuals get AIDS from infected persons of any sex.
5. Avoid sex with male or female prostitutes (Redfield et al., 1985).
6. Avoid all types of sexual expression with infected persons, including fellatio and cunnilingus. Cuts and sores in the mouth offer an avenue for the virus to enter or exit. Avoid anal intercourse since this is a major means of transmission of AIDS (Goedert et al., 1984). Avoid oral contact with the anus (called "rimming").
7. Avoid intravenous drug use and especially sharing syringes and needles (boiling does not guarantee sterility).
8. Do not share personal items such as razor blades, toothbrushes, nail clippers, ear piercing tools, tattoo equipment, and douche or enema equipment.
9. Avoid oral, vaginal, or anal contact with semen.
10. Avoid inserting fingers or fist into the anus either as a passive or active partner. Small tears allow direct access to the bloodstream.
11. Do not allow another's urine to enter open sores or cuts, your mouth, anus, vagina, or eyes.
12. Just in case AIDS may be transmitted via saliva, avoid sustained, open-mouthed kissing and French kissing unless you are certain you are both free of the virus.

AIDS virus antibodies has been exposed to the virus, is infected, and can transmit it to others. The latest evidence suggests that at least 50 percent of those infected will get the full-blown disease (Wallis, 1987). Persons may spread the virus without knowing they are infected. The incubation period may be from several years to as long as 10 years.

The AIDS virus is found in semen, blood, urine, vaginal secretions, saliva, tears, and breast milk and is transmitted from male to female, female to male, male to male, and female to female during the exchange of body fluids (Communicable Disease Summary, 1985). Transmission is through direct sexual contact and use of infected needles or syringes. The AIDS virus can also pass from mother to fetus during pregnancy and through breast milk to a nursing infant (Koop, 1986). Although the AIDS virus has been found in tears and saliva, no instance of transmission from these body fluids has been reported. AIDS is *not* transmitted through casual, nonsexual social contact such as occurs at home, in offices, restaurants, or schools (Friedland et al., 1986). It is *not* transmitted through touching, holding, shaking hands, or playing together, nor by sneezing, breathing, or coughing, nor through food or biting insects, nor through towels, toilet seats, eating utensils, or water fountains ("Health Service . . .", 1985). AIDS is a disease of heterosexuals as well as homosexuals and bisexuals. It is also frequent among intravenous drug users (Smilgis, 1987). The more sex partners one has, male or female, the greater the risk of becoming infected.

SUMMARY

1. There is a positive relationship between orgasm and happy marriage. It is harder for wives to be happily married without orgasm, and it is harder for them to have orgasm without a happy marriage.

2. Masters and Johnson have divided the human sexual response cycle into four phases: the excitement phase, the plateau phase, the orgasm phase, and the resolution phase.

3. Physiological responses during the cycle include vasocongestion and erection; myotonia; lubrication; an increase in heart and pulse rate, blood pressure, respiration, and perspiration; sex flush, and orgasm.

4. The responses of the male and female are similar even though the actual sexual organs are different.

5. One important difference between men and women is that the latter are able to have multiple orgasms. Some men can also have multiple orgasms if they tighten the PC muscles during orgasm to prevent ejaculation so that continued stimulation will result in excitation to orgasm over again.

6. Kaplan outlined a three-stage model of human sexual response that included the desire stage, excitement, and orgasm.

7. Sources of sexual arousal include tactile stimulation, visual stimulation, audio stimulation, verbal stimulation, olfactory stimulation, and mental stimulation through fantasy and erotic dreams.

8. Some helpful lovemaking principles include the following:
   - The man and woman ought to both feel free to initiate sex.
   - The couple needs to communicate their desires to one another.
   - Both men and women show variations in sexual desire over a period of time and ought to allow themselves an uninterrupted period of time to make love.
   - The physical setting either enhances or retards lovemaking.
   - Couples can learn to let themselves go and be completely uninhibited consistent with their mutual feelings and desires.
   - It is helpful to take a leisurely bath or give body massage before sex to relax and get in the mood.
   - To achieve sexual satisfaction, couples need to be willing to try and to learn.
   - Frequency of intercourse varies with each couple and with age. The important consideration is for both persons to feel satisfied with the frequency with which they are participating.

9. Male sexual dysfunctions include premature ejaculation, erectile dysfunction, ejaculatory inhibition, and inhibited sexual desire.

10. Female sexual dysfunctions include general sexual dysfunction, orgasm dysfunction, dyspareunia (painful intercourse), and vaginismus.

11. The causes of sexual dysfunction are either physical or emotional or both. Causes include: ignorance or lack of knowledge and understanding; negative environmental or situational circumstances; inadequate stimulation; psychological blocks, negative feelings toward one's partner or disturbance in the relationship; and physical abnormalities, illness, surgery, or drugs.

12. Four types of help are available: (1) medical help for physical problems, (2) psychotherapy for emotional problems and hang-ups, (3) marriage counseling, and (4) sex therapy that concentrates on the immediate sexual problem. Most therapists agree that conjoint therapy involving both the man and woman is desirable.

13. Sexually transmitted diseases may be arranged into three categories according to their cause: those caused by viruses (AIDS, herpes, hepatitis B, and genital warts), those caused by bacteria (chlamydial infections, gonorrhea, and syphilis), and those caused by parasites (pubic lice and scabies).

14. Any of the sexually transmitted diseases caused by viruses or bacteria can be serious if left undetected and untreated.

15. AIDS is of special concern not only because it is incurable, but also because it is always fatal once a person really contracts it.

SUGGESTED READINGS

Belliveau, F., and Richer, L. (1970). *Understanding Human Sexual Inadequacy*. New York: Bantam. A lay explanation of Masters' and Johnson's treatment of sexual dysfunctions.

Brecher, R., and Brecher, E. (1966). *An Analysis of Human Sexual Response*. New York: New American Library. A simplified explanation of Masters' and Johnson's findings on human sexual response.

Chase, A. (1983). *The Truth About STD*. New York: Morrow. Nontechnical overview.

Comfort, A. (1972). *The Joy of Sex*. New York: Crown. The most popular sex manual for the layperson.

Kaplan, H. (1983). *The Evaluation of Sexual Disorders*. New York: Brunner/Mazel. Medical and psychological evaluation of sexual dysfunctions.

Kilman, P. R., and Mills, K. H. (1983). *All About Sex Therapy*. New York: Plenum Press. A layperson's guide to sex therapy.

Koop, C. E. (1986). *Surgeon General's Report on Acquired Immune Deficiency Syndrome*. Washington, DC: U.S. Department of Health and Human Services.

Lumiere, R., and Cook, C. (1983). *Healthy Sex and Keeping It That Way*. New York: Simon and Schuster. Genital health and disease.

Masters, W., and Johnson, V. (1966). *Human Sexual Response*. Boston: Little, Brown. The classic work on sexuality written from a technical point of view.

Masters, W. H., and Johnson, V. E. (1970). *Human Sexual Inadequacy*. Boston: Little, Brown. The classic work on their approach to and treatment of sexual dysfunction.

Rice, F. P. (1978). *Sexual Problems in Marriage*. Philadelphia: Westminster Press. The author's explanation of sexual response, dysfunctions, and treatment for the layperson.

10

TRANSITION TO MARRIAGE AND NONMARITAL COHABITATION

KEY TERMS

consanguinity
affinity
common-law marriage
void marriage
voidable marriage
cohabitation
POSSLQ
Rites of passage

The transition from singlehood to marriage is not accomplished all at once, but ordinarily takes place over several years. Whether the transition is successful or not depends on a number of factors. One factor is marital readiness. To what extent are two people really ready for marriage? What legal requirements must be fulfilled in order to marry, and is the couple able to meet them? What is involved in entering into a marriage contract, and how can such a contract become more meaningful and helpful? What can the couple do to prepare for marriage ahead of time? What kinds of marital education, assessment, and counseling might be considered? Does living together before marriage aid in preparing for successful marriage? How can engagement become a constructive period of preparation? What functions do rites of passage fulfill in aiding the transition to marriage? This chapter attempts to answer these questions.

MARITAL READINESS

A number of important factors determine marital readiness. Based upon the research information we have, the following considerations may be significant:

- Age at the time of marriage
- The level of maturity of the couple
- The particular time when marriage takes place
- How long two people have gone together before marriage
- The amount of dating and social experience
- Willingness to assume the responsibility of marriage
- Readiness for sexual exclusiveness
- Emotional emancipation from parents
- Level of education and vocational aspirations and the degree of their fulfillment

Age and Maturity

Age and level of maturity are important considerations in evaluating marital readiness. Teti, Lamb, and Elster (1987) found that males who married in adolescence (before they turned 19) were more likely to divorce or separate than were individuals who married later. Booth and Edwards (1985) found that marital instability was higher for men and women who married while in their teens.

There are a number of reasons for the greater instability of teenage marriages. Teenagers are usually emotionally immature and not able to deal with the problems and stresses of early marriage. They do not have the social skills necessary to deal with a sustained intimate relationship. Their lack of skills leads to dissatisfaction with the way the spouse fulfills certain marital obligations. This leads to friction and marital instability. Booth and Edwards (1985) found that the principal sources of marital dissatisfaction among couples who married young were the spouses' lack of faithfulness; the pres-

Age and level of maturity at the time of marriage are important factors that determine marital readiness. What other considerations may be significant?

ence of jealousy; the lack of understanding, agreement, and communication. Attempts to dominate or refusal to talk made communciation difficult.

Early marriages are often precipitated by premarital pregnancies, which often result in couples abandoning educational pursuits in favor of parenthood and/or full-time (and lower-status) employment (Haggstrom, Kanouse, and Morrison, 1986). The result is low income and increased stress trying to deal with the strains of adolescence, marriage, and parenthood. Long-term consequences are especially negative for women, who more frequently are compelled by circumstances to make a career-inhibiting life choice (Lowe and Witt, 1984). Kellam, Adams, Brown, and Ensminger (1982) found also that teenage mothers tend to be the only adult in their households. Many remain alone for years after a child's birth. They often have little help with child rearing and participate less in community organizations than do older mothers. This mother-aloneness is hard on the young mother and has been found to have detrimental consequences for the child's psychological well-being and early success in school (Kellam, Adams, Brown, and Ensminger, 1982).

Maneker and Ranking (1985) did find that among divorcing couples those married youngest were married somewhat longer when they did divorce than those married at a later age. The reasons may be complex. The younger persons lacked financial and emotional resources to pursue the process of divorce. They may have been less aware of the alternatives to stressful marriage. There were some, no doubt, who were very miserable during the years of marriage. Marriage duration is not synonymous with marital quality. All couples in this study divorced eventually.

There is some evidence that postponing marriage too long may also have a negative effect on marital stability and quality. From the standpoint of marital stability, men who wait to marry until 27 years of age and women who wait until 25 have waited as long as practical to maximize their chances of success (Rice, 1983). After age 30, the chances of marital success begin to decline (Booth and Edwards, 1985; Vaillant, 1977a).

Another factor in marital readiness is the extent to which people really choose to get married at the particular time they do. One husband explained:

> Margie and I could not have picked a worse time to get married. I was laid off work a week before we got married. Her mother was sick and later diagnosed as having terminal cancer. Margie and I didn't really give ourselves time enough to know one another well. (Author's counseling notes)

One wife felt she and her husband got off to a bad start because she let him talk her into marriage before she was ready. Such people become disenchanted, not because they are not in love or because they don't want to get married eventually, but because they are not ready when they do marry.

Motives for Marriage

The motives for marriage are also important in marital success or failure. Most people in our culture get married for love and companionship, some for security. Other people get married for essentially negative reasons. We have mentioned that the number one reason for marriage while still in high school is *pregnancy*. It is hard, however, to make a success of marriage forced by pregnancy (Bishop and Lynn, 1983).

Other people marry to try to *escape* — an unhappy home, school failure, personal insecurity, or an unhappy social adjustment with peers (Rice, 1987). But people take their unhappiness and problems with them into marriage, and so escape is futile. Sometimes people marry to try *to hurt others* — parents, an ex-boyfriend or girlfriend, or even themselves. One way people have of showing contempt for themselves is to marry a completely unsuitable partner.

People sometimes marry on the *rebound* from one failed relationship to try to heal their damaged ego and raise their self-esteem. They are especially hurt if they didn't want to break off the relationship. They may marry hastily to show themselves and their ex-partner that someone still wants them. The mate they choose may not be a suitable person for them at all.

Other individuals want *to prove their worth and attractiveness.* Some men marry to prove their manhood, to prove that some woman wants them, or to show that they are not homosexuals.

It is not unusual for people to believe they are in love with those who have helped them. Clients often "fall in love" with their counselors, patients with their doctors, parishioners with their clergy, or students with their teachers. Such persons mistake *gratitude* for love.

Similarly, very paternal or maternal people are attracted to those for whom *they feel sorry.* Men marry women who seem defenseless, alone, in trouble, or who need a strong shoulder on which to lean. Such marriages build the egos of the men involved. Some women are invariably attracted to men who are maladjusted and problems to themselves and others. One woman married an alcoholic because she thought he needed her and she wanted to take care of him.

In a society that overromanticizes marriage and overcriticizes staying single, it's hard to resist the temptation to get married simply *as a means of avoiding condemnation.* When her friends are announcing their engagements and getting married, the individual woman feels left out if she doesn't do likewise.

Dating and Social Experience

Generally speaking, those who have a number of successful friendships, who have participated in a variety of social activities, who are members of social organizations, are better able to establish successful marriages than are those who are social isolates with a minimum of social experience (Grover, Russell, Schumm, and Paff-Bergen, 1985). Social participation helps one to develop socials skills, poise, and the ability to get along with others — all traits that are needed in successful marriage (Burgess, Locke, and Thomas, 1971).

Dating and social experience help people develop social skills, poise, and the ability to get along with others. How do young adults know when they are ready for a permanent relationship?

An additional consequence of social experience needs to be recognized. It is helpful if individuals feel they have enough dating and social life before assuming the responsibilities of marriage. Most young adults want a period of carefree fun after emancipation from parents: a chance to come and go as they please, to go to new and different places, to make new friends or enjoy themselves with their present ones. If they marry before they have a chance to do these things, some regret it afterwards and wish they had waited. Later in marriage some of these individuals seek to "have the fling" they feel they were deprived of earlier.

Problems develop if husbands or wives continue to spend most of their leisure time with old friends rather than with one another. One wife complains:

> All my husband wants to do is go partying with his old buddies like he used to do before he was married. I don't expect him to give up his friends, but he never spends any time with me. He expects me not to complain when he leaves me home all alone. (Author's counseling notes)

Such problems are common occurences among young couples who have not developed beyond the "going partying with the guys (or gals) stage" before marriage.

Willingness to Assume Responsibility

Many marriages fail because the couple is not yet able or willing to assume responsibility. The parents who are suddenly faced with the financial responsibility of supporting an infant child as well as themselves have to be quite ready to assume this responsibility at the time of marriage or they may grow to regret the marriage and resent the child. Many young marriages could work if the couple didn't have children right away. They feel they are too tied down, too busy with the baby, and are not able to go out like they used to. Some young mothers show their resentment of their children by their impatience and intolerance of them. One wife complained about her husband's immaturity, "Should I expect my husband to love our child?" (Reiner and Edwards, 1974). It is evident from these comments that marriage and parenthood require a great deal of maturity and that many young couples have difficulties only because they haven't yet grown up enough to assume the responsibilities required.

Readiness for Sexual Exclusiveness

Ordinarily, monogamous marriage in our society means that husbands and wives desire sexual exclusiveness. While many adults are quite tolerant of premarital sexual intercourse, most are insistent upon the marital fidelity of their mate. Marital readiness for the majority of couples requires an attitude of sexual exclusiveness.

Emotional Emancipation from Parents

Another indication of marital readiness and maturity is emotional emancipation from parents. Individuals who still seek emotional fulfillment primarily from their

One study shows that women in their twenties who have career aspirations marry later in life than those who plan to stay at home and raise families.

parents are not yet ready to give their chief loyalty and affection to their spouse, as is necessary for a successful marriage. No wife or husband wants to play "second fiddle" to an in-law or to compete with the in-law for affection. Of course, sometimes an immature husband or wife is so emotionally insecure that any affection the spouse gives to parents is resented. In such cases, the problem is not caused by the spouse's immaturity, but by personal insecurity or feelings of inadequacy of the spouse's mate.

Educational and Vocational Readiness

There are some significant relationships between educational-vocational aspirations and the time of marriage. The lower the educational and vocational aspirations of youths, the more likely early marriage will occur. Those youths who have no post–high school educational plans are likely to feel that, since they have completed their education, marriage is the next possibility. A study of graduate students in engineering and science showed that the higher their educational level, the longer after college graduation before they married. Once married, the higher their educational level, the longer after college graduation they began their families (Perrucci, 1968). One study of women in their twenties showed that those who had career aspirations married later in life than did those who planned to stay home and raise families (Cherlin, 1980).

The results of dropping out of school to marry or because of marriage are most often negative (Marini, 1978). The husband or wife who drops out is seriously limiting his or her earning ability and income — which, in turn, creates marital problems and instability. If the wife drops out of school to put her husband through college, as some women do, there is a possibility that her husband will "grow away from her" and that an intellectual gap will be created between them. Even more important, as the years pass, the wife may resent more and more the fact that she gave up her education for marriage. She may need to work for financial reasons or because of a need for personal fulfillment, yet she is limited in what she can do because of an inadequate education.

One of the unfortunate results of premature marriage is its interference with personal mobility. When persons are relatively free of responsibilities, they have the option of changing major fields of study if in school or of changing jobs if working. If they're married and supporting a family, by the time they discover who they are and what they want to become, they are already "locked in" doing a job just because it's a way of making money.

CLASSROOM FORUM
Marriage While in College

Discuss the following questions in class:

1. What is your attitude toward getting married while still an undergraduate in college?

2. Would you personally want to get married while still an undergraduate in college? Why? or Why not?
   To married students: Are you glad or sorry you married while in college? Explain reasons for your feelings.

3. What are some disadvantages of marrying while in college?

4. What are some advantages of marrying while in college?

5. In general, do married students do better or worse academically than single students?

6. *To single students*: Do you know any married students? How do they feel about marriage while in college? What are the principal problems they experience?
   To married students: What are some important problems and adjustments you experience?

7. Is it "easier and better" if both the husband and wife are going to school or if only one is attending?

8. Should married students accept financial help from parents? Explain.

9. Is the social life of married students better or worse than that of single students while in college? Is it possible to participate in college social, extracurricular, and sports activities and still be married? Explain.

10. How do you feel about a married couple having children while still in college? Explain the reasons for your feelings.

MARRIAGE AND THE LAW

Marriage as a Civil Contract

All persons who get legally married enter into a civil contract. This means that their marriage is not just a personal affair. It is also of social concern; and each state has set up laws defining one's eligibility to marry and the procedure by which a contract may be established, as well as laws governing the maintenance of the contract once it is made.

© Rothco Original

Legal Requirements for Marriage

Since marital regulation is the responsibility of each state rather than of the local or federal government, marital laws differ. However, the following outline includes most of the major legal requirements regulating getting married (Rice, 1979a).

AGE Most commonly males and females may marry without parental consent at age 18. Puerto Rico and Mississippi require both the male and female to be 21. The most usual minimum ages for marriage with parental consent are 16 for females and males. However, Rhode Island permits marriage with parents' and the judge's consent at 12 for females and 14 for males. New Hampshire permits marriage with the parents' and the judge's consent at age 13 for females and 14 for males. A few other states permit marriage as young as 14 or 15 for males and females. The majority of states allow marriage at young ages under special circumstances such as pregnancy or childbirth. Parental consent does not seem to be much of a deterrent to early marriage. Some states do not require documentary proof of age, and in such cases lying is frequent. Youths often cross state lines to be married at younger ages than are required by their own state.

CONSANGUINITY The term **consanguinity** refers to a blood relationship or descent from a common ancestor. All states forbid consanguineous marriage with one's son, daughter, mother, father, grandmother, or grandfather, sister, brother, aunt, uncle, niece, or nephew. About half the states forbid marriages to first cousins. Some states also forbid marriages of second cousins or marriage to a grandniece or grandnephew.

AFFINITY   The term **affinity** refers to a relationship resulting from marriage. Some states forbid marriages to stepparents, stepchildren, mother-in-law, father-in-law, son-in-law, daughter-in-law, aunt- or uncle-in-law. Critics argue that the law has gone completely overboard in forbidding such marriages, since no biological harm can result from such a marriage.

MENTAL DEFICIENCY   Since some mentally handicapped persons are not able to meet the responsibilities of marriage, a number of states forbid their marrying. Other states have no acceptable definition of feeblemindedness so cannot prevent such marriages. In other instances, sterilization or placement in institutions prevents these persons from reproducing.

INSANITY   Most states prohibit marriages of the insane, the reason being that the insane person is incapable of giving his or her consent. Additionally, such a marriage could create severe problems for both the family and society.

PROCEDURAL REQUIREMENTS   Couples must have the legal permission of the state before marriage can take place. This is accomplished through issuance of the marriage license, but the couple must fulfill certain requirements before obtaining the license. About one-half of the states will issue the license the same day the couple applies, but the rest have a waiting period. This allows a "cooling off" period for couples who may be making hasty decisions. It is estimated that as many as 20 percent of couples never use the license or return to pick it up. The most common waiting period is three days; two states require two days, a few four or five days, and two require eight days. Six states also require a waiting period (from 24 hours to five days) after issuance of the license before the wedding can take place.

About three-fourths of the states require a blood test for syphilis. However, in most cases a more complete physical examination, which would reveal other sexually transmitted or infectious diseases or any other serious health problems such as tuberculosis or psychosis, is not required. Many examinations that are given are superficial and perfunctory unless couples are careful to get a complete physical checkup.

COMMON-LAW MARRIAGES   A **common-law marriage** is marriage by mutual consent, without a license, and without being solemnized by any particular form. Thirteen states plus the District of Columbia still permit common-law marriages if the couple can prove they have lived as husband and wife for seven or more years (Clark, 1980).

Generally, those states recognizing common-law marriages do so if three legal conditions are met. The couple must be legally marriageable. They must live together and hold themselves out to the community as husband and wife. They must intend to be legally married at some future date. In cases of dispute — usually involving the legitimacy of children or inheritance rights — it is sometimes difficult to prove intent to wed unless reliable witnesses are available or unless it is in writing. In frontier days, when a preacher or other person with legal authority to perform weddings was not readily available, common-law marriages fulfilled a real need while the couple were waiting for the "wedding" to take place. Today, however, such relationships create legal tangles and difficulties and are slowly being eliminated.

VOID OR VOIDABLE MARRIAGES   If the legal requirements have not been met, a marriage may be defined as void or voidable. A **void marriage** is never considered valid in the first place, so a court decree is not necessary to set it aside. Marriages may be considered void in cases of bigamy (where a prior marriage still exists), where the marriage partners are related to each other within certain prohibited degrees, or if either party is an adjudged lunatic or mental defective. Some states consider marriage to lunatics or mental defectives voidable but not void.

Voidable marriages require an action of annulment to set them aside, after legal action has been instituted by one party. Only one person (either the husband or the wife) needs to have the marriage voided, and action must be brought during the lifetime of the individuals. The most common grounds for voiding a marriage are if either party is under the age of consent, either party is physically incapable of having intercourse, either party consents to the marriage through fraud or duress, or either party lacks the understanding to consent to the marriage.

Fraud as grounds for annulment may include many different things such as concealment of a previous marriage or divorce, financial misrepresentation, concealment of pregnancy, misrepresentation as to chastity, concealment of disease, misrepresentation of character, refusal to have children, or breaking a promise to have a religious ceremony after a civil ceremony. The injured party must act within a reasonable period of time to have the marriage set aside. If the injured party voluntarily cohabits with the guilty spouse after the fraud is known, the suit may be barred.

MARRIAGE AS A PERSONAL CONTRACT

In recent years, personal marriage contracts have been used increasingly in addition to the usual legal agreements (Weitzman, 1981). Part of the impetus has come from the women's movement, whose members seek complete sex-role equality in marriage (Vander Mey and Roser, 1981). The feeling has been that if a couple draws up a written agreement prior to marriage or even after marriage, outlining husband and wife roles, relationships, and responsibilities, the marriage is more likely to be an egalitarian partnership, wives are less likely to be second-class citizens, to play only the traditional female role of housewife and mother, and to be expected to perform all of the menial chores. When a couple supports and signs such an agreement, husbands are more likely to share in these chores, to look upon their wives as equal partners, and to be relieved of the entire responsibility of earning family income. Advocates also point out that issues are clarified and conflicts are minimized. There are marriage counselors who use the contract principle of negotiation and reciprocity to assist couples in working out their problems.

The personal marriage contract is usually written by the individual couple, for themselves. Other parties are involved as witnesses only if the couple seeks legal sanction. In some cases, a contract may be only verbal.

Areas of Concern

The following categories of provisions in the contract are both salient and relevant. These categories are those most frequently found in contracts (Sussman, 1974):

Economic — could include a discussion of ownership, distribution, and management of property before and after marriage. It also specifies the contribution of each person to the total family income and support.

Children — would discuss the decision to have children, the responsibility for birth control, the attitude toward abortion, and the support and custody of the children in event of divorce.

Career and domicile — discusses the intention of the partners to maintain their individual careers outside the home, with equal importance attached to careers of the wife and husband in deciding on moving the domicile.

Relationships with others — would include a discussion of friendships, time devoted to individual interests and to each other.

Division of household responsibilities — would discuss how household responsibilities are divided.

Renewability, change, and termination of contract — discusses the provisions and means for periodic reevaluation and change of the contract as needed. Provisions for contract termination could be discussed, and agreements reached on arrangements in case of a divorce.

Other provisions — might include a discussion of the woman's name after marriage, religion, relations with in-laws or families of previous marriages, or items dealing with decision making.

The categories may be divided in other ways. Marriage imposes both rights and duties in four major areas—*sexuality, children, domestic and economic services*, and *property*. The rights and duties in these four areas could be spelled out in the personal contract.

A comprehensive marital contract may also include such things as a declaration of marital intent; the past history and present status of the two people; future expectations with respect to support, residence, religion, work, sex life, and children; present assets; the future ownership of property; and matters of estate. One forceful argument given in favor of writing such a comprehensive contract is that it may enable the partners themselves to make the rules before there is trouble.

Rationale

Another advantage of a personal contract prior to marriage is that it can serve as a springboard for fruitful discussions. The contract can stimulate couples to talk about everything with one another, to develop their decision-making capability, and to develop negotiating skills as well as personal and social identities. Couples can derive real security from knowing what to expect in the future.

One of the chief advantages of having a personal contract in marriage is that it can motivate the couple to reexamine and realign sex roles and to effect innovative changes in roles and behavior.

The contract can also become a communicative tool for dealing with situations. As problems emerge, contract making becomes part of the means of finding solutions, since the contract itself can specify negotiation procedures.

One disadvantage of the contract is that it is hard to legislate human behavior. Even provisions agreed upon may not be compatible with the real nature of the couple and so may be beyond their capability of keeping. A contract might be used to try to control or force behavior. One couple reports that after the contract was signed, it was hung on the refrigerator and the wife became a nag trying to enforce it (Author's counseling notes).

Another disadvantage is that it is hard to anticipate all marital problems and contingencies, and so the contract never covers everything. Furthermore, couples, relationships, and situations change over a period of time; the contract may become dated easily if not rewritten after every major change.

Whether the contract is a help or hindrance will depend on the maturity of the people writing and using it. The fearful, immature, selfish person may use the contract to protect his or her own ego, to satisfy neurotic needs, or to gain advantage. A completely irresponsible person may never abide by any agreement.

A contract that is interpreted literally according to the letter of the law may become as much a source of conflict as a disputed situation. Whenever the contract becomes more important than the relationship, the contract has ceased to serve a useful purpose.

At the present time, the personal benefits and social functions of a contract are a matter of long-term study. Whether personal contracts will enhance successful marriage and reduce divorce remains to be seen (Wells, 1976).

Couples need to recognize that any provision in the personal contract that attempts to change the marriage contract as defined by law is contrary to public policy and is unenforceable (Slovenko, 1983). The American Law Institute's *Restatement of the Law of Contracts* (sec. 587) gives these examples:

1. A and B who are about to marry agree to forgo sexual intercourse. The bargain is illegal.

2. In a state where the husband is entitled to determine the residence of a married couple, A and B who are about to marry agree that the wife shall not be required to leave the city where she lives. The bargain is illegal (Slovenko, 1983, p. 277).

In recent years, there has been a tendency to uphold personal marriage contracts relating to property provisions provided they are "fair and reasonable" and "not unconscionable" (Slovenko, 1983, p. 277). However, courts will not uphold provisions relating to life-style agreements, sexual performance, or other unenforceable orders. An important advantage of a personal marriage contract is its value as a consciousness-raising instrument, stimulating couples to think about many aspects of their relationship.

PREPARING FOR MARRIAGE

The Need for Preparation

It seems ironic that couples will spend dozens of hours over months and months planning a wedding, but spend little time preparing for their marriage. One young man revealed his priorities: "We aren't going to have much of a wedding, but we're going to have a wonderful marriage" (Author's counseling notes). This young man was acknowledging his order of priorities: marriage was more important than the wedding. Why spend thousands of dollars and many hours planning a wedding, only to have the marriage break up shortly after?

The basic theme here is that we can prepare ourselves for marriage in such a way that marital success is more certain. There are no guarantees, of course, but we feel that if we are going to be successful in a vocation, we need to prepare ourselves ahead of time. Why do we feel that vocational preparation is important and possible, but marital preparation is not? People aren't born with innate knowledge of how to be good husbands and wives and how to succeed in marriage. These things must be learned. But how?

We have mentioned elsewhere in this book, especially in Chapter 3, that much of what we learn about marriage and family living is acquired while we are growing up in our family of origin. This is the most important means of learning. But there are other, more formal ways of preparing for marriage. Here we will discuss premarital education, premarital assessment, and premarital counseling.

Premarital Education

Premarital education takes many forms. It may include an academic course at the college level in marriage and family living. It may include short courses offered by individual counselors or by community agencies and organizations: child and family service agencies, mental health clinics, community counseling centers, extension service groups, women's clubs, service organizations, churches, or schools. Usually, such courses extend over a period of weeks, with six weeks quite common. Classes are usually held once a week. Attendance is by enrollment, with a small registration fee required. Required reading and loan materials may be made available. Sessions may include lectures, audiovisuals, discussions, role-playing, and self-evaluation by taking tests and filling out inventories; these are often supplemented by premarital counseling opportunities.

Nickols, Fournier, and Nickols (1986) report on preparation for marriage workshops that have been offered for the past 10 years. The workshops combine the approaches of counseling and education and provide direction and opportunities for couples to discuss topics important to married persons and to learn and practice skills that enhance relationships.

These workshops include six, two-hour sessions, with a variety of procedures and materials used. Each topic is introduced in a "mini-lecture." Following each presentation are activities designed to teach interpersonal skills or to facilitate couple communication and clarification of information, attitudes, and opinions on the topics.

An important part of the workshop was administration of the PREPARE inventory, which provides an objective assessment of personal and relationship issues in 12 content areas related to marriage (Olson, Fournier, and Druckman, 1979; 1982). A more detailed discussion of the PREPARE inventory is found in the next section.

Individual counselors, community agencies, and organizations may offer classes and workshops in premarital education.

Other types of programs are sometimes offered to develop specific skills. Once such training program was designed to train married couples in listening skills (Garland, 1981). Although the program was used with married couples, a similar approach could be used with engaged couples.

Clergymen and churches often require couples to come for instruction before weddings are performed. Such programs are most often designed to interpret the religious meaning of marriage. The programs might be enhanced by including sexual, emotional, economic, social, and familial aspects of marriage also.

Physicians and nurses have done an excellent job of offering childbirth education classes to expectant mothers and their partners. Concerned community leaders might well consider doing as thorough a job on a regular basis by offering programs on preparation for marriage to couples.

Premarital Assessment and Counseling

Marriage preparation includes assessment; that is, an evaluation of the extent to which the couple is fit and ready for marriage. The most common form of assessment is health assessment: a physical examination and blood tests for sexually transmitted diseases. In addition to the usual blood test for syphilis, many couples are now including tests for AIDS, gonorrhea, and herpes. Certainly, if either partner has a sexually transmitted disease, both persons need to know about it.

Premarital assessment is broader than just health education. It may profitably include an overall assessment of a couple's total relationship. Such an assessment is difficult for the couple to do themselves because it's hard for them to be objective. A couple can go to a marriage counselor for the express purpose of premarital counseling that might explore important areas of the relationship; the purpose of the counseling would be to determine the level of adjustment and any possible unresolved difficulties that need attention. Premarital counseling also helps couples to solve difficulties that have been revealed. It may be used with individual couples or with couples in groups (Gleason and Prescott, 1977).

Since 1970, Los Angeles County in California has required premarital counseling when at least one partner is under 18 years of age (Shonick, 1975). The goal of the program has been an ambitious one: to increase the chances of success in teenage marriages. There are not enough data to determine if the goal has been accomplished, but the experiences so far have indicated that the concept is a good one and that "the entire marriage and family counseling profession should give much more thought than it already has regarding premarital counseling for all age groups" (Elkin, 1977, p. 443). One of the problems in the Los Angeles program is the lack of uniform requirement regarding the content and length of the program. Many clergy require only one counseling session in contrast to the three sessions offered by Community Health Service and other agencies (Shonick, 1975).

Buckner and Salts (1985) report on a fairly comprehensive premarital assessment program conducted by a marital and family therapy training center. The program includes an introductory session and six assessment sessions over a period of at least 12 weeks. In addition, a post-wedding check is done after the couple has been married three months. The main goal is to enable each partner to examine himself or herself, the partner, and their relationship in order to reevaluate and confirm that indeed each wants to marry the other. A second goal is to examine some of the frequent problem areas for couples. These areas include friends, family and in-laws, religion, values, recreation, finances, children, sex, and affection. A third goal of the program is to help the couple feel comfortable in seeking professional help in the future if they are having marital or family problems.

Initial assessment of the couple is enhanced with *Stuart's Premarital Counseling Inventory* (Stuart and Stuart, 1975). In the sessions, discussion between the couple and the therapist and use of dyadic structured and unstructured exercises provide information for assessment. Homework is assigned for each session. Couples and therapists report that partners get to know one another better, their expectations of the relationship are clarified, and the couples develop a better understanding of the dynamics of their relationship (Buckner and Salts, 1985).

Special mention needs to be made of a new instrument for predicting marital success. It is a premarital inventory called *PREPARE* (Olson, Fournier, and Druckman, 1979, 1982). PREPARE is a 125-item inventory designed to identify relationship strengths and work areas in 11 relationship areas: Realistic Expectations, Personality Issues, Communication, Conflict Resolution, Financial Management, Leisure Activities, Sexual Relationship, Children and

Marriage, Family and Friends, Equalitarian Roles, and Religious Orientation. Additionally, the instrument contains an *Idealistic Distortion Scale* (Fowers and Olson, 1986). For each scale, an Individual Score is provided for each spouse; furthermore, an individual's score on a category is revised based on that person's idealistic distortion score and the correlation of that scale with idealistic distortion. In addition, a *Positive Couple Agreement* (PCA) score is provided for each category; it measures the couple's consensus on issues in that area (Flowers and Olson, 1986).

Validity tests of PREPARE have shown that the inventory can be used to correctly predict happily married couples from those who will end up divorcing in 81 percent of the cases, happily from unhappily married in 79 percent, and happily married from those who cancel marriage in 78 percent of the cases. When both individual and positive couple agreement scores are used for predicting successful marriages, they can correctly discriminate satisfied from dissatisfied marriages, and satisfied marriages from those who cancel, in over 80 percent of the cases. Furthermore, these combined scores can correctly discriminate successful marriages from those that end in divorce in 91 percent of the cases (Fowers and Olson, 1986, p. 410, 411). This is really exciting news, since it gives counselors a very useful tool to use in premarital and marital counseling. Figure 10.1 shows the positive couple agreement

FIGURE 10.1 Happily Married versus Divorced/Separated: Positive Couple Agreement (PCA) Scores on PREPARE Categories.

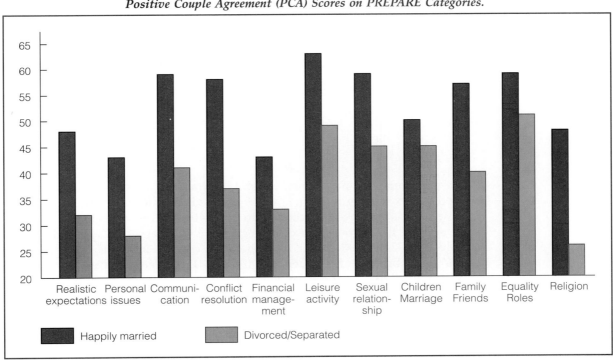

From Fowers, B. J. and Olson, D. H. (1986). Predicting marital success with PREPARE: A predictive validity study. *Journal of Marital and Family Therapy, 12,* (4), 409.

ASSESSMENT
Assessment Instruments

Instead of offering an assessment instrument in this chapter, the following is a partial list of assessment instruments that counselors and their clients might use in premarital assessment and counseling. Readers who go for premarital counseling may want to ask their counselors if they can take any of the following tests as an aid to evaluation.

Dyadic Adjustment Scale. Spanier, G. B. (1976). Found in Spanier, G. B. (1976). Measuring dyadic adjustment: New scales for assessing the quality of marriage and similar dyads. *Journal of Marriage and the Family, 38,* 15–28.

Marriage Role Expectation Inventory. Dunn, M. S. (1979). Saluda, NC: Family Life Publications, Inc., P.O. Box 427, Saluda, NC 28773.

Pre-marital Counseling Inventory. Stuart, R. B., and Stuart, F. (1975). Champaign, IL: Research Press.

PREPARE. Olson, D. H., Fournier, D. G., and Druckman, J. M. (1979, 1982). *PREPARE-ENRICH Counselor's Manual* (rev. ed.). Available from P.O. Box 1363, Stillwater, OK 74076.

A Religious Attitudes Inventory. Crane, W. E., and Coffer, J. H., Jr. (1964). Saluda, NC: Family Life Publications, Inc., P.O. Box 427, Saluda, NC 28773.

Sex Knowledge Inventory. McHugh, G. (1979). Saluda, NC: Family Life Publications, Inc., P.O. Box 427, Saluda, NC 28773.

A Sex Attitude Survey and Profile. McHugh, G., and McHugh, T. G. (1976). Saluda, NC: Family Life Publications, Inc., P.O. Box 427, Saluda, NC 28773.

(PCA) scores of happily married versus divorced or separated couples on various PREPARE categories.

NONMARITAL COHABITATION

Percentages

The government now defines **cohabitation** as two unrelated adults of the opposite sex sharing the same living quarters in which there is no other adult present (Spanier, 1983). According to this definition, referred to as **POSSLQ** (Persons of the Opposite Sex Sharing Living Quarters) (S. Davidson, 1983), there were 2,334,000 unmarried cohabiting couples in the United States in 1987 (U.S. Bureau of the Census, 1989), a 47 percent increase since 1980. Thirty-one percent of these couples had some children in the household under 15 years of age. A little over half (56 percent) had never been married; about a third had been divorced, and a few (11 percent) were married to someone else or widowed. Twenty-three percent of all the householders were under 25 years of age. Sixty-one percent were 25-44 years old. Eleven percent were age 45-64. Six percent were 65 years old or older.

These figures tell us the total number of couples cohabiting and their marital status prior to living together, but the figures do not indicate what percentage

Nonmarital cohabitation has increased rapidly in the 1980s, reflecting changes in social norms. One factor associated with the increase in cohabitation may be the increase in the average age at first marriage.

of couples who marry have lived together beforehand. A study of marriage license applications in Lane County, Oregon, in 1980 revealed that 53 percent of all applicants gave identical home addresses and were presumed to have been cohabiting prior to marriage (Gwartney-Gibbs, 1986). There is no evidence that these figures are higher than for the nation as a whole, since the incidence of cohabitation has increased similarly across the nation (Spanier, 1983).

Studies of the incidence of cohabitation among college populations indicate that about 25 percent of students live with a dating partner at some point in their college career (Macklin, 1978); Risman, Hill, Rubin, and Peplau, 1981). However, the rates vary depending upon the type of school, housing, parietal policies, the sex composition and ratio of the student body, as well as the researchers' sample and definition of cohabitation (Glick and Spanier, 1980).

Reasons for the Increase

The increase in nonmarital cohabitation reflects widespread changes in social norms regarding the acceptability of sexual relations prior to marriage (Tanfer and Horn, 1985). The new sexual freedom has partly eliminated the pressure

Tanfer (1987) conducted a study of heterosexual cohabitation among a national sample of women 20–29 years old to determine how these women compared with those who did not cohabit. The findings may be summarized as follows:

Women who cohabit are more likely to be older than noncohabiters.

White women are nearly one and one-half times more likely than black women to cohabit. Part of the reason is the relative scarcity of black men in the eligibility pool.

Cohabiters tend to be less educated and less likely to be employed than noncohabiters.

Women whose mothers have not completed high school are also somewhat more likely to be cohabiters.

Cohabiters tend to be concentrated in large metropolitan areas and are more likely to be living in the West than are women who have not cohabited. Women in the West are one-third more likely to cohabit than are women in the rest of the country.

Cohabiters have lower rates of church attendance and higher percentages of them have no religious affiliation (Newcomb and Bentler, 1980).

Women who grew up in single-parent families are about one-third more likely to cohabit than are women who grew up in intact families.

Cohabiters have intercourse at a relatively younger age; and because cohabiters are more likely to have had a pregnancy, early marriage to legitimize the pending birth is more common among cohabiters than noncohabiters.

Virtually all cohabiting women are sexually active and have intercourse more frequently than women who have never cohabited. Nearly one-half reported having intercourse more than once a week on average, compared with one-fourth of never-cohabiters.

Cohabiters use contraceptives less frequently than noncohabiters, partly because some want to have a child.

One-half of the cohabiters, compared with less than one-fourth of noncohabiters, have ever been pregnant. Furthermore, the proportion of unwed mothers among cohabiters is two and one-half times larger than among never-cohabiters.

The odds of having ever cohabited are about 85 percent higher among women who ever had a birth than they are among nulliparous women (those who have never had a child). Among nonvirgins, the probability of lifetime cohabitation is about 60 percent higher for multiparous women (those who have had multiple births) than among nulliparous women.

Cohabiters are more likely than noncohabiters to engage in unconventional behavior and to espouse more liberal attitudes. "Liberated" women appear to be more disposed toward cohabitation. Liberated women are more likely to perceive themselves as liberated from traditional sex-role characteristics and are more likely than noncohabiting women to describe themselves as extroverted, assertive, and independent (Newcomb and Bentler, 1980; Macklin, 1978).

A significantly larger proportion of cohabiters than noncohabiters want to get married. Furthermore, cohabiters are no more likely than noncohabiters to perceive their singleness as permanent. In other words, cohabiting women are more likely to be involuntary and temporary singles than are their counterparts who never marry.

These comparisons suggest that *cohabitation is an advanced stage of courtship, rather than a substitute for marriage. There is no evidence of rejection of marriage nor of the likelihood of choosing singlehood as a permanent way of life.*

From Tanfer, K. (1987). Patterns of premarital cohabitation among never-married women in the United States. *Journal of Marriage and the Family, 49*, 483–497. Copyright © 1987 by the National Council on Family Relations. Reprinted by permission.

to marry in order to find sexual fulfillment (Cargan and Melko, 1982). The increased availability and efficiency of contraceptives have made it more possible to have sexual relations without the risk of pregnancy.

The general population has become more accepting of those who do cohabit, so cohabitors find greater acceptance among family members, peers, and other community members. Changing attitudes toward women — their roles and sexuality — also permit them to cohabit outside of marriage.

The high divorce rate has resulted in a growing pool of previously married adults who have the option of living with someone as an unmarried couple or remarrying. The period of time between divorce and remarriage is also increasing, adding to the pool of previously marrieds (Spanier, 1983). Another factor associated with the increase in cohabitation may be the increase in the average age at first marriage. Thus, unmarried cohabitation may be seen as a contemporary extension of the courtship process, contributing to the postponement of marriage itself.

Some persons who cohabit have become disenchanted with traditional courtship and the superficiality of the dating game. Some are searching for more intimate, meaningful relations with a high degree of emotional involvement. The human need for love and affection and the need to belong to someone who cares is an especially powerful need in an impersonal society.

Some persons have become doubtful or even cynical about traditional marriage. The majority still approve of marriage and want to be married, but increasing divorce rates and the unhappiness of many friends' marriages have made some people more cautious about entering such relationships unprepared and uninformed. Many desire to experiment with living with someone before making more permanent commitments. Others feel that cohabitation offers the best means of personal preparation and growth; still others want to test their compatibility with a particular person. Some feel that nonmarried cohabitation is far more enjoyable and meaningful than steady dating and is less risky than marriage. Others look upon it as a permanent substitute for legal marriage.

Breaking up can be painful and traumatic, but it is less devastating than legal divorce. For the short term at least, cohabitation appears to be attractive to a good many persons and carries a minimum of risk and responsibility (Rice, 1983).

Patterns of Relationships

One of the most important considerations is what the relationships mean to the couple involved. Actually, there is no single pattern, no set meaning that can be applied to cohabiters. Any one relationship may fall along a continuum from friendship to a substitute for marriage. For purposes of analysis, the relationships may be grouped into five basic types (Rice, 1983):

Utilitarian arrangements

Intimate involvement with emotional commitment

A trial marriage

Prelude to marriage

An alternative to marriage

A good number of cohabiting adults do so for utilitiarian reasons. They save money by sharing living quarters and expenses. They are able to share the work of housekeeping, laundry, and general maintenance. Some adults don't want to get married because they will lose some financial benefits: alimony, welfare, or pension payments. In such cases, they may or may not have an intimate relationship. They may be lovers or only friends.

Intimate Involvement with Emotional Commitment

This group includes those who love one another, want to have sex together, and want to be together in a monogamous relationship. They usually have a strong commitment to one another, but there are no plans for marriage. They do not consider themselves married and are content to wait and see what happens. *Risman and colleagues' (1981) study of cohabitation in college found no statistically significant association between cohabitation and the type of relation that eventually evolved (that is, whether the couple married or not).* Cohabiting couples were not less likely to have married or more likely to have broken up by the end of the two-year study in comparison to couples that had not cohabited.

A Trial Marriage

Other adults love one another, but want to live together as a test of their compatibility to decide "if they are meant for each other" and if they want to get married. The arrangement is considered "the little marriage to see if a big marriage will last."

Prelude to Marriage

A number of adults move in together before they get married. They have already committed themselves to marriage and see no reason to be apart in the meantime.

An Alternative to Marriage

Those in this category are cohabiting not as a prelude to marriage, but as a substitute for it. This includes those who are married to someone else and separated but not divorced, who have been unhappily married and have become very skeptical about the viability of legal marriage. Others have seen their friends' unhappy marriages and have concluded that legal marriage is not for them or that it is destructive to real love and intimacy. Those with this philosophy can offer numerous and strong legal or ideological arguments why they do not believe in marriage.

In order to avoid misunderstanding, those contemplating cohabitation would be wise to discuss their feelings ahead of time to ascertain the meaning associated with the decision to live together. If one considers cohabitation paramount to engagement and the other is doing it without love and commitment, hard feelings and hurts result.

Intimacy, Communication

One of the motives of some cohabiting couples is to find a deeper level of intimacy than is possible in dating relationships (Perlman and Abramson, 1982). Generally speaking, in comparison to dating couples, cohabiters do report greater intimacy. Not surprisingly, they see each other more often, have sexual intercourse more often, see their relationship as closer and indicate greater love for each other as measured by the Rubin (1970; 1973) Love Scale. Risman et al. (1981) reported cohabiters self-disclosed more to their partner and received more self-disclosure. Thus, *cohabiters were more intimate than dating couples* not only in terms of frequency of interaction and sex, but in other ways as well. Table 10.1 shows the results.

TABLE 10.1 *COMPARISON OF INTIMACY—COHABITERS
AND COUPLES GOING TOGETHER*

	WOMEN'S RESPONSES		MEN'S RESPONSES	
	Going Together	Living Together	Going Together	Living Together
Interaction (percent seeing partner daily)	52.6	100.0	48.9	100.0
Frequency of intercourse (percent 6+ times/week)	11.8	37.5	11.6	43.7
Closeness (means) (9-point scale)	7.5	8.4	7.5	8.3
Love scale (means) (9 items, 9 maximum)	7.0	7.5	6.9	7.4
Self-disclosure given (17 items; 34 maximum)	25.0	28.3	24.7	27.8
Self-disclosure received (17 items; 34 maximum)	24.6	27.6	24.2	27.2

From Risman, B. J., Hill, C. T., Rubin, Z., and Peplau, L. A. (1981). Living together in college: Implications for courtship. *Journal of Marriage and the Family, 43,* 77–83. Copyright © 1981 by the National Council on Family Relations.

Reactions to Cohabitation

Generally speaking, *the majority of cohabiting couples report no regret at having cohabited.* Among those who later married, Watson (1983) reported that only 9 percent of the women and 4 percent of the men expressed regrets. The proportion of dissatisfied couples is higher for those who do not marry. A few are devastated by relationships that fail. Some are very unhappy living together and experience tension and conflict. Yllo and Straus (1981) found a much higher rate of violence among cohabiting couples than among married couples, especially among the young.

Some people are hurt, either because the relationship didn't work out or because they expected that it would result in marriage and it did not. Several studies have shown that men and women have somewhat different reasons for cohabitation. For many males, cohabitation is no different from dating (Abernathy, 1981). Males most often cite their need for sexual gratification as the reason, whereas females state that marriage is their most important motive (Newcomb, 1979). When the relationship doesn't lead to marriage, some women feel used and exploited. The men expect them to pay half the expenses, do many of the household chores, and provide regular sexual privileges without a commitment to marry. As a result, many cohabiting females develop negative views of marriage and the role of the husband. They begin to see themselves as a source of sex, not as a source of affection. Then there is anxiety about pregnancy, in spite of contraception. If pregnancy occurs, some say they will marry, yet marriage because of pregnancy is one of the worst motives in relation to marital success. *All that can be said with*

CLASSROOM FORUM
Differences Between Living Together and Marriage

E. Mansell Pattison (1982), professor of psychiatry at the Medical College of Georgia, organized a marital therapy group for six young couples whose marital problems began when they got married, even though each couple had lived happily together for several years before marriage. Involved was a paradox: a happy union before marriage and an unhappy union as soon as they married. What had happened? What change had occurred when no overt change had taken place in their lives except a legalizing ceremony?

The following are personal accounts of the couples.

Joe: She had her job and I had mine. We got along swell. It was like magic. The day after we got married, it all fell apart.

Jane: Sex was great. But as soon as we got married, he couldn't and I didn't want to.

Question: Did you emotionally share your lives together?

Answers: *Peter*: Yes, in a superficial sort of way. We enjoyed our company together. *Pat*: Sure we had a lot of fun together.

Question: Did you really get to know each other living together?

Answers: *Alice*: I knew what he thought, and there was the excitement of intellectual exploration. But those were his thoughts. I didn't have to take them seriously. *Art*: I knew what she thought. But I really didn't know the value imperatives that lay behind her thinking.

Question: Did you trust each other while living together?

Answers: *Al*: Well, yes, but trust is a function of time. You can't develop deep trust without the passage of many events in a relationship. *Amy*: Sure you trust each other, but without a permanent commitment you only trust for the moment, you can't really count on each other.

Question: What changed in your relationship when you got married?

Answers: *Arthur*: I had to start being honest with her about myself. *Sarah*: We had to start making real decisions about money, careers, where we lived, what we did. *Zeke*: Living together was like time out. When we got married, it was like the clock started running. This was real life in real time. *Susan*: We discovered the real persons we were. We couldn't stand it. We just started to really get to know each other. *Frank*: I suddenly had relatives. I had to take them seriously. There were implicit responsibilities and expectations. *June*: I thought, now I could start *demanding* that he change, and I found he could now *refuse* to change. *George*: There was

certainty now is that cohabitation has been harmful to some and helpful to others. The effect depends upon the individuals involved, on how they feel, and on what happens.

Effect on Dating and Courtship Patterns

There is some evidence that living together has an influence on dating and courtship patterns. In their study of cohabitation in college, Risman et al. (1981) found that living together was a factor in the transition to marry for those who did marry. Those who had lived together before marriage had a shorter interval between the time of first dating and the time of marriage. Those who had lived together said they had been under a great deal of pressure from parents either to marry or to end the cohabiting relationship. Either cohabitation sped up the need to make a commitment decision, or couples who decided to live

---

CLASSROOM FORUM
(continued)

the expectation of success. We couldn't just play around. We each had serious expectations of what each would do that we were supposed to live up to. *Marie:* We didn't have separate resources anymore. It wasn't just sharing; now it was a question of what was fair and *we couldn't agree on the rules. Albert:* When you live together, your friends and social relations sort of let you go. When you get married people expect you to behave like married people.

Question: Did living together prepare you for marriage.

Answers: Alan: No! It doesn't prepare you for anything. *Betty:* I thought so, until I got married. I had magical fantasies about marriage, only reinforced by living together. But there was no magic in marriage—just a lot of hard work.

Question: Overall what is the basic difference between living together and being married?

Answers: John: Having a real relationship, not a phony one. *Mary:* Working out a true partnership of mutual understanding. *Eric:* Having someone who accepts you for what you are, without pretense. *Joyce:* Sitting in the kitchen on Saturday morning—slightly unkempt, and burping—and knowing that he loves you sitting there.

Excerpts: Patterson, E. M. (1982). Living together: A poor substitute for marriage. *Medical aspects of human sexuality, 16,* 71–91. Reprinted with permission from Medical Aspects of Human Sexuality © Cahners' Publishing Company. Published May 1982. All rights reserved.

QUESTIONS FOR CLASS DISCUSSION

1. What are the most important differences between nonmarital cohabitation and marriage as revealed by these couples?

2. For those of you who cohabited before marriage: How do these observations compare to your own experiences?

3. Is it possible to sort out a compatible mate through cohabitation? If so, what would have to be accomplished?

4. Are there are disadvantages to cohabitation that might affect marriage negatively?

5. How do you feel about cohabiting before marriage? Explain your feelings and why you feel that way.

together had already made the decision to marry. Cohabiting couples who later married were less likely to take a honeymoon and were likely to have fewer wedding guests. Overall, those who cohabited had less elaborate marital rituals.

Effect on Marriage

One of the important questions we can ask is, To what extent has cohabitation resulted in greater satisfaction in subsequent marriage? Actually, there is no evidence that premarital cohabitation weeds out incompatible couples and prepares people for successful marriage (Macklin, 1983). Newcomb and Bentler (1980) conducted a longitudinal study examining the effects of premarital cohabitation on subsequent marital stability. After four years, they found no significant difference in marital stability between couples who had previously cohabited and those who did not. Interestingly, cohabiters who divorced initially had a slightly higher level of marital adjustment or fewer problems in their marriage than couples who did not cohabit before marrying and divorcing. Among all who continued to be married in the fourth year, the level of marital adjustment of the cohabiters was lower than that for noncohabiters, though not significantly. This study was limited; it included only 77 couples and the sample was drawn from only one geographic area (California). It would be unwise, therefore, to conclude from it that cohabitation has no effect on subsequent marriage.

In fact, there is some evidence to suggest that there may be differences between cohabiters and noncohabiters, though this evidence is indirect and is not always consistent. Moeller and Sherlock (1981) studied 139 recently married, college matriculating young adults and found that the marriages of previous cohabiters were more egalitarian and less husband-dominated, but there were no significant differences in the levels of conflict between the two groups. Similarly, Markowski and Johnston (1980) found some differences in temperament between those who had cohabited and those who had not, but they concluded that cohabitation "did not seem to greatly benefit nor harm the marriage relationship" (p. 125).

Clatworthy and Scheid (1977) felt cohabitation was a negative factor in preparing people for marriage. "Premarital cohabiters . . . were less likely to acquiesce in disagreement; disagree more often in such things as finances, household duties, and recreation; were less dependent on their spouses; considered their marriages a less intrinsic part of their lives; had broken up more often; and a higher percentage had sought marriage counseling" (cited in Macklin, 1978, p. 231). Premarital cohabitation was no guarantee of selecting a more congenial partner nor of a better marriage.

The results seem to be affected partially by how long people have been married at the time of the evaluation. Most research indicates that a period of disillusionment in relation to marriage occurs after the initial glow and excitement have worn off and couples have settled down to daily living. Presumably, the longer couples have lived together before marriage, the earlier in the marriage relationship the period of disillusionment sets in. Thus, DeMaris and Leslie (1984) studied couples in the second year of marriage and Watson (1983) evaluated them in the first year of marriage. Comparisons of married couples who had cohabited with those who had not found that cohabiters scored significantly lower in marital communication, consensus, and satisfaction. However, the researchers could not establish with clear cause and effect that cohabitation caused lower marital quality. There were too many other variables that might have influenced results. In fact, Watson and DeMeo (1987) did a follow up in the fourth year of their marriages of couples who had earlier taken part in the original studies of Watson and found that the premarital relationships of the couples, whether of cohabitation or traditional courtship, did not appear to have had a long-term effect on the marital adjustment of intact couples. Watson explained that his first study measured the relationship of couples who had been married for one year. At that time, the noncohabiting couples had entered marriage more slowly; that fact and the newness of the experience of living together had led them to a more positive evaluation and higher adjustment scores than those of cohabiters. Because of the small numbers of subjects, Watson and DeMeo (1987) were not able to determine the effects of cohabitation or noncohabitation on divorce, but what they did find was that after four years of marriage, marital adjustment was no longer affected by the living arrangement in the months leading up to marriage. Rather, the relationship the couple had subsequently built with one another was the important thing.

One large-scale study conducted among Canadians needs to be mentioned. White (1987) investigated data from a probability sample of 10,472 ever-married Canadians and found that premarital cohabitation had a positive effect on staying married. This positive effect remained when length of marriage and age at marriage were controlled. The odds for staying married were much better for cohabiters than noncohabiters. This study used a large sample of Canadians; previous studies in the United States used much smaller, non-representative samples from specific regions. *Until more representative data are available, we cannot conclude at this time that nonmarital cohabitation increases or decreases subsequent marital satisfaction and stability.*

Effect on Children

There are practically no data available on the effects of nonmarital cohabitation on children. The latest census report shows that 31 percent of cohabitors had children under 15 years of age in the household (U.S. Bureau of the Census, 1987a). The effect on them will depend a great deal on the quality and harmony of the cohabiting relationship — and on the quality of the relationship that nonparent as well as parent cohabiters establish with the children. Children need love, affection, security, stability, and guidance in their lives. If the cohabiting relationship supplies these needs, children will likely benefit. If the relationship does not meet children's needs, they will be affected negatively. This is one reason why cohabiters who are parents need to choose partners very carefully. What effect will their live-in partner have on the children involved? The most difficult adjustment remarried couples make is in establishing harmonious relationships with children of previous marriages (F. P. Rice, 1978b). It is assumed this will also be true of cohabiting couples.

Children also need stability in their lives. What will be the effect on them of developing attachment to a nonparent cohabiter only to have that person leave after a while? And certainly a series of cohabiting experiences would create insecurity in the lives of children.

Rites of passage are rites or ceremonies by which people pass from one social status to another. In our culture, the rites of passage from a single to a married status include:

- Engagement
- Prenuptial celebrations, including a possible engagement party, bridal shower, bachelor's party, and rehearsal dinner.
- Wedding ceremony
- Wedding reception
- Honeymoon

Engagement

An engagement to be married is an intermediate stage between courtship and marriage at which time a couple announces the intention to marry. Engagement may be informal, at least for a while, during which time the two people have an understanding to marry. Marriage is still too far off to make a formal announcement, or the couple wants a further testing of their relationship. Since many engagements are broken, a couple is probably wise to be very certain before formalizing an announcement. Some couples move from informal engagement to marriage without ever formalizing the engagement period at all.

A formal engagement announcement is usually made in the newspaper. An engagement party or dinner is another formal way of making the announcement and introducing the couple to friends and family. It serves notice to all of the couple's intention to marry and gives everyone an opportunity to adjust to the idea.

The couple should have become well acquainted with one another's immediate family (especially parents) long before becoming engaged, since this is an important part of the mate selection process. See Chapter 8. However, the couple may not have met some family members, and so an engagement get-together becomes a good opportunity for introductions. Without such an occasion, couples may want to visit relatives or have them come to visit in order to get acquainted. The couple will be wise to build friendly relationships with as many family members as possible, since a friendly network of social support after marriage can become a positive factor in their relationship.

Engagement also becomes a final testing of compatibility and an opportunity to make additional adjustments. Some problems, such as planning finances or making housing arrangements, are difficult to resolve unless a date has been set for the wedding. One woman commented:

> Sam owns a lot of property. I didn't feel free to bring up anything about ownership until after we were engaged. As it happens, he's going to put my name on all of it too. But I can see how the whole subject could have caused a lot of problems. (Author's counseling notes)

If any problems that have arisen in the couple's relationship have not been worked out before engagement, this period allows an additional opportunity

An engagement to marry may be informal, marked only by the couple's understanding to marry. A more formal announcement, accompanied by the traditional engagement ring may provide a further testing of the relationship, giving everyone an opportunity to adjust to the idea.

PERSPECTIVE
When Are Engagements Broken?

At one time, engagements were almost never broken. Engagement represented an irrevocable promise to marry. By the middle of the twentieth century, however, broken engagements were common. In a study of 1,000 couples in 1953, Burgess and Wallin (1953) found that between one-third and one-half of the individuals had been engaged more than once.

Today, engagements are more of a testing period than an irrevocable commitment to marry, and so are often broken. In a study of 810 college students who had broken one or more engagements, the following reasons were given for broken engagements (Landis and Landis, 1977).

Cause of Breakup	Men N=240	Women N=570
Parents	11.0%	12.0%
Mutual loss of interest	8.0	8.0
Partner lost interest	13.0	10.0
I lost interest	18.0	22.0
Separation	19.0	19.0
Contrasts in background	11.0	14.0
Incompatibility	10.0	15.0
I was not ready for marriage	18.0	25.0
Partner was not ready for marriage	7.0	18.0

From Landis, J. T., and Landis, M.G. (1977). *Building a successful marriage* (7th ed.). Englewood Cliffs, NJ: Prentice-Hall. Reprinted by permission.

for testing. The more things are worked out prior to marriage, the fewer adjustments and surprises arise afterwards.

The engagement period affords a time for planning the wedding and the honeymoon. Dates must be set. Arrangements are made with whomever is officiating at the wedding. Facilities for the wedding, rehearsal dinner, and reception are reserved. Booking the honeymoon may have to take place far in advance. Dozens of decisions regarding the size and type of wedding need to be made. Members of the wedding party need to be invited. Wedding invitations are sent out. Wedding planning ordinarily takes much longer and more effort than people anticipate.

The engagement period also involves preparation for marriage itself. A most important part of this, but one often neglected, is premarital education. Premarital assessment and counseling may also be employed. Marriage preparation also involves applying for a marriage license and a physical examination and blood tests for sexually transmitted diseases. The couple may want to include a blood test for AIDS if they have risked exposure.

Bridal Showers and Bachelor Binges

The bridal shower has come to be regarded as an American rite of passage that emphasizes the transition from single to married (Casparis, 1979). It has several functions. It allows some participation of persons who might otherwise not be able to attend the wedding. It enables friends to participate in the passage of the bride from singlehood to married life. Most friends and relatives are merely observers at the wedding. They can be participants in the shower,

The bridal shower is one of the rites of passage that emphasizes the transition from single to married life.

since it is they, not the mother and the bride, who give the shower. The traditional gift giving, gender segregation, and jokes at the expense of the bride, are ritual devices to reinforce female solidarity and express ambivalent feelings associated with the passage from single to married life (Berardo and Vera, 1981).

Showers serve a traditional function. The emphasis on gifts that contribute to the couple's outfitting their new home makes showers comparable to other customs associated with weddings, such as the European tradition of hope chests (Casparis, 1979).

The traditional bachelor's party becomes a rite of passage to lament the groom's giving up bachelorhood as he makes the transition to married life. The party is also a rite of initiation that serves to give last-minute advice to the marital novice. The rite is also an "ordeal" during which the guest of honor has to put up with a number of jokes at his expense (Berardo and Vera, 1981).

Some parties serve a positive function. They are an opportunity for friends to wish their buddy well as he moves from the status of eligible bachelor to husband. They are losing a friend whom they could call on without prior notice. The party helps all deal with ambivalent feelings. The festive atmosphere and lighthearted and warm mood that prevails emphasizes the support and friendship among participants. Most grooms feel that the event has been successful and a lot of fun (Berardo and Vera, 1981).

The Wedding as a Religious and Civil Rite

Eighty percent of all persons who marry are married by the clergy (Knox, 1985). This means that the majority of marriages are performed under the auspices of a religious group and that the wedding itself is a sacred rite. The Roman Catholic church considers marriage a sacrament, with special graces bestowed by God through the church to the couple. The marriage bond is considered sacred and indissoluble. Both Judaism and Protestantism consider marriage a covenant of divine significance, sanctified by God, and contracted between the spouses and the religious group with God as the unseen partner. While lifelong marriage is considered ideal, divorce and remarriage are allowed under certain circumstances.

Any religious rite is rich in meaning and symbolism (Chesser, 1980). While the rites vary among different religious groups, there are certain things they all have in common. Four parties are represented in each of the services: the *couple, the religious group* (clergy), the *state* (witnesses), and the *parents* (usually through the father). Each party to the marriage rite covenants (enters into an agreement) with the other parties in fulfilling his or her obligations so that the marriage will be blessed "according to the ordinances of God and the laws of the state." The denomination, through the clergy, pledges God's grace, love, and blessing. The man and woman make vows to one another "in the presence of God and these witnesses." The state grants the marriage license once the law has been fulfilled (the witnesses are present to see that the law is obeyed). The parents (through the father) pledge to give up their daughter to her new husband, no longer coming between the bride and groom. After giving the bride away, the father sits down beside his wife, leaving the couple standing together.

כשושנה בין החוחים

While practices vary among different religious groups, all have certain things in common. Four parties are normally represented in the religious wedding rites: the couple, the religious group, the state (witnesses), and the family.

In this rite, the couple must indicate their complete willingness to be married; they must make certain pledges to one another; they indicate to the clergy their agreement to abide by divine ordinance and civil law. They join hands together as a symbol of their new union. Rings are a sign of eternity (having neither beginning nor end) and so symbolize the eternal nature of love. They are also a sign, seal, and reminder of the vows taken. The license is signed and witnessed as evidence that state law has been fulfilled.

In the traditional Jewish wedding, the Ketubah, or marriage contract, is read aloud and handed to the bride. Many modern-day-Jewish young people object to the traditional words of the Ketubah because they reflect stereotyped sex roles of the husband and wife. As a general rule, Reform rabbis do not use the traditional Ketubah. In Reform services, more contemporary versions may be written. In these new versions both the bride and groom make the same promises with traditional Jewish husband and wife roles eliminated.

Since Vatican II, Catholic couples are also freer to rethink the content of their wedding service. The modern Protestant couple may also want to rethink the vows they make to one another. The authors of the book *Write Your Own Wedding* (Brill, Halpin, and Genne, 1973) suggest that the couple consult their priest, minister, or rabbi to discuss the wedding. Different religious groups have different rules and customs regarding weddings, but more and more clergy of all faiths are giving each couple an opportunity to share in some of the decisions that are made and even to help design their own individual service if they so desire (Rice, 1979a).

Honeymoons

In one study, 60 percent of couples who lived together before marriage took a honeymoon, whereas more than 95 percent of couples who had not lived together took a honeymoon (Risman, Hill, Rubin, and Peplau, 1981). The honeymoon can serve some useful personal and social functions. The couple has been so caught up in a whirlwind of activities that they have not had time to be alone. They may be physically and emotionally exhausted. The honeymoon best serves its functions when it affords privacy and an opportunity for rest and relaxation together. It can be a wonderful experience. Sometimes it's exasperating. One husband commented: "My bride was so exhausted that she became sick for most of our honeymoon. I spent most of my time just taking care of her" (Author's counseling notes). A bride recalls: "We spent most of our honeymoon at his parents' house. What a let-down. There was no privacy, and no opportunity just to be alone" (Author's counseling notes). Another bride remarked: "We went camping on our honeymoon. It rained the whole week. We had a miserable time. I don't know why he insisted on playing Daniel Boone. I was glad to get home" (Author's counseling notes).

Couples need to plan jointly and make careful preparations ahead of time. Some couples prefer just spending time together in their new home.

SUMMARY

1. The transition from singlehood to marriage ordinarily takes place over several years. The transition is more successful if couples are ready for marriage.

2. Getting married involves entering into a civil contract. Each state has its own laws regarding marriage. Laws include age requirements, restrictions on consanguinity and affinity, on marrying mental defectives and insane persons. Procedural requirements include obtaining a marriage license and required blood tests and observing a waiting period.

3. Only 13 states and the District of Columbia permit common-law marriages.

4. Increasing numbers of couples are drawing up personal contracts that outline agreements in relationship to economics; children; careers and domicile; relationships with others; division of household responsibility; provisions for renewing, changing, or terminating the contract; and other potential conflicts.

5. A personal contract can serve as a springboard for discussion, motivate couples to reexamine and realign sex roles, and become a communicative tool.

6. A personal contract has a number of disadvantages. It's hard to legislate human behavior; it's hard to anticipate all situations and problems ahead of time. A contract's value depends partially on the maturity of the people using it. If interpreted literally, it can become a source of conflict itself.

7. Civil law says that it is unlawful to include provisions in the personal contract that are contrary to public law or that are unenforceable.

8. Couples need to prepare for marriage through marriage education, assessment, and premarital counseling.

9. A number of instruments, usually inventories, have been developed to help couples assess their relationship. One of the most valid is PREPARE.

10. Nonmarital cohabitation has increased 47 percent from 1980 to 1987. Thirty-one percent of cohabiters have children under 15 years of age in their household. A little over half have never been married. The largest group according to age is 25–44-years old, although 23 percent of cohabiters are under 23 years of age.

11. The reasons for the increase include wider acceptability of premarital sexual relations; increase of availability and efficiency of contraceptives; more accepting attitudes; changing attitudes toward women; the high divorce rate; increase in average age at marriage; and disenchantment with traditional courtship, dating, and traditional marriage. Some couples do not cohabit for a variety of reasons.

12. The relationship may mean different things to different persons. A relationship may be a utilitarian arrangement, an intimate involvement with emotional commitment, a trial marriage, a prelude to marriage, or an alternative to marriage.

13. Generally speaking, cohabiters report deeper intimacy and better communication than do dating couples.

14. Cohabitation seems to be harmful to some persons, helpful to others.

15. Cohabitation tends to speed up the time between first dating and time of marriage. Cohabiters also tend to follow less elaborate marital rituals than do those who have not cohabited before marriage.

16. At the present time, we cannot conclude that nonmarital cohabitation increases or decreases subsequent marital satisfaction and stability.

17. The effect of marital cohabitation on children will depend upon the quality and stability of the relationship and the extent to which it meets children's needs.

18. Engagement is an intermediate stage between courtship and marriage. It serves as an announcement of the couple's intention to marry. It is also a period of final testing of compatibility. It can be a time for planning the wedding and honeymoon.

19. The wedding is both a religious and civil rite, rich in meaning and significance. Four parties are often represented in the service: the couple, the religious group, the state, and the parents. Many couples prefer writing their own wedding service.

20. The honeymoon is another rite of passage that best fulfills its function when it affords privacy and an opportunity for rest and relaxation.

Eekelar, J. M., and Katz, S. N. (Eds.) (1980). *Marriage and Cohabitation in Contemporary Societies*. Toronto: Butterworth. Interdisciplinary overview of legal, social, and ethical issues.

Knox, D. (1975). *Marriage: Who? When? Why?* Englewood Cliffs, NJ: Prentice-Hall. Assessment growth in relationships.

Macklin, E. D., and Rubin, R. H. (1983). *Contemporary Families and Alternative Lifestyles*. Beverly Hills, CA: Sage. Explores a variety of alternatives to traditional marriage.

Seligson, M. (1974). *The Eternal Bliss Machine: America's Way of Wedding*. New York: Bantam. A discussion and examination of wedding ceremonies.

Trost, J. (1979). *Unmarried Cohabitation*. Vasteras, Sweden: International Library. Experiences in Sweden.

Warner, R. (1984). *Living Together Kit*. Occidental, CA: Nolo Press. Helps for couples living together.

Weitzman, L. (1981). *The Marriage Contract: Spouses, Lovers, and the Law*. New York: Free Press. The law and marriage contracts.

PART III
MARRIAGES AND FAMILY RELATIONSHIPS: GROWTH AND CHALLENGES

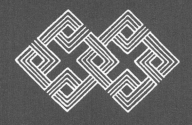

11

MARRIAGE AND FAMILY RELATIONSHIPS OVER THE FAMILY LIFE CYCLE

KEY TERMS

family life cycle
marital adjustment

marital adjustment tasks
postparental years

developmental tasks

Marriage relationships are never static but rather are constantly changing, developing, and growing. Sometimes relationships become meaningless, frustrating, unsatisfying, and troublesome. At other times they become more fulfilling and vital as the years pass.

The adjustments that people face early in marriage are unique because the relationship is so new. The adjustments during parenthood are different still. Adjustments during middle age relate to the aging process and to children growing older and leaving home. Late adulthood requires establishing new roles in the family, as married people, older parents of adult children, and as grandparents. The elderly have to make peace with their past and be able to accept their lives as they have lived them.

Most people face the prospect of separation from their spouse for some part of their lives. A small percentage of older people get divorced at this stage of life; more live out their lives as widows or widowers. Being alone requires special adjustments that married people do not face.

The extent to which the elderly are able to overcome their problems and make the adjustments that life requires will determine their sense of well-being and life satisfaction during this stage of their life. Each phase of life has its own joys and its own problems. Knowing what some of these are helps everyone to pass through each stage successfully.

MARRIAGE AND PERSONAL HAPPINESS

Few married people would disagree with the thesis that the quality of marriage has a strong effect on their happiness and satisfaction with life (Zollar and Williams, 1987). Data from six national studies conducted in the United States revealed that marital happiness contributed more to personal global (overall)

The quality of marriage has a strong effect on personal happiness and life satisfaction. Since the marital relationship is seldom static, most couples will experience periods of instability as well as periods of harmony.

happiness than did any other kinds of satisfaction, including satisfaction from work (Glenn and Weaver, 1981). At the same time, an unhappy marriage can also have a negative effect on life satisfaction and subjective well-being (SWB) (Haring-Hidore, Stock, Okun, and Witter, 1985). People who are having severe marital problems may not be able to eat properly; they often can't sleep; they may become debilitated and run down during the period of upset.

Marital relationships are seldom static. Partners may report a period of harmony during which everything seems fine, only to have "all hell break loose" to the point where the couple is talking about divorce. The more unstable the couple, the more variable the relationship. Most couples have some ups and downs in their relationship. What is important, however, is the general quality of the relationship over periods of time and the extent to which partners report satisfaction with it.

THE FAMILY LIFE CYCLE

Stages

One of the most helpful ways of examining marital relationships over periods of time is to look at them over various phases of the family life cycle. The **family life cycle** divides the family experience into phases or stages over the life span and seeks to describe changes in family structure and composition during each stage. The cycle can also be used to show the challenges, tasks, and problems that people face during each stage, and the satisfactions derived.

Figure 11.1 shows the family life cycle of a husband and wife in an intact marriage. The ages of the husband and wife are median ages for the U.S. population. Thus, the husband is married at 26, the wife at 24. They wait two years and have two children. The husband is 50 and the wife 48 when the youngest child is 20 and leaves home. The empty-nest years until retirement are from age 50 to 65 for the husband and age 48 to 65 for the wife. The wife lives to be age 78, the last nine years as a widow (U.S. Bureau of the Census, 1989). The husband dies at 71.

The traditional family life cycle has been criticized because it does not apply to divorced couples. Figure 11.2 shows separate cycles of a husband and wife, each of whom marry, have two children, divorce, and remarry a spouse with two children. In each case, the children reside with their mother after the divorce. Note that the median age of first marriage is one year younger than the age of couples who never divorce. The husband is 32 and the wife is 30 when they divorce. Their children are 3 and 5 years old. The father remarries four years later, at age 36, to a woman who is 33, with two children 6 and 8 years old who reside with her and her new husband. The husband is 50 when his youngest stepchild is 20 and moves out of the house. He and his wife have 15 empty-nest years until he retires at age 65 and an additional 6 years together before he dies at age 71.

The wife is 30 when she divorces. Her two children are ages 3 and 5. She remarries three years later when her children are 6 and 8. She is 47 years old when her youngest child is 20 and moves out of the house. She spends 18 empty-nest years with her husband until she retires at age 65, has three more years with her husband until he dies at age 71. She spends the last 10 years of her life, from age 68 to 78, as a widow (U.S. Bureau of the Census, 1989).

FIGURE 11.1 Family Life Cycle — Intact Marriage.

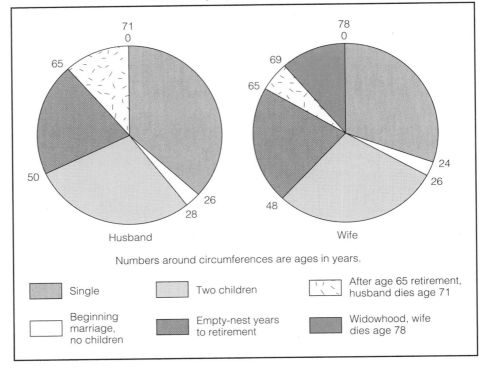

Statistics from U.S. Bureau of the Census. (1989). *Statistical Abstract of the United States, 1989* (109th ed.). Washington, DC: U.S. Government Printing Office.

Of course, the family life cycle of individual couples may vary from these norms, but these give us a fairly clear picture of what happens to the majority of people.* Eighty percent of the men and 75 percent of the women who divorce remarry, so there are substantial numbers of individuals who don't remarry (Furstenberg and Spanier, 1984; Glick, 1984). Others may remarry more than once, and others may have much larger families.

Marital Satisfaction

How does marital satisfaction change over various phases of the family life cycle? The studies are quite consistent in showing a decline in marital satisfaction during the early years of marriage, particularly following the birth of the first child and continuing to the end of the preschool or school age period (Schumm and Bugaighis, 1986). A few studies show the decline extending to the end of the teenage period. Practically all studies show an overall increase in marital satisfaction after children have reached school age or finished their teenage years. Some also show another slight decline in satisfaction prior to

*For a discussion of the family life cycle in Canada, see Rogers, R. H., and Witney, G. (1981). The family cycle in twentieth century Canada. *Journal of Marriage and the Family, 43,* 727–740.

*FIGURE 11.2 Family Life Cycle —
Marriage, Divorce, Remarriage; Children Reside with Wife.*

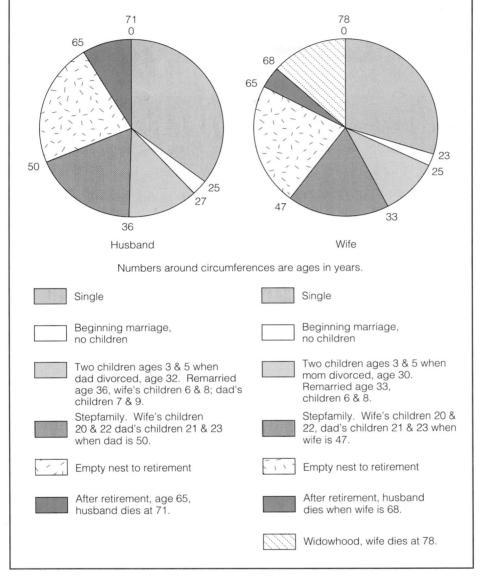

Numbers around circumferences are ages in years.

Single — Husband

Single — Wife

Beginning marriage, no children

Beginning marriage, no children

Two children ages 3 & 5 when dad divorced, age 32. Remarried age 36, wife's children 6 & 8; dad's children 7 & 9.

Two children ages 3 & 5 when mom divorced, age 30. Remarried age 33, children 6 & 8.

Stepfamily. Wife's children 20 & 22 dad's children 21 & 23 when dad is 50.

Stepfamily. Wife's children 20 & 22, dad's children 21 & 23 when wife is 47.

Empty nest to retirement

Empty nest to retirement

After retirement, age 65, husband dies at 71.

After retirement, husband dies when wife is 68.

Widowhood, wife dies at 78.

Statistics from: U.S. Bureau of the Census. (1989). *Statistical Abstract of the United States, 1989* (109th ed.). Washington, DC: U.S. Government Printing Office.

retirement (Anderson, Russell, and Schumm, 1983; Feldman and Feldman, 1975; Lupri and Frideres, 1981); Rollins and Cannon, 1974; Spanier, Lewis and Cole, 1975). *The general trend is for marital satisfaction to be somewhat curvilinear — to be high at the time of marriage, lowest during the child-rearing years, and higher again after the youngest child has passed beyond the teens* (Schram, 1979). Apparently, bearing and rearing children interferes with marital satisfaction (Anderson, Russell, and Schumm, 1983).

Some couples breathe a sigh of relief when the last child leaves home, and many couples report a noticeable increase in marital satisfaction.

The common assumption that couples, and particularly wives, are affected negatively by the children's leaving home cannot be substantiated by research (Glenn, 1979). In fact, data from six United States national surveys indicate that women whose children have left home are happier, enjoy life more themselves, and have greater marital satisfaction than do women whose children are still at home (Glenn and McLanahan, 1982).

When the question is raised as to why marital satisfaction is at an ebb when the children are of school age, the most plausible explanation seems to be that the demands placed upon the couple during these years are at their greatest. The couple is under increased financial pressure because of the needs of a growing family. Usually, job responsiblities outside the home are at a maximum. The children make increasing demands as they get older, and community responsibilities also increase during the middle years of marriage. In more technical language, "the number and intensity of social roles of an individual gradually increase until the middle years" (Riley and Foner, 1968). As a result, the partners experience greater role strain because they cannot perform all these roles as well as they and others might expect. This role discrepancy results in less satisfaction with the marital relationship. After the children are grown, however, role expectations and strain decrease in these later years, with a concomitant increase in marital satisfaction (Olson, McCubbin and Associates, 1983; Rice, 1983).

MARITAL ADJUSTMENTS EARLY IN MARRIAGE

All couples discover that their marriage never lives up to all of their expectations. As a result, couples go through a series of adjustments in which they try to modify their behavior and relationship to achieve the greatest degree of satisfaction with a minimum degree of frustration.

Marital adjustment may be defined as the process of modifying, adapting, and altering individual and couple patterns of behavior and interaction to achieve maximum satisfaction in the relationship. According to this definition, adjustment is not an end in and of itself. It is a means to an end. The end is satisfaction in and with the marriage. It is quite possible for couples to "adjust" to one another but still be quite unhappy and dissatisfied with the relationship. For example, people who like sex may accept the fact that their mates seldom want to go to bed with them. They learn to adjust to this situation, but this does not mean they really like it or that they are satisfied with this accommodation. Or people may learn to "adjust" to a mate's bad temper and try to overlook it, but this does not mean they approve. They have learned how to avoid overt conflict, but this adjustment gives them very little real comfort or joy. *The goal of adjustment is to achieve the greatest degree of marital satisfaction and success.*

Sometimes a particular adjustment may not be the best that one would like, but it may be said to be successful to the extent that it provides the highest positive satisfaction possible under the circumstances. Obviously, adjustment is not a static achievement to be done just once. It is a dynamic, ongoing process that takes place throughout married life.

Marital Adjustment Tasks

All couples discover that they have to make adjustments in one or more areas. These areas of adjustment might be called **marital adjustment tasks** and may be divided into 12 areas as shown in Table 11.1. The extent to which couples need to make adjustments after marriage will depend partially on the extent to which some of these tasks are confronted during courtship.

Beginning Adjustments

All couples who enter into a serious relationship are faced with most of the adjustments listed in Table 11.1. Some couples make many of them before marriage and so have fairly smooth sailing afterward. Other couples make few adjustments ahead of time and are faced with nearly all of these marital adjustment tasks afterwards. These tasks can be overwhelming if encountered all at once. This often leads to a period of disillusionment and disenchantment in couples who have not realized what marriage really involves (Breiner, 1980).

Tremendous Trifles

In the beginning, couples notice every minute detail about the way the other person walks, talks, dresses, eats, sleeps, bathes, and so on. Everything one does comes under the close scrutiny and observation of the other. The newness of the experience makes the two people very observant and sometimes critical. One husband complained because his wife never wanted to sleep with a window open, whereas he liked a lot of fresh air. One meticulous wife

TABLE 11.1 Marital Adjustment Tasks

Emotional fulfillment and support
Learning to give and receive affection and love
Development of sensitivity, empathy, closeness
Giving emotional support, building morale, fulfilling ego needs

Sexual adjustments (Greenblat, 1983)
Learning to satisfy, fulfill one another sexually
Working out mode, manner, timing of sexual expression
Finding, using acceptable means of birth control

Personal habits (Walters, 1982)
Adjusting to one another's personal habits, speech, cleanliness, grooming, manners,
    eating, sleeping, promptness
Reconciling differences in smoking, drinking, drug habits
Elimination or modification of personal habits that annoy one another
Adjusting to differences in body rhythms, schedules
Learning to share space, time, belongings, work

Sex roles (Bahr, Chappell, and Leigh, 1983; Ericksen, Yancey, and Ericksen, 1979)
Establishing husband-wife roles in and outside the home
Working out sex roles in relation to income production, housekeeping, household
    maintenance, homemaking, caring for children
Agreement on division of labor

Material concerns, finances (Rice, 1986)
Finding, selecting a residence: geographical area, community, neighborhood, type of
    housing
Equipping, maintaining a household
Earning adequate income
Managing money

Work, employment, achievement (Blumstein and Schwartz, 1983)
Finding, selecting, maintaining employment
Adjustment to type, place, hours, conditions of employment
Working out schedules when one or both are working
Arranging for child care when one or both are working

(continued)

discovered that her husband never liked to take a bath or to use deodorant. Another discovered that her husband always threw his dirty socks and underwear in a corner of the room. One husband was annoyed because his wife always lounged around the house in her bathrobe until after lunch. Gradually, couples begin to get used to one another, to overlook some of these little things, and to learn how not to annoy one another. Early in the marriage, however, these "tremendous trifles" can be quite aggravating (Rice, 1983).

Material Roles

One major marital adjustment concerns husband-wife roles in relation to material concerns and money. Earning an adequate income is not easy; the couple begins to realize that an enormous task has been taken on. Of course, where the husband and wife observe less traditional sex role separation, they can be of real help to one another in earning the income and in performing household duties. Still they both have assumed heavy responsibilities in getting married or have considerable adjustments to make before performance is adequate. Most young couples feel like this one: "We both had a lot of growing up to do after we got married" (Author's counseling notes).

Social life, friends, recreation (Mancini and Orthner, 1978)
Learning to plan, execute joint social activities
Learning to visit, entertain as a couple
Deciding on type, frequency of social activities as individuals and as a couple
Selecting, relating to friends

Family, relatives
Establishing relationships with parents, in-laws, relatives
Learning how to deal with families

Communication (Mace, 1982)
Learning to disclose and communicate ideas, worries, concerns, needs
Learning to listen to one another and to talk to one another in constructive ways

Power, decision-making (Scanzoni and Szinsvacz, 1980)
Achieving desired balance of status, power
Learning to make, execute decisions
Learning cooperation, accommodation, compromise
Learning to accept responsibility for actions

Handling conflict, solving problems
Learning to identify conflict causes, circumstances
Learning to cope with conflict constructively
Learning to solve problems
Learning where, when, how to obtain help if needed

Morals, values, ideology
Understanding and adjusting to individual morals, values, ethics, beliefs, philosophies, and goals in life
Establishing mutual values, goals, philosophies
Accepting one another's religious beliefs and practices
Decisions in relation to religious affiliation, participation

Independence, Decision Making

Some young people have never lived away from their parents before marriage. Some get homesick and want to go back home quite often to visit parents. Becoming emotionally independent of parents and learning to depend on one another for guidance, moral support, and emotional fulfillment is a major task (O'Neill and O'Neill, 1972). Learning how to make joint decisions becomes an important part of the early months of marriage. In the process, the couples work out their own balance of status and power and the process by which decisions are made. When differences and conflict arise, the couple must deal with them constructively not only to solve problems but also to strengthen rather than weaken their relationship.

Friends and Social Life

Selecting and relating to friends and establishing the type and frequency of social life sometimes causes trouble. A common complaint is "I don't like his (or her) friends." Being married does not mean one has to give up all of one's old friends, but neither does it mean that one can maintain the same social

Most persons have disagreements in their relationships. Please indicate below the approximate extent of agreement or disagreement between you and your partner for each item on the following list.

	Always agree	Almost always agree	Occasionally disagree	Frequently disagree	Almost always disagree	Always disagree
1. Handling family finances	5	4	3	2	1	0
2. Matters of recreation	5	4	3	2	1	0
3. Religious matters	5	4	3	2	1	0
4. Demonstrations of affection	5	4	3	2	1	0
5. Friends	5	4	3	2	1	0
6. Sex relations	5	4	3	2	1	0
7. Conventionality (correct or proper behavior	5	4	3	2	1	0
8. Philosophy of life	5	4	3	2	1	0
9. Ways of dealing with parents or in-laws	5	4	3	2	1	0
10. Aims, goals, and things believed important	5	4	3	2	1	0
11. Amount of time spent together	5	4	3	2	1	0
12. Making major decisions	5	4	3	2	1	0
13. Household tasks	5	4	3	2	1	0
14. Leisure time interests and activities	5	4	3	2	1	0
15. Career decisions	5	4	3	2	1	0

	All the time	Most of the time	More often than not	Occasionally	Rarely	Never
16. How often do you discuss or have you considered divorce, separation, or terminating your relationship?	0	1	2	3	4	5
17. How often do you or your mate leave the house after a fight?	0	1	2	3	4	5
18. In general, how often do you think that things between you and your partner are going well?	5	4	3	2	1	0
19. Do you confide in your mate?	5	4	3	2	1	0
20. Do you ever regret that you married (or *lived together*)	0	1	2	3	4	5
21. How often do you and your partner quarrel?	0	1	2	3	4	5
22. How often do you and your mate "get on each other's nerves?"	0	1	2	3	4	5

(continued)

	Every day	Almost every day	Occa-sionally	Rarely	Never	
23. Do you kiss your mate?	4	3	2	1	0	

	All of them	Most of them	Some of them	Very few of them	None of them	
24. Do you and your mate engage in outside interests together?	4	3	2	1	0	

How often would you say the following events occur between you and your mate?

	Never	Less than once a month	Once or twice a month	Once or twice a week	Once a day	More often
25. Having a stimulating exchange of ideas	0	1	2	3	4	5
26. Laugh together	0	1	2	3	4	5
27. Calmly discuss something	0	1	2	3	4	5
28. Work together on a project	0	1	2	3	4	5

There are some things about which couples sometimes agree and sometimes disagree. Indicate if ether item below caused differences of opinions or were problems in your relationship during the past few weeks. (Check yes or no)

	Yes	No	
29.	0	1	Being too tired for sex
30.	0	1	Not showing love

31. The dots on the following line represent different degrees of happiness in your relationship. The middle point, "happy," represents the degree of happiness of most relationships. Please circle the dot which best describes the degree of happiness, all things considered, of your relationship.

0	1	2	3	4	5	6
Extremely *Unhappy*	Fairly *Unhappy*	A Little *Unhappy*	Happy	Very Happy	Extremely Happy	Perfect

32. Which of the following statements best describes how you feel about the future of your relationship?

5   I want desperately for my relationship to succeed, and *would go to almost any length* to see that it does.

4   I want very much for my relationship to succeed, and *will do all I can* to see that it does.

3   I want very much for my relationship to succeed, and *will do my fair share* to see that it does.

2   It would be nice if my relationship succeeded, but *I can't do much more than I am doing* now to help it succeed.

1   It would be nice if it succeeded, but I *refuse to do any more than I am doing* now to keep the relationship going.

0   My relationship can never succeed, and *there is no more that I can do* to keep the relationship going.

(*continued*)

life one had while single. The challenge is to develop joint friendships and social activities in which a couple can participate together (Rice, 1983).

Sharing and Cooperation

It is not easy for individuals who have been single and independent for a number of years to begin to think in terms of "we" instead of "I." Even such things as time schedules and decisions about when to go to bed and when to get up in the morning involve some degree of cooperation and consideration for one another (Adams and Cromwell, 1978). Couples now share belongings, space, work, and time and have much to get used to in adjusting to individual differences. Throughout it all, they also need some individual privacy and space in their togetherness.

ADJUSTMENTS TO PARENTHOOD

Parenthood as Stress

"First pregnancy," says psychiatrist Eldred, "is a nine-month crisis. Thank God it takes nine months, because a child's coming requires enormous changes in a couple's ways of adjusting to each other" (Maynard, 1974, p. 139). In recent years, there has been less of a tendency to refer to the addition of a first child as a crisis and more of an inclination to refer to it as a period of stress and transition (Bell, Johnson, McGillicuddy-Delishe, and Sigel, 1980; Boss, 1980; Miller and Sollie, 1980). The amount of stress will vary from couple to couple. *The more stressful a couple's marriage before parenthood, the more likely it is that they will have difficulty in adjusting to the first child.*

The addition of a first child is a period of transition and stress, but successful adjustments are measures of parenting readiness.

Sometimes stress arises if the pregnancy was not planned (Hobbs and Wimbish, 1977). *Part of the stress comes from the fact that most couples are inadequately prepared for parenthood.* As one mother states, "We knew where babies came from, but we didn't know what they were like." When their first child is born, many parents have absolutely no experience in caring for infants. One study showed that men who had been prepared for parenthood by attending classes, reading books, and so forth found far greater satisfaction in being a parent than did those who had not been so prepared (Russell, 1974).

Part of the stress arises, also, because of the abrupt transition to parenthood. Rossi (1968) writes:

> The birth of a child is not followed by any gradual taking on of responsibility, as in the case of a professional work role. It is as if the woman shifted from a graduate student to a full professor with little intervening apprenticeship experience of slowly increasing responsibility. The new mother starts out immediately on twenty-four-hour duty, with responsibility for a fragile and mysterious infant totally dependent on her care. (p. 35).

For this reason, it is of great help to the mother if her husband will share this care with her. Direct assistance from relatives in the early days after birth can also minimize stress.

May (1982) studied 100 expectant fathers and their partners to determine what factors were important to a subjective sense of readiness for pregnancy and fatherhood. She found four factors that were most important to these men:

1. Whether or not they had intended to be a father at some time in their lives

2. Stability in the couple relationship

3. Relative financial security

4. A sense of closure to the childless period of their lives. In other words, they had to feel they had met most of the goals they had set for themselves, goals that were necessary to accomplish before fatherhood.

The timing of the pregnancy was extremely important to the men in this study. These men commented (May, 1982):

"I would have preferred to have the baby later." (p. 357)

"I really don't think the father should be rushed . . . Men are not insensitive. It's not that they don't care about the baby. It's just that they are going to care at the right time, when it's right for them." (p. 359)

Stress will vary from child to child depending upon each child's temperament and how easy each child is to care for. Some children never give any trouble. Others, such as hyperactive or sick children, require an abnormal amount of care (Balkwell and Halverson, 1980).

ADJUSTMENTS DURING MIDDLE ADULTHOOD

Midlife Issues

The most noticeable changes of midlife are physical ones. These changes are gradual, but increasing wrinkles, graying hair, and balding pates remind us of the aging process. Muscle tone declines, weight increases, strength and endurance ebb. "Body-monitoring" increases as individuals concern themselves with the dimensions of their middle-aged bodies (Kets deVries, 1978).

Perhaps for the first time, *adults are confronted with their own mortality*. Until now, they have counted the years past. Now, they begin to count the years ahead. The midlife crisis is precipitated by the awareness that years are numbered. The paradox is that people are entering the stage of fulfillment, the prime of life, but the prime and fulfillment are dated (Jaques, 1965). Brim (1976) explains that the "indices of aging are nothing compared to the vivid sudden confrontation with the fact of one's own mortality" (p. 5).

This personalization of mortality leads to an awareness that time is finite, that life is a race against time; and there is a sense of urgency to accomplish all that we want to achieve (Neugarten, 1976). Many middle-agers intensify efforts to live life while they can before it is too late. Baruch, Barnett, and Rivers (1983) found that some women are concerned about living too long (longer than their husbands) and not being able to function as adults.

This crucial shift of time orientation in the life cycle may lead to introspection, self-analysis, self-appraisal, and stock-taking. Middle-agers engage in an existential questioning of self, values, and life itself (Gould, 1979). They

The most noticeable changes at midlife are physical. But within the individual, it can be more profound with a new awareness of one's own mortality.

ask: Who am I? What have I done with my life? Where is my life going? What is the purpose of life? What am I here for? Is there anything else for me? (McIlroy, 1984).

This assessment of self extends to an examination of responsibilities, career, and marriage. As one middle-ager expressed it: "I'm tired of doing what is expected, what I'm supposed to do. I'd like to find out what I want to do, and start thinking of me for a change" (Author's counseling notes). Financial responsibilities tend to be heavy in middle age. Lowenthal, Thurnher, Chiriboga, and associates (1975) found that men at midlife became obsessed with financial security for themselves and their wives in retirement. The total family income becomes an important contributor to feelings of mastery and power over one's life (Baruch, Barnett, and Rivers, 1983).

Many middle-agers are under considerable stress. This is the time of heaviest responsibilities at work and in the community (Merriam, 1979). The main stresses for men are work and economics (Levinson, 1978). The man may be stoic, rigidly scheduled, and compulsive. Middle-aged women who are stressed are concerned about lack of companionship with their husbands, their own work, and the possibility of their young adult children making bad marriages. As far as work is concerned, however, Baruch, et al. (1983) found that employed middle-aged women scored higher on mastery and pleasure (two indices of well-being) than did single or divorced women. Employment seemed to be a buffer against stress for them.

Thus, midlife is a time when personal, practical and existential issues are all in focus. It can become a time for reexamination, a time to chart new courses for life ahead.

As we have discussed, marital satisfaction tends to be at its lowest ebb when the children are of school age or in their teenage years. On the average, the wife is 41 and the husband is 43 when the youngest child is age 13 (See fig. 11.1). If the husband and wife have been busy working and raising children, and being active in community affairs, they may have drifted apart, spending less time communicating, playing, and being together (Swensen, Eskew, and Kohlhepp, 1981). It is easy to get so absorbed with other activities that the marriage suffers from lack of attention. Parents who stayed together until their children were grown now feel freer to dissolve their relationship. Some do.

For others, however, *middle age can become a time for revitalizing a tired marriage, for rethinking their relationship, and for deciding that they want to share many things in life together.* Goldstine (1977) suggests that there are three cycles in most marriages — falling in love, falling out of love, and falling back in love — and that the last cycle is the most difficult and rewarding. If the couple can learn to communicate and express tender feelings, especially feelings of love and affection that they have neglected, they can develop greater intimacy than they have experienced in a long time (Swensen, 1983). This improved communication can also uncover troublesome issues that have been denied. Once faced and resolved, they need no longer prevent improved companionship and togetherness (Appleton, 1983).

The Postparental Years

The term **postparental years** usually refers to the ages after the last child leaves home and until the husband's and wife's retirement. As shown in figure 11.1, if the woman gets married at the median age of 24 and has two children, she is 48 when the last child leaves home. The husband who married at age 26 and has two children will be 50 when the last child leaves. Some writers prefer the term the *empty-nest years*; for once children are born, one is always a parent.

The biggest adjustment for the wife whose whole life has been wrapped up in her children is in filling the gap after the children leave. One woman comments:

> My daughters were both 19 when they married. I didn't want them not to marry, but I missed them so much. I felt alone. I couldn't play golf. I couldn't even play bridge. I don't have a profession, and I couldn't take just any job. I just didn't have a chance to learn anything. (Author's counseling notes)

While these comments are not unusual, *even greater numbers of women breathe a sigh of relief after the last child leaves* (Cooper and Gutmann, 1987; Rubin, 1979). At last, these women are now free to live their own lives. Many go back to school, take up postponed careers, establish businesses, and become involved in hobbies and personal interests or in community affairs of one kind or another. These women can now enjoy the pleasures of their own lives and/or of being grandmothers, with only a minimum of child-care responsibility (Rice, 1983). Many husbands don't feel too great a loss when the children leave, especially if they have reasons to be proud of them and their accomplishments (Lewis, Frenau, and Roberts, 1979).

When the last child leaves home, the postparental years begin. Although most couples report a noticeable increase in marital satisfaction, today's empty nest doesn't always stay empty. What effect might the returned child have on marital satisfaction?

There is considerable evidence to show that adults in the postparental period are happier than are those earlier or later in life. The period has been described as "a time of freedom" This new-found freedom was described by one wife in this way:

> There's not as much physical labor. There's not as much cooking and there's not as much mending and, well, I remarked not long ago that for the first time since I can remember my evenings are free. And we had to be economical to get the three children through college. We're over the hurdle now; we've completed it. Last fall was the first time in 27 years that I haven't gotten a child ready to go to school. That was very relaxing. (Deutscher, 1964, p. 55)

One husband showed his relief at not having such a great financial burden. "It took a load off me when the boys left. I didn't have to support 'em anymore" (Deutscher, 1964, p. 55). It would appear, therefore, that while there are adjustments to be made during the empty-nest years, there are increased opportunities to enjoy life as a couple (Harkins, 1978; Rice, 1983).

One postscript needs to be added. The empty nest may not stay that way. High divorce rates and financial need have resulted in increasing numbers of adult children returning home to live with their parents. The fledglings are returning to the nest.

This has important ramifications for parents, the adult children, and grandchildren. Most parents do not welcome the return of their children and view their stay as a short-term arrangement (Clemens and Axelson, 1985). The areas of the greatest potential conflicts include everyday maintenance of self and clothing, the upkeep of house and yard, the use of the family car, and the life-style of the child, including sexual expresssion, drinking, drugs, and friends. Grandparents sometimes resent babysitting grandchildren while a parent goes out to work or play. Sometimes the adult child reverts to the role of the dependent child, and the parents return to superordinate roles of earlier times. Increasing evidence points to a lessening of life satisfaction for all parties involved (Clemens and Axelson, 1985).

CLASSROOM FORUM
The Midlife Crisis

Bill was 40. That fact suddenly dawned on him when the people at the office gave him a party for his fortieth birthday and presented him with a cane! He had never considered himself old, but now he began to wonder if the quickly passing years meant life was passing him by.

He had always been a hard worker — going to work early in his office at the bank, and coming home in time for supper. He had been a "good family man." He had helped guide his son through school and Little League. But he was now graduated from high school and away at college. Bill and his wife lived a fairly normal married life like other couples. But they lived somewhat separate lives. They rarely talked about anything important. Their sex life had dropped off to once a month. They spent little time together socially. Bill's wife, Dot, was a real estate agent and spent a lot of time out of their house with clients. Bill didn't mind because she made good money.

Now Bill began to change his behavior. He had always been a conservative dresser. He bought several flashy sports coats and light jerseys with crew necks. He purchased a high-speed sports car. Instead of coming right home after work, he began stopping off at a local lounge for a few drinks. He was arrested twice for speeding, and once for DUI. Most of Bill's drinking buddies were divorced or single, and he envied their freewheeling life style.

One day, out of the clear blue, he told his wife he wanted a divorce. He wanted to find out what life was like out there, and he realized he could not as a married man. "Seems like I've been married all my life," he explained. "There must be more to life than going to work and coming home every day. I have to find more than this for me" (Author's counseling notes).

DISCUSSION

1. How would you describe Bill's feelings about himself and his life? What precipitated his midlife crisis?

2. Bill's wife told her counselor, "I can't understand what's happened to him. He's not the man I married. He's changed." If you were her counselor, what would you say to her?

3. If you were Bill's counselor, what approach would you use? What would you say and do?

4. What are some ways that Bill might solve his problem? What are the alternatives?

5. Would getting a divorce help Bill and his situation?

6. If you were Bill's wife, what would you do?

*"I'm of an age when one begins
to realize that one's mid-life crisis
is never going to amount to
much."*

'Punch Original

ADJUSTMENTS DURING LATE ADULTHOOD

Developmental Tasks

The major adjustments (**developmental tasks**) facing elderly persons may be grouped into nine categories:

1. Staying physically healthy and adjusting to limitations
2. Maintaining an adequate income and means of support
3. Adjusting to revised work roles
4. Establishing acceptable housing and living conditions
5. Maintaining identity and social status
6. Finding companionship and friendship
7. Learning to use leisure time pleasurably
8. Establishing new roles in the family
9. Achieving integrity through acceptance of one's life

We'll discuss each of these briefly before turning to a more detailed discussion of the marriage and family relationships of the elderly.

Staying Physically Healthy and Adjusting to Limitations

The task of staying physically healthy becomes more difficult as people age. It requires good health habits and the practice of preventive medicine. Older people dread physical problems that impair mobility, their senses, and the capacity

Older people dread physical problems that impair mobility and independence. One of the developmental tasks of late adulthood is to stay physically healthy.

to care for themselves (Quinn, 1983). As a consequence, maintaining good health is one of the most important predictors of life satisfaction in the elderly (Baur and Okun, 1983).

Maintaining Adequate Income and Means of Support

Many adults face the problem of having adequate income in their old age. One study revealed that the elderly who felt they were better off financially than their relatives reported higher life satisfaction than did those who were not so well off (Usui, Keil, and Durig, 1985). Most older adults want financial independence, but this requires careful long-term planning (Strate and Dubnoff, 1986).

Adjusting to Revised Work Roles

Retirement at age 65 is no longer compulsory, but many workers must retire at 70. *Forced retirement has been ranked among the top ten crises in terms of the amount of stress it causes the individual* (Sarason, 1981). People who elect retirement, plan for it, and look forward to it feel they have directed their own

CLASSROOM FORUM
The Elderly and Adult Children Living Together

Do you have any elderly grandparents or parents living with you in your own home? How does this arrangement work out?

Are you living with elderly parents or grandparents in their home? How does this arrangement work out?

How does living together affect your life?

What special problems arise because of this living arrangement? What could you do to alleviate these problems?

Are the elderly happy with the present living arrangements?

Do you have any suggestions for others that would minimize the problems that arise?

Are there any alternative solutions to the arrangement?

Why aren't the alternatives implemented?

What do you think of nursing homes for the infirmed elderly?

Would you consider putting an elderly parent or grandparent in a nursing home?

If you were elderly and disabled, would you want to go to a nursing home?

Are any of your relatives in a nursing home? With what results?

What are some alternatives to nursing home care?

If you had adult married children, and your daughter divorced, would you consider letting her and her two preschool children move back into your home?

If you had two children and were divorced, would you consider moving back into your parents' house if you could not afford a place of your own? Explain the reasons for your answer and the pros and cons of the situation as you perceive them.

lives and are not being pushed or manipulated (Kilty and Behling, 1985, 1986). Those most satisfied with retirement are those who have been preparing for it for a number of years (Evans, Ekerdt, and Bosse, 1985).

Certainly, *retirement should be retirement to, not from*. Retirees who are most satisfied seem to be those most involved in meaningful activity following retirement (Hooker and Ventis, 1984).

Establishing Acceptable Housing and Living Conditions

For some of the elderly, being able to keep their own home is of great importance. It allows them independence and usually more satisfactory relationships with their children (Hoyt, Kaiser, Peters, and Babchuk, 1980). Statistics from 1986 revealed that almost three out of four households maintained by persons 65 years old and over were owned by them. In the remaining households, the elderly were *renting*. Of course, many older people (about one out of ten men and one out of five women 65 and older) are not heads of households, since they go live with married children (U.S. Bureau of the Census, 1980).

Maintaining Identity and Social Status

The aged have high status and prestige in primitive societies because they possess the greatest knowledge of traditions and ceremonies considered essential for group survival. The elderly also have high status in agricultural societies because they control the property, have the greatest knowledge of farming skills, are able to perform useful tasks, and are the leaders of the extended family. But as our society becomes more industrialized and modern, the elderly lose their economic advantages and their leadership roles in industry and in the extended family. Consequently, *they lose their status and prestige* (Balkwell and Balswick, 1981; Ishii-Kuntz and Lee, 1987).

Part of the loss of status comes when people retire. People find status through their occupation (Hurst and Guldin, 1981). When they leave that role, they have the feeling that they have lost their main identity. As Bell says; "A former mechanic is no longer a mechanic—he is occupationally nothing" (Bell, 1975, p. 332). Those who are able to develop a meaningful identity through avocations, social life, their marriage, their children, or other activities adjust more easily.

Finding Companionship and Friendship

Loneliness is one of the most frequent complaints of older people, especially of the formerly married (Creecy, Berg, and Wright, 1985); Essex and Nam, 1987). Their challenge is to find meaningful relationships with others. *Developing and maintaining friendships with peers seems to be more important to the emotional well-being of the elderly than interaction with kin* (Lee and Ellithorpe, 1982). The elderly who are able to find a dating partner can likely satisfy their need for companionship and emotional fulfillment (Adams, 1985). One 73-year-old woman stated:

> It was a lot harder when my boyfriend, Ted, died than when my husband of 40 years passed away. I needed Ted in a way I never needed my husband. Ted and I spent so much time together; he was all I had. And at my age I know it will be hard to find someone else . . . I would like to date someone like Ted again . . . but, well, let's face it; how many men want a 73-year-old woman? (Bulcroft and O'Connor, 1986, p. 401).

Learning to Use Leisure Time Pleasurably

Late adulthood offers most people an opportunity to enjoy themselves. As work roles decline, more leisure time is available for preferred pursuits. Life satisfaction in late adulthood is very much dependent on social activity. *People need worthwhile, pleasurable activities to help them feel good about themselves and about life in general* (Glass and Grant, 1983; McClelland, 1982).

Establishing New Roles in the Family

Several events bring about the adjustment of family roles: children marrying and moving away, grandparenthood, retirement, the death of a spouse, or becoming dependent on one's children. All of these circumstances require major adjustments and a realignment of family roles and responsibilities. Family relationships during late adulthood will be discussed in more detail later in this chapter.

At the heart of
marriage and family
relationships is the need
for companionship,
communication,
and compassion.

For every human being, life begins with the union of a mother's ovum and a father's sperm. From the moment of conception, a unique human being develops through stages of simple cell division, the emerging complexity of form and function, as seen in a seven-week-old fetus, to a fully formed fetus capable of surviving outside the mother's womb.

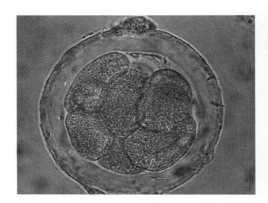

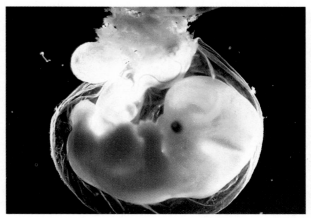

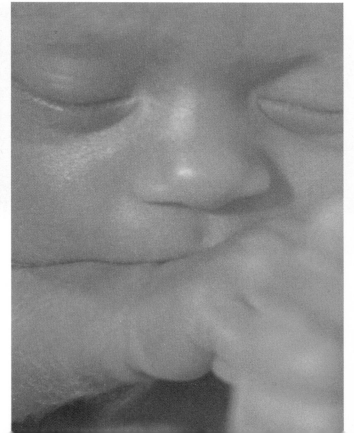

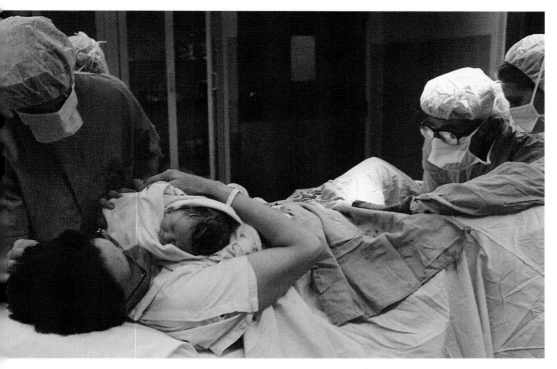

The birth of a child will dramatically alter the daily life of the family. The reality of the changes brought on by the child's birth, however, is fully felt once the child comes home and is recognized by the community as a new family member.

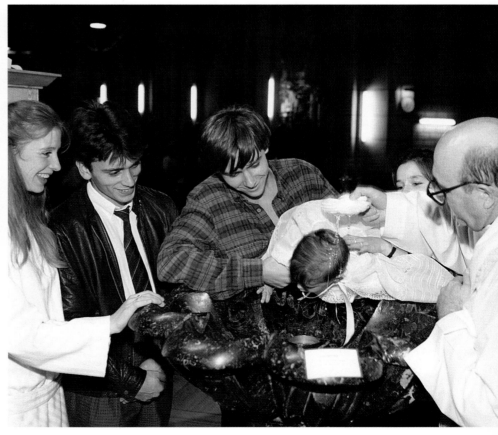

What is a perfect family? In most societies, the ideal family is often seen as large, patriarchal, and multi-generational. The American ideal is still influenced by the image of the farm family even though less than two percent of Americans live on farms or ranches. More recently, a popular image of American families is the suburban single family home with the two-car garage.

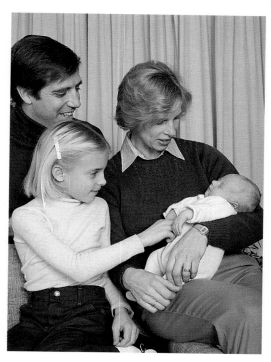

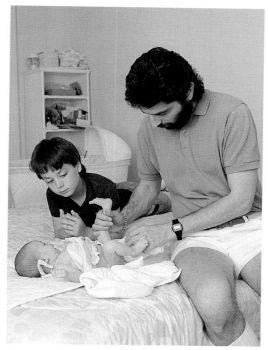

Today's family is being redefined by new social arrangements. A modern household containing only a married couple and their children often exists without the supports and advantages of the large, multi-generational family. New parenting roles, such as fathers caring for very young children, are breaking old stereotypes. Housing costs and housing shortages are forcing many young families to expect less of the American ideal of home ownership than did their parents. Remarriage is also common, often forming a new family that includes children from previous marriages.

Regardless of a family's cultural, ethnic, or economic identity, the most intimate joys of family living include caring for each other, basing daily routines on good communication and respect, enjoying simple pleasures, and sharing an active life together.

Despite all the joys and pleasures, few families escape moments of stress such as the death of a loved one or arguments over family finances. Faced with stressful events or changed circumstances, many families now turn to counselors and therapists for help.

What is a perfect relationship? What sustains and nurtures the intimate bonds between people? While the sense of newness and the prospects for growth are clear, it is the best of times to explore these questions.

Late adulthood offers an opportunity to pursue leisure activities. Knowing how to enjoy such activities and having appropriate settings available in which to pursue them is not always the reality for many individuals.

*Achieving Integrity Through
Acceptance of One's Life*

Erikson (1959) says that the development of ego integrity is the chief psychosocial task of the final stage of life. This includes life review, being able to accept the facts of one's life without regret, and being able to face death without great fear. It entails appreciating one's own individuality, accomplishments, and satisfactions, as well as accepting the hardships, failures, and disappointments one has experienced. Untimately, *it means contentment with one's life as it is and has been* (Reker, Peacock, Wong, 1987; Ryff, 1982).

MARRIAGE AND FAMILY RELATIONSHIPS
OF THE ELDERLY

Marital Status

As health and longevity of the elderly increase, an increasing proportion of adults over age 65 are still married and living with their spouse. In 1989, 82 percent of men 65–74 years old and 69 percent of men 75 and older were married. Figures for women of comparable ages were 53 percent and 24 percent respectively. Obviously, there are far greater numbers of widowed women than men. Table 11.2 shows the figures (U. S. Bureau of the Census, 1989).

TABLE 11.2 *The Marital Status of Older Americans*
by Age and Sex, in Percentage: 1989

	MALE			FEMALE		
Marital Status	55–64	65–74	75+	55–64	65–74	75+
Never-married	5.8	4.7	4.3	4.2	4.8	6.4
Married	84.1	81.5	68.8	70.1	53.0	23.8
Widowed	2.9	9.0	23.6	16.7	36.7	67.0
Divorced	7.3	4.8	3.2	9.0	5.5	2.7

From U.S. Bureau of the Census (1989). Statistical Abstract of the United States, 1989. Washington, DC: U.S. Government Printing Office.

Marital Satisfaction

For many older adults, marriage continues to be a major source of life satisfaction (Kozma and Stones, 1983). *Marital happiness and satisfaction usually increase during a second honeymoon stage after the children are launched and after retirement.* The spouses usually have more leisure time to spend together and with adult children and grandchildren. The adults may still be in good health. They depend more on one another for companionship (Zube, 1982). As one wife remarked; "I feel closer to Bill than I have for years. We had forgotten what it meant to have real companionship" (Author's counseling notes).

Sometimes during the last stages of old age, marital satisfaction again declines (Gilford, 1984). Some wives complain that their husbands are always underfoot and expect to be waited on. Keating and Cole (1980) report that wives were busier than ever completing and reorganizing household tasks so they had little time to respond to their husband's needs as well. Some retired husbands take on a few additional household tasks, but others don't share more than when they were working (Arling, 1976). Much of a retired husband's time at home is spent in his own pursuits. So while the retired couple is together more, retirement does not ensure that the husband will spend that much additional time in household chores.

There is some evidence that there is a reversal of sex roles in relation to authority in the family as people get older. The man who retires loses some status and authority in family governance. The woman often assumes a more dominant role as an authority figure (Liang, 1982). This is especially true in relation to planning activities for herself and her husband and in assuming a nurturing role that has not been possible since the children were launched (Keating and Cole, 1980).

Declining physical health and financial resources begin to take their toll. The couple finds it harder to cope with their life situation. Declining status and involuntary disengagement from society result in increasing discontent. Spouses now have fewer physical, social, and emotional resources to reward one another in mutual marital exchange (Dowd, 1980). Figure 11.3 shows the trend.

FIGURE 11.3 *Mean Levels of Marital Satisfaction by Age Group (N = 318).*
Group sample sizes are shown in parentheses.

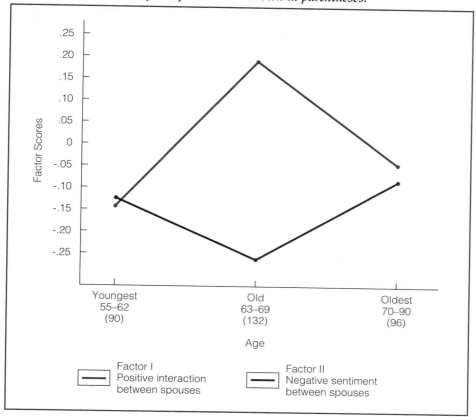

From Gilford, R. (1984). Contrasts in marital satisfaction throughout old age: An exchange theory analysis. *Journal of Gerontology, 39*, 331.

Parent–Adult Child Relationships

The image of parents growing older without contact and concern of their adult children does not coincide with the facts (Montgomery, 1982). A national survey by Shanas (1980) revealed that half of the aged with children had seen one of them on the day of the interview or the day before. If the time period covered the previous week, the proportion of elderly parents in contact with children increased to three-fourths. Similar findings appear in a 1984 survey of the elderly (Kovar, 1986). Thus, "the finding that most older persons are *not* isolated from their children is well supported in the existing literature" (Bengtson, Cutler, Mangen, and Marshall, 1985, p. 319).

Aldous (1987) did a study of the relationships between 124 older couples and their adult children. The couples were in their early and mid-sixties. Some were retired, some not. On the average, the couples had been married 30 years or more. About a third of the fathers were professional, technical, or managerial people. The parents had an average of 3.6 children, most of whom had left home and lived, on the average, 487 miles away. The parents' relationships with their children exhibited certain common characteristics.

A study of 38 housewives whose husbands had recently retired revealed both positive and negative aspects of their husband's retirement (Hill and Dorfman, 1982).

Percentage of Wives Mentioning this Aspect	Things Wives Liked
81	Time available to do what we want
67	Increased companionship
33	Flexibility
28	Increased participation of husband in household tasks
22	Decrease in home responsibility
22	Husbands were happier

Percentage of Wives Mentioning this Aspect	Things Wives Didn't Like
36	Financial problems
31	Husband didn't have enough to do
22	Too much togetherness

The wives also had suggestions for others.

Percentage of Wives Mentioning this Aspect	Suggestion
33	Try to keep husband busy
31	Try to continue their own preretirement activities
25	Sacrifice own interests for husband's sake
22	Do more together as a couple
22	Preserve own privacy by having own part of house

Adapted from Hill, E. A., and Dorfman, L. T. (1982). Reaction of housewives to the retirement of their husbands. *Family Relations, 39,* 195–200. Copyright ©1982 by the National Council on Family Relations. Reprinted by permission.

Contacts were frequent. Parents and children kept in touch with each other by letter, or telephone, more than weekly in the past year. They visited in one another's homes more than once a month and celebrated holidays together at least once every two months.

They helped one another. Because parents had greater resources than children, parents had made loans, given gifts, or paid bills for each child about once every two months. They also provided child care, house care, shopping, transportation, and help in times of illness. Parents were most in touch with those adult children who were most in need. For example, the never-married and divorced were of special concern to parents. Divorced daughters with children most often received household help and child care from parents.

The children reciprocated as able. They provided gifts and financial aid of $50 or less in value about four times a year. They were most able to provide help requiring physical energy, giving assistance with house and yard work six times per year.

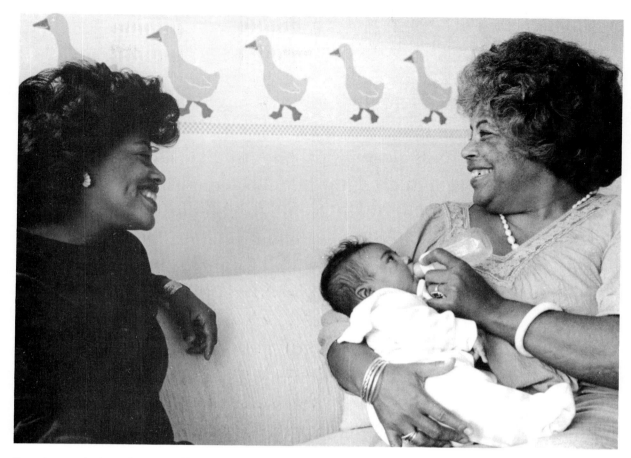

Recent research shows that most older persons are not isolated from their children and grand-children, and becoming a grandparent brings about a welcome new status.

Both mothers and fathers reported some disagreement with their adult children over rearing grandchildren, treatment of siblings, treatment of themselves, and how often get-togethers took place. Generally, both parents and adult children were very satisfied with their relationship with each others.

Other studies have reported important factors in parent–adult child relationships:

- The frequency of contact is not the key factor in satisfactory relationships.

- Emotional support is important and can be more significant than whether adult children provide financial support (Houser and Berkman, 1984).

- The morale of the elderly is higher if they feel they can reciprocate some of the help their children or friends give them (Stoller, 1985; Roberto and Scott, 1986).

- Providing extensive care for severely functionally impaired parents causes extreme stress and hardship for the caregivers. Community personal care services, day care, home nursing, and homemakers' services are needed (Archbold, 1983).

Divorce, at whatever time of
life, is a very distressing
experience, but research
shows that the degree of
unhappiness over divorce
increases steadily with age.

Divorce

Divorce at whatever time of life is a very upsetting experience. If it comes during late adulthood, it is even more difficult. Chiriboga (1982) found that *the proportion of divorced adults who were unhappy increase steadily with age.* In comparison to those who were middle-aged at the time of divorce, adults who were 50 and over stand out as the more maladapted group. The older subjects were lower in morale and overall happiness. They averaged more symptoms of psychological disturbance and reported they were troubled by the separation.

WIDOWHOOD

Sex Ratios

Couples who marry and have children in the 1980s and whose marriages are not broken by divorce or separation can expect to live together for 45 years. From birth, the female's life expectancy is 78 and the husband's is 72, but the husband is two years older than the wife when they marry; so she can expect to be a widow for eight years (U.S. Bureau of the Census, 1989). The greater longevity of women means that the number of widows exceeds widowers at all age levels. Table 11.3 shows the ratios at different ages (U.S. Bureau of the Census, 1989). Partly as a result of these ratios, the remarriage rates for

TABLE 11.3 Ratio of Widows to Widowers at Different Ages

Age	Ratio of Widows to Widowers
45–54	5.3 to 1
55–64	6.6 to 1
65–74	5.2 to 1
75 years and over	4.9 to 1

Adapted from U.S. Bureau of the Census. (1989). *Statistical Abstract of the United States; 1989* (109th ed.). Washington DC: U.S. Government Printing Office, 41.

widows is lower than for widowers. The younger a person when a mate dies, the greater the chances of remarriage.

The Trauma

The death of a spouse is recognized as one of life's most traumatic events. The survivor often confronts emotional, economic, and/or physical problems precipitated by the spouse's death. We will look at just a few of these problems (Smith and Zick, 1986).

Relationships with Friends and Family

Older people, especially widows, have a consistently high degree of contact with other family members, including married children. Usually, the elderly female is closer to her children, especially daughters, than is the elderly male. However, the woman is more likely to depend on them for material aid. The more dependent elderly people become, and the more that helping roles are reversed, the lower their morale. All research findings stress the positive importance of peer support in helping widows and widowers adjust. Morale is positively associated with involvement with friends (Bankoff, 1983).

Problems of Widows

An in-depth study of 72 women of middle socioeconomic status, all widowed for fewer than five years, showed that *the most frequently cited problem was loneliness* (Wyly and Hulicka, 1977). Some idealized their husbands, making it even harder to get over their loss (Lopata, 1981). Widows miss their husbands as companions and partners in activities (Kivett, 1978). This problem is accentuated if the woman has low income and cannot afford many social activities outside the home. Widows report that social participation is a problem because so many activities are couple oriented (Keith, 1986). Sexual frustration is common among the widowed (Goddard and Leviton, 1980). The problem of loneliness is accentuated because large numbers of widowers and

Loneliness is the most frequently cited problem of widowhood, most extreme for widows whose social activities were highly couple oriented.

widows live alone. The problem is minimized if the widow has peers, friends, and confidantes who are available as social companions (Balkwell, 1985).

A second problem cited by widows in Wyly and Hulicka's study was home maintenance and car repair. Other problems cited frequently by younger widows were decision making, child rearing, and financial management. Widows in the oldest group mentioned such problems as learning basic finance, lack of transportation, and fear of crime. The only advantages of widowhood, mentioned by the younger women, were increased independence and freedom of choice (Wyly and Hulicka, 1977).

Financial problems plague both widows and widowers (Balkwell and Balswick, 1981). In every age category, however, widowed females earn less than widowers (Morgan, 1981). The most impoverished females are widows older than 65, even though they may be receiving social security or pensions of some sort (Warlick, 1985). Blacks and other minorities in rural areas or areas of urban blight are the poorest. If they are to have the basic necessities of life, a variety of social supports are needed (Scott and Kivett, 1980).

Widows indicate that one of their major adjustments is related to role changes. Widowhood, at all ages, changes the basic self-identity of a woman. This is especially true of the traditionally oriented woman whose role of wife was central to her life. This woman has to reorient her thinking to find other identities. Therefore, specific role changes depend on what roles were emphasized before widowhood. The childless career wife who was not very close to her husband may not have to change her role performance at all. In fact, she may welcome the increased freedom (Rice, 1986).

Widowers

Whether the adjustments for widowers are easier or more difficult than for widows is a matter of dispute. Because they have not been as close to their families as have their wives, widowers have fewer contacts with them and receive less social support from their families following the death of their spouse (Longino and Lipman, 1981). Men with dependent children may have difficulty caring

Do you have any elderly relatives with whom you are fairly close? Who are they, where do they live, and how far are they from you?

What are the most important problems that they face? What can they do about these situations? What factors prevent these problems from being solved?

Do you or other members of your family try to help them? What do you or others do? With what result?

Are you receiving and accepting help from older members of your family? Explain. What what results?

Do you feel that parents ought to continue to give aid to their children after the children are married?

What can be done to improve the economic situation of the elderly? What do you think of compulsory retirement at age 70? Explain. Is it possible to prepare for retirement? How?

Do you know well an elderly married couple? What kind of relationship do they have? Explain. What do they do that you admire? What do they do that you do not admire?

Why are some people so prejudiced against the elderly? What factors in our society encourage prejudice against the elderly? How do you feel about elderly people? Why do you feel that way?

Who has the harder time after a spouse dies: a widow or widower? Give the reasons for your answer.

TABLE 11.4 *Relative Scores of Primary Problem Areas*
of Widowers Following Death of Spouse

Problem Area	Relative Score*
Loneliness	55
Acceptance of loss	18
Going places/Doing things alone	17
Housework	10
Cooking	7
Personal care	7
Child care	3
Financial	3

From Clark, P. G., Siviski, R. W., and Weiner, W. (1986). Coping strategies of widowers in the first year. *Family Relations*, 35, 428. Copyright ©1986 by the National Council on Family Relations.

*A global indication of the relative importance attributed to various problems was obtained by assigning values between 0 and 3 to each response, corresponding to decreasing levels of importance (0 = no problem) and summing the scores across the subjects.

Kohn, J. B., and Kohn, W. K. (1978). *The Widower*. Boston: Beacon. Problems and adjustments of the widower.

for them. Bischof feels that widowers without parental responsibilities, however, have a greater degree of freedom than do widows without dependent children (Bischof, 1976). Their primary disruptions are in learning to cook, keep house, and care for themselves, although many men already do these things. Some may be able to hire help. In such cases, the major adjustment is to the loss of their wife's companionship and love (Clark, Siviski, and Weiner, 1986). Table 11.4 shows the primary problem areas as revealed in a study of 27 widowers (Clark, Siviski, and Weiner, 1986). Clearly, loneliness was cited as the major problem for these widowers. Accepting the loss of their spouse and going places/doing things alone were apparently problem areas of secondary importance (Clark, Siviski, and Weiner, 1986).

SUMMARY

1. The quality of marriage has an important effect on happiness and satisfaction with life, but marriage relationships are seldom static. Their quality varies over periods of time.

2. The family life cycle divides the family experience into phases or stages, each with its own challenges, tasks, and problems.

3. In general, the graph of marital satisfaction is curvilinear: high at the time of marriage, lowest during the child-rearing years, and higher again after the youngest child is beyond the teen years.

4. Marital adjustments may be defined as the process of modifying, adapting, and altering individual and couple patterns of behavior and interaction to achieve maximum satisfaction in the relationship. The goal of adjustment is to achieve the greatest degree of marital satisfaction and success that is possible.

5. Marital adjustment tasks early in marriage may be grouped under a number of different categories: emotional fulfillment and support; sexual adjustments; personal habits; sex roles; material concerns; work, employment and achievement; social life, friends and recreation; family and relatives; communication; power and decision making; handling conflict and solving problems; and morals, values, and ideology.

6. Beginning marriage may lead to a period of disillusionment when immature couples have not realized ahead of time what marriage involves.

7. In the beginning of marriage, couples notice and are annoyed by tremendous trifles, because they notice every detail of the way their mate walks, talks, dresses, eats, sleeps, bathes, and so on. Gradually, they begin to get used to one another, and they don't notice these things as much.

8. Material roles include earning income and learning to manage it, responsibility for cooking and homemaking, and physical care.

9. Learning to be independent and make one's own decisions is hard for those who have never been away from parents and on their own.

10. Selecting friends and establishing a joint and satisfactory social life is another task to be accomplished.

11. Learning to share and cooperate and to begin to think in terms of "we" rather than "I" is another important adjustment.

12. The transition to parenthood is a time of stress and requires considerable adjustment.

13. Midlife issues include adjusting to physical changes and to the increasing awareness of one's mortality. This leads to a shift in time orientation; to introspection, self-analysis, self-appraisal, and stock-taking; and to asking basic questions about the purpose and goals of life.

14. The assessment of self extends to an examination of the responsibilities of one's career and marriage. Midlife can become a time for reexamination, for charting new courses for life ahead.

15. Middle age can also become a time for revitalizing a tired marriage, for rethinking the relationship, and for deciding what things in life the couple wants to share together.

16. The postparental years are usually happier for couples. They have a greater chance to do what they want without the responsibility of children.

17. Sometimes the empty nest doesn't stay that way. Children move back home for various reasons, resulting in potential conflict.

18. The task of staying physically healthy becomes more difficult as people age. It requires good health habits and the practice of preventive medicine.

19. Many adults face the problem of having adequate income in their old age. Most people face a significant drop in income when they retire.

20. Forced retirement creates stress. People ought to be able to decide for themselves when they should retire. Partial retirement and part-time employment is a happy solution for some people. Certainly, retirement need not be a time of idleness and uselessness. People ought to retire to something, not from; they need worthwhile things to do after retirement.

21. Having acceptable housing and living conditions is a problem for many elderly. Many want their own residence, which allows them independence.

22. Maintaining identity and social status after retirement becomes a problem in industrial societies where people have position because of the work they perform. The elderly need to find identity through avocations, social events, marriage, their children, or other activities.

23. Finding companionship and friendship is one important key to life satisfaction in late adulthood.

24. Learning to enjoy leisure time contributes to well-being in late adulthood.

25. Roles in the family change as people get older, but new ones need to be established in relation to grown children and grandchildren.

26. The achievement of ego integrity through a life review and acceptance of one's life as it has been is the chief psychosocial task of the last stage of life.

27. Marital happiness and satisfaction usually increase after the children are launched and immediately after retirement, and then decrease again as age takes its toll.

28. The image of parents growing older without contact and concern of adult children does not coincide with the facts. Contacts are frequent. Emotional support is more important than financial help, and morale is higher if the elderly can reciprocate. Considerable stress is created if adult children have to provide extensive care for severely functionally impaired parents.

29. Divorce is more stressful in late adulthood than it is earlier in life.

30. Because of the greater longevity of women, and because men are on the average two years older than women when they marry, the average married woman can expect to live the last eight years of her life as a widow. The death of a spouse is recognized as one of life's most traumatic events.

31. Widows face a number of problems: loneliness, home maintenance and car repair, financial problems, and role changes in the family.

32. Widowers are usually not as close to their families as widows are and so have less social support. Widowers may have more difficulty in caring for dependent children, cooking, and doing household chores.

MARRIAGES AND FAMILY RELATIONSHIPS: GROWTH AND CHALLENGES

Dangott, L. R., and Kalish, R. A. (1979). *A Time to Enjoy: The Pleasures of Aging.* Englewood Cliffs, NJ: Prentice-Hall. Encourages people to realize that they have choices and ought to take advantage of and enjoy the pleasures of aging.

Fiske, M. (1979). *Middle Age: The Prime of Life?* New York: Harper and Row. Stress and coping in middle age.

Fried, B. (1976) *The Middle-Age Crisis.* New York: Harper and Row. A lucid, witty study of the problems that plague men and women entering the middle years.

Fuch, E. (1978). *The Second Season.* Garden City, NY: Anchor Press/Doubleday. Life, love, and sex for women in the middle years.

Hunter, W. W. (1976). *Preparation for Retirement.* Ann Arbor, MI: Institute of Gerontology, The University of Michigan–Wayne State University. Life after retirement can be more than a postscript. People need to prepare for new roles.

Jorgensen, J. (1980) *The Graying of America: Retirement and Why You Can't Afford It.* New York: McGraw-Hill. All the reasons why people shouldn't retire completely.

Kalish, R. A. (1975). *Late Adulthood: Perspectives on Human Development.* Monterey, CA: Brooks/Cole. Part of life-span human development series, emphasizing biology, cognition, personality and the self, relating to others, and physical and social environment.

Kohn, J. B., and Kohn, W. K. (1978). *The Widower.* Boston: Beacon. Problems and adjustments of the widower.

Levinson, D. J. (1978). *The Seasons of a Man's Life.* New York: Ballantine. Popular results of research on the adult life cycle.

Peterson, J. A., and Briley, M. L. (1977). *Widows and Widowhood.* New York: Association Press. A creative approach to being alone.

Ragan, P. K. (Ed.). (1979). *Aging Parents.* Los Angeles: USC Press. A series of articles by experts.

Rubin, L. G. (1979). *Women of a Certain Age: The Midlife Search for Self.* New York: Harper and Row. The challenges facing middle-aged women in our society.

Sheehy, G. (1976). *Passages.* New York: Dutton. The adult life cycle during young and middle adulthood and the predictable crises of adult life.

Silverstone, B., and Hyman, H. K. (1976). *You and Your Aging Parent.* New York: Pantheon. The modern family's guide to emotional, physical, and financial problems of aging parents.

Steinberg, L. D. (Ed.). (1981). *The Life Cycle: Readings in Human Development.* New York: Columbia University Press. An academic presentation.

Stevenson, J. S. (1977). *Issues and Crises During Middlescence.* New York: Appleton-Century-Crofts. Significant issues and crises of young adulthood and middle adulthood with special emphasis on the middle years.

Troll, L. E., Israel, J., and Israel, K. (1977). *Looking Ahead: A Woman's Guide to the Problems and Joys of Growing Older.* Englewood Cliffs, NJ: Prentice-Hall. Issues such as sexuality, menopause, marriage, friendships, and jobs.

Van Hoose, W. H., and Worth, M. R. (1982). *Adulthood in the Life Cycle.* Dubuque, IA: William C. Brown. Various aspects of adulthood development.

12

SEX AND GENDER: IDENTITY AND ROLES*

*Part of the material in this chapter is taken from the author's book *Human Sexuality* © 1989 by William C. Brown Co. Used by permission of the publisher.

Sex describes more than what we do. It describes who we are as biological males or females. We also manifest personality traits and behavior that characterize us as men or women. These are largely acquired as learned behavior while we grow up. The purpose of this chapter is to examine the concepts of gender, gender identity, and gender roles and to describe some of the influences on their development. Traditional masculine-feminine stereotypes are also discussed to show their effects on human potential, relationships, and roles. Gender roles in interpersonal relationships, in the family, and over the life cycle are examined along with children's roles and the importance of spouse gender role consensus. The chapter concludes with a discussion of the present trend toward more androgynous personalities and roles.

SEX AND GENDER

Sex

From a physical viewpoint, **sex** may be defined as our biological identity, whether male or female. The definition sounds simple. "He" is a boy; "she" is a girl, based upon biological characteristics. The usual method for determining a child's biological sex is through external genital examination. Thus, a child is assigned a **genital identity** (Waltner, 1986). But this method of sex assignment may be in error in cases of **pseudohermaphroditism** when a boy or girl has external genitalia characteristic of the opposite sex. The true **hermaphrodite**, of course, has genitalia, gonads, and internal reproductive organs of both sexes. The only sure way to determine if an individual is a biological male or female is a microscopic examination to determine whether a child has female (XX) or male (XY) chromosomes.

Gender and Gender Identity

Gender includes not only our biological sex, but also those psychosocial components that characterized us as a male or female (Lips, 1980). **Gender identity** has been defined as a person's personal, internal sense of maleness or femaleness, which is expressed in personality and behavior. This is our subjective sense of being a male or female. Most children accept cognitively their assigned sex as a boy or a girl and then strive to act according to the expectations of the society and the group of which they are a part. Some children, however, have difficulty establishing their gender identification. The most notable examples are **transsexuals**, who cannot accept their assigned gender even though it is biologically correct. Psychologically, they consider themselves to be the opposite of their biological sex.

Gender Roles

Gender role is our sex role as the outward manifestation and expression of our maleness and femaleness in a social setting (Scanzoni and Fox, 1980). It is expressed in our personality and behavior and is related to and influenced by cultural expectations of what is considered socially appropriate. Behavior thought to be appropriate for a male is considered masculine. That which is thought to be appropriate for a female is considered feminine.

ENVIRONMENTAL INFLUENCES

Masculinity and Femininity

Sex is determined by biological factors. Gender identities and gender roles are influenced by the environment. Certain qualities of maleness are defined and become "masculine" because of society's view of what being male means. Society prescribes how a male ought to look and behave, what type of personality he ought to have, and what roles he should perform. Similarly, a female is created not only by genetic conception but also by those psychosocial forces that mold and influence her personality. When we speak of a masculine man, we express a value judgment based on an assessment of the personality and behavioral characteristics of the male according to culturally defined standards of "maleness." Similarly, a feminine woman is labeled according to culturally determined criteria for "femaleness." In this sense, the development of **masculinity** or **femininity** is education in what it means to be a man or a woman within the context of the culture in which one lives (Rice, 1989).

Concepts of masculinity and femininity vary with different human societies and cultures. Margaret Mead (1950), in studying three primitive tribes, discovered some interesting differences. *Arapesh* men and women displayed "feminine" personality traits. Both males and females were trained to be cooperative,

Certain qualities of maleness are defined and become "masculine" because of society's view of what being male means.

unaggressive, and responsive to the needs and demands of others. In contrast, *Mundugumor* men and women developed "masculine" traits; they were ruthless, aggressive, and positively sexed, with maternal cherishing aspects of personality at a minimum. In the third tribe, the *Tchambuli*, the sex attitudes and roles prescribed by American culture were reversed: the woman was dominant and impersonal; the man was less responsible and more emotionally dependent.

Concepts of masculinity and femininity have undergone considerable change in the United States. In early colonial days, a "true man," especially a gentleman, could wear hose, a powdered wig, and a lace shirt without being considered unmanly. Today he would be considered quite feminine. Thus, the judgments made about masculinity or the extent of "manliness" are subjective judgments based on the accepted standards of "maleness" as defined by the culture. These standards vary from culture to culture or with different periods of history in the same society (Rice, 1989).

Societal Expectations

Because society plays such an important role in the establishment of the criteria for masculinity and femininity and in the development of maleness or femaleness, it is important to understand how gender identification and gender role learning take place. *After assessment of sex, society expects the child to begin thinking and acting like a boy or like a girl, according to its own definitions.* If a child is a girl, she is dressed like a girl. She is expected to wear girls'

Concepts of masculinity or femininity have undergone considerable change over the centuries. Still, this 19th century dandy shows some striking similarities to the contemporary image of the "true man."

underwear, shoes, and stockings; girls' blouses; and girls' coats. She is given
dolls and other toys considered appropriate for little girls. She is expected to
act like a "little lady." She is encouraged to play girls' games and, as she gets
older, to help her mother around the house in doing traditionally feminine
chores.

As a girl grows up, she is encouraged to enter occupations that are considered feminine (such as nursing) or to avoid others that are considered
masculine (such as manual labor in heavy industry) (Kenkel and Gage, 1983).
While these definitions are changing somewhat, there are still sex-typed occupations, and the girl is expected to abide by social expectations. She is also
pressured to get married. If she does marry, all of her family and friends keep
asking her when she is going to become a mother.

Thus, what society expects a girl to be and do becomes the basic influence
in molding her into a woman. She also observes her older sister, her mother,
and other females acting like women, and so she begins to identify with them,
to imitate them, and to model her behavior after others (Klein and Shulman,
1981). Thus, once sex is assigned and accepted by her and others, the more
she is programmed to become a woman. The same process applies to boys:
once sex is assigned, the boy is expected to dress, talk, think, and act like a
man; manifest masculine traits; enter masculine occupations; and do masculine things. He is programmed to become a man.

Various social influences play a role in gender identity and gender role
development. Three of these influences will be discussed here: *parental influences, influences of television,* and *school influences.*

Parental Influences

*One of the ways that children develop gender identification and appropriate gender
roles is through identification with parents and modeling their behavior.* (Lueptow,
1980; Smith and Self, 1980). **Parental identification and modeling** is that
process by which the child adopts and internalizes parental values, attitudes,
behavioral traits, and personality characteristics (Korman, 1983b). Identification begins soon after birth because of children's early dependency upon
their parents. This dependency, in turn, normally leads to emotional attachment. Gender identification and gender role learning take place almost unconsciously and indirectly in this intimate parent-child relationship. The child
may learn that his or her mother is soft, warm, and gentle, that she is affectionate, nurturing, kind, and sensitive. Others learn that their mother is
rough, loud, and rejecting. Not only does each child receive different care
from each parent; but he or she also listens and observes that each parent
behaves, speaks, dresses, and acts differently in relation to the other parent,
to other children, or to persons outside the family. Thus, the child learns
what is a mother, a wife, a father, a husband, a woman, or a man through
the parental example set and through daily contacts and associations.

Usually young boys and girls both identify more closely with the mother
than with the father, primarily because they are more often with their mothers.
As a result, young boys often show more similarity to their mothers than to
their fathers. As a result, they may have greater difficulty in achieving same-
sex identification than do girls and are often more anxious than females
regarding their gender identification and roles (Currant et al., 1979). On the

305

SEX AND GENDER:
IDENTITY AND ROLES

Is cooking the family dinner a sex-typed role? The ability to perform any family task without concern for its sex appropriateness can affect the child's marital role later in life.

one hand, they are more severely punished for being "sissies" than girls are for being masculine; and, on the other hand, they have more difficulty breaking away from feminine influences and finding suitable male role models. When the father is absent from the home, the male child may have even more difficulty because of the lack of masculine influence.

Influence of Television

Television plays a significant role in the socialization process for young and old alike. Children's television and its commercials contain considerable gender bias and sexism (Mayes and Valentine, 1979; Welch et al., 1979). However, children do not watch children's programs only. Prime-time television draws the largest numbers from every age group. Hoyenga and Hoyenga (1979) studied some 300 prime-time television commercials with an eye to how gender roles were presented. The results are shown in Table 12.1.

In general, TV commercials portray women almost solely in the helping role, waiting on others and living out their lives in service to others, never really taking charge of their own lives (Walstedt, 1977). Such a view perpetuates traditional views of women's role in society (Doyle, 1985).

In the television shows packaged in between the commercials, women generally are excluded or portrayed in very narrow and traditional roles (Hashell, 1979). Two rather exhaustive government-sponsored studies of television programming (U.S. Commission on Civil Rights, 1977, 1979) concluded

TABLE 12.1 Gender Roles in 300 Television Commercials

Role or Occupation	Percentage Male	Percentage Female	N*
Baby and infant care	—	100	12
Inmate in nursing home	—	100	7
House cleaning	3	97	35
Washing clothes and dishes	3	97	32
Shopping	3	97	32
Cooking and serving food	6	94	80
Store owner	50	50	8
Salesperson	71	29	14
Product expert	74	26	82
Builder	80	20	25
Riding motorcycle	88	12	8
Farmer	90	10	10
Engaging in sports	93	7	72
Driving a vehicle	94	6	32
Office worker (not secretary)	100	—	15
Soldier	100	—	25
Service station worker	100	—	11
Miscellaneous occupations (secretary, nurse, doctor, etc.)	51	49	57

Source: The question of sex differences: Psychological, cultural, and biological issues (p. 216) by Katharine Blick Hoyenga and Kermit T. Hoyenga, 1979, Boston: Little Brown. Copyright © 1979 by Katharine Blick Hoyenga and Kermit T. Hoyenga. Reprinted by permission of the authors.

*N is the total number of people participating in that particular role. People not performing a particular task (those standing or walking, for instance) were not counted. The only overlapping role was "product expert"; those people sometimes had another role.

that television portrayed most women as having no definable occupation or means of support. Of those women employed outside the home, a majority held positions — such as nurses and household workers — associated with traditional "women's work" (Kalisch and Kalisch, 1984). Besides showing women performing traditional female tasks, the studies also found that women, for the most part, were portrayed as being dependent on men for their livelihood; men were generally portrayed as being more independent and in charge of a variety of situations (Dominick, 1979). Male TV characters were shown in ambitious, adventuresome, strong, and dominant roles, whereas females were more often cast in dependent, submissive, and weak or auxiliary roles. In the most general sense, male TV characters are either heroes or villains, and females appear as either adulterers or victims of men's actions (Goff, Goff, and Lehrer, 1980; Doyle, 1985).

Television affects the value system of those who watch it. The messages beamed into the living rooms of millions of people every day shape their attitudes, beliefs, and gender roles. With regard to television's influence on gender roles, the research of Fruch and McGhee (1975) is most revealing. Basically, these researchers found that children who were "heavy" television viewers (25 or more hours a week) held more traditional gender stereotypes and values than did those who were "light" viewers (10 or fewer hours a week). Others have also found that "heavy" television viewing, as well as how television portrays gender roles, has a relationship to conceptions about gender stereotypes among preschool viewers (Gross and Jeffries-Fox, 1978) and young adult viewers (Eisenstock, 1984). A word of caution, however. These studies

Television plays a significant part in the sex role socialization of children.

do not prove cause and effect, but they do show there is a relationship between TV viewing and gender stereotypes. Either television influences a person's gender attitudes, or people who hold traditional gender stereotypes watch more television, or there is some other factor that influences both variables (Doyle, 1985).

School Influences

Gender concepts and roles are taught both informally at home and more formally in school as the child grows up (Brody and Steelman, 1985; Rosen and Aneshensel, 1978). Giving children gender-specific toys may have considerable influence on vocational choices. Such toys influence boys to be scientists, astronauts, or football players and girls to be nurses, teachers, or stewardesses (Kacerguis and Adams, 1979). Publishers have made a considerable effort to remove sexual stereotypes from reading materials. Without realizing it, however, many teachers still develop traditional masculine-feminine stereotypical behavior in school. Studies of teachers' relationships with boys and girls reveal that teachers encourage boys to be more assertive in the classroom (Sadker and Sadker, 1985). When the teacher asks questions, the boys often call out comments without raising their hands, literally grabbing the teacher's attention. Most girls sit patiently with their hands raised, but if a girl calls out, the teacher reprimands her: "In this class, we don't shout out the answers; we raise our hands." The message is subtle and unintentional, but powerful: boys should be assertive academically; girls should be quiet (Rice, 1989).

Much has also been done to try to change school courses and programs that promote gender-typed roles. Traditionally, physical education courses for boys emphasized contact sports and competition; those for girls promoted grace, agility, and poise. Home economics was offered only to girls; shop and auto mechanics only to boys. Guidance counselors urged girls to become secretaries and nurses, boys to become business managers and doctors. Females were usually prepared for marriage and parenthood, boys for a vocation. Gradually these emphases are declining, so that both males and females are free to choose the programs they want (Rice, 1989).

Implications

Social learning theory thus emphasizes that boys develop "maleness" and girls "femaleness" through exposure to scores of influences — parents, television, school, and others — that indoctrinate them in what it means to be a man or a woman in the culture in with they are brought up (Goffman, 1977). They are further encouraged to accept the appropriate gender identity by being rewarded for one kind of behavior and punished for another (Flake-Hobson, Skeen, and Robinson, 1980). Thus, gender-role concepts and stereotypes of a particular culture become self-fulfilling prophecies (Snyder, 1982). Those who have lived up to societal expectations are accepted as normal; those who do not conform are criticized and pressured to comply. Society ostracizes nonconformers and forces them to seek those with similar concepts or identities.

MASCULINE-FEMININE STEREOTYPES

Many people develop stereotyped concepts of masculinity and femininity (Albrecht, Barr, and Chadwick, 1977). The word stereotype first appeared in 1798 when Didot, a French printer, designed printing blocks to duplicate pages of type. The essential feature of these stereotypes, or printing blocks, was their permanence and unchangeableness (Naffziger and Naffziger, 1974, p. 252). Gradually, the term began to be used for any rigid concept or idea held about others, whether or not those ideas were current. Today, **gender stereotypes** are assumed differences, norms, attitudes, and expectations about men and women.

Masculinity

According to typical masculine stereotypes, men are suppose to be:

Aggressive	Adventurous
Dominant	Courageous
Strong	Independent
Forceful	Ambitious
Self-confident	Direct
Rugged	Logical
Virile	Unemotional
Instrumental	

These stereotypes of masculinity are considered socially desirable by some elements (but certainly not all) in our society today. The stereotypical American businessman is supposed to be aggressive and ambitious. The man in "Marlboro Country" ads is rugged, tattooed, and virile.

A good description of masculine stereotypes in our culture is given by David and Brannon in their book *The Forty-nine Percent Majority: The Male Sex Role* (David and Brannon, 1976). They emphasize three dimensions of the traditional male sex role.

To be a man, the male has to avoid all sissy stuff or anything feminine. This rule is applied to every aspect of life. If the male buys cosmetics, these have to have names like *Brut, Command,* or *Hai Karate.* The male has to avoid hobbies and pastimes like knitting, flower arranging, or poetry. He is never to be emotional or to reveal tender emotions or weaknesses. Above all, men are never to express affection toward other men so as to avoid all suspicion of homosexuality (Tognoli, 1980).

To be a man, the male must be a big wheel: he must be successful, have status, and be looked up to. This means achieving wealth or fame or other symbols of success such as being able to afford fancy clothes or expensive cars. Men who do not make it in business have to prove themselves in other ways: by being stronger and tougher than anyone else, by being able to seduce and dominate women, or even by becoming the champion dart thrower at the neighborhood bar.

To be a man, a male must be a sturdy rock with an air of toughness, confidence, and self-reliance. The great heroes are John Wayne in *True Grit,* Clint Eastwood in *Dirty Harry,* or Sylvester Stallone in *Rocky.* Real men must sometimes hurt, conquer, humble, outwit, punish, or defeat others. An aura of sex and violence pervades much of life and is one symbol of misconceived masculinity.

Femininity

What are the traditional concepts of femininity as taught by the middle and upper-middle strata of our society? In the past, women were supposed to be:

Unaggressive	Warm and affectionate
Submissive	Sentimental
Weak	Softhearted
Sensitive	Dependent
Gentle, tender	Aware of feelings of others
Kind	Emotional and excitable
Tactful	Somewhat frivolous, fickle, illogical, talkative

A "feminine" female was never too aggressive, too boisterous, loud, or vulgar in speech or behavior (Hall and Black, 1979). She was expected to be tender, softhearted, and sensitive and to cry on occasion and to sometimes get upset over small things (Balswick and Avertt, 1977). It was all right for her to like laces, frills, and the frivolous. She was expected to be submissive and dependent and interested primarily in her home (Dweck et al., 1978; Soltz, 1978).

Concepts of femininity often vary. Who is to say that one woman is more or less "feminine" than another woman? How much room is there for individual differences and choices?

Today, there are few social groups where these stereotypes of femininity are rigidly held, indicating the significant changes that have already taken place in our concepts.

Problems with Stereotypes

One problem with stereotypes is that whenever rigid gender standards are applied to all members of one sex, individual personalities can become distorted. Everyone is expected to conform, regardless of individual differences or inclinations. Furthermore, gender identity and gender role stereotypes place serious limitations on the relationships that people are capable of forming and on career or personal achievements. The traditionally unaggressive, submissive, weak female was not able to stand up for herself at home, so her husband and children took advantage of her. If she was considered emotional, frivolous, or illogical, she was thought to be unworthy to assume positions of leadership in government or business. (In spite of women's advances, only two of the Fortune 500 corporations are headed by women.) If our daughters are expected to be breadwinners, if many women remain single, or if some women are required to raise their children alone, then they need the same assertiveness, independence, and rational thinking that we seek to develop in our sons. If women are to succeed, new roles require acceptance of different traits.

What about the traditional gentler female traits: tenderness, kindness, softheartedness, sensitivity, and awareness of the feelings of others? These traits have always been needed in all types of human relationships, a fact that qualified women to play the role of nurturer. Traditionally men were not supposed to exhibit these traits. They were not supposed to show feelings, to cry; they were supposed to be impervious to sorrow, pain, and tragedy, and to be able "to take it like a man." As a result, some men considered it unmanly to tell their wives "I love you" or to give their children (especially boys) a big hug and kiss. Men were encouraged to be interested in sex because "real men" were virile, but they were often encouraged to be indifferent to love.

The result has been insensitive men and sensitive women trying to learn to live together in the same world (Notarius and Johnson, 1982). The very traits that women were supposed to exhibit and men were expected to suppress exposed women to the hurts and upsets of intimate living and isolated men from being able to understand why their partners were so upset in the first place. It was also difficult for men and women to become real friends and companions.

As far as family life is concerned, being openly aggressive, dominant, independent, and unemotional is distinctly disadvantageous. The over-aggressive male gets in trouble with friends, family, and society. An earth populated by aggressive males results in wars and destruction. Modern men need to be less aggressive and more cooperative. Modern women need to be more assertive and less passive. Both need to be sensitive and tender in their feelings and relationships with one another.

As far as roles in the family are concerned, *highly segregated gender roles result in lack of cooperation, companionship, and intimacy in the family.* Cooperative sharing of roles results in greater contentment and companionship among all family members and in greater opportunities for meaninfgul relationships.

1. Should young boys be allowed to play with toys traditionally designed for girls, such as dolls, baby carriages, housekeeping toys, and dishes? Explain.
2. Should young girls be allowed to play traditional boy's games, such as football, baseball, basketball, and hockey? Explain.
3. How do you feel about traditional concepts of masculinity? Explain.
4. How do you feel about traditional concepts of femininity? Explain.
5. What changes need to be made in traditional concepts of masculinity? Why? Will men become too "sissy" if taught to be more emotional?
6. What changes need to be made in traditional concepts of femininity? Why? Will women become too aggressive?

GENDER ROLES IN INTERPERSONAL RELATIONSHIPS

Men as Initiators; Women as Followers

Typically, the assertive male was supposed to be the initiator in relationships between the sexes, and the woman was expected to follow. He was expected to ask *her* out on a date and to decide where to go, what to do, and when to meet. He was expected to court *her* while she demurely, but coquettishly responded. He was expected to ask for *her* hand in marriage. The woman who was too bold or forward was regarded as a threat to the traditional relationship.

After marriage, the male continued his dominant role as decision maker and initiator. He was supposed to have the last word over that of both his wife and children. Today, the male who tries to play this dominant role may find himself in conflict both with himself and with his female companion.

Complaints about male dominance are frequent among women of all ages and statuses: "Everything is his way. We always do what he wants. When is he going to consider my feelings?" Sometimes, these same men complain because it is they who always have to initiate sex. One man commented: "I can remember only one time when my partner initiated foreplay. I'm the one who always has to start. Why can't she be the aggressor? I'd like her to seduce me sometimes" (Author's counseling notes). This man was inconsistent in his expectations, however. He wanted a woman who followed his lead in most daily activities, but who seduced him in bed. Actually, he was unsure about his role.

Double Standards of Behavior

Stereotyped concepts of gender roles also result in double standards of behavior. Men as aggressors have been encouraged to express their sexual desires, women to inhibit theirs. Men were supposed to "need sex," but not women. As a result, men sought multiple partners, but the woman who did so was considered a "loose" woman. Men were taught to express sexual desire, but not to show feelings. As a result, the male was likely to have sex without warmth and emotional feeling. Women were allowed to be emotional, but not erotic. Consequently, women showed emotions and feelings but inhibited their sexual desire and expression. Wives complained that their husbands were unfeeling. Husbands complained that their wives weren't interested in sex. Men and women aren't born that way. Men can learn to be warm and loving, women to be erotic.

Women as Givers, Men as Receivers

As another consequence of stereotypical gender roles, women have been taught that their role is to please the man, regardless of their own needs and desires. Nowhere is this more evident than in intimate relationships. Some women go through years of marriage attending to their husband's wants.

If women are to achieve true equality in intimate relationships, they can no longer be the passive, pleasing partners who consider their partner's needs without regard for their own. This means learning to communicate their needs to their partner. Their full satisfaction requires that their partners reciprocate in kind and be as giving as they are demanding.

GENDER ROLES IN THE FAMILY

Beliefs About Gender Roles

Beliefs about men and women profoundly affect the roles they play in the family. Some adults believe that gender roles are innate; that men and women are "born" to perform certain roles (Mirowsky and Ross, 1987). The male chauvinist, for example, considers women subordinate, without equal authority, destined to care for husbands and children, not suited for many kinds of jobs because of their physical, emotional, and mental nature. According to this view, if employed, they cannot expect equal pay for equal work, because men are meant to be the primary breadwinners.

Not surprisingly, men more often than women believe in innate gender roles. Subjects who are older, less educated, and more traditional in their religious beliefs also hold more traditional beliefs about gender roles (Cherlin and Walters, 1981; Duncan, 1982; Hartman and Hartman, 1983; Huber and Spitze, 1983; Peek and Brown, 1980; Ransford and Miller, 1983; Rogler and Procidano, 1986; Thornton, Alwin, and Camburn, 1983). One important goal of the women's movement has been to motivate women to achieve true egalitarian rights and roles. As long as sexist views persist, women will be placed in subordinate, inferior roles. Feminists have been insistent, however, that the emphasis on equality does not mean they desire or expect women and men to be and act identically (Margolin, Talovic, Fernandez, and Onorato, 1983). Rather, the emphasis has been on freedom—the freedom to choose one's own destiny and status.

Housework and Child-Care Roles

With over half of all married women gainfully employed outside the home, fairness would require a willingness on the part of husbands to assume shared responsibilitity for housework and child care. *Significant progress has been made, but egalitarian roles have not been achieved fully* (Bird, Bird, and Scruggs, 1984). Marital satisfaction depends partly on partners perceiving themselves and their spouses as each doing a fair share of family work (Yogev and Brett, 1985). When women work outside the home and then have to come home and do most of the work around the house and care for the children, they experience considerable role conflict and strain (Elman and Gilbert, 1984; Katz and Piotrkowski, 1983; Van Meter and Agronow, 1982). A study of dairy farm wives in New York revealed that when husbands offered support to their wives in the performance of both farm and home roles, the wives reported far less role conflict and stress in fulfilling their dual roles (Berkowitz and Perkins, 1984).

Individual psychological well-being has also been equated with less traditional sex-role orientation (Markides and Vernon, 1984). Furthermore, the quality of child care is related negatively to the amount of housework mothers are expected to perform (Olson, 1981). In families where husbands and wives share household chores, mothers have more time to respond to their children's personal and social needs. Sharing is important, therefore, to individual well-being, to the marital relationship, and to quality parent-child relationships (Haas, 1980).

Several studies reveal, however, that mothers still spend significantly more time doing housework and caring for children than do their husbands. One study of 1,565 white couples, some of whom were dual-earner families and others of whom were single-earner families, revealed that overall the wives performed about

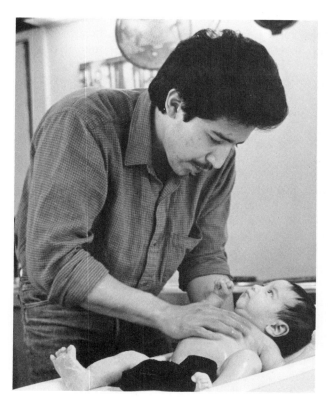

In families where husbands help with child care and household responsibilities, working wives report considerably less role conflict and stress.

Fathers' willingness to participate in child care is influenced by a number of variables. Barnett's and Baruch's (1987) research with 160 Caucasian, middle-class parents revealed the following:

The more hours the wife worked per week, the more likely the fathers participated in child care tasks. (A few studies disagree with this.)

Liberal mothers who expected the help of their husbands were more likely to get it than were traditional mothers who did not expect such help.

Fathers who reported dissatisfaction with the quality of fathering they received as children tended to compensate by providing more care for their own children.

Fathers did a higher proportion of child-care tasks when their child was small.

Fathers spent more time in interacting with their children when the children were younger than when they were older. (The same is true of mothers.)

Fathers' proportionate interaction time was greater when there were more children in the family.

Fathers spent more time caring for their children when the fathers worked fewer hours per week.

79 percent of the housework that was done in their homes (Berardo, Shehan, and Leslie, 1987). Even in dual-earner families the wives performed 69 to 71 percent of the housework, the percent depending on the types of jobs husbands and wives held. Another study of 40 upper-middle-class families in metropolitan Boston revealed that mothers spent significantly more time in child care and did more of the traditionally feminine child-care tasks and household chores while fathers did more of the traditionally masculine household chores (Levant, Slattery, and Loiselle, 1987). Another study over a 10-year period (from 1965–1975) revealed few changes in the amount of time men spent in housework and child care even though wives' participation in the labor force increased considerably during that same period (Coverman and Sheley, 1986).

Roles over the Family Life Cycle

There is some evidence that *perceived equity in family roles tends to increase over the family life cycle* (Schafer and Keith, 1981). A study of 364 community-dwelling older adults revealed that most of these persons described flexible roles in their relationships and, furthermore, that this group obtained higher scores on mental health items that were used as behavioral measures of successful aging (Sinnott, 1982). Apparently, life situations and learning resulted in a trend toward dual masculine-feminine roles as people got older.

Children's Roles

As more and more women join the labor force, the question arises as to what extent children, as well as fathers, are expected to participate in household tasks. Because working spouses are facing time pressure, one solution is to enlist the help of children. A study of 105 two-parent, two-child families,

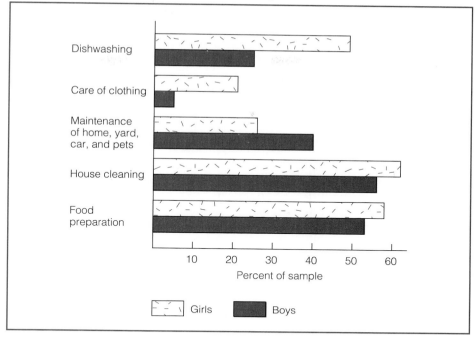

FIGURE 12.1 Participation Rate
in Household Tasks by Children.

Adapted from Gogle, F. L., and Tasker, G. E. (1983). Children and housework. *Family Relations, 31,*
395–399. Copyright ©1983 by the National Council on Family Relations. Reprinted by permission.

where the children were 6 through 17 years of age revealed some interesting findings (Cogle and Tasher, 1982). The majority of children (88 percent) participated in at least one household task. Both boys and girls participated most often in house cleaning and food preparation. Boys participated least often in care of clothing and in dishwashing, girls least often in care of clothing and in maintenance of home, yard, car, and pets. Figure 12.1 shows the results. Apparently, there was some sex-role stereotyping in children's participation in the home.

Whether stereotyping occurs depends partly on the sex of the children in the family. Brody and Steelman (1985) found that the more daughters in a family, the more likely sex-typing of traditional female chores increased. As the number of sons increased, the sex-typing of traditional female chores decreased. Also, when there were more sons in the family, they were expected to do traditional male chores, regardless of the number of girls in the family.

Some parents overlook their children as one of the best sources of household help available. *Participation in housework plays an important role in teaching children family responsibility, home living skills, and accompanying attitudes that carry over into their adult lives.*

Gender Role Consensus

If husbands and wives agree on gender role expectations and performance, couples report higher marital quality than if there is disagreement (Bowen and Orthner,

1983). A wife who wants her husband to fulfill certain roles, but whose spouse does not live up to her expectations, will not be completely satisfied with the relationship. Husbands too have certain preconceived expectations about the roles their wives should fulfill. If their wives do not live up to expectations, marital satisfaction is less (Bahr, Chappell, and Leigh, 1983; McNamara and Bahr, 1980). The need for **gender-role congruence** is an important consideration in selecting a mate with whom one will be compatible.

ANDROGYNY

What seems to be emerging is a gradual mixing of male and female identities and roles to produce **androgyny** (male and female in one). Androgynous persons are not gender-typed with respect to roles, although they are distinctly male or female in sex (Bem, 1975). They match their behavior to the situation rather than being limited by what is culturally defined as male or female. An androgynous male feels comfortable cuddling and caring for a young boy; an androgynous female feels comfortable pumping gas and changing the oil in her car. Androgyny expands the range of acceptable behavior,

Androgyny expands the range of acceptable behavior. Clothes and hairstyles do not express either maleness or femaleness.

allowing individuals to cope effectively in a variety of situations (Flake-Hobson, Skeen, and Robinson, 1980).

319

SEX AND GENDER:
IDENTITY AND ROLES

Advantages

The mixing of roles is advantageous to both sexes. Traditional men lack sensitivity and emotional warmth and so encounter difficulty in forming close attachments and friendships. They see danger in intimacy, are afraid of a smothering relationship or rejection and hurt. Traditional women see danger in isolation, independence, and achievement, are afraid of being set apart by success, being ridiculed, or being left alone. Men's aggressiveness leads to conflict and violence. Women's passive submission leads to exploitation (Gulligan, 1982). Both sexes are restricted in their behavior and relationships by narrow and constricting sex-typed roles (Rice, 1989). Research has indicated that both masculine and androgynous people are more independent and less conforming than those identified with femininity, and that both feminine and androgynous individuals are more nurturing than those who are traditionally masculine (Bem, Martyna, and Watson, 1976).

In recent years, a number of studies have asked: "Can a man or woman possess androgynous traits and be psychologically healthy and well-adjusted?" This is an important question since, historically, psychologists taught that mental health depended on a clear-cut separation between male and female roles (Cook, 1985). *Now, some studies reveal that androgynous individuals have better social relationships and superior adjustments than others* (Avery, 1982; Wells, 1980). A study of the relationship of sex roles to physical and psychological health of 180 men and women with an average age of 18.3 revealed that androgynous individuals always showed a more favorable adjustment (Small, Teagno, and Selz, 1980). They possessed adaptive capabilities and resources such as effective coping techniques, emotional integration, communication skills, and a well-defined self-concept with a high level of ego strength and integration. Another study, this of 195 new mothers, showed that those classified as either androgynous or masculine scored lower on dimensions reflecting psychological distress than did their feminine or undifferentiated counterparts (Bassoff, 1984). A study of military wives indicated that androgynous gender role orientation influenced coping patterns positively, aiding in their adjustment to long-term separation (Patterson and McCubbin, 1984).

Other studies show that androgynous persons evidence more flexible behavior, higher levels of self-esteem, and more social competence and motivation to achieve than do gender-typed people (Bem, 1979; Bem and Lenney, 1976). As far as sexual behavior is concerned, Walfish and Myerson (1980) found that androgynous people, both men and women, have more positive attitudes sexually than do those who were traditionally gender-typed. Other studies found more tolerance of various types of sexual behavior in androgynous people (Garcia, 1982) and greater incidence of orgasm and sexual satisfaction in adrogynous women (Kimlicka, Cross, and Tarnai, 1983; Radlove, 1983). Androgynous men have been found to feel less pressure to perform sexually and to have a lower incidence of sexual dysfunction than do masculine, sex-typed males (Spencer and Zeiss, 1987).

ASSESSMENT
Masculine, Feminine, or Androgynous?

The purpose of this assessment is to determine the extent to which you and/or your partner are traditional or androgynous in your gender-role expectations in the family. For each of the following items, draw a circle around the answer that best describes who should be primarily responsible for each task. Assume both the husband and wife are working full-time.

Task	Wife	Husband	Both
Cleaning house	W	H	B
Washing dishes	W	H	B
Washing clothes	W	H	B
Vacuuming rug	W	H	B
Washing floor	W	H	B
Dusting	W	H	B
Washing windows	W	H	B
Mowing lawn	W	H	B
Weeding garden	W	H	B
Planting flowers	W	H	B
Taking car for repairs	W	H	B
Cleaning car	W	H	B
Emptying trash	W	H	B
Writing checks for bills	W	H	B
Planning vacations	W	H	B
Balancing checkbook	W	H	B
Helping children with homework	W	H	B
Bathing baby	W	H	B
Changing baby's diaper	W	H	B
Playing games with children	W	H	B
Attending PTA meetings	W	H	B
Cooking food and preparing meals	W	H	B
Disciplining children	W	H	B

Development

How and when is androgyny developed? *College students who score low in traditional sex typing and high in socialization show a pattern of androgynous identification,* or modeling of a parental pair in which neither parent exemplifies the typical gender-role stereotypes. Instead, both parents provide models for their children: of competence, tolerance, consideration of others, and sharing of responsibilities (White, 1980). As a result, the children identify with the characteristics of both parents.

Two different studies of young adolescents showed that girls were more androgynous than boys early in their development (Mills, 1981; Nicholson and Antill, 1981). In seventh and eighth grades, girls viewed intellectual achievement more positively than did the same-age boys. Only later were girls socialized into a more feminine role that viewed achievement as a "masculine" pursuit. Boys appeared to be more sex-typed, so that intellectual pursuits were not part of the male role until later. Thus, *society tended to encourage a more androgynous sex role for boys as they got older but reinforced a more traditionally defined feminine sex role as the girls aged.* Nicholson and Antil (1981) describe the result: the number of problems reported by females

Sending out birthday cards	W	H	B
Planning social life	W	H	B
Initiating sexual intercourse	W	H	B
Maintaining contact with relatives	W	H	B
Selecting house to buy	W	H	B
Decorating house	W	H	B
Taking children to church	W	H	B
Driving car on trips	W	H	B
Feeding dog	W	H	B
Calling doctor	W	H	B
Calling bank	W	H	B
Deciding on investments	W	H	B

Totals

The man and woman should fill out the questionnaire separately to see how their views agree. There are 35 items in all. Add up the number of W's, H's, and B's for each partner. The most androgynous couples are those with the most B's. The degree of androgyny can be determined with the following scale:

Number of B's	Extent of Androgyny
19–23	Slightly androgynous
24–29	Somewhat androgynous
30–35	Very androgynous

The more W's, the more the person believes the items listed are the wife's responsibility. The more H's, the more the person believes the items listed are the husband's responsibility. If there is an imbalance between W's and H's, the person may be expecting an unequal division of responsibility in the family.

remained at a high level as they got older, primarily because of pressures to conform to a feminine gender role identity. But since the gender role demands on boys declined as they got older, they reported fewer problems.

SUMMARY

1. Sex is one's biological identity, male or female. Gender includes not only biological sex, but also those psychosocial components that characterize one as a male or female. Gender identity is an individual's personal, internal sense of maleness or femaleness that is expressed in personality and behavior. Gender role is one's sex role as the outward manifestation and expression of one's maleness and femaleness in a social setting.

2. Environmental influences are a major determinant of gender identities and gender roles. Society defines the qualities of maleness and femaleness needed to be a man or woman. Three of the major influences on children that mold their individual gender identities and roles are parental influences, influences of television, and school influences.

3. One of the problems is that people develop stereotyped concepts of masculinity and feminity. The problem with stereotypes is that by forcing everyone to conform to the same mold, the development of individual personality is severely limited, as is personal achievement. New demands require women to be more assertive and less passive and men to be less aggressive and more cooperative. Both sexes need the traditional female traits of tenderness, kindness, softheartedness, sensitivity, and awareness of the feelings of others in all types of human relationships. Cooperative sharing of roles results in greater contentment and companionship among family members.

4. Stereotypical gender role concepts affect interpersonal relationships between men and women. Men are supposed to be the initiators, women the followers. Double standards of behavior are encouraged. Women become the givers, men the receivers. These concepts make it difficult to build egalitarian relationships.

5. Beliefs about men and women affect profoundly the roles they play in the family. Those who believe that sex roles are innate are more likely to subscribe to traditional concepts that teach the subordinance of women. Feminists have been working to achieve egalitarian rights and roles for women.

6. Egalitarian roles have not been achieved fully, even though marital satisfaction, individual psychological well-being, and child-care quality are improved when husbands and wives share in family tasks. Mothers still spend significantly more time than their husbands doing housework and caring for children, even when the women work full-time outside the home.

7. Roles tend to become more equitable over the family life cycle as persons get older.

8. The majority of children participate in at least one household task. Participation in housework plays an important role in teaching children family responsibility, home living skills, and accompanying attitudes that carry over into their adult lives.

9. If husbands and wives agree on gender role expectations and performance, couples report higher marital quality than if there is disagreement. Gender role congruence is an important consideration, therefore, in selecting a mate with whom one will be compatible.

10. The present trend is toward androgyny, where people are not sex-typed with respect to roles, although they are still male or female in gender. A mixing of roles is advantageous to both sexes. Androgyny is most likely to develop in children who model after a parental pair where neither parent exemplifies the typical sex-role stereotypes.

SUGGESTED READINGS

David, D., and Brannon, R. (Eds.). (1976). *The Forty-nine Percent Majority: The Male Sex Role*. Reading, MA: Addison-Wesley. Various aspects of man's changing roles.

Deckard, B. S. (1983). *The Women's Movement: Political, Socioeconomic, and Psychological Issues*. New York: Harper and Row. Feminist discussion of the issues.

Forisha, B. L. (1978). *Sex Roles and Personal Awareness*. Morristown, NJ: General Learning Press. Research and case studies on changing roles of men and women.

Lipman-Blumen, J. (1984). *Gender Roles and Power*. Englewood Cliffs, NJ: Prentice-Hall. Sex and gender roles in society and in the family.

Lips, H. M. (1988). *Sex and Gender*. Mountain View, CA: Mayfield. Comprehensive discussion.

Margolis, M. (1984). *Mothers and Such: View of American Women and Why They Changed*. Berkeley, CA: University of California Press. Issues on reasons and process of change in attitudes and behavior.

Pogrebin, L. C. (1980). *Growing Up Free*. New York: McGraw-Hill. Sex-role development of children and adolescents.

Richmon-Abott, M. (1983). *Masculine and Feminine: Sex Roles Over the Life Cycle*. Reading, MA: Addison-Wesley. Sex-role socialization and male-female relations from birth to death.

Schaffer, K. F. (1981). *Sex Roles and Human Behavior*. Cambridge, MA: Winthrop. General discussion.

Stockard, J., and Johnson, M. (1980). *Sex Roles: Sex Inequality and Sex Role Development*. Englewood Cliffs, NJ: Prentice-Hall. Social, economic, and political factors that contribute to difference in opportunities for men and women.

Weitzman, L. J. (1979). *Sex Role Socialization*. Palo Alto, CA: Mayfield. Socialization to sex roles from early childhood through the college years.

13

WORK AND FAMILY ROLES

In the majority of today's families, both husbands and wives are employed outside the home. That employment has a profound effect on the family life of individuals involved as well as on individual satisfaction. In turn, family life can influence the work environment.

In this chapter, we explore the interrelationships between work and family living to show how each influences the other. We are particularly concerned about some effects on the woman herself and on her family when the woman becomes involved in three major roles: those of wife, mother, and employee. What are the effects on her life satisfaction and marital adjustments, and what roles might her husband play to increase her personal well-being and that of their family?

We are also concerned here with dual-career families: both the benefits and the adjustments that are required. What are some of the advantages, and what are the major problems that dual-career couples face? What effects do dual-career marriages have on the husband-wife relationship and on the family? Opportunity is also presented in this chapter for you and your partner to assess your personal attitudes toward dual-career marriage.

MAN'S WORK AND THE FAMILY

The Provider Role

In our society, the key male role is the provider role. The male who successfully fulfills that role is more likely to be happy with himself and to feel adequate as a husband and father than is the male who feels he is not a good provider (Osherson and Dill, 1983). Draughn (1984) found that men judge their own job competence and satisfaction according to four criteria.

The "good provider" role can be rewarding, but it can be stressful if it takes away time from the marital relationship.

Personal achievement: the extent to which they feel important, capable, and adequately rewarded; have received income increases; have promotion opportunities and a sense of achievement; and find their job interesting.

Income achievement: the extent to which they feel their level of income is satisfactory, compares favorably with others, reflects their personal worth, includes cost-of-living raises, and enables them to save money.

Task and work environment: the extent to which they are challenged, but not burdened, by job difficulty, job pressure; the extent to which they are satisfied by the physical surroundings and facilities in which they work, other people on the job, and the amount of time the work requires.

Perception of wife and friends: the extent to which their wives make a favorable assessment of their success, salary, and workplace; the extent to which their friends assess their success favorably; and the impact of home problems on the job, and job problems on the marriage.

Feelings of inadequacy in fulfillment of the provider role are likely to be disastrous for both the man and his family (Draughn, 1984). It is difficult for a man to feel good about himself or his role performance if he can't supply the bare necessities of life. If family housing is a dilapidated shack, if the children have to go to school in shabby clothes, if he can't afford a dependable car, or a birthday present for his wife, he may feel he has failed as a man in the principal area in which others expect him to be competent: that of provider.

In their study of the relationship between marital adjustment and work identity of blue-collar men, Gaesser and Whitbourne (1985) found that satisfaction with extrinsic work factors (wages, security, work setting and hours, and company policies) were the most important considerations related to marital adjustment. Workers who were satisfied with their job had more energy to devote to the marital relationship.

Work That Puts Stress on the Family

Many men have jobs that are particularly stressful for the family. Included are jobs that are so difficult for the husband that he is under constant strain at work and harder to live with when he is home. Also included is work that requires periods of separation and work that is so demanding of the man's time that he can't spend any quality time with his wife and children.

The man who is a workaholic and who gives 80 hours a week to his job has no time or energy left to devote to his family. He and his wife seldom go out together or spend time alone; they seldom communicate; they seldom make love. He hardly knows his children since he's rarely home during waking hours. The more ambitious the man is and the harder he works, the less likely he will be to take the time to develop close family relationships.

In the case of the workaholic, the compulsion to work so hard and long comes from within the man himself. His compulsion is to succeed, often for personal ego fulfillment, to bolster his self-image as he tries to become a "somebody." He is a perfectionist who demands complete mastery and control over his situation. He becomes absorbed with details and is unable to delegate responsibility. When unrealizable goals are not reached, he suffers anxiety, guilt, anger, and depression, which he attempts to overcome by further attempts at control. He may become irritable and abusive toward his spouse, offspring, and fellow employees (Rosenthal and Rosenthal, 1983). Leisure is a burden,

Some work requires periods of separation from home and family. What can separation do to a relationship?

an empty time during which nothing is accomplished. A workaholic shows signs of anxiety and depression if he is deprived of something to do for just a few hours. If he takes vacations or retires, he may develop ulcers, asthma, or colitis. His work addiction may bring high blood pressure or heart disease (Morris and Charney, 1983).

The causes of workaholism are psychological, originating in the psyche of the individual. But there are ways of finding fulfillment other than through work. Meaningful family relationships can meet real needs too. Men need to sort out their priorities and ask themselves if their job is worth sacrificing their family for. Marriages and family relationships require time and attention like anything else worthwhile if close relationships are to be maintained.

At other times, the demand to work so hard comes from the employer, who displays a callous disregard for a man's mental health or personal life. The man has to satisfy his boss or lose his job.

> Such was the case of Berman who joined a company as a management trainee soon after he graduated from high school. A hard worker, he put himself through college at night while rising steadily through the ranks of the giant corporation. Eventually he became manager of a large department, with a salary of about $50,000, plus substantial fringe benefits. In time, however, the job became increasingly difficult for him, demanding more and more of his evening and weekend hours. The pressure became so great that he asked several times to have his work load lightened. His superiors promised to ease up on him, but nothing changed.
>
> Approaching 50, and with 30 years of service to the company, Berman decided

PERSPECTIVE
*Graduate Student Management of Family
and Academic Roles*

Many graduate students are married. Some are parents. They are confronted with the responsibilities of their family role in addition to their academic role. Often they also work at least part-time. Interrole conflict exists when expectations in one of these roles are incompatible with the expectations of the other (Dyk, 1987).

Greenhaus and Beutell (1985) have identified two major forms of interrole conflict: time-based conflicts and strain-based conflicts.

Time-based conflicts arise when time pressures from one role make it physically impossible to meet expectations arising from another. Time-based conflicts may arise from any one or more of the following sources:

Workaholism—compulsion to work long hours
Children—having a number of small children
Husband—with traditional gender-role attitudes
Spousal absence—on business trips
Job—inflexible work schedules
Class—schedules and required study hours

Strain-based conflicts arise when strain in the student role affects participation in the family role or vice-versa. There is a "negative emotional spillover" (Bartolome and Evans, 1980) from work to nonwork. Stressful events in school such as pressure of assignments, exams, or term papers due affect family life; child-care responsibilities at home or marital conflict may affect school work.

Beutell and Greenhaus (1980) have found the two most effective coping strategies: Type 1, structural role redefinition, and Type 2, personal role redefinition.

Type 1, **structural role redefinition**, involves attempts to lessen the conflict by mutual agreement on a new set of expectations. Thus, the graduate student spouse and parent might give up part of a role—such as reducing course load, limiting volunteer efforts with organizations outside the home, sharing study with other students, coordinating child care with other parents who take turns, hiring assistance for domestic chores or for babysitting, or enlisting the help of other family members. The goal is to reduce the load one carries personally.

Type 2, **personal role redefinition**, involves reducing the standards of role performance. It may be done in at least three ways: *prioritization, compartmentalization, and reduction of standards*. First, individuals set priorities for school, work, and family, and perform only those with the highest priority. Ranking lists help to arrange the order of importance. Identifying short-range and long-range priorities helps to uncover those things that are urgent and must be done now, versus those things that may be done later. "To-do" lists and planning calendars help to get things done.

Compartmentalization is the strategy of not attending to one role while performing another. A student blocks out family demands while focusing on studies and leaves books and manuscript in the office to focus attention on the family.

Reduction of standards at school involves deciding to do what one can to be well-prepared and leaving the rest. At home, it may mean lowering one's standards of house cleanliness.

It is important to anticipate role strains and to develop strategies for dealing with potential conflicts (Dyk, 1987).

to take early retirement, largely to escape from the strain of his job. His superior talked him into staying on, promising to ease his work load. Relying on those promises, he agreed, but again, no relief came. Some time after that, Berman discovered that he would not become eligible again for early retirement and pension for another five years.

With escape by retirement thus effectively blocked, Berman became increasingly anxious about his ability to accomplish his work. A psychiatrist warned that Berman's position was precarious and would be further impaired without some relief in the conditions of his work. Still, nothing changed.

Berman's colleagues found him sitting at his desk in a dazed stupor. They could not snap him out of it, nor could the company doctor. During this catatonic episode, he was not sent to a hospital, he was not sent home, no one called his wife. After a few hours, he came out of it on his own. He stayed in the office for the rest of the day, and left for home alone. Three weeks later he committed suicide. His widow is suing the company, claiming it caused her husband's death by failing to respond to repeated complaints and pressure (B. Rice, 1981a).

One barrier to family closeness is a job schedule that makes it difficult for family members to be together. Some jobs require rotating shifts. If the husband and wife both work, and on different shifts, they rarely have any time to be together. Other jobs, such as being a police officer, are very stressful in and of themselves and require a lot of time on weekends and holidays (Maynard, Maynard, McCubbin, and Shao, 1980). Other work, such as being in the armed services or merchant marine, requires long periods of separation (Jones and Butler, 1980). Whenever there is conflict between family and job demands, such competition becomes a source of individual and family stress.

EMPLOYED WOMEN AND THE FAMILY

Facts and Figures

The numbers and percentages of wives and mothers in the labor force are increasing and have been well-documented (See Chapter 1). In 1988, 57 percent of all married women over age 16, 73 percent of women with the youngest child 6 to 17 years of age, and 57 percent of married women with the youngest child under 6 years of age were in the labor force (U.S. Bureau of the Census, 1989). In the same year, 52 percent of women with babies under one year old were also in the labor force (Hock, Christman, and Hock, 1980). The effect on children will be discussed in detail in Chapter 20.

Life Satisfaction

But what about the impact of this employment on women's lives? Are employed wives more fulfilled, satisfied with life, and just plain happier than housewives? Wright (1978) has pointed out that work is described as an alienating force in the lives of men, but is somehow transformed into a liberating force in the lives of women. This position assumes that any sort of paid employment is preferable to full-time housewifery.

The research on life satisfaction of married women who work versus those who do not work shows slightly greater satisfaction among those working, but the results depend upon a number of variables. In a study of working-class wives in a North-east suburb, Ferree (1976) determined that employed wives were more satisfied than housewives. However, women who worked part-time were more satisfied than either housewives or wives who worked full-time. An examination of life satisfaction of upper-middle-class wives of Canadian professional men showed that employment outside the home produced greater satisfaction with life in general and with marriage in particular. Housewives reported lower satisfaction scores and poorer mental and physical health (Burke and Weiz, 1976). A comparison of a national sample of wives of blue-collar and white-collar husbands showed that working wives of both socioeconomic statuses reported only slightly more satisfaction than did housewives (Wright, 1978).

In an effort not to place all housewives in the same category, Freudiger (1983) divided women into three groups: working wives, formerly employed housewives, and never-employed housewives. The purpose of her research was to determine the most important sources of life satisfaction for these three groups of women. Table 13.1 shows the results, with the variables listed in decreasing order of importance. *For both the working wives and formerly employed housewives, marital happiness was by far the most important source of life satisfaction.* Occupational prestige was second in importance for working wives. Financial satisfaction was second in importance for formerly employed housewives. *For never-employed wives, financial satisfaction was first in importance and marital happiness second.*

The never-employed housewife most likely views her spouse as the traditional breadwinner and herself as the traditional wife. Her husband's contribution to her financial satisfaction may be more important to her than his role as a lover and companion. Lacking an occupation, she also derives satisfaction from her marriage, from voting, religious participation, and her education, which allows her to pursue interests stimulated by her knowledge. Surprisingly, the presence of preschool children detracted from her life satisfaction, while the presence of teenagers exerted a positive influence on the never-employed woman's life.

TABLE 13.1 *Effect of Selected Variables
on Life-Satisfaction Index of Wives*

Working Wives	Formerly Employed Housewives	Never-Employed Wives
Marital happiness	Marital happiness	Financial satisfaction
Occupational prestige	Financial satisfaction	Marital happiness
Age	Race	Voted last election
Perceived health	Religious participation	Education
Financial satisfaction	Age	Presence of preschooler (– factor)
Race	Perceived health	
Religious participation		Religious participation

Adapted from Freudiger, P. (1983). Life satisfaction among three categories of married women. *Journal of Marriage and the Family*, 45, 213–219.

In comparing these three groups, the working mother, even with all her problems, enjoys occupational prestige. The formerly employed wife appears more free to follow her own activities, to see acquaintances, and to pursue interests acquired while in the labor force. The never-employed woman may perceive herself as trapped in the mother role and gains no satisfaction from this role until her children are teenagers. For all three categories of women, marital happiness is important. *This finding is in agreement with other studies that view marital happiness as more important to overall happiness than job satisfaction* (Benin and Neinstedt, 1985).

Role Conflict and Strain

One of the important considerations in the life satisfaction of working wives is whether they have been able to integrate their work life with their home life. A study in Ohio of life satisfaction among employed mothers of adolescents revealed that in addition to job satisfaction, the most important influence on life satisfaction of rural employed mothers was the lack of conflict between family and job roles (Walters and McKenry, 1985). Because these women were mothers of adolescents, the adolescent children gave some important assistance with household tasks, thus relieving some of the role strain of the mothers. Also, the majority of these rural mothers were employed in low-paying, low-skilled occupations. It is possible that they were very capable of handling the demands of family and job roles. The majority of these mothers also said they were working for personal rather than economic reasons, so they were not a threat to their husband's provider role, nor were they dependent upon his support of their working. The mothers were dependent upon their adolescents' support, however, indicating that *the maternal role holds the most potential conflicts with employment outside the home.* If children's needs are not met satisfactorily, then role conflict and dissatisfaction could easily result.

A number of factors influence role strain of working women. Basically, there are three major sources of strain: *individual sources* (those that originate within the individual), *family-related sources* (those that come from the family), and *work-related sources* (those that originate from the work situation (Kelly and Voydanoff, 1985; Voydanoff and Kelly, 1984).

One invididual source of role strain is the woman's own conflict over the fact that she is working. If she prefers being at home, but has to work for various reasons, her ambiguous feelings become an inner source of conflict and tension. One mother remarked; "I hate working. I'd rather be home, but George and I can't make it financially unless I do, so I have no choice" (Author's counseling notes). This wife came home from work very tired at night, partly because she had to push herself to work in the first place.

A family-related source of strain is the presence of young children in the family. The more young children in the family, the more stress is introduced (Katz and Piotrkowski, 1983). Some women feel guilty about leaving their children, especially when the children are small. However, mothers feel less stress if they are satisfied with the quality of substitute child care (Van Meter and Agronow, 1982).

Another source of conflict is the strain of having to fulfill too many roles at once (Berkowitz and Perkins, 1984; Gilbert, Holahan, and Manning, 1981). If a woman works full time, is raising one or more children, and tries to be a good wife, she has taken on the responsibility of at least two and one-half full-time jobs. If her job is demanding, and her husband is not very sympathetic and helpful at home, or if he demands a lot from her, along with the children, she is under constant pressure to give and give. If she feels she can't fulfill her own or her family's expectations, she may get upset or depressed (Keith and Schafer, 1985). One husband remarked; "I don't mind your working, but I expect my supper when I get home." Some husbands don't mind their wives working as long as it doesn't inconvenience them. Other more thoughtful husbands expect their wives to work to help out financially, but these husbands also are very willing to share the household and other tasks. Husband support and help alleviates part of the stress (Spitze and Waite, 1981).

The job itself may be a source of stress and strain (Kelly and Voydanoff, 1985). Inflexible job demands, inconvenient schedules, long hours, and job pressures all create strain. If a boss or co-workers are hard to get along with, or if the job requires unreasonable hours and a lot of responsibilities, the woman is exhausted by the time she gets home. The last thing she needs is to have to spend the rest of her waking hours trying to satisfy the demands of a husband and children. This is why assistance from a considerate husband, older children, or hired help is so important. One woman remarked; "I'd love to be able to come home from work and have someone have *my* supper on the table for *me*" (Author's counseling notes).

In contrast to these negative reactions, some women love their job and have husbands and children who help or are able to hire some assistance. Some of these women are more relaxed at work than at home. In fact, some go to work to get away from their families. One mother remarked:

> I can't wait to get out of the house in the morning. Work is the only place I have any peace and quiet. I'd go absolutely crazy if I had to stay home all day. My children could drive me crazy. (Author's counseling notes)

There are all kinds of people and all kinds of needs. Some women are far better wives and mothers because they go to work. They're more patient, more giving, and more attentive during the time they are home than they would be if their only full-time job was that of wife, homemaker, and mother.

Marital Adjustment

Social science has devoted considerable effort to comparing employed wives with nonemployed wives to determine effects on the husband-wife relationship. Some investigators report a positive relationship between wife employment and marital adjustment (Burke and Weir, 1976). Still other researchers show no effect (Locksley, 1980). Others report a negative relationship (Ladewig and McGee, 1986). A comprehensive summary of findings of 27 studies was made by Smith (1985). He summarized 2,018 comparisons between husbands of employed women versus husbands of nonemployed wives, and 2,584 comparisons between employed versus nonemployed wives to determine the degrees of marital adjustment. Marital adjustment was divided into five categories: *physical, companionship, communication, tensions and regrets,* and *one global (overall)* measure. As seen in Table 13.2 and Table 13.3, *most of the*

TABLE 13.2 *Cumulative Results of Effects of Wife's Employment on Five Categories of Marital Adjustment for Wives*

Criterion Variable	Number of Comparisons	RESULTS (%)		
		Favor Employed Wives	Show No Difference	Favor Nonemployed Wives
Global/overall	1,376	5	86	9
Tensions and regrets	440	4	82	14
Communication	309	7	72	21
Companionship	285	14	59	27
Physical	174	8	60	32
Total Comparisons	2,584	6	79	15

From: Smith, D. S. (1985). Wife employment and marital adjustment: A cumulation of results. *Family Relations, 34*, 483–490. Copyright ©1985 by the National Council on Family Relations. Reprinted by permission.

TABLE 13.3 *Cumulative Results of Effects of Wife's Employment on Five Categories of Marital Adjustment for Husbands*

Criterion Variable	Number of Comparisons	RESULTS (%)		
		Favor Employed Wives	Show No Difference	Favor Nonemployed Wives
Global/overall	1,066	4	93	3
Tensions and regrets	303	2	91	7
Communication	252	2	54	44
Companionship	253	6	43	51
Physical	144	1	19	80
Total Comparisons	2,018	3	76	21

From: Smith, D. S. (1985). Wife employment and marital adjustment: A cumulation of results. *Family Relations, 34*, 483–490. Copyright ©1985 by the National Council on Family Relations. Reprinted by permission.

comparisons showed no difference in adjustment between husband groups and wife groups. The very few differences that existed tended to favor the nonemployed groups. However, when the results were controlled according to wives' education level, family income, social class, the presence and age of children in various stages of the life cycle, and husbands' education, the basic finding of no difference between employed and nonemployed groups remained. What this means is that the wife's employment status alone appears to have little or no effect on marital adjustment (Smith, 1985). This does not mean there aren't problems in two-earner families. There may be. But it does mean that whether the wife works is not *the* key to marital adjustment. Other factors are more significant. For example, one study found that the couples' belief

CLASSROOM FORUM
Should a Married Mother of an Infant
Work Outside the Home?

1. How do you feel about a mother of an infant under one year of age working outside the home?
2. What would be your primary concerns?
3. Under what circumstances would you do it and under what circumstances would you not?
4. What kind of substitute care would you prefer?
5. If the couple did not need the money, would the decision to work be justified?
6. If the wife had to work, what are some of the things the husband could do that would make things easier for the mother and would also benefit the child?

in their ability to resolve disagreements was the best predictor of marital adjustment, not the wife's work status (Meeks, Arnkoff, Glass, and Notarius, 1986). Another study found that whether couples had an equitable relationship — that is, whether there was a fair balance of rewards and constraints for both the husband and wife — was the key factor in marital adjustment (Rachlin, 1987). Thus, either single-earner or dual-career couples may have poor or good marriages.

DUAL-CAREER FAMILIES*

Two-Earner Versus Dual-Career Families

The problems of role strain and conflict have been highlighted by extensive studies of two-earner families. There are basically two types of these families. The **dual-earner family** is one where both spouses are involved in the paid labor force. One of the spouses may be pursuing a career while the other views his or her employment as a job, or both spouses may see themselves as having jobs (Rachlin, 1987). Ordinarily, just having a job does not involve as extensive a commitment, as much continuity of employment, or as much responsibility as the pursuit of a career. Most people would find it easier to give up one job and get another than to change careers.

The **dual-career family** is a specific subtype of the broader category of dual-earner families (Rachlin, 1987). In the two-career family, there are two career-committed individuals, both of whom are trying to continue professional and family roles (Skinner, 1980). But the pursuit of a career requires a high degree of commitment and a continuous developmental life (Holmstrom, 1973; Pendleton, Poloma, and Garland, 1980; Rapoport and Rapoport, 1971, 1978). Individuals pursue careers by undergoing extensive education and preparation, and then moving upward from one job level to another. A career ordinarily requires full-time employment, especially if one is working for someone

---

*Part of the material in this section has been taken from the author's book *Contemporary Marriage*, 1983, and is used by permission of the publisher, Allyn and Bacon.

Often when both members of a couple work, they are career-committed individuals who are trying to balance professional and family roles.

else. The greater the responsibility and the higher the position achieved, the greater is the commitment of the individual — leaving less time to devote to mate and child. Many married men and women who work do not pursue a career. Only about one in six married couples in the United States has both spouses working at year-round, full-time jobs. Even then, these jobs cannot all be described as careers. *The dual-career marriage, then, is actually a minority pattern in spite of the millions of working wives and mothers.* As a minority occurrence, the dual-career marriage is also difficult to achieve from a strictly managerial point of view. It is difficult to rearrange husband-wife and father-mother role relationships and responsibilities; it is difficult to find adequate child-care help in a society that expects parents to assume the major burden; and it is difficult to maintain the expected husband-wife intimacy and companionship so that the marriage itself becomes a viable relationship.

In spite of difficulties, some couples are able to succeed in pursuing careers and in being good mates and parents. Other couples try to succeed at all three roles and fail. Looking at both the successes and failures of others helps in understanding the satisfactions, adjustments, and problems of dual-career marriage (Huser and Grant, 1978; Jones and Jones, 1980; St. John Parsons, 1978).

The Wives

Career women tend to be energetic, competitive, and ambitious, and have a need for personal recognition and achievement (D. G. Rice, 1978). Quite typically the marriage rate among career women is lower than among women in general. Many who do marry remain single until age 35 or 40 (Allen and Kalish, 1984). They frequently turn down proposals from men who are opposed to careers for women. Often they have long courtships to see how their two careers will mesh (Holmstrom, 1973).

The issue of the wife's career does not always come up prior to marriage. In marriages where the couples are younger, this may be because the wife decides to pursue a career only *after* she is married. In marriages where the partners are older and both are working, it may just be assumed that the wife will continue in her long-established career. In Holmstrom's (1973) study, most of the husbands said that prior to meeting their wives they had not thought much about whether they wanted to marry a woman devoted to homemaking or one who had career interests. Those who had thought about it said they preferred a woman with intellectual interests and a professional orientation.

Apparently, *establishing a two-career marriage does not always happen by deliberate choice and planning, especially on the part of the husband.* Perhaps even without formal discussion, the wives are able to sense that their fiancés will approve of their career after marriage, and so they feel free to go ahead. Certainly, after marriage, all wives agree that it is absolutely essential that they have the complete support and understanding of their husbands (Bird and Bird, 1987; Houseknecht and Macke, 1981).

The majority of career women say that having children is important to them (Epstein and Bronzaft, 1972). In spite of their desire for children, career women are atypical in several ways:

1. They tend to have small families, with fewer children than the average couple (Bryson, Bryson, and Johnson, 1978; Tickamyer, 1979).

2. There is usually a long interval between marriage and the birth of the first child (Skinner, 1980).

3. Because of the delay of both marriage and childbearing, most of the wives have their first child at a relatively late age, usually not until their thirties.

The Husbands

The attitude of the husbands toward their wives' having careers ranges from relaxed detachment and willing acceptance because "I knew what I was getting into," to positive involvement and facilitation of their wives' career roles. Holmstrom reports several characteristics of husbands of career wives (Holmstrom, 1973, p. 135):

1. Husbands took their wives' work seriously, often showing deep admiration and respect for their wives' accomplishments.

2. Husbands wanted their wives "to be happy" or "to be the kind of person she was."

3. Husbands not only showed positive attitudes toward their wives' careers, but they also translated this into concrete, practical acts of support. These dual-career husbands changed their own behavior and way of life to accommodate two careers. They took their wives' needs into account before moving. They considered their wives' time when setting up schedules. They helped with domestic and child-rearing duties.

All research shows that *the husband's attitude is an important factor in making a dual-career marriage workable* (Jones and Jones, 1980). Because of the importance of the husband's attitude, career wives caution: "Be careful whom you marry. The choice of a husband is very important in making a career possible; if you don't have a husband who supports you and is interested in your work, you can't survive."

Dual-career husbands tend to be secure, well-adjusted men whose identities are not threatened by their wives' working, nor by the nontraditional division of labor within the household. The husband who has to feel psychologically superior to his wife, who feels threatened if his wife achieves a position of prominence, who has strong feelings of competitiveness, or who has to "put down" his wife cannot tolerate a dual-career marriage. Competition and jealousy can be a real threat to the relationship (Hiller and Philliber, 1982).

Benefits of a Dual-Career Marriage

There are some real satisfactions and gains in a dual-career marriage. *The financial rewards in a dual-career marriage are considerable*, especially if both persons are earning salaries as professional people. The standard of living is relatively high, with couples able to provide for expensive leisure activities and holidays. In addition, the extra expenses for clothes, transportation, domestic help, and child care because both are working, make it necessary for couples to have a relatively high income. This high income contributes to marital quality (Thomas, Albrecht, and White, 1984).

Career-oriented women often report the need for challenging family and couples-only activities in order to maintain high levels of marital satisfaction.

One frequently mentioned reason why any highly qualified woman wants a career in addition to a family is because of a need for creativity, self-expression, achievement, and recognition. A woman who is trained for a profession wants the satisfaction of using that training (Hall and Gordon, 1973). Many such women are dissatisfied with confining their energies to their husbands and children, with just being "John's wife" or "Susan's mother." Such women find a large part of their identity in their career life (Gannon and Hendrickson, 1973). Many feel that they would experience a real loss if the satisfactions of a career were removed. There are also indirect benefits to the husband and the family. A woman who is getting satisfaction from her career is a happier wife and mother.

The most successful dual-career marriages are those in which the husband and wife treat one another as equal partners. As a result, *they share not only in earning the income, but also in caring for children and in performing household tasks* (Scanzoni, 1980). Wives are far less satisfied and under more strain in those marriages where the responsibility for homemaking tasks rests primarily on their shoulders (Pendleton, Poloma, and Garland, 1980).

Moving

The pressure to move about frequently while one's career is becoming established presents difficulty for the two-career family (Gilliland, 1979; Kilpatrick, 1982; Wallston, Foster and Berger, 1978).

The expectation of frequent moves is based primarily on the assumption that there is only one such professional per family and that this person is the husband (Voydanoff, 1980). The wife and children are supposed to tag along. If there were a choice between the husband's and wife's career, *traditionally it was expected that the wife would follow the husband* (Bird and Bird, 1985; Heckman, Bryson, and Bryson, 1977). Under such circumstances, it would become difficult for the wife to pursue an uninterrupted career, and so the competing job requirements of two careers may threaten to separate the couple geographically and maritally (Ammons, Nelson, and Wodarski, 1982).

It is not always easy for both partners to find suitable employment in one area, especially in less populated areas where there are fewer opportunities. Also, some firms and employers have rules against **nepotism**: hiring two people from the same family. Even the U.S. Department of Health, Education and Welfare's Office of Civil Rights has declared rules against nepotism discriminatory (Pingree et al., 1978). The rule falls hardest on the husbands and wives who are in the same field, since employers are especially reluctant to hire two people in the same administrative department or section. If the rule is enforced, it is usually enforced against the wife. She is the one who is denied employment, permitted to work only part-time to circumvent the rule, or forced to work outside her field (Cherpas, 1985).

In her study of dual-career families, Holmstrom (1973) found that 15 out of 20 couples said that the issue of moving had arisen since their marriage. In every case, the wife's decision about where to live was influenced by the career needs of her husband. Sometimes the wife wanted to move but could not because the husband could not or would not move. In 12 out of 15 cases, however, the husband's decision about where to live was also significantly influenced by his wife's career. The couple negotiated for a set of positions,

Moving day can cause special strains in any family. In the dual career marriage, the decision about where to live and about when to move must take into account the career requirements of both the husband and the wife.

taking into account the occupational needs of both; or the husband followed the wife; or the couple decided to postpone the move. Sometimes one remained behind to finish up some work and then rejoined the other later.

Travel

The issue of travel arises in dual-career marriages because professionals often attend out-of-town meetings or conferences or consult with others in different locales. Professional wives are expected to travel on brief business trips, usually from two to ten days. Some have to travel monthly or more often; a few have to make extended trips abroad. Generally, husbands travel even more than their wives; some are away for long periods of time each year.

Occasionally, couples commute long distances when home and the base for their careers are in different locations (Gross, 1980; Kirschner and Walum, 1978). They may work all week in separate places and get together on weekends. Actors and actresses commonly follow this pattern. Most couples report that they feel lonely and have more difficulty being emotionally close and intimate (Kirschner and Walum, 1978). The one left home often resents the added burden of running errands and caring for the house and children alone (Gross, 1980). The only advantage is the increased freedom to work hard at one's job while away from home.

The difficulties in combining a career with parenthood become apparent after the first child is born. In the nuclear family, the husband, wife, and children live in their own household separate from their relatives, and so there is no other family member available to care for the children while the parents are working.

One solution being considered by increasing numbers of career couples is to remain childless. This actually makes a dual-career marriage easier (Houseknecht and Macke, 1981; Reading and Amatea, 1986). Those who do have children end up finding their own solutions to the child-care dilemma. Wealthier parents hire a nurse, a *governess*, or some other full-time person to live in and take care of the child on a 24-hour-a-day basis. Actually, this is one of the better solutions to a difficult problem if one can afford the enormous expense and if the right person can be found. The wrong person can be extremely harmful to children. Another solution of the wealthy is to send their children to *private boarding schools* and to *camp* in the summer.

Parents who work days, seldom travel, and are usually home weekends, often end up getting a regular *babysitter* every day during the week and then taking care of their own children during other times.

The parents can send their child to a *day-care center*, if one is available (which is unlikely in some communities), but care is provided only during the day. The child must still be taken to the center and brought back home each day, an arrangement that further complicates the lives of any two busy career people, especially if they have to drive miles each way. What happens when the parents are out of town? Usually one or the other parent is available,

For the dual career family, finding quality child care is often a crisis. The availability of quality day care for children is becoming recognized as a national concern.

but providing transportation is only part of the problem. The parent who is home must still get the child ready for day care and care for him or her after the center has closed. What if a child is sick or if the parent has an important evening meeting? Obviously, a babysitter is still needed, preferably one who can get home by herself or himself.

One of the crucial considerations, of course, is the kind of substitute care provided the child when parents are gone (Chantiny, Kagan, and Crowell, 1973; Papousek, 1973). The quality and consistency of the substitute care provided is paramount. In one study, 93 adolescents who grew up in dual-career families were asked to rate their families on various components of family strength (appreciation, concern, respect, support, esteem, commitment, positive communication, and conflict management). An average of 68 percent said they were satisfied or very satisfied with their families on these components of family strength. Eighty-three percent were satisfied or very satisfied with having grown up in a dual-career family (Knaub, 1986). Apparently, their parents didn't do too bad a job in combining careers with child rearing.

Overload

The strains of a dual-career marriage are considerable. One source of strain is overwork (Keith and Schafer, 1980). The demands of the marriage, children, career, and home are great and often leave couples tense and exhausted.

Most couples try to hire some sort of domestic help on a regular basis. Couples report considerable difficulty in getting competent help, however. Some become so discouraged with hired help that they just decide to split the work between them. Most try to purchase various labor-saving machines to cut down on the time required. Some use other means for increasing the efficiency of housework and for streamlining tasks. For example, some couples buy more prepared foods. Others are careful to buy clothing that never needs ironing. Others report that they have lowered their standards of housekeeping and cleanliness. Some, however, are disturbed by their own untidiness (Holmstrom, 1973). Some couples assign definite chores to children in the family (Rapoport and Rapoport, 1971).

Scheduling

Most couples admit that they have to budget their time very carefully. If job requirements allow the individual considerable flexibility in controlling his or her own schedule, it is easier to mesh job and home responsibilities. If an individual works for himself or herself, scheduling may be considerably easier. Some businesses have **flexitime** that allows workers to choose the eight hours during the day when they will work (Meer, 1985c).

Husbands and wives also try to mesh their schedules so that one or the other is available to care for children and so that they will be able to spend time together as a couple. Most couples admit that they have to give up a number of activiites just to have time for necessary things. Career couples usually do not entertain as often as some others do. The wife does not as often play the hostess role for her husband. There is not as much time or need for involvement in community activities or for such things as gardening or leisure time reading.

Career husbands and wives each sacrifice a great deal to make it possible for the other to pursue a career. For this reason, if each does not accept the high value that the other places on career pursuit, conflict is bound to arise. *If two people compete, each trying to outperform the other, the relationship may become tense.* If two people are certain of their own identities and secure within themselves, they are able to work out compromises so that each is not threatened by the demands and successes of the other (Atkinson and Boles, 1984; Rubenstein, 1982).

Quality of Marriages

Like any marriage, dual-career marriages can be of high or low quality, depending on many factors. Thomas, Albrecht, and White (1984) discuss a framework for an analysis of marital quality, illustrated in figure 13.1. The

FIGURE 13.1 *A Theory of Marital Quality.*

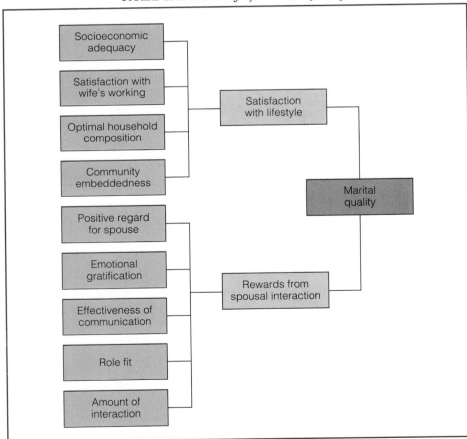

researchers divided marital quality into two major components: *satisfaction with life-style* and *rewards from spousal interaction*. Satisfaction with life-style included four requirements for marital quality: *socioeconomic adequacy*, *satisfaction with wife working*, *optimal household composition* (older children in the family rather than younger), and *community embeddedness* (maintaining an adequate and desired level of satisfying social life).

Rewards from spousal interaction included five requirements for marital quality: *positive regard from spouse*, *emotional gratification* (expression of affection, sexual satisfaction, encouragement of personal growth from spouse, and congruence between ideal and actual spouse), *effective communication*, *role fit* (absence of role conflict and presence of role complementarity and role sharing), and *amount of interaction* (sharing activities and companionship).

The researchers emphasized that the quality of marriage of dual-career couples depended on the extent to which the spouses found that these requirements were met in their life-style and their relationship.

ASSESSMENT
Attitudes Toward Dual-Career Marriage

1. Would you want to have a dual-career marriage? Explain your feelings. Would the benefits outweigh the disadvantages?

2. Are there any special conditions that would have to exist before you entered into a dual-career marriage?

3. If you were in a dual-career marriage, would you want to have children?

4. Are there any special circumstances under which you would not want to be in a dual-career marriage?

5. *To men:* Would it bother you if your wife earned more than you? Would it bother your female partner?

6. *To women:* Would it bother you if you earned more than your husband? Would it bother your male partner?

7. In case of moving to a new job in a different location, whose work should take precedence, the man's or the woman's? Explain your feelings.

8. Suppose you are in a dual-career marriage and your partner is earning more than you. If your partner gets another and even better job offer, do you feel you should move for the sake of your partner's career?

9. *To men:* How would you feel about your wife's having a career in which she had to be away from home several nights a week? For a week at a time? For several weeks at a time?

10. *To women:* How would you feel about your husband's having a career in which he had to be away from home several nights a week? For a week at a time? For several weeks at a time?

11. *To men and women:* How would you feel about your mate's having to travel overseas as part of her or his work?

12. How would you feel about working in different cities, and being able to come home to your spouse only on weekends?

13. Would you want a dual-career marriage if you had to put your infant in an infant-care center during working hours?

14. If you were a career person and had a new baby, how old do you feel the baby should be before the mother returns to work?

(continued)

344

MARRIAGES AND FAMILY
RELATIONSHIPS:
GROWTH AND
CHALLENGES

ASSESSMENT (*continued*)

15. Do you feel your marriage could be happy if you and your mate both had full-time careers? Compare the degree of happiness that you feel you might have if one spouse had only a part-time job, as compared to both of you having careers.

16. *To men:* Would you be willing to switch traditional roles with your wife and be a househusband while she went to work? Explain your feelings.

17. If you and your spouse both had full-time jobs and had preschool age children, what type of substitute child care would you prefer and why?

Instructions: You and your partner answer these questions individually (write the answers out) and then read your answers to one another as a basis for your discussion. In what ways do you agree? In what areas do you disagree? The important consideration is not whether you do or do not approve of dual-career marriages, but how your feelings compare with those of your partner.

SUMMARY

1. In our society, the key male role is the provider role. Feelings of inadequacy in fulfillment of the provider role are likely to be disastrous for both the man and his family.

2. Some types of work are particularly stressful for the family. This includes work that is quite difficult, that requires periods of separation from family, or that is too demanding of a man's time.

3. The workaholic's compulsion to work comes from within the man, who has a strong need to succeed for ego fulfillment. He is a perfectionist who drives himself to try to find feelings of importance and control over his life.

4. Sometimes the demand to work so hard comes from an employer who has a callous disregard for a man's mental health or personal life. One of the barriers to family closeness is a job schedule that makes it difficult for family members to be together.

5. Married graduate students have two major forms of interrole conflict: time-based conflicts and strain-based conflicts. The two most effective ways of coping with these conflicts are through structural role redefinition and through personal role redefinition.

6. The numbers and percentages of wives in the labor force are increasing. The research on life satisfaction of married women who work versus that of those not working shows only slightly greater satisfaction among those working.

7. Marital happiness is the most important source of life satisfaction for both working wives and formerly employed housewives. For never-employed wives, financial satisfaction is first and marital happiness second as sources of life satisfaction.

8. One of the most important determinants of life satisfaction of working wives is whether they have been able to integrate their work life with their home life. The maternal role has the most potential conflicts with employment outside the home.

9. There are a number of major sources of role strain on working women: individual sources, family-related sources, and work-related sources. One individual source is the woman's own conflict over working. Family-related sources include the presence of young children in the family and the strain of having to fulfill too many roles at once. The job itself may also be a source of stress and strain.

10. Most of the comparisons of employed versus nonemployed mothers show no difference in marital adjustment between the two groups. Thus, the wife's employment status alone appears to have no influence on marital adjustment.

11. The dual-career family is a specific subtype of the dual-earner family and usually requires full-time employment, a high degree of commitment, and a continuous developmental life.

12. Career women tend to be ambitious and have a need for personal recognition and achievement. The issue of the wife's career does not always arise before marriage and does not always happen by deliberate planning ahead of time. The majority of career women say that having children is important to them, in spite of the fact that pursuing a career is easier in childless marriages.

13. The attitude of the husband toward his wife's working is important. Dual-career husbands tend to be secure, well-adjusted men whose identities are not threatened by their wives' working.

14. The benefits of a dual-career marriage include financial rewards; an outlet for creativity, self-expression, achievement, and recognition; and sharing child care and household tasks.

15. Problems arising in dual-career marriages include: pressures to give all for one's career and to put it ahead of family; the problems of having to move frequently, of making the decision of whose career takes precedence, or of how to find jobs for both persons; the need to travel away from home; the problem of finding adequate substitute child care; the problem of overload; the problem of scheduling family life activities and work requirements; and the problem of jealousy and competition between spouses.

16. Like any marriage, dual-career marriages can be of high or low quality, depending on many factors. Marital quality arises from two major components: satisfaction with life-style and rewards from spousal interaction. Satisfaction with life-style arises from socioeconomic adequacy, satisfaction with wife's working, optimal household composition, and maintaining an adequate and desired level of satisfying social life. Rewards from spousal interaction include positive regard from spouse, emotional gratification, effective communication, role fit, and the amount of interaction. The quality of marriage depends on the extent to which spouses find these requirements met in their life-style and their relationship.

17. Dual-career marriage can present problems and strains, but the possibility is there for satisfaction or for dissatisfaction.

Aldous, J. (Ed.). (1982). *Two Paychecks: Life in Dual-Earner Families*. Beverly Hills, CA: Sage. A series of articles.

Beer, W. R. (1982). *Househusbands: Men and Housework in American Families*. New York: Praeger. A study of 56 part-time and full-time househusbands.

Bohen, H. C., and Viveros-Long, A. (1981). *Balancing Jobs and Family Life: Do Flexible Work Schedules Help?* Philadelphia: Temple University Press. Impact of flexible schedules on the family.

Gilbert, L. A. (1985). *Men in Dual-Career Families: Current Realities and Future Prospects*. New Jersey: Lawrence Erlbaum. Comprehensive discussion.

Hall, F. S., and Hall, D. T. (1979). *The Two-Career Couple*. Reading, MA: Addison-Wesley. Managing a two-career marriage.

Hood, J. G. (1983). *Becoming a Two-Job Family*. New York: Praeger. How 16 working, middle-class couples worked out the job, housework situation.

Pepitone-Rockwell, F. (Ed.). (1980). *Dual-Career Couples*. Beverly Hills, CA: Sage. A series of articles.

Rapoport, R., and Rapoport, R. (Eds.). (1978). *Working Couples*. New York: Harper and Row. Selected articles.

Rice, D. G. (1978). *Dual-Career Marriage: Conflict and Treatment*. New York: Free Press.

Voydanoff, P. (Ed.). (1984). *Work and Family: Changing Roles of Men and Women*. Palo Alto, CA: Mayfield. A series of articles.

14

MANAGING MATERIAL RESOURCES

KEY TERMS

variable mortgage interest rates
points
condominium

The way we use money is a reflection of our basic values. The proportions we spend on different things reflect not only needs, but also priorities, and so reveal what we value the most. The way in which we manage money can also be a revelation of our basic character: our degree of maturity, responsibility, and unselfishness and our ability to cooperate. People who buy things they don't need often do so as a means of gaining status or prestige or to allay fears and anxieties. Others never spend money at all, preferring instead to save it "for their old age." The classic example of extreme insecurity is the elderly person who dies alone in a shack, living like a pauper, with $50,000 tucked away under the mattress.

Other people reveal basic emotional needs in their efforts to use money to gain power or love. They use money to manipulate and force others to do their bidding or to buy affection. For some parents, material indulgence of children becomes a substitute for neglect.

Whatever our value system or basic character, we all can benefit ourselves and others by improving our money management skills. Even if we don't care much about money, necessity forces us to learn to manage on what we have and to be willing to show consideration for other family members. The better managers we become, the better we are able to follow the order of priorities we have established and the more we are able to get and give what we want in life (Rice, 1983).

MONEY AND THE FAMILY

Financial Needs

Couples quickly discover that two can't live as cheaply as one. Table 14.1 shows the percentage of families at different income levels. In this case, the

TABLE 14.1 *Income Levels and Percent Distribution of Families in Each Level*

Income Levels (dollars)	Percent of Families at Each Income Level, 1987	INCOME LEVELS PER YEAR	
		1987	1990 (Projected)
All income levels	100		
Less than 5,000	4.4		
5,000 to 9,999	7.3		
10,000 to 14,999	9.1		
15,000 to 19,999	9.5		
20,000 to 24,999	9.2		
25,000 to 34,999	17.5		
35,000 to 49,999	20.2		
50,000 and over	22.9		
Families below poverty level	10.8		
Median income		$30,853	$35,530

Adapted from U.S. Bureau of the Census. (1989). *Statistical abstract of the United States; 1989* (109th ed.). Washington, DC: U.S. Government Printing Office.

figures represent gross income (before deductions). The median income level of families was $30,853 in 1987, meaning that 50 percent of all families were above and below that figure (U.S. Bureau of the Census, 1989). By 1990, median family income should rise to around $35,530 per year.

In spite of the rise in family income, however, real income or purchasing power now remains about constant. Because of inflation, the cost of living has increased, by percentage, as much as wages have increased during the last 15 years, so families are no better off now than they were 15 years ago (U.S. Bureau of the Census, 1989).

Various estimates have been given on how much it costs to bear and rear a child to maturity. Regardless of price levels, the costs may be figured roughly as requiring three years of the family's income (not including costs for a college education). Thus, a family with two children can expect to spend more than $200,000 to rear them to age 18. If college costs are included, total costs will

Basic emotional needs are often expressed in the way people use money (or credit) to gain power or love in a relationship. Do some people acquire such a form of expression in childhood, and is it healthy to their adult relationships?

349

MANAGING MATERIAL
RESOURCES

be closer to $250,000 to raise both to maturity and to send them to a state university for four years. The total will be closer to $380,000 if the children go to more expensive private colleges.

Poverty and Family Life

Obviously, millions of persons will never reach median income levels. In 1987, 11 percent of persons living in families were below the poverty level, which was $11,611 for a non-farm family of four (U.S. Bureau of the Census, 1989). For these families, daily life is a struggle just to pay the bills for rent, groceries, a pair of shoes, a winter coat, or a TV set (Komarovsky, 1964).

The effects of poverty on the family are many: increased tension and unhappiness in the marital relationship; high rates of illegitimacy, desertion, separation, or divorce; and children brought up without a stable father figure in the home. Low income results in cultural and social deprivation with accompanying lower aspiration and educational levels (Gabriel and McAnarney, 1983; Rank, 1987). Limited resources also leave few opportunities for contacts with the outside world, resulting in isolation and provincialism. Increased problems and the lack of resources result in much higher rates of mental and physical illnesses (Komarovsky, 1964). Limited alternatives and feelings of helplessness and powerlessness leave little hope for the future or few prospects for getting ahead. The poor are at the mercy of life's unpredictable happenings: sickness, injury, loss of work, or trouble with the law. If the husband is home, his lack of status creates more tension and antagonism

Eleven percent of U. S. families live below the official poverty level. Poverty implies high rates of illegitimacy, desertion, separation, and divorce. Why, then, do many mothers living in poverty view motherhood with satisfaction?

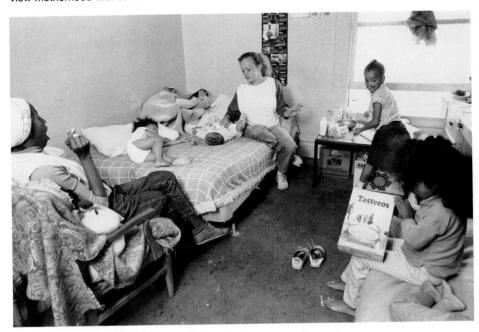

between the husband and wife. Low-income mothers tend to view motherhood as their chief satisfaction in life in compensation for the lack of companionship in marriage and the poverty of their lives (Dill, 1980).

Money and Marital Satisfaction

Family income has a close relationship to marital satisfaction (Schaninger and Buss, 1986). Financial complaints are consistently cited as a major problem by couples seeking divorce (Kitson and Sussman, 1982). However, *marital satisfaction is not always greatest when income is the highest* (Jorgensen, 1979). *For most couples, marital satisfaction is dependent on their feelings that income is adequate* (Berry and Williams, 1987). If the husband and wife are not earning as much as they feel they need, and if they feel their earnings aren't adequate, their marriage satisfaction is lessened because of financial pressures and tensions over money.

The management of money, even more than the level of income, is a major source of harmony or discord in the marital relationship. Couples who can agree on handling finances report more satisfactory marriages than do couples who have conflict over money (Berry and Williams, 1987); Keith and Whitaker, 1982). When conflict occurs, it arises because of immature or unrealistic attitudes toward earning, saving, or spending money. The emotional use of money to control or punish a spouse or to compensate for inadequacies, guilt, or inability to give love also causes difficulty.

Some 400 physicians, mostly psychiatrists, were asked their opinions about the prime reasons for money's being the source of marital quarrels (Mace, 1982). Figure 14.1 shows the results. This study revealed that the primary reason money was a source of marital quarrels was its use as a means to dominate and control a spouse.

FIGURE 14.1 *What is the Prime Reason for Money Being the Source of So Many Marital Quarrels?*

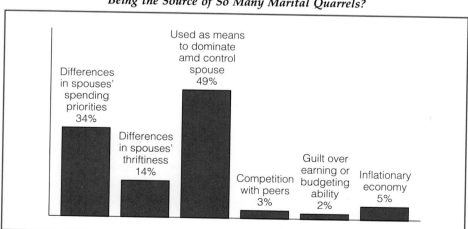

Source: Mace, D. R. (1982). Current thinking on marriage and money. *Medical Aspects of Human Sexuality, 16,* 109–118.

Barbara and Walter were in their middle thirties when they went to their minister to make arrangements for their wedding. They had been going together for over three years and were anxious to get married. The arrangements were made over four months before the date of the wedding.

Two weeks before the wedding date, Barbara went back to see the minister.

"I'm very worried," she confided. "I keep telling Walter to go on and get fitted for his tux. He's supposed to select the suits for the best man and ushers, also, and to make a deposit. I keep reminding him, but he puts it off."

The minister agreed to talk to Walter. "Is something bothering you that you haven't told Barbara?" the minister inquired.

"Well, you know, those tuxes are awfully expensive," Walter explained. "It's going to cost me over $200 for rentals. And by the time I get through paying for the bridal bouquet, and the church and organist expenses, this wedding will cost me a bundle."

"Do you have the money?" the clergyman inquired. Walter replied that he did have it in the bank, but he hated to deplete his account.

Several days later, Walter called off the wedding. He explained to Barbara that he could not afford to get married. Barbara was devastated, contacted all wedding guests to tell them the wedding was off, and canceled all the arrangements that she had made with the church and the caterers for the reception.

The clergyman did get another chance to talk to Walter. The clergyman found out that Walter actually owned over one million dollars of real estate around town. He had started out as a paper boy when he was 10 years old and had saved and

(continued)

Money is sometimes used as a tool for personal attacks. Kieren, Henton, and Marotz (1975) write:

> One partner may use his or her spending habits as a tool to attack the other for dissatisfactions in their relationship . . . A wife may continually go on spending sprees in order to punish her husband for his sexual indifference to her . . . In another example, a husband may keep tight control over money because he sees this as a way to legitimize his power in the family . . . Emotionally immature spouses who see money as a means of compensating for their personal limitations will in all probability encounter difficulty in money management.

The authors go on to say that money can be a valuable resource to the marital system, but it can also be a source of irritation to that system.

Masculine-Feminine Differences

One of the reasons couples have disagreements over money is because of traditional masculine-feminine differences in socialized priorities. A traditional wife who was brought up to feel that she is primarily responsible for the home and children and for family care is going to be more interested in decorating the house, buying clothing for the children, paying for food, or investing in a new sewing machine. The traditional husband may be interested in impressing others at work with his new car or clothes or in getting a boat or snowmobile. His wife can't understand why he wants to get ski equipment for the children when she would rather spend the money on music lessons. Conflict arises because invested his money. The chief topic of conversation around the dinner table when Walter was growing up was the Dow Jones Industrial average and how the family stocks were doing.

Following the wedding cancellation, Walter packed his secondhand car, and took off by himself for a vacation trip to Washington, D.C.

DISCUSSION

1. Some adults, like Walter, are very miserly when it comes to spending money, whereas others are spendthrifts. Why are people this way? What are some of the reasons for their behavior in relation to money?

2. Have you ever known people who were extreme in the way they manage money? Describe them and their characteristics. Can you explain the psychology of their behavior?

3. If a couple finds that they are very different in their spending habits, what are some of the things they could do to work things out?

4. Can habits in the way people handle money be changed? How?

5. Describe the spending habits of your parents. In what ways are you like them, and in what ways are you different? Were your parents good money managers? Why or why not?

the husband and wife have different priorities according to the way they were socialized. If the husband and wife were socialized to have similar values, however, their conflicts over the way their money is spent will be minimal.

If both the husband and wife are employed, the couple may disagree over the use of their two paychecks. Some couples put one check into a checking and one into a savings account. Others use one of the checks for important things they couldn't afford otherwise: a downpayment on a house, new furniture, or a vacation. In some cases, both checks are needed to pay basic living expenses.

Some people who earn the money feel a special right to it. "It's my money, I earned it." In such cases, if the other person feels that the money should be spent and used by all, conflict is bound to result.

WHY PEOPLE GO INTO DEBT

No matter how much money they make, some couples are always in debt. They estimate that if they had a little more each month they would be able to balance their budget, but when "the little more" is obtained, the couple still can't make do. They never seem able to meet all their obligations. The more income increases, the greater the indebtedness incurred (Bagarozzi and Bagarozzi, 1980).

The families that are most in debt are not the poor but those in middle-income brackets. The poor less frequently have mortgages, charge accounts, or large installment debts, although they might if they were able to establish credit. Level of income is not the reason why couples do or do not go into debt. The reasons relate more to the life-style of the couple and their ability to manage their money wisely.

Couples go into debt because of: (1) credit spending, (2) crisis spending, (3) careless or impulsive spending, and (4) compulsive spending.

Credit Spending

Many couples go into debt because of excessive and unwise use of credit. Credit can be a helpful thing: few couples can afford to pay cash for a home, automobile, or other large purchases. But habitual and unthinking use of credit often leads to excessive indebtedness that couples can ill afford.

Crisis Spending

Many people go into debt because of crisis spending (Moen, 1979). That is, unexpected but important events occur that throw the family budget off completely, and couples are forced to go into debt to meet the emergency. Unemployment is the most common crisis (Anderson, 1980; Moen, 1983; Thomas, McCabe, and Berry, 1980). Uninsured illness is another crisis. Other couples, such as farm couples, have variable incomes. They never know from one year to the next what their earnings will be, so it is very hard to plan ahead (Rosenblatt and Keller, 1983).

Careless or Impulsive Spending

Many couples go into debt because they buy things carelessly or impulsively. As a possible consequence, they pay more than is necessary, get merchandise of inferior quality that doesn't last as long as it should, or get things they don't need.

Some couples see things they want and buy them without ever stopping to think whether or not they can afford them. Mrs. G. says:

> My husband loves to go to auctions. Whenever he reads about someone selling the contents of their home in an auction, he always shows up. He loves the crowds and the excitement, but he gets carried away. Once he brought home a cement mermaid. I don't know what he expected to do with it since we don't have a fish pond or swimming pool. But he likes it. It's still down in the family room where he put it. (Author's counseling notes)

Couples who buy without careful planning or thought waste money needlessly.

Compulsive Spending

Other people are compulsive buyers. They can't say no. Their buying habits may be an expression of their emotional insecurity; they can't say no to a salesperson for fear of hurting that person's feelings or because they are afraid

"At what point would you say we stopped pursuing the finer things in life and settled for just keeping our heads above water?"

Source: *Dynamic Years.* (1978). November/December, p. 61. Drawing by Joseph Farris.

that person won't like them. Or they buy to try to gain status and recognition. Some people try to make up for basic insecurities by collecting things:

> My husband Frank is a compulsive collector. He spends a fortune on his coin collection, will travel hundreds of miles to see a rare coin, and will always end up outbidding everyone else to buy it. He shows his collection to everyone who comes into the house and derives great satisfaction from owning a coin that other collectors have never seen. (Author's counseling notes)

Frank's wife called him "incurable."

A lot of purchases are made to satisfy deep-seated needs for recognition or status rather than out of physical necessity. One husband relates: "We don't have much else, but we're the only family on the block to own two color TV sets, a fact of which we're very proud" (Author's counseling notes).

MONEY MANAGEMENT

Management Systems

Four different systems exist for managing money in the family. *One system is for the wife to exercise complete control.* She makes the major decisions, pays the bills, and gives her husband an allowance for spending money. This system is often preferred by the husband who is financially irresponsible or who doesn't want to be bothered with the responsibility of money management. One husband commented, "I admit I don't know how to handle money. That's why I let my wife have the paycheck and pay all the bills."

The second system is for the husband to exercise complete control. He pays all the bills, decides how much is spent on what, and doles out allowances to his wife for "housekeeping money" and to his children for incidentals. One modern variation of this system is for the husband to allot a portion of family income to his wife, who is responsible for certain expenditures and bills.

The third method is joint control, where the husband and wife have joint bank accounts, where both have free access to the accounts, and where most decisions are shared, including the responsibility for making purchases and paying the bills. The wife may or may not work; but if she does, her wages

Joint control of family
finances, with most decisions
shared, is often cited as
important to the survival of
the marriage; yet it is only
one system of management a
couple may choose to adopt.

become joint property, as are the husband's earnings. There is no separate "his money" or "her money." All is their money. A longitudinal survey of 311 couples revealed that happily married couples demonstrated more joint husband and wife influence in handling family finances than did unhappy couples. Establishment of equality and equity early in the marriage was important for survival of the marriage (Schaninger and Buss, 1986).

The fourth method is autonomous control, where the husband and wife keep their wages, financial planning, accounts, and expenditures completely separate. He has his money; she has hers. They each may be responsible for a certain proportion of all expenses, or they each may have particular areas over which they are responsible. The only joint decision is over who pays what and how much. The following is such an arrangement:

> Amanda was a career woman. When she married, she insisted on keeping all finances and accounts completely separate, each person contributing 50 percent of all expenses. However, she earned slightly less than her husband, so she would run out of money before he did. When this happened, she might borrow from her husband, but she always insisted on paying him back. She paid for everything she needed for herself: her own car, clothes, and personal expenses. She did not want to be financially dependent on her husband in any way. (Author's counseling notes)

The chief advantage of this system is that the wife can feel independent. One disadvantage is that the couple learns to rely on two incomes. One husband felt that his wife was so independent that she really didn't need him in any way: "Sometimes I feel she could walk out that door tomorrow and never miss me." Actually, the wife was not financially dependent, but she was emotionally dependent. She loved her husband very much, but it bothered him that she didn't need to depend on him for money.

Most couples adopt variations of these four systems. The husband may control some things, the wife others. They may plan jointly in some cases; in other instances they prefer to manage their money separately.

There is no right or wrong money management system. *The best system is what works for the individual couple.* Who actually manages the money is not as important as the skill with which it is done and the extent of the responsibility and agreement of both spouses in relation to its use. The person who has the most interest and skill in money management might be the one to exercise the most control, as long as the other person is in agreement. Marital adjustment is smoother when couples adopt a "we" attitude in relation to making financial decisions.

Establishing Goals

Few families have so much money that they can do without a system of priorities in their spending plans. *The first step in effective management is to make a list of basic goals* so the couple can decide how to plan their finances to accomplish their objectives (Pershing, 1979). Goals can be arranged under four headings: *long-term goals* (over five years), *medium-term goals* (two to five years), *short-term goals* (one year), and *immediate goals* (one month). Objectives can be placed under appropriate headings together with estimated costs. If desired, goals can be listed in order of decreasing priorities.

Budgeting

Budgeting is the allocation of expenses on a regular basis. This requires an examination of personal values plus knowledge of actual costs. How much is required for food, clothes, shelter, and so forth? How much does the couple have and want to spend on entertainment, eating out, or personal improvement? Expenses may be allocated under major headings that the spouses establish for themselves.

The actual amounts allocated under these different categories will depend partially upon level of income. The lower the income, the greater the percentages that have to be allocated for housing and food, and the lower are the usual percentage allocations for taxes, savings, insurance, and donations. Higher-income families spend smaller percentages of their total income on food and housing, but greater percentages on clothing, transportation, taxes, and savings.

Of course, some expenses are fixed. These include all financial commitments already made or occurring on a regular basis. Other expenses are flexible and vary according to a couple's needs and priorities. Since the flexible expenses can be controlled to a certain extent, the couple has to decide on the allocations among the various categories. Again, the actual decisions will reflect the couple's values and priorities.

The allocations will be tentative. *The next step is to keep careful financial records of where the money goes.* To do this, some sort of bookkeeping system has to be set up. The most convenient system utilizes the same categories as in the budget, so that entries may be made under the categories. Daily entries can be made, along with notations of each, indicating what money was spent for. The husband and wife may want to keep individual expense books to jot down daily entries so they won't forget them, until such time as they can transfer the information to the account pages. It is not necessary to account for every penny, such as the way personal allowances and expense money are spent, but overall amounts can be recorded.

PERSPECTIVE
A Record-Keeping System

As discussed, one important step in budgeting is to keep careful financial records of where the money goes. Table 14.2 is a helpful account sheet enabling the couple to record expenditures daily and by category. Totals under each category can be computed at the end of each month to see what was spent.

Analyzing Expenditures

After records have been kept over a period of time, *the couple can begin to analyze expenditures by categories* (Kieren, Henton, and Marotz, 1975). Is the money going where the partners want it to go? How do actual expenditures compare with budget estimates? The couple will discover that the regular, fixed expenses cause little trouble. It's the variable expenses that create difficulties. By analyzing expenditures, however, the couple can determine what things they want to cut out so they can have more money available for something else. Budget estimates need to be revised periodically to reflect actual needs, priorities, and changing income.

HOUSING

Residence and the Family Life Cycle

Housing needs vary over different stages of the family life cycle. The housing requirements of a family with several children are obviously different from those of a newly married couple or an older widow. Studies of residential satisfaction at different stages of the family life cycle show that *satisfaction with housing is at the lowest level among young married couples with preschool children* (McAuley and Nutty, 1985). See figure 14.2. Couples of this age are caught in a housing squeeze (McLeod and Ellis, 1983). Their income is low at the same time that they need increased space for a growing family. Because of the high cost of housing, many receive financial assistance from their families (Kennedy and

TABLE 14.2 Account Sheet.   *Month of* _____ , 19 ___ .   *Gross Monthly Income* _____ .

Date	Housing	Food	Transpor-tation	Clothing, personal care	Medical, dental	Personal improve-ment	Work expenses	Recrea-tion	Personal expenses	Charity	Savings	Taxes	Insurance, retirement	Miscella-neous	Totals daily
1															
2															
3															
4															
5															
6															
7															
8															
9															
10															
11															
12															
13															
14															
15															
16															
17															
18															
19															
20															
21															
22															
23															
24															
25															
26															
27															
28															
29															
30															
31															
Total															

Totals can be made horizontally (daily) and vertically (monthly). At the end of each month check horizantal and vertical totals. They should agree. Allocation of expenses can be made by comparing expenses under each category.

FIGURE 14.2 *Residential Satisfaction and the Life Cycle.*

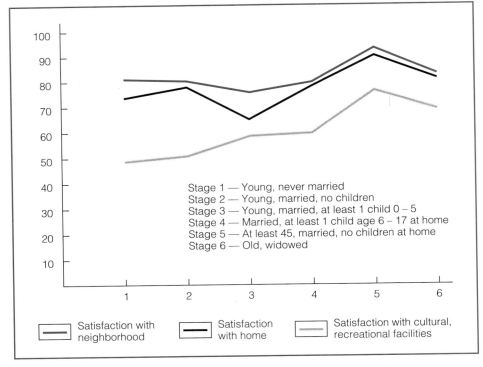

Source: McAuley, W. J., and Nutty, C. L. (1985). Residential satisfaction, community integration, and risk across the family life cycle. *Journal of Marriage and the Family, 47,*125–130.

Stokes, 1982). Most young families move frequently in the early years as their needs grow and their financial situation improves. Also, changes in family status (getting married, having children, separating, getting divorced) are accompanied by residential changes. It is estimated that five of the eight or nine moves that the average person makes in a lifetime are immediately associated with life-cycle changes (Speare and Goldscheider, 1987).

There are a number of qualities that people consider most important in selecting new housing. Preferences may vary somewhat at different stages of the family life cycle. However, *at all stages of the cycle, the number one consideration is the cost of housing.* People have to ask: Can we afford it? Married couples with children also look for the quality of the schools, adequate income, and job security. As people get older, they want convenience to medical facilities, peace and quiet, and high-quality local services. The elderly also look for low property taxes, public transportation, and convenience to church (McAuley and Nutty, 1982). Table 14.3 shows the results of one study.

Housing and Family Life Changes

One change in family life affecting housing needs has been the rapid increase in one-parent families due to the high rate of divorce and the increased number of out-of-wedlock births. Most of these families consist of a mother and one or

TABLE 14.3 Qualities Considered Important in Selecting Housing

Life-Cycle Stage	Most Often Mentioned as most important			Most Often Mentioned as second in importance	
I	1) Housing costs	15.1*		Healthiness of environment	10.7
	2) Peace and quiet	10.3		Housing costs	9.2
	3) Opportunities for advancement	8.3		Convenience to medical facilities	8.6
II	1) Housing costs	21.4		Housing costs	10.6
	2) Convenience to work	8.2		Quality of local services	8.5
	3) Job security	7.5		Friendliness of neighbors	7.5
III	1) Housing costs	31.4		Quality of schools	12.9
	2) Quality of schools	7.3		Healthiness of environment	9.0
	3) Job security	6.7		Earnings or salary	8.9
IV	1) Housing costs	24.1		Quality of schools	12.0
	2) Quality of schools	9.7		Housing costs	11.9
	3) Job security	9.4		Job security	8.9
V	1) Housing costs	27.4		Convenience to medical facilities	11.9
	2) Convenience to medical facilities	12.4		Housing costs	8.4
	3) Peace and quiet	7.6		Quality of local services	6.3
VI	1) Housing costs	24.3		Property taxes	8.0
	2) Convenience to medical facilities	11.1		Peace and quiet	7.2
	3) Public transportation	6.7		Convenience to church	6.9

Source: McAuley, W. J., and Nutty, C. L. (1982). Residential preferences and moving behavior: A family life-cycle analysis. *Journal of Marriage and the Family, 44*, 301–309. Copyright ©1982 by the National Council on Family Relations. Reprinted by permission.
*Numbers reflect proportions within each life-cycle stage.

more children. Some move back in with parents; others live in the house of other adults (Scheirer, 1983). Overcrowding is common, creating additional friction in the family. Some of those who live separately cannot afford to pay much for housing, and so either live in public subsidized housing or in substandard living spaces in poor neighborhoods. Overcrowding creates its own problems.

A substantial number of persons live alone. About one-third of never-marrieds live alone. The number of people who live alone increases with each age group, reaching a maximum of about 75 percent of widowed persons (Alwin, Converse, and Martin, 1985). These persons require living spaces in areas that provide maximum social support and integration through contacts with friends. This is why many never-married persons often find condominium or apartment living attractive. As we saw in Chapter 11, three out of four elderly most often stay in their own homes where they have friends and/or relatives nearby.

Housing Costs

Housing expenses constitute one of the largest items in the family budget at all income levels. Considerable thought needs to be given, therefore, to the type of housing chosen. Should a couple buy or rent? For couples who can afford the

TABLE 14.4 *Annual Costs To Buy Versus To Rent a House*

1	2	3	4	5	6	7	8
Year	Value of house, (6% appreciation per year)	Taxes, insurance, maintenance (5.5% of value of house per year)	Annual payment on 25-year $80,000 mortgage at 10.5% interest	Lost interest on $21,951 down payment at 8%	Total yearly costs to buy (columns 3,4,5)	Landlord's profit: 10% of appreciated value of house each year	Total annual rent (columns 3,7)
1990	$101,951	$5,607	$9,064	$1,756	$16,427	$10,195	$15,802
1991	108,068	5,942	9,064	1,756	16,763	10,807	16,751
1992	114,552	6,300	9,064	1,756	17,120	11,455	17,755
1993	121,425	6,678	9,064	1,756	17,498	12,142	18,821
1994	128,710	7,079	9,064	1,756	17,899	12,871	19,950
1995	136,432	7,504	9,064	1,756	18,324	13,643	21,147
1996	144,617	7,954	9,064	1,756	18,774	14,461	22,416
1997	153,294	8,431	9,064	1,756	19,283	15,329	23,760
1998	162,491	8,937	9,064	1,756	19,757	16,249	25,186
1999	172,240	9,473	9,064	1,756	20,293	17,224	26,697

down payment, buying is by far the first choice if the decision is made strictly on the basis of cost.

Let us assume you buy an existing one-family house at the beginning of 1990. The house has 1600 square feet, which is the median size in the United States; and you pay the median price for that, which is estimated at $101,951. You pay $21,951 down and take out an $80,000 mortgage at 10.5 percent interest for 25 years. Your yearly payments are $9,064. Let us further assume that your property taxes, insurance, and maintenance costs are 5.5 percent of the appreciated value of the house each year. The first year, these costs are $5,607. Let us further assume you could have earned 8 percent interest on the $21,951 down payment if you had not bought the house. That figure is $1,756 per year for every year you own the house. The total costs of home ownership, exclusive of utilities, for the first year are $16,427 ($9,064 + 5,607 + 1,756).

But the house appreciates in value each year so that your insurance, taxes, and maintenance costs go up. The mortgage payments remain the same. If the house appreciates in value 6 percent per year, your yearly cash costs are as found in Column 6 of Table 14.4.

Buying Versus Renting

How do these figures compare with renting the identical space and house? Let us assume the landlord has to pay the same 5.5 percent of the value of the house for taxes, insurance, and maintenance; he also earns 10 percent profit each year on the appreciated value of the house. During the year, 1990, he would have to charge a rent of $15,802 ($5,607 + 10,195 profit). If the house appreciates at 6 percent per year, the rents would be as listed in Column

TABLE 14.5 Annual Costs To Buy a House If House Sold During Year

1 End of Year	2 Selling Price (6% appreciation per year)	3 Selling Price − 6% brokers fee	4 Appreciation for year (after paying broker's fee)	5 Total yearly cost to buy (taxes, insurance, maintenance, mortgage, loss of interest)	6 Payment on Principal this year	7 Net cost for year sold (columns 5 − [4 + 6])
1990	$108,068	$101,584	$−367	$16,427	$ 696	$16,098
1991	114,552	107,678	6,094	16,763	776	9,803
1992	121,425	114,140	6,462	17,120	856	9,802
1993	128,710	120,987	6,847	17,498	952	9,690
1994	136,432	128,246	7,259	17,899	1,064	9,576
1995	144,617	135,939	7,693	18,324	1,176	9,955
1996	153,294	144,096	8,157	18,774	1,304	9,313
1997	162,491	152,741	8,645	19,283	1,448	9,190
1998	172,240	161,906	9,165	19,757	1,608	8,984
1999	182,574	171,620	9,714	20,293	1,874	8,795

8 of Table 14.4. *As you can see, it is slightly cheaper to rent than to buy during the first two years.* After that time, costs to rent go up much faster than costs to buy, so that by the end of 1999, your rent would be $26,697 versus $20,293 per year to buy.

The real savings in buying a house are realized when the house is sold. Let's use the same 1600-square-foot, $101,951 house. Table 14.5 shows the cost of home ownership each year the house is sold. The net costs each year are calculated by subtracting the appreciation and payment on the principal during the year from the total yearly costs. As you can see by comparing figures in Tables 14.4 and 14.5, the first year the net cost of home ownership ($16,098) is greater than the cost of renting ($15,802). After that, the yearly costs for buying are substantially lower than for renting. If the house is sold the tenth year of ownership, the cost that last year is only $8,795 compared to a cost of $26,697 for rent. Thus, it is wise to rent only on a short-term basis. *Buying is far more economical in the long run whether you keep the house or sell it.*

Of course, you can get by much more cheaply by renting a smaller place; but if we're going to compare values, we have to compare comparable spaces.

In addition to costs, there are other considerations in deciding whether to buy or rent. Table 14.6 shows the advantages and disadvantages of home ownership versus renting an apartment.

Variations in Costs

Purchase costs as well as rent costs vary tremendously across the United States. Table 14.7 shows the 1987 prices in different sections of the country for a 2000-square-foot house with 3 bedrooms, 2 baths, and a two-car garage. The percent

TABLE 14.6 Home Ownership or Renting: Advantages and Disadvantages

HOME OWNERSHIP

Advantages	Disadvantages
1. Builds equity in house, so ownership is a form of savings.	1. May require expensive down payment that many couples can never accumulate.
2. Providers a tax shelter, since taxes and interest are deductible.	2. Yearly payments ordinarily greater than renting the first couple of years.
3. Usually more space, outside yard.	3. Sometimes hard to sell. Lack of fluidity of investment sometimes forces homeowner who has to move to sell at a loss.
4. More privacy than apartment.	
5. Greater freedom to live as one wishes.	4. Requires expensive, time-consuming maintenance.
6. Value appreciates, helping to offset negative effects of inflation.	5. Overall price is so high it is beyond reach of many Americans.
7. Pride in owning property.	6. Interest rates are high and expensive over the years.
8. Fixed price and mortgage payment schedule (exclusive of taxes and insurance) that does not increase over the years (unless loan is drawn up with escalation clause).	7. Requires considerable knowledge of construction quality, housing values, and costs if people are to avoid a poor buy.
9. Usually found in better neighborhoods than apartment buildings.	8. May have to buy in locations a long distance from place of work.
10. Is cheaper in the long run than renting.	

APARTMENT RENTAL

Advantages	Disadvantages
1. Allows for flexibility of movement. Can move on 30-day notice if lease allows escape clause with minimum penalty for leaving before lease is up.	1. More limited as to geographical area in which to live since apartments are restricted to certain areas.
2. Do not have to assume long-term cost.	2. No accumulation of equity.
3. Lower initial cost; lower costs per month for first couple of years.	3. Lack of privacy, may be noise and confusion.
4. No expensive and time-consuming maintenance.	4. Usually smaller, less convenient living space.
5. Gives couples time to evaluate community, neighbors, and costs before they make any decisions.	5. Subject to restriction on building use and to rules for governing property. May not allow children, pets.
6. Opportunity to invest and to make profit on money that would otherwise go to down payment on house.	6. May be subject to nonrenewed lease or to eviction.
7. Minimum investment in furniture and furnishings. Laundry services often available.	7. Raise in rent uncertain from lease year to lease year. Hard to calculate future costs.
8. Close to other people, so opportunity to meet others. Children have friends to play with.	8. Less control over who neighbors are.
9. Sometimes provides recreational facilities: playgrounds, tennis courts, swimming pool.	9. Subject to performance of landlord in maintaining property.

Adapted from Rice, F. P. (1979). *Marriage and parenthood*. Boston: Allyn and Bacon, 382, 383.

figures show the change in prices from 1986 to 1987. As you can see, costs in Oklahoma and Texas, where declining oil prices hurt the economy, are relatively low. Costs in the most affluent areas of California, Massachusetts, or Connecticut are as much as ten times those of the least expensive areas. How much you pay will depend on where you live. Also, some costs have

TABLE 14.7 1987 Housing Prices in Select Areas*

Five Most Expensive Areas

Beverly Hills, CA	$636,667	up 8.4%
Greenwich, CT	599,667	down 1.2%
La Jolla, CA	472,333	up 8.3%
Los Altos, CA	440,000	up 13.9%
Menlo Park, CA	420,000	up 15.9%

Five Least Expensive Areas

Oklahoma City, OK	$66,833	up 1.3%
Charleston, WV	66,967	up 5.6%
Tulsa, OK	74,167	down 3.4%
Corpus Christi, TX	74,833	up 2.6%
Eugene, OR	75,833	up 3.9%

Selected New England Areas

Burlington, VT	$133,167	up 12.4%
Portland, ME	144,167	up 21.9%
Springfield, MA	173,233	up 20%
Manchester, NH	178,967	up 12%
Hartford, CT	197,133	up 29.6%
Rhode Island suburbs	218,333	up 23%
Framingham, MA	224,167	up 31.9%
Newton, MA	296,000	down 0.7%
Stamford, CT	349,833	up 7.6%

Source: "Housing Costs in State Still Below U.S. Average." (1988). *Portland Press Herald*, April 19. Portland, Maine.

*Prices based on a 2,000-square-foot home with three bedrooms, two baths and a two-car garage. Percent figures show change from 1986.

started to level off or decline, whereas costs in other sections of the country (part of New England) are still rising extremely fast. General trends for the area need to be taken into consideration in timing your purchase. The wisest move is to buy a house in an area where prices are beginning to rise, but have not yet peaked. Those who pay inflationary prices may lose money on their house once prices start to come down. One man from Texas explained: "Before the oil bust, I was offered $130,000 for my house and I didn't take it. Now I can't get rid of it at $65,000."(Author's counseling notes)

Interest Rates

The mortgage interest rates you have to pay are another crucial factor in house buying. Table 14.8 shows the monthly mortgage payments on a $60,000 mortgage for 25 years at various rates of interest. It also shows the total payments over the life of the loan. Each percentage point increase in interest rates amounts to an increase in monthly payments of over $40. Over the life of the loan, each percentage point increase in interest rates results in a total additional charge of over $12,000 to $13,000.

**TABLE 14.8 *Monthly Mortgage Payments and Total Payments
on a $60,000 Mortgage for 25 Years
at Various Interest Rates***

Interest Rate	Monthly Payments	Total Payment over Life of Loan
8	$463.09	$138,927
8.5%	483.14	144,942
9 %	503.52	151,056
10 %	545.23	157,266
10.5%	566.51	163,569
11 %	588.07	169,953
11.5%	609.89	176,421

**TABLE 14.9 *Monthly Payments on a $60,000 Mortgage
at 10.5% Interest over Different Loan Periods***

Life of Loan (years)	Monthly Payments	Total Payment over Life of Loan
15	$663.24	$119,383
20	599.03	143,767
25	566.51	169,953
30	548.85	197,586

Variable mortgage interest rates *are always lower in the beginning than are fixed interest rates.* In times of increasing interest rates, it might be better to take out a mortgage with fixed rates. In times of falling interest rates, variable mortgages are an advantage. No one can predict with certainty what interest rates are going to do over the long term, so all you can do is select a rate schedule that seems most advantageous to you at the time.

Points

In addition to interest, lenders charge "**points**" up front as a loan charge. Each 1 point charged means you pay 1 percent of the total cost of the mortgage. This amount is deducted from the mortgage money available to you, unless you pay the points in cash. Thus, if a lender charges you 3 points on a $60,000 loan, you are paying $1,800, leaving $58,200 available for your mortgage. Some institutions seem to have lower interest rates, but they charge more points in compensation. Ask your lender what the total interest rate is, including the cost of paying points.

Life of the Loan

The life of the loan also has a significant influence on total payments. Table 14.9 shows the monthly payments on a $60,000 mortgage at 10.5 percent interest over a period of 15, 20, 25, and 30 years; it also shows the total payments

The condominium, a house or apartment that is purchased as part of a cluster of units, has become increasingly popular in the last two decades as the price of the free-standing family house has risen beyond the reach of many young couples and families.

over the life of the loan. The total difference in monthly payments between a 30-year loan and a 25-year loan is only $17.66 per month, yet this amounts to a difference of $27,633 over the loan life. The difference between a 30-year loan and a 20-year loan is $50.18 per month or $53,819 over the loan life. *If you can afford it, it's to your advantage to take out a loan for as short a period as possible.* Also, interest rates are lower on loans for a fewer number of years.

The only situation in which you might not try to pay off the mortgage quickly is when you can get a higher rate of interest by investing the money that you have to pay on the mortgage. At the present time, long-term savings pay about 8 percent interest, but mortgages are staying higher than 10 percent. In spite of the fact that interest is deductible from your income tax, you save money by paying off the mortgage.

Buying a Condominium

A **condominium** is a house or apartment that you buy as part of a cluster of units. A few condos are free-standing structures, and others are built side by side: some are part of an apartment complex. When you buy a condo, you get legal title to your own dwelling and are responsible for paying property taxes, insurance on your personal furnishings and belongings inside your residence, and your own utilities. You are also responsible for maintenance inside your unit.

At the same time, you pay a monthly condo fee that covers maintenance cost of community facilities and the maintenance of the outside of all the units. Condo fees, along with mortgage, interests, and property taxes are deductible from income tax. Since you own your own condominium, you may resell it or rent it as you choose. You may finance a condominium as you would a house, so you build up equity in your property. Many people buy condos to avoid having to mow lawns, shovel snow, and maintain the outside of their building. Also, they usually can take extended trips away from their residence with some assurance that their property is safe. Some people enjoy the community living and the chance to have friends close by.

There are some pitfalls and disadvantages to condominium ownership.

1. You have less privacy.

2. You are subject to the rules of the association, which may have restrictions against pets, renting, children, or other things. You cannot make additions or alterations to the outside of your structure without approval.

3. Your monthly fee is set by the association, and it may become higher than you anticipated. Some builders subsidize the fee during construction, so the figure is unrealistically low to attract buyers. After construction ends, the association may be forced to raise the fee very rapidly.

4. If you buy during construction, the integrity of the developer is important. If the person is highly reliable, well-financed, and experienced, you may get what is promised. A disreputable builder who makes idle promises or employs shoddy workmanship creates real problems for subsequent owners. Buyers need to investigate the developer, thoroughly examine the charter and rules of the association, and make certain they know their entitlements before buying. Some developers retain ownership to parking or other facilities and charge rent to subsequent buyers. Find out who owns and controls what.

5. Any money deposited should be put in escrow with interest in your name, not mixed with other developer funds. Find out from the town office exactly what your taxes are. Get reliable estimates of prospective utility costs from the utility companies. Condominium buying is great for some people, but you have to know ahead of time what you're getting into.

The potential resale value of your condo depends upon the area. Like houses, condominium values are depressed in some areas and accelerating rapidly in others.

AUTOMOBILES

Costs

The automobile is another major expense in most families. Yet, because of rapid depreciation, the value declines very rapidly in only a few years. For this reason, a car is the poorest "investment" one can make. It may be necessary, but it is costly.

Table 14.10 shows the estimated 12-year cost of owning and operating an automobile, by size of car, in 1990. The total cost to own and operate a large automobile is $3,883 per year ($46,000 ÷ 12). A passenger van is the most

TABLE 14.10 *Estimated* 12-Year Cost of Owning and
Operating an Automobile, by Size of Car, in 1990*

Car	Total	Taxes and Fees	Costs Excl.[1] Taxes
Total cost ($1,000)			
Large[2]	46.6	3.3	43.3
Intermediate[3]	42.3	2.8	39.5
Compact[4]	35.4	2.4	33.0
Subcompact[5]	34.5	2.3	32.2
Passenger van[6]	59.6	4.2	55.4
Cents per mile cost			
Large[3]	38.7	2.8	35.9
Intermediate[3]	35.2	2.3	32.9
Compact[4]	29.5	2.0	27.5
Subcompact[5]	28.7	1.8	26.9
Passenger van[6]	49.6	3.4	46.2

*Estimates calculated from data from the U.S. Federal Highway Administration. Based on a vehicle operated in Baltimore, Maryland, area with an assumed life span of 12 years, 120,000 miles.
[1]Includes depreciation, repairs and maintenance, tires, gasoline, accessories and oil, insurance, and parking
[2]Fully equipped 4-door sedan, price $14,619
[3]Two-door coupe, price $13,055
[4]Four-door sedan, price $11,131
[5]Five-door (hatchback), price $8,885
[6]Passenger van, price $16,177

expensive ($4,966 per year). A subcompact is the cheapest but still costs $2,875 per year ($34,500 ÷ 12). Owning an automobile is not cheap.

Figure 14.3 shows costs in cents per mile over the 12-year life of a large car (purchase price $14,619). Note that the depreciation is by far the largest expense during the first four years, after which repairs and maintenance become more expensive than depreciation. After the first year, total costs per mile are greatest during the fourth through the seventh years. Ordinarily then, to save money, you ought to trade in your car before it is four and one-half years old. However, if you do decide to keep it for its total life, costs go down very rapidly after the seventh year because depreciation is small and people usually stop doing some repairs and maintenance.

Used Cars

If you want to buy a used car to save on depreciation expenses, but still keep repairs to a minimum, buy a low mileage car two years old and keep it about two and one-half years, or buy a car three years old and keep it about a year and a half before trading it in. *Based on actual costs, it is cheaper to buy a secondhand car than a new one, provided you get a good used car at a fair price.*

New Cars

No buyer has to pay the sticker price for a new car. This is only the starting point for negotiations. Most cars are sold for less than the sticker price, depending

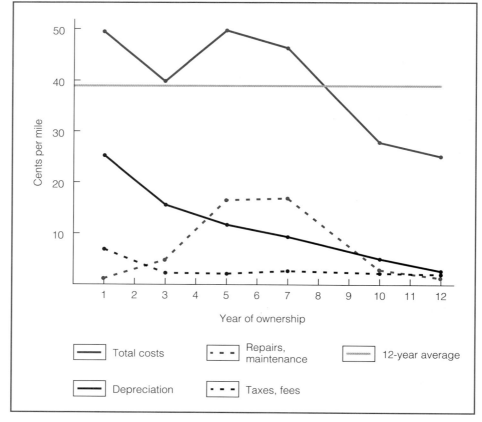

*FIGURE 14.3 Estimated Costs of Owning and Operating
a Large Automobile, 1990, Cents per Mile.*

Estimates calculated from data from the U.S. Federal Highway Administration. Based on a vehicle operated in Baltimore, MD, area with an assumed lifespan of 12 years, 120,000 miles. Original purchase price $14,619.

ASSESSMENT
My (Our) Personal Spending Habits

Using the account sheet shown earlier in this chapter, keep track of your actual expenditures for a period of one, two, or three months. At the end of the period, go over the totals under each category, noting the ones for which you spent more money than you would prefer, and noting the categories where you spent less money than you would like. The next month, try to adjust your spending so you're cutting down in those areas in which your expenditures have been excessive and so you're increasing your expenditures in areas where you need to increase the amount of money you spend. If you repeat this conscientiously over a period of months, you should see some improvement in the budgeting of your money. You should be getting more of what you want for your money's worth.

upon the total cost of the car and the trade-in allowance for one's old car. The higher the price of the new car, the greater the total discount dealers allow. The buyer can check the *Bluebook* to find out what the old car is worth as a trade-in. *Consumers Union Buying Guide* for the current year can be consulted for recommendations on new car buys and the precise steps to take in buying a used car.

SUMMARY

1. By 1990, median family income is estimated at $35,530 per year. In spite of rising income, real income remains about constant because of the effects of inflation.

2. About 11 percent of persons living in families have incomes below the poverty level. The effects of poverty on families are higher rates of illegitimacy, desertion, separation and divorce; tensions and unhappiness in the marital relationship; higher rates of mental and physical illness; higher rates of alcoholism and drug abuse; and other problems.

3. Family income has a close relationship to marital satisfaction, but satisfaction depends most on the feelings that income is adequate, not on having a high income per se.

4. Money management is also a source of harmony or discord in the family.

5. Conflict over money occurs in part because men and women have been socialized to emphasize different priorities in making purchases. Also, some people who earn money feel that it's theirs because they earned it, and other family members do not have a right to it.

6. People go into debt because of credit spending, crisis spending, careless or impulsive spending, and compulsive spending.

7. There are four different systems for managing money in the family: (1) the wife exercising complete control, (2) the husband exercising complete control, (3) joint control, or (4) autonomous control. The best system is what works for the individual couple.

8. There are several requirements for effective money management: (1) establish goals and priorities, (2) allocate spending under different categories (budget), (3) keep careful records of expenditures, (4) analyze expenditures, and (5) adjust spending according to preferences.

9. Housing needs vary over different stages of the family life cycle. Satisfaction with housing is usually at its lowest when children are young, because needs are the greatest and income to buy adequate housing is low. At all stages, the number one consideration in selecting housing is cost.

10. One of the changes that affect housing needs is the rapid increase in one-parent families. There are also a large number of persons who live alone. These persons need affordable housing that also permits a maximum of social support and contact with friends.

11. Housing costs constitute one of the largest items in the family budget at all income levels. Based strictly on costs, it is cheaper to rent than to buy for the first two years; after that rental costs go up faster than the costs to buy. The real savings in buying a house are realized when the house is sold. Because of appreciation on the house, the longer the home is owned, the less expensive it is per year to live there.

12. House costs vary tremendously across different regions of the United States.

13. Mortgage interest rates, points charged to service the loan, and the mortgage loan life also need to be considered when buying a house.

14. A condominium is a house or apartment that you buy as part of a cluster of units. A monthly condo fee is charged to maintain the outside of the units and the community-owned spaces. There are both disadvantages and advantages to condo ownership.

15. The automobile is another major expense in most families. Because of rapid depreciation, the value of the car declines rapidly in only a few years.

16. Cost of auto ownership may be kept to a minimum by keeping a new car four and one-half years and then trading it in. At the end of four and one-half years, the costs of repairs and maintenance become greater than the costs of depreciation.

17. In buying a used car, purchase one that is two or three years old, keep it two and one-half or one and one-half years and trade it in. In buying a new car, never pay the sticker price for the car; this is only the starting point for negotiations to see what one can get for a trade-in on the old car and the discount one can get on the new car.

SUGGESTED READINGS

Ginsberg, L. G. (1981). *Family Financial Survival*. Millbrae, CA: Celestial Arts. Financial planning.

Miller, R. L. (1981). *Economic Issues for Consumers* (3rd ed.). St. Paul, MN: West. Consumer-related issues.

Porter, S. (1979). *Sylvia Porter's New Money Book* (Rev. ed.). New York: Doubleday. Comprehensive reference book.

Stein, B. J. (1985). *Financial Passages*. New York: Doubleday. Financial planning during particular stages of life.

Westfall, D. (1984). *Every Woman's Guide to Financial Planning*. New York: Basic Books. What every woman should know about finances.

15

COMPANIONSHIP IN AND OUTSIDE THE FAMILY

KEY TERMS

joint companionship
parallel companionship
segregated companionship

In an impersonal world, the family becomes even more important as a center of companionship and love. Family members seek fulfillment of their basic human needs for affection and belongingness.

In this chapter we are concerned with family interaction and togetherness versus separateness. We are concerned also about companionship in leisure, the need for recreation, the types of leisure-time activities people enjoy, and how personality differences affect social life as related to marital satisfaction. Family vacations and television viewing habits are discussed in relation to family relationships.

We look beyond the family also to friendships, some basic male-female differences in relationships with friends, and some of the benefits and pitfalls of both same-sex and opposite-sex friendships.

This chapter also provides an opportunity for assessing personal loneliness and friendship potential.

COMPANIONSHIP AND THE FAMILY

Companionship as a Motive for Marriage

If we were to ask couples why they want to get married, most would say, "for love and companionship." In a *Playboy* survey, just two reasons for marriage were rated "very important" by a clear majority of men: 74 percent responded, "having another person to share one's life with," and 62 percent said, "having someone to share important life experiences with" (Hunt, 1974). When Cargan and Melko (1982) asked both marrieds and singles what was the greatest advantage of being married, most replied in terms of sharing and companionship: "companionship and someone to share decisions with," "someone to share with the good and bad of life," "the opportunity to converse with someone every day," "being able to share your life with someone you love." The word that turned up most frequently was *companionship*.

We all need companionship — the company of someone to love, to talk to, and to share life experiences with — whether those experiences be play, work, joy, or sadness. Most of life's happiest experiences are more fun when we are in the company of someone else. Most of life's saddest moments are less difficult if we have a companion to help ease the burden.

Research indicates that couples who share interests, who do things together, who share some of the same friends and social groups, derive more satisfaction from their relationship than do couples who are not mutually involved (Argyle and Furnham, 1983). However, it's not just the amount of time that couples spend together that is the criteria of marital satisfaction, but the quality of the relationship they enjoy when they are together (Osmond and Martin, 1978).

When Companionship Doesn't Develop

Although people say they choose to marry for companionship, marriage counselors hear couples complaining over and over:

"We never spend any time together."

"We don't talk to one another."

What is the greatest advantage of being married? Some studies show that both married and single people respond to that question by answering that sharing and companionship are important motives for marriage.

"We don't have any interests in common."

"We've drifted apart."

These comments come from couples who in the beginning of their marriages said the primary reason for getting married was "companionship and love."

Obviously, something has gone wrong. Usually, one of several things has happened:

- The husband and/or wife spend most of their time on the job, with little left over for the family. (See Chapter 13 for a full discussion.) It's easy under these circumstances to drift apart.

- The husband and/or wife have separate friends and spend most of their leisure time with their own friends rather than with joint friends as a couple.

- The husband and/or wife have individual hobbies and leisure time activities that they pursue separately rather than together. If these activities take up most of the leisure time, the couple is separated during leisure hours. One husband described his situation: "My wife is a marathon runner. She works out several hours a day and works full-time in addition. It doesn't leave us any time together as a couple" (Author's counseling notes).

- The husband and wife spend most of their free time outside the house attending paid amusements. They are always on the go — attending movies, concerts, or athletic events — but they spend little time alone together just talking. They are in one another's company, but they are not finding real intimacy based on emotional closeness.

- The husband and/or wife spend their free time with the children rather than devoting some of it to being together as a couple. One husband complained: "Since the baby was born, my wife's whole life has been wrapped up in Sarah. My wife has no time for me" (Author's counseling notes).

- The husband and/or wife vegetate in front of the television, rather than spending quality time together. One wife described her situation: "Our routine is always the same. He comes home from work, has a couple of beers, eats supper, sits down to watch television, and falls asleep. I'm sick of never going out" (Author's counseling notes).

- The husband and/or wife don't enjoy being together. They are embarrassed by what the other person does when they do go out. One wife commented: "Whenever we have company my husband uses the occasion to put me down and say something critical about me. He says he's only kidding, but I'm tired of being the brunt of his jokes. I've quit going out with him" (Author's counseling notes). One husband explained: "When we go to another couple's house my wife totally monopolizes the conversation. She interrupts. She turns the conversation around to talk about something she's interested in. It's very embarrassing" (Author's counseling notes).

In each of these situations, either the husband or wife didn't spend enough time with the other, or when they were together their activities were not conducive to companionship.

Styles of Companionship

Researchers have identified three different styles of companionship that characterize relationships: *joint companionship, parallel companionship,* and *segregated companionship* (Orthner, 1981).

Joint companionship *is characterized primarily by jointly shared interests and activities* (Rogler and Procidano, 1986). The emphasis is on interaction during leisure pursuits. There is close emotional involvement as well. One husband described his situation: "It just so happens that my wife is also my best friend. We do everything together and have most things in common. I can't understand people who get married and then go their separate ways" (Author's counseling notes).

Parallel companionship *is characterized by parallel activities where couples do things in the company of one another* because they want to "be together," but where they each do their own thing as individuals. Watching TV, reading, doing individual house projects, or pursuing separate hobbies are all examples of parallel companionship. There may be some conversation, some visiting, or playing with the children, but most of their attention is focused on their individual pursuits. While it is nice to have company, if there is lack of meaningful conversation or of real involvement, much emotional closeness may be lost. Some couples go out to dinner together, for example, but then never say anything to one another during the whole meal.

Segregated companionship *involves participating primarily in activities outside the dyadic relationship.* Each spouse spends time with his or her own circle of friends or kin, excluding the other from activities. One wife observed:

When my husband bought a boat I thought it would be something we could do together. He takes his friends sailing, but he doesn't want me along. He really doesn't want to be with me. One reason may be because I don't drink and his friends do. He knows I disapprove of their behavior. (Author's counseling notes)

In such relationships home may be little more than a meeting place where spouses pass one another on their way to other activities.

There are advantages and disadvantages to each of these companionship styles, depending on what couples expect. Those who want joint companionship but who are segregated may become very disenchanted. As one wife expressed it, "If I wanted to be alone all the time, I would never have gotten married" (Author's counseling notes).

Togetherness Versus Separateness

People differ in their need for closeness. The couple who wants close companionship will be miserable if separated. In fact, some men give up promotions or change jobs so they won't have to be separated from their families so much. One man remarked:

> I cheerfully . . . passed up two good promotions because one of them would have required some traveling and the other would have taken evening and weekend time — and that's when Pat and I *live*. The hours with her (after twenty-two years of marriage) are what I live for (Cuber and Haroff, 1965, p. 56).

There are, however, couples who get on one another's nerves if they are together too much. They welcome time spent apart. One wife complained:

> I nearly go crazy when my husband is home on vacation. He makes too much work for me and demands something all the time. I'm glad when he goes back to work and especially when he's away on business. I get a lot more things done and have time to do what I want for a change. (Author's counseling notes)

Generally speaking, couples who have utilitarian marriages, who stay together for convenience, for the sake of the children, or for financial or social reasons rather than for companionship, don't mind enforced separation as much. In fact, some *want* to spend a lot of time away from one another. But couples who really enjoy one another's company, who have a fulfilling sex life, and who seek a vital, close relationship, hate anything that keeps them apart.

There is a difference between closeness and possessiveness, however. Some people want to so possess their spouse that they cannot tolerate any spaces in their togetherness. The discussion in the classroom forum in this chapter is an example of a marriage based on possessiveness.

Loneliness

Loneliness is not simply being alone. It's being alone when we'd rather be with someone; or it's the feeling we have when we are with someone and do not feel close to them, or when we are with someone and would rather be with someone else. Loneliness is the distressing feeling we have when there is a discrepancy between the kind of social relations we want and the kind of social relations we have (Perlman and Peplau, 1981). It involves dissatisfaction with our present social relations (Brehm, 1985). *Loneliness can be due to either social isolation or emotional isolation.*

CLASSROOM FORUM
Togetherness or Possessiveness?

After four years of marriage, John and Ruth are in marital therapy. They each agree that things were better before the wedding. Now they complain of feeling smothered. They have few couple friends and no separate friends. Ruth is possessive and feels anxious when John tries to take time apart for himself. She is home most of the time with their two-year-old daughter and feels resentment about this. She has not worked since the third month of her pregnancy, and complains of being lonely and that she and John don't "do things together" as they used to. John resents what he calls Ruth's "clinging." "She won't make other friends," he complains. Their sex life is faltering. He asserts that Ruth just isn't interested; she makes excuses and withdraws.

Ruth had grown up in a home where her father was very much the "boss" and her mother complied with his wishes. The model of marriage she learned from her parents was one in which the spouses would have no separate friends. They were, after all, a couple. Her father's activities around the house were appropriate for "man's work." Her mother had the bulk of the household responsibilities. Outside the house, except for his work, they went everywhere and did everything together. Because of the role stereotypes they accepted and their possessiveness, they placed strict limits on any privacy for each other.

Marriage for Ruth and John is a closed system. The partners consider themselves a unit rather than two persons who also interact independently with others in the orbits of their lives. They have little or no personal privacy and no sense of freedom to make independent choices and separate friends. Their activities and experiences are curtailed because they are restricted to what both would like. For one to move outside this "couple front" might result in a feeling of guilt and inhibition, with resultant threats, anger, and resentment in the other.

QUESTIONS

1. How does Ruth really feel toward John? Why is she resentful?

2. On the one hand, Ruth is possessive and jealous when John tries to take time apart from her; but on the other hand, she rejects sexual and emotional intimacy. Why is she unable to display affection when John comes home? Why is she jealous of his outside interests?

3. John and Ruth have no freedom to make independent choices and separate friends. Is this good or bad for marriage? Explain your views.

4. Why do some people become overly possessive of their mates? What are the possible effects on the marriage?

5. Solomon and Minor (1982) write: "Partners in a healthy, rewarding relationship need individual privacy to function as autonomous persons and to experience the sort of personal growth that will bring freshness, zest, and motivating power into the marital relationship" (p. 107).

   How do you feel about this point of view? Explain your feelings.

Source: Solomon, K., and Minor, H. W. (1982). Need for privacy in marriage. *Medical Aspects of Human Sexuality, 16,* June, 104–111.

Social isolation is situational (e.g., geographical separation) whereas *emotional isolation* is relational (feeling estranged from a person who is physically nearby).

In their survey, Rubenstein and Shaver (1982) found five major reasons people gave for feeling lonely.

Loneliness can be either social or emotional isolation. Which form of loneliness is more likely to be related to personality attributes of the lonely person?

Being unattached: having no spouse; having no sexual partner; breaking up with spouse or lover.

Alienation: feeling different; being misunderstood; not being needed; having no close friends.

Being alone: coming home to an empty house.

Forced isolation: being housebound, being hospitalized; having no transportation.

Dislocation: being far from home; starting in a new job or school; moving too often; traveling often.

In the preceding categories, loneliness is ascribed to either social or emotional isolation. But *it may also relate to personality attributes, to the kind of people we are*. For example, lonely people are likely to have low self-esteem and to feel unworthy and unlovable; as a result, others have difficulty accepting them because they cannot accept themselves (Peplau, Miceli, and Morasch, 1982).

Lonely people expect others not to like them (Jones, Freemon, and Goswick, 1981; Jones, Sansome, and Helm, 1983). They may be passive and shy, and so seldom take the initiative in social situations (Cheek and Busch, 1981). They also engage in relatively little self-disclosure that would allow others to get to know them (Solano, Batten, and Parish, 1982).

Lonely people tend to be socially unresponsive and insensitive to others, and so they have difficulty relating appropriately to others (Jones, Hobbs, and Hackenbury, 1982). The focus of their concern is themselves, which means they have difficulty establishing rapport and intimacy based upon genuine concern for their partner.

The following summarizes some important research findings on loneliness.

1. In general, adolescents and young adults are lonelier than older adults. Loneliness declines with age until well into old age, at which time it begins to increase (Ostrov and Offer, 1980; Rubenstein and Shaver, 1982).

2. In general, married people are less lonely than the separated, divorced, or widowed (Perlman and Peplau, 1981; Rubenstein and Shaver, 1982). Loneliness is derived from loss of marriage rather than from its absence.

3. Among married couples, females report greater loneliness than do males (Freedman, 1978; Peplau, Bikson, Rook, and Goodchilds, 1982). This is because marriage is more likely to reduce a woman's than a man's social networks. A married woman may quit her job to stay home, or she may leave her relatives to follow her husband (Fischer and Phillips, 1982).

4. Among the separated, divorced, or widowed, males report greater loneliness than females (Rubenstein and Shaver, 1982). This is because the unattached man may have more trouble forming close emotional relationships than does the unattached woman.

5. People whose parents have divorced report feeling more lonely than those whose parents have not divorced. The younger the person when parents were divorced, the more loneliness the person experienced as an adult (Rubenstein and Shaver, 1982).

Family Interaction

Most married people need privacy and time to do their own thing as individuals. They also need time together as a married couple. And they need time to be with their children as a whole family. It's not easy to keep things in balance. When the children are young, it's easy to become absorbed in taking care of them and neglect the marital relationship. Marriage relationships have to be nurtured to stay alive.

One study of family interaction in 126 families with one, two, or three children between the ages of 6 and 11 revealed some interesting findings (Davey and Paolucci, 1980). Only 12 percent of family interaction was between just the husband and wife. Nineteen percent of family interaction involved just the children with each other. Only 18 percent of family interaction involved the whole family. Twenty-nine percent of family interaction was between the mother and one or more children. Nineteen percent of family interaction involved just the father and one or more children.

What type of activities did family members participate in? Sixty-two percent of interaction involved socializing. The next most frequent activity was eating (15 percent of the total interaction). Interestingly, only 10 percent of all family interaction involved household work: meal preparation and cleanup, house and yard care, ironing and laundry, and marketing. This revealed little cooperation in sharing household work. Most of the remainder of the time was spent in care of family members.

For each question below, circle the most appropriate answer. Then add up the numbers that correspond to the answers you chose. Your total scores should fall between 80 (not at all lonely) and 320 (very lonely).

1. When I am completely alone, I feel lonely:

Almost never	(10)
Occasionally	(16)
About half the time	(24)
Often	(32)
Most of the time	(40)

2. How often do you feel lonely?

Never, or almost never	(10)
Rarely	(11)
Occasionally	(17)
About half the time	(23)
Quite often	(29)
Most of the time	(34)
All the time, or almost all the time	(40)

3. When you feel lonely, do you usually feel:

I never feel lonely	(10)
Slightly lonely	(13)
Somewhat lonely	(20)
Fairly lonely	(27)
Very lonely	(33)
Extremely lonely	(40)

4. Compared to people your own age, how lonely do you think you are?

Much less lonely	(10)
Somewhat less lonely	(16)
About average	(24)
Somewhat lonelier	(32)
Much lonelier	(40)

5. I am a lonely person

Strongly disagree	(10)
Disagree	(20)
Agree	(30)
Strongly agree	(40)

6. I always was a lonely person

Strongly disagree	(10)
Disagree	(20)
Agree	(30)
Strongly agree	(40)

7. I always will be a lonely person

Strongly disagree	(10)
Disagree	(20)
Agree	(30)
Strongly agree	(40)

8. Other people think of me as a lonely person

Strongly disagree	(10)
Disagree	(20)
Agree	(30)
Strongly agree	(40)

Loneliness scores on this scale:

Average loneliness among respondents to newspaper surveys was about 170. Rubenstein and Shaver suggest that

80–132 = least lonely	171–206 = more lonely than average
133–170 = less lonely than average	207–320 = most lonely

Source: Rubenstein, C. M., and Shaver, P. (1982). *In search of intimacy*. New York: Delacorte Press.

The findings of this study did reveal that most family interaction took place at home and increased on weekends and during vacations. Overall, however, *there was not a lot of time spent in either husband-wife interaction, or parent-child interaction.* Father-child interaction was noticeably lacking. *Without adequate parent-child interaction, socialization of the child by the parent cannot take place* (Bronfenbrenner, 1978).

Family interactions involving the whole family are important, but they are not the most common type of interaction within the home. What type of activities do family members participate in most often and when?

COMPANIONSHIP IN LEISURE

Need for Recreation

Recreation is a necessary part of a balanced life. It's purpose is to re-create, to refresh body and spirit, to soothe jangled nerves and relieve tension, to provide relaxation and pleasure away from the cares of the world. It really is not so important what type of recreation people prefer, as long as it affords a break from work-related activity, a change from one's usual routine, and a chance to do something different that one enjoys.

Types of Leisure Activities

A national sample surveyed by the Gallup Organization revealed the percentage of people who participated in different leisure-time activities. *Flower gardening* was listed by a greater percentage of respondents (44 percent) than was any other activity. *Swimming* (41 percent), *fishing* (34 percent), *bicycling* (33 percent), and *bowling* (25 percent) were among the top five activities. Table 15.1 shows the results (U.S. Bureau of the Census, 1987b).

There is a difference, however, in the percentage of people participating in different activities, and the percentage of those who say the activities are their favorites. *Some people engage in certain activities for health benefits, not because*

It is not so important what type of recreation people prefer, as long as it affords a break from work related activity, a change from one's usual routine, a chance to do something enjoyable.

TABLE 15.1 *Adult Participation in Leisure Time Activities,*
by Selected Type: 1985

Type of Activity	Number (mil.)	Per-cent[1]	Type of Activity	Number (mil.)	Per-cent[1]
Flower gardening	77	44	Hunting	25	14
Swimming	72	41	Golf	23	13
Fishing	60	34	Baseball	23	13
Bicycling	58	33	Tennis	23	13
Bowling	44	25	Ping pong/table tennis	21	12
Jogging	40	23	Canoeing/rowing	16	9
Softball	39	22	Roller skating	16	9
Camping	37	21	Horseback riding	16	9
Weight-training	33	19	Target shooting	16	9
Billard, pool	33	19	Skiing	14	8
Aerobics	32	18	Racquetball	14	8
Motor boating	28	16	Waterskiing	12	7
Volleyball	28	16	Touch football/flag	11	6
Calisthenics	26	15	Sailing	9	5
Basketball	26	15			

Source: U.S. Bureau of the Census. (1987). *Statistical abstract of the United States, 1987* (107th ed). Washington, DC: U.S. Government Printing Office.
[1]As of early Dec. 1985. Based on national sample survey of 1,500 households conducted by the Gallup Organization, Inc.

they are so fond of them. Swimming, bicycling, and jogging are among the most frequently engaged-in activities. But in a nationwide study of 5,000 people, only 18 to 30 percent of the bicyclers, swimmers, and joggers listed these activities as their favorites. The favorite activities were hunting and outdoor team sports, with nearly 75 percent of the participants saying they enjoyed these sports. About half the fishers, snow skiers, and campers said these activities were among the most enjoyable for them, followed closely by people who participated in golf, horseback riding, and tennis (Bridgewater, 1985).

Personality Characteristics, Social Life, and Marital Satisfaction

The quality and type of social life people participate in depends partially on their personality characteristics and individual preferences. Some people are gregarious and outgoing, make friends easily, like to be with others, and feel comfortable in a variety of social situations. Other people are shy and withdrawn and avoid many kinds of social involvements. *Filsinger and Lamke (1983) found that interpersonal competence in general social relationships is a predictor of interpersonal competence in marriage.* This means that those who score low in social anxiety tests also score highest on marital adjustment.

Filsinger and Wilson (1983) found that both individual social anxiety and couple social anxiety were related to marital adjustment. The higher the husband's social anxiety, the lower his adjustment to marriage. The higher the wife's social anxiety, the lower her adjustment to marriage. And when the husband's and wife's individual society anxiety scores were combined, the higher their total social anxiety was, the lower their marital adjustment. Apparently, the characteristics that enable people to feel comfortable in social situations are also helpful in getting along in marriage.

Vacations

Vacations can be a great help in building companionship if the spouses get along when they are together and if they both enjoy similar types of experiences. However, most marriage counselors hear from couples who have just come back from vacation. What was designed for fun and relaxation turned out to be a source of conflict and upset. One wife reported:

> My husband and I saved money for a long time to take our dream trip to Jamaica. But all we did was fight. Steve spent his time ogling at the bikini-clad girls on the beaches, making insulting remarks to me, and drinking too much and becoming argumentative. We had a miserable time. I couldn't wait to get home. (Author's counseling notes)

One of the problems with vacations is that spouses aren't used to being together 24 hours a day. When they're home and working they don't see one another much and may get along reasonably well. But when given the time to be together continuously, unresolved issues may come up that they have previously avoided. If they aren't used to communicating or problem-solving, tensions become worse and tempers explode, ruining whatever companionship they have (Rosenblatt, 1983).

Vacation planning is often a mixture of fantasy and reality. Why do people take vacations? Do most people realize their vacation goals?

Psychology Today (Rubenstein, 1980) did a survey of readers to find out their views on vacations. Some of the highlights of the survey are as follows:

- Men and women envision vacations that will bring dramatic and positive changes in their lives: in themselves or in their relationships. However, there is often a gap between fantasy and reality. Most people carry the same psychological baggage wherever they go. Workaholics bring their briefcase along to catch up. Health nuts play tennis, jog, and swim even more than at home. Those who enjoy their vacations the most are the same people who enjoy their work most.

- The main reasons for taking vacations were: (1) for rest and relaxation, to get unwound; (2) for intellectual enrichment, having a genuine curiosity about the world and wanting to explore it; (3) for family togetherness; (4) for erotic adventure, a chance to meet new friends, or to find sexual escapades; (5) for self-discovery, to solve personal problems; and (6) to escape routine, boredom, and problems. Those who believe they can escape from themselves on vacations are not being realistic.

- The most popular vacation activities were sightseeing, eating, going to the beach, outdoor activities, being with friends, or going shopping. The most popular vacation spots were beaches, parks, or forests.

- Men had a stronger sense of vacation excitement than women, but they enjoyed vacations less and were more eager to return to work after vacations.

- About half of the respondents spent most of their vacation time with a spouse or friend. Those who enjoyed their vacations most spent time not with a prearranged partner, but with people they met while on vacation. Those who enjoyed their vacations the least spent most of their time alone.

- A number of married people said they dreamed of ditching their spouses for vacations: the men to engage in sexual adventures, the women because they said their husbands didn't know how to enjoy themselves.

One of the most common family pastimes is watching television. One Nielsen survey in 1984 found that *the average American television set is on approximately 44 hours per week* (re: act, 1984). In some families, the set is turned on the first thing in the morning and not turned off until late at night. This does not mean family members are always watching it; sometimes it's there for background noise. However, one survey indicated that *the average American child aged 2 to 11 views television 27.5 hours per week* (Tooth, 1985). Children spend more time watching television than going to school.

The effects on the family are of some concern. *One negative effect of watching television is to decrease communication and interaction among family members.* The more family members watch, the less they talk (Brody, Stoneman, and Sanders, 1980). Fathers especially seem to become absorbed in television viewing, so that the quality of their interaction with their children and wives may suffer (Hopkins and Mullis, 1985). Mothers often do family chores simultaneously while watching television, so may not become totally absorbed in watching. One frequent complaint of wives is: "My husband and I never have a chance to talk. He's watching television and doesn't want to be distracted."

Watching television is a passive activity. Absorption in the "boob tube" may result in a decrease in family communication, frequency of sexual relations, less time devoted to activities and work around the house, and less

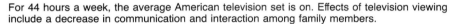

For 44 hours a week, the average American television set is on. Effects of television viewing include a decrease in communication and interaction among family members.

physical activity and social interaction among children (Grzech and Trost, 1978; Rosenblatt and Cunningham, 1976). In one experiment, families who voluntarily gave up television viewing reported that their children played and read more, that siblings fought less, that family activities became more common, and that mealtimes were longer (Chira, 1984). Other effects of television watching on children are discussed in Chapter 20 on parenting.

BEYOND THE FAMILY

Friendships

No family is a self-contained social unit that can exist apart from other people. No matter how well-developed the companionship within the family, family members need friends. Children need friends of their own age, couples need friends to talk to and to do things with. Life is more interesting and fun when it involves compatible friends. *One study of the chief sources of life satisfaction revealed that having friends ranked third in importance (after spouse and parents) as the most important source of satisfaction* (Argyle and Furnham, 1983). Studies of dimensions of psychological good health have revealed that achieving mutual friendship is one of the most important components of mental health (Rosenthal, 1984; Vaillant, 1977a). Friends also call on one another for assistance, for both instrumental and emotional support (Roberto and Scott, 1986).

Making friends is not always easy, especially if couples move to a city where neither of the spouses knows anyone. Large-scale industrialization and urbanization have resulted in an anonymity where couples can live alongside of one another for months without ever really getting acquainted (Allan, 1985).

The challenge is to overcome the anonymity of city life by developing friendship networks, if not with one's neighbors, then with others whom one meets through work, through other people, through one's children, through social organizations, or activities. One study of 92 graduate students who moved either to New York City or to upstate rural areas revealed that two months after their arrival students who moved to small towns had an average of 6.3 friends. Students who moved to New York City had 3.5 friends. Seven months later, however, the numbers were, respectively, 5.3 and 5.1. The newcomers in both environments got together with most of their friends at least once a week (Horn, 1981).

In the beginning, the urban students reported higher levels of fear, distrust, and uncertainty in meeting strangers. They were more vigilant in taking safety precautions. As they became acquainted, however, the city people were more likely to invite friends home. One city student explained, "You need close relationships because of the cold nature of the city" (Horn, 1981, p. 100). The urban students also reported a broadened perspective as a consequence of exposure to and interactions with other people.

In a study of social networks of both black and white rural families, the black mothers reported significantly fewer supportive networks than white mothers reported (Gaudin and Davis, 1985). In comparison to the black mothers, the white mothers reported over twice as many neighbors they could call on. The primary social network of the black mothers consisted of their relatives. In general, the blacks had more relatives living close by. The researchers concluded that many of these disadvantaged black families were isolated nuclear family units and that

> without the strong, ready available support from kin, neighbors, and friends, the family is a high risk for child neglect, abuse, crime, and delinquency or less obvious indicators of family breakdown. (p. 1020)

Gender Differences

There is a difference between friendships based primarily on emotional sharing and those based on engaging in common activities. Though all close friendships have both elements, *female friendships are characterized more by emotional sharing and male friendships more by engaging in common activities* (Caldwell and Peplau, 1982). The following examples illustrate the differences:

> Sally and Susan were good friends. They would tell one another all about their boyfriends, how they felt about them and details of their relationships. Whenever they had any problems they called one another to discuss the situation. They asked one another's advice and gave consolation and moral support.
>
> Chuck and Hank were good friends. They played racquetball together, worked on their old cars in one another's garages, attended movies, went to bars together, and always called one another to plan something to do or when they needed a ride.

In these examples, *the women revealed feelings and intimacies; the men shared interests and activities.* Men seldom talk about personal, intimate things with their buddies. Wright (1982) observed that females have "face-to-face" friendships, while male friends are "side-by-side." When men do talk about intimate things, it is usually with women, since the men feel less anxiety with women and less competition with them than with other males (Peretti, 1980). Many men still have the notion that to reveal emotions is unmanly (Tognoli, 1980). Women are still more at ease than men with emotional intimacy in friendships.

Same-Sex and Opposite-Sex Friendships

One study revealed that same-sex friendships among married spouses were more satisfactory than cross-sex friendships. Same-sex friends were able to share more interests, to do things together, to give emotional support (Argyle and Furnham, 1983). Conflict was higher among opposite-sex friends who were not able to understand one another.

In addition, there is the factor of jealousy of one's spouse over cross-sex friendships. Certainly, most spouses will not tolerate cross-sex friendships if those friendships include sexual intimacy. Suspicion of extramarital emotional involvement and/or physical involvement is one of the most frequent problems presented to marriage counselors. In some cases the spouse insists that the other person is "just a friend." In some cases this is true; at other times the spouse is lying when there has been an involvement that goes beyond friendship. Spouses can usually tell when there is romantic interest that goes beyond friendship. One wife remarked:

Same sex friends typically share interests, do things together, and give emotional support to each other. Why are the same factors sometimes problematic in friendships between people of the opposite sex?

> My husband has a good friend, Pauline, whom he met at work. He says they are just friends, but he really sparkles when he talks about her. I've seen the way they look at one another when they are together. I don't think he's slept with her, but he certainly is attracted to her. He has lunch with her several times a week, by themselves, and I'm getting very upset by it. (Author's counseling notes)

In this case, the husband had slept with Pauline and the wife had cause for concern.

In other situations, the relationship is quite platonic, or strictly a business relationship, and certainly is no threat to the marriage; but the other spouse is almost pathologically jealous and accuses his or her mate of affairs with every acquaintance of the opposite sex. One husband complained:

> My wife accuses me of being attracted to every woman I meet. If I even talk to a woman, whether at work or in the neighborhood, she gets very angry and upset and accuses me unjustly. (Author's counseling notes)

Fifty percent of the people in the world are of the opposite sex, and some of them will be friends — at work, in the neighborhood, and in community organization. But since successful marriage involves sexual exclusiveness, fidelity, and commitment to one person only, to allow friendships to go beyond the just-friends stage is to court problems.

Married people can do several things to avoid difficulty with opposite-sex relationships.

1. Keep business relationships on a professional basis.
2. Make a point of introducing friends to your spouse.
3. Let your spouse know of occasions when you have seen or met with the other person, whether at a business lunch or on a social occasion.

4. Never try to hide anything from your spouse and don't have anything to hide.

5. Avoid one-to-one dates for social purposes.

6. Prefer groups of mixed company rather than dyadic encounters.

7. Recognize that many affairs develop without people intending things to happen, simply because people place themselves in compromising situations.

8. Make certain that other persons whom you meet know your monogamous, no hanky-panky attitude.

ASSESSMENT
Friendship Potential Inventory

This questionnaire is designed to measure your friendship potential. To complete this questionnaire, assign a value to each statement by choosing the answers below the number (from +2 to −2) which indicates the extent to which you agree or disagree with the statement. For example, if you "completely agree" with a statement, you would write "+2" in the blank before it, or, if you moderately disagree, you would write "−1" in the blank. Be sure to fill in all the blanks.

+2 = Completely agree
+1 = Moderately agree
 0 = Neither agree nor disagree
−1 = Moderately disagree
−2 = Completely disagree

_____ 1. Most people seem to have more friends than I do.*

_____ 2. I often compliment my friends on their nice appearance.

_____ 3. I'd rather use public transportation than ask a friend for a ride.*

_____ 4. I shy away from meeting new people because I'm afraid they won't like me.*

_____ 5. I'm the type of person who likes people.

_____ 6. In times of trouble I count on my friends for help.

_____ 7. People tend to feel good when they are around me.

_____ 8. I'd help a friend who was in a jam even if it was inconvenient for me to do so.

_____ 9. I hold back from criticizing people and their ideas.

_____ 10. When I like someone, I try to let them know it.

_____ 11. I'm too busy to have many friends.*

_____ 12. When I see someone I know, I greet them with a smile and a cheerful "hello."

_____ 13. I am reluctant to confide in others.*

_____ 14. I'll occasionally give a gift to a friend just because I want to.

_____ 15. Very seldom will I call a friend just to chat.*

_____ 16. I'm reluctant to lend money no matter how small the amount.*

_____ 17. I like to spend my free time socializing with friends.

_____ 18. If a close friend told me a confidential secret, there's a good chance that I would tell someone else.*

(continued)

9. You and your spouse develop your social life with other couples, where you both know and enjoy both the husband and wife.

10. If you're having marital difficulties, get help from a professional person. Many extramarital affairs develop because of a whole series of unresolved problems in the marriage, making the partners vulnerable to outside encounters and relationships.

ASSESSMENT (continued)

_____ 19. I'm not likely to help a person if it involves much trouble for me.*

_____ 20. There are other things that are more important to me than making friends.*

_____ 21. If a friend asked my opinion about an unflattering hairstyle, I would give an honest answer.

_____ 22. One or a few close friends are worth many not-so-close friends.

_____ 23. I believe that most people really don't need or want my friendship.*

_____ 24. When in a group, I let others keep the conversation going.*

_____ 25. I'll go out of my way to keep in touch with old friends, even if they live far away.

_____ 26. My friendships tend to get better with the passage of time.

_____ 27. I tend to be a "wallflower" at parties.*

_____ 28. One of my difficulties in making friends is my fear of rejection.*

*Reverse score.

Scoring: You determine your friendship potential score by:

1. Reverse the sign (+ or − on questions 1, 3, 4, 11, 13, 15, 16, 18, 19, 20, 23, 24, 27, and 28).

2. Add up all *positive* scored questions and write this figure below.

3. Add total of all positively answered questions to factor of 56.

4. Add up all negative scored questions and subtract this number from the total.

5. The resultant number is your friendship potential score.

Total Positive Score	_____
Plus Correction Factor	56
Equals	_____
Subtract Total of Negative Score	_____
Your Friendship Potential Score	_____

People with scores of 85 and above are defined as having above average friendship potential. Scores between 67 and 85 are in the average range. People with scores of 67 or below fall in the category of below average in Friendship Potential.

Source: Dawley, H. H. (1980). *Friendship*. Englewood Cliffs, NJ: Prentice-Hall. Reprinted by permission of the author.

1. The primary motive for marriage in our culture is for love and companionship. Couples who share interests, do things together, and who share some of the same friends and social groups derive more satisfaction from their relationship than do couples who are not mutually involved.

2. Sometimes companionship doesn't develop. There are various reasons: one or both spouses spend most of their time on the job, spend most of their leisure time with separate friends, pursue individual hobbies or leisure time activities, spend most of their free time out of the house attending paid amusements, spend their free time with their children rather than with one another, vegetate in front of the TV, or don't enjoy being together.

3. Three different styles of companionship characterize relationships: joint companionship, parallel companionship, and segregated companionship. There are advantages and disadvantages to each of these companionship styles.

4. People differ in their need for closeness. There is a difference between closeness and possessiveness. Some people so want to possess their spouse that they cannot tolerate any spaces in their togetherness.

5. Loneliness is not simply being alone; it is the distressing feeling we have when there is a discrepancy between the kind of social relations we want and have. Loneliness can be due to either social isolation or emotional isolation. Social isolation is situational; emotional isolation is relational.

6. There are five major reasons for being lonely: being unattached, alienation, being alone, forced isolation, and dislocation.

7. Loneliness may also result from negative personality attributes.

8. Married people need time for privacy and to do their own thing; they need time together as a couple; they need time to be with their children.

9. Recreation is a necessary part of a balanced life. It is important to achieve a healthy balance between physical and nonphysical activities.

10. According to a national survey, the five most popular recreational activities were flower gardening, swimming, fishing, bicycling, and bowling. However, some people engage in certain activities for health reasons, not because they are so fond of them. In one study, the favorite activities were hunting and outdoor team sports. Other most popular sports were fishing, snow skiing, camping, golf, horseback riding, and tennis.

11. Interpersonal competence in general social relationships is a predictor of interpersonal competence in marriage.

12. Vacations can help to build companionship if the spouses get along when together so much and if they can enjoy similar types of experiences. However, some spouses fight because they aren't used to being together so much, and unresolved problems come out while on vacation.

13. One of the most common family pastimes is watching television. There may be some negative effects of excessive watching of television, the most important being less communication and interaction among family members.

14. Having friends is also one of the chief sources of life satisfaction and is important to psychological and social well-being. Making friends is not easy, especially if couples move to the city where they do not know anyone. The challenge is to overcome the anonymity of city life by developing friendship networks.

15. There are some differences between friendships men develop and those women develop. Female friendships are characterized by emotional sharing, male by sharing interests and activities. Men are still afraid of revealing emotions.

16. Same-sex friendships among married spouses are more satisfactory than cross-sex friendships. Same-sex friends are able to share more interests, to do things together, and to give emotional support. In addition, there is the factor of spousal jealousy over cross-sex friendships. Certainly, most spouses will not tolerate extramarital sexual intimacy. Married people need to avoid letting cross-sex friendships lead to physical and emotional involvement.

SUGGESTED READINGS

Bell, R. R. (1981). *Worlds of Friendship*. Beverly Hills, CA: Sage. What we know about friendships of both men and women of different ages and marital status.

Brenton M. (1974). *Friendship*. New York: Stein and Day. Friendship through the life cycle.

Iso-Ahola, S. E. (1980). *The Social Psychology of Leisure and Recreation*. Dubuque, IA: William C. Brown. The meaning of leisure and the way in which it affects people's lives.

16

POWER AND DECISION MAKING

Educated, middle-class marital ideology in the United States emphasizes an egalitarian exercise of family power. "Husbands and wives are equal and should share everything 50–50." But exactly what does this mean in relation to making decisions, in influencing one another, and in governing the family? Does this mean that both the husband and wife share in every decision? Does it mean they each make half of the decisions?

Actually, this ideology isn't often worked out in practice. Some people want more power and control than others. Even when husbands and wives are equals, they usually don't share all decisions and control.

We are concerned here with patterns of power and with what gives some people power over others. We are concerned also with the applications of power, the processes of power, and the ways that power are applied in intimate relationships. We are concerned with the outcomes of power: the effect of various power patterns on individuals and on marital satisfaction. And finally, we emphasize the need for equity and fairness in the use of power in interpersonal relationships.

THE MEANING OF POWER

In broad terms, **power** has been defined as the ability of an individual within a social relationship to carry out his or her will, even in the face of resistance by others (McDonald, 1980). Thus, power can be defined as Person A's ability to influence the behavior of Person B and to resist the influence of Person B. We have power over others when we can get them to do what we want when we want it, and when we can avoid giving them what they want from us.

Family Power

Power may be exercised in social groups and organizations and in all kinds of interpersonal relationships. We are concerned here only with family power. Figure 16.1 shows the different units of family power. As can be seen, the

FIGURE 16.1 Different Units of Family Power.

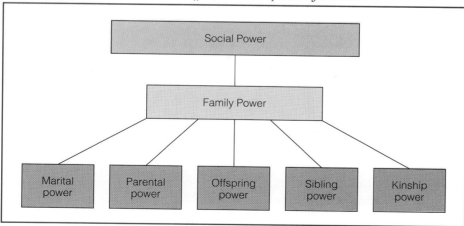

From McDonald, G. W. (1980). Family power: The assessment of a decade of theory and research, 1970–1979. *Journal of Marriage and the Family, 42,* 841–854. Copyright ©1980 by the National Council on Family Relations. Reprinted by permission.

power exerted by different family members is partly derived from social power, that which society exerts or delegates. Power within the family involves marital power, parental power, offspring power, sibling power, or kinship power. We are concerned especially with marital power — the power relationship in the marital dyad — and to a lesser extent with power exercised by children over parents. Other power relationships — those of parents over children, brothers and sisters over one another, and relatives over other family members — will be discussed in subsequent sections of this book.

WHY PEOPLE WANT POWER

Self-Actualization

From one point of view, all people want to feel that they have some control over their own life, that they have the power to change, influence, or direct what happens to them personally. This desire is expressed in a variety of ways:

> *Wife:* "I like to have my own money so my husband can't tell me what to buy."
>
> *Husband:* "I like to make my own decisions. I hate anyone else telling me what to do."

Rollo May (1967) has observed that people who are unwilling or unable to use power condemn themselves to a life of frustration. They never get to do what they want to do or to carry out their own desires and plans. Hundreds of seminars and classes are conducted yearly to teach people how to become more assertive.

Eventually, asserting the self results in locking horns with someone else who has other ideas, and so a power struggle may ensue to see whose wishes are carried out. Even people who are not ordinarily combative find that they sometimes have to exert power over other persons to be able to fulfill themselves. One wife comments:

> I'm bound and determined that I'm going to have a career. My husband doesn't want me to, but I've been adamant. He knows I won't change my mind, so he's had to give in. (Author's counseling notes)

Without some personal power, it's difficult to survive as an independent individual. Even two-year-old toddlers need to learn how to say no and how to influence parents, if they are ever to grow up as autonomous adults.

Social Expectations

Often people exert power because that is what they feel they are supposed to do, and they want to avoid criticism for not fulfilling expectations. Friends admonish the husband-to-be: "Let her know from the beginning who's boss and who's wearing the pants in the family." Mother tells her daughter, who is soon to be married: "Remember, don't spoil him. Let him know you expect his help around the house. If you don't, he will walk all over you." Each society has its own institutionalized norms that prescribe the domains of

The role expectation of the woman as homemaker still persists, but the way in which the role is fulfilled may vary depending on her other obligations.

authority that husbands and wives control. This is referred to as **legitimate power**, that which is bestowed by society on husbands and wives as their right according to social prescription. Thus, in some societies, the husband is granted the right to be "head of the family," and the wife is given the right to direct homemaking. Szinovacz (1987) writes:

> Social norms and role expectations set the context within which marital exchanges and power relations are evaluated. What is judged to be fair or acceptable depends not only on the partner's personal values, but also on social norms and contingencies. (p. 614)

What society prescribes may not always be fair, but it still may exert considerable influence on the behavior of individuals.

Family-of-Origin Influences

Patterns of power can often be traced to experiences in one's family of origin. Children tend to model their behavior after their parents. A son growing up under the influence of a dominant father may adopt the same pattern and have difficulty establishing a more democratic relationship with his wife. Galvin and Brommel (1986) quote one man:

> My German father and my Irish mother both exercised power over us in different ways. My father used to beat us whenever we got out of line, and that power move was very obvious. On the other hand, my mother never touched us, but she probably exercised greater power through her use of silence. Whenever we

did something she did not approve of, she just stopped talking to us — it was as if we did not exist. Most of the time the silent treatment lasted for a few hours, but sometimes it would last for a few days. My brother used to say it was so quiet you "could hear a mouse pee on a cotton ball." I hated the silence worse than the beatings. (p. 135)

The family of origin serves as the first power base from which the child learns to function. Methods used there are often repeated in the children's adult life. Certain types of power applications, such as physical violence and abuse, are passed from generation to generation at an early age. Even techniques of control, such as silence, are learned behavior.

Psychological Need

Sometimes the need for power and the way it is expressed go far beyond ordinary limits. A man who has deep-seated feelings of insecurity and inferiority may try to hide these, or compensate for them by becoming autocratic and dictatorial. He can't let his wife win an argument or get her way, because if she does he'll feel weak and ineffective. His facade of power depends upon not letting any cracks develop in his armor. A longitudinal study of male undergraduates who were interviewed first in college and then again 14 years later found that those who were high in the need for power when they were undergraduates were less likely to have wives with full-time careers than were men who were low in need for power during their undergraduate days. Men who were particularly secure when they were in college were more accepting of an economically egalitarian marital life (Winter, Stewart, and McClelland, 1977).

DECISION MAKING

Patterns

One of the important measures of power is decision-making power: the extent to which a person has the final say or choice when a decision is made. Blood and Wolfe (1960) were among the most influential of the early researchers studying the question. They identified four types of decision-making patterns:

1. *Husband dominant.* A traditional patriarchal family form in which the power is exercised by the husband.
2. *Wife dominant.* A matriarchal family form in which power is exercised by the wife.
3. *Autonomic.* A form in which the husband and wife have equal power, which they choose to exercise individually and separately. Husbands and wives who make decisions without consulting the other, or who divide spheres of influence over which they each preside, come under this category.
4. *Egalitarian or syncratic.* A democratic family form in which a fairly equal distribution of power is shared between the husband and wife.

CLASSROOM FORUM
Mr. G.

Mr. G. was brought up in a family with a passive, alcoholic father who was always sick or hurt. He had no hobbies and interests, and never took his son hunting or fishing. His whole life was his whiskey bottle. His wife was strong and domineering. She took care of everything at home. Mr. G. thought his mom was terrific.

Mr. G. had no respect for his father. On the one hand, he held contempt for him; on the other hand, he felt sorry for him. He vowed that when he grew up he would not be like his father.

Mr. G. comments:

My father was passive. I'm just the opposite. I feel I have to wear the pants. I never want my boys to get the upper hand. I haven't included my wife in most of the decisions I've made. I've taken it on myself to do it. I know I haven't been there to support her in things she's interested in. She does a great job in so many ways, but I've never told her. When we'd go out to a party, I'd make her the brunt of my jokes. I knew it bothered her, yet I did it. She has the opinion that everything we have is mine, not hers. I'd tell her: "You didn't pay for it, I did."

After 18 years of marriage, Mrs. G. is almost ready to call it quits. She explains:

I give and give, and don't get anything in return. I get no emotional support from him. I support him morally all the time. Yet, if things get tough for me, all he does is criticize. We'll discuss something, and then he'll do the opposite of what I wanted him to do. He doesn't care at all about my feelings. He's sometimes physically abusive. He once threw me across the room. I ended up in the hospital. He calls me names, and the boys too. He says I'm an idiot, a jerk, and I'm stupid.

I don't think I deserve it. Up to now, I've been stupid enough to stay. Now, I don't want to be married any longer. I don't want him to touch me. I just want to be left alone.

QUESTIONS

1. What was Mr. G.'s main problem?

2. Why was Mr. G. the way he was?

3. In what ways was he trying to solve his own problem?

4. What are some other ways Mr. G. could overcome his problem?

5. If you were a marriage counselor, what approach would you use to help this couple?

6. If you were Mrs. G., what would be some possible alternatives? What would you do? Why?

Early Research

Blood and Wolfe (1960) interviewed 731 urban wives in metropolitan Detroit and asked them who made the final decision in eight areas: what job the husband should take, what car to buy, whether to buy life insurance, where to go on vacation, what house or apartment to take, whether the wife should go to work (or quit work), what doctor to have when someone is sick, and how much money the family could afford to spend on food (p. 19).

The results indicate that the largest percentage of families were autonomic (41 percent). About 31 percent were labeled syncratic. Twenty-five percent were husband-dominant, and only 3 percent were wife-dominant. Two decisions (his job and the car) were primarily the husband's province. Two decisions (her work and how much money to spend for food) were primarily the

FIGURE 16.2 Allocation of Power in Decision-Making Areas (731 Detroit Families).

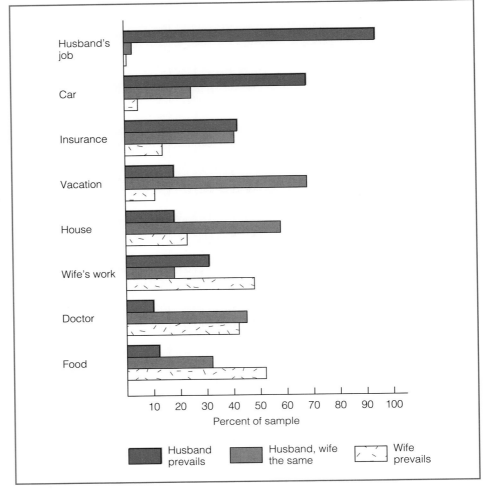

Adapted from Blood, R. O., Jr., and Wolfe, W. M. (1960). *Husbands and wives: The dynamics of married living.* New York: Free Press, 21.

wife's province. Two decisions (life insurance and doctor) were made either by the husband or by the husband and wife sharing them. The other two decisions (vacation and house) were shared authority. Figure 16.2 indicates the allocation of power in these decision-making areas (Blood and Wolfe, 1960).

Methodological Issues

Blood and Wolfe's (1960) study raised a number of methodological issues that are still relevant.

First, wives only were asked these questions. The answers were given on the basis of wives' self-reports: their perceptions of who had the power. Self-report studies tend to show that both husbands and wives overestimate their partner's power, while underestimating their own power (Bokemeier and Monroe, 1983; Monroe, Bokemeier, Kotchen, and McKean, 1985). Since spouses' responses may differ, both need to be questioned to get a more complete picture (Quarm, 1981).

Second, the results depend on what decisions are included in the questionnaire. Blood and Wolfe (1960) tended to include an overrepresentation of masculine areas of decision making. Centers, Raven, and Rodriques (1971) added six decision areas to those originally included by Blood and Wolfe (1960) and found that the husband's power was 10 percent less. The six added areas were whom to invite to the house or to go out socially with, how to decorate or furnish the house, which TV or radio program to tune in, what the family will have for dinner, what clothes will be bought, and what type of clothes the spouse will buy. The reason for the indicated drop in the husband's power is that some of these six new decision areas were considered the wife's prerogative.

Third, another criticism is that each of these decision-making areas was treated as equally important. Certainly what job the husband should take or whether the wife should work or not are major decisions that influence a number of different lesser ones: car, house or apartment, vacation, life insurance, and food. A family might be labeled husband-dominant even though he made a number of decisions that were not considered important to his wife, and vice versa. Also, husbands may delegate minor, everyday decisions to their wives, reserving important decisions for themselves. Wives may make more decisions, but husbands make more important ones (Johnson, 1975).

Fourth, Blood and Wolfe's results came from urban Detroit housewives. The results cannot be applied to all other population groups. Rural husbands and wives may divide up responsibilities differently from city families. A study of decision making of farm husbands and wives in Wisconsin (Wilkening and Bharadwaj, 1967) showed some specialization between husbands and wives in decision-making patterns. Husbands were more involved in such decisions as whether to buy or rent more farm land, whether to borrow money for the farm, what specific make of machinery to buy, how much fertilizer to buy, or whether to try out a new crop variety. Wives were more involved in such decisions as whether to take a job in town, how much money to spend for food, when to invite people for dinner, when to make household repairs, when to buy major household equipment, whether to paint or paper in the home, as well as in decisions relating to the children such as when children visit friends and how much money children get for allowances. Interestingly enough, these farm wives were often involved in whether to buy a different car, probably because the car was often used by the wife. Also, the wives were more often involved in areas pertaining to buying a car, household maintenance, food and entertainment, wife's working, and child training than their husbands wanted them to be, indicating more of a patriarchal attitude on the part of the husbands than the wives were willing to accept.

Fifth, the results of any study are influenced by the methods of gathering the information and the way that information is analyzed (Allen, 1984; Hill and Scanzoni, 1982). The three most popular ways of measuring marital power are self-reports on questionnaires, information from interviews, and observation of couples in the laboratory while the couples carried out assigned decision-making tasks. When Johnson (1975) asked Japanese-American wives in Hawaii to fill out a questionnaire about who makes decisions in a number of different areas, they did not indicate a single area in which their husbands dominated. However, when interviewed in detail, these same women indicated a great deal of husband dominance, especially in relation to major decisions. Apparently, the interviews brought out their real feelings.

Corrales (1975) found that when decision-making of wives was observed in the laboratory, they had a lot more power than was indicated when husbands and wives answered questionnaires. Apparently, both spouses were influenced by sex-norms, by "authority expectations," so that when answering the questions, they put down what would be most socially acceptable: male dominance. In "real life," however, wives actually had a lot more power than they or their husbands realized.

Sixth, Blood and Wolfe (1960) were also criticized for their emphasis on resources as a source of power, leaving out other influences. According to Blood and Wolfe (1960), those spouses who possessed the greatest resources — occupational prestige, income, education, or superior ethnic and social class background — had more power to make family decisions. They found also that the relative resources of the husband and wife were found to be important. For example, the wife with small, dependent children has less power. The wife who is gainfully employed has more power. The resource theory will be examined in greater detail in the next section. What is important is that a large number of bases of power besides resources need to be considered. Let's look at various ones.

SOURCES OF POWER

Power Bases

Various efforts have been made to sort out the origins of power. What gives husbands and wives power in the marital relationship? Various sources have been identified. These are:

Legal sources — rights as prescribed by law

Cultural norms — in relation to class, racial, and ethnic expectations

Gender norms — rights accorded because of sex

Economic resources — primarily money, property, and position

Education and knowledge — education is referred to as expert power, knowledge as informational power

Personality differences — individual characteristics such as self-esteem or age that determine one's influence

Communication ability — verbal and language skills and ability to talk and persuade

Emotional factors — the ability to bestow or withhold love and affection

Physical stature and strength — these give a person the ability to coerce another

Circumstances — life situations such as the stages of the family life cycle that provide or limit alternatives

Children — their influence on parents

Let us examine each of these bases of power.

Part of the authority or power of spouses in the marriage relationship is prescribed by law. For example, state laws require husbands and wives to live together; and ordinarily it is the wife's duty to follow her husband wherever he decides to work and live. The wife's domicile is presumed to be her husband's domicile (Weitzman, 1981). The laws of most states view the husband as the primary breadwinner. As such, he is responsible for the wife's support. In return, most states give him control of the family resources. However, eight states have passed community property laws. These laws allow each spouse to lay claim to half of all the property acquired during the marriage in case of divorce. Also, most other separate property states now require a fair and equitable distribution of property in case of divorce (Sonenblick, 1981).

Most state laws also say that in exchange for his financial support, the husband is entitled to his wife's household and domestic labors, child care, love, affection, companionship, and sexual services (Weitzman, 1981, 60). Because the wife is legally obligated to provide these services, the law does not allow her to be compensated for her work in the home, nor is she entitled to compensation in money, goods, or a share of assets she helped accumulate during the marriage should the marriage fail (Weitzman, 1981, 64).

According to the marital rape exemption law, first passed in Massachusetts in 1857, a husband could not be prosecuted for forcing his wife to have sex with him. Several states have struck down the marital exemption law and now allow the wife to prosecute for marital rape. Other states allow prosecution under certain circumstances.

When the law says that a spouse has certain authority or rights, this becomes an important basis for assumption of such power. One of the important contributions of the women's movement has been to give women a firmer legal basis for power in the family.

Cultural Norms

The power structure of families varies among different social classes, races, and ethnic groups (Rodman, 1967, 1972). Most studies indicate that lower-socioeconomic-status husbands try to be more dominant and authoritarian than do middle-class husbands. They are often concerned about their masculine image and so demand deference as men and rely on tradition to support their patriarchal authority (Rubin, 1976; Willie and Greenblatt, 1978). They often use physical force and coercion in maintaining control. In actual practice, however, while higher-status husbands espouse an egalitarian philosophy, they control more resources, have greater prestige, and are voluntarily given more deference and control than are lower-status husbands. Thus, they tend to exercise more power than blue-collar husbands. Blue-collar husbands allow their wives to make more decisions than do middle-class men. Partly because of lower income, less education, and fewer skills, the position of the lower-class husband is tenuous at best, especially if his wife earns a substantial proportion of the family income.

Traditionally, the black family has been considered *matriarchal*, with wives and mothers dominant. Recent research tends to contradict this view. Black marriages tend to be more egalitarian than white, with middle-class black

The greater the wife's education and earnings, the more
likely she is to share decision
making power with her
husband.

families being more egalitarian than middle-class white families (Willie and
Greenblatt, 1978). A number of studies indicate the black matriarchy is a myth
and that egalitarian decision-making patterns predominate (Gray-Little, 1982;
McDonald, 1980). Black marriages cannot be stereotyped any more than white
marriages can. Black couples show variations in power structure at the same
socioeconomic level just as white marriages do (Gray-Little, 1982).

Puerto Rican and Mexican American families have always been considered
patriarchal. The Mexican American male was expected to prove his "machismo"
(manhood) by being dominant over his wife and children. (See Chapter 2.)
Mexican American families still emphasize male dominance, but the most
prevalent pattern is one in which the husband and wife share in decision
making as equals (Cromwell and Cromwell, 1978). Thus, the concept of Chicano patriarchy lacks validity.

An intensive study of decison making in Puerto Rican families in the New
York City area also contradicted the male-dominant image of such families
(Cooney, Rogler, Hurrell, and Ortez, 1982). A substantial majority of husbands
and wives shared decisions regarding their place of residence, insurance,
vacation plans, and home improvements. Roughly one-third also shared decisions regarding the husband's job or the wife's employment.

There were some noticeable variations among Puerto Rican families, however. Parent generations more closely adhered to the modified patriarchal
norms associated with Puerto Rican culture, while the child generation more
closely adhered to the transitional egalitarian norms associated with American
culture. The greater the wife's education, the greater the probability of shared
decisions.

Power relationships are also influenced by stereotyped gender norms. Sex-role socialization that emphasizes women's passivity, submissiveness, and dependence reinforces patriarchal power structures and hinders women's authority (Thompson, 1981). Traditionally, the husband was given legitimate power, and the wife and children were taught to submit to his authority (Scanzoni and Szinovacz, 1980). Gender norms often specified a rigid division of responsibility. The husband dominated financial policy; the wife cared for the children. The husband did rugged, heavy chores outside the house; the wife did less-strenuous maintenance inside the house (Appleton, 1982).

As more egalitarian gender norms develop and as interest spheres and power domains overlap, more family issues become subject to negotiation and compromise.

There seem to be some gender differences in the way that men and women exert power. Men use more coercion and direct, aggressive approaches. Women counterbalance this with more subtle, indirect, emotional methods of control (Falbo and Peplau, 1980). Women can withhold love and affection, evoke sympathy, and control through guilt. Whenever sex is viewed as something women do for men, women can offer or withhold sexual favors in bargaining (Komarovsky, 1964). Women who assume a position of learned helplessness are also able to request services and evoke feelings of responsibility in a way that becomes a powerful influence.

Economic Resources

According to resource theory, those who control valued resources needed by other family members hold power over them (Blood and Wolfe, 1960; deTurck and Miller, 1986). Money and property are two such valued resources. Some husbands feel that because they are the primary breadwinner, they have a right to dictate family decisions. One husband remarked, "It's my money, I earned it; therefore I have the right to spend it as I please."

Women who have no source of income of their own may not have equal power in their marriages if it is not relegated by their husbands and if they don't demand it. Some men keep tight reins over the money, doling it out or withholding it as they see fit, leaving their wives in a position of childish dependency. Much worse, there are women trapped in unhappy marriages who want to escape, but cannot because they have no means of support. Lack of economic power is lack of control in the marriage, a helplessness that puts some women at their husband's mercy (Klagsburn, 1985).

When the wife is gainfully employed, she gains more power in decision making in the family (Hiller and Philliber, 1978; Lee and Petersen, 1983). One study showed that the more the wife's income equalled that of her husband, the more likely that the spouses were equal partners (Scanzoni, 1980). Her power increased as she gained more income and more ownership of property (Osmond, 1978; Salamon and Keim, 1979).

In the case of one second marriage, the husband moved into his wife's house. Whenever an argument ensued, she reminded him that if he didn't like something, it was her house, and he could just leave. Owning the property gave her power in their relationship (Author's counseling notes).

In a society in which education is valued, a person who has superior education has an important source of power. One wife who didn't finish high school is awed by her husband, a college graduate. She looks up to him and follows his lead, because she feels "he is smarter than I am." This type of power is referred to as **expert power** in which a person is acknowledged as generally superior in intelligence and knowledge.

The influence of education on power depends partly on the cultural context and partly on the relative differences between the husband and wife. In the United States, both low- and high-education white-collar husbands and high-education blue-collar husbands gain power if they exceed their wife's education, and they lose power if they fall short. However, low-education blue-collar husbands tend to have more power even when their wives have superior education. Komarovsky (1964) attributes the greater power of some blue-collar husbands to cultural norms that emphasize patriarchal attitudes among the less-educated blue-collar classes.

Information is also a source of power. One husband commented: "My wife decorates the house. She knows much more about these things than I do." This type of power is referred to as **informational power** because it involves superior knowledge of a specific area.

The **theory of primary interest and presumed competence** says that the person who is most interested and involved with a particular choice and who is most qualified to make a specific decision will be more likely to do so (Conklin, 1979). Often these two aspects, interest and competence, go together. If the wife will be using the kitchen utensils more than her husband, and is more interested in which ones to buy, and if she has had more experience in the use of different utensils, presumably she will be the one who will exert the most influence in making this decision. If the husband does most of the driving and knows more about cars, presumably he will take more interest and exert more influence in this decision.

Personality Differences

Personality characteristics also relate to power. Considerable age differences between spouses influence power, with the older spouse exerting power over the younger one (Scanzoni and Polonko, 1980). Regardless of age, some people seem to be more domineering and forceful than others, exerting considerable influence on all with whom they come in contact. Shy, introverted, fearful people who don't dare express opinions are often controlled by those who are more forceful.

The degree of power depends partly on how motivated people are to gain strength and control. Some people strive for power to overcome inner feelings of weakness and insecurity (Veroff and Veroff, 1972). Others are just the opposite: they have high self-esteem and are very self-confident, and so are able to exert more influence. The converse also occurs: those with the greatest conjugal power also report higher levels of self-esteem (deTurck and Miller, 1986). The two seem to go together. Then, too, charming people with a lot of charisma may be natural leaders whom others follow very readily.

Some people are better talkers than others. They have superior verbal skills, are able to explain their ideas clearly and to convince others through the power of their words. Cross-sex investigations of communication patterns reveal that husbands often dominate the wife: they more often start the discussion, more often interrupt their female partners or shout them down, and more often have the last word. Males seem to have more active control over the conversation than do females (Zimmerman and West, 1975).

Some men, however, do not fit this description. They are relatively nonverbal, sometimes because they have been brought up in a home where problems were never discussed. Some wives do all the talking and complain that their husbands don't talk to them. Other people were brought up in conflicting homes and don't like to argue, and so keep quiet rather than cause trouble. Safilios-Rothschild (1973) found that women more often than men use nonverbal influence techniques such as anger, crying, pouting, or the silent treatment. Educated women tended more often to use sweet talk and affection as a way of exerting influence, as well as other verbal techniques.

Emotional Factors

Wives do have an important source of psychological power: the ability to bestow or withhold affection. Some wives use sex as a weapon: withholding it if their husbands do not do what they want. One woman made her husband promise to buy her a new dress before she'd have sex with him. Another remarked, "First clean the garage, and then we'll make love" (Author's counseling notes).

Of course, love or sex must be valued before it is a power source. When loves dies, so does its power. In his novel *Endless Love*, Scott Spencer (1980) writes:

> There had been a time when Rose had felt she could protect her position in the marriage . . . by simply (and it *was* simple) withholding her love. But now that her love was no longer sought, there was no advantage to be gained in rationing it. It was clear that the power she once had was not real power — it had been bestowed upon her, assigned. It had all depended on Arthur's wanting her, depended on his vulnerability to every nuance of rejection. He had, she realized now, chosen her weapon for her. He had given her a sword that only he could sharpen. (pp. 66, 67)

According to social exchange theory, *those with the greatest love and emotional need have the least power.* Because they are so dependent, they have the most to lose if the relationship breaks up. They are so afraid of losing love that they often do everything possible to please their partner (McDonald, 1980).

> Kathy was a college sophomore when she fell in love with Andy, a senior. She thought by letting him use her car, and granting other favors, that he would love her even more. Instead he became rejecting and unfeeling. He'd take her car and wouldn't let her have it. He'd ignore her on weekends so he could go out with his friends. He treated her rudely and with indifference. She became desperate, doing everything she could to keep his love. (Author's counseling notes)

Withholding or bestowing love can be one of the most powerful means of exerting influence, but only when the other person is emotionally dependent on that source of affection (Warner, Lee, and Lee, 1986).

Physical Stature and Strength

Coercive power is based on the belief that one spouse can punish the other for noncompliance. One type of coercion is the threat of physical punishment. One wife commented:

> My husband is a big man, and very strong. When he gets mad I never know what he's going to do. I'm afraid he'll hurt me. He once threw me down the front steps, just because I didn't have his lunch ready. (Author's counseling notes)

This wife realized what her husband could do to her if he decided to strike her. The physical beating of a wife is used by some males as a means of punishment or control. (See Chapter 17.) Kalmuss and Straus (1982) found that wives who were most dependent economically were also those who were most likely to stay in severely abusive marriages. Occasionally, one hears of wives who use physical violence against their husbands as a means of getting their own way.

Coercive power is based on the belief that one spouse can punish the other for noncompliance. An economically dependent spouse is more likely to stay in a severely abusive situation.

The more limited their alternatives, the less power people have in relationships. If a husband feels that his wife can't leave because she has no one to
turn to, no place to go, and no money to do it with, he has more power in
a relationship than would be true otherwise. The stage in the family life cycle
is an important consideration. Women who have the most dependent children, who are the most dependent economically and socially, have less power
over their situation than do women who are not yet parents or those whose
children are grown up.

Alternatives affect power, but the reverse is also true (Huston, 1983). High-
power individuals can prevent people with low power from developing alternative sources of the resources they need. For example, an economically
powerful husband can insist that his wife not pursue a career; thereby he
maintains the primary power in their relationship.

Circumstances may change power balances; or a crisis may occur that
results in a realignment of power in a relationship. Physical incapacitation or
illness of one spouse may force an otherwise submissive partner to take a
more active role. If a husband loses his job and remains unemployed over a
long period of time, his power and authority may diminish. Egalitarian couples, because they are more fluid and flexible, are able to shift and exchange
roles in order to meet the demands of a stressful situation.

Children

The presence of dependent children can render one more powerless, but
children themselves can also be a power source. That is, children themselves
exert considerable influence over their parents and other family members
(Grusec and Kuczysiski, 1980; McGillicuddy-DeLisi, 1980). Even the cry of a
baby has considerable influence. Children can gang up on parents and render
them powerless if they are able to divide the parents and get one to disagree
with the other. For this reason, therapist Jay Haley (1982) emphasizes the
need for parents to discuss issues and present a united front to avoid
confusion.

POWER PROCESSES

We have discussed power bases; that is, the sources of power. **Power processes** refer to the way that power is applied. Safilios-Rothschild (1976) makes
a distinction between orchestration power and implementation power.
Orchestration power is the power to make the overall important decisions
that determine family life-styles and the major characteristics and features of
the family. **Implementation power** sets these decisions in motion. For example, a wife may decide how much money her husband can spend on a new
appliance (but he is the one who actually makes the purchase). Conflicts arise
only when the implementing spouse tries to modify the guidelines and boundaries established by the orchestration (McDonald, 1980).

410

MARRIAGES AND FAMILY
RELATIONSHIPS:
GROWTH AND
CHALLENGES

Power Tactics

Power tactics are those means that people use to get others to do what they want. Some tactics help to build better relationships. Others are destructive.

Discussing, Explaining, Asking, Telling

Discussing, explaining, asking, and telling are positive ways of power implementation (Falbo and Peplau, 1980). Couples who can explain things in a rational, intelligent way, or who ask directly and clearly, are using a gentle or "soft" form of power that is effective. It also builds positive feelings and satisfaction in the relationship (Kipnis, 1984).

Persuasion

Persuasion is a stronger form of discussion. Its purpose is to try to convince the other person to believe or do something that he or she is reluctant to accept. Sometimes, the person is genuinely convinced and accepts willingly. At other times, the person acquiesces, but against his or her inclinations.

> Bill wanted to go to Hawaii on his vacation. Sally was reluctant because she did not want to go so far away. Bill got all the brochures and for months talked to his wife about how wonderful it would be to go to Hawaii. He finally convinced her that Hawaii was *the* place to go. (Author's counseling notes)

Couples who are able to communicate thoughtfully with one another build positive feelings and satisfaction in the relationship.

Bargaining is the process by which two parties decide what each shall give and receive in arriving at a decision. The process involves *quid pro quo*, which means "something for something." The purpose of bargaining is to reach an agreement or compromise solution to a problem. Bargaining is a process of position modification and convergence. For bargaining to take place, several conditions have to exist:

- Each party has some power to withhold or grant something that the other person wants. If one person wields a disproportionate amount of power over the other, the dominated person has little to negotiate with.
- Each party wants something from the other, for which he or she is willing to give something else.
- Each party is motivated to reach an agreement.
- Each person is flexible enough and fair enough to make compromises and grant concessions.

It's helpful if both partners are flexible and willing to compromise, without being too tough or too soft (Scanzoni and Polonko, 1980).

Being Nice

Being exceptionally nice, attentive, and considerate when one wants something may put people in a good mood and make them feel so grateful that they can't refuse a request. Some wives are better at "buttering up" their husbands than others. Men too learn how to flatter a woman and "hand her a line" to win her favor. Sincere flattery and consideration are much appreciated. If they are false efforts to win favors, they are deceitful and create distrust.

Being Helpless, Dependent

Some persons try to control by being helpless or dependent. If they present themselves as powerless, unable to do something, they may evoke the sympathy of the other person, who is glad to show off his or her expertise:

> Whenever Helen wants her husband to do a project around the house, she starts it herself, gets in trouble, and appeals for her husband's assistance. The tactic always seems to work. (Author's counseling notes)

> Don hates yard work, house repairs, painting, and every kind of physical chore in and outside the house. Several times, his wife asked him to do something. He was all thumbs, completely inept, and did such a terrible job that his wife took over and did it herself. Don explained, "If she knows I'll do a terrible job, she doesn't ask me." (Author's counseling notes)

Some men are flattered by "coming to the rescue" of dependent females. For this reason, some women have been brought up to pretend to be helpless (Johnson, 1976). Other women find such tactics demeaning to themselves and to all women. Many women also have no respect for a man who is not capable in many areas, especially in doing traditional men's chores.

Some husbands and wives play the weakling, helpless role to evade responsibility themselves. They are usually insecure and lack self-confidence. They manipulate their mate into taking charge; then they criticize him or her for not doing the job right, and also complain because the spouse is such a take-over person.

Overprotection

The overprotective husband or wife does not allow his or her spouse to mature or become independent, thus rendering the spouse powerless. An example is the wife who plays mother hen to her husband, treating him like a helpless child, so she can "rule the roost."

Deceiving, Lying, Outwitting

Some people seek to control others by deceiving, lying, and outwitting them. They make promises they don't keep in exchange for concessions. They pretend to be someone they are not. They become habitual liars to try to avoid responsibilities.

> Jim told Mary he couldn't get married at this particular time because he couldn't afford it. He agreed to marriage when Mary told him that she would continue to work after marriage to help out, but she quit her job two weeks after the wedding. (Author's counseling notes)

> Harry told Sylvia that he didn't want to discontinue their affair and that he would divorce his wife and marry her. Five years have passed, and he has never filed divorce papers. (Author's counseling notes)

Criticizing

One of the most personally destructive forms of gaining power is the constant use of criticism to undermine and demean the other person. Some spouses wait until other family members or company are present and then point out the wrongdoing and failures of their spouse. It's difficult for the criticized spouse to defend himself or herself without creating an embarrassing scene. One wife complained:

> According to my husband, I never do anything right. It doesn't matter how hard I try, or what I do, he finds fault. He's beaten me down so I don't have any self-respect or self-confidence at all anymore. (Author's counseling notes)

Comparing one person with another, with friends, or with brothers or sisters is another way of making them feel inept and inadequate.

Scapegoating is a way of blaming someone else for every bad thing that happens. The attempt is to make the other person feel responsible and guilty so the controller doesn't have to accept the blame.

> Mary is married to an insensitive, cruel husband. When she decides to leave, he blames her for separating him from his infant daughter. He insists it's all her fault that she is leaving. (Author's counseling notes)

Bach and Wyden (1970) use the term **gaslighting** to describe the process by which one person destroys the self-confidence, perception, and sense of reality of the other. The term comes from the movie *Gaslight*, in which the husband attempts to drive his wife insane by turning down the gaslights and then telling her she's imagining things when she says they are growing dimmer. In gaslighting, one partner denies the truth of what the other is saying, sarcastically criticizes the other for his or her feelings or opinions, or turns things around to make the other partner feel guilty for having any doubts.

> One example is a husband who is having an affair that the wife suspects. He stays away all night Friday, and has become very indifferent toward his wife. When she questions him, he accuses her of imagining things, that the only thing wrong with their marriage is that she doesn't trust him. He tells his wife that she is too jealous, too suspicious, and tries to possess him and run his life, and that if she gives him more freedom maybe things would work out. He insists she's imagining things and that the affair is all in her mind. (Author's counseling notes)

Punishing

Some spouses use a variety of punishments to influence the behavior of the other. Whenever she gets in a bad mood, one wife does a variety of things she knows her husband doesn't like. She cooks spaghetti because her husband hates it; she starches the collars of his shirts because he likes them soft. She goes out and buys things she doesn't need and charges them to his account. Her techniques are very childish, but her husband is really afraid of what she'll do if he crosses her (Author's counseling notes).

Silent Treatment

Using the silent treatment can be very punishing. Some couples live in silence for days as tension continues. Silence, however, prevents reconciliation and perpetuates misunderstandings (Galvin and Brommel, 1986).

Blackmail

Threatening blackmail is a coercive tactic that creates fear and anger.

> Bill's parents hated alcoholic beverages and told him and their other children that if they ever drank they would disown them. Bill wanted to divorce his wife Shirley, but she threatened to tell his parents about his drinking if he ever left her. (Author's counseling notes)

Anger, Temper

Emotionally unstable people may become violently angry, throw temper tantrums, punch out walls, break furniture, or use other power tactics to try to get their own way.

The silent treatment can be very punishing. Some couples live in silence for days as tension continues.

When Dick found out that his wife wanted to divorce him, he started throwing furniture around the house. "If you leave me, there won't be anything left of this house. You'll get nothing," he threatened. (Author's counseling notes)

Some spouses report that living with their partner is like waiting for a bomb to explode. They never know what will set it off. Some people are very much afraid of their partner's temper, which has become an effective means of control.

Cruelty, Abuse

The most extreme forms of control are cruel and abusive treatment. The husband who beats up his wife and pushes her around terrorizes her so that he can keep control over her. It takes a strong person to separate herself from such treatment, especially if her husband tries to make her believe that it is all her fault and that she deserves it.

OUTCOMES OF POWER STRUGGLES

Effects on Individuals

One of the most important considerations in evaluating patterns of power in relationships is the effect that different patterns have on the individuals involved. Some people strive to gain control, but at what cost? If they gain the upper hand at the cost of alienating their partner, stimulating anger and hostility, or destroying their relationship, what's the point? Some spouses are so intent on winning the battle that they lose the marriage.

Generally speaking, extreme imbalances of power between two people tend to have a negative effect. Horowitz (1982) found that lack of power was associated with psychological distress for both men and women. Men, espe-

PERSPECTIVE
Power Neutralization Strategies

People use various strategies to neutralize the power of another person.

1. *Refuse to do it.* Listen, don't argue or disagree, but don't take any action. One husband commented, "My wife never argues with me. She just goes ahead and does what she wants anyhow."

2. Whenever the issue comes up, *change the subject. Refuse to listen. Show no interest.* One wife complained that every time she's bring up her husband's drinking, he'd start to do something else, or he'd walk away. Of course, couples never really solve anything using these tactics.

3. *Become emotionally detached from the situation. Don't care.* If a husband threatens to leave, the wife's attitude will be, "Go ahead, there's the door."

4. If a partner refuses to do something, *obtain the needed services elsewhere.* "If you won't paint the kitchen, I'll hire someone else to do it."

5. *Resign to do without, perhaps finding a substitute.* If an insensitive husband threatens to withdraw love and affection, the wife can neutralize his action by saying: "I really don't need your affection. I get all I need from the children." This really doesn't solve the problem except to prevent the husband from using withdrawal of love and affection as a weapon.

6. *Change the balance of power through self-improvement.* One husband treated his wife badly when she was obese and dependent and as long as he felt she was powerless in the relationship. She went on a diet and lost 55 pounds, returned to school, earned her degree, and got a job earning more money than he. Now, he's very, very nice to her. He's afraid she's going to leave him.

7. *Beat the other person at his or her own game.* This means replying with coercive tactics, or withholding a reward until the other person complies. Sometimes this tactic works. It may be the only way of preventing the other person from bullying. At other times, this kind of power struggle will create a standoff with neither partner willing to give in. Two stubborn people playing this game can wreck a relationship.

cially, who were without power, who were socially castrated because of lack of employment or status, suffered enormously. Unemployed married women, especially those who did not have children, were also more distressed than those who were breadwinners and who were mothers. In contrast, possessing economic and social power led to lower levels of psychological stress for both men and women.

At the other extreme, high levels of power can also be destructive. Power can corrupt. This means that power produces strong psychological changes in power holders and they start to exploit those they control. They become puffed up with their own importance. Their moral values become self-serving. They become self-centered and selfish. They may become unfeeling and quite abusive. The person dominated becomes an "it" to use, rather than a person to cherish (Kipnis, 1984).

An extreme example is the literary figure of Don Juan, who uses the sexual conquest of women to prove his manhood and flaunt his power. A study of couples in the Boston area revealed a group of males who were modern equivalents of Don Juan (Stewart and Rubin, 1976). They flitted from relationship to relationship, never fully satisfied with one woman. This study revealed that for males, a high need for power was associated with low relationship satisfaction (both their own and that of their partners), low love for their partner, and a high number of problems in the relationship.

One of the consequences of power imbalances in relationships is that the person who feels coerced or manipulated and who often gives in becomes frustrated and resentful. A person may accept coercion for awhile; but as frustrations and hostility increase, the relationship worsens. Couples who habitually deal with decisions on a win-or-lose basis often discover that winning a marital conflict becomes an illusion. The victory turns into loss for both when feelings of anger and hurt develop between the partners.

Marital Satisfaction

Marital satisfaction is maximized when couples achieve a balance of power that is acceptable to them. This balance may vary with different couples. Very few women can respect a man that they can order around or who will not assume a fair share of responsibility. One wife commented:

> My husband depends on me for everything. I control the money. I pay the bills.
> I call the repair man. I arrange our nights out. I invite friends over. I have to
> decide when to paint the house and who's going to do it. I have to plan our
> vacations. I'm the one who guides the children. I wish my husband would make
> some of the decisions and take part of the responsibility. I'm getting tired of
> doing it. (Author's counseling notes)

This wife became more and more disenchanted with her husband. The feeling developed: "I'd like a man who can take care of me for a change."

One study of black couples showed that, in general, the husband-led power pattern was associated with the highest levels of marital quality and that the egalitarian and wife-led couples reported lower levels of marital quality. In spite of the espousal of egalitarian patterns as most desirable, greatest satisfaction was found for couples in traditional relationships (Gray-Little, 1982).

In contrast to this finding, however, there is a body of social science research that emphasizes that equitable relations tend to be more stable and satisfying (Walster, Walster, and Berscheid, 1978). Madden and Janoff-Bulman (1981) found that wives who felt they had power to control the outcome of marital conflicts were more satisfied with their marriages than were women who had little control. If the wives blamed their husband for the conflict and had little control over the situation, they found their marriages very unsatisfying.

It is difficult for a wife to feel good about herself if she feels she has lost control over her life (Doherty, 1981). It is also hard for a man to respect the powerless woman. Men too tend to devalue and lack respect for women whom they can push around. One man explained, "My wife does everything I tell her to do. Just once, I wish she'd tell me to go to hell" (Author's counseling notes). Very few people admire those they can manipulate and control, but neither do most people want to be married to a dictator who does not respect their feelings and wishes.

The Need for Equity

Exchange theorists suggest that satisfaction in marriage hinges on the perception of fairness or equity in exchanges, rather than on the existence of a particular power structure. However, cultural norms influence their perceptions. Individual preferences vary. What is important is that spouses feel that the power relationships they have achieved are fair and equitable according to their own expectations. According to this viewpoint, there are no rigid hierarchical patterns within stable marriages. Spouses alternate in their role of power subject and power holder as the task and personal preferences of family members dictate (Beckman-Brindley and Tavormina, 1978).

ASSESSMENT
Our Scale of Decision-Making Power

This scale will help you assess who makes the decisions in your relationship. For each item, circle the answer according to who makes the *final* decision. Select your answer according to the following scale:

1 — Woman always makes the final decision.
2 — Woman makes the final decision more often than the man.
3 — Man and woman have exactly the same power in making the final decision.
4 — Man makes the final decision more often than the woman.
5 — Man always makes the final decision.

Note that there is a separate scale for dating couples and for married couples. After you have completed the scale, have your partner answer it also, without seeing your answers. After answering, add up the total score for the eight items, then divide by 8 to get your average score. The higher the score, the more your relationship is male dominated. (An average score of 5 would mean that the man always makes the final decisions. A score of 1 would mean that the woman always makes the final decisions.) If you and your partner have different scores, you have different perceptions of who has the decision-making power.

For Dating Couples

Who makes the final decision

1. About how often to see one another?	1	2	3	4	5
2. About what to do on dates?	1	2	3	4	5
3. About how to dress on dates?	1	2	3	4	5
4. About how far to go sexually?	1	2	3	4	5
5. About which restaurant, night spot, or lounge to go to?	1	2	3	4	5
6. About what movie to see?	1	2	3	4	5
7. About how often to visit family members?	1	2	3	4	5
8. About which friends to select?	1	2	3	4	5

For Married Couples

Who makes the final decision

1. About what car to buy?	1	2	3	4	5
2. About whether or not to buy life insurance?	1	2	3	4	5
3. About what house or apartment to take?	1	2	3	4	5
4. About how much money to spend per week on food?	1	2	3	4	5
5. About what doctor to have when someone is sick?	1	2	3	4	5
6. About where to go on vacation?	1	2	3	4	5
7. About whom to invite to the house or go out socially with?	1	2	3	4	5
8. About how to decorate or furnish the house?	1	2	3	4	5

418

MARRIAGES AND FAMILY
RELATIONSHIPS:
GROWTH AND
CHALLENGES

SUMMARY

1. Power has been defined as the ability of an individual within a social relationship to carry out his or her will, even in the face of resistance by others.

2. People want power for a variety of reasons: to feel that they have control over their lives, because society expects them to, because they are following the pattern modeled by their parents, or because of a psychological need to compensate for inferiority feelings and insecurity.

3. One of the most important measures of power is decision making: the extent to which a person has the final say or choice when a decision is made.

4. Studies by Blood and Wolfe and others have raised some methodological issues: the need to question both husbands and wives, the need to include a variety of decisions and those important to both husbands and wives when making out the questionnaire, the need to classify decisions and weigh them according to their importance, the need to be cautious about generalizing from findings in relation to a specific group, the need to use a variety of methods of gathering information to obtain a true picture, and the need to recognize that there are a wide variety of sources of power.

5. Power is based on legal and cultural sources, gender norms, economic resources, education and knowledge, personality differences, communication ability, emotional factors, physical stature and strength, circumstances, and children.

6. Power processes refer to the way that power is applied. Orchestration power is the power to make the overall important decisions that determine family life-styles and the major characteristics and features of the family. Implementation power sets these decisions in motion.

7. People use various means to get what they want. Some of these tactics help to build better relationships. Some do not.

8. Power tactics include discussing, explaining, asking, telling; persuasion; bargaining and negotiation; being nice to get what one wants; being helpless and dependent as a means of control; overprotection to keep people from gaining power; deceiving, lying, outwitting; criticizing to keep a person subjugated; scapegoating; gaslighting (destroying their validity and integrity); punishing; using silent treatment as a means of punishment; blackmail; control through anger, temper, cruelty, and abuse.

9. There are various means for neutralizing power: refuse to do it, don't listen, become emotionally detached, obtain services elsewhere, resign to do without or find a substitute, change the balance of power through self-improvement, or beat the other person at his or her own game. The problem with some of these methods is they don't completely solve the problem, or they create a power struggle, resulting in a standoff with neither party willing to give in. Two stubborn people playing this game can wreck a relationship.

10. One important consideration is what effect power relationships have on individuals and marital satisfaction. Generally speaking, extreme imbalances of power between two people tend to have a negative effect. Lack

of power is associated with psychological distress for both men and women. At the other extreme, high levels of power can be destructive, resulting in negative psychological changes in the power holder and hurting the power subject.

11. Marital satisfaction is maximized when couples achieve a balance of power that is acceptable to them. This balance may vary with different couples. What is important is that spouses feel that the power relationships that they have achieved are fair and equitable according to their expectations.

SUGGESTED READINGS

Bramson, R. M. (1981). *Coping with Difficult People*. New York: Ballantine Books. Includes how to cope in a variety of situations.

Cromwell, R. E., and Olson, D. H. (Eds.). (1975). *Power in Families*. New York: Wiley. An interdisciplinary reader focusing on major conceptual, theoretical, methodological, and substantive issues.

LaRoe, M. S., and Herrick, L. (1980). *How Not to Ruin a Perfectly Good Marriage*. New York: Bantam. A popularized approach.

Phelps, S., and Austin, N. (1975). *The Assertive Woman*. San Luis Obispo, CA: Impact. Assertiveness training for women.

Scanzoni, J. (1982). *Sexual Bargaining: Power Politics in the American Marriage* (2d ed.). Motivations to marry, marital conflict, and marital change in the past and future.

17

COMMUNICATION AND CONFLICT

KEY TERMS

communication
body language
double-bind communication
feedback
intrapsychic sources of conflict

intrasomatic sources of conflict
interpsychic sources of conflict
ventilation
catharsis

constructive arguments
destructive arguments
family violence
child abuse
wife abuse

Years of experience in marriage counseling have convinced me that the two most important requirements for a satisfying marriage are ability to communicate, and ability to handle conflict. If couples can do these two things, they are usually able to handle most problems that arise.

We aren't born with these abilities. Communication is a fine art that must be learned. Learning how to handle conflict requires years of experience and effort.

In this chapter, we are concerned with both tasks: improving communication skills and learning to deal with conflict constructively. And, finally, we are concerned with conflict that erupts into family violence, which becomes so destructive to family members.

COMMUNICATION

The Process

Communication *between human beings may be defined as a message one person sends and another receives.* It is also the process of transmitting feelings, attitudes, facts, beliefs, and ideas between persons. Communication is not limited to words, but also occurs through listening, silences, facial expressions, gestures, touch, body stance, and all other nonlanguage symbols and cues used by persons in giving and receiving meaning. In short, it may include all the means by which people exchange feelings and meanings as they try to understand one another and as they try to influence one another (Rice, 1983).

Importance in Marriage

Understanding one another is an important element in marital satisfaction (Honeycutt, 1986; Tiggle, Peters, Kelley, and Vincent, 1982). Understanding, in turn, depends on the extent and nature of the communication among the parties involved (Allen and Thompson, 1984; Montgomery, 1981). Many authorities contend that *good communication is the key to intimacy and to family interaction and is the lifeblood of the marital relationship* (Powers and Hutchinson, 1979; Stephen, 1985; Witkin, Edleson, Rose, and Hall, 1983). One couple writes:

> There is no area of our married life that isn't affected by communication: our bed, our job, our children, our social life, our leisure time, our relationship with relatives and friends. All could become potential areas of discontent and friction when there isn't good communication between us. (Herrigan and Herrigan, 1973, p. 149)

Considerable research evidence substantiates these statements. Some researchers have found that for wives, especially, *good communication is more related to general satisfaction with marriage than is sexual satisfaction* (Wachowiak and Bragg, 1980). Clinicians talk about the psychologically deserted wife who is denied the comfort of discussing her problems with her husband and whose constant lament is "he never talks to me" (Mace and Mace, 1974; Mornell, 1979). Women are more satisfied with their marriages when they can talk about their problems with their husbands and have control over the resolution of conflicts (Madden and Janoff-Bulman, 1981).

Good communication is the key to intimacy and family interaction and is the lifeblood of the marital relationship.

This does not mean, however, that all communication is helpful to marriage. The act of communicating does not always lead to a resolution of problems. Talking things over and expressing feelings may make things worse. As one author expressed it: "Engagement . . . can result in escalation" (Raush et al., 1974, p. 307). Couples who openly share negative feelings the other can't handle may increase tension and alienation (Billings, 1979). As a result, some couples avoid such disclosure, feign agreement, or deliberately lie as a means of maintaining marital harmony. Just communicating is not enough; communication must be constructive, with words and timing carefully selected. One study showed that marital happiness was greater when couples employed relaxed, friendly, open, attentive, expressive and precise styles of communication (Honeycutt, Wilson, and Parker, 1982).

Verbal and Nonverbal Communication

Both verbal and nonverbal communication are strongly associated with good marital adjustment. However, nonverbal communication, the language of signs and signals, is more subject to misinterpretation.

> Barbara comes downstairs dressed only in her bikini panties and bra. Her husband, Chuck, interprets this as a signal that she's interested in going to bed. Right away, he becomes aroused and starts to make advances. She becomes annoyed: "Will you leave me alone! I'm trying to get my dress out of the dryer." It is obvious that Barbara's signal was only that she was without her dress and needed to get it, but Chuck interpreted it as asking for him.

One study found that when husbands were able to read their wives' nonverbal cues, the wives were more satisfied with their marriages than when the husbands were not able to interpret them (Gottman and Porterfield, 1981).

One of the most important uses of words is what Berne calls "the stroking function" (Berne, 1964, p. 13). By this he means words that soothe, that give recognition, acceptance, and reassurance and that fulfill emotional needs. Words can heal hurt egos or satisfy deep longings. What husband is immune to the words: "I think you're a handsome, wonderful man"? Words are also used to solve problems, to convey information, or to reveal emotions. One of the most important functions is to provide companionship; or, as expressed by John Milton, "In God's intention, a meet and happy conversation is the chiefest and the noblest end of marriage."

Nonverbal communication comes in many forms. **Body language** includes such things as posture, facial expressions, still or tense muscles, blushing, movement, panting breath, tears, sweating, shivering or quivering, an increased pulse rate, or a thumping heart. "The message 'I love you' may be communicated in a gesture (outstretched arms), facial expression (pleasant smile), tone of voice (whisper), speed of speech (slow), eyes (attentive), and touch (gentle)" (Knox, 1975, p. 162). The manner of dressing and the use of cosmetics are forms of communication. Emphasizing the mouth with cosmetics highlights sex appeal; playing up the eyes gives an ethereal or spiritual message.

Direct actions are another form of communication; this allows the florist to remind us, "Say it with flowers." Some nonverbal communication is symbolic communication. A surprise gift may symbolize infinite care and love.

Sometimes the messages transmitted verbally and nonverbally contradict one another. The O'Neills write:

> Bill may say to his wife, "I'm listening, I'm listening," but his body is hunched over attentively in front of the television set. Arthur may tell his wife, "I love you," over and over, but she has good cause to wonder if he means it when he never listens to her attentively, gives her only a peck on the cheek, and is perfunctory in bed (O'Neill and O'Neill, 1972, p. 100).

When words and actions are inconsistent, often referred to as **double-bind communication**, stress between partners is increased as anxiety grows (Roy and Sawyers, 1986).

BARRIERS TO COMMUNICATION

Barriers to communication may be grouped under five categories: physical and environmental, situational, cultural, sexual, and psychological.

Physical and Environmental Barriers

There is a close relationship between physical proximity and social interaction. In general, *closer physical distances are associated with more intimate relationships.* This means that such factors as the size and arrangements of living spaces and the location of furniture in those spaces has an influence on interaction. The closer people sit around a table the more likely that they will be friendly, talkative, and intimate. Whether couples sleep together in the same bed or in separate bedrooms influences the extent of their interaction.

Physical confinement is associated with accelerated self-disclosure, particularly in intimate areas of exchange. This means that the longer couples are

"A gun, Harvey? I thought we had agreed—no more major purchases."

together the greater the possibility that intimacy will develop. Of course, there is also the possibility that conflict and tension will arise.

Situational Barriers

Situations can also enhance communication or make it more difficult. If employment separates couples frequently or for long periods of time, the tendency is for communication to break down, with a resultant loss of intimacy. When couples live together with others in the same spaces, lack of privacy becomes a major factor in making intimate communication more difficult. The situational context changes during different periods of marriage and affects communication. For example, husbands tend to make far more effort to give emotional support to their wives during pregnancy; but, following childbirth, they often feel that their wives do not require the same special support. As a result, the increased closeness reported during pregnancy then declines, resulting in the increased dissatisfaction that some wives feel after childbirth (Raush et al, 1974).

Cultural Barriers

Wide cultural differences impose difficulties in communication (Hawkins, Weisberg, and Ray, 1977). Such factors as educational and age differences affect the ability of the couple to communicate with one another. The graduate student and elementary school graduate think on different levels and about different things. One graduate student commented:

> During these years I've been in college, my wife and I have drifted apart. I learn all about these new things in school, come home and tell my wife about them. But she isn't interested and doesn't know what I'm talking about.

One possibility, of course, would be for the wife to enroll in college too.

Couples with divergent ethnic backgrounds also have more difficulty understanding one another. Words have different meanings, as do actions. People are also socialized differently. Persons who are taught to be more reserved have more difficulty communicating in marriage than do others. One wife of a blue-collar husband comments:

> He can clam up and not talk for a long time. Sometimes I ask, "What are you so clammy for; spit it out and you'll feel much better," but he'll answer me coarsely or just say, "Oh yeah." Sometimes I can worm it out of him, but I believe in leaving him alone (Komarovsky, 1964, p. 157).

Gender Barriers

Some barriers to communication are a result of socialized masculine-feminine differences. Men and women are socialized to be interested in different things. Not as many wives as husbands are interested in talking about the Sunday afternoon football game. One husband confessed that he was bored with his wife.

> What does she have to talk about? Dirty diapers and stuff. I don't care about that. She talks about the children, but we both see what is happening. We are both there, it's no use talking about it all the time. (Komarovsky, 1964, p. 149)

This same husband liked to read; when he came across an interesting article he tried to "talk her into reading the magazine, but she doesn't like reading, so I stopped bringing up these things" (Komarovsky, 1964, p. 149). Men and women are also socialized to express different degrees of sensitivity. When those who are emotionally sensitive and responsive try to communicate with those who are not, the results can be frustrating.

Psychological Barriers

The most important barriers to communication are psychological: fear of rejection, ridicule, failure, or alienation, or lack of trust between two people (Larzelere and Huston, 1980). Husbands and wives will not share experiences if they are unrewarding, threatening, or downright painful. They need to be sure of an empathetic reply.

IMPROVING COMMUNICATION SKILLS

Requirements

Skill in communication has five requirements:

1. *A positive feeling between spouses* where they value and care for one another and *are motivated* to want to develop sympathetic understanding
2. *A willingness to disclose* one's own attitudes, feelings, and ideas
3. *An ability to reveal attitudes, feelings, and ideas clearly and accurately*
4. A talent for being a *good listener* and for receiving messages accurately
5. *A reciprocal relationship* where disclosure and feedback originate with both partners and there is a free flow of information from both directions

Communication is most possible when couples really show they care about one another and when they are motivated to try to understand one another. It is not just the communication itself that is important but also the spirit behind the message and a couple's feelings for one another. The tone of voice used and the words selected are also important. Most authors also talk about the importance of *empathy* — experiencing the feelings, thoughts, and attitudes of another person. Couples who frequently make positive statements about one another have much higher marital satisfaction than do those who are very negative or disparaging in what they say. In addition, supportive communication stimulates reciprocal supportiveness, increasing the degree of marital integration (Alexander, 1973).

Self-Disclosure

Communication depends partly on the *willingness of the persons involved to disclose their real feelings, ideas, and attitudes.* People cannot really get to know others unless they are willing to talk about themselves. Some people can be classified as high revealers, others as low revealers. High revealers are more prone to reveal intimate facets of their personalities and to do so earlier in their relationships than are low revealers. They are also able to make a more accurate assessment of the intimate attitudes and values of their friends than are low revealers (Taylor, 1968). In general, dyads where both persons are high revealers are more compatible than are pairs of low revealers or pairs that differ in the level of disclosure (Davidson, Balswick, and Halverson, 1983).

Other research has shown a direct correlation between satisfaction in marriage and disclosure of feelings to one's partner (Hansen and Schuldt, 1984; Jorgensen and Gaudy, 1980). However, it's not just the amount of disclosure that is important, but also what is said, when it is said, and how (Schumm, Barnes, Bollman, Jurich, and Bugaighis, 1986). People who are hostile may be wise not to talk until they can discuss a situation more rationally. Satisfied couples infrequently discuss negative feelings pertaining to their mates. The negative feelings they disclose usually relate to external events such as a bad day at work. Feelings about their spouses are usually positive and pleasant. Thus, as in other facets of communication, it is not disclosure alone that builds satisfaction but the fact of selective disclosure of feelings that seems more beneficial to marital harmony than indiscriminate catharsis.

Clarity

Couples differ in their *abilities to convey messages clearly and accurately.* Some couples have few verbal skills and so make greater uses of nonverbal techniques. But saying what one means and interpreting accurately can be learned. Clarity and accuracy are enhanced by the following:

1. Avoiding "double-level" messages where words say one thing and actions and innuendos another.
2. Speaking clearly and to the point; saying what one really means; avoiding vagueness, ambiguity, and indirect approaches.

ASSESSMENT
The Quality of Our Communication

Draw a circle around the number that best describes your communication with your partner. You can each answer separately and then compare your evaluations or you can decide jointly the best answer for each of the items.

Evaluate according to the following scale:

1 — All of the time
2 — Much of the time
3 — Some of the time
4 — A little of the time
5 — None of the time

Our discussions foster our relationship.	1 2 3 4 5
When we discuss we stick to the point.	1 2 3 4 5
We listen and seldom interrupt one another.	1 2 3 4 5
We share equal speaking time or one of us chooses to listen only.	1 2 3 4 5
The speaker's tone of voice conveys caring and interest.	1 2 3 4 5
We believe our opinions are simply different, not right or wrong.	1 2 3 4 5
We engage in mutual personal information sharing and/or mutual problem solving.	1 2 3 4 5
The person speaking asks for information or a response from the person listening.	1 2 3 4 5
Each of us shares his or her personal point of view (thoughts and feelings).	1 2 3 4 5
Each of us is tolerant of the other person's point of view and responds without judging that point of view.	1 2 3 4 5

Add the total score and divide by 10. The average will tell you where you are on the scale. The lower the number, the better your communication. High scores on particular items indicate the need for improvement.

3. Avoiding both exaggeration or understatement of the case one is presenting.

4. Avoiding flippant, kidding remarks that mask one's feelings and opinions. How many times have you heard: "I didn't really mean that. I was only joking. Don't take everything so literally."

5. Asking the other person to repeat what was said if there is any doubt about it.

6. Talking about important things when there is a minimum of distraction and when the other person can focus his or her attention completely on what is being said.

Good Listening

Good communication also involves *open listening and hearing* and being able to receive what has been said (Garland, 1981). Sometimes people pretend to listen when they do not. This can become a habit that discourages the speaker from talking. Other people find it useful not to listen to those things that make them uncomfortable or that they don't want to hear. They figuratively turn off their hearing aids:

> George D. always started to play with the children every time his wife tried to talk to him about spending too much money on his hobbies. This made Mrs. D. furious, because she knew he was trying to shut her out so she could not get through to him. (Author's counseling notes)

Some people are so interested in talking themselves that they don't really listen. They are so concerned about what they're going to say next that they aren't really listening to what is being said.

Feedback and Reciprocity

Feedback *involves responding to what the other person has said as well as disclosing one's own feelings and ideas.* This type of marital interaction has been correlated with marital satisfaction (White, 1983). In technical terms, feedback involves receiving the output of a computer and feeding it additional information to correct its errors (Sollie and Scott, 1983). In human communication, feedback involves paraphrasing the other person's statement to make sure it is understood, asking clarifying questions, and then giving one's own input or response telling how one feels about the matter.

CONFLICT IN RELATIONSHIPS

The Inevitability of Conflict

A certain amount of conflict and discord may be considered a normal part of every relationship. Two people will never agree on everything. Tensions build up and misunderstandings occur in the process of living. The numerous decisions that couples must make and the disappointments, frustrations, and adjustments they must face will result, at some time, in a hurt look, an angry word, or a more overt quarrel. Some couples have more conflict than others; some are able to deal with it more constructively than others, but the potential for conflict is there in every human relationship. In fact, *those couples who are the closest to one another, who have the greatest potential for satisfaction in their relationship, also have the greatest potential for conflict* (Argyle and Furnham, 1983).

Mace and Mace (1974) compare the relationship of marriage to that of two people who are confined in a delineated space. If the space were a mile-square field, the couple could coexist fairly well. If they wanted to talk or needed one another's help, they could easily get together. If they wanted to be alone or had a quarrel, they could quickly get out of sight and sound of each other. But reduce this space to 150 square feet — the area of an average bedroom — and there would be a very different situation. Now the two people would be fully conscious of each other during every waking moment. They would see and hear every move, cough, sneeze, grunt, and groan. If a disagreement arose, there would be no chance to get away to gain perspective or to cool off. Solving the problem would be painful. Mace and Mace conclude: "That's what intimacy means — great when two people are in harmony with one another, terrible when they're in conflict."

Some conflict and discord may be a normal part of every relationship. Research suggests that couples who are closer and have the greatest potential for satisfaction in their relationship also have the greatest potential for conflict.

The Need To Understand Conflict

But while some conflict may be inevitable, it does not mean it is always desirable or helpful. Conflict can destroy love and even an otherwise good marriage. But it can also relieve tensions, clear the air, and bring two people closer together than ever before. It depends upon the total circumstances, the focus of the conflict, the way it is handled, and the ultimate outcome.

There is a need, therefore, to understand as much as possible about conflict. What are its causes? What are its functions in marriage? What are some of the ways couples deal with conflict? Which ways help and which ways hurt the marriage? What factors influence a couple's conflict-solving abilities? How can conflict become a more constructive means for bringing a couple closer together?

SOURCES OF CONFLICT

Conflict may have its origin in (1) intrapsychic sources, (2) intrasomatic sources, (3) interpsychic sources, (4) situational or environmental sources (Rice, 1983).

Intrapsychic Sources

Intrapsychic or inner sources of conflict *refer to those that originate within the individual when inner drives, instincts, and values pull against each other.* The conflict is, basically, not with one's mate but with one's self, so that inner tensions arise because of the inner battle. As a result of these inner tensions, the individual has disagreements or gets into quarrels in situations that stimulate that tension.

Mr. M. was brought up by parents who rejected him and made him feel unwanted and unloved as a child. As a result, he became the kind of man who was afraid to show love for his wife or to let her get close to him. He needed her and wanted her attention and companionship; but whenever she tried to develop a close, loving, intimate relationship, he became anxious and fearful and would end up rejecting her or pushing her away. She was very hurt and became frustrated and angry, which, in turn, made him mad. They always ended up in a fight when they started getting close to one another. (Author's counseling notes)

Whenever any person has irrational fears, anxieties or neurotic needs, these can be the basic sources of husband-wife friction. For example, a wife who has a deep-seated fear of losing her husband becomes terrifically jealous of other women, even if her husband has only superficial contacts with them. She gets in an argument with her husband whenever she sees him talking with any member of the opposite sex.

In each of these examples, the basic cause of the conflict lies deep within the psyche of the individuals involved. Usually, the anxieties have their origins in childhood experiences and early family relationships. For this reason, troubles that arise in marriage because of these previous experiences are difficult to deal with. Permanent solutions can be found only when the internal tensions within the individual are relieved (Feldman, 1982).

Intrasomatic Sources

Intrasomatic sources *refer to inner tensions having a physical origin*. Physical fatigue is one such source. Fatigue brings irritability, emotional upset, impatience, distorted reasoning, and a low frustration tolerance. It causes people to say and do things that they wouldn't do ordinarily. Hunger and a low level of blood sugar are also potential sources of tension. A painful headache may be just as much a source of conflict as a serious disagreement. Emotional illness also is a major source of friction and arguments. Mentally ill people often behave in disruptive, bizarre ways, with the result that their marriages are often threatened (Rushing, 1979). Even emotionally healthy men and women have fluctuations of mood that influence their behavior.

Interpsychic Sources

Interpsychic sources *of conflict are those that occur in relationships between people*. All couples have marital problems, but unhappily married couples are more likely to complain of neglect and lack of love, affection, sexual satisfaction, understanding, appreciation, and companionship than are the happily married. Furthermore, their self-image is attacked; their mate magnifies their faults, makes them feel worthless, belittles their efforts, and makes false accusations. These complaints become the focus of the conflict that ensues. Lack of communication, inability to resolve differences, and withdrawal from one another also perpetuates the difficulties (Dhir and Markman, 1984).

The intimate interaction patterns and relationships between mates far outweigh other major sources of conflict. Couples begin to feel hurt, resentful, and frustrated when they are not meeting one another's sociopsychological needs. Relationships with kin, the community, or others outside the family do not affect the couples as much as their relationships with one another do. When 108 couples who had come for marriage counseling were asked what they

CLASSROOM FORUM
Mr. and Mrs. A.

Mr. and Mrs. A. are in their early forties. They came for marital therapy because of increasingly frequent destructive conflicts. These conflicts were marked by a high degree of verbal abuse (mutual blaming, insults, name calling) and, on a few occasions, physical violence (pushing, hitting, throwing objects at each other). The process of conflict initiation between Mr. and Mrs. A. was highly predictable. Mr. A. would behave in a way that his wife experienced as inattentive or neglectful — being preoccupied with his work, for example. She would complain to him about his behavior. Sometimes her complaints were delivered in a relatively nonhostile manner; at other times, they were delivered in a hostile manner. To some degree, Mr. A. experienced her complaints as assaults even when they were delivered in a nonhostile way, but this was especially so when they were delivered hostilely. He reacted with rage and verbal abuse. Mrs. A. then retaliated with an equally destructive barrage of verbal abuse, and the conflict began to escalate. After a variable period of escalation (minutes to hours) they withdrew from each other and then maintained a cold distance for a period of days to weeks. Eventually, one person would make a reconciling move, the other would respond, and they would resume a more cordial relationship until the next outbreak of conflict.

Family Background: Mr. A.'s father had never expressed overt approval of his accomplishments, including his performance as a high school basketball player. He grew up with feelings of inadequacy and a longing for approval and admiration from his father. Unconsciously, he never wanted his wife to disagree with him or to criticize him.

Mrs. A. felt very hostile toward her father for ignoring her while she was growing up and for "abandoning" her and her mother by having a long-standing extramarital affair. She unconsciously expected her husband to pay total and complete attention to her at all times.

QUESTIONS

1. In what ways were Mr. and Mrs. A. alike? How did they get that way?

2. What was Mrs. A. seeking in the marriage that she was not getting from her husband? Why was she the way she was?

3. What was Mr. A. seeking in the marriage that he was not getting from his wife? Why was he the way he was?

4. Why would Mrs. A. get so angry at her husband? What could she do instead of yelling at him and still find at least part of her needs fulfilled?

5. Why would Mr. A. get so angry at his wife? What could he do instead of getting so mad and still find at least part of his needs fulfilled?

6. When Mr. and Mrs. A. withdrew from one another and maintained a cold distance, how did this make the problem worse?

7. If you were a marriage counselor to this couple, what goals would you try to achieve to solve this problem?

Adapted from Feldman, L. B. (1982). Dysfunctional marital conflict: An integrative interpersonal-intrapsychic model. *Journal of Marital and Family Therapy, 8,* 417–426.

considered to be their basic problem in marriage, 38 percent of the husbands and 46 percent of the wives indicated they had one or more unsatisfied sociopsychological needs, such as the need for understanding, communication, love, affection, or companionship as their basic problem (McMillan, 1969).

Stressful living conditions or unexpected events that disturb family functioning affect every member of the family, not just the adult members. The more children in a family, the more strain, stress, and conflict are naturally introduced.

Research also indicates that *it is difficult to sort out cause and effect of conflict because of the interrelationship of multiple problems.* A husband's lack of sexual interest in his wife has been found to be correlated with quarreling, lack of communication, his social habits, infidelity, his wife's loneliness, and his mental health problems, and can be an indicator of his general alienation (Krupenski, Marshall, and Yule, 1970). A wife's lack of sexual interest in her husband correlates with her dislike of her husband and personal indifference, lack of communication, and her mental health difficulties. Her sexual disinterest appears as an indicator of a nervous, upset, and alienated wife who has difficulty coping in a situation of stress. Similarly, this same study showed that economic difficulties were related to all other factors (McMillan, 1969).

Every marriage counselor knows that the problems couples complain about in the beginning of counseling may be only symptoms or the focal point of conflict. The real causes of difficulties often run much deeper. Sometimes, couples themselves may not realize the basic reasons for their difficulties. These causes often are found only in the underlying psyche of the individual or in the pattern of their interpersonal relationship with one another.

Situational or Environmental Sources

Situational, societal, or environmental sources of conflict include such things as living conditions in the household, societal pressures on family members, or unexpected events that disturb family functioning. For example, the more children in a family, the more strain, stress, and conflict is introduced.

The methods of managing and resolving conflict are important to the family.

Sometimes a marital relationship remains in a state of relative equilibrium until some traumatic event occurs to disrupt the relationship. One study of couples who had lived together in basically neurotic relationships for a number of years showed that specific events could disrupt this neurotic equilibrium by interfering with the neurotic need gratification patterns of the couples. One wife seemed to get along fairly well with her husband as long as he paid a lot of attention to her by berating her for sexual affairs she had prior to marriage. When he stopped because he wanted "to treat her better than before," she had an affair with a man next door to give him new evidence of her sexual promiscuity. The wife's real motive was that she missed the attention her husband had shown through his criticism of her sexual affairs. In another case, the husband and wife started having conflict when the wife expressed a desire to stop having children after the birth of the tenth child (the same number her mother had). The husband did not wish to stop having children until after the twelfth child (McGee and Kostrubala, 1964).

In each of these instances, a specific event triggered the conflict, although the seeds of tension were already present in the relationship. Unexpected events such as unemployment, change of jobs, war, disaster, illness, an unplanned pregnancy, death, or a forced separation or move may be enough to trigger a crisis. Couples who are emotionally insecure or unstable usually have far more difficulty coping than do other couples (McCubbin, Joy, Cauble, Comeau, Patterson, and Needle, 1980). One study showed that couples who have high levels of tension between them have even more conflict when they are together because of vacations, retirement, illness, or reduced hours of employment (Rosenblatt et al., 1979).

It is not the existence of conflict per se that is important to the family, but the methods of managing and resolving the conflict (Straus, 1979). Some couples have a lot of conflict, but keep it under control, and resolve their tensions and problems. Other couples are never able to minimize tension or solve anything, and so small problems grow into very big ones.

Avoidance

Some couples try to deal with conflict through *avoidance* (Fitzpatrick, Fallis, and Vance, 1982). That is, they try to prevent conflict by avoiding persons, situations, and issues that stimulate it. The following comments illustrate avoidance techniques:

"My husband really growls when he gets up in the morning, so it's better if we don't say anything."

"My wife and I try to avoid controversial issues."

"My wife is very sensitive about her kinky hair, so I never say anything."

"If I complain about my husband's drinking, it just leads to an argument, so it's better not to say anything."

In each of these cases the couples were trying to avoid conflict.

Sometimes a person becomes too upset to think straight. In such instances, positive solutions can be found only after the intense negative feelings have subsided. Physical activity through work or recreation, distraction by going to a movie or by visiting a neighbor, or discussion with a counselor may be necessary to drain off negative feelings to the point where the individual can talk more rationally with his or her mate.

What about conflict in front of the children? Disagreements that concern the children may have to involve them, such as decisions about what time to come in at night, doing family chores, school work, appropriate dress, and others. But in these instances, children have to learn that there is a fair way and a foul way to fight, that conflict can be constructive or destructive, that there are certain rules to the game that should be observed even during times of anger. When children are small, to expose them to frequent and/or violent arguments will stimulate a great deal of fear and insecurity, and it is certainly detrimental to their mental health. Furthermore, these negative effects persist into adulthood. Young adults who had witnessed parental marital violence when they were children were significantly more anxious than were those from more harmonious households. Women who had viewed violence were also more depressed and more aggressive than were women who had not viewed violence when they were growing up (Forsstrom-Cohen and Rosenbaum, 1985).

Children growing up in an atmosphere of tension become anxious, tense, and insecure people. One study showed that the more children were exposed to family fights, the lower their self-concept was. This was as true in intact as in broken families (Raschke and Raschke, 1979).

In some instances, however, couples try to avoid discussing controversial issues even though they are important in the marriage. In these cases, keeping quiet might be counterproductive. By so doing, the couple avoids conflict, but also never solves the problem. Couples who never face important issues in their efforts to avoid controversy gradually withdraw from one another. There is a gradual disengagement and alienation where couples stop communicating and caring about one another. As a result, there is increased loneliness, less reciprocity in settling issues, a loss of intimacy, and a decline in other forms of interaction, such as sexual intercourse (Altman and Taylor, 1973).

One of the most common complaints of wives is that their husbands won't talk to them about problems. Such husbands seek to prevent conflict by avoiding issues. As a result, the wives become even more frustrated and either put pressure on in their efforts to confront their husbands with the problems, or withdraw more and more. The problems are not solved.

Ventilation and Catharsis

The opposite of avoiding conflict is to ventilate it. **Ventilation** *means draining off negative emotions and feelings so these can be replaced by more positive emotions.* This concept has been used in psychotherapy for years. It involves encouraging persons who are disturbed to talk out or to act out their feelings to get them out in the open where they can look at them, understand them, and channel them in less destructive directions. This therapeutic approach, which emphasizes the importance of leveling or letting it out, is based on the idea of **catharsis**. Catharsis theories, also called ventilation theories, assume that all persons have built into their nature a tendency toward aggression that cannot be bottled up. If they attempt to repress this tendency, it will only result in a more destructive explosion at some later time. Hence it is better to "let it out" through a series of minor explosions than to let negative feelings accumulate until they become a potential bomb. The authors of *The Intimate Enemy* state in their book that "couples who fight together are couples who stay together — provided they know how to fight properly" (Bach and Wyden, 1968). The authors go on to note that 80 percent of the couples who come to them don't fight at all; they avoid conflict. The result is emotional divorce.

In commenting on *The Intimate Enemy*, Straus writes:

> In fairness, it must be pointed out that Bach and Wyden's book makes a sharp distinction between procedures for rational conflict and what they call "kitchen sink" or "Virginia Woolf" type fighting, characterized by insults and personal attacks designed to hurt the husband or wife. However, although Bach and Wyden reject Virginia Woolf type fights, they do advocate dropping inhibitions and "outmoded notions of etiquette" — what I will call "civility" later in this paper. Their emphasis on "leveling," "honesty," "having it out," "overcoming inhibitions," and venting aggressive feelings contradicts their rejection of Virginia Woolf type fights (Straus, 1974, p. 13).

Actually, in his audiotape course on "therapeutic aggression," Bach makes much stronger statements about expressing aggression. During one group sesssion on "aggressive dating" Bach urged the women participants, "Don't be afraid to be a real shrew, a real bitch! Get rid of your pent-up hostilities! Tell them where you're really at! Let it be totally vicious, exaggerated hyperbole" (Bach, 1973). Other authors urge symbolic acts of physical aggression such as punching pillows, biting a plastic baby bottle, smashing a board. One author insists that the only way to have a vital marriage is to maintain a fairly high level of tension but without physical attacks (Charny, 1972). The emphasis is on leveling, "gut-level communication," and "letting it all hang out."

Evaluations of this approach to dealing with conflict admit that such methods have proved to be helpful psychotherapy for those with hostile feelings and emotional problems. But venting one's hostilities on the psychiatrist's couch, in the counseling center, or in other psychotherapeutic environments, and in the presence of a trained therapist, is far different from doing the same in one's own home where the hostilities are directed toward one's spouse or children. In therapy, the hostilities toward family members are given verbal expression or, in the case of children, physical expression (such as symbolically shooting baby sister with a gun) in the presence of the therapist, but not actually in the physical presence of that person. To tell a therapist, "I hate my wife" is far different from telling the wife, "I hate you." In the first instance, the hostilities have been drained off harmlessly, so that when the husband gets back home he feels less hateful; but in the second instance, even though the husband feels better, the wife feels worse and will usually retaliate in some fashion, which may result in an increase of hostile feelings between the two people. Reviews of the effects of catharsis in the family situation suggest that *almost none of the research with any pretensions to scientific rigor supports the idea of catharsis and some show the reverse; that is, opportunities to observe or give vent to anger, hostility, and violence tend to produce greater subsequent levels of aggressions and violence* (Berkowitz, 1973; Steinmetz and Straus, 1973, 1974; Tavris, 1982). The reason is that the family is an intimate, closely confined group, with members intensely involved with one another. If excessive hostility is directed at other family members, they feel angry, hurt, or misunderstood. If this reactive emotion is not dealt with, additional disagreements arise and tension mounts, sometimes to intolerable levels. Furthermore, family members can't get away from the source of friction without splitting up the family, if only temporarily.

In a revealing piece of research, Straus found a strong, positive association between the level of verbal and physical aggressions between husbands and wives. He discovered that *as the level of verbal aggression increases, the level of physical aggression accelerates even more rapidly.* Figure 17.1 shows the relationship. The facts as presented provide no evidence of the beneficial effects of "leveling," letting it out," releasing inhibitions, or expressing one's anger toward one's mate. On the contrary, the results suggest that "gut-level communication," rather than helping to avert physical aggression, is associated with physical violence (Straus, 1974). Furthermore, the more often aggression is expressed, the more often it is likely to occur in the future. The persons are learning to assume aggressive roles.

What about more intellectual, rational approaches to problem solving? Straus's evidence suggest that *families that take the calm, rational, intellectual, emotion-suppressing approach show much lower levels of physical violence.* This is even more true for working-class families than for those of middle-class socioeconomic status. This means that intellectual approaches that observe "civility" and "etiquette" in interpersonal relationships are more helpful in the long run in promoting marital harmony and stability and in resolving conflicts (Martin, Schumm, Bugaighis, Jurich, and Boleman, 1987).

FIGURE 17.1 *Relationship Between Verbal and Physical Aggression.*

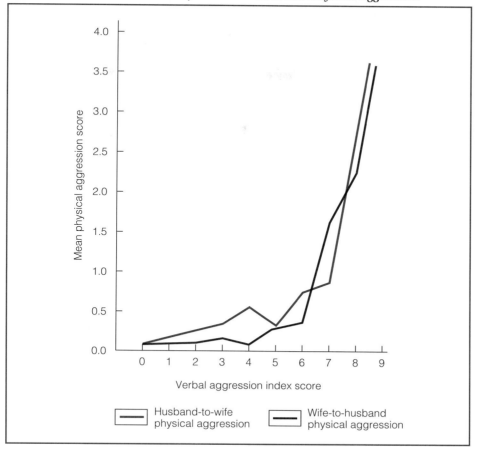

Source: Strauss, M. A. (1974). Leveling, civility, and violence in the family. *Journal of Marriage and the Family, 36,* 17. Copyrighted 1974 by the National Council on Family Relations. Reprinted by permission.

Constructive Conflicts

A distinction must be made, therefore, between conflicts that are constructive and those that are destructive (Brandt, 1982). **Constructive arguments** *are those that attack the problems, stick to the issues without being sidetracked, and lead to a more complete understanding, to consensus, compromise, or other acceptable solutions to the problem* (Gottman, Markman, and Notarius, 1977). They minimize negative emotions, build respect and confidence, and bring a couple closer together. They take place in a friendly and trusting atmosphere in a spirit of goodwill where honest disagreements may be discussed and understood and where the argument progresses according to fair rules. The following is an example of a constructive quarrel.

He (testy): The bank called and said we're overdrawn again.

She (skeptical): Gee, darling, I can't believe it. I thought we had plenty of money in our account. Have they made an error?

He: I don't know, but let me see the bank book.

She (after retrieving the checkbook from her purse): We had plenty of money in last week.

He (examining the book): Didn't you write a check for the insurance? I don't see it.

She (shocked): Oh, my gosh. I forgot to deduct the $340. No wonder we're overdrawn. I wrote another check to the oil company on top of that.

He (sighing): What am I going to do with you?

She (putting her arms around him and kissing him): Love me.

He (squeezing her hard): I do. I sure do.

While the problem in the preceding example was not a serious one, it could have resulted in a heated argument if not handled correctly. As it was, the discussion stuck to the point without bringing in extraneous issues or belittling anyone; it was conducted in a friendly, rational manner so that the wife could admit her mistake without any threat; the husband accepted her explanation — and her — and the result was a feeling and expression of closeness and love.

If couples are able to think rationally about a problem, they can take six steps toward constructive problem solving. These steps are:

1. Identification and definition of the problem
2. Collection of information about the problem
3. Production of alternative solutions
4. Deciding among alternatives
5. Taking action
6. Evaluating the action

One revealing study of 52 different families revealed the outcome of conflict among family members on 64 different occasions around the family dinner table. The study asked about who started and stopped the conflict in these families and with what result (Vuchinich, 1987). The mother, father, son, or daughter were about equal in the number of times each initiated a conflict. Conflict was stopped most often by the mother and least often by the father. Daughters stopped conflict more often than sons, indicating that women functioned as peacemakers.

Conflicts were not often resolved. Table 17.1 indicates the means by which each conflict episode was closed and the roles played by each family member. Sixty-one percent of the conflicts ended in a standoff whereby family members dropped the conflict without any resolution. In 21 percent of the conflicts, the conflict ended with one person's agreeing or going along with another (submission). In 14 percent of the conflicts, participants each gave a little and accepted a compromise. In 4 percent of the conflicts, one party withdrew by refusing to talk or by leaving the room. About a third of the conflicts were "nipped in the bud" before they started, either by accepting corrections or by ignoring challenges.

TABLE 17.1 *Conflict-Closing Formats and Family Roles*

Family Role	Submission	Compromise	Standoff	Withdrawal	Total
Mother	3	10	25	2	40 (38.1%)
Father	2	1	9	1	13 (12.4%)
Son	8	2	11	1	22 (21.0%)
Daughter	9	2	19	0	30 (28.5%)
Total	22 (21.0%)	15 (14.2%)	64 (61.0%)	4 (3.8%)	105

From: Vuchinich, W. (1987). Starting and stopping spontaneous family conflicts. *Journal of Marriage and the Family, 49,* 591–601. Copyright ©1971 by the National Council on Family Relations. Reprinted by permission.

Note: Data presented here include conflicts where mother, father, and at least two children were present.

Destructive Conflicts

Destructive arguments *are those that attack the ego of the other person rather than the problem.* They seek to shame, belittle, or punish the other person through name calling or by attacking sensitive issues in a spirit of hatred, revenge, or contempt. They are characterized by real lack of communication and by suspicion, and they often rely on interpersonal strategies that involve threat or coercion. The argument brings up many side issues, and it seeks to relieve the attacker's individual tensions at the expense of the other person. Destructive arguments increase resentment and hostility toward the other person; undermine confidence, trust, friendship, and affectionate feelings; result in loss of companionship; and engender greater alienation. The following phrases are examples of destructive ways of quarreling.

"How would you know? You never went to college. You're just a dumb slob." (labeling)

"Other husbands earn enough to pay their bills, but not you. You're too lazy." (comparison, labeling)

"You're the worst housekeeper I have ever seen." (Comparison, overgeneralization)

"Do you always have to be so obnoxious?" (sarcasm)

"I refuse to give you your dinner until you fix my vacuum cleaner." (blackmailing)

"If you don't sleep with me, then to hell with your allowance." (threat, coercion, withdrawal)

In these examples of destructive quarreling, efforts were made to shame and hurt the other person through deprecating remarks, coercion, and threats to try to force compliance. There was a great deal of distrust, contempt, and hostility revealed in the husband-wife relationships.

One of the characteristics of destructive arguments is the way they get off the track and bring in irrelevant issues. The following is a recapitulation of a family fight in the Smith domicile on a Sunday morning following a Saturday night dance. *The scene*: around the kitchen table. *The characters*: Sue and Bill Smith.

Sue (sarcastically): You were quite a ladies' man at the party last night.

Bill (casually): What do you mean?

Sue (raising her voice): Get off it. You know damned good and well what I mean. You danced with Joan half the night. I thought you'd squeeze her so hard you'd smash her boobs.

Bill (cuttingly): Well, at least she's got some to squeeze; that's more than some people I know.

Sue (starting to yell): Look who's talking, lover boy. You couldn't even make it last night could you? What's the matter, losing your zip?

Bill (angrily): Not really, you're getting so goddamn fat, you're disgusting to look at. Why in the hell don't you go see your doctor and lose some weight?

Sue (very sarcastically): Speaking of doctors, your mother says it's time for your annual checkup. Can't you even go to your doctor without mama reminding you? When are you going to grow up and do something yourself for a change? I never heard of a grown man who calls his mama every day the way you do.

Bill (stomping out of the room): You s.o.b., everytime we get into a discussion, why do you have to bring in my mother? I'm going to play golf.

Sue (yelling after him): Maybe you can score at the country club. You sure can't in bed.

Certainly, this quarrel did not solve any problems. Sue was jealous and hurt by her husband's dancing with Joan, but he did nothing to relieve her anxiety or hurt. Instead, he attacked her ego by trying to belittle her. She struck back, using destructive approaches, bringing up completely different problems. Such a quarrel only increased their misunderstanding, tensions, hostilities, and alienation in relation to one another.

VIOLENCE IN THE FAMILY

Family violence *generally refers to any rough and illegitimate use of physical force or aggression or of verbal abuse by one family member toward another.* Violence may or may not result in the physical injury of another person. Thus, a husband who throws and breaks dishes, destroys furniture, or "punches out walls" when he is angry may not injure his wife or children, but he is certainly being violent.

Family violence is not easily defined, since there are disagreements over what is a legitimate and illegitimate use of force (Dibble and Straus, 1980). There is often a discrepancy between husbands' and wifes' perceptions of family violence (Browning and Dutton, 1986; Szinovacz, 1983). Attitudes toward violence have a significant effect on whether people act violently toward a spouse or children. In our society, men are more often socialized to accept violence. Early in their lives, boys are encouraged to behave belligerently and aggressively, and to use physical force (Scher and Stevens, 1987).

Violence may or may not result in physical injury of another person. Family violence refers to any rough and illegitimate use of physical force or aggression or verbal abuse of one family member by another.

Unlike Sweden, where a parent can be imprisoned for a month for striking a child, many Americans believe that spanking children is normal and necessary and "good." In fact, a high percentage of families use corporal punishment to discipline their children (Steinmetz, 1978). This prerogative has been extended to bus drivers and school teachers in many states. Yet, many spankings verge on beatings. Some men and women believe that it is acceptable for a man to hit his wife under some circumstances (Gelles, 1980). Most wife beaters deny they have "beaten" their wives: "I just pushed her around a little bit, but I didn't really hurt her," is a common assertion, yet many of these wives are badly injured (Szinovacz, 1983). Even civil authorities hesitate to interfere in family quarrels, because of the difficulty of distinguishing between legitimate force and illegitimate violence in the family (Ford, 1983). As violence continues, however, public tolerance seems to be declining and people are demanding preventative and remedial action (Gross and Robinson, 1987).

Spouse and child abuse are more limited and specific terms, usually referring to acts of violence that have a high probability of injuring the victim. An operational definition of **child abuse**, however, may include not only physical assault that results in injury, but also malnourishment, abandonment, neglect, emotional abuse, and sexual abuse (Finkelhor and Araji, 1986; Gordon and O'Keefe, 1984; Hodson and Skeen, 1987; Martin and Walters, 1982). Sexual abuse by a relative is incest (Nelson, 1986; Stark, 1984; Vander Mey and Neff, 1984). **Wife abuse** may include not only "battering," but sexual abuse and marital rape as well (Gelles, 1980). Violence often starts during courtship and continues after marriage (Bernard, Bernard, and Bernard, 1985; Flynn, 1987; Makepeace, 1986, 1987; Roscoe and Benaske, 1985). Studies of both victims and offenders of courtship violence reveal relatively "problematic" social profiles: minority races; no religion or infrequent church attendance; very low or very high income; social stress; isolation; disrupted home; emotionally distant and harsh parenting; early dating; and school, employment, and substance abuse problems (Makepeace, 1987).

A Cycle of Violence

Studies of family violence show that individuals who have experienced violent abusive childhoods are more likely to grow up and become child and spouse abusers than are individuals who have experienced little or no violence in their childhood years (Conger, Burgess, and Barrett, 1979; O'Leary and Curely, 1986). Also, teenagers who are most exposed to violence are more likely to use violence against their parents (Peek, Fischer, Kidwell, 1985). Violence begets violence, which means it is passed on from generation to generation (Giles-Sims, 1985). One study of a national probability sample of men and women showed that men are more likely to approve of violence against women if they observed their fathers hitting their mothers (Ulbrich and Huber, 1981). Data from another nationally representative sample of 2,143 adults showed that the modeling of marital aggression did not appear to be sex specific. Observing one's father hitting one's mother increased the likelihood that sons would be victims as well as perpetrators and that daughters would be perpetrators as well as victims of severe marital aggression (Kalmuss, 1984). Some batterers have experienced abuse not only from parents, but from siblings as well (Gully, Dengerink, Pepping, and Bergstrom, 1981). The greater the frequency of violence, the greater the chance that the victims will grow up to be violent parents or partners (Gelles, 1980). Evidence indicates that both abused children and their siblings who witness the abuse exhibit severe emotional pathology: shy, gloomy, and passive dispositions (Halperin, 1981).

Factors Related to Violence

Early studies attempted to show that abusive parents suffered from *mental or emotional illness*, that the reason people abused their spouses or children was that they evidenced various psychiatric defects: psychoses, neuroses, or psychopathic problems of one kind or another. Empirical evidence shows, however, that child abusers are not necessarily emotionally ill. However, they usually are parents who exhibit *more psychological problems* than other parents do (Martin and Walters, 1982). Abusive behavior is triggered by irritating behavior that the parents neither expect nor understand. They often have *negative concepts of self*, which they project onto the child. When parents feel negative about themselves, the abuse is magnified. Once begun, abuse continues because of the parents' continuing *lack of knowledge about children and parenting* and the parents' growing contempt for themselves. Abusive parents see themselves as unworthy people and allow the abuse to continue as a method of ensuring their unworthiness (Otto and Smith, 1980).

Spouse abusers may seem to be ordinary citizens in other aspects of their lives (Steinmetz, 1978). But a positive social facade frequently conceals *disturbing personality characteristics* (Bernard and Bernard, 1984). They have been described as having Dr. Jekyll and Mr. Hyde personalities. There is evidence here, too, that they very typically have *poor self-images* that they express by being outwardly violent (Gelles, 1982; Goldstein and Rosenbaum, 1985). They also *rank higher in general aggression* than mates who do not engage in such action (Rosenbaum and O'Leary, 1981). Excessive *jealousy* and *alcohol or drug abuse* are also common (Feazell, Mayers, and Deschner, 1984).

Family violence may be related to *stress* of one kind or another. One study showed that Vietman veterans who had been exposed to combat, death, and acts of cruelty were likely to return to society with psychological problems that had a direct effect on the likelihood of divorce and heavy drinking (Laufer and Gallops, 1985). Unplanned pregnancies or premarital pregnancies cause emotional stress and strain on the limited financial resources of both the mother and father. Wives report being the victims of beatings before and after the birth of their child. Attacks during pregnancy are especially brutal, with wives being kicked or punched in the stomach.

Financial problems, unemployment, or job dissatisfaction that are perceived by husbands as incompetency in fulfilling their roles as providers are linked to child abuse and wife beating. *Social isolation* also raises the risk that severe violence will be directed at children or between spouses. Families who lack close personal friendships and who are poorly integrated into the community lack support networks during times of stress. They also feel less influenced by the social expectations of friends and family. Certainly, a battered wife is less likely to become friendly with neighbors because of embarrassment or fear of discovery, but this only compounds her problem (Steinmetz, 1978).

Domestic violence may be found among families of all socioeconomic status groups. Physical abuse between spouses is also a part of middle- and upper-class marriages. The horror stories include that of a physician who jumped on his wife's spine, causing paralysis, because she had left a door open and allowed air-conditioned air to escape; a divorce lawyer who designed a special weapon to beat his wife that would not make marks; and a space-age scientist who hit his wife in the stomach so severely that she vomited for several days (Langley and Levy, 1977). *However, abuse seems more frequent among lower-class families* (Lockhart, 1987). This may be due partly to the underrepresentation of reported violence among middle-class families, and partly to the reliance of lower-class families on social controls such as the police and social service agencies. Furthermore, lower-class women are more dependent economically on their husbands and so feel locked into an abusive relationship (Strube and Barbour, 1983, 1984). Middle- and upper-class families have many more resources to mediate stress, such as greater financial resources, greater access to contraception and abortions, greater access to medical and psychological personnel, more opportunities to utilize babysitters, nursery schools, and camps to provide relief from child-rearing responsibilities (Dibble and Straus, 1980).

There is evidence, however, that *spousal incompatibility with respect to status contributes to marital satisfaction and to violence.* Couples in which the wife's educational attainments are low relative to the husband's experience a high incidence of spousal violence. In contrast, overachievement by the woman in relation to her husband is also associated with marital dissatisfaction and a high incidence of spousal violence. Either extreme creates tensions (Hornung, McCullough, and Sugimoto, 1981).

A lot of family violence is related to *alcohol and drug abuse*. Some people never get abusive until under the influence. The question arises: Do they drink or take drugs and lose control because of the alcohol or drugs, or do they drink or take drugs to give them an excuse for their abusive behavior? Either one or both may occur.

Parent-child interaction is reciprocal, so that one affects the other. Children with certain characteristics have a greater potential for being recipients of parental abuse than do others (Watkins and Bradbard, 1982). Those who are hardest to take care of and who impose the greatest stress on the parents are most likely to be abused, as are those who are perceived to be "different." These include *premature babies* and those of *low birth weight* who are more likely to be *restless, fretful, and require intensive care*. It includes children with *physical handicaps* or those who are *mentally retarded* whose development is delayed. Couples with larger-than-average families, especially if the children are unwanted, are more likely to abuse them. If there is a *lack of emotional-attachment behavior between parents and child*, the children are more likely to be abused (Gelles, 1980).

Prevention and Intervention

There are three major treatment approaches to help child-abusing families. The *psychiatric approach* uses individual, family, and group therapy (Otto, 1984). The *sociological approach* emphasizes family planning programs, abortion services, family life education (Marion, 1982), and support services such as day-care centers, nursery schools, and homemaker services. The *social situation approach* tries to modify distressing social situations and to change interaction patterns among family members.

Crisis shelters (Berk, Newton, and Berk, 1986), transition houses, "hot line" services, police intervention teams, legal intervention, trained social service workers, family therapy services and teams (Gelles and Maynard, 1987), and many other organizations (Hughes, 1982) are involved in dealing with spouse abuse. Considerable progress has been made in treating both abused and abusive spouses, and every effort ought to be made in individual cases to get professional help for these persons (Cook and Frantz-Cook, 1984).

Authorities such as medical personnel, and the general public are being encouraged to report cases of child or spouse abuse so that intervention begins as soon as possible. The natural inclination of people "not to interfere" allows much abuse to go unreported and untreated. However, in recent years, the media have focused increasing attention on spousal and child abuse. Apparently, there have been some positive results. There was a decline in both parent-to-child violence and marital violence rates between 1975 and 1985 (Straus and Gelles, 1986).

SUMMARY

1. Communication between human beings may be defined as a message one person sends and another receives. It is accomplished both through verbal

PERSPECTIVE
Common Characteristics of Battered Women

Numerous studies of the profiles of battered women have revealed some common personality traits (Gellman, Hoffman, Jones, and Stone, 1984; Ibrahim and Herr, 1987; Wetzel and Ross, 1983).

1. Accepts traditional male and female roles and values regarding the home and family.

2. Accepts male dominance and the myth of male superiority; equates dominance with masculinity.

3. Is passive and placating; easily dominated.

4. Feels she has no basic human rights — often not even the right not to be hit. She may feel: "It's a man's right to strike his wife and children."

5. Accepts guilt even where there has been no wrongdoing: "I must have done something to deserve this."

6. Accepts her partner's view of reality and what he says.

7. Feels that she must help her mate: "This man needs me."

8. Acts as a buffer between her partner and the rest of the world. Makes excuses for him: "He was drunk when he did it."

9. Has strong needs to be needed; is emotionally and psychologically dependent on her abuser.

10. Underestimates or downplays the dangerousness of her situation. Denies her terror and her anger.

11. Has unshakable faith that things will improve: "He will change." Or, feels that there is absolutely nothing she can do about her situation.

12. Bases her feelings of self-worth on her ability to "catch" and hold a man.

13. Fears divorce and doubts her ability to make it on her own.

14. Is economically dependent on her abuser.

15. Uses sex to establish intimacy.

16. Suffers low self-esteem.

17. Doubts her own sanity.

18. Suffers from depression and severe stress reactions with psychosomatic complaints.

and nonverbal means. It is one of the most important requirements for marital satisfaction. But it can be helpful or harmful depending on how it is conducted.

2. Barriers to communication can be classified into five categories: physical and environmental, situational, cultural, sexual, and psychological.

3. The five requirements for good communication are motivation and concern, willingness to disclose oneself, the ability to transmit messages clearly, good listening, and feedback to clarify what is being transmitted.

4. Conflict is probably inevitable in every relationship. It arises from various sources: intrapsychic, intrasomatic, interpsychic, and situational or environmental.

5. There are various methods for dealing with conflict. One is avoidance. The opposite of avoidance is ventilation catharsis: letting out all feelings in an unrestrained manner. Rational, tactful, thoughtful, and considerate approaches to conflict solving work better. Conflict is constructive if it sticks to issues, generates solutions, and builds better feelings between people. Conflict is destructive if it attacks the ego rather than the problem, if the discussion gets off track and increases tension and alienation.

6. Family violence refers to any rough and illegitimate use of physical force or aggression by one family member against another. It includes both spousal abuse and child abuse.

7. Violence tends to run in cycles, with those who have been abused as children growing up to be abusers themselves. Abusers are often people with poor self-images that they project onto the abused person, whom they blame for their own problems. They typically have more psychological problems than other people and are explosive, aggressive persons, who react violently to stress. They are often social isolates without significant friendships. Alcohol and drug abuse may play an important role in violence.

8. There are three approaches to helping child-abusing families: psychiatric approaches, sociological approaches, and social situation approaches. Crisis shelters, transition houses, hot line services, police intervention, legal intervention, social services, family therapy, and aid through various organizations are all a part of the help available for abusers and their abused families.

SUGGESTED READINGS

Broderick, B. (1979). *Couples: How to Confront Problems and Maintain Loving Relationships.* New York: Simon and Schuster. Practical advice from a counselor.

Coulson, R. (1983). *Fighting Fair.* New York: Free Press. Basic principles in handling conflict.

Derlega, V. J., and Chaiken, A. L. (1975). *Sharing Intimacy: What We Reveal to Others and Why.* Englewood Cliffs: NJ: Prentice-Hall. Self-disclosure in communication.

Garbarino, J., Stocking, S. H., and associates. (1980). *Protecting Children from Abuse and Neglect.* San Francisco: Jossey-Bass. Individual and social responsibilities for children.

Gelles, R. J. (1979). *Family Violence.* Beverly Hills: Sage. Written by an outstanding authority on the subject.

Gottman, J. M., Notarius, C., Gonso, J. and Markman, J. (1976). *A Couple's Guide to Communication.* Champaign, IL: Research Press. A practical guide.

Millar, D. P., and Millar, F. E. (1982). *Messages and Myths: Understanding Interpersonal Communication.* Palo Alto: Mayfield. An academic approach.

Miller, S., Nunnally, E., and Wackman, D. (1975). *Alive and Aware: Improving Communications in Relationships.* Minneapolis, MN: Interpersonal Communications Programs. Textbook in marital communications programs. Communication skills.

Rubin, L. B. (1983). *Intimate Strangers: Men and Women Together.* New York: Harper and Row. Helpful approach.

Sager, C. J., and Hunt, B. (1979). *Intimate Partners: Hidden Patterns in Love Relationships.* New York: McGraw-Hill. Psychological approach.

Scoresby, A. L. (1977). *The Marriage Dialogue*. Reading, MA: Addison-Wesley. Elements of effective dialogue. Managing marital conflicts.

Straus, M. A., Gelles, R. J., and Steinmetz, S. K. (1980). *Behind Closed Doors: Violence in the American Family*. New York: Anchor. A definitive work by an outstanding authority.

Thorman, G. (1980). *Family Violence*. Springfield, IL: Charles C. Thomas. A helpful discussion.

Walker, L. E. (1979) *The Battered Woman*. New York: Harper and Row.

PART IV
PARENTHOOD

18

DECISIONS: PARENTHOOD AND FAMILY PLANNING

We are fortunate to live at a time when efficient and safe methods of contraception are available. Without birth control, couples would have to resign themselves to having one child after another or to avoiding sexual relations after they'd had the number of children they desired. A walk through an old cemetery reveals the difference between yesteryear and today. Dozens of tombstones contain the names of women who died at young ages from the burden of bearing one child after another. Beside them are the names of many of their children who also did not get a chance at life because of ill health.

Contraception has improved the lives of millions of people. Most importantly, it helps them to plan the number of children they want and to have them at the time that is best for all concerned.

To acquaint couples with the options available, this chapter includes an overview of contraceptive methods and their use. Final decisions about methods need to be made by couples in consultation with a physician.

An additional choice available to couples is the choice of whether to have children, and it is also discussed here.

TO PARENT OR NOT TO PARENT

The Options

One of the options that has become increasingly available to couples is the choice of whether to have children (Veevers, 1980; Whelan, 1980). This choice has become possible because adequate means of contraception are available to prevent unwanted pregnancies and because social-cultural norms relating to parenting are undergoing profound changes. While the vast majority of couples want to have children, voluntary childlessness is increasing and society is more accepting of this lifestyle.

Who Wants to Remain Childless?

A study conducted by the Census Bureau in 1980 revealed that the incidence of lifetime childlessness could reach 25 percent among women aged 25 in 1990 (Bloom and Trussell, 1983). Women who had a post–high school education were far less likely to have children than were those who had less education. Race was not a significant determinant of childlessness, but childhood residence was. Rural women were less likely to remain childless than were those growing up in nonrural areas. Other research indicates little difference in happiness in the family of origin between those who want to remain childless and those who do not. However, the childless are less traditional and sexist in their views of women (Feldman, 1981).

Surveys among youth reveal similar results: women who want to remain childless have higher social mobility goals, are less likely to want to be "housewives only," are more likely to prefer an urban residence and to expect to marry at later ages than women who want children (Kenkel, 1985). Interestingly, another survey among black and white adolescents revealed that both black and white males placed more value on having children than did their female counterparts (Thompson, 1980).

Voluntary childlessness is increasing, and society is more accepting of those who choose to remain childless. What role does level of education, race, type of community, or age at marriage have to do with the decision to remain childless?

In a June 1982 population survey, an examination of lifetime birth expectations of all women 18 to 34 years old revealed that 12 percent expected to have no children at all. Among those currently married, only 7 percent expected no children, while among single women, the figure was 21 percent (U.S. Bureau of the Census, 1983).

Smaller Families

The number of children desired is also declining. Among 18- to 24-year-olds, the average number of children desired is now 1.9. White women expect fewer births than blacks or Hispanics; women in the labor force expect fewer births than those not in the labor force; white-collar workers expect fewer children than blue-collar workers, service workers, or farm workers (U.S. Bureau of the Census, 1983).

Delayed Parenthood

The timing of birth of the first child has also been delayed (Soloway and Smith, 1987). In 1980, on average, women then aged 25 to 29 had been 24 at first birth ("Young American women delaying motherhood," 1983). Between 1970 and 1982, there was a doubling in the rate of first births to women in the 30–34 age group. This delay in parenthood may be attributed to delayed marriage, financial situations, increased pressure for women to get more education and get started in a career, and use of the time for individual development. In 1982, the largest proportion of women who had their first baby after age 30

In a recent survey, the larger proportion of women who have their first baby after age 30 were highly educated, professional women in dual career marriages.

were highly educated, professional women, in dual-career marriages (Baldwin and Nord, 1984).

The long-term effect of delaying first birth is decreasing fertility. Women who delay childbearing end up having fewer children (Wilkie, 1981). The effect on families is probably positive. Couples have more time to adjust to marriage before becoming parents. They are usually more emotionally mature, stable, and responsible. Late bearers are more settled in jobs and careers, more likely to have greater insight, own their own homes, and have more savings. They are usually better able to handle the competing demands of work and parenthood. Thus, a new stage appears to be developing: a transition stage between marriage and parenthood during which couples are free for personal development, to build a stable marriage, and to become financially secure before taking on the responsibility of children (Wilkie, 1981).

Choosing Child-Free Marriages

Couples who are voluntarily childless and those who would like to see more couples consider the possibility use some convincing arguments against having children. Problems of *overpopulation* continue to increase. Other couples frankly admit that *they don't want to accept the gamble*. One wife writes:

Something prevents us from making the final decision to go ahead. I believe this something could be called fear. For one thing, life is so good right now that we hesitate to change it in any way . . . We view children as an unknown risk. . . .

What if, in spite of our best efforts, our child turned out to have severe emotional problems, to be a drug addict or a criminal? (Michels, 1970, pp. 166, 167)

Another of the principal arguments against having children is the *restriction on freedom* that rearing children entails. Having children means readjustment of one's total life-style to take into account their needs and activities. A mother from Ann Arbor, Michigan, commented: "Suddenly I had to devote myself to the child totally. I was under the illusion that the baby was going to fit into my life, and I found that I had to switch my life and my schedule to *fit him*." It's a simple fact that *no children means no childwork and less housework*. No children means freedom for the couple to do what they please (Katz, 1972, p. 163).

There is no question that *the woman who is seeking self-fulfillment through a career of her own finds it much easier when she doesn't have children* (Faux, 1984). Movius calls voluntary childlessness "the ultimate liberation":

> Career-oriented wives may increasingly consider the child-free state as a liberating alternative. Freed from child care responsibilities, a woman who is committed to a career may benefit from greater mobility, fewer family commitments and more time for professional development. (Movius, 1976, p. 57)

As a result, women brought up to find personal fulfillment primarily through career pursuits do not often feel dissatisfied or threatened if they do not also have children (Reading and Amatea, 1986). It depends on what women are socialized to do and become.

One of the motherhood and marital myths is that married women with children are happier than women in childless couples. As shown in Chapter 11, marital satisfaction is at its lowest ebb during the child-rearing years (Schumm and Bugaighis, 1986). Furthermore, there is a rather large body of accumulating evidence that indicates that, on the average, children adversely affect marital quality (Glenn and McLanahan, 1982; Hoffman and Levant, 1985; Miller and Sollie, 1980). Couples who expect that the presence of children will solve their marital problems are in for a rude awakening. Having children usually aggravates marital tensions.

Judging from the thousands of cases of child abuse in the United States each year, large numbers of people should not become parents. *Many people have neither the interest nor the aptitude to be parents*; the resultant performance is at best marginally competent and at worst blatantly irresponsible (Veevers, 1980).

One of the arguments that people use for having children is that they don't want to be alone in their old age. There is some evidence that widows who are childless report lower well-being than those who are not (Beckman and Houser, 1982). However, *among older married women, childlessness has no significant effect on well being*. The degree of loneliness has no relationship to parent status (Kivett and Learner, 1980). Glenn and McLanahan (1981) found that having children had little impact on "global happiness" of people 50 and older. Friendships with people of the same age was far more important to

Parents of adult children are a frequent source of pressure on young couples to have children of their own, perhaps so they can become grand-parents; but while the pressures can be intense, the reasons are not always so clear.

the happiness of older adults. The researchers concluded that the decision to have children should not be based on the assumption that parenthood will lead to psychological rewards in old age.

Social Expectations

Certainly, *childless couples report that there are pressures on them to have children.* One source of pressure is from the negative attitudes that some people have toward those who are childless (Calhoun and Selby, 1980; Callan, 1985). Wives report that they are stigmatized to some extent because they do not have children. Other persons try to make them feel that they are abnormal, selfish, immoral, irresponsible, immature, unhappy, unfulfilled, or nonfeminine. Wives report that family members and friends generally accept their child-lessness for the first 12 months. Then after the first year the pressure to have a baby grows, reaching a peak during the third or fourth years. After the fifth year, the pressure diminishes; family and friends give up trying to persuade (Veevers, 1973a, b).

The Decision To Have or Not To Have Children

The decision to have children is an important one. *It is helpful if prospective mates can choose one another partially on the basis of whether they want children or not* (Callan, 1983; Oakley, 1985). However, in her study of 52 voluntarily childless couples, Veevers (1974a, 1974b, 1973b) found that only one-third of the couples had agreed *before* marriage not to have children. With the other two-thirds, remaining childless came not as an agreement ahead of time, but as a series of postponements that took place in four stages.

In the *first stage*, couples postponed having children for a definite period because of work, graduating from school, traveling, buying a house, saving a nest egg, or adjusting in marriage.

It is helpful if prospective mates choose one another partially on the basis of their desire to have children or not.

During the *second stage*, the couple remained committed to parenthood but postponed the event indefinitely because they said they "couldn't afford it now" or needed "to feel more ready," for example.

In the *third stage*, there was open acknowledgment that they might remain permanently childless, since they had already experienced many of the social, personal, and economic advantages of remaining childless.

In the *fourth stage*, the couple had made a definite decision not to have children. For some, this involved a change in attitude or a recognition that an implicit decision had already been made and that it now ought to be acknowledged openly.

Most of the couples in this study were well defended against the pressures to have children. They considered many of their friends' arguments with detached amusement and were no longer hurt or intimidated by them. Many said they told friends that they were "willing to consider adoption" and that this took the pressure off of them since others now considered that they were "normal" and "well adjusted" (Veevers, 1973b).

Couples who are married and have not yet decided whether they want children can find various types of help available (Skovholt and Thoen, 1987). Daniluk and Herman (1984) report that after participation in a 20-hour workshop on parenthood decision making, 42 percent of the female participants had made a decision regarding parenting. Those couples who search for information and thoroughly discuss alternatives before making parenthood decisions are more likely to make decisions that they really want and can live with afterward than are those couples who never really consider the alternatives (Holahan, 1983).

Ask yourself the following questions about having children:

1. Do you want children? Why or why not? Make a list of the reasons you can think of for having children. Then make a list of the reasons why you wouldn't want to have children. Which group of reasons seems more compelling?

2. How do your views of having children compare to the views of your boyfriend, girlfriend, fiance, or spouse? Do any significant differences need to be worked out?

3. Do you feel under any pressure to have children whether you want to or not? Where is this pressure coming from?

4. What do you feel is the ideal age for a woman to have children? Why do you choose this age?

5. Ideally, how many children do you feel a couple should have? Why?

6. How far apart do you feel children should be spaced? Explain the reasons for your answer.

7. How old should a man be before he becomes a father?

8. Do you approve or disapprove of the trend for women to have children at older ages? Explain.

9. How many children did your parents have? Were they happy with this number? Why or why not? Were you happy growing up with the number of brothers or sisters you had? Has this influenced your feelings about the number of children you want?

THE IMPORTANCE OF FAMILY PLANNING

Obviously, if parenthood is to become optional and childbearing is by choice, then adequate birth control measures become a necessity. There are several additional compelling reasons why **family planning** is desirable.*

Health Aspects

One is to protect the *health* of the mother and of children. Births to mothers who are too young, too old, or births that are too close together create extra health dangers to both mothers and children.

Emotional Considerations

Becoming a parent is a significant, irrevocable, and stressful event that requires preparation and considerable adjustments. *Timing* is especially

---

*Some of the material in these sections on family planning and birth control is taken from the author's book *Human Sexuality* and is used by permission of the publisher, William C. Brown Co. © Copyright 1989.

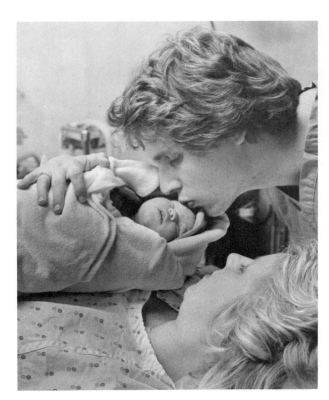

Family planning means having children by choice and not by chance. Becoming a parent is a significant, irrevocable, stressful, and joyful event that requires preparation and considerable adjustment.

important, since *when* childbirth occurs is a major determinant of the effect on individuals involved. Thus, the birth of a child to an unmarried 17-year-old may generate a personal, social, and economic crisis, whereas a planned birth to a happily married 28-year-old would certainly not have similar effects. The *psychological impact* on the mother and father are lessened considerably if parenthood is chosen and welcomed (McLaughlin and Micklin, 1983).

Effects on Marriage, Family, and Children

Family planning is necessary also for the good of the *marriage and the family*. Having children imposes strains on the marriage. Having children early in a relationship adds additional stress. Yet a majority of teenage couples have a baby within one year after marriage (Marini, 1981). Unfortunately, the younger the bride and groom, the more likely that the woman is premaritally pregnant; and brides who are pregnant have the poorest prognosis of marital success (Furstenberg, 1976). Because both premarital pregnancy and early postmarital pregnancy are followed by a higher-than-average divorce rate, large numbers of children grow up without a secure, stable family life or without both a mother and a father (Gershenson, 1983).

Not only do young couples begin having children at an early age, but they also have more children (Marini, 1981; Peabody, McKenry, and Cordero, 1981). The more they have, the greater the strain on them and their marriage (Abbott and Brody, 1985; Figley, 1973).

The Department of Agriculture estimates it costs about $5,714 per year (1987 figures) for an average middle-class family to raise a child to age 18 (Edwards, 1987). This does not include obstetric and maternity costs, babysitting and child-care costs, and the income that a mother would have earned if she had not stayed home to take care of her children. If all expenses, plus the costs of a four-year college education at a state university are included, Olson (1983) estimates total costs to raise a child born in 1980 to age 22 would be $215,000, or an average of $9,772 per year. This does not include any wages the mother might lose from not working. This represents about 23 percent of family income of $42,000 per year. Raising two children would cost 38 percent of the family income and three children 53 percent. It doesn't take much imagination to realize that having a large number of children imposes a great *strain on the family budget*.

In recent years, much emphasis has been placed on the *humanitarian and ecological importance of family planning* (Corman and Schaefer, 1973). At the present rate of population growth, which is about 2 percent per year, the world will double in population every 35 years. The world now has over 5 billion people. Can it support double that number by the year 2022? Already the world is polluted from overpopulation. Already more than half the world's people live in cities that cannot house, feed, or support them. Older cities —

PERSPECTIVE
Why Some People Don't Use Contraceptives

David A. Grimes (1984) has written an interesting article outlining some of the reasons why people fail to use contraceptives.

1. *Lack of knowledge* of the contraceptives that are currently available, of the efficiency of each, and of when and how to use them.
2. *Lack of preparedness* ahead of time. Some people think they are promiscuous if they plan to have intercourse and prepare for it.
3. *Denial*. The notion that "it won't happen to me."
4. *Lack of personal responsibility*. Unwillingness to take responsibility because of immaturity or desire to put the responsibility onto one's partner.
5. *Intentional risk taking*. Playing the "game of coital chicken" in pursuit of a not-so-cheap thrill.
6. *Guilt or hostility*, with a subconscious desire for pregnancy as a punishment of self or partner.
7. *Shame and embarrassment*. Fear that family members or others will find out.
8. *Gamesmanship*. The attempt to control a sexual relationship.
9. *Problem with sexual identity*, so that fertility is equated with sexuality and vice versa.
10. *Nihilism*. Fatalism about one's plight in life and socioeconomic status, feeling of hopelessness and helplessness.
11. *Fear* of side effects, health consequences, risks, and of loss of control of sexual drive.
12. *Lack of understanding* of the need to take prompt action, and of what to do when there has been a contraceptive omission or failure.

such as Calcutta, Delhi, Mexico City, or São Paulo — have become urban nightmares. Family planning then becomes one of the most important humanitarian problems the world faces.

HORMONAL CONTROL

Use and Action

Oral contraceptives contain two synthetically produced female sex hormones that are chemically similar to ones the woman already produces in her body. These natural hormones are estrogen and progesterone (progestogen is the artificially produced equivalent). When these two hormones are present in sufficient quantities in the woman's bloodstream, conception is prevented in three ways:

1. Ovulation is prevented in about 90 percent of the menstrual cycles.
2. When a woman takes a birth control pill, the cervical mucus remains thick and sticky throughout the month, blocking the entrance to the uterus and making penetration by the sperm difficult.
3. The pill also alters the endometrium, the inner lining of the uterus, so that successful implantation and nourishment of a possible fertilized ovum is difficult (Guttmacher, 1983).

Effectiveness

All of these effects make the birth control pill the single most effective chemical contraceptive used. Since some users are careless, however, the actual pregnancy rate for combination pills is 7 unplanned pregnancies per 1,000 women per year (Guttmacher, 1983).

Advantages

The pill is convenient and easy to use. Uneducated, low-socioeconomic-status women as well as higher-status women can take the pill reliably and faithfully. This is important, since no contraceptive is effective if it is not used.

Types and Administration

There are several types of pills. **Combination pills** contain estrogen and progestogen. The woman begins taking the pill on the fifth day of her period, counting the first day of menstruation as day one. She takes the pill for 21 days, then omits the medication for 7 days. Some brands have a different color pill, a **placebo** (sometimes containing iron), which the woman takes each day for 7 days before recommencing the 21-day regimen. Since the pill is a prescription drug, it should never be taken without a prior physical examination and a doctor's prescription and guidance.

A **morning-after pill** is seldom given because it has not been approved by the Food and Drug Administration for general use. (There are possible risks

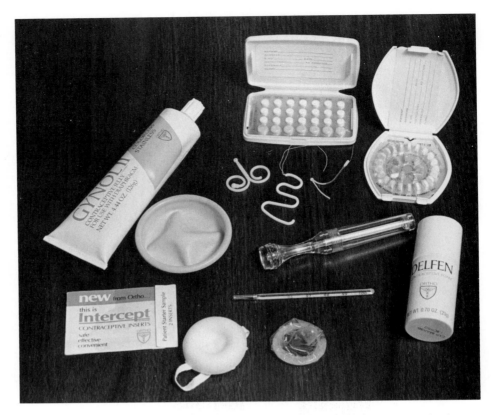

The variety of contraceptives from which to choose is considerable. How does one make the best choice? What are the risks of pregnancy, and what are the health risks associated with each type of contraception?

associated with regular use.) It is used mostly in hospital emergency rooms for rape victims and on college campuses in a few pilot programs. However, it has now been approved for general use in England ("Post-coital pills . . . ," 1984). The treatment consists of four ordinary contraceptive pills (Ovral) containing estrogen and progestogen taken over a 12-hour period. For this method of postcoital contraception to be effective, treatment must begin within 72 hours of intercourse. The patient initially takes two pills, and 12 hours later takes two more pills (Johnson, 1984). One way in which the method is believed to work is by blocking hormone receptors in the endometrium, making implantation impossible. The treatment may also act upon the corpus luteum to induce early onset of the next period; or if treatment is administered early in the cycle, the alteration in hormone levels may have an antiovulatory effect.

Another form of contraception is the **once-a-month pill**. The combination of estrogen and progestogen is rapidly absorbed by body tissues and then released slowly into the bloodstream. A monthly injection of combined hormones has been tested in Egypt, Cuba, Mexico, and Sweden; and trials showed that the injection effectively stops ovulation (Fotherby et al., 1982). Neither the injection nor the pill is yet available in the United States because authorities are not certain it is safe over a long period of time.

A newer form of pill, called the **minipill** because it contains only progestogen, is now being sold. This pill is taken daily with no break, but the small dosage does not prevent either ovulation or menstruation. Yet the likelihood of impregnation is greatly reduced by maintaining a mucous barrier in the cervix, by altering the sperm cells within the tubes, or by interfering with the passage of the egg down the tube. Minipills do produce fewer side effects. They have a one percent higher failure rate than the combination pills. They are prescribed very infrequently at the present time.

Another form of contraception is the **progestogen capsule** implanted under the skin of the forearm. The capsule can remain in place for several years, and in a five-year test in Chile no pregnancies occurred. The major side effect is an irregular menstrual cycle (Diaz, Pavez, Miranda, Robertson, Sevin, and Croxatto, 1982). The capsule is not available to the general public in the United States. A long-lasting **progestogen injection** that is needed only four times a year is *Depo-Provera*. It is used in more than 80 countries and is being considered in the United States. Authorities are hesitant because it has produced cancer in some laboratory animals (Boffey, 1983).

A number of other hormonal methods are being tested. These include IUDs (intrauterine devices) and **vaginal rings** that release progestogens, and **prostaglandin tampons** that can be inserted by the woman herself, causing early abortion ("Development of six new birth control methods . . . ," 1983).

Risk of Thromboembolism

One of the most serious worries about using the pill is the worry that it may cause blood clots (*thrombosis*). There is a marked increase in risk with age. Deaths per 100,000 users from blood-clotting diseases, including coronary thrombosis, that are attributable to the pill are 1.3 for women 20 to 29; 4.8 for women 30 to 34; 7.8 for women 35 to 39; and 46.4 for women 40 and over ("About new report on 'the pill,'" 1975). On the basis of these findings the FDA sent a warning bulletin to doctors suggesting they advise patients older than 40 to change to some other contraceptive. It was also found, however, that *the chief risk was among those older women who also smoked cigarettes*. If women who use the pill would not smoke, at least one-half of the deaths could be averted (Layde, Ory, and Schlesselman, 1982).

Risk of Cancer

Research into the full relationship of the pill to various forms of cancer is revealing. *Women who have used oral contraceptives appear to be about half as likely to develop ovarian and endometrial cancer* as are women who have never used the pill ("Women who never used pill . . . ," 1982). The protective effects of the pill against two of the most common cancers in American women appear to be long-lasting.

What about breast cancer? This is of particular concern since it is a leading cause of cancer death in women. In general, it may be said that *the pill itself does not seem to increase a woman's risk of getting breast cancer* (Lincoln, 1984; "Pill does not increase risk . . . ," 1982). Scientists seek to sort out different variables. But all that can be said now is that no certain cause and effect relationships have been established between the pill and breast cancer (Lincoln, 1984). Nevertheless, all women, users or not, are urged to get annual breast examinations.

There does not seem to be any overall increase in the risk of cervical cancer among pill users, but there is an increased risk among long-term users, especially women who initiate sex early and have multiple sex partners (Lincoln, 1984). It is difficult to sort out variables. Those women who have had sex longest and the most frequently and with the most partners show increased risk. But it has also been shown that pill users have intercourse more frequently than those who don't use the pill, so which is the cause of cervical cancer: the pill or sexual activity? This is why it is necessary for researchers to consider the sexual histories of the women in their research population (Lincoln, 1984). Doctors still recommend that women receive annual examinations, including Pap smears, to help detect cervical cancer.

Sexual Drive and Frequency of Intercourse

The effect of taking the pill on sexual drive and frequency of intercourse is variable. There seems to be some evidence that long-term usage of the pill may decrease sexual drive. Masters and Johnson (1967) report a reduction in women's sex drive after taking the pill for 18 to 36 months. They suggest that other methods be substituted from time to time to give the woman's system a chance to restore its hormonal balance. However, there are some women who report increased sexual drive while on the pill.

Overall, the frequency of sexual relations of women on the pill seems to increase, because the fear of pregnancy is alleviated and the mechanical unpleasantness of other birth control methods is eliminated.

Fertility

One of the questions that arises is the effect of the pill on subsequent fertility after the patient stops taking it. *Generally, the woman reverts back to her pre-pill condition.* A minority of women who have been on the pill become more fertile after ceasing to take it, usually because of more regular menstruation and ovulation.

Other Side Effects

Other side effects of the pill are variable, differing with different persons and with different brand names of the pill. Many of the unpleasant effects disappear after a patient becomes adjusted to the pill or after the doctor adjusts brands or dosage.

Positive Effects

There are some noncontraceptive health benefits in taking oral contraceptives. Too often these beneficial effects have been ignored, especially by the media, which seem to emphasize the negative. Eight health problems may be prevented by oral contraceptive use. For five of these, the pill's positive effects are well documented; for the other three, further confirmation is needed. The five health problems are (Ory, 1982):

Benign breast disease. Oral contraceptives reduce benign breast disease. The longer the pill is used, the lower the incidence of the disease.

Cysts of the ovary. The combination pills suppress ovarian activity and reduce ovarian cysts.

Iron-deficiency anemia. Oral contraceptive users suffer approximately 45 percent less iron-deficiency anemia than do nonusers.

Pelvic inflammatory disease (PID). Pill users have only half the risk of developing pelvic inflammatory disease. When the pill is used for one year or longer, the reduction is 70 percent.

Ectopic pregnancy. Current users of oral contraceptives have nearly complete protection against this condition.

The three other problems that the pill offers protection against, but with less substantiating evidence are:

Rheumatoid arthritis. Pill users are only one-half as likely to develop this condition.

Endometrial cancer. Users of combination pills have about one-half the risk as nonusers.

Ovarian cancer. Pill users have about one-half the incidence of this as nonusers.

Conclusions

Overall, if women are under 35, don't smoke, and are in good health, they can use oral contraceptives with only a very small risk. They may also derive some positive benefits. The pill prevents 50,000 hospitalizations annually in the United States, not counting the hundreds of thousands of pregnancies it prevents (Ory, 1982).

CHEMICALS AND SPERMICIDES

Foams, Creams, Jellies

Contraceptive foams, suppositories, creams, or jellies are chemicals that are used to prevent conception. *They work in two ways: by blocking the entrance to the uterus and by immobilizing the sperm.* To be most effective, they are inserted in the very back of the vagina, over the cervix, and not more than 5 to 15 minutes before ejaculation (see Figure 18.1) Additional applications must be made each time intercourse is repeated. Foam that comes in an aerosol can is the most effective of the four types since it spreads more evenly and blocks the cervix more adequately than the other types. It has a failure rate during one year of 22 percent (Hatcher, Stewart, Guest, Schwartz, and Jones, 1980). Some women can't use chemicals because of burning and other adverse reactions. Urinary tract infections also become a problem for some women.

FIGURE 18.1 *Insertion of Spermicidal Preparation with a Plastic Applicator.*

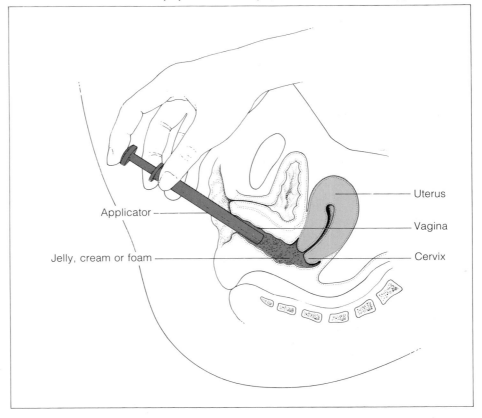

Insert the spermicide at the very back of the vagina so as to cover the opening to the cervix.

Douching

Douching is used to try to flush sperm from the vagina. At best, it is not a very effective means of contraception since (1) the sperm may already have entered the cervix or (2) the jet of water may push them up into it. Douching has one of the highest rates of failure of any contraceptive technique (Guttmacher, 1983).

MECHANICAL DEVICES

IUD

The **IUD**, or intrauterine device, is usually made of plastic, but sometimes of metal, and is placed in the uterus to prevent pregnancy. It comes in various sizes and shapes: coils, rings, loops, bow, double S., T-shape, springs, and others. The IUD must be inserted by a physician. He or she loads an inserter with an IUD and threads the device through the cervical canal and into the uterine cavity. The IUD is "unwound" into a straight line while in the inserter but resumes its former shape when released in the uterus (Guttmacher, 1983).

In September 1985, the Ortho Pharmaceutical Corporation stopped manufacturing and marketing its Lippes Loop; and in January 1986, G. D. Searle stopped U.S. distribution of its two IUDs, the copper-bearing Cu-7 and TCu 200. Together, these IUDs accounted for almost all of these devices sold in this country. Only one IUD, the hormone-releasing Profestasert, is currently available; but this accounted for only three percent of total sales of all IUDs when all were available. The companies withdrew their devices from the market because of financial risk posed by lawsuits against the companies. The high cost of defending liability suits and of insurance made continuing manufacture of the IUDs unfeasible (Forrest, 1986).

Condom

The **condom** or "safe" is usually made of thin, strong latex rubber or, less frequently, of animal gut and is inserted over the end of the penis and then unrolled to enclose the penile shaft. Condoms come in different styles (and now even in different colors). Some have a teat on the end to receive the ejaculate. If the condom doesn't have this feature, it can be unrolled on the penis so as to leave a half-inch space or overlap at the end to receive the semen. One of the latest styles has an adhesive to seal the top of the condom to the penis, thus preventing leakage of semen. Other models come packaged singly in fluid, which provides lubrication and allows the penis to be inserted into the vagina easily. If a condom is not lubricated, a contraceptive jelly or cream may be used to aid intromission and to prevent the condom from tearing on insertion.

The failure rate of condoms as a contraceptive has been calculated at about 10 percent (Hatcher et al., 1980). When failure occurs, it is due to one or more of several reasons: the condom has a hole in it; it ruptures; or it slips off. Users are urged to hold onto the top of the condom when the penis is withdrawn to prevent leakage or the condom's slipping off. When used together with a spermicidal foam, jelly, or cream, the contraceptive efficiency of the condom is increased and the spermicide is damaging to a possible AIDS virus.

Condoms have been widely promoted as the best method, except abstinence, of preventing the spread of sexually transmitted disease. But *a U.S. government inspection program conducted in 1987 has revealed that one of every five batches of condoms failed to meet minimum standards for leaks* (Parachini, 1987). Eleven of 106 batches of American-made and 30 of 98 imported condoms flunked the test. To add to the uncertainty, some of the imports are repackaged and sold under U.S. labels.

Government officials and others were shocked at these results. In addition, it was found that lambskin condoms, often preferred by gays, allow the leakage of AIDS, herpes, and hepatitis B viruses through the membrane itself. Syphilis and gonorrhea bacteria are too large to pass through. Latex rubber, however, does not allow leakage of small virus organisms unless it is torn or improperly used.

Despite the AIDS scare, there are still no mandatory manufacturing quality requirements for condoms. Dr. Gerald Bernstein, who is working on a government-funded condom evaluation, says, "Using condoms is not what people are talking about when they say 'safe sex.' It may be safer sex, but I think it's a misnomer to say condoms are 'safe' sex" (Parachini, 1987).

The **diaphragm** is a thick rubber latex dome-shaped cap stretched over a collapsible metal ring, designed to cover the mouth of the cervix. It comes in a variety of sizes and must be fitted by the physician to each woman. A snug fit is especially important, since its effectiveness as a contraceptive depends on its forming an impenetrable shield over the entrance to the uterus (see Figure 18.2). If the fit is not right, the sperm can get around the edges of the diaphragm and enter the cervix. For this reason, the largest diaphragm a woman can wear comfortably is advised, since under sexual excitement the back portion of the vagina enlarges (Masters and Johnson, 1966). After childbirth, a woman always requires a larger size diaphragm. Also, a size change may be in order whenever a woman gains or loses 15 pounds. To add to its effectiveness, about a spoonful of spermicidal cream or jelly is smeared in the cup fitting against the cervix and about the rim to create a protective seal. For additional protection, foam should be inserted into the vagina after the diaphragm is in place and before each act of intercourse (Tyrer, 1984). When fitted and placed correctly, and when a spermicide is used, the failure rate is only 3 percent. Overall, however, the actual failure rate over a period of one year is 17 percent (due primarily to incorrect placement). The diaphragm should not be removed until at least six hours after intercourse.

Vaginal Sponge

In 1983, the U.S. Food and Drug Administration approved a disposable **vaginal sponge** as a nonprescription contraceptive (Kafka and Gold, 1983). The sponge is approximately two inches in diameter, is made of a soft polyurethane foam saturated with the same spermicide used in most creams, jellies, and foams. It may be worn for up to 24 hours and may be used for more than one act of intercourse without requiring additional applications of spermicide. It is less messy than creams, jellies, and foams and is easier to insert and remove than the diaphragm. Before insertion, the sponge is moistened with water to activate the spermicide. *It prevents conception in three ways: it releases the spermicide, blocks the cervix, and absorbs the sperm.* It must be left in place for at least six hours after coitus and may not be reused. The 12-month pregnancy rates are slightly higher than those of the diaphragm. The use of the sponge during menstruation is not recommended by the FDA (Kafka and Gold, 1983). It is advisable not to leave it in place for longer than 24 hours.

STERILIZATION

An estimated 100 million couples worldwide have chosen **sterilization** as their means of birth control; this is about twice as many as have chosen the pill (Johnson, 1983). An estimated 1.1 million sterilizations (455,000 male and 622,000 female) were performed in the U.S. during 1983 ("Sterilizations exceed one million in 1983").

Vasectomy

Male sterilization or **vasectomy** has become increasingly popular as a means of birth control. It is a simple operation, requires only 15 to 30 minutes in the

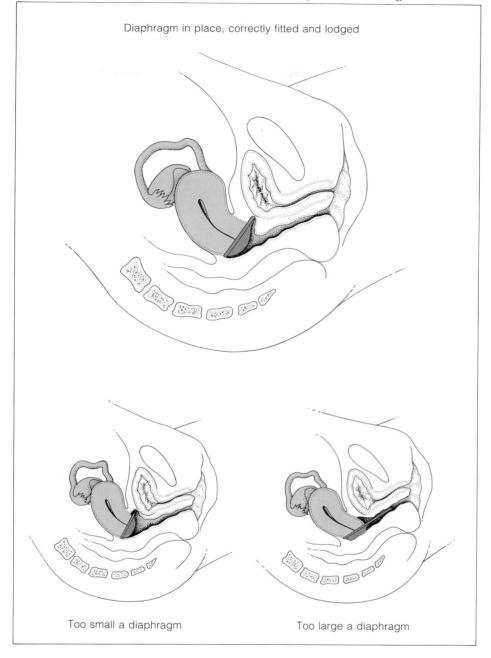

Diaphragm in place, correctly fitted and lodged

Too small a diaphragm

Too large a diaphragm

doctor's office, is relatively inexpensive, and is effective in 99 percent of the cases. It involves either cutting and tying or cauterizing the vas deferens ("Electro-cautery . . . ," 1984). When failure occurs, it is due to a spontaneous rejoining of the two severed ends of the vas deferens, to a failure on the part of the doctor to tie an accessory vas (some men have three or four), or to intercourse without using other contraceptives while there are still residual sperm in the tubes. Occasionally, an apparent failure has been due to infidelity on the part of the wife rather than the failure of the surgical technique.

There are a number of misconceptions regarding vasectomies. A vasectomy does not involve **castration**, which is the removal of the testicles. In vasectomy, the man continues to ejaculate semen, but it contains no sperm. His physical ability to have sexual relations is not in any way affected. He still has erection, orgasm, and ejaculation as usual. His masculinity is in no way affected; his voice, body hair, musculature, beard growth, and so on remain unchanged. Male hormones are still produced and released by the testicles into the bloodstream as usual (Fleishman and Dixon, 1973).

The latest research indicates no adverse health consequences of vasectomy ("Study of some 20,000 men . . . ," 1984). Vasectomy should be considered permanent, since the chances of rejoining the vas through surgery (vasovasostomy) are unpredictable. Experiments are being conducted in inserting various obstructions into the tubes, which can later be removed to allow the sperm to pass once again. One clinic is experimenting with a screw valve that can be turned on or off by the physician (Guttmacher, 1983). An overwhelming majority of males who have vasectomies report they are glad they did and would recommend it to their friends.

Salpingectomy

Salpingectomy, or **tubal ligation**, is female sterilization by severing and/or closing the fallopian tubes so that mature egg cells and sperm cannot pass through the tube. Since the ovaries and the secretion of female hormones are in no way disturbed, there is no change in the woman's femininity, physique, menstrual cycle, sexual interest, or sexual capacity ("Menstrual changes . . . ," 1984; "Most women find . . . ," 1984). In most cases, her interest in sex and her sexual responsiveness improve because the fear of unwanted pregnancy has been removed. Hypothetically, salpingectomy is reversible in 50 to 66 percent of the cases; but it is not easily accomplished, since it requires a second major operation. Most women who request reversal were sterilized young and subsequently divorced and remarried ("Requests . . . ," 1984).

The most widely used method of tubal ligation is **laparoscopy** (Johnson, 1982). With this method, the physician introduces a tubular instrument through the abdominal wall, usually through the navel, and closes the fallopian tubes with *tubal rings* or a *spring-locked clip*, or through *electrocoagulation* ("For safety . . . ," 1983). This method is successful and is far simpler than older methods since the woman can leave the hospital the day of the operation or the following morning; there are no cosmetic scars remaining. (Bean, Clark, Swicegood, and Williams, 1983).

Existing literature indicates that approximately 2.5 women out of every 1,000 will get pregnant after the operation. When pregnancy occurs it is due to one of three reasons: (1) the woman had an undetected pregnancy at the time of the operation, (2) improper surgery, and (3) the tubes reopen as a result of the body's healing process (Grimes, 1984; Johnson, 1982).

The Rhythm Method

The **rhythm method** of birth control relies upon timing coitus so that it occurs only during the so-called "safe period" of the month, that period when the woman is most likely to be infertile. Although authorities differ in their time estimates, one can say with fair certainty that the ovum can be fertilized no longer than 48 hours after it is released and that the sperm can fertilize an ovum no longer than 48 hours after being ejaculated (McCary and McCary, 1982). However, to be cautious one should add an extra 24 hours to these figures. The average woman ovulates 14 days before her next menstrual period, with a common range of 12 to 16 days. A few women ovulate regularly outside this common range, other women occasionally. Some have very irregular ovulation. Ovulation has been known to occur on any day of the cycle, even during menstruation itself. It is suspected that women may occasionally ovulate twice during a cycle—perhaps because of the stimulus of sexual excitement itself. While not completely substantiated in humans, coitus-induced ovulation is a distinct possibility (Clark and Zarrow, 1971). For these reasons, *there really is no completely "safe period" of the month when a woman can't get pregnant.*

Careful attention to one's individual cycle, by whatever means, can only minimize the possibility of pregnancy. Figure 18.3 illustrates schedules of fertile and infertile periods on a regular 26- and on a 31-day cycle and the schedule of a woman whose cycle is irregular from 26 to 31 days. Since the woman who is irregular on a 26- to 31-day cycle never knows exactly when ovulation occurs, nor when her next period will be, she is safer to abstain for 15 days instead of the usual 10. A woman whose cycle is irregular from 24 to 33 days can never find any "safe" period except during menstruation. Of course, these are only statistical calculations. As has been mentioned, one can't really be sure of any infertile period during any cycle. For this reason, the average failure rate is 30 percent (Westoff and Westoff, 1971). As can be seen from Figure 18.3, possible times for intercourse are severely limited, especially on the irregular cycle.

There are, however, two principal methods by which couples can improve upon the rhythm method (Klaus, 1984). One is the *basal body temperature method*. The method relies on the fact that body temperature rises a fraction of a degree at the time of ovulation and remains higher for the rest of the cycle. The woman records her temperature daily, looking for the rise. However, such a temperature rise can occur 72 hours prior to ovulation and as long as 72 hours afterward. It is not specific in pinpointing ovulation, but it indicates that ovulation is in process and that by the third sustained day of the rise it is in fact complete.

The *ovulation method* (also called the *cervical mucus method*) relies on cervical mucus as the predictor of ovulation. Sometime before the middle of the menstrual cycle, cervical mucus becomes detectable at the vulva when follicular estrogen rises. At this point, the mucus is sticky and gummy and appears yellow or white. With progressive ripening of the follicle, the mucus becomes increasingly slippery, clear, and stringy, like raw egg white. The vagina becomes increasingly lubricated. The last day of lubrication is called "peak" and is followed in no more than 24 hours by ovulation. Abstinence is required

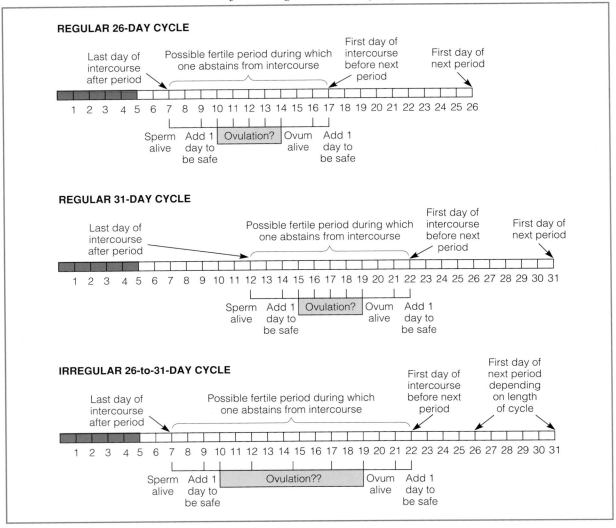

FIGURE 18.3 Fertile and Infertile Periods During a 26-Day, 31-Day, and Irregular (26-31 Day) Cycle.

from the first day of mucus discharge until the fourth day after peak (Klaus, 1984). There are also a number of ovulation predictor kits on the market that attempt to pinpoint the time of ovulation.

Coitus Interruptus

Coitus interruptus refers to the practice of withdrawing the penis from the vagina before ejaculation occurs. While this method is better than nothing, its success depends upon a high degree of self-control on the part of the man. Under sexual excitement, the normal man reaches a point beyond which ejaculatory control is impossible (Masters and Johnson, 1970). If he doesn't withdraw in time, he will ejaculate whether he wants to or not. Also, before orgasm, the male discharges a small amount of lubrication fluid that has been secreted by the Cowper's glands. The male is not aware of when this pre-ejaculate is discharged; and since it often contains sperm cells that have been residing in the urethra, the sperm may be deposited before the man withdraws. While the sperm count is low and fertilization is less likely than in actual orgasm, it can occur. Depending upon the care and timing of the man, withdrawal has a high failure rate. The greatest disadvantage to coitus interruptus is its interference with sexual satisfaction and pleasure of both the man and woman.

Noncoital Stimulation

Couples can use techniques of stimulation to orgasm other than intercourse. *Mutual masturbation* has been used for years as a substitute for intercourse. If the man gets semen on his fingers and introduces sperm into the vaginal canal, however, conception can happen (McCary and McCary, 1982). *Interfemoral stimulation* is a method whereby the man places his penis between the woman's closed thighs and rubs back and forth along the length of the clitoris. Climax may be reached in this way, but if the male ejaculates near the vaginal opening, there is a possibility the sperm may find their way inside. *Oral-genital stimulation* is sometimes used, not only as a method of precoital love play but also as a technique of arousal to orgasm.

WHICH METHOD?

To be ideal, a contraceptive would be (1) 100 percent effective, (2) inexpensive, (3) convenient to use without any fuss or bother and without interfering with lovemaking, and (4) without any risk or adverse side effects. As of now, no one method is ideal. In deciding on a method, couples might consult their physician, weigh all factors, and make a choice based upon information that is as complete as possible.

One interesting question is what contraceptive methods are currently in use among women in the United States. The National Center for Health Statistics (NCHS) collected nationally representative data on contraceptive practices among women 15–44 years of age. The data were collected between August 1982 and February 1983 and included currently married, never married, and widowed, separated, or divorced women. The results of the survey are shown in Table 18.1.

Overall, it was found that pill use had declined sharply among married women when compared with frequency of use from earlier surveys. At the same time, prevalence of female contraceptive sterilization rose sharply, especially among wives 35 and older. There was also a slight increase in the use of barrier methods — the condom and diaphragm in particular — among married women.

Contraceptive status and method of choice of never-married and previously married women differed sharply from those of wives. Sexually active never-married women were less likely than married to practice contraception and were more likely to choose the pill when they did. Later figures would probably reveal an increase in condom use because of fear of AIDS. Previously

TABLE 18.1 *Number and Percentage Distribution of Women Aged 15–44 Practicing Contraception, by Current Method, According to Marital Status, 1982*

Method	Total	Never married	Currently married	Widowed, divorced or separated
No. of users (thousands)	29,498	6,727	19,187	3,584
% distribution				
Sterilization	32.7	5.0	41.0	40.5
Female	21.9	3.3	25.6	37.0
Male	10.8	1.8*	15.4	3.5*
Pill	28.6	53.2	19.8	29.5
IUD	7.3	5.5	7.1	12.0
Barrier	22.9	26.4	24.0	10.5
Diaphragm	8.3	13.5	6.7	6.9*
Condom	12.2	11.7	14.4	1.6*
Foam	2.4	1.2*	2.9	2.0*
Periodic abstinence	4.0	2.5*	4.7	2.5*
Withdrawal	2.0	3.4	1.7*	0.6*
Douche	0.2	0.3*	0.2*	0.2*
Other	2.3	3.7	1.5*	4.3*
Total	100.0	100.0	100.0	100.0

From Bachrach, C.A. (1984). Contraceptive practice among American women, 1973–1982. *Family Planning Perspectives, 16*, November/December, 255–259. Copyright © The Alan Guttmacher Institute.
*Denotes percentages with relative standard errors of 0.30 or more.

married women were also less likely than wives to practice contraception but, when using a method, were more likely than either never-married or currently married users to depend on one of the more effective methods — sterilization, the pill, or IUD.

ABORTION

Need for Understanding

If contraceptives are not used or a given method fails, then a woman or a couple is faced with the issue of an unplanned pregnancy and needs to decide what should be done. One of the alternatives is **abortion**. Abortion raises some difficult questions to which there are no simple answers. Abortion issues may be divided into five categories, which are discussed in the following sections: legal, physical and medical, moral, social and realistic, and psychological and personal considerations.

Legal Considerations

On January 22, 1973, the United States Supreme Court ruled that *a state could not inhibit or restrict a woman's right to attain an abortion during the first trimester*

PERSPECTIVE
Mistakes People Make with Contraceptives

The following are some of the common errors in using various contraceptives.

THE PILL

1. Forgetting to take the pill for one or more days
2. Taking the pill only at the time of intercourse
3. Running out of pills, being unable to fill prescription
4. Taking the wrong pills on particular days
5. Discontinuation because of side effects such as withdrawal bleeding

IUD

1. Failure to detect expulsion
2. Confusing the pain from PID with pain caused by the IUD itself
3. Failure to notify physician if pregnancy occurs so that the IUD can be removed

CONDOMS

1. Using deteriorated condoms
2. Failure to put them on soon enough
3. Failure to withdraw soon enough after ejaculation so that penis becomes flaccid and condom slips off
4. Reusing a soiled condom
5. Using petroleum jelly, which deteriorates rubber, as a lubricant

DIAPHRAGM

1. Improper fit
2. Improper insertion
3. Removal too soon after coitus; if additional spermicidal jelly is desired, removal of diaphragm to put more in
4. Use of wrong kind of jelly (grape jelly or other nonspermicidal jelly)

SPERMICIDES

1. Wrong application or insertion. For example, taking a spermicidal suppository orally, or failure to remove wrapper from suppository before insertion, or insertion in wrong body orifice.
2. Confusing feminine hygiene suppositories and spermicidal suppositories.
3. Impatience; not waiting long enough for suppository to melt (Grimes, 1984).

of pregnancy (first 12 weeks) and that the decision to have an abortion was the woman's own in consultation with her doctor (*Doe v. Bolton*, 1973; *New York Times*, 1973; *Roe v. Wade*, 1973; Sarvis and Rodman, 1974). The major ground for the court's decision was the woman's *right to privacy*.

The court further declared that *during the second trimester of pregnancy (13 to 26 weeks) — when abortion is more dangerous — "a state may regulate the abortion procedure to the extent that the regulation relates to the preservation and protection of maternal health"* (*Roe v. Wade*, 1973). Reasonable regulation might include such things as outlining the qualifications or licensure of the person who performs abortions or the licensing of the facility where the abortion is performed. The court went on to say that the state's interest in protecting the life of the fetus arises only after viability (after 24 to 28 weeks, when the fetus is potentially capable of living outside the mother's womb). However, the state "may go so far as to proscribe (forbid) abortion during that period except when it is necessary to preserve the life or health of the mother" (Reed, 1975, p. 205). The reasons the court rejected the state's interest in protecting human life from the moment of conception were (1) that the "unborn have never been recognized in the law as persons in the whole sense," (2) that the rights extended to the unborn, in law, are contingent upon live birth, and therefore, (3) a state's interest in protecting fetal life cannot override the woman's right to privacy (Sarvis and Rodman, 1974).

In the meantime, *Congress passed the Hyde Amendment sharply restricting the use of federal Medicaid funding to pay for abortions for low-income women.* This ban on federal funding of abortions has been renewed every year since (Henshaw and Wallison, 1984). *The Supreme Court has also ruled that a state may require an unmarried minor who seeks an abortion to notify or obtain consent of her parents; if she does not wish to do so, she must be able to obtain permission from a judge* (Donovan, 1983). The judge's authorization is to be based on a determination either that the minor is mature enough to make her own decision or that it is in the minor's best interest to have the abortion without informing her parents.

This decision, which took effect in July 1982, has had wide-ranging implications. Ideally, all unmarried minors would get parental advice about their pregnancies. But *it is precisely because of the lack of good family relationships that minors refuse to talk to parents.* Agencies in three states report that 20–55 percent of their minor patients are going to court rather than confiding in their parents (Donovan, 1983). This puts these minors through an emotionally difficult and sometimes traumatic experience.

In January 1989, the United States Supreme Court agreed to hear a case brought to it by the state of Missouri (*Webster et al. v. Reproductive Health Services et al.*, 1989). The court was asked to rule on four sections of the Missouri act:

1. A preamble to the act which stated that "the life of each human begins at conception" and that state laws be interpreted to provide unborn children "with all the rights, privileges, and immunities available to other persons, citizens, and residents of this state" subject to the Constitution and the Court's precedents (*Webster et al. v. Reproductive Health Services et al.*, 1989).

2. A prohibition on the use of public facilities or employees to perform abortions.

3. A prohibition on public funding of abortion counseling.

4. A requirement that physicians conduct viability tests prior to performing abortions (Rehnquist, 1989).

In a 5–4 decision announced on July 3, 1989, the court upheld the constitutionality of sections 2 and 4 of the Missouri act and returned to the states the right to enact restrictions on abortion. The court refused to pass on the constitutionality of the preamble and contended that it represented only a value judgment of the state of Missouri which did not restrict abortions in any way (Rehnquist, 1989).

According to the findings of the U.S. Supreme Court, public hospitals or other taxpayer-supported facilities may not be "used for the purpose of performing or assisting an abortion not necessary to save the life of the mother" and "it shall be unlawful for any public employee within the scope of his employment to perform or assist an abortion, not necessary to save the life of the mother." This latter finding is not intended to direct the conduct of any physician or health care provider, private or public, but "is directed solely at those persons responsible for expending public funds" (Rehnquist, 1989). The finding did not declare illegal, as such, the performance of abortions in privately-supported facilities by physicians who are paid privately. However, critics do point out that the decision severely restricts the availability of abortions to the poor.

One of the most controversial parts of the decision is the overthrow of the trimester provisions of Roe v. Wade and the substitution of medical tests for viability. According to the findings of the court, medical tests must be performed on any fetus thought to be at least 20 weeks old to determine its viability before an abortion can be performed. The court reaffirmed the provision in Roe v. Wade that states may pass laws regulating or proscribing abortion after viability "except where it is necessary . . . for the preservation of the life or health of the mother" (Rehnquist, 1989).

This decision has been criticized because, according to some, determination of viability is expensive, sometimes unreliable and inaccurate, and may impose significant health risks for both the pregnant woman and the fetus. Various tests can be made to find gestational age, fetal weight, and lung maturity. As a result of the tests, viability is determined by the judgment of the responsible attending physician. In defending its position, the majority of the court said: "We are satisfied that the requirement of these tests permissibly furthers the State's interest in protecting potential human life" (Rehnquist, 1989).

Both Right to Choose and Right to Life advocates predict that the court's decision will lead to a 50-state battle to determine whether additional restrictions will be enacted. Faye Wattleton, president of the Planned Parenthood Federation of America commented: "Now a woman's access to abortion will become hostage to geography as states enact a patchwork of laws and regulations aimed at blocking abortions" (Dionne, 1989, p. 1). Archbishop John May, president of the National Conference of Catholic Bishops, observed: "The biggest winners today are the tiniest people of all — children within the womb" (Dionne, 1989, p. 1).

The U.S. Supreme court has already agreed to hear three more cases: two that concern the rights of teenagers to obtain abortions without parental involvement in Ohio and Minnesota and a third case from Illinois that requires abortion clinics performing abortions in the first three months of pregnancy to meet standards similar to those required for operating rooms in full-care hospitals (Greenhouse, 1989). The stage is set for further battles.

Physical and Medical Considerations

Certainly, from every viewpoint *if a pregnancy is to be terminated, it should be terminated as soon after conception as possible.* This is of special necessity from a biological and medical point of view. Many physicians and hospitals refuse to give abortions to women who are more than 12 weeks pregnant ("After a conviction," 1975).

What are the possible aftereffects of abortion on the mother's health and future childbearing? Overall, *induced abortion is safer for women than childbirth itself* ("Researchers confirm . . . ," 1982). *In general, abortion doesn't impair the ability of women to become pregnant again* ("Abortion doesn't impair . . . ," 1985).

Moral Considerations

Much of the controversy about abortion has centered on the moral issues involved. For many individuals and churches, *abortion is wrong because it represents the murder of a human being* (Adamek, 1974). This point of view holds that the soul enters the body at the moment of conception so that the new life is immediately a human. The Christian church in the first centuries after Christ forbade abortion under all conditions from the beginning of pregnancy.

Opponents of this view argue that to say that a group of human cells, however highly differentiated at the early stage of growth, is a person is to stretch the point. There is neither consciousness, nor any distinctly human characteristics and traits. Advocates of this view point to the teachings of the thirteenth-century church father, Thomas Aquinas, who said that there was neither life nor ensoulment until the fetus moved and, therefore, abortion was not sinful in the first 16 weeks of pregnancy. This view lasted for three centuries following Aquinas; then the church fixed ensoulment at 40 days after conception, following Aristotle's teaching. Abortion during the first forty days of pregnancy was not considered sinful until the Council of Trent in 1869, when it was once more ruled that life begins at the time of conception and that abortion at any time is a grave sin. This view was reaffirmed by the Second Vatican Council and made official Catholic doctrine by Pope Paul in December 1965 (Mace, 1972a). In recent times, Protestant thought has become more liberal, permitting abortion under certain circumstances.

Members of the *right-to-life movement and others emphasize the rights of the unborn child.* They emphasize the right to life of the fetus and say that no individual or state should deprive the fetus of its constitutional and moral right to live (Sarvis and Rodman, 1974). Legally, of course, the Supreme Court has never established the fact that the fetus is a person, enjoying full protection under the Constitution and the Bill of Rights. *Right-to-choose proponents emphasize that the moral and legal rights of other parties must also be considered,* not just those of the fetus (Mace, 1972). What about the rights of the mother, the father, other family members (Finlay, 1981)? Should these lives be sacrificed for the sake of the fetus?

The Supreme Court ruling establishes the legal principle that the mother's right takes precedence, at least before viability. It is obvious that the moral dilemmas raised by the abortion issue are not easy to solve (Allgeier, Allgeier, and Rywick, 1981; Silber, 1980).

Social and Realistic Considerations

Those advocating the right to choose emphasize the realistic position that *strict laws against abortion, such as those that permit abortions only when the mother's physical life is threatened, have never worked.* If a woman is determined not to

The Supreme Court has repeatedly been asked to consider when life begins. Who has the right to decide when and if a pregnancy can be terminated? The dilemmas raised by the abortion issue are not easily solved by anyone.

have her baby, she will attempt, however foolishly (and sometimes futilely), to abort her own child. Or she will go to an unqualified person and get an illegal abortion that may threaten her life. Various estimates place the number of illegal abortions before 1967 at around 1 million per year or about 20 percent of total pregnancies. Maternal death rates from illegal abortions in New York City were about 19 times higher than those from legal abortions. Legalized abortion, therefore, saves lives by reducing the number of illegal attempts (Guttmacher, 1983).

Strict laws against abortion discriminate against the poor and against deprived minority groups. The low-income woman who gets pregnant is either forced to bear her child, to try to abort her own child, or to go to a completely unqualified abortionist. The high-income woman who has "been careless" or who has "made a mistake" receives the attention of the private physician. Data from New York City during the first nine months after the liberalization of its laws showed that the problem of differential access according to race was largely eliminated (Steinhoff, 1973).

In reply to these social and realistic considerations, *right-to-life groups empha-size their fears that without any restriction, except the individual woman and her conscience, an "abortion mentality" develops so that abortions become too common-place.* The majority of abortions today are not for medical reasons, but for personal, social, and economic reasons. *Most thoughtful advocates of abortion agree that it should be only a backup measure,* not the primary method of birth control. They urge fuller use of contraceptives among all sexually active persons (Zelnik and Kantner, 1978).

1. Do you generally agree with the right-to-choose or the right-to-life groups? Explain your views.
2. Explain your feelings about the U.S. Supreme Court's rulings concerning abortion.
3. What do you think of forbidding the use of federal Medicaid funds for abortion?
4. Do you feel teenagers should have to get consent from parents before having an abortion? Why? Why not? What do you think of requiring teenagers to go to court to get the court's permission to have an abortion?
5. How do you personally feel about abortion?
   In general?
   In case of rape?
   In case of birth defects?
   For underage minors?
   For unmarried women?
   For middle-aged married women?

Psychological and Personal Considerations

Right-to-life proponents have often pointed to the *negative psychological effects* on the woman who has had an abortion. *But the incidence of psychological aftereffects is a major subject of dispute.* Both sides cite facts to support their views. Those advocating the right to choose point to the fact that *many women are far more depressed before the abortion is performed than they are afterward.* When abortions were illegal, much of the anxiety was over the illegality of the act. These feelings have now been eliminated.

In contrast, right-to-life proponents point to the realistic fact that *some women do suffer psychological scars* as an aftermath of an abortion. For this reason, abortion counseling, which assists the woman in working through her feelings ahead of time (and afterward if needed), is a must. *For some, abortion provides great relief with little if any disturbance. For others, the experience is upsetting.* The key factor seems to be whether the woman wants an abortion or whether she is reluctant. Being refused an abortion and forced to bear an unwanted child can lead to psychiatric symptoms. But the woman who has health problems and has to have an abortion, or who is persuaded to have an abortion against her better judgment, is also more likely to show negative psychological reactions (Pare and Raven, 1970). This is why, if the decision is hers, adverse psychological reactions are minimized.

SUMMARY

1. One of the options that has become increasingly available to couples is the choice of whether to have children. Women who want to remain childless are more likely to be well-educated, urban, less traditional in their sex roles, upwardly mobile, and professional; they are also more likely to marry at later ages than women who want children.

2. The number of children desired by U.S. families is also declining, with 1.9 children being the average goal.

3. More women are also delaying parenthood so they can complete their education, get established in their jobs, have more time to adjust to marriage, and have greater opportunity for personal freedom before having their first baby.

4. There are a number of arguments against having children: world overpopulation, restriction on freedom, the lack of interest or aptitude for parenthood, and the fact that children really don't increase personal happiness and satisfaction in old age. Without children there is less work at home, more opportunity for self-fulfillment, and less strain on the marriage.

5. In spite of some change in atittudes, society, friends, and parents still put a lot of pressure on couples to have children.

6. The decision not to have children is an important option that couples may want to consider.

7. Planned parenthood means having children by choice and not by chance: the number wanted when they are wanted. Family planning is necessary to protect the health of the mother and children, to reduce the negative psychological impact and stress of parenthood, for the good of the marriage and the family, for economic and social reasons, and out of humanitarian and ecological considerations.

8. Oral contraceptives are efficient, convenient, and easy to use. They are of several types: combination pills containing estrogen and progestogen, the morning-after pill (regular pills taken in large dosages postcoitally), the once-a-month pill (injections of large dosages of estrogen and progestogen), the minipill (progestogen only), progestogen capsules (implanted under the skin), progestogen injection, IUD and vaginal rings containing progestogen, and prostaglandin tampons that cause early labor. Pill users worry about thromboembolism (there is a small risk), cancer (users are less likely to develop ovarian and endometrial cancer, no more likely to develop breast cancer, somewhat more likely to develop cervical cancer), fertility (little effect), and various other side effects. Pills have a number of positive health effects: they reduce benign breast disease, ovarian cysts, iron-deficiency anemia, PID, ectopic pregnancy, rheumatoid arthritis, and endometrial and ovarian cancer. Overall, if women are under 35, don't smoke, and are in good health, they can use oral contraceptives with only a very small risk.

9. Contraceptive foam, suppositories, creams, or jellies are chemicals that are used to prevent conception by blocking the entrance to the uterus and by immobilizing and killing the sperm. Douching has one of the highest failure rates of any contraceptive technique.

10. Mechanical devices include the IUD, condom, diaphragm, and vaginal sponge.

11. Over one million sterilizations (more female than male) are performed yearly in the United States. Male sterilization or vasectomy is the easiest to perform, is the cheapest, and is highly effective with no adverse health consequences. Salpingectomy or tubal ligation is now most often done by laparoscopy.

12. Attempts at birth control without devices include the rhythm method, which relies on intercourse during the so-called safe period of the month

when the woman can't get pregnant (there is really no completely safe period), coitus interruptus (withdrawal), or various means of noncoital stimulation, such as mutual masturbation, interfemoral stimulation, or oral-genital stimulation.

13. In considering the pros and cons of abortion, there are five important considerations: legal considerations, physical and medical considerations, moral considerations, social and realistic considerations, and psychological and personal considerations. The abortion controversy and dilemma have no easy answers.

SUGGESTED READINGS

Dornblaser, C., and Landy, U. (1982). *The Abortion Guide: A Handbook for Women and Men*. New York: Berkley. All aspects of abortion.

Faux, M. (1984). *Childless by Choice*. Garden City, NY: Doubleday. The implications of the decision not to have children. Dispels the myths that surround motherhood and nonmotherhood.

Hatcher, R., et al. (1986). *Contraceptive Technology: 1986–1987*. New York: Irvington. Up-to-date book on birth control.

Montreal Health Press. (1979). *A Book About Birth Control*. Montreal: MHP. For the lay person.

Veevers, J. E. (1980). *Childless by Choice*. Scarborough, Ontario: Butterworth. Factors to consider in decision making.

Whelan, E. (1980). *A Baby? . . . Maybe*. New York: Bobbs-Merrill. Raises the question and possibility of childlessness.

19

PREGNANCY, CHILDBIRTH, AND TRANSITION TO PARENTHOOD

Most couples want to have children sometime in their lives. But having children raises some important questions. How does a couple know if the woman is pregnant? How can the birth date be calculated? What are some typical reactions to parenthood and pregnancy, and what major adjustments do men and women face? What do they need to know to protect the health of the baby? What are the possible complications of pregnancy? How can couples prepare themselves for the experience of childbirth? What happens during labor and childbirth itself? What about the use of anesthesia? What about natural childbirth methods? What about induced or accelerated labor? Delivery by cesarean section? The Leboyer method? What do couples need to know before and after the baby is born? What do you do if the woman can't get pregnant?

These are some of the important questions discussed in this chapter.*

PREGNANCY

Signs and Symptoms

One of the first questions the prospective mother asks is: "How can I tell when I'm pregnant?" The signs and symptoms of pregnancy may be divided into three categories. **Presumptive signs** indicate a possibility of pregnancy. They are the first that are noticed by the woman; but they are subjective, so she may only presume pregnancy from them. The presumptive signs are:

Cessation of menstruation

Morning sickness

Increase in size, tenderness, and fullness of the breasts, along with development of dark coloration of the areola (the ring around the nipple)

Frequent urination

Quickening or feeling of movement by the mother

Overpowering sleepiness (McCary and McCary, 1982).

Probable signs of pregnancy are more objective than presumptive signs, since they must be interpreted by the physician. Some of them occur later in pregnancy than the presumptive signs, but they still are not absolute proof. The probable signs include:

Positive pregnancy tests

Darkening of vaginal tissues and of cervical mucous membranes: so-called *Chadwick's sign*

Softening of cervical tissue: Hegar's sign

Enlargement of abdomen and uterus

Mapping of fetal outline

Intermittent contractions of uterus

An increase in basal body temperature (from 98.8° to 99.9° F for more than sixteen days)

---

*Part of the material in this chapter is taken from the author's book *Human Sexuality* © 1989 and is used by permission of the publisher, William C. Brown Co.

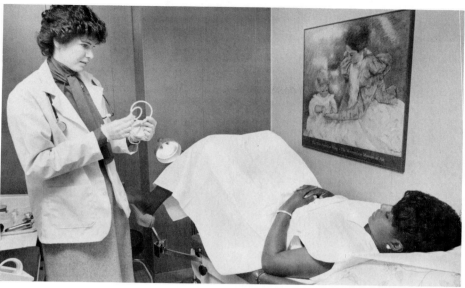

How does a woman know when she might be pregnant? What signs may tell her that she is?
Signs of pregnancy can be detected, interpreted, and confirmed by a physician.

Positive signs of pregnancy are indisputable, since no other condition except pregnancy causes them. There are five of them: *the examiner feels the fetus move, hears the fetal heartbeat, detects the fetal skeleton by x-ray, gets an electrical tracing of the fetal heart, and maps the fetal outline* by means of special ultrasonic equipment. When these signs are discovered, the mother and her physician *know* she is pregnant.

Tests

Since most women don't want to wait several months to determine if they are pregnant, pregnancy tests are administered. The two basic categories of tests are *biologic* and *immunologic*. There are numerous types of tests under each category, but all are based on detecting the presence of **HCG (human chorionic gonadotropin)**, which is secreted by the placenta. In the older biologic tests, a woman's urine was administered to test animals such as mice, frogs, toads, or rabbits. If HCG were present in the urine, it caused ovulation in female animals. Pregnancy was detected by killing the animal and examining the ovaries. The disadvantages were that pregnancy could not be detected for four to six weeks after the last menstrual period and that many animals were killed.

The immunologic tests are easier to perform and are reliable earlier. They involve adding the woman's urine to anti-HCG chemicals to see the reaction. The immunologic tests are easier to administer than the biologic tests, but they are not 100 percent accurate, especially in the first few weeks of pregnancy. They can give either false positive or false negative readings. The woman with a negative test who does not menstruate within another week should repeat the test. Furthermore, these tests will not detect ectopic pregnancies.

Home pregnancy tests are convenient and relatively inexpensive, but they are not always accurate. In addition, most home pregnancy test kits advise women to see their physician after they have examined the results of the test.

Home pregnancy tests sold under various brand names are immunologic tests designed to measure the presence of HCG. These tests are convenient and relatively inexpensive. Their major fault is the high rate of false negatives (20 percent of the time they tell the woman she is not pregnant when she is). They also have a 3 percent rate of false positives (indicating pregnancy when it doesn't exist).

A newer type of immunologic test called the *beta subunit HCG radioimmunoassay* measures HCG in a blood sample and is sensitive enough to detect pregnancy eight days after conception or five days before a missed period. It is very accurate; but only some hospitals have the facilities to do this procedure, and it is more costly than the other methods (Saxena, 1980).

Calculating the Birth Date

The duration of the pregnancy is ordinarily estimated at 280 days, or 40 weeks from the beginning of the last period. This is approximately equivalent to 267 days from the time of conception. Of course, these are average figures. One study showed that 46 percent of women had their babies either the week before or the week after the calculated date and 74 percent within a two-week period before or after the anticipated day of birth. Occasionally, pregnancy is prolonged more than two weeks beyond the calculated date, and usually an error in calculation is involved. At the most, 4 percent of pregnancies are actually carried two weeks or more beyond the average time (Guttmacher, 1983).

The expected date of birth may be calculated using **Naegele's formula** as follows: subtract three months from the first day of the last menstrual period, then add seven days. Thus, if

- the date of first day of last period was November 16
- subtracting three months gives the date August 16
- adding seven days gives the birth date as August 23.

This is really a shortcut for counting 280 days from any fixed date. In other words, a woman ordinarily delivers nine months and seven days from the beginning date of her last menstrual period (Guttmacher, 1983).

Emotional Reactions to Prospective Parenthood

How men or women react to prospective parenthood depends upon a large number of factors. A most important one is *whether the pregnancy is planned or not*. Does the couple want a child at this time? Do they feel ready to accept the responsibilities? Are the mother and father of appropriate ages? (The mortality rate of infants born to adolescent mothers is substantially higher than that of those born to women aged 20 or older ("Substantially higher morbidity . . .," 1984).

Another important factor is *the status of the couple relationship*. Do they have a harmonious relationship? (The more stressful the couple relationship, the more difficulty they will have adjusting to parenthood.) Are they married? If not, how do they feel about raising a child out of wedlock? Does the woman want to be a single or unmarried parent? Does the woman want to bear *his* child? Does the man want her to bear his child? Will they assist each other in the rearing of the child? Will he accept responsibilities as a father? Will she as a mother? How will the child affect their relationship?

May (1982) studied 100 expectant fathers and their partners to determine what factors were important to a subjective sense of readiness for pregnancy and fatherhood. She found four factors that were most important to these men:

1. Whether or not they had intended to be a father at some time in their lives
2. Stability in the couple relationship
3. Relative financial security
4. A sense of closure to the childless period of their lives. In other words, they had to feel they had met most of the personal goals they felt were necessary to accomplish before fatherhood.

The timing of the pregnancy was extremely important to the men in this study. One man commented (May 1982):

I really don't think the father should be rushed . . . Men are not insensitive. It's not that they don't care about the baby. It's just that they are going to care at the right time, when it's right for them. (p. 359)

Pregnancy affects the man and woman differently. The woman has to carry the child for nine months, accompanied by varying degrees of physical discomfort or difficulties and sometimes by anxiety about impending childbirth. Many women want to be mothers, but hate the period of pregnancy. The following are typical comments:

> I don't like being pregnant. I feel like a big toad. I'm a dancer, used to being slim, and can't believe what I look like from the side. I avoid mirrors.

> I had insomnia. I couldn't get comfortable. I couldn't sleep, he'd kick so much. (Boston Women's Health Collective, 1984, pp. 346, 351)

Other women are extremely happy during pregnancy. One woman comments:

> I was excited and delighted. I really got into eating well, caring for myself, getting enough sleep. I liked walking through the streets and having people notice my pregnancy. (Boston Women's Health Collective, 1984, p. 346)

Part of the woman's reaction to her pregnancy depends upon the reactions of her mate to her and her changing figure. One study emphasized that a woman accepts her pregnancy well when it brings her closer to her husband, but she rejects pregnancy when she feels it serves to exclude her from her

The wife's reaction to pregnancy is strongly related to the emotional support and help she receives from her husband.

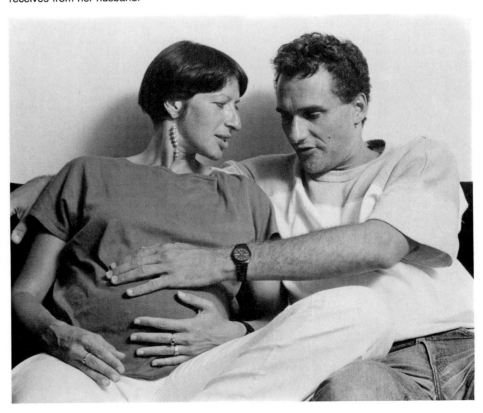

husband. If the husband is fully employed so that the wife feels confident of her husband's ability to provide for the baby, she also feels better about having a child (Meyerowitz, 1970). The wife's reaction to pregnancy is also strongly related to the emotional support and help she receives from her husband (Leifer, 1980).

Some men who resent the pregnancy can be extremely cruel. One husband refused to walk alongside his pregnant wife when on the street, forcing her to walk a number of paces behind him. It is important, therefore, that the husband as well as the wife be ready for parenthood.

In contrast, however, some husbands are more attentive and loving toward their wives during pregnancy than at any other time, leading one wife to remark: "I'm always sorry when my pregnancy is over, because Bob and I are closer then than at any other time. He is absolutely wonderful to me." Some husbands identify so closely with their wives' pregnancies that they experience some of the same physical symptoms as their spouses (Lipkin and Lamb, 1982).

PERSPECTIVE
Developmental Tasks of Pregnancy

According to Valentine (1982), every pregnancy requires prospective parents to perform a significant amount of psychological work in order to prepare themselves physically and emotionally for the arrival of their new child. She describes developmental tasks that must be mastered before postpartum adjustment and parental roles are accomplished.

Valentine outlines four developmental tasks confronted by the expectant woman and four others by the expectant father. The pregnant woman's tasks are:

1. *Development of an emotional attachment to the fetus.* The facilitation of this process affects later maternal feelings toward the new infant.

2. *Differentiation of self from the fetus.* This enhances her commitment to her child as an individual.

3. *Acceptance and resolution of the relationship with her own mother.* If the woman's relationship with her mother is problematic, her relationship with her child may be affected adversely.

4. *Resolution of dependency issues.* These are centered on the relationship with her mother and her husband/partner. At some point, she needs a shift in dependency from those of primarily daughter/wife to the attainment of role as mother.

The developmental tasks of the expectant father are:

1. *Acceptance of the pregnancy and attachment to the fetus.* This is necessary in finding a satisfactory role as father before parenting responsibilities begin.

2. *Evaluation of practical issues such as financial responsibilities and living arrangements.* This is necessary in the development of a sense of being a good provider for one's family.

3. *Resolution of dependency issues* (in relation to their wives). Some men have a heightened sense of dependency during pregnancy and develop greater anxiety about rejection or being unimportant because they receive less of the wife's attention or because sexual relations lessen.

4. *Accepting and resolving the relationship with his own father.* A father's feeling toward his own father condition his own ability to express loving and tender feelings toward his own child.

Medical and Health Care

Ordinarily, the fetus is well protected in its uterine environment, but the expectant mother needs to put herself under the care of a physician as soon as she suspects she is pregnant. Time is of the essence, since the first three months of development are crucial to the good health of the child. Initial visits to the doctor include a complete physical examination. It is helpful if the prospective father goes to the doctor with his wife, since the father needs to be involved. The physician will want a complete medical history, will perform various tests, and will make recommendations regarding health care during pregnancy, sexual relations, dealing with minor complications, and danger signs to watch for in avoiding major complications.

Minor Side Effects

No pregnancy is without some discomfort. Expectant mothers may experience any one or several of the following discomforts to varying degrees: *nausea* (morning sickness), *heartburn, flatulence, hemorrhoids, constipation, shortness of breath, backache, leg cramps, uterine contractions, insomnia, minor vaginal discharge,* and *varicose veins* (Hern, 1971). The physician will give suggestions regarding the best ways of minimizing these discomforts.

Major Complications

Major complications arise only infrequently, but when they do they present a more serious threat to the health and life of the baby than do the minor discomforts already discussed. Major complications may include any of the following.

Pernicious vomiting is prolonged and persistent. One patient in several hundred suffers from this condition to such an extent that hospitalization is required.

Toxemia is characterized by waterlogging of the tissue (edema) as indicated by swollen limbs and face, or rapid weight gain; albumin in the urine; headache; blurring of vision; hypertension; and eclampsia (convulsions). It can be fatal if not treated and is most commonly a disease of neglect because of lack of proper prenatal care. It ranks as one of three chief causes of maternal mortality (Guttmacher, 1983).

Spontaneous abortion may be indicated by vaginal bleeding. Studies indicate that about one in six pregnancies is spontaneously aborted before the fetus is of sufficient size to survive. Most occur early in pregnancy. Three out of four happen before the twelfth week, and only one in four occurs between the twelfth and twenty-eighth weeks (Guttmacher, 1983).

Placenta previa happens about once in 200 pregnancies and is the premature separation of the placenta from the uterine wall, usually because the placenta is growing partly over or all the way over the opening to the cervix. It usually occurs in the third trimester of pregnancy. If given proper treatment, 80 to 85 percent of the cases result in the baby's surviving. About 60 percent of affected babies are delivered by Cesarean section (Guttmacher, 1983).

FIGURE 19.1 Possible Implantation Sites for Ectopic Pregnancy.

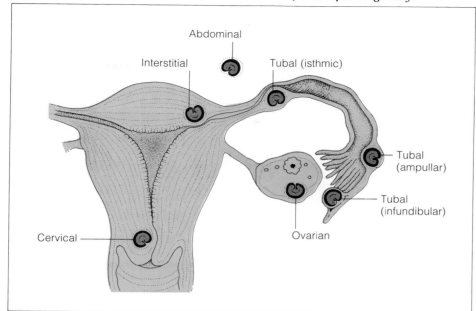

Tubal pregnancy occurs when the fertilized ovum attaches itself to the wall of the fallopian tube and grows there rather than within the uterus. Sometimes the pregnancy, termed **ectopic**, is situated in the ovary, abdomen, or cervix. Figure 19.1 shows possible implantation sites ("Ectopic pregnancy . . .," 1984). All such pregnancies have to be terminated by an operation. Surveys indicate that the number of such pregnancies has been climbing steadily (Curran, 1980; Rubin, 1978). This may be due to a number of factors: the postponement of childbearing, during which time the fallopian tubes age; previous abortion; pelvic inflammatory disease (PID); sexually transmitted diseases; frequent douching with commercial preparations; and previous surgery. Any condition that affects the tubes and impedes transport of the fertilized ovum will contribute to an ectopic pregnancy ("Increasing rates . . .," 1984, p. 14). In spite of the increase in such pregnancies, the mortality rates have fallen, indicating that women are getting prompter and better treatment ("Annual ectopic totals . . .," 1983).

Rh incompatibility involves an expectant mother with Rh negative blood who carries a fetus with Rh positive blood.

Illness of the mother, depending upon the illness and its severity, can create major complications.

Sexual Relations

Masters and Johnson (1966) have reported the results of a study of the changes in sexual tensions and performances through the three trimesters of pregnancy. The female subjects were divided into two groups: (1) those going through a first, full-term pregnancy (referred to as nulliparous women) and (2) those going through at least a second full-term pregnancy (referred to as

TABLE 19.1 *Changes in Female Sexual Interest and Performance During Pregnancy*

	FIRST TRIMESTER OF PREGNANCY	SECOND TRIMESTER OF PREGNANCY	THIRD TRIMESTER OF PREGNANCY
Nulliparous Women (N = 43)			
Increase in sex interest and performance	9%	74%	
No change	14	26	
Decrease	77		83%
Parous Women (N = 68)			
Increase in sex interest and performance	6%	88%	
No change	84	12	
Decrease	10		67

Source: Adapted from W. H. Masters and V. E. Johnson, *Human Sexual Response* (Boston: Little, Brown, 1966), pp. 156–160.

parous). As a group the nulliparous women showed a marked reduction in sexual interest and effectiveness of sexual performance during the first trimester of pregnancy and a marked increase during the second trimester (Table 19.1). During the third trimester there was usually a loss of sexual interest as well as a marked decline in sexual intercourse because of medical contraindications for periods of from four weeks to three months. As a group, the parous women showed no change in sexual tension or in effectiveness of sexual performance during the first trimester of pregnancy, a marked increase during the second trimester, and a marked decrease in sexual interest and performance during the third trimester, primarily because of chronic exhaustion from the pregnancy and from taking care of other children, and/or because of prescribed medical contraindications for periods of from four weeks to three months.

Among both the nulliparous and parous groups surveyed by Masters and Johnson, 70 percent of the women had been told by their physicians that intercourse was medically contraindicated during the last four weeks to three months. Many wives did not believe that sexual continence was really necessary and expressed concern with the proscribed period (Masters and Johnson, 1966).

There are several conditions that may make intercourse late in pregnancy unsafe. Those conditions are a history of previous miscarriages, some degree of dilation of the cervix, vaginal or uterine bleeding, rupture of the bag of waters, and premature labor (Herbst, 1979). When intercourse is contraindicated couples may find mutual masturbation a pleasurable alternative. In one study, only half as many husbands as wives said that declining sexual activity during pregnancy was due to a decline in their wife's sexiness or attractiveness (LaRossa, 1979). Apparently, many wives felt less attractive than their husbands felt they were and so withdrew from sexual activity because of negative feelings about themselves.

Most other studies confirm Masters' and Johnson's finding that sexual activity declines during the third trimester. However, two different studies found a gradual, persistent decline in sexual activity through the three trimesters of pregnancy (Calhoun, Selby, and King, 1981; Solberg, Butler, and Wagner, 1973). Apparently, there is no one pattern that can be applied to all women. Many women don't feel as great a need for intercourse, but have an increased desire for nonsexual affection during pregnancy (Walbroehl, 1984).

What about sexual interest and activity after childbirth? Forty-seven percent of the women in Master's and Johnson's study described low or negligible levels of sexual activity when interviewed early in the third postpartum month. The reasons for low levels of sexuality were fatigue, weakness, pain, irritative vaginal discharge, or a fear of permanent physical harm if coitus were resumed too soon. Fifty-three percent reported varying levels of sexual interest. The nursing mothers reported sexual stimulation from the sucking activity of their infants and wanted to begin having intercourse with their husbands as soon after childbirth as possible. All of the women interviewed, except those for whom intercourse was medically forbidden for three months, returned to full coital activity within six weeks to two months after delivery. Despite the fact that intercourse was medically forbidden for at least six weeks by most physicians, there frequently was a return to prepregnancy coital activity within three weeks of delivery, especially among higher tensioned women and by those who were actively nursing.

What about the reaction of husbands? Thirty-nine percent had withdrawn slowly, almost involuntarily, from active coital demand upon their wives during the end of the second trimester or early in the third trimester. Some were afraid of injuring the fetus; others just weren't interested. Only one-third of the men whose wives were medically prohibited from having intercourse from four weeks to three months prior to confinement understood, agreed with, and honored the prohibition. One-third did not understand the reasons, were not sure the doctor had said it, or wished they had had it explained to them. All of the husbands interviewed expressed concern over how soon after delivery intercourse could be resumed (Masters and Johnson, 1966).

Mental Health

Prolonged nervous and emotional disturbance of the mother may result in a hyperactive, irritable, neurotic child. Emotional disturbance may also have negative effects upon the mother herself. Women who suffer from pernicious vomiting during pregnancy have been found to be under considerable emotional stress, usually because of conflict between wanting and not wanting the unborn child.

There is a close relationship between personality and emotional factors and spontaneous abortion. Women who are prone to bearing premature infants may show similar upset. Emotional disturbance has also been shown to be related to difficult and prolonged labor and to such physical complications of pregnancy as toxemia, which has already been discussed.

Pregnancy is not always the euphoric, blissful experience that romantic literature describes. It can be a happy, healthful time, but it can also be a period of stress and anxiety, especially for the immature and unprepared. Bell

(1975) writes: "It does sometimes happen that arrival of pregnancy interrupts a pleasant dream of motherhood" (p. 453). This is why preparation for childbirth and for parenthood is so important.

CHILDBIRTH

Prepared Childbirth

The term *prepared childbirth* as used here means physical, social, intellectual, and emotional preparation for the birth of a baby. It means physical care of the body to provide the ultimate physical environment for the growing fetus and physical conditioning so that the body is prepared for labor and childbirth. It means social preparation of the home, the husband, and the children so the proper relationships exist within the family in which the child will be growing up. It means intellectual preparation: obtaining full knowledge and understanding of the process of birth and what to expect before, during, and after the hospital stay. It also means adequate instruction in infant and child care (Hicks and Williams, 1981). It mean psychological and emotional conditioning so that fear, anxiety, and tension are kept to a minimum, making childbirth as pleasant and pain-free as possible.

The term *prepared childbirth,* as used here, does not insist upon labor and delivery without drugs and medication, although it may include that if the mother desires. In other words, the emphasis is not just on what is called *natural childbirth* (all childbirth is natural), but on whether the woman, her husband, and family are really prepared for the experience of becoming parents.

The Lamaze Method

The *Lamaze method* originated in Russia and was introduced to the Western world in 1951 by Fernand Lamaze (1970), a French obstetrician (Boston Women's Health Collective, 1984). The important elements of the Lamaze method include:

1. Education about birth, including teaching the importance of releasing uninvolved muscles
2. Physical conditioning through exercises
3. Learning controlled breathing and how to "let go": how to relax the muscles and release muscular tension. These techniques are useful in pain prevention.
4. Offering emotional support to the wife during labor and delivery, primarily by teaching the husband how to coach her during the process. The importance of the husband-wife relationship and communication are emphasized. In this method as well as other natural childbirth methods, the attendance of the husband or another support person in childbirth education classes is essential (Bean, 1974). One important feature is that the

mother is taught that she can be in control during the experience (Felton and Segelman, 1978).

Critique of Prepared Childbirth

Prepared childbirth, by whatever method, is not without its critics, especially if a particular advocate emphasizes that drugs or medication of any kind should not be used. Also, some physicians and nurses object to husbands in the delivery room, especially those who are more hindrance than help. However, a majority of obstetricians accept most of the concepts of prepared childbirth. "The patient is calm and relaxed. Without fear, she has less pain," one said. Part of the value of prepared childbirth is the benefit not only of psychological suggestion but also of physical conditioning.

LABOR, DELIVERY

When Labor Begins

Real **labor** is rhythmic in nature, recurs at fixed intervals, usually begins with contractions about 15 to 20 minutes apart, and decreases to three- to four-minute intervals when labor is well under way. In addition, the total length of each muscular contraction increases from less than half a minute to more than a minute. One of the signs that labor is about to begin or has already begun is the discharge of the blood-tinted mucous plug that has sealed the neck of the uterus. The plug is dislodged from the cervix and passes out of the vagina as a pinkish discharge; it is termed **show**. Its appearance may anticipate the onset of labor by a day or more, or it may indicate that dilation has already begun.

Sometimes the first indication of the impending labor is the rupture of the **bag of water** (**amniotic sac**), followed by a gush or leakage of watery fluid from the vagina. In one-eighth of all pregnancies, especially first pregnancies, the membrane ruptures *before* labor begins. When this happens, labor will commence in 6 to 24 hours if the woman is within a few days of term. If she is not near term, labor may not commence for 30 or 40 days or longer. This delay is actually necessary, because the longer the baby has to develop completely, the greater the chance of being born healthy. About half the time, however, the bag of water doesn't rupture until the last hours of labor.

Duration of Labor

Bean (1974) reports a study of 10,000 patients who delivered at Johns Hopkins Hospital. The study showed the total length of labor of each patient from the onset of the first contraction until the extrusion of the afterbirth. The median number of hours of labor for *primiparous* women (first labor) was 10.6, for *multiparous* (refers to all labor subsequent to the first) was 6.2. One woman

Around 1900 about 95 percent of babies were born at home. Birthing was a family event. Today, that ratio has been reversed: 95 percent are born in the hospital and only 5 percent at home (Gordon and Haire, 1981). The switch has been at the urging of physicians, who prefer delivery in sterile, well-equipped, more convenient hospital settings.

Some expectant parents are concerned that hospital practices are too rigid, impersonal, and expensive. They object to the separation of family members and want more control over the childbirth process. If the mother is not in good health, has a history of previous birth complications, or if there is a chance of prematurity, **breech** or **transverse** birth, multiple births, blood incompatibility, or disproportion between the sizes of the baby's head and the mother's pelvis, the National Association of Parents and Professionals for Safe Alternatives in Childbirth (NAPSAC) advises against home delivery.

The mother must locate a pediatrician who will see the infant soon after birth. Many physicians will not deliver babies at home. Even those who approve may lose hospital privileges or insurance coverage. Many couples also find that their health insurance policies will not cover home deliveries.

Certainly, even with careful screening, there are risks and disadvantages. The couple must weigh the benefits against the risks.

QUESTIONS

1. Have you even known a mother who had a home delivery? What were the circumstances? How did she feel about it? How did she get along?
2. Would you ever consider delivering your baby at home? Why? Why not?
3. Have any of you had a home delivery?
4. To nurses: What is your opinion of home delivery? Have you ever assisted in delivering a baby in any location other than the hospital. Describe.

in a hundred may anticipate that her first child will be born in less than three hours. Every ninth woman requires more than 24 hours.

Going to the Hospital

The doctor will give instructions as to when he or she wants to be notified. Most want to be called as soon as rhythmic contractions are established. The doctor will also determine when the mother should go to the hospital. Admission procedures vary somewhat after arrival at the hospital.

The Father's Role

Medical opinion is also changing gradually in relation to the role of the father. Since fathers are encouraged to attend classes with their wives and to act as coaches during labor and delivery, many couples are insisting that the father be present during labor and even at the delivery. Certainly, a husband's willingness to participate in childbirth can be critical for the physical comfort and satisfaction of his wife with the birth experience (Block, Norr, Meyering,

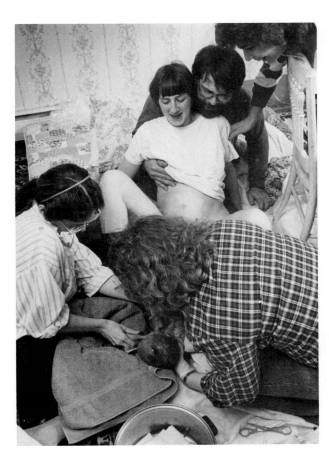

Around 1900, about 95 percent of babies were born at home, and birthing was a family event. In today's changed circumstances, what are the benefits and risks of home birthing?

Norr, and Charles, et al., 1981). One study showed that fathers who were present at delivery showed more interest in looking at their infants and talking to them than did fathers who were not present at delivery (Miller and Bowen, 1982). These considerations need to be worked out between the couple and the physician beforehand to avoid misunderstanding.

Stages of Labor

The actual process of labor can be divided into three phases. The *first* is the dilation stage, during which the force of the uterine muscles pushing on the baby gradually opens the mouth of the cervix, which increases from less than four-fifths of an inch in diameter to four inches. This phase takes longer than any other. There is nothing the mother can do to help except relax as completely as possible to allow the involuntary muscles to do their work.

The *second* stage begins upon completion of dilation and ends with the birth of the baby. It involves the passage of the baby through the birth canal. During the phase when hard contractions begin, the mother alternately pushes and relaxes to help force the baby through the birth canal. After the baby is delivered and tended to, the obstetrician again turns his/her attention to the mother for the third stage of labor.

Expectant fathers are encouraged to attend birth preparation classes and act as coaches during labor and delivery. One study indicates that fathers who were present at delivery showed more interest in looking at their infants and talking to them than did absent fathers. What might be the reasons for this difference?

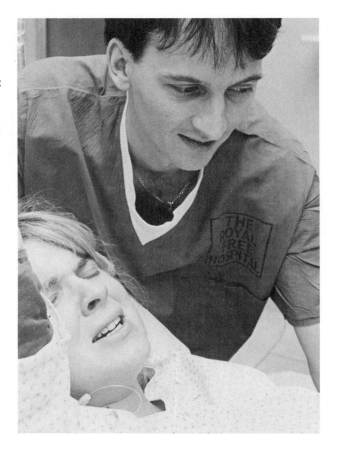

The *third* stage involves the passage of the placenta or *afterbirth*. The mother may be kept in the delivery room for an hour or so after delivery while her condition is checked. When her condition is considered normal, she is usually placed in a recovery room for a while before being returned to her own room.

Use of Anesthesia

Anesthesia used to alleviate pain in childbirth may be divided into two categories: **general anesthesia** and **local** or **regional anesthesia.** General anesthesia affects the whole body by acting on the nervous system. It can slow or stop labor and lower maternal blood pressure (Wilson, Carrington, and Ledger, 1983). It crosses the placental barrier and affects the fetus as well as the mother, decreasing the responses of the newborn infant. Local or regional anesthesia blocks pain in specific areas and has minimal effect on the baby.

Induced or Accelerated Labor

There are various reasons why physicians sometimes induce labor: Rh blood problems, diabetes, medical problems such as toxemia, overdue baby, ruptured membranes, labor stopping too soon, or insuring that trained personnel

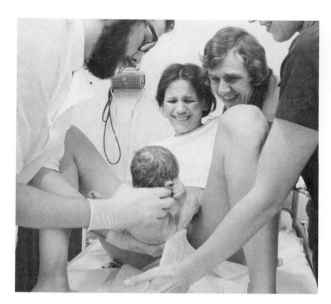

The second stage of labor ends with the birth of the baby. Within the next few minutes, the baby's physical condition will be carefully evaluated.

will be available (especially in remote areas). In 1978, the FDA came out against elective induction (that which is solely for the woman's or physician's convenience). Risks of induced labor include internal hemorrhaging, uterine rupture, hypertension, oxygen deprivation to the fetus, premature birth, or excessive labor pain.

Cesarean Section

Medical complications may require a **Cesarean section**, which is direct removal of the fetus by incision of the abdomen and uterine wall. Some medical indications include: small pelvic opening, difficult labor, breech or other malpresentation, placenta previa, heart disease, diabetes, or sexually transmitted disease in the mother (Andrews, 1983; Amirikia, Zarewych, and Evans, 1981). Although Cesareans are major surgery, the risk of maternal death is less than 2 percent. It is regarded as one of the safest of all abdominal surgeries (Stichler and Alfonso, 1980).

POSTPARTUM

The Leboyer Method

In his book *Birth Without Violence*, the French obstetrician Leboyer (1975) emphasizes gentle, loving treatment of the newborn. Not all of his ideas are accepted by American obstetricians, but those ideas include dim lights, gentle voices, and delaying cutting the cord until the naked newborn is soothed, massaged, and stroked while resting on the mother's abdomen. After the cord is cut, the baby is bathed in water similar in temperature to that of the environment inside the mother.

The theory behind the method is that bringing a newborn into a world of blinding lights and loud voices, where it is jerked upside down, spanked, treated roughly, and immediately separated from its mother, is a terrifying, traumatic experience after the secure, warm world of the womb. "Why do we do it?" Leboyer asked. "Because we never really thought of the infant as a person. The newborn is a sensitive, feeling human being, and in the first few moments after birth, he should be treated that way. We must introduce him to the world gradually" (Braun, 1975, p. 17).

Advocates of the Leboyer method are highly enthusiastic. "I've been absolutely amazed by the results," says Davis, a family doctor in Carson City, Nevada. "I've delivered at least thirty-five babies with the Leboyer method in the last five months — and I can't say enough about it. These babies are so different from the others, so graceful in their movement. They seem to be reaching out instead of protecting themselves" (Braun, 1975, p. 19).

Care of the Newborn

As soon as the baby emerges, the most important task is to get the baby breathing. The physician swabs or suctions the nose and mouth with a rubber bulb to remove any mucus. The **umbilical cord** is clamped in two places — about three inches from the baby's abdomen — and cut between the clamps. There are no nerve endings in the cord, so neither the infant nor the mother feels the procedure. Drops of an antibiotic or silver nitrate are put in the infant's eyes to prevent bacterial infection, since the infant could be blinded by gonorrhea bacteria if the mother is infected. An exemption may sometimes be obtained if the physicain is certain there is no gonorrhea.

At one minute after delivery, the baby will be evaluated by a widely used system developed by pediatrician Virginia Apgar and called the **Apgar Score**. The test assigns values for various signs and permits a tentative rapid diagnosis of problems. The five signs of a baby's physical condition at birth that are measured are *heart rate, respiratory effort, muscle tone, reflex response* (response to breath test and to skin stimulation of the feet), and *color*. Each sign is given a score of 0, 1, or 2.

Parent-Infant Contact, Bonding

There is important evidence to show that parent-infant contacts during the early hours and days of life are important (Klaus and Kennel, 1982). Studies at Case-Western Reserve University in Cleveland confirmed the maternal feeling that the emotional bonds between mother and infant are strengthened by intimate contact during the first hours of life. This is referred to as **bonding**. One group of mothers was allowed 16 extra hours of intimacy during the first three days of life — an hour after birth, five hours each afternoon. At one month of age and again at a year, these mothers were compared with a control group that had gone through the usual hospital routine. The differences were striking. The mothers who had more time with their babies fondled them more, sought close eye contact, responded to their wails. The researchers concluded that *keeping the mother and baby together during the first hours after birth strengthened a mother's "maternal sensitivities"* and that prolonged infant-mother separation during the first few days would have far-reaching negative effects (Salk, 1974).

It is an understandable desire for new parents, fathers as well as mothers, to want to hold their baby, yet policies and rules at less progressive hospitals keep parents and baby separated during much of the hospital stay. Fathers are permitted to see their baby only through the nursery room window. The mother is brought her baby on a fixed schedule only at feeding time, even if the infant has been crying for an hour because it was hungry before. As a result, the parents are frustrated and their child is denied the benefits of *"contact comfort,"* which psychologists emphasize is so important in the development of love (Harlow and Suomi, 1970).

Rooming In

In order to avoid this separation, many hospitals are equipped with **rooming in** facilities where the baby is cared for most of the time by the mother in her own room or in a room the mother shares with several others. A big advantage to rooming in is that the new father and siblings can share in the baby's care also, so that child care becomes family centered from the beginning. Another big advantage is that new mothers learn much about infant care while still in the hospital, thus avoiding the panic and anxiety that occurs if they are given the total responsibility all at once (Salk, 1974).

One advantage of rooming-in arrangements is the new father's opportunity to share in the baby's care from the very beginning.

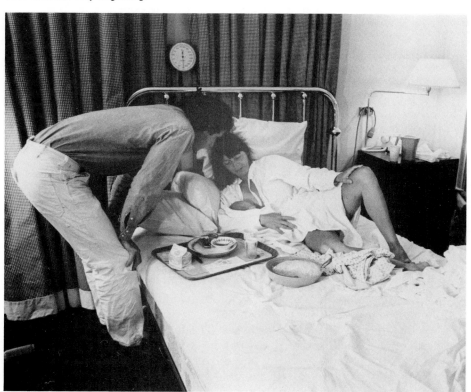

One of the questions every mother faces is whether or not to breast-feed her baby. Actually, if the decision to breast-feed is made during pregnancy, the mother can massage her nipples and toughen them for the experience. One consideration is how the mother feels about nursing. Both bottle- and breast-fed babies do well emotionally, depending upon the parents' relationship with their child. Each child needs physical contact and warmth, the sound of a pleasant voice, and the sight of a happy face. A warm, accepting mother who is bottle-feeding her baby helps her infant feel secure and loved. The important thing is the total parent-child relationship, not just the method of feeding.

Whatever type of milk is given has to be of sufficient quantity and has to agree with the baby. Most doctors would agree that there is usually nothing nutritionally better for the baby than mother's milk, provided the supply is adequate. Babies less frequently develop allergies to the mother's milk, have a lower incidence of intestinal infections, and a lower incidence of crib death (Macfarlane, 1977). Sometimes, however, the mother's supply is not adequate, or her nipples become cracked and sore so that nursing is too painful. Because of the effort involved, nursing mothers may become excessively fatigued by three months postpartum. Such problems can usually be overcome. One way is to supplement the breast with a bottle. Most nutritionists feel that babies need supplementary solid foods no later than six months of age and earlier in most cases (Waterlow and Thomson, 1979). It is important also that the nursing mother watch her diet carefully, since the baby receives necessary nutrients from her. Furthermore, drugs taken by her are usually passed along to the baby in her milk (Platzker, Lew, and Stewart, 1980).

Some women find breast-feeding to be a challenge, and they become very upset if they can't manage it. Others really want to breast-feed but let medical personnel dissuade them. Individual mothers can follow their best instincts and do what they really want to do and what seems best for the baby. If needed, they can receive support and consultation from the La Leche League, which has chapters all over the world. Overall, there has been a definite incease during the past decade in the percentage of mothers who are breast-feeding their babies (Martinez and Dodd, 1982).

Postpartum Adjustments

The period following childbirth is one of conflicting feelings (Leifer, 1980). The long period of pregnancy is over. There is a feeling of relief. If the baby is wanted and healthy, there is considerable happiness and elation. Within several days after delivery, however, the woman may experience various degrees of "baby blues" or postpartum depression, characterized by feelings of sadness and periods of crying, depression, insomnia, irritability, and fatigue (Hopkins, Marcues, and Campbell, 1984).

These feelings have numerous causes. The mother may have been under emotional strain while she anxiously awaited her baby. Once the tension is over, a letdown occurs, resulting in feelings of exhaustion and depression. Childbirth itself may impose considerable physical strain on her body, which requires a period of rest and recovery. Following childbirth, there is a rapid

Most doctors would agree that nothing is better for the baby than mother's milk. Breast feeding has also been shown to lower the incidence of intestinal infections and crib death.

decline in estrogen and progesterone in the bloodstream, which may have an upsetting, depressive effect on her (Waletzky, 1981).

Upon returning home, the mother feels the strain of wanting to do everything right in caring for the baby. One young mother remarked: "I never imagined that one small baby would require so much extra work. I'm exhausted" (Author's counseling notes). If the mother does not have much help from her husband, or if he continues to make personal demands upon her, she may become exhausted from lack of sleep, from physical and emotional strain of caring for the baby, from the work around the house, and from caring for other children, in addition to attending to her husband's needs. Clearly, she needs help and understanding. Conscientious husbands who do everything they can to assist also complain about their lack of sleep, interference with regular work, and the strains imposed upon them.

INFERTILITY

Incidence

One-third of all couples in the United States experience some difficulty in having a child, either because they are unable to conceive or because the mother has difficulty carrying the child long enough to produce a live birth (McCary and McCary, 1982; Westoff and Westoff, 1971). Approximately 15 percent of couples would never be able to have children without medical help (Porter and Christopher, 1984). With help, about half of these couples do have children (Rao, 1974).

How long does it ordinarily take for couples to achieve pregnancy? In one study, Guttmacher (1983) found that one-third of couples were able to achieve pregnancy the first month, more than half within the first three months.

Answer the following True-False questions to determine how much you know about childbirth. The correct answers are found at the end of the quiz.

T F   1. Fertilization of the ovum usually takes place in the uterus.

T F   2. Pregnancy tests involve a check for the presence of the hormone estrogen in the blood or in the urine.

T F   3. The major function of the placenta is to transfer nutrients and oxygen from the mother to the fetus and to eliminate waste from the fetus.

T F   4. After the child is born the placenta is absorbed into the mother's body.

T F   5. The baby's sex is determined by the sex of the egg.

T F   6. The time of the month when the woman ovulates and is most likely to get pregnant is 14 days before the onset of the next menstrual period.

T F   7. An ectopic pregnancy is the implantation of the egg cell outside of the uterus.

T F   8. Missing a menstrual period is a certain sign of pregnancy.

T F   9. Babies born in the second trimester of pregnancy have a poor chance of survival.

T F   10. Almost every drug a pregnant woman uses will cross the placenta and enter the circulation of the fetus.

T F   11. If a mother smokes during pregnancy the result is excessive birth weight of the baby.

T F   12. An episiotomy is performed to prevent the ova from reaching the uterus.

T F   13. During the second stage of labor the baby is born.

T F   14. The injection of vitamin D immediately after birth prevents transmission of infection from the mother's vaginal passage to the newborn's eyes.

T F   15. A fetus is suspended in antibiotic fluid.

T F   16. Morning sickness is commonly experienced in the second trimester of pregnancy.

T F   17. One of the advantages of breast-feeding is that the infant receives disease-preventing antibodies in its mother's milk.

T F   18. When a mother produces antibodies against the blood of her fetus she has Ph incompatibility.

T F   19. The longest stage of labor is the first stage.

T F   20. Sexual intercourse is not safe after the third month of pregnancy.

Answers: 1–F; 2–F; 3–T; 4–F; 5–F; 6–T; 7–T; 8–F; 9–T; 10–T; 11–F; 12–F; 13–T; 14–F; 15–F; 16–F; 17–T; 18–F; 19–T; 20–F.

Fifteen percent required four to six months; 13 percent seven to twelve months, and 8 percent one to two years. More than 6 percent of those who eventually had a baby took two or more years to achieve pregnancy. The median time for conception was two and one-half months. Generally speaking, if couples are younger than 35 years of age, they should wait for a full year of attempting pregnancy before consulting a physician. If they are older than thirty-five, they should see a doctor after six months of unsuccessful attempts. Psychological and physical factors that work against conception grow stronger with time, so the older couple should get help sooner. For the younger couple, waiting a reasonable period of time (one year) improves the chances of fertility.

If help is to be obtained, the active cooperation of both the man and woman is essential, since either one may be the cause of infertility. The important thing is to explore all possible causes and to find out what is wrong and if the problem can be remedied.

Psychological Effects

A couple who is desirous of having a child, but is not successful, may develop an anxiety-ridden emotional state that may lead to a crisis (Menning, 1979). The woman may feel barren, ashamed, deprived of motherhood, and disappointed in herself if she is infertile; or she may blame her husband if he is sterile. Intercourse becomes a baby-making chore, and so she may lose the gratification of her sex life.

The male may have been looking forward to securing his "immortality" and proving his virility. When he can't do these, he becomes depressed. He is required to perform sexually when told to, so spontaneity is lost. Erectile dysfunction or ejaculatory incompetence may become a problem. Medical help may correct the problem; if not, therapy may help the couple work through the adjustments required (Falik, 1984).

SUMMARY

1. The signs and symptoms of pregnancy may be divided into three categories: presumptive signs, probable signs, and positive signs. Suspicions of pregnancy may also be confirmed by taking a pregnancy test, the most common of which are immunologic tests.

2. The birth date may be calculated by using Naegele's formula, a short way of counting 280 days from the beginning of the last period.

3. How men and women react to prospective parenthood and pregnancy depends upon a large number of factors, including their desire and readiness to be parents and the status of the couple relationship. The developmental tasks of pregnancy for a couple are: developing an emotional attachment to the fetus, solving practical issues such as financial and living arrangements, resolution of dependency issues in relation to one another, and resolving the relationship with their parents. In addition, the woman needs to learn to differentiate herself from her fetus.

4. Couples are wise to get good prenatal care as soon in the pregnancy as possible. Women may experience minor discomforts. Major complications such as pernicious vomiting, toxemia, threatened abortion, placenta previa, ectopic pregnancy, Rh incompatibility, or certain illnesses of the mother require expert medical help. Sexual relations usually continue during pregnancy up until the later part of the third trimester. Despite the fact that intercourse is medically forbidden for six weeks after childbirth by some physicians, many mothers, especially those who are nursing, return to full coital activity soon afterwards. The mental health of the mother is also important during pregnancy since her emotional state affects the pregnancy, the childbirth experience, and the emotions of the child.

5. Couples can prepare themselves for childbirth; physical, social, and intellectual preparation for the baby is necessary. Preparations may include education about birth, physical conditioning, learning relaxation and proper breathing, and preparing the husband to give emotional support and help to the wife during labor and delivery. The most popular natural childbirth method is the Lamaze method.

6. Couples may want to consider all factors before deciding on home delivery rather than a hospital delivery. Labor may be divided into three stages: dilation, childbirth, and passage of the afterbirth. Anesthesia may be general, which affects the whole body and that of the baby, or local or regional, which blocks pain locally or regionally and doesn't have as much negative effect on the fetus. Induced or accelerated labor and Cesarean sections are warranted only with sufficient medical reasons.

7. Leboyer has developed a method of birth without violence that has a positive, soothing effect on the baby. Following birth, the infant is evaluated and given an Apgar score as a measure of physical condition.

8. Bonding between parent and child is more likely to take place if parents maintain intimate contact with their infant from the time of birth. Rooming in allows the mother and the father to have this contact and to take care of the baby themselves.

9. Either breast- or bottle-feeding, properly done, may meet both physical and emotional needs of the baby.

10. Postpartum blues are common after birth.

11. Some couples are infertile; that is, they are unable to conceive or complete a pregnancy, and so they need medical help. The cause may be in the couple relationship, or with either the man or woman. Many causes can be corrected.

SUGGESTED READINGS

Ashford, J. (1983). *The Whole Birth Catalog: A Sourcebook for Choices in Childbirth.* Trumansburg, NY: The Crossing Press. Different methods of childbirth today.

Gerson, K. (1985). *Hard Choices.* Berkeley, CA: University of California Press. Choices about work, career, motherhood.

Glass, R., and Ericsson, R. J. (1982). *Getting Pregnant in the 1980s.* Berkeley, CA: University of California Press. A nontechnical presentation.

Grad, R., Bash, D., Guyer, R., Acevedo, Z., Trause, M. A., and Reukauf, D. (1981). *The Father Book — Pregnancy and Beyond.* Washington, DC: Acropolis Books. Questions and concerns of the expectant father.

Grossman, F., Eickler, L., and Winickoff, S. (1980). *Pregnancy, Birth and Parenthood.* San Francisco: Jossey-Bass. Pregnancy and postpartum adjustments in the first year.

Herzfeld, J. (1985). *Sense and Sensibility in Childbirth.* New York: Norton. Childbirth concerns.

Leboyer, F. (1975). *Birth Without Violence.* New York: Random House. The classic on the subject.

Parke, R. (1981). *Fathers.* Cambridge, MA: Harvard University Press. Becoming an involved and caring father.

Rubin, S. (1980). *It's Not Too Late for a Baby.* Englewood Cliffs, NJ: Prentice-Hall. For the prospective parent over 35.

20

PARENTING

KEY TERMS

latchkey children
psychosocial task
cognition
socialization
discipline

Being parents has many rewards and pleasures. For some persons, to live childless — even with a loving mate — is unthinkable. They want children as a creative expression of themselves: to love and to be loved by them. They find their own lives enriched by having children (Chilman, 1980). These are very real feelings and very much a part of being parents (Rice, 1983).

But learning to become parents is not an easy task. New parents soon learn that taking care of an infant involves long hours of physical labor and many sleepless nights. One mother commented: "No one told me a baby wakes up four or five times a night." Parents soon learn that their life as a couple isn't the same. They don't have the same freedom of movement and the opportunities to do what they want to do. Furthermore, the parental task is a 24-hour job seven days a week for years and, once begun, is irrevocable. You can't give the baby back. "I think I made a mistake" was one mother's first reaction as she came out from under the anesthetic. A baby changes things; in fact, it changes everything, and so couples need to give considerable thought to the responsibilities involved. If they devote themselves to learning how to be the best possible parents, they and their children are better able to enjoy the experience (Vukelich and Kliman, 1985).

PHILOSOPHIES OF CHILD REARING

Changing Emphases

Child-rearing philosophies — like fashions — seem to go in cycles (McGillicuddy-De Lisi, 1980). Yesterday's parents, feeling their own parents were too strict, turned to self-demand schedules, child-centered homes, progressive education, and more indulgent concepts of child rearing. Now some parents are worried that today's children are too spoiled and are reacting to what they feel has been overpermissiveness. It is evident that *child-rearing philosophies change from one generation to the next and that parents often have to sort out conflicting advice* (Dail and Way, 1985).

Husband-Wife Differences

Husband and wives often differ with one another on their basic philosophies of child rearing, a situation that can create marital conflict and confusion for the child (Gilbert, Hanson, and Davis, 1982). Each parent may feel that the way he or she was reared is the "right way" and that other methods will not achieve as good a result. Parents may sometimes repudiate the methods by which they themselves were reared and resolve to do differently with their own children (Reis, Barbara-Stein, and Bennett, 1986).

Life Circumstances

Not only is family background important in the way parents relate to their children, but *life circumstances affect parent-child relationships as well.* Parents who experience a great deal of stress in their lives have more difficulty being patient and relaxed with their children. One study of black and Hispanic

The parental role sounds so simple—to meet the needs of children so they can grow. In what way does a child need to grow? What must parents do to satisfy all of the child's needs?

mothers who were on welfare found that these mothers were less emotionally and verbally responsive to their children, spanked them more, and were generally less likely to avoid restriction and punishment than were those not on welfare (Philliber and Graham, 1981). However, welfare was not the cause, per se; rather it was the combined frustration of their lives that affected the quality of parenting.

Another study found that maternal age at first birth related to the degree of supportive maternal behavior. The older a mother was when she had her first child the more likely she was to give praise and physical affection to her child. The younger a mother at first birth, the more likely she was to criticize her child and use physical punishment (Conger, McCarty, Yang, Lahey, and Burgess, 1984). When pregnancy occurs early in a mother's life, this event may have long-term negative consequences for her social, psychological, and material well-being and for her child (McLaughlin and Micklin, 1983).

Differences in Children

No one method can be considered "best" for all children. Children are individuals; what works for one may not work for another. What is important is the quality of the parent-child relationship, the total climate of the family setting rather than the particular philosophy of child rearing that is followed (Walters and Walters, 1980).

Meeting Children's Needs

The parental role sounds simple; it is to meet the needs of children so they can grow (Amato and Ochiltree, 1986; Ballenski and Cook, 1982). Within all children are "the seeds of growth"; that is, a natural inclination to develop to maturity. Parents don't have to teach children to grow physically, for example. The tendency to grow is so strong that only by extreme physical deprivation can parents prevent physical development; and even then, some development takes place. This means that the parental task is to discover the *physical needs* of their child and to fulfill those needs.

Similarly, the parental task is to fulfill *emotional needs* so that children can grow to become emotionally secure and stable persons. If children's needs for love, affection, security, understanding, and approval are met, they are more likely to develop positive feelings (Cooper, Holman, and Braithwaite, 1983). But if they are deprived of their emotional needs, the children may become fearful, hostile, insecure, anxious, and rejecting persons.

Children also have *social needs.* They are born naturally gregarious persons. They want to be with others, generally like other people, and ordinarily try to please them and be accepted by them. But these natural tendencies are unsophisticated. Children want friends but don't know how to relate; they want others to like them, but don't know how to please. Their need, therefore, is for socialization — to build on their normal desire to belong and to relate by learning group mores, customs, manners, and habits so they can fit into the group. The parental task is to provide their children the necessary opportunities for socialization so that they can become a part of society.

The capacity for intellectual growth is also inborn. Children are born naturally curious. They want to learn about everything. They desire a variety of new experiences by which this learning can take place. The parental role is to encourage cognitive growth and to fulfill these *intellectual needs* by providing sensory stimulation and a variety of learning experiences involving observation, reading, conversation, and a maximum amount of contact with others and with the natural world (Smith, 1982). As long as the environment in which children are placed is a stimulating one, as long as the curiosity of children is encouraged, their cognitive development proceeds at an unbelievably fast rate. But once their surroundings become sterile, unchanging, and uninteresting, or their human contacts and experiences are limited, growth stops or slows down because of intellectual deprivation.

Children also have the capacity for moral growth. They are born trusting persons and only become disbelievers and mistrusting when they learn they can't depend upon people around them. They are born with a capacity to develop a sensitive conscience and with an ability to distinguish different moral values once these are taught. But their ability is only a potential one; it has to be developed through educated reasoning, by imitating the example of others, and through the trial and error of living. The parental role here is to fulfill their children's *moral needs* for trust and for values to live by (Hoge, Petrillo, and Smith, 1982).

Sometimes, of course, children's needs aren't met, either because parents can't or won't fulfill them. The childen aren't given proper food and rest; they aren't loved; they aren't socialized; they are deprived intellectually and spiritually. When this happens, growth stops or slows down, so the children remain physically, emotionally, socially, intellectually, or morally retarded. *Growth takes place by fulfilling needs; retardation occurs because of deprivation.*

Sharing Responsibilities

When children have two parents, the children benefit if both parents share in meeting their needs (Atkinson, 1987). The needs of dependent children are not easily met by the mother or father alone, especially if there is more than one child. To expect the mother alone to fulfill the exhausting parenting role is unfair (Levant, Slattery, and Loiselle, 1987).

A child benefits by being cared for by more than one parent. Every parent has strengths and weaknesses. Most fathers can contribute something positive to a child's life (Cardell, Parke, and Sawin, 1980). The best fathers are almost indispensable (Hanson and Bozett, 1987). One mother relates:

> I do an awful lot for the children, but there are some things that John can do better. He can put the baby to bed, rock her, and get her to sleep a lot more calmly and easily than I can. I'm too impatient. He teaches our oldest son how to fish, roller skate, and play baseball. I never could do those things. And John is very affectionate. He hugs and kisses Maurine and holds her. I do too, but not like John. She is in seventh heaven when she is in his arms. You don't have to tell me that my children need their father. I know they do. (Author's counseling notes)

We must not omit the fact that the father also benefits from caring for his children.

The modern father's minimal participation in the day-by-day care of children has been well documented (Coverman and Sheley, 1986; Levant, Slattery, and Loiselle, 1987). While middle-class fathers take a more active role than lower-class fathers, the major responsibilities for child care still fall most heavily on the mother. This situation is slowly changing. There is increasing recognition that fathers can and should participate in the child-rearing facets of family life and that, if they do not, their children miss much and they themselves are missing out on a chance for self-actualization (Barnett and Baruch, 1987).

Latchkey Children

The term **latchkey children** *refers to unsupervised youngsters who care for themselves before or after school, on weekends, and during holidays while their parents work.* They commonly carry keys to let themselves in and out of their homes (Robinson, Rowland, and Coleman, 1986). *Some studies cite benefits of self-care:* independence, self-reliance, less stereotyped sex-role views of mothers, peer interaction, greater participation in household duties, greater ability to care for self (Long and Long, 1981; Stroman and Duff, 1982). Other experts claim that those reports reflect inaccurate judgments made to ease parents' guilty feelings (Sparks, 1983).

Numerous studies emphasize the negative aspects of self-care. In a study in Charlotte, North Carolina, fear and apprehension at being left alone was the most frequently mentioned negative effect (Council for Children, 1984). A long-term study of 1,000 current and former latchkey children and their parents revealed that 50 percent of those adults who were former latchkey children

The following guidelines represent minimum requirements that parents may use to evaluate the readiness of their child for self-care:

Physical. A child should be able to:

1. Control his or her body adequately so that he or she is not susceptible to injury while moving around the home.
2. Manipulate locks and doors so that he or she will not be locked in or out.
3. Operate safely any equipment to which he or she will have access while alone. This might include stove, blender, or vacuum cleaner. If it isn't safe to operate, he or she shouldn't have access to it.

Emotional. The child should:

1. Be able to comfortably tolerate separations from adults for the length of time required without much loneliness or fear.
2. Not exhibit a pattern of withdrawn, hostile, or self-destructive behavior.
3. Be able to handle usual and unexpected situations without excessive fear or upset.
4. Be able to follow important rules without always "testing the limits."

Cognitive. The child should:

1. Be able to understand and remember verbal and written instructions.
2. Solve problems without relying on irrational solutions.
3. Be able to read and write well enough to take telephone and other messages.

Social. The child should:

1. Be able to solicit help from friends, neighbors, and designated helpers when appropriate.
2. Understand the role of police, fire fighters, rescue squads, and other community resources.
3. Be willing and able to call on those resources when needed.
4. Be able to maintain friendships with other children and adults.

Assessing Family Readiness for Self-Care
The family may or may not be ready and suitable for self-care. Ideally, parents or guardians should be able to:

1. Maintain some level of communication with and supervision of their children, even if they are not physically present.
2. Be available for emergencies or designate several other adults who will be.
3. Be stable enough to provide emotional security for their children.
4. Provide training for their children in the special issues that may arise in self-care.

Assessing Community Suitability for Self-Care
For best results, the community should:

1. Be reasonably safe in fact and perceived as safe by all family members.
2. Provide a variety of care options so that families can make appropriate choices based on their changing needs and circumstances.

Source: Cole, C., and Rodman, H. (1987). When school-age children care for themselves: Issues for family life educators and parents. *Family Relations, 36,* 92–96. Copyright © 1987 by the National Council on Family Relations. Reprinted by permission.

said they were still afraid to be alone (Long and Long, 1983). These adults reported that as latchkey children they suffered loneliness, boredom, resentment toward parents, increased fears, and social isolation. However, most of the subjects in the study were living in inner-city, black, ghetto areas. Other studies of white, middle-class children in rural or suburban settings have not found these disadvantages (Galambos and Garbarino, 1983; Rodman, Pralto, and Nelson, 1985). Overall, however, the environmental context is the single most important factor in how well latchkey children adjust to self-care (Galambos and Garbarino, 1983). Whether the children are in a relatively safe, crime-free setting or in environments where the potential for crime is higher makes a difference in reported fear levels (Robinson, Rowland, and Coleman, 1986).

MEETING EMOTIONAL NEEDS

The Infant's Emotional Needs

The basic emotional needs of infants are for security, trust, love, and affection, as well as self-esteem. The psychoanalyst Erikson (1959) concluded through psychotherapy with children that developing trust is the basic **psychosocial task** during the first year of life. If infants are well-handled, nurtured, and loved, they develop trust and security and a basic optimism. Badly handled, they become insecure and mistrustful. During the first year of life, parents can best meet these needs by fostering their children's feelings of dependency, helping them feel totally secure. This is accomplished in several ways. The *home environment* is important. If it is fairly relaxed and free of tension and anxiety, if it is a pleasant, happy place, children develop a feeling of well-being just by living there. The *emotional tone* that parents convey is also important. Warm, loving, pleasant parents who are themselves calm and relaxed convey these feelings to their children. Being able to depend on parents for *need fulfillment,* whether it be for food when hungry or for comfort when upset, also develops children's sense of security and trust. *Physical contact and closeness* is also important. Children feel secure when held close to one's own warm body, when they can feel their hand on one's face, or feel the comfort of loving arms. Children also need several hours of sucking daily apart from their nutritional requirements. Above all, children *need to feel they are wanted and accepted,* that their parents truly like them and approve of them. These feelings, when transmitted to them, build their own sense of self-esteem (Schaper, 1982).

Emotional Attachments

Research has shown that *children begin to make emotional attachments to other people very early in their development* (Daly and Wilson, 1980). Even though many babies are able to distinguish the mother from other persons by one month of age, they begin to develop emotional attachments to persons in general before they become attached to one person. A study of 60 infants focused on their protest at being separated from objects of attachment by

If the home environment is relaxed, free of tension and anxiety, and a pleasant, happy place, children develop a feeling of well being just by living there.

ascertaining the extent of their crying and whimpering (Schaffer and Emerson, 1964). The situations were everyday, ordinary occurrences, such as being left alone in a room, being left in a pram (this was a British study) outside a store, and being put down from arms or lap. It was found that *half of the specific attachments, including attachments to mother, occurred most often between 25 and 32 weeks.* Strongly attached infants were found to have mothers who responded quickly to their indications of need. If the infant was left outside on the street with other persons around and things happening, the protest was less than if the infant was left alone in a room. If the infant was ill, in pain, fatigued, or afraid at the time, the protest was stronger in seeking the mother's presence. When the attached object returned, such as when the father returned from work, the infant demanded more attention for a while. Figure 20.1 shows the development of the infant's attachments at different ages (Schaffer and Emerson, 1964).

Effects of Separation and Rejection

These findings regarding attachment mean that if a parent has to absent herself or himself from a child in the early months of the infant's life, the child will not usually be too upset if there is a competent substitute, especially one to whom the infant has also formed an attachment. Upset can be avoided by leaving children only with sitters to whom they have become attached. When a new sitter is hired, a parent should stay until the child gets used to

FIGURE 20.1 *Development of infants' attachments.*

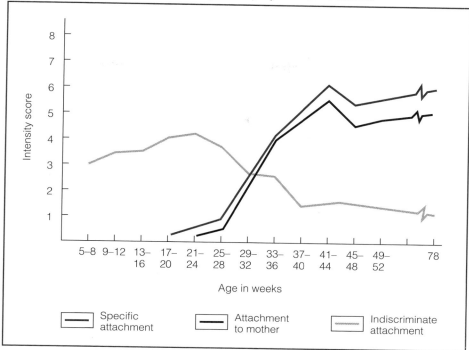

Adapted from Schaffer, H. R., and Emerson, P. E. (1964). The development of social attachments in infancy. *Monographs of The Society for Research in Child Development, 29,* 3. Reprinted by permission of The Society for Research in Child Development, Inc.

that person. Maximum upset occurs when children are left with persons to whom they are not attached (Bowlby, 1969).

Group Care

Some authorities feel that group care is more appropriate after two and one-half to three years of age — at the time the child needs contact with peers (Salk, 1974). If day care at younger ages is necessary, however, it is less upsetting if a child is cared for at the center by the same adult each day.

Fears of Spoiling

One of the most frequent worries of new parents is that they will spoil their children. Because of this fear, they sometimes don't give children as much care as they really need. The fact remains that *no child is spoiled by love, by being given appropriate affection and attention as needed.* Children who are starved for affection do either of two things. Either they withdraw and become calloused and indifferent to whether they are loved or not or they become even more demanding. Current psychology suggests that the syndrome of spoiling, characterized by excessive demands, sulking, pouting, crying, or temper tantrums to get one's own way may occur from overindulgence, but may also occur from (1) a lack of emotional support and affection and (2) a family environment that is authoritarian or that fails to be demonstrative in its affec-tional interaction. *Emotional deprivation increases anxiety and stimulates further demands from the child.*

Autonomy

One of the emotional needs of children beginning at about age 18 months and continuing for more than two years is the need for autonomy; that is, the need to assert independence and self-will and to assert their rights as individuals (Erikson, 1959). "No, I don't want to" becomes a familiar sound throughout the house during this period.

If children are to function as individuals, they want to learn to do things for themselves: to walk, to pick up and manipulate objects, to feed themselves, to hang on to things to prevent falling. As soon as children can move around, they will push adults away, protest against them. This is the child's way of trying to become a person. "Me do" is the key phrase during this period.

Since children of this age are not as capable as they would like to be, frustration and anger are frequent and temper outbursts increase. Figure 20.2 shows the results of a classic study by Goodenough (1931) from *Anger in Young Children.* As can be seen, there was a marked peak in anger outbursts during

FIGURE 20.2 *Number of anger outbursts in 10 hours by age and sex.*

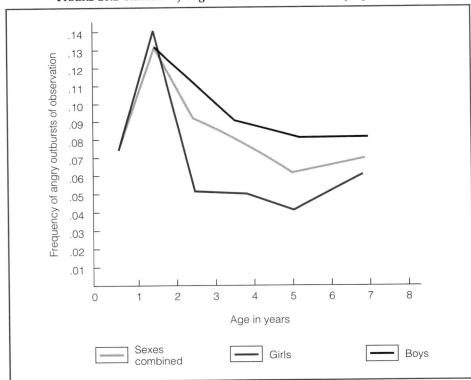

Adapted from Goodenough, F. L. (1931). *Anger in young children* (Monograph #9). Minneapolis: University of Minnesota Press, Institute of Child Welfare. Reprinted by permission.

the second year and a decline thereafter. Physical factors were found to influence anger responses: hunger before mealtime, illness, even slight colds or constipation.

The parent's role is to encourage independence in such things as eating, playing with toys, walking, and so forth, and to guide through substitution, distraction, and tactful control, trying to avoid direct confrontations as often as possible.

FOSTERING COGNITIVE AND INTELLECTUAL GROWTH

Cognition

The word **cognition** is derived from the Latin **cognoscere**, "to know." It refers to individuals becoming acquainted with the world and objects in it, including themselves. They do this by taking in information through the sense of vision, touch, taste, hearing, and smell; processing this information; and acting on it. This process goes on daily so that the infant is developing cognitively all the time (Piaget and Inhelder, 1969).

Parental Contributions

Parents can assist in this development in several major ways. *One way is by providing secure human relationships from which exploration can take place.* Cognitive development proceeds faster when the child feels emotionally secure.

In addition to providing a secure base, *parents can enhance cognitive development by offering a stimulating and intellectually rich environment* (Parks and Smeriglio, 1986). This means talking and singing to babies; playing music; offering objects that vary in shape, texture, size and color; propping babies up so they can see; taking them places so as to expose them to a variety of sights, sounds, and people; offering toy and play material to look at, hold, squeeze, suck, bite, taste, smell, hear, examine, climb onto, crawl under, push, pull, drag, ride, swing, jump, float, and splash.

Sensorimotor Deprivation

Children who are culturally deprived do much more poorly on IQ tests because of cognitive retardation. The theory of the Head Start program is to compensate for this cultural deprivation by offering an environment rich in sensorimotor experiences. While Head Start helps, the one disadvantage of the program is that it is offered too late. Intervention by 18 months is recommended for infants who are markedly culturally deprived.

Language Development and Cultivation

In the beginning, human babies utter vowel-like sounds that are expressions of emotional distress or comfort. The median time for uttering the first word is around 11 months. By 12 months, the average vocabulary is two words.

Parents who read stories to their children enable them to produce significantly more sounds and so learn to talk earlier than do other infants. Early literacy experiences strongly influence a child's later performance in school.

From 12 to 18 months, babies begin to combine words. The earliest sentences are usually two words: a noun and a verb or predicate such as "Daddy all gone." Between 9 and 12 months, babies show they understand words and respond and adjust to them. A baby may open its mouth in response to the word "cracker" or accept a glass of water in response to the word "drink."

The rapidity of language development has a definite relationship to environment and human relationships. Slowness in starting to talk, defective articulation, and stuttering are all associated with certain kinds of disturbing parent-child relationships. Parents who read stories to their children enable them to produce significantly more sounds and so learn to talk earlier than do other infants. Both the amount and warmth of the vocalization of mothers with their infants are related to their children's vocalization. These studies offer convincing proof that *the infant's early experiences with people's talking have definite effects on his or her own language behavior.*

Education Defining and Modeling

As children get older, parents serve as models and definers of their children's educational aspirations and attainment (Cohen, 1987). Parents transmit their educational values to their children. Parents who are educated themselves serve as examples of what they hope their children will achieve. Those who take an interest in their children's schooling are teaching them that education is important and that they are expected to do well. In his study of parents as educational models and definers, Cohen (1987) found that mothers and fathers were about equal in their modeling influence, although whichever parent was higher in education tended to have more influence. Because of their superior education, white-collar parents were more effective educational models than blue-collar parents.

SOCIALIZATION AND DISCIPLINE

The Family's Role in Socialization

Socialization is the process by which persons learn the ways of society or social groups so that they can function within it or them. The dictionary says it is "to make fit for life in companionship with others." Children are taught the ways and values of their society through contact with already socialized individuals, initially the family.

If parents choose to be absent from the home a great deal, other adults may exert more socializing influence on small children than do the parents. As the children get older and are able to maintain contacts with their peers, the peer group may take over and begin to exert more influence in developing values. Bronfenbrenner (1975) suggests that in many urban and suburban homes, where the parents of school-age children are not often home and the children themselves are with their peers most of the time, peer contacts exert the greatest influence on values. Ordinarily, it is adults who are able to teach such values as cooperation, unselfishness, consideration for others, and responsibility. Peer values often emphasize aggressive, antisocial behavior. In an interview Bronfenbrenner commented:

> If parents begin to drop out as parents even before the child enters school, you begin to get children who become behavior problems because they haven't been "socialized . . ." They haven't learned responsibility, consideration for others. You learn that from adults. There's no way that you can learn it from kids of your own age. (Bronfenbrenner, 1975, p. 49)

Bronfenbrenner is pointing to an important trend: the trend in which fewer parents spend the time with their children necessary for them to make their influence felt. When this happens, other persons or groups assume this important role of the family.

Meaning and Goals of Discipline

The word **discipline** comes from the same root as does the word *disciple*, which means "a learner." *Discipline, therefore, is a process of learning, of education, a means by which socialization takes place.* Its purpose is instruction in proper conduct or action rather than a means of punishment (Petersen, Lee, and Ellis, 1982). *The ultimate goal of discipline is to sensitize the conscience and to develop inner self-controls,* so that individuals live according to the standards of behavior and in accord with the rules and regulations established by the group.

In the beginning, control over the child is established by external authority; but gradually children are encouraged to adopt these principles for themselves so that the standards they strive to follow become a part of their own lives, not because they have to, but because they want to. When this happens, these internalized truths become their own standard of conduct (Elkind, 1970).

"Don't Kevin—you'll fall off and hurt yourself."

© Rothco Original

Principles of Discipline

If discipline is to accomplish its goal of developing inner controls, there are a number of principles that, if followed, enhance this development. These may be summarized as follows:

1. *Children respond more readily to parents within the context of a loving, trusting relationship of mutual esteem.* Children who receive nurturance and emotional support from parents show lower levels of aggression than do those who do not receive this support (Zelkowitz, 1987).

2. *Discipline is more effective when it is consistent rather than erratic.*

3. *Learning is enhanced if responses involve rewards and punishments;* that is, if reinforcement is both positive and negative.

4. *Discipline is more effective when applied as soon after the offense as possible.*

5. *Severe punishment, especially if it is cruel and abusive, is counterproductive because it stimulates resentment, rejection, and similar harsh, cruel behavior on the part of children* (Herzenberger and Tennen, 1985).

6. *Discipline becomes less effective if it is too strict or too often applied.* A parent who continually criticizes a child no matter what the child does is teaching the child that it is impossible to please the parents.

7. *All children want and need external controls in the beginning, since they are not yet mature enough to exert self-control over their own behavior.* Appropriate methods of discipline will vary according to the child's age and level of understanding. *However, extremes of either permissiveness or authoritarianism are counterproductive.* At very young ages discipline may be accomplished

through wise management: providing interesting toys and activities, equipping sections of the residence such as a play room or play yard, or childproofing the house by keeping dangerous things out of reach. Young children may be disciplined through distraction and offering substitute activities. Sometimes the wisest discipline is through environmental manipulation: removing the child from the situation or the situation from the child. Parents can discuss issues with older children and arrive at joint decisions, whereas instruction to preschoolers necessarily involves more imperatives. Even then, explanations and reasons are helpful, depending upon the children's level of understanding.

8. *Methods of discipline to be avoided are those that threaten the child's security or his development of self-esteem.* In some cases, parents threaten to give children away if they aren't good or to call a policeman to put them in jail. Similarly, threats to withdraw love if children aren't good is a harmful means of disciplining, but it is one that middle-class parents often employ in subtle ways to control their children's behavior. It may work to control behavior, but it is devastating to the child's security if regularly employed.

PERSPECTIVE
Children's Work Around the House

A study of 790 Nebraska homes in which there was at least one child age 18 revealed some interesting data on the extent to which children were regularly required to do chores around the house or yard. Apparently, assigning chores was a developmental process. In some households, chores were assigned to very young children (about a third of boys and girls four years of age or under were assigned work). The older children became, the more work was assigned, so that by age 9 or 10, well over 90 percent of the children were involved in regular chores. The median number of hours spent on chores was four hours per week. Even among the older, hardest workers, only six hours per week was required (White and Brinkerhoff, 1981).

In the beginning, children were responsible for themselves: picking up their own toys, making beds, cleaning their rooms. By 10 years of age children moved beyond self-centered chores and were now required to help the family.

Parents gave five reasons for assigning chores.

1. *Developmental* — doing chores builds character, develops responsibility, helps children learn.

2. *Reciprocal obligations* — it is their duty to help the family.

3. *Extrinsic* — parents need help.

4. *Task learning* — children need to learn to do these tasks.

5. *Residual* — miscellaneous reasons, including earning an allowance or needing to keep busy (White and Brinkerhoff, 1981).

Another study of 105 children, ages 6 through 17, revealed that the majority of children (88 percent) participated in at least one household task. Children participated most often in house cleaning and food preparation, with older children assuming the most responsibility. Sex-role stereotyping was evident with girls assuming more traditionally feminine tasks. The authors conclude that some parents are overlooking their children as one of the best sources of household help, and that such parents may not fully realize the important role that housework plays in teaching children family responsibility and home living skills (Cogle and Tasher, 1982).

Occurrence

So far, the discussion in this chapter has implied that there are two persons at home who are able and willing to meet children's needs. In many families this is not the case. In 1980, nearly 4 percent of children were living with neither parent (Montemayor and Leigh, 1982, Fischer, 1983). *In 1987, 27 percent of all families with children living at home were maintained by one parent.* Of this total number, 88 percent were maintained by mothers; only 12 percent were maintained by fathers. These figures continue to grow. Between 1970 and 1987, there was a 142 percent increase in the number of one-parent families (U.S. Bureau of the Census, 1989). High divorce rates mean that these families will increase even more in the years ahead. The one-parent family, therefore, represents a major segment of the population, especially among black families and especially among the poor. Fifty-five percent of all black children under 18 are currently living with a lone mother as compared with 17 percent of white children under 18 (U.S. Bureau of the Census, 1989). Large numbers of these single mothers have never been married (Campbell, Breitmayer, and Ramey, 1986).

Single parents have special needs, and so increasing attention needs to be given to offering them support and education to help them with their tasks (Johnson, 1986; Porter and Chatelain, 1981). Research has indicated that these families may be very healthy or unhealthy, depending on the total situation (Hanson, 1986).

Special Problems of the Female-Headed Family

One of the most important problems of the female-headed family is limited income (Blechman, 1982; Pett and Vaughn-Cole, 1986). The median income of families headed by a woman is 50 percent of the income of families with a male head. As a consequence, one-third of these families live below the poverty level (U.S. Bureau of the Census, 1989).

These women also have to cope with inadequate child care (Turner and Smith, 1983). Relatives and family day-care homes (homes of nonrelatives) are the primary care providers for children under age three. Eighty-eight percent of infants and 74 percent of toddlers of mothers employed full-time receive these types of care. For preschoolers (3–5), group care programs (nursery schools and day-care centers) are the most important, followed by relatives and family day-care homes. Among school-age children (6–12), relatives are the most important source of care, followed by family day-care homes, nonrelatives in home, and group care. Table 20.1 shows the percentage of children of full-time employed mothers receiving each type of care. In the years ahead, more family and group-care programs will need to be made available to children of working mothers (Hofferth and Phillips, 1987).

The mother who is left alone to bring up her children herself may have difficulty performing all family functions well (Burden, 1986; Sanik and Mauldin, 1986). There may be little time or energy left to perform household tasks, which means either the house is less clean, little time is available for food preparation, or the physical and emotional care of the children is neglected.

After the first year or so following separation, problems of communication, showing affection, and spending time with the children tend to diminish for the custodial parent and the children.

TABLE 20.1 *Percent Distribution of U.S. Children
in Four Types of Nonparental, Nonsibling Care Arrangements
While the Mother Is Working Full-time, 1982*

Age Group	Relative	Nonrelative in Home	Family Day-Care Home	Group Care
Less than 1	43.3	5.6	44.4	6.7
1–2	28.4	8.4	45.3	17.9
3–5	30.1	7.5	28.0	34.4
6–8	41.3	7.6	35.9	15.2
9–12	52.7	13.2	25.3	7.7
Total	38.0	8.7	34.0	19.6

Source: Bachrach, C., Hown, M., Mosher, W., and Shimizu, I. (1985). National survey of family growth, cycle III: Sample design, weighting, and variance estimation. *Vital and Health Statistics.* Ser. 2, no. 98. Hyattsville, MD: National Center for Health Statistics.

Several studies have shown that, *after divorce, custodial mothers have more trouble communicating with their children, don't show affection, have trouble controlling their children, spend less time with their children because of demands on their time, and are often too absorbed with their own problems to help their children* (Hetherington, Cox, and Cox, 1982; Colletta, 1985; Dornbusch et al., 1985; McLanahan, 1985). Some of these problems in mother-child relationships improve and stabilize after the first year or two following separation (Wallerstein and Kelly, 1980).

The mother must also deal with her own emotional needs for affection and adult companionship. She often feels isolated from the mainstream of social life, which is organized for couples (Smith, 1980). One widow remarked, "I still haven't got used to it. You can be alone in a big crowd." Some of these mothers turn to their children for emotional gratification. At times, mothers relate to their children as peers, treating them as chums, turning to them as confidantes and friends, thus depriving their children of a mother figure (Glenwick and Mowrey, 1986). As one teenage daughter expressed it, "Instead of my mother taking care of me, I ended up taking care of her."

Some solitary parents seek social outlets outside of the home through a variety of groups. *Parents Without Partners* was organized not only to help parents with problems with their children but also to meet the social and emotional needs of adults who are alone. Single parents also establish a variety of social networks and receive social support from their family of origin, friends, and extended family networks (Gladow and Ray, 1986). These networks are important to their psychological well-being (McLanahan, Wedemeyer, and Adelberg, 1981).

Relationships between the noncustodial parent (usually the father) and children are also affected because of separation and divorce. Commonly, immediately after divorce, noncustodial parents spend considerable time with their children and treat them in an indulgent and permissive manner (Amato, 1987). Furstenberg and Nord (1985) found that relationships between noncustodial fathers and their children were primarily social and recreational, and that fathers rarely laid down rules or disciplined their children. This "every day is Disneyland" situation does not last long, however. Contact between father and children tends to decline over time and relationships become less close (White, Brinkerhoff, and Booth, 1985). Grief (1986) found that noncustodial mothers who were paying child support were also more involved with their children than were mothers who were not paying:

> Even if it is the payment of only a dollar a month, the message is still given to the children and the father that the mother wants to help and is caring for them in a variety of ways. (p. 92)

Special Problems of the Male-Headed Family

Solo fathers usually do not suffer poverty to the same extent as do solo mothers (Norton and Glick, 1986). However, *financial pressure* is still one of the most common complaints (Barry, 1979). Most have a greater income than do their female counterparts but still not as large an income as do married men (U.S. Bureau of the Census, 1987b). Most solo fathers do not hire housekeepers. Many receive considerable help with housework from older children (Grief, 1985). The most successful become adept at housekeeping and child care responsibilities before becoming single fathers.

Typically, most single fathers are concerned about not *spending enough time with their children.* If the children are of preschool age, fathers are faced with the same dilemma as are solo mothers who must work, that of finding adequate *child-care services.* Even if the man can afford household help and child care, he experiences *a profound change in his daily maintenance and care and that*

Many noncustodial fathers are concerned about not spending enough time with their children.

of the children. Single fathers undergo considerable *intrapersonal stress* as they take on the responsibility of raising their children. Marital separation often gives rise to feelings of anger, loss, loneliness, failure, and lack of self-esteem and self-confidence. Single fathers are under additional intrapersonal pressure to prove their competency as parents. Part of their stress arises because they are often forced to change their circle of friends and to rebuild their social life.

Overall, however, the evidence suggests that many are satisfied with their new life-styles. They tend to be stable, rather traditional, and established men with a strong motivation to be with their children (Pichitino, 1983). Most feel comfortable and competent as single parents (Resman, 1986). Most can be successful parents, but many would benefit from family life education and child development classes (Smith and Smith, 1981).

Effects of Paternal Absence on Sons

The important question that plagues both parents and professionals is whether or not the children grow up to be maladjusted because of the lack of two parents in the home (Blechman, 1982). The findings reveal that *the earlier a boy is separated from his father and the longer the separation is, the more affected the boy will be in his early years.* One study of fifth-grade boys who were father-absent before age two found them to be less trusting, less industrious, and to have more feelings of inferiority than did boys who became father-absent between the ages of three and five (Santrock, 1970a). *Father absence also affects the development of masculinity.* Father-absent boys are more likely to score lower on measures of masculinity (Biller and Bahm, 1971); to have unmasculine self-concepts and sex-role orientations; and to be more dependent, less aggressive, and less competent in peer relationships than their father-present counterparts (Santrock, 1970b).

As boys grow older, however, the earlier effects of father absence decrease (Santrock and Wohlford, 1970). By late childhood, lower-class father-absent boys appear to score as high as their father-present counterparts on certain measures of sex role preference and sex role adoption. In fact, one study of male teenagers from disrupted families reports that they have less conflict in their homes and a better self-image than did those from intact homes. With father gone, the son stepped in and assumed a "man of the house" role, giving him a new status (Slater, Stewart, and Linn, 1983).

There is one fairly common difference, however, between boys raised in single-parent and dual-parent families. *Those in single-parent families have a lower level of educational attainment and consequent lower income as adults* (Mueller and Cooper, 1986). One study showed that the proportion of young men from single-parent families who did not finish high school was more than twice the proportion of those who always lived in two-parent families. The proportion who received a bachelor's degree or went on to graduate school from two-parent families was almost double that for single-parent families (Krein, 1986).

The effect of father absence is dependent partially on whether or not boys have other male surrogate models. Father-absent boys with a father substitute such as an older male sibling are less affected than those without a father substitute (Santrock, 1970b). Young father-absent male children seek the attention of older males and are strongly motivated to imitate and please potential father figures (Biller, 1971).

Effects of Paternal Absence on Daughters

The effect of paternal absence on daughters has not been as extensively studied as has been the effect on sons. The reasoning has been that children make a same-sex identification, and so daughters would be affected less by the father's absence than would sons. *Girls aren't affected as much when they are young, but they are definitely affected during adolescence.* Lack of meaningful male-female relationships in childhood can make it more difficult to relate to the opposite sex. One study showed that father-absent girls showed greater frequency and extent of heterosexual involvement, but also greater anxiety in dating than did women from father-present homes (Fleck, Fuller, Molin, Miller, and Acheson, 1980). Case studies of father-absent daughters are often filled with details of problems concerning interactions with males. In one study of a group of girls who grew up without fathers, Eberhardt and Schill (1984) found few effects during preadolescence; but during adolescence the girls of divorced parents who had lived with their mothers were inappropriately assertive, seductive, and sometimes sexually promiscuous. Having ambivalent feelings about men because of their negative memories of their fathers, they pursued men in inept and inappropriate ways. They began dating early and were likely to engage in sexual intercourse at an early age. Hepworth, Ryder, and Dreyer (1984) reported two major effects of parental loss on the formation of intimate relationships: *avoidance of intimacy* and *accelerated courtship.*

In summary, therefore, *fathers appear to play a significant role in encouraging their daughters' feminine development.* The father's acceptance and reinforcement of his daughter's femininity greatly facilitates the development of her self-concept. Interaction with a competent father also provides the girl with basic experiences that help in her relationship with other males. Girls who have positive relationships with their fathers are more likely to be able to obtain satisfaction in their later heterosexual relationships (Biller, 1971).

Nevertheless, a father-present home is not necessarily always better for the children than a father-absent home. Some fathers, though home, spend little time in caring for their children or relating to them (Levant, Slattery, and Loiselle, 1987). In such families, father absence would not have as much effect as in homes where the father spent more time with his children.

Some fathers are also inappropriate models. If there is a father at home who is rejecting, paternal deprivation may be a significant cause of emotional problems and/or antisocial behavior. There is some evidence too that girls who over-identify with their fathers may develop high levels of masculinity and low femininity, and become more homosexually oriented than those who only moderately identify with their fathers (Heilbrun, 1984). Thus, *either very distant or very close relationships can cause problems in sex-role and heterosexual orientation.*

The effect of paternal absence on the mother is crucial in determining the influence on the children. (Brandwein, Brown, and Fox, 1974). Many father-absence studies have failed to take into account the mother's changed position following a divorce, separation, or the death of her husband. If the mother is quite upset, if her income is severely limited, if her authority and status in the eyes of the children is significantly reduced, if she must absent herself frequently from the home because she has to work, or if she has inadequate care for her children when she is gone, the children are going to be affected — not because of their father's absence, as such, but because of the subsequent effect on their mother and their relationships with her. Furthermore, the presence of surrogate father figures exerts a modifying influence on both boys and girls.

CLASSROOM FORUM
Growing Up in a One-Parent Family

1. Are your parents separated or divorced? What effect did this have on you?
2. Were you brought up in a one-parent family? How did you feel about it? What were the most important problems you experienced from being brought up in a one-parent family?
3. If you were brought up in a one-parent family, which parent did you live with? How did you and your parent get along? What was your relationship with the parent with whom you were not living?
4. What effect does a one-parent family have on daughters? On sons?
5. How does father absence affect sons? Daughters?

SUMMARY

1. Child-rearing philosophies change from one generation to the next, so parents need to sort out conflicting advice. Husbands and wives often differ on basic philosophies of child rearing.

2. Life circumstances also affect parent-child relationships, particularly the amount of stress people experience. Maternal age at first birth also affects the degree of supportive maternal behavior.

3. Children are different, and so no one method can be considered best for all children.

4. The parental role is to meet the needs of children so they can grow. The parental task is to fulfill physical, emotional, social, intellectual, and moral needs of children. Growth takes place by fulfilling needs; retardation occurs because of deprivation.

5. If there are two parents with children, the children benefit if both parents share in meeting their needs.

6. The term *latchkey children* refers to unsupervised children who care for themselves while parents work. Numerous studies emphasize the negative aspects of self-care; other studies emphasize the positive aspects. A number of factors ought to be considered in evaluating a child's readiness for self-care.

7. The infant's emotional needs include the need for trust, love, affection, security, and self-esteem. The home environment; emotional tone between parents and child; the willingness of parents to fulfill emotional needs, to offer physical contact and closeness, ample time for sucking, and to help children feel wanted and accepted are all important in helping children build self-esteem.

8. Children begin making emotional attachments to people in general before developing specific attachments to caregivers. Children are upset by separation from or rejection by caregivers unless a substitute caregiver to whom the child is attached is provided.

9. Some authorities feel that group care is more appropriate after two and one-half to three years of age.

10. Parents worry about spoiling their children, but no child is spoiled by love and affection.

11. One of the emotional needs of children beginning at age 18 months and continuing for more than two years is the need for autonomy.

12. Cognition means to know and understand. Parents can assist in cognitive development by providing secure human relationships from which exploration can take place and by offering a stimulating and intellectually rich environment. Sensorimotor deprivation retards cognitive development. Language development is enhanced by talking and reading to children. Parents also serve as models and definers of children's educational aspirations and attainment.

13. Socialization is the process by which persons learn the ways of a given society or social groups; it means to make fit for life in companionship with others. Parental influence in socialization is enhanced by maintaining close, warm, affectionate relationships with children and by providing appropriate role models.

14. The purpose of discipline is to teach. It is a means of learning, of education, a means by which socialization takes place. The goal is to sensitize the conscience so that children internalize truths and standards.

15. Twenty-five percent of all families with children living at home are maintained by one parent. This figure continues to rise. Ninety percent of these homes are maintained by the mother and only 10 percent by fathers. Larger percentages of black children than white children are growing up in one-parent families.

16. Special problems of the female-headed family are limited income, inadequate child care, role strain, difficulty in communicating with and controlling children, little time to spend with children, and often being too absorbed with their own problems to help their children. Mothers must also deal with their own emotional needs for affection and adult companionship.

17. Some single mothers turn to their children for emotional gratification. The result may be maternal possessiveness and overprotection. At other times, mothers relate to their children as chums, thus depriving their children of a mother figure.

18. *Parents Without Partners* and other social networks and social supports are important to single parents.

19. Relationships between the noncustodial parent and children are also important to children. Some non-custodials tend to be too indulgent; others to neglect their children.

20. Single fathers face a number of different problems: financial pressure; housework; not spending enough time with children because of work responsibilities; finding adequate child-care services; intrapersonal stress and pressure arising from marital failure and separation, from proving competency as a parent, and from having to change their circle of friends and to rebuild their social life.

21. Some of the effects of paternal absence on sons are psychological maladjustments of various kinds and difficulty in the development of masculinity. The earlier a boy is separated from his father, the more negative the effect will be, but the early effects of father absence decrease as adolescence approaches. One major effect is that boys reared in father-absent homes attain a lower level of educational and occupational attainment.

22. Girls are affected by paternal absence during adolescence more than they are affected at younger ages. Father-absent girls often have difficulty with their heterosexual adjustment or feminine development.

23. Father-present homes are not always better than father-absent homes. Some fathers, though at home, spend little time with their children or are inappropriate models for children. The effect of paternal absence on the mother is crucial in determining the influence on the children. The more negatively the mother is affected, the more negative the effect on children.

SUGGESTED READINGS

Atlas, S.L. (1981). *Single Parenting: A Practical Resource Guide.* Englewood Cliffs, NJ: Prentice-Hall. A practical guide based on personal experiences and insights.

Barnes, B. C., and Coplon, J. (1980). *The Single Parent Experience: A Time for Growth.* New York: Family Service Association of America. Advantages and demands of being the sole custodial parent.

Children's Bureau. (1980). *Infant Care* (13th rev. ed.). U.S. Department of Health and Human Services Publication (OHDS) 80-30015. Washington, DC: U.S. Government Printing Office. The classic governmental work on this subject.

Clarke-Stewart, A. (1982). *Daycare.* Cambridge, MA: Harvard University Press. Research-based discussion of the effects of day care on children's development. Guidelines for parents on selecting day care.

Gatley, R. H., and Koulack, D. (1979). *Single Father's Handbook.* New York: Anchor Books. Written by two psychologist single fathers.

Kliman, G. W., and Rosenfeld, A. (1980). *Responsible Parenthood.* New York: Holt, Rinehart and Winston. A general guide for parents.

Knight, B. M. (1980). *Enjoying Single Parenthood.* New York: Van Nostrand Reinhold. Social and personal areas of single parenthood.

LaRossa, R., and LaRossa, M. M. (1981). *Transition to Parenthood: How Infants Change Families.* Beverly Hills, CA: Sage. Research based.

Murdock, C. V. (1980). *Single Parents are People Too.* New York: Butterick. A single parent gives viewpoints from various helping professions.

Rowlands, P. (1982). *Saturday Parent: A Book for Separated Familes.* New York: Crossroad Continuum. Practical advice illustrated with anecdotes.

Sears, W. (1982). *Creative Parenting.* New York: Everest House. A positive approach to being parents.

Weiss, R. S. (1979). *Going It Alone.* New York: Basic Books. For men or women who are left to care for the children.

21

PARENTS AND EXTENDED FAMILY RELATIONSHIPS

KEY TERMS

positive identification
negative identification

The couple relationship in marriage does not exist in isolation. Not only do the husband and wife continue to maintain relationships with their own parents, but each has inherited a whole new set of in-laws as well. How the husband and wife relate to their own parents and to one another's parents has important influences on their marriage.

In this chapter, we are concerned with these extended family relationships and influences and how they affect the couple. We are also concerned with some special situations: parental rejection, positive and negative parental identification, over-dependency on parents, mother-daughter and mother-son relationships, and problems created by parental disapproval of choice of mate.

Special attention is given to in-law and grandparent relationships. What kind of in-laws and grandparents do people like? What are some problems that arise, and what are the important roots of conflict? What are some special considerations when couples live together with in-laws and grandparents? This chapter focuses on some positive aspects of such relationships: what grandparents can do for children and what children can do for them. Emphasis is placed on working out harmonious relationships among generations.

PARENT ADULT-CHILD RELATIONSHIPS

Family-of-Origin Influence

The relationship a child experiences with parents while growing up continues to exert a profound influence on that person as an adult. The feelings, attitudes, and reactions engendered in the parent-child relationship continue to affect current emotions, relationships, and behavior, at either an unconscious or conscious level (Henker, 1983). If the relationships with parents have been satisfying, pleasant emotional reactions and memories are carried into marriage and usually cause no trouble as time passes. However, disruptive relationships involving frustration, deprivation, fear, or hurt produce unpleasant emotional experiences and memories that reemerge from time to time, producing varying amounts of stress. In some cases, time moderates the distress. In other cases, parent-child misunderstandings emerge and influence the family relationships after the adult child marries.

Parental Rejection

One common experience is that of the child brought up in a family where the needs for approval and affection are not met. If dependency needs are unfulfilled and the child is made to feel undervalued as a person, feelings of inferiority and unworthiness may be carried over into all areas of life. Sometimes a wife marries because of her need for an affectionate father figure. Or, a husband marries a woman who becomes the substitute mother he needs to love him.

> A case in point is that of Sue who was the eldest child in a farm family. She had two younger brothers. The father felt that only males could work with crops and machinery. Also, the father often took the boys fishing, or to football or baseball games. He never took his daughter. Sue enrolled in high school and won a scholarship to college. Her mother expressed her pride in Sue's achievements, but her father paid little attention.

The relationship a child experiences with parents while growing up continues to exert a profound influence on that person as an adult.

At 23, Sue married a professional man who came from a financially comfortable family that stressed creative and artistic success. After the first year of marriage, Sue complained that her husband neglected her and seldom paid attention to her needs. She began demanding frequent dinners out, lovely gifts, and a new and larger house. His protests finally led to marriage therapy that made them both realize that she was projecting her childhood feelings of being undervalued into the marriage. (Messer, 1983, p. 137)

When children grow up with emotional deprivation, they may transfer their needs for attention, love, recognition, and approval to the marriage relationship and expect their spouse to fulfill all the emotional needs that were not met in their own family during childhood. The most frequent example of marriage for neurotic reasons is that of the spouse with exaggerated dependency needs. Such spouses may become clinging, smothering, insatiable in their demands for attention. Such people may need constant reassurance: "I won't be rejected by you as my parents rejected me" (Messer, 1983).

Parental Identification

Identification with parents also influences marital expectations and behavior. **Positive identification** is the attachment of the child to images of desired loving behavior. The songs "I Want a Girl Just Like the Girl Who Married Dear Old Dad" and "She's Daddy's Little Girl" illustrate these desires in marriage. In this situation, the child seeks to duplicate family-of-origin relationships in his or her own marriage.

Such situations become troublesome when the spouse is not like the beloved parent: when the wife cannot be like her husband's mother or the husband like his wife's father. The wife who expects her husband to play the same role as her father did in his marriage is being unrealistic. As one husband said, "I'm not like your father, so don't expect me to be." Or the husband who expects his wife to play the same role in their marriage that his mother did in hers is really saying, "I can't love you as you are. I can only love you if you're like my mother." People often develop unrealistic marital expectations from the example set by their own parents.

Negative identification results in an effort to avoid being like the parent. One man reared in a family with three sisters was always wary lest a female dominate him. In marriage, two personalities interact. How they deal with the mate's conscious and unconscious needs will partly determine the success of the marriage.

Over-Dependency on Parents

Another situation is that of the child who forms an overly dependent attachment to the parent of the opposite sex. If, after marriage, the adult child remains as dependent on the parent as before, the other spouse may feel excluded and resentful (Abramson, 1986).

One example of neurotic dependency is the following case:

Susan married at age 28. She had always been "Daddy's girl." Whenever she had a problem she went to Daddy for help and advice. She never made a decision without consulting Daddy first.

Several weeks before her wedding she became panicky at the thought of leaving her father, but he reassured her that he would still be around and that everything would be "all right."

She married, had a child, but continued to call her father every day, consulting him about every aspect of her life. She never did establish the closeness with her husband that he always wanted. Her Dad remained the central figure in her life. (Author's counseling notes)

History is filled with examples of famous national figures who remained "Mama's boys" and who led the nation with Mama at their sides. Franklin Roosevelt's mother Sara remained in the center of his life. As a child, he was her pampered darling, with his golden long curls and his ponies and pets on the 1,000-acre Hyde Park estate, and on the frequent trips abroad. The involvement of Sara Roosevelt in her son's life was unending. She moved to a Boston apartment while her Franklin was at Harvard. She never gave up trying to manage him; and her position was powerful, since she held the purse strings. As might be expected, Franklin's wife, Eleanor, saw Sara as a thorn in her flesh, usurping her place by Franklin's side. Sara also had a poor marriage. Her own husband James was twice her age when she married him, a retiring man who had poor luck in business; she ignored him while doting on Franklin.

General Douglas MacArthur had a high-powered mother, "Pinky," who accompanied him to West Point and stayed on to keep watch over him for

The primary relationship between a husband and wife can be weakened by conflicting loyalties and by the interference of parents. What can happen when a mother-son relationship takes precedence over the husband-wife relationship?

the next four years, living in a hotel adjacent to the campus. She tutored him in history; and the morning of his West Point examination, she went with him as far as the door, where she gave him a pep talk: "You must believe in yourself, my son, or no one else will believe in you. Be self-confident, self-reliant . . . now go to it." (McCullough, 1983, p. 36). Throughout his career, Pinky maneuvered to be near her son, or to live with him, until her death in Manila in 1935. Her own husband, a celebrated general, had long been dead, and she decided her son must surpass him.

Both of these men became forceful, self-confident, egotistical leaders whose mothers treated them as supermen and taught them to believe in themselves. The efforts succeeded; but in both situations, the mother-son relationship took precedence over the husband-wife involvement, and was shaky at best.

After marriage, the primary loyalty of a husband and wife should be to one another, rather than to parents, or else the primary relationship is weakened by conflicting loyalties and by the interference of parents.

Mother-Daughter Relationships

Jessie Bernard (1975) once quipped: "In the name of tidiness . . . motherhood ought to end when children leave home." Yet, *parental and filial sentiment and responsibility persist into adulthood, with the mother-daughter relationship the most enduring and active of intergenerational bonds* (Cicirelli, 1980; Leigh, 1982). Typically, married daughters see their mothers more often than sons do (Guinzburg, 1983), and maternal grandparents see their grandchildren more than paternal grandparents do. Fischer (1983) found that the mother-daughter bond was even closer and less strained after the daughter's baby was born. Living nearby was associated with less conflict with their own mothers, but more conflict with mothers-in-law. Daughters were much more likely to ask their mothers than their mothers-in-law for child-rearing advice. Daughters with children, compared to those without children, were more likely to have more contact with their own mothers — more telephone contact with near and far mothers and more visiting with near mothers (Fischer, 1983).

When there is strain in the mother-daughter relationship, it is usually because of the mother's criticism of the daughter's person: her weight, temper, or past and present behavior. Mothers also sometimes criticize home managment issues such as the way the daughter keeps house or the way she cooks. *Mothers also like to give their daughters advice on child rearing* — what to feed a child, or how to toilet train a child. *Sometimes the mother's criticism focuses on the daughter's husband.* However, in Fischer's (1983) study, 42 percent of daughters reported no sources of irritation or annoyance with their mothers, but only 17 percent expressed no irritation or annoyance with mothers-in-law.

Other research has suggested that similarity in education and values between mothers and daughters enhances communication, intimacy, and understanding. Not surprisingly, Suitor (1987) found that well-educated mothers were more likely to react favorably to their married daughters' return to school than were less-educated mothers, and the well-educated mothers were consistently more likely to be used as confidantes. Less-educated mothers expressed fear and disapproval of their daughters' return to school. One daughter whose mother had only an elementary education reported:

> She doesn't care for [my going to school]. She feels I should be home where I belong . . . I wouldn't have any trouble if I was home here all of the time. (Wouldn't have any trouble with what sorts of things?) Marriage, kids, any problems. She attributes anything that goes wrong [to my being away from home] . . . I'm married, so my husband should feed me and clothe me and I should sit home and have dinner ready on the table. (Suitor, 1987, p. 439)

Other factors affect mother-daughter attachments. One of these is the aid pattern between the two generations. Thompson and Walker (1984) identified four basic patterns of aid exchange between mothers and daughters:

Mother dependent. The flow of assistance is greater from daughter to mother than from mother to daughter.

High reciprocity. Mothers and daughters are exchanging high levels of aid.

Low reciprocity. Mother and daughter are exchanging low levels of aid.

Daughter dependent. The flow of assistance is greater from mother to daughter than from daughter to mother.

The researchers studied two generations of mother-daughter relationships: young adult women (students) and their middle-aged mothers and these same middle-aged women and their mothers. They found that the typical aid patterns from parent to child continued until the elderly parent was unable to reciprocate and the aid pattern was reversed. Among younger pairs, the daughter-dependent pattern was the model, while it was the least typical pattern among older pairs.

The aid patterns also were significantly related to the degrees of mother-daughter attachment. In general, among young pairs, those most materially dependent (usually the younger daughters) reported lower levels of emotional dependency and attachment. In other words, the middle-aged mothers usually provided more aid and reported more positive evaluations of attachment than their younger daughters, who may have been rebelling against parental authority. However, among older pairs, high reciprocity of aid patterns were most conducive to attachment for both mothers and daughters so that high material interdependence was associated with high emotional interdependence. However, among all groups, the need to maintain independence continues throughout life. *The ability to give aid remains more important to attachment than receiving aid* (Thompson and Walker, 1984).

When Parents Disapprove of Choice of Mate

Parent-child relationships become particularly important in the mate selection process. Parental influence may begin when the child first starts dating (Johnson and Milardo, 1984). The parent may try to influence choice of friends and dating partners. Parents are understandably concerned, but how they express that concern is the key to maintaining harmonious relationships and to continued dialogue between them and their youth. If the parents object to the

Parent-child relationships become particularly important in the mate selection process. If parental objections exist, they may be based on factors such as significant age differences, family background differences, or personality traits. When are such objections valid?

choice, the couple is sometimes pushed into one another's arms for comfort and solace. This "Romeo and Juliet" effect may result in hasty, poor mate choices that would not happen if parents would let the relationship alone to evolve or dissolve naturally.

Parental objections are usually based on one or more of the following:

1. *The parents don't like the person their son or daughter has chosen.* "He's rude." "He's crude." "She's impolite." "She has a bad reputation." "He's not a very nice person." "She's too domineering." "She's been divorced." These objections are based on dislike of the other person's personality.

2. *The parents feel the other person has a problem.* "He drinks too much." "She's too emotional." "He can't hold a steady job." "She can't get along with anybody."

3. *The other person is different from the parent's family.* "Her family are rather common people." "She's not educated." "He's not of our faith." "Why couldn't he have picked some fine Italian (or Irish, Jewish, Swedish, or Spanish) girl?"

4. *There is a significant age difference.* "She's too young." Or "She's too old for him."

5. *The person has been married once or more before.* "This is his third time around. There must be something wrong with him." "She has three children by a previous marriage. Why does he want to get stuck with her?"

6. *The couple is in too much of a hurry.* "They've only known one another for three months." "They don't even know one another." "We don't even know him (her)."

Of course, *some parents would object no matter whom their son or daughter selected.* Such parents may be possessive of their offspring and unwilling to let go or let them grow up. Or parents want to keep them home to help the family. An only daughter who was still at home was expected to care for her widowed mother. She explains:

> I had to take my mother into consideration. No, I couldn't do anything. She had to be my prime concern . . . so there was just no question about it . . . It was my responsibility because my older brother was married, and my other brother was in school, so I was elected. (Allen and Pickett, 1987, p. 522)

A survey of 400 psychiatrists revealed that 81 percent of them felt that marrying someone to whom one's parents objected tended to affect marriage adversely (Gadpaille, 1982). The negative effect is felt in a number of ways. Parents who object before marriage may not be able to back off, so they continue to object and criticize, exerting an adverse influence. Parents may come between the husband and wife by taking sides in disputes. The choice of spouse in opposition to parental acceptance may be indicative of problems in the parent-child relationship, and so the resultant pathology in the child finds disruptive expression in the marriage. Furthermore, the selection of a mate to whom parents object is often motivated by rebellion against parental values, a motivation that impairs judgment in choosing a spouse (Gadpaille, 1982).

There are several approaches to take. Individuals can try to get their parents to like their choice of mate. If objections are based on lack of knowledge, given time and opportunity to get acquainted, some parents end up approving. Parents are not always wrong. The situation needs to be discussed. If

The following questionnaire is used to assess your relationship with your mother and father. Indicate the strength of your feelings on the following scale:

1 — Not at all
2 — Very mild feelings
3 — Mild feelings
4 — Average feelings
5 — Much
6 — Very much
7 — Very, very much

	PARENT	
	Mother	Father

Emotional Support

1. How much do you feel that you are close to your . . .?
   Mother: 1 2 3 4 5 6 7 Father: 1 2 3 4 5 6 7

2. How much do you feel that your views on life are similar to those of your . . .?
   Mother: 1 2 3 4 5 6 7 Father: 1 2 3 4 5 6 7

3. How much do you feel that you are understood by your . . .?
   Mother: 1 2 3 4 5 6 7 Father: 1 2 3 4 5 6 7

4. How much do you feel friendly and relaxed when you are with your . . .?
   Mother: 1 2 3 4 5 6 7 Father: 1 2 3 4 5 6 7

5. How much do you feel your ideas and views are respected by your . . .?
   Mother: 1 2 3 4 5 6 7 Father: 1 2 3 4 5 6 7

Active Help and Support

6. How much do you feel that you can turn to your . . . when you are in need of help or guidance?
   Mother: 1 2 3 4 5 6 7 Father: 1 2 3 4 5 6 7

7. How much do you feel that you can discuss your work and activity with your . . .?
   Mother: 1 2 3 4 5 6 7 Father: 1 2 3 4 5 6 7

Parental Leadership

8. How much do you feel that you are inspired to develop your abilities by your . . .?
   Mother: 1 2 3 4 5 6 7 Father: 1 2 3 4 5 6 7

9. How much do you feel that you are told what to do by your . . .?
   Mother: 1 2 3 4 5 6 7 Father: 1 2 3 4 5 6 7

10. How much do you feel that you are protected against difficulties and dangers by your . . .?
    Mother: 1 2 3 4 5 6 7 Father: 1 2 3 4 5 6 7

EXPLANATION

The first group of questions (1–5) measures your feelings about the degree of emotional support your parents give you. The second group of questions (6–7) measures your feelings about the degree of active help and support your parents give you. The third group of questions (8–10) measures your feelings about the leadership role your parents assume in relationship to you.

There are no right or wrong answers. Most people want the emotional support of parents. The degree of active help and support or parental leadership desired varies. Some parents give too much help or exercise too much leadership authority according to the feelings of their adult children. This quiz helps you to compare the roles of your mother and father and evaluate your feelings about your parents' roles.

Adapted from Cicirelli, V. G. (1980). A comparison of college women's feelings toward their siblings and parents. *Journal of Marriage and the Family, 42*, 111–118. Copyright © 1980 by the National Council on Family Relations. Reprinted by permission.

there are serious differences, this may be a warning signal to go slowly, to take more time and not to rush into marriage. Premarital counseling may also help clarify issues.

The time to resolve problems is before marriage, if possible, else troublesome issues will carry over into the marriage. One wife explained:

> When my husband was courting me, I tried in every way to get his parents to like me, but they would never accept me. They seemed to resent everything I did. I knew I was going to have in-law problems after marriage, and we certainly did. (Author's counseling notes)

IN-LAWS

In-Law Adjustment and Marital Happiness

How important are in-laws in their effect on marital success or failure? *In-law disagreements are more common in the early years of marriage* (Landis and Landis, 1977). Some young couples are able to work out their relationships with in-laws so that a good understanding with them is reached. Others are not able to make acceptable adjustments, and their marriages fail for this and other reasons. Still others settle into a permanent state of friction with their in-laws. This friction may not break up the marriage, but it can cause much unhappiness (Fischer, 1983).

The Kind of In-Laws People Like

One of the most comprehensive studies on in-laws was by Duvall (1954). Her study is an old one, but the best available to date. The results are the basis for the discussion that follows.

About one-fourth of all couples had a very fine relationship with their in-laws. Couples gave the following reasons for liking their in-laws.

> *They are the kind of people we admire:* sincere, interesting, young in spirit, good-natured, pleasant and fun, generous, tolerant, and understanding.
>
> *They do many things to help us.* They take care of the baby; they help us when we're sick or when my husband is away in the service; they give us so many things like furniture, clothes, and money.
>
> *They are more like parents to us than our own parents.* (Orphans and persons from broken homes may be especially close to their in-laws.)
>
> *They are loved because they are the parents of my spouse, who is a fine person.*
>
> *We're in-laws ourselves so we can appreciate what it means.* (Such couples objected to stereotyped prejudices against in-laws, which they felt were very unfair.)

In-Laws People Dislike

In her book, *In-Laws: Pro and Con,* Duvall (1954) grouped undesirable traits of in-laws into a number of categories. Of all complaints, the one noted more frequently than any other about the *mother-in-law* was that she meddled, interfered, and intruded on privacy. She was also criticized frequently for

About one-fourth of all couples have a fine relationship with each other's families. How important are in-laws in their effect on marital success?

being possessive, overprotective, and demanding and for nagging and criticizing. More than half of all complaints about the mother-in-law were in these three categories: being meddlesome, possessive, and nagging.

Sisters-in-law were also condemned for meddling, nagging, and criticizing. But they were also sometimes accused of being indifferent and aloof or thoughtless, inconsiderate, and selfish. Some were also childish and immature, jealous and envious, or gossipy. These types of sisters-in-law may have had trouble sharing their younger brother with his wife and may also have been competitive and immature persons who carried their sibling rivalry into adulthood.

Most people didn't find *brothers-in-law* difficult to get along with; but when they did, they often found them incompetent and lazy, childish and dependent, or thoughtless and selfish. There seemed to be a tendency for brothers-in-law to use their relatives in inconsiderate ways. Like sisters-in-law they were also sometimes criticized for being too indifferent and aloof.

The top-ranking difficulty with *fathers-in-law* was their being meddlesome, followed by nagging, critical, possessive, and overprotective. They were also often accused of being old-fashioned and intolerant, resistant to change, and self-righteous and smug. They sometimes evidenced quite annoying overt behavior: boastfulness, talkativeness, and drinking. Some were accused of being too indifferent and aloof, however, and of ignoring their children.

The Roots of Conflict

There are many reasons for in-law conflicts. Sometimes the problem is with the parents-in-law. More frequently, it is with the couple themselves, who in most cases are more critical of their in-laws than the in-laws are of them.

Many couples are conditioned to expect trouble. Children hear mother-in-law jokes at a young age even before they are old enough to understand them. By the teens, the children laugh with others when jokes are made about her. By the time of marriage, they already expect that the mother-in-law will be all the terrible things they had been taught.

Immaturity of the married couple may contribute to conflict with in-laws. In fact, there is a negative correlation between age at marriage and in-law adjustment. Those who marry young take longer to achieve a good understanding with in-laws and have more frequent disagreements than do those who marry later.

It is not surprising that young couples are more vulnerable to in-law problems than older couples. If the young are still rebelling against their parents, they may transfer a part of this revolt against authority to their in-laws (Goodrich, Ryder, and Raush, 1968). A lack of confidence and experience invites more parental interference or help. A young husband may not be able to carry the full financial responsibility for his family, even with the wife working. The responsibility shifts back to parents. A young wife has a tendency to "run home to mother" when marital problems arise.

It takes time for young couples to shift their primary loyalties from parents to one another. *If the marriage is to succeed, however, the couple's first loyalty is to one another.* Time is also required to get used to the different patterns and habits of the other family members. Good relationships with parents-in-law require maturity, time, and patience; as a result, young couples seldom adjust to their in-laws without difficulties.

The following examples illustrate the problems of immature couples in dealing with in-laws (Rice, 1983).

> *A young husband*: My wife complains of being homesick. She calls her mother up nearly every day and wants to spend every weekend with her folks.

> *A wife*: My husband ignores me when his mother is around. He seems so wrapped up in her that I feel left out.

Some parents create problems because they resent the mate their son or daughter married. Some parents find it hard to accept a son- or daughter-in-law who comes from a different national, religious, economic, or social background. Others resent anyone a son or daughter married because the mate "is not the right one" or "is not good enough." In these cases, the intolerance of the parents is the primary problem.

Parents who are emotionally insecure and who have difficulty adjusting to the loss of their child create problems by being overprotective and meddling. Sometimes the dependent children encourage this overprotection and continue to look to parents rather than to their mates for guidance. In such cases, the mates rightly feel left out and find it unbearable to have to play "second fiddle" to their in-laws.

Living With Parents or In-Laws

Most young couples do not want to live with their parents after marriage; but the younger they are when they first get married, the greater the likelihood that they will do so for a while, since they cannot afford living quarters of their own. This doubling up adds to the stress of family relationships.

CLASSROOM FORUM
Concern About Future In-Law Interference

A young woman is worried because her fiance appears to have more than usual filial attachment to his mother.

1. Should she be concerned? Why? Why not?
2. What approach might she use in talking to her fiance? What might be her goal in talking to her fiance?
3. Should she talk to his mother? Why? Why not? If so, what might she say to her?
4. If you were this young woman and were sure that the mother would be an interfering mother-in-law, would you break the engagement? Why? Why not?
5. Should she *not* marry the man because of his mother? Why? Why not? Explain.

When doubling up is necessary, a variety of living arrangements is used. If doubling up takes place under one roof — but in a house where there are two separate apartments — the situation is not any more stressful than if the two families lived next door. When families live in the same house or apartment, the must share more spaces — kitchen, bathroom, living room, garage, and other areas — and there is a greater likelihood of conflict. Some families even end up sharing the same sleeping quarters. If at all possible, it is helpful if each couple has at least one room they can call their own and to which they can retreat for privacy.

It may not be possible, however, to be completely separate (Komarovsky, 1964). When this situation exists, couples find it necessary to develop a clear understanding of financial obligations ahead of time. Who is to pay for what and how much? The same thing applies to the division of household and yard work. What are each husband and wife expected to do? If the young couple is living in their parents' house, a common complaint of parents is that the children are messy; that they aren't careful of walls, rugs, or furniture; or that they abuse privileges they have been granted. The persons owning the house feel that they are entitled to set the rules and regulations for living there (Rice, 1983).

Sharing Residence with the Elderly

In recent years, there has been an upswing in the numbers and percentage of persons who accept the idea of an elderly person sharing a home with an adult child (Okraku, 1987). According to a survey of a national sample, in 1973, less than one-third (31.4 percent) thought it was a good idea. By 1983, however, the proportion approving unconditionally had gained over 11 points to 43 percent. In general, the younger the age group, the more approval of multigenerational residence. Evidently, younger adults had become more sensitized to the plight of increasing numbers of elderly persons and saw shared residence as a viable option for assisting elderly parents, and especially for keeping them out of institutions (Poulshock and Deimling, 1984). Young adults also were faced with economic pressures and the high costs of housing and welcomed the benefits of pooled resources and assistance in domestic and child-rearing tasks (Okraku, 1987).

Many elderly people will give up their independence and share residence with an adult child. One advantage, confirmed by research, is the unique emotional attachments between grandparents and grandchildren.

The oldest cohorts showed the greatest disapproval and confirmed the conclusion that older people will give up their independence and share residence with an adult child only when forced to do so by circumstances. So *even though there has been some softening in attitudes, in actuality fewer generations double up today than previously.*

GRANDPARENTS

The Changing Grandparent

Recent demographic trends have contributed to a rise in the number of living grandparents and fewer grandchildren per grandparent (Sprey and Mathews, 1982). For most, grandparenthood begins in middle age and spans several decades, lasting well into the grandchild's adulthood (Thompson and Walker, 1987). *Adults today can expect to spend nearly one-half of their lives as grandparents* (Barranti, 1985).

Today's grandparents are usually much different from the stereotyped picture of grandmother in her shawl, rocking idly before the fireplace. Shawls and fireplaces are not standard equipment for the modern grandmother. She

Stereotypical images of grandparents as lacking in vitality do not agree with current realities.

is more apt to be young, vigorous, alert, and energetic, with plenty of ideas and enthusiasm.

There are several reasons why modern grandparents are different. *For one thing, they are actually much younger in body than those of previous generations.* The median age for men when the last child leaves home is 50. For women it is 48. By these ages the children have left to get married or otherwise have become independent, leaving mom and dad alone at home. Many become grandparents before reaching their fortieth birthday. A man or woman in the forties is still a very young person. One investigation of black, working-class families in Southern California included interviews with 18 grandmothers who were in their late twenties through their late thirties (Stark, 1986).

Modern nutrition and improved medical care have made it possible for people to stay younger and healthier. Thus, a woman of 40 today may be as healthy as a woman of 30 was in the eighteenth century. The life expectancy of today's woman in the United States is 78, of today's man is 71. In many cultures and countries, the majority of people still do not live beyond 40. These countries are in the same situation today as was our country in its earliest years.

Modern grandparents have a chance to be younger in mind and spirit. "Mother" is judged by her ability to keep up in appearance, taste, vitality, and knowledge with her daughters and daughters-in-law. "Dad" is judged in business by his new, refreshing, creative ideas, and the extent to which he has taken refresher courses in his field of knowledge. Furthermore, modern mass media and increasing opportunities for adult education in the community help middle-aged and older citizens keep up with modern trends and ideas. Many grandparents learn a great deal by traveling.

Stylists, cosmeticians, and beauticians enable the modern woman to maintain a stunning, fashionable, youthful figure and appearance, so that real age is concealed. Today's grandmother can often pass for a woman 20 or more years younger. Her situation is completely different from that of the lady described in Gilbert and Sullivan's *Trial by Jury* who "could easily pass for forty-three in the dusk with a light behind her."

Grandparents People Like

Many couples appreciate grandparents:

"Grandmother helps the baby to really feel loved and secure because she rocks, cuddles, and sings to him."

"She is much better about teaching the childen to pick up and put things away than I am."

"She has more time to listen and talk to the children."

"Granddad fixes all the broken toys."

"He is able to take our son fishing — something his dad never has any interest in doing."

"During the past four years, my wife and I have saved over a thousand dollars in babysitting expenses because her mother was willing to care for the children."

Busy wives and mothers especially appreciate the help grandmothers give with children and household chores. This help is most appreciated when the mother is sick or in the hospital having another baby.

Most mothers feel that there are many advantages in having the maternal grandmother, rather than someone else, as helper.

"She is more dependable. I don't have to watch her closely."

"I can talk to her more freely and ask questions."

"She cooks the same way I do."

"We like the same things."

"She is more understanding when I'm tired and cranky."

"It's best for the children to have their own grandmother."

Other mothers qualify their own preference for the maternal grandmother by saying:

"It depends on how your husband gets along with her."

"It's easier to ask paid help to do things than to ask your own mother."

"I don't want her to feel I'm taking advantage of her."

Generally speaking, couples like grandparents with these qualities:

"Young in ideas and spirit."

"Someone you can depend on."

"They love and enjoy children."

"They are willing to take suggestions."

"They try to back up what we say and expect."

"They don't undermine our authority."

"They do not overindulge the children."

"They don't offer unwanted advice."

What Grandparents Can Do for Children

The importance of the grandparent/grandchild relationship in the lives of children has been confirmed in research (Baranowski, 1982; Kornhaber and Woodward, 1981) and writings (Cherlin and Furstenberg, 1986). The emotional attachments between grandparents and grandchildren have been described as unique because the relationship is exempt from the psycho-emotional intensity and responsibility that exists in the parent/child relationship (Barranti, 1985).

Grandparents can do a number of things for children:

Grandparents can help children feel secure and loved. Children can never have too much of the right kind of love — love that helps children grow and develop, that eliminates anxiety, tension, and hurt. Love that adds security and trust, that accepts and understands, is always needed. The modern role of grandparents is less associated with authority and power and more associated with warmth and affection (Wilcoxon, 1987).

Grandparents can help children to know, trust, and understand other people. Children can learn that grandma's arms can be just as comforting as mother's. They discover grandfather's house to be a safe and happy home away from home. They learn how to be flexible and to adjust to the ways grandmother thinks, feels, and behaves, which are different from the way mother does.

Grandparents help children to bridge the gap between the past and the present, to give children a sense of history (Kornhaber and Woodward, 1981). Most children enjoy hearing grandparents tell about life when they were growing up. Grandparents who are able to share the rich heritage of the past with children, give them a deeper, broader, more understanding foundation upon which to base their own lives and to build new knowledge. This also helps adolescents identity development as they learn about their cultural and family heritage (Baranowski, 1982).

Grandparents can provide children with experiences and supervision that their own parents do not have time or money to provide. In this sense, the grandparent acts as a surrogate parent (Neugarten and Weinstein, 1964). This is especially important with so many marriages failing and with the subsequent increase in one-parent families. Grandparents now help to take care of the home and children while parents work (Gould, 1982).

Grandparents can give children a fine sense of values and a philosophy of life that is the result of years of living. Valuable experiences and lessons learned by living need to be shared. In this regard, grandparents play the traditional role of valued elder (Kivnick, 1982).

Grandparents can give children a wholesome attitude toward old age. In Western culture, especially, where youth is almost worshipped, children need to know

Grandparents can be important in the lives of adolescents and young adults. Research shows that grandparents share family history and help the young to understand their parents.

and learn to respect their elders. Older people who live rich, fruitful, meaningful lives are a good example for children. They provide a role model for the future role of grandparent, for aging, and for family relationships.

Adolescents, Young Adults, and Grandparents

Research has also indicated that grandparents can be important in the lives of adolescents and young adults. Grandparents share family history and help adolescents and young adults to understand their parents (Baranowski, 1982). Grandparents also function as confidantes and provide outlets when parent/ teen relations become tense (Updegraff, 1968). By observing grandparents and talking with them, adolescents are better able to understand the behavior and attitudes of parents (Streltzer, 1979).

Research on the relationship between college-age men and women and their grandparents reveals the following:

- *When there is high contact between generations, the maternal grandmother/granddaughter bond is the strongest* (Hoffman, 1979–1980; Thompson and Walker, 1987).

- *Young adults have more contact with maternal grandmothers than other grandparents, express a desire for more contact, and indicate that the relationship is important to them* (Hartshorne and Manaster, 1982).

- *Maternal grandmothers describe a closer relationship with grandchildren than do grandfathers.* Grandfathers often have a narrower view of what they have to offer grandchildren than grandmothers and perceive young granddaughters as not needing or wanting their advice (Hagestad and McDonald, 1979). However, *paternal grandfathers and grandsons have a more intense bond than do maternal grandfathers and grandsons* (Kivett, 1985).

- When grandchildren do not have close contact with their grandparents, parents transmit their own feelings and attitudes about their own parents to their children. Therefore, *parents are very influential in determining the grandparent/grandchild relationship* (Gilford and Black, 1972; Robertson, 1976; Thompson and Walker, 1987).

What Grandchildren Can Do for Grandparents

The value of grandparent-grandchild relationships is not all a one-way street with benefits flowing from grandparent to grandchild. Grandchildren also enhance the lives of grandparents. Baranowski (1983) outlines five ways that grandchildren contribute to the lives of grandparents.

1. *Biologic community.* Grandchildren are a source of biologic continuity and living evidence that the family will endure. All individuals wish a part of themselves to survive after death, and grandchildren are in a perfect position to play this part. In a sense, grandchildren allow a grandparent to glimpse his/her own immortality.

2. *Self-esteem.* Grandparents' self-concept is enhanced by playing the role of mentor, historian, and resource person.

3. *Vicarious accomplishment.* Grandparents feel a sense of pride when their grandchildren achieve something of significance. Whether it be a grandchild's first steps, an outstanding athletic performance, or graduation from high school or college, the grandparent has an event to boast about to friends.

4. *Social contact.* The lives of some older people are characterized by social isolation and loneliness, especially if they are physically incapacitated. The frequent presence of grandchildren can help overcome the isolation that can all too easily turn the older individual into a bored and boring person. A key function of grandchildren in this sense is to help keep the grandparent up-to-date by introducing the new ideas, new customs, and new traditions of the younger generation.

5. *Physical assistance.* Grandchildren who have grown past early childhood can provide a variety of types of assistance to help grandparents maintain an independent life-style. In one study, over half the adolescents surveyed had done work of some kind with or for a grandparent in the last year — lawn care, shoveling snow, household chores, and many other forms of help with the physical aspects of maintaining a home. Such help plays a crucial role in supporting the growing trend toward helping able older adults remain in their homes as long as possible as an alternative to institutionalization (Baranowski, 1983, pp. 117, 118).

Grandparents as Problems

Some persons would say that grandparents spoil children, pamper them, never discipline them, or give them too many gifts (Kivnick, 1982). Other persons would say that grandparents undermine parental authority, try to buy children's affection, or cling to children to satisfy personal needs.

Newspaper and magazine articles occasionally deal with the problems of raising children when there is an aged person in the home. One such article was entitled "Grandma Made Johnny Delinquent." This article traced the cause of juvenile delinquency back to the presence of the father's mother in the home and urged that for the sake of the children the grandmother be asked to leave the house (Rice, 1966).

Such a view is extreme. Grandparents are not all alike; they are as different as are different parents. Some grandparents are problems. Others are not. However, problems arise over one or more of the following five situations.

Grandparents may have different ideas about raising children. Sometimes grandparents' ideas are sound; but if their ideas conflict with those of parents, disagreements develop.

Some grandparents have a tendency to preach and give unsolicitied advice to parents and grandchildren. This may cause resentment, especially in adolescent grandchildren who need the space to seek their own identity. As one 15-year-old girl remarked: "Granddad can give good advice, but I wish he'd talk *with* me instead of *at* me. He tries to act like he always knows what's best for me, but I want to make my own decision sometimes." A comment such as this clearly indicates that the era of the autocratic grandparent is over. This may take some adjustment on the part of grandparents who were raised in the more authoritarian family system of times past and feel that the only alternative to autocracy is a laissez-faire or overly permissive approach that results in undisciplined grandchildren (Baranowski, 1983, p. 123).

Some grandparents become too possessive of their grandchildren. Grandparents who are lonely, in need of love, affection, and attention, may use their grandchildren to fill their own empty life. When grandparents start competing with the child's own parents for affection and loyalty, friction and resentment develop.

Sometimes parents deeply resent the affection that children develop for their grandparents. A mother wants grandma to babysit; but when she discovers that her child seems to like grandma better than her, she may become resentful. Such a mother is not emotionally mature or secure in her child's love, and she does pose a problem for the grandparent.

Grandparents often are puzzled about the roles they are expected to play in relation to their grandchildren. Most grandparents are very busy with their own lives. Others need to feel useful in relation to their grandchildren. This need is particularly acute for the widowed grandmother who does not work outside the home or for the retired grandfather left alone with few responsibilities or interests.

Feeling lost, useless, in the way, is a frequent complaint of older people. Many want to be useful to their grandchildren, but they are uncertain how best to fit into the modern family. Sometimes couples take advantage of grandparents. They use them to excess as babysitters, often "dumping" the grandchildren on them without forewarning. At other times, couples expect gifts of clothes, money, and many favors, without really showing appreciation. And sometimes, grandparents are criticized for showing too little or too much interest, or for the way they do try to help.

Is it any wonder that grandparents ask, "I wonder what kind of grandparent they really expect me to be?" Such a question points to the need for couples and grandparents to discuss feelings and expectations and the role of the grandparent in the family.

Grandparents need to be careful not to undermine the authority and discipline of the parents. If grandma interferes while parents are disciplining or lets the grandchildren break the rules of the house when the parents are away, the parents have a right to be upset. Grandparents need to play a supportive role to parents and should be careful not to undermine or contradict them.

PERSPECTIVE
A Code for Grandparents

Accept the fact that the parents have the final responsibility for your grandchildren. This holds true unless you care for the grandchildren day after day in the absence of their own mother or father. Except in this last instance, parents should have the final word on how children are to be raised.

In case of disagreements, talk things over with your children. They can learn from you; but in the final analysis, they have to make their own decisions, even if you feel they are making a mistake.

Don't try to win the loyalty and love of your grandchildren above their parents. It is always dangerous and unethical to come between children and their mother or father or to try to draw children close to you at the expense of their loyalty to their own mother or father. Don't try to turn grandchildren against their parents or try to recast them in your image.

Remember that being a grandparent is not a full-time career. You should continue to live a separate life of your own. Get a job if you like. Keep up with friends. Pay attention to your looks and dress. Cultivate some personal interests: reading, music, a course of study, crafts, club membership, volunteer service work, visiting shut-ins, paid labor, or community projects.

Keep up to date. Don't look back to the old days by telling your children how much better things were then. Make an effort to keep up with the ways life has changed or even improved.

Don't demand consideration because of your age or status in life. Try to earn it by winning respect and contributing to the well-being of the family. Help with chores; offer gifts if you can afford them. Do your share to ease burdens and to generate cheerfulness. Don't lean on others more than needed or expect that your married children owe you a living. The more you can give to others, the more you will receive from life (Rice, 1966).

SUMMARY

1. The relationship a child experiences with parents while growing up continues to exert a profound influence on that person as an adult. Both satisfying and disruptive memories and emotions may be carried into marriage, either at a conscious or an unconscious level.

2. If children grow up with emotional deprivation, they may transfer their needs for attention, love, recognition, and approval to the marriage relationship and expect their spouse to fulfill all the emotional needs that were not met in their own family while they were growing up.

3. Parental identification also influences marital expectations and behavior. Positive identification results in the child's seeking to duplicate family-of-origin experiences in his/her own marriage. Negative identification results in an effort to avoid being like the parents.

4. Children who form overly dependent, neurotic attachments to their parent of the opposite sex weaken the primary marriage relationship through conflicting loyalties and by the interference of parents.

5. The mother-daughter relationship is the most enduring and active of intergenerational bonds. When there is a strain in the mother-daughter relationship, it is usually because of the mother's criticism of the daughter as a person, of her home management, the way she raises her children, or her husband. Similarity in education and values between mothers and daughters enhances communication, intimacy, and understanding.

6. There are four basic aid patterns between mothers and daughters: mother dependent, high reciprocity, low reciprocity, and daughter dependent. Aid patterns are significantly related to the degree of mother-daughter attachment, with those giving the most aid reporting the closest attachment.

7. Parent-child relationships become particularly important in the mate selection process. Parents may try to influence choice of mate. Parental objections to a choice of mate may drive the couple into one another's arms. Rebellion against parents also impairs judgment in choosing a spouse.

8. There are several things that couples can do when parents disapprove of mate choice. They can try to get their parent to like their choice of mate and can give parents time and opportunity to get acquainted. They can discuss the situation with parents; premarital counseling may help. The time to resolve problems is before marriage, or else trouble carries over into the marriage.

9. In-law disagreements are most common in the early years of marriage.

10. About one-fourth of all couples have a fine relationship with in-laws and like them for a variety of reasons.

11. The mother-in-law is mentioned most frequently as troublesome. The most frequent criticism is that she meddled; interfered; nagged; criticized; intruded on privacy; was possessive, overprotective, and demanding.

12. Sisters-in-law were condemned for meddling, nagging; criticizing; being indifferent and aloof, thoughtless, inconsiderate, childish and immature, jealous, envious, or gossipy.

13. Brothers-in-law were not often difficult to get along with; but when they were, they were incompetent and lazy, childish and dependent, thoughtless and selfish.

14. Troublesome fathers-in-law were meddlesome, nagging, critical, possessive, overprotective, old-fashioned and intolerant, resistant to change, self-righteous, smug, boastful, talkative, indifferent and aloof, and convinced that their own ideas were right and others wrong; they also drank too much.

15. The roots of conflict may include the following: negative conditioning to expect trouble and immaturity of the couple; the parents' resentment of the mate the child selected, or emotionally insecure parents who can't let their child go, who are overprotective and meddling.

16. Most young couples do not want to live with their parents after marriage, and parents don't want to live with them. When doubling up is necessary,

each couple needs its own space; obligations and responsibilities should be discussed ahead of time.

17. There has been an upswing in the numbers and percentages of young persons who accept the idea of sharing a home with an elderly person, but older people will give up their independence and share residence with an adult child only when forced to by circumstances. In actuality, fewer generations double up today than previously.

18. Demographic trends have resulted in more living grandparents and fewer grandchildren per grandparent.

19. Today's grandparents are younger in body, mind, and spirit than those of previous generations.

20. Many couples appreciate grandparents for all they do for them and their children.

21. Grandparents can help children feel secure and loved; can help children to know, trust and understand other people; can provide children with supervision and experiences that parents do not have the time or money to provide; can give children a fine sense of values and philosophy of life based upon the result of years of living; and can give children a wholesome attitude toward old age.

22. Grandparents can be important also in the lives of adolescents and young adults. The maternal grandmother/granddaughter bond is the strongest of the grandparent–grandchild bonds, but paternal grandfathers and grandsons have a more intense bond than do maternal grandfathers and grandsons. Parents are very influential in determining the grandparent/grandchild relationship.

23. Grandchildren can also do many things for grandparents: provide a source of biologic continuity and a sense that the family will endure, enhance grandparents' self-esteem, give grandparents a sense of vicarious accomplishment through their achievements, help grandparents overcome social isolation, and provide physical assistance.

24. Grandparents sometimes are problems in the family if they express different ideas about raising children, tend to give unsolicited advice to parents and grandchildren, or become too possessive; if parents resent affection that children give grandparents; if grandparent roles have not been clearly defined; or if they undermine the authority and discipline of parents.

SUGGESTED READINGS

Albin, M., and Cavalo, D. (Eds.). (1981). *Family Life in America, 1620–2000*. St. James, NY: Revisionary Press. A series of readings using a historical approach in analyzing the changes in the family.

Cherlin, A. J., and Furstenberg, F. F., Jr. (1986). *The New American Grandparent*. New York: Basic Books. Their place in the family, and their life apart.

Farber, B. (1981). *Conceptions of Kinship*. New York: Elsevier North Holland. A study of kinship with emphasis on kinship as an element in maintaining social continuity.

PART V
FAMILIES UNDER STRESS

22

FAMILY CRISES AND CRISIS MANAGEMENT

KEY TERMS

crisis
crises overload
comarital sex
alcohol abuse
alcoholism

problem drinking
rationalize
project
repress
blackouts
trajectory of our life

living-dying interval
sudden infant death syndrome, crib death
involuntary manslaughter
post-traumatic stress disorder

Family crises include the death of a parent, spouse, child, or other close relatives; critical, acute, or chronic illness; unemployment; disability of family members; marital difficulties; separation or divorce; natural disasters such as flood, hurricane, or fire; mental illness; and arrest or imprisonment.

We are going to discuss typical patterns of family adjustment to crises and to describe the process. In addition, we shall discuss three major crises that illustrate the types of experiences families face. The crises discussed here are the crisis of infidelity, the crises of alcohol abuse, and the crises of death and grief.

FAMILY CRISES

A **crisis** *may be defined as a drastic change in the course of events; it is a turning point that affects the trend of future events.* It is a time of instability, necessitating decisions and adjustments. Sometimes the crisis develops because of events outside the family: a hurricane, earthquake, flood, war, national economic depression, or the closing of a plant where a family member works (McCubbin et al., 1980). At other times, a crisis occurs within the family system: the loss of a family member, conflict that erupts in family violence, divorce, or alcoholism (Weigel, Weigel, and Blundall, 1987). Internal crises tend to demoralize a family, increasing resentment, alienation, and conflict. Sometimes a crisis develops out of a whole series of smaller external and internal events that build up to the point where family members can't cope. Broderick (1984) explains:

> Even small events, not enough by themselves to cause any real stress, can take a toll when they come one after another. First an unplanned pregnancy, then a move, then a financial problem that results in having to borrow several thousand dollars, then the big row with the new neighbors over keeping the dog tied up, and finally little Jimmy breaking his arm in a bicycle accident, all in three months, finally becomes too much. (p. 310)

Broderick calls this situation **crises overload**.

Patterns of Family Adjustment to Crises

There are definable stages to a family crisis (Boss, 1987; Hansen and Hill, 1964; Lavee, McCubbin, and Patterson, 1985; Walker, 1985). The *first stage* is the onset of the crisis and the increasing realization that a crisis has occurred (Figure 22.1). An initial reaction may include disbelief. Family members may define a situation differently; what is a major crisis to one person may not be to another. One spouse, for example, may be on the verge of a divorce; the other refuses to accept the fact that there is a problem, believing that the spouse is "making too big a deal out of it." The first step, therefore, involves defining the problem and gradual acceptance that a crisis exists: for example, the gradual realization and acceptance of a child's disability. Therefore, the impact of the crisis will depend upon the nature of the precipitating event and the interpretation and cognitive perception of it, the degree of hardship and stress the crisis produces, and the existing resources available to handle the problem.

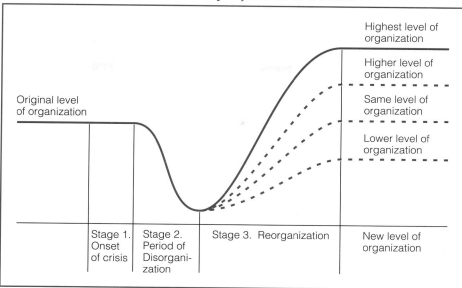

The *second stage* of a crisis is a period of disorganization. Shock and disbelief may make it impossible to function at all in the beginning or to think clearly. "I don't know what I'm going to do" is a common reaction. The period of disorganization may last for only a few hours or it may stretch into days or weeks. During this period the family's normal functioning is disrupted. Tempers are short, loyalties are strained, tension fills the air, friction increases, family morale declines. When it occurs, child and spousal abuse is more likely to develop during the time of maximum disorganization than at any other time (Watkins and Bradbard, 1982). When Mount St. Helen erupted on May 18, 1980, thousands of people felt the stress. Associated Press reports from Washington after the eruption indicated that criminal assaults rose 25 percent, suicide threats and attempts doubled, and the number of cases of battered wives increased 45 percent (Blumenthal, 1980). The situation was particularly stressful because of the violence of the explosion (500 times the force of the atom bomb at Hiroshima) and the uncertainty of subsequent explosions. People did not know what would happen next or how long the catastrophe would last. The effects of stress were delayed, however. The greatest increase in spouse-abuse cases did not occur until about 30 days after the major eruption.

Other studies have shown that the use of alcohol and other drugs sharply increases during times of stress and may lead to a deeper level of disorganization or serve to handicap the family's capacity to bounce back from the crisis (Miller, Turner, and Kimball, 1981).

The *third stage* is one of gradual reorganization during which family members try to take remedial action. If the crisis is a financial one (Larson, 1984), family members borrow money, sell the family car, or cash in on some savings. Other family members get temporary employment to help out, or a breadwinner starts drawing unemployment. If the financial crisis persists, the stock of resources begins to run out. The family has to think about a second mortgage, selling the house, or moving to another neighborhood.

What are the definable stages of a family crisis? At what stage do family members try to take remedial action? If the crisis is financial, what actions are likely?

Once the crisis "hits bottom," things begin to improve. The family breadwinner gets a new job, and bills are gradually paid off; the family begins to recoup its emotional and physical resources. Eventually, after a period that may range from days to months, the family is reorganized at a new level. Sometimes the new level is never as satisfactory as the old; at other times the level of organization is superior to the old. (In the case of a financial crisis, family money management improves and/or total income is higher). At any rate, the level is high enough and stable enough to mark the end of the period of crisis. (See Figure 22.1.)

Crisis theory such as that just described is helpful as a model for understanding what happens when families have various kinds of crises. While this theory can be applied to a wide variety of crises, three types have been selected here for detailed discussion. These are the crisis of *infidelity*, the crisis of *alcoholism*, and the crisis of *death and grief*.

THE CRISIS OF INFIDELITY

Trends and Reasons

The majority of Americans still enter marriage expecting and committed to sexual fidelity. Americans place a high value on sexual exclusiveness as important to a healthy marriage relationship (Stayton, 1983). A survey among 321 undergraduate college students revealed that only 15 percent found extramarital sexual involvement, necking, and petting acceptable (Weis and Slosnerick, 1981).

In spite of these attitudes, the meager data available indicate an increase in extramarital sexual relationships since the 1960s (Elbaum, 1981; Reiss, 1973; Saunders and Edwards, 1984). Reviews of the research literature indicate that from 40 to 50 percent of married men report having affairs (Thompson, 1983).

The figures are slightly lower for women (Reiss, Anderson, and Sponaugle, 1980).

Why do adults become involved in extramarital affairs even though they say they don't believe in them? There are a variety of reasons.

Emotional Need

For some people, extramarital affairs are an effort to fulfill emotional needs. Affairs are an expression of personality problems. A woman may unconsciously seek an older father figure (who is already married) to comfort her and love her and to replace the Daddy whom she lost in childhood or who rejected her as a child (Jeffress, 1982). A man may want an older woman who will mother him because he never felt loved and cared for by his mother while he was growing up. Richardson (1986) says that many professional women fall in love with their married bosses because the bosses offer a safe harbor, a relationship where the women can be vulnerable, weak, and dependent, a luxury denied them in their professional role.

Extramarital affairs can be an important validation of attractiveness and self-esteem. Some women find married men a special challenge because they are already spoken for and presumably harder to get. Affairs may result from fear about one's self-worth or sexual attractiveness. The affairs become an effort to feel better about oneself. Elbaum (1981) writes:

> The need for validation that is absent in marriage is a common cause of extramarital coitus. In fact, some affairs are not sexual in nature but revolve around a man or woman seeking affection and comfort from a significant other. (p. 491)

Infidelity may be a symptom of emotional difficulties in the individual and an attempt to resolve these difficulties (Saul, 1983).

Unresolved Marital Problems

Infidelity can also be a symptom of unresolved problems in the marriage itself. These problems build up year after year and are never dealt with (Saunders and Edwards, 1984). Sometimes the marital problems are sexual. The husband and/or wife is sexually frustrated and so seeks sexual fulfillment outside the marriage bond. A husband explains, "My wife doesn't enjoy sex; she's seldom willing. Why should I go through life frustrated? My girlfriend gives me everything I need and want" (Author's counseling notes). At other times the problems are social or emotional. A wife explains, "My husband never talks to me. My lover and I talk for hours about everything. He's interesting and so much fun to be with" (Author's counseling notes).

Many times business people meet others of the opposite sex through their work and are attracted to those who share similar career interests. One husband explains:

> Sarah and I have absolutely nothing in common. She's a wonderful person, but I can't talk to her about my work. It's different with Kathy. We are in the same profession, and we can have serious discussions about everything. (Author's counseling notes)

Eventually, this husband divorced his wife and married Kathy.

Unresolved issues, such as the lack of communication, the efforts of one person to dominate another, the lack of demonstration of affection, and the lack of social life and companionship build up over the years. People repress their feelings because they don't like to be upset and frustrated all the time. Eventually, they shut off their positive feelings of warmth and affection as well. However, they are still vulnerable to respond to those persons who fulfill the needs not being met in their primary relationship.

If hostility builds up between marital partners, an extramarital affair becomes a way of balancing the animosity felt toward a spouse or a way of "getting even" for the hurts suffered in the marriage (Saul, 1983). Most people aren't interested in extramarital relationships when everything is going smoothly in their marriage. *For this reason, an affair is a symptom of problems, often not the problem, even though it compounds the difficulties.*

Ambivalence About Marriage

People who are ambivalent about being married themselves may seek sexual partners who are already married because they feel "safer" knowing they won't have to make a permanent commitment. They escape the responsibilities of being a spouse, but gain the benefits of being a lover (Jeffress, 1982).

Pleasure, Excitement

Some people have affairs simply because they want the excitement of sexual variety. Other people like the competition with a married spouse, and the married person's unavailability only serves to increase the challenge. They like the excitement of forbidden sex. There is risk, of course. One is the possibility that they might become emotionally involved whether they have intended to or not. To other people, a one-night stand provides excitement and freedom from the responsibilities of an emotional commitment (Elbaum, 1981). The risks here include the possibilities of AIDS or another sexually transmitted disease, as well as the negative effects on the marriage because marital vows have been violated.

A new relationship may seem more exciting than an old one, primarily because it is different and new. But the initial flush of intense emotions declines, leaving the couple empty unless something deeper has developed in the meantime.

Permissive Values

Some individuals don't really see anything wrong with extramarital sex — as long as their spouse doesn't find out or "it doesn't hurt anyone." One husband became involved with another woman with whom he continued to have sex. He couldn't understand why his wife was so upset when she found out. As far as he was concerned, he ought to have been allowed to have a wife and a mistress. Some people have numerous partners before marriage and continue to do so afterwards because permissiveness is a part of their value system.

Some couples accept and practice **comarital sex**, which is extramarital sex about which the other partner knows and consents prior to the involvement

(Macklin, 1980). Sometimes, emotional involvement with the other partner is a part of comarital sex, at other times not (Thompson, 1984). Couples report more positive evaluations of comarital sex if love is involved, but that involvement also constitutes a threat to the marriage (Harnett, Mahoney, and Bernstein, 1977).

Ulterior Motives

Having a lover who is also a supervisor or mentor sometimes offers other advantages. One management trainee explained: "I know he gave me special help and attention he wouldn't have otherwise. That's why I've been able to move up so fast" (Richardson, 1986, p. 26). *Having an affair with a married person who is in a position of authority is one way an individual may advance a career* (Colp, 1982). Of course, some people may not be interested in advancing their careers. *They may just want to be allied to someone who is wealthy and powerful.*

Opportunity

The reason some single women give for having affairs with married men is that there are not enough single men to go around; however, this is true only at older ages. Figure 22.2 shows the ratio of unmarried men to unmarried

FIGURE 22.2 Ratio of Unmarried Men to Unmarried Women, by Age: 1987.

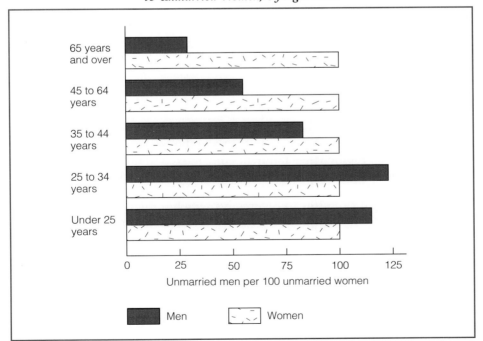

From U.S. Bureau of the Census. (1989). Statistical Abstract of the United States, 1989. Washington, DC: U.S. Government Printing Office.

women by age in 1987. Young adults age 25 to 34 had a ratio of 123 unmarried men for every 100 unmarried women. However, at age 35 to 44, there were 88 unmarried men for 100 unmarried women, and this dropped to 55 per 100 for the age group 45 to 64 years (U.S. Bureau of the Census, 1989). Thus, *only after ages 25 to 34 is there a shortage of single men.*

However, the more educated the woman and the more advanced in her career, the more selective she becomes, and the more she associates with men who are also older, educated, and professional. The majority of these men are married. Rather than opt for relationships with men who do not seem as attractive, some single women opt for involvement with married men. They are the new "Other Women" (Richardson, 1986).

Of course, we can also discuss this from the man's point of view. *Many married men are opting for affairs with single, younger women.* The men find an ego boost to weather their middle-age crisis, and they find sexual excitement and pleasure without the responsibilities of marriage.

Affairs as Crises for Single Women

However valid or invalid the reasons for having an affair, *extramarital affairs are often a crisis for the single woman.* Part of the problem stems from the fact that the affair must be kept secret. Like spies or members of secret organizations, the couple must be discreet about when and where they meet. They cannot be seen together in public, unless it is at a business meeting or on a casual basis. Even out-of-town rendezvous become dangerous. One married man who lived in Maine met his girlfriend at O'Hare airport in Chicago, only to discover that his boss was getting off the same plane as his friend!

Another problem stems from the fact that the single woman gradually loses control of how her time is spent. Her married lover has family obligations, which he often puts ahead of her. He spends holidays and important occasions with his wife and children. The girlfriend has to fit her schedule to that of the married man. One woman comments:

> The flaw was that he really was in charge, even when I thought I was. When it finally came down to it, he thought I should stop what I was doing when he came over. (Richardson, 1986)

Once a woman has accepted male initiative in the relationship, she sacrifices control over life's moments — moments that stretch to hours, days, months, and years. She sacrifices independence and is unable to hold onto her image of a woman with mastery and control; the result is a subsequent loss of self-esteem. If the man promises to divorce his wife but never does, the woman is hurt and disappointed unless she has been successful in limiting her emotional involvement — although many times, she hasn't. The woman who becomes dependent in an affair that goes nowhere ends up deriving more pain than pleasure (Richardson, 1986). Guilt, anxiety, and the burden of deception can take a terrible toll (Elbaum, 1981). One woman explains:

> Worst was the energy drain, the psychological energy that went into keeping the relationship at bay, and then dealing with the unexpected hurt. It ended up being very costly to me, to my career, and my life in general. (Richardson, 1986, p. 27)

Extramarital affairs have varying effects on married people and their marriages. Some marriages are never the same afterward. Guilt, anger, jealousy, distrust, loss of respect, and the destruction of love and intimacy are common (Buunk, 1982; Elbaum, 1981). One wife remarked: "I don't know if I can ever trust him again. Every time he's out of town I wonder what he is doing and who he's with" (Author's counseling notes). Another wife commented: "All I can think of is that he was doing this with that other woman. I can't give myself to him" (Author's counseling notes). In these cases, extramarital affairs may be a major factor in precipitating divorce.

Sometimes, however, the crisis of an affair stimulates the couple to finally accept the fact that their marriage is in deep trouble and that they need help. One wife explained:

> I've been trying to tell my husband for years that I was unhappy in our marriage, but he didn't listen. Now, I've met someone else, and for the first time my husband is listening and is willing to go to a marriage counselor. (Author's counseling notes)

In this case, the affair had a positive value.

Many people who become involved in an affair never intended it to happen. "I never thought it would happen to me" is a frequent comment. Such people don't have an affair just for the thrill of it. Their physical, emotional, and social needs are not being met in their marriage, and so they become very vulnerable to another person who offers what they lack. The way to straighten out the difficulty is to find out what needs are not being met in the marriage and to find ways and means of fulfilling them.

There are some couples whose marriages are not affected very much by an affair. One of the spouses is having an affair, but the other doesn't care. These are often marriages where the emotional bonds between the couples are already broken, so the extramarital relationship is just evidence of the fractured marriage. These couples have either lost or never had a meaningful relationship with each other (Voth, Perry, McCranie, and Rogers, 1982).

In some situations, a wife discovers that her husband is unfaithful but chooses not to confront him with his actions because she has children and does not feel equipped to support herself and her children (Saul, 1983).

Husbands are not the only participants. The author has numerous female clients who have had long-standing affairs. Most of the time, however, the husbands did not know. Or, if they found out, they demanded the affair be stopped. If the wife wanted to maintain her marriage, she usually broke off the affair. Sometimes she did not, usually because she had already decided to divorce her husband.

One of the significant differences between husbands and wives is that more husbands than wives who are involved in meaningful affairs don't want to give them up. They expect that they'll be allowed to stay married at the same time that they are involved in the affairs. One husband spent every weekend for seven years with his girlfriend, leaving on Friday night and not returning until Sunday evening, with the full knowledge of his wife. Finally, his wife asked him to leave, permanently, but felt very guilty afterward that she was the one who broke up the marriage!

The affairs that are most threatening to the marriage are ongoing affairs that include emotional involvement as well as sexual relations (Thompson, 1984). Persons who believe that they have fallen deeply in love don't want to give up the affairs. The affair seems so meaningful and exciting. Clients report: "I haven't felt like this for years. I can't give up something that makes me feel alive again" (Author's counseling notes). Of course, what people don't realize in the beginning is that the intense emotional excitement will pass; and if the relationship is to endure, the couple needs to have many other things going in the relationship.

From many points of view, extramarital relationships become a crisis in the marriage that requires considerable effort to resolve.

PERSPECTIVE
Preventing Infidelity

The following guidelines are helpful in preventing extramarital affairs (Voth, Perry, McCranie, and Rogers, 1982; Stayton, 1983).

1. Keep the lines of communication open in your marriage relationship. Share feelings, disappointments, and unmet expectations, as well as positive reactions. Major problems arise usually as whole series of small, unresolved issues that build up over a period of time. Solve small problems as they arise by learning to discuss them rationally, calmly, and sympathetically.

2. Strive to fulfill one another's physical, social, emotional, and intellectual needs through your relationship. Find out what the needs of your partner are, take them seriously, and strive to meet those needs.

3. Learn to be loving and affectionate, frequently expressing warmth and physical affection. Hugging, cuddling, kissing, caressing, and physical closeness are as important to emotional fulfillment as is sexual intercourse.

4. If you have personality faults and problems that are unresolved, get therapy to help you work through these. Remember, extramarital sex usually creates more problems than it solves.

5. Strive for variety and imagination in your lovemaking. If your sexual relationship has become too routine, spruce it up, perhaps by changing the times, places, manner, and mode of sexual expression.

6. Resolve to make your sexual relationship a mutually satisfying experience, by being concerned about one another's preferences and desires, and by giving as well as receiving pleasure.

7. Commit yourself to sexual fidelity and live by that commitment.

8. Show respect, appreciation, approval, and acceptance of your spouse.

9. Avoid heterosexual situations that are conducive to involvements. Keep your business associations on a professional basis. Avoid one-to-one meetings for social purposes. Avoid compromising situations. Recognize that people sometimes do and say things when they have been drinking or taking other drugs that they wouldn't ordinarily say and do.

10. When you find yourself physically attracted to a person not your spouse, tell your mate and discuss the situation. Be honest and aboveboard, and don't try to hide anything.

Definitions

Alcohol abuse is a generic term that includes both **alcoholism** (addiction to alcohol characterized by compulsive drinking) and **problem drinking** (functional disability as a result of alcohol consumption) (U.S. Department of Health, Education and Welfare, 1980a). Both alcoholism and problem drinking create problems in and for the family. A Gallup Poll revealed that about one-fourth of Americans reported that alcohol had been a cause of trouble in their families (Gallup, 1979). Alcohol is a major factor in marital disruption, domestic violence, and child abuse. In a high proportion of cases of wife abuse, or in cases where a parent beats a young child so severely that he or she is hospitalized, the parent is drunk at the time. More than 200,000 premature deaths each year are associated with alcohol misuse (U.S. Department of Health, Education, and Welfare, 1980b). Countless thousands more children are born with various defects, especially mental deficiencies, associated with heavy drinking during pregnancy.

Development of Chronic Alcoholism

One of the finest descriptions of how alcoholism develops is included in *I'll Quit Tomorrow* (Johnson, 1973). The information that follows, presented in abbreviated form, is taken from that book.

Johnson divides the process of becoming an alcoholic into four phases:

Phase One: Learns mood swing

Phase Two: Seeks mood swing

Phase Three: Harmful dependence; acute, chronic phase

Phase Four: Drinks to feel normal

Phases one and two, represented by Figures 22.3 and 22.4 are discovering and learning phases during which people learn that taking a drink will give them a warm, good feeling and may even cause giddiness, depending upon the amount. The initiation is interesting and pleasant, and people learn that they can make themselves feel better. They can turn on the feeling of euphoria any time they drink, and they can control the degree of mood swing by the amount. And it works every time! One drink will do this, two or three will do that. So every time they come home tired, or when they are depressed or upset, they seek a drink or more because they have learned through experience that alcohol will do the trick. Thus, they have developed a relationship with alcohol. They have learned that it works, that it is a positive experience, and that they can trust it; and so they seek mood swings in more or less regular and appropriate ways.

There is no acute problem yet. When the effects of the alcohol wear off, the drinker returns to normal. Unless people drive while drinking and have an accident, or get in some other kind of trouble, there is no damage and no emotional cost.

Up to this point, drinkers follow self-imposed rules, one of which is perhaps: "Don't drink until five o'clock." But the day comes when they look at

FIGURE 22.3 *Phase One: Learns Mood Swing.*

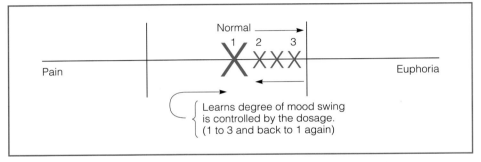

From Johnson, V. E. (1973). *I'll quit tomorrow.* New York: Harper and Row, 11. Reprinted by permission of the publisher.

FIGURE 22.4 *Phase Two: Seeks Mood Swing.*

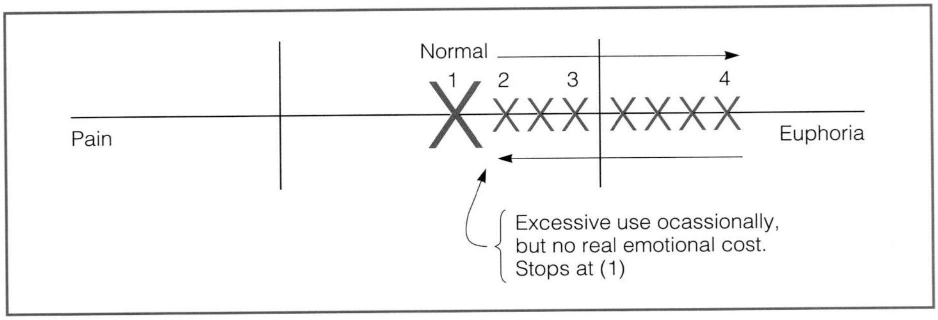

From Johnson, V. E. (1973). *I'll quit tomorrow.* New York: Harper and Row, 13. Reprinted by permission of the publisher.

their watch and it's only two o'clock: three hours before time to get out of work. Waiting becomes too painful, so they have a drink with lunch or while watching Saturday afternoon television. From this point on, the feeling of relief may be sought earlier and earlier in the day, with larger and larger amounts of alcohol.

As social drinkers get deeper into their chemical, getting drunk begins to have a very different effect on them. They are caught in a habit that carries them beyond social drinking. *They enter phase three which is alcoholism, by becoming harmfully and chemically dependent.* They think everything is all right and are unaware that they have crossed an invisible line that they cannot get back across by themselves (Figure 22.5).

As drinking becomes more and more excessive, the mood swings become more pronounced. Drinkers go from euphoria to negative emotional reactions and pain. They feel remorse at their excesses, and at their foolish behavior: "I was stupid last night. Nobody stands on a table and leads cheers at the club. I'll have to call Harry and Jane and apologize." With each drinking experience, drinkers feel more remorse and develop a reduced self-image (Figure 22.6). Their ego strength ebbs as drinking produces painful and bizarre behavior. They begin to feel self-hatred: "I'm just no damn good" is the reaction.

But no one can live forever with self-hatred, anxiety, guilt, shame, and remorse, so *drinkers begin to build up their defenses. Through various defense mech-*

FIGURE 22.5 *Phase Three: Harmful Dependence.*

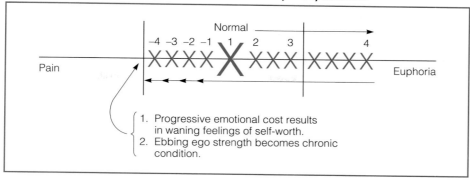

1. Progressive emotional cost results
   in waning feelings of self-worth.
2. Ebbing ego strength becomes chronic
   condition.

From Johnson, V. E. (1973). *I'll quit tomorrow.* New York: Harper and Row, 17. Reprinted by permission
of the publisher.

FIGURE 22.6 *Phase Three: Harmful Dependence (Deterioration of Self-Image).*

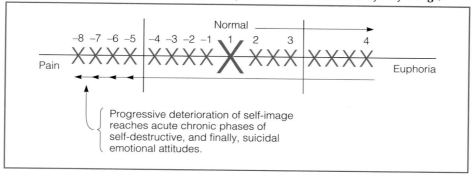

Progressive deterioration of self-image
reaches acute chronic phases of
self-destructive, and finally, suicidal
emotional attitudes.

From Johnson, V. E. (1973). *I'll quit tomorrow.* New York: Harper and Row, 19. Reprinted by permission
of the publisher.

*anisms they build a wall around their negative feelings, to the point where they become
unaware that such destructive emotions exist.* For one thing, they begin to make
excuses for drinking, to **rationalize** their behavior: "I don't feel well." "I'm
tired." "I'm under pressure at work." "It's my birthday and I need a drink."
Whatever happens becomes an excuse for drinking (Figure 22.7).

For another thing, they begin to blame others for their drinking problem,
to **project** their own self-hate on them (Figure 22.8). Alcoholics do not know
this is happening. It occurs unconsciously. Because alcoholics hate themselves, they must vent their hate by attacking others. "They are always trying
to run my life." "If you would straighten up, everything would be all right."
Of course, those whom the alcoholic attacks may end up blaming themselves
and do all they can to try to remedy the situations that they feel may be
causing the drinking. They fix dinner earlier. They hide the bottle. They plead,
they get angry. Nothing works. As their failures mount, they become more
anxious, guilty, frantic, and emotionally distressed. This reinforces the alcoholic's view that others are to blame.

Alcoholics also use another defense mechanism to hide their guilt, shame,
and remorse. They **repress** their feelings, which helps them not to feel at all
(Figure 22.9). As a result, they may become very apathetic, indifferent, or
emotionless about everything: their family, friends, even their own drinking.

FIGURE 22.7 Phase Three: Harmful Dependence (Rational Defenses).

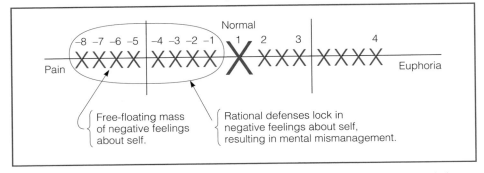

From Johnson, V. E. (1973). *I'll quit tomorrow.* New York: Harper and Row, 25. Reprinted by permission of the publisher.

FIGURE 22.8 Phase Three: Harmful Dependence (Projection).

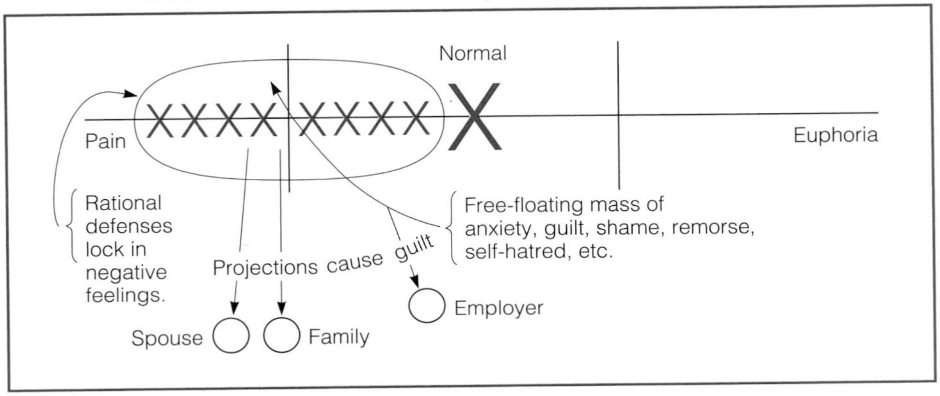

From Johnson, V. E. (1973). *I'll quit tomorrow.* New York: Harper and Row, 29. Reprinted by permission of the publisher.

As the disease progresses, **blackouts** *may become more frequent.* These are not to be confused with "passing out" or drinking to the point of losing consciousness. The chemically induced blackout involves a permanent and complete loss of memory for a given period of time. Afterward, alcoholics ask:

"How did I get home last night?"

"Where am I? How did I get to this motel room?"

Drinkers go on functioning during the blackout as though they are aware of what is going on around them, but they actually remember none of it again. They suffer real *amnesia.* Other people assume they are in control of themselves and are rational, and resume relations with them following these memory lapses on the assumption that they have shared common experiences. Alcoholics are generally so embarrassed by the loss of memory that they try to bluff it out. Confusion is likely to result.

But the actual loss of memory hides from alcoholics what they have done. They might have drunk a quart, but honestly remember only two drinks. They may have acted obnoxiously or violently, but remember only their euphoria. "I had a few drinks, but I was perfectly all right" is all they remember. Alcoholics cannot understand why others look askance at them or shun them after a while. And friends cannot understand why drinkers do not see

FIGURE 22.9 Phase Three: Harmful Dependence (Repression).

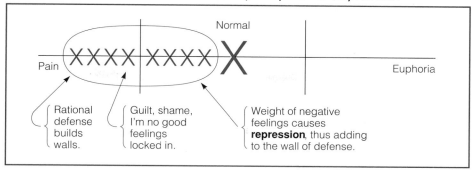

From Johnson, V. E. (1973). *I'll quit tomorrow.* New York: Harper and Row, 69. Reprinted by permission of the publisher.

FIGURE 22.10 Phase Four: Drinks to Feel Normal.

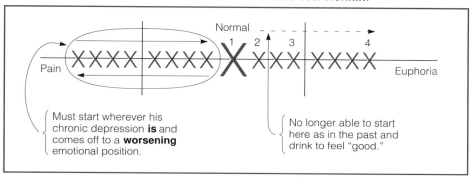

From Johnson, V. E. (1973). *I'll quit tomorrow.* New York: Harper and Row, 26. Reprinted by permission of the publisher.

what they are doing to themselves and others. The reason is that alcoholics don't remember. *Between blackouts and repression, their judgment is seriously impaired.*

In the acute stage, alcoholics are no longer emotionally able to start any given drinking episode from the "normal point." They no longer feel "good," "great," or euphoric. They feel chemically depressed on the painful side of the figure (see Figure 22.10) *and have to drink just to feel normal.* Thus, they drink in the morning when they wake up. They drink on the job (if they still have one). They drink at home. They drink because they have been drinking. Drinking at this stage is thoroughly compulsive.

Two obstacles prevent alcoholics from getting the attention they need. First, most people do not understand their helpless condition and so deal with them judgmentally. "Can't you see how sick you're getting?" When alcoholics don't see this, people react by turning away. They may even have a false expectation that alcoholics will gain insight when they hit bottom! This makes alcoholics even more isolated and defensive. And *second,* their rigid behavior and distorted memory patterns prevent alcoholics from getting help. Their impaired judgment and their chemical dependency keep them locked into the self-destructive pattern. The sicker they get, the more actively they resent intervention.

Alcoholism is a progressive illness and is always fatal unless arrested. But to arrest it requires intervention from the outside, by knowledgeable persons who are trained to perform the function.

Treatment consists of several aspects. *First*, alcoholics must be confronted with the reality of their illness so they will realize their condition. Even at their sickest, they can accept some reality if it is presented to them by persons they can trust in forms they can receive (see Johnson, 1973, on "The Dynamics of Intervention," p. 43.)

Second, once the alcoholic is willing to receive treatment, chemical dependency is dealt with in a carefully phased detoxification program. Intensive medical treatment is begun to care for the acute symptoms of the disease.

Third, education is necessary to teach alcoholics the facts about their disease. They are taught through lectures, films, reading, discussion, and other means. The primary goal is to make them realize intellectually what chemical dependency is and to accurately describe to them the symptoms and consequences of their disease.

Fourth, through individual and group psychotherapy they are helped to identify their defenses and to break them down so they can become feeling persons again. As their defense wall is breached, they are encouraged to ventilate negative attitudes and feelings, so they can have realistic insights into their condition and gradually rebuild their own feelings of self-worth as the disease is arrested (see Figure 22.11).

Fifth, alcoholics are assisted with the process of rehabilitation: finding jobs, repairing broken family and personal relationships where possible, and becoming accepted members of society again. Rehabilitation requires involving meaningful persons who have suffered because of the alcoholic's illness and helping them to develop the attitudes that are conducive to healing.

Coping with an Alcoholic Husband

We have outlined the stages of alcoholism: how it develops, how the alcoholic reacts, and some principles of treatment. We also need to develop a better understanding of the disease from the point of view of family members who live with the alcoholic. *Alcoholism is a family crisis because the disease affects the whole family* (Downs, 1982; Smith, 1982). Like the alcoholic, family members also go through various stages as they attempt to cope with the crisis (Parades, 1983). We are going to discuss these stages from the point of view of the wife of an alcoholic husband, recognizing that the same principles are applicable to the husband of the alcoholic wife.

In the initial stages of alcoholism, the husband's drinking may be sporadic, alternating between periods of sobriety and intoxication. During this stage, the amount of stress in the family depends upon the frequency of the drinking bouts. Family members are constantly adapting and readapting first to an intoxicated husband and then to a sober one (Downs, 1982).

When drinking becomes heavy enough and frequent enough, the wife attempts to get the husband to cut down (Wiseman, 1980). She believes that her husband's drinking is voluntary, so she talks things over with him to persuade him to cut down before it leads to trouble.

FIGURE 22.11 The Process of Therapy.

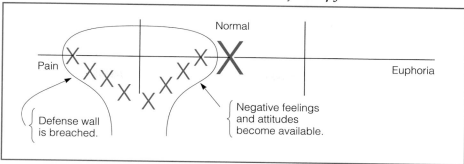

From Johnson, V. E. (1973). *I'll quit tomorrow.* New York: Harper and Row, 72. Reprinted by permission of the publisher.

ASSESSMENT
Are You an Alcoholic?

The following questions were developed by Johns Hopkins University Hospital for deciding whether a patient is an alcoholic.

Do you lose time from work due to drinking?

Is drinking making your home life unhappy?

Do you drink because you are shy with other people?

Is drinking affecting your reputation?

Have you ever felt remorse after drinking?

Have you found yourself in financial difficulties as a result of drinking?

Do you turn to lower companions and an inferior environment when drinking?

Does your drinking make you careless of your family's welfare?

Has your ambition decreased since drinking?

Do you crave a drink at a definite time daily?

Do you want a drink the next morning?

Does drinking cause you to have difficulty in sleeping?

Has your efficiency decreased since drinking?

Is drinking jeopardizing your job or business?

Do you drink to escape from worries or trouble?

Do you drink alone?

Have you ever had a complete loss of memory as a result of drinking?

Has your physician ever treated you for drinking?

Do you drink to build up your self-confidence?

Have you ever been to a hospital or institution on account of drinking?

Three "yes" answers may well mean alcoholism. If there are four "yes" answers, alcoholism is almost certain to be present. There are also many other signs that indicate whether a serious drinking problem exists.

From Keller, J. E. (1971). *Drinking problem?* Philadelphia: Fortress Press, 17, 18. Copyright © 1971 Fortress Press. Reprinted by permission.

The following are excerpts from interviews which Dr. Jacqueline Wiseman conducted with wives of alcoholic husbands. "Usually, when we are alone, I tell him, 'You gonna start to drink again, you better be careful'" (Wiseman, 1980, p. 544). The husband's response is predictable: "I'm taking care of myself. I'm not drinking so much now. Don't worry."

When the gentle nudge doesn't work, the wife's arguments escalate:

> You'd better realize you have a drinking problem, that it has gotten out of hand. Your drinking is affecting our family life. If you continue drinking, you'll be out of a job and it will ruin your health. (Wiseman, 1980, p. 544)

The husband may make promises to cut down, but these promises are rarely kept for very long. One wife explains:

> He was very intelligent, and he would always agree. Then he would really get drunk and get a big hangover and say, "That's it. You are right, honey, no more."
> I live in hope until the next time (he starts drinking again).

The wife experiences great disappointment and strain because of a succession of broken promises. She begins to move from logical discussion to nagging. One wife admits: "I've become a screaming, nagging bitch, that's what I've become" (Wiseman, 1980, p. 544). The husband's response becomes more defensive: "The reason I drink is because you've become so nasty. Who wants to come home to a nasty woman?" (Wiseman, 1980, p. 544). Some men use counter-criticism: "You're too fat. Stop eating and I'll stop drinking" (Wiseman, 1980, p. 544).

When these efforts don't work, the wife may turn to emotional pleading and threats to leave: "I begged him. I pleaded, I cried. I threatened to leave. I was very emotional and said that if he loved me, he wouldn't do this to me and the children" (Wiseman, 1980, p. 545). Many husbands respond to these threats with lack of interest, not taking them seriously. "Maybe you're right, maybe we should give up and quit and get a divorce" (Wiseman, 1980, p. 545). Note that, in all of these efforts, the wife assumes that the husband can quit drinking or can cut down if he wants to try.

Wives use a variety of other strategies. When nagging, pleading, or threats don't work, some try the opposite strategy: act normal or natural, and then maybe he won't want to drink. One wife comments:

> I just talked to him like I'm talking to you. I just pretend like nothing is wrong. Sometimes it would work and at other times he would keep at me 'til I got mad. (Wiseman, 1980, p. 546)

Another strategy is to try to take over all household responsibilities and to make everything at home better in the hope that an extremely pleasant, burden-free atmosphere will reduce their husband's need to drink.

Wives also try other strategies: select safe, nondrinking companions or visitors for social occasions; hide or restrict the money available for alcohol; pour out the liquor or smash the bottles; keep him out of trouble by keeping him busy with household chores or a variety of hobbies and free-time activities. Some wives even try drinking along with him to stop the nagging or to show him what it's like to be living with an alcoholic. Others drink at home with him so he won't go out to drink. The strategy usually fails when the wife discovers she can't match the husband's intake (Wiseman, 1980, pp. 541, 548). Other wives use coercion: they withhold sex, or threaten to tell his boss or his parents.

Gradually, the wife begins to realize that she can't control her husband's drinking. At that point, she may decide she wants to divorce her husband, or she may opt for staying married by creating separate worlds and spaces between them. One wife explained:

> I figure after trying everything out, I figure let me leave him alone. It will either kill him or cure him, or something, but let him do it on his own. I cannot fight him. (Wiseman, 1980, p. 548)

If the wife gets professional help, she may also begin to realize that alcoholism is a disease, that her husband can't control his drinking, and that he needs help (Peele, 1983). *The most important role she can play is to get help herself and through professional assistance to discover what type of treatment is available to her husband that he might be motivated to seek.* Sometimes, the husband is never willing to accept help. At other times, he enters treatment, but achieves only temporary sobriety. Still other husbands enter therapy and achieve permanent sobriety. If that happens, rebuilding the family relationships is still a long-term task, since trust, admiration, and affection develop only slowly, especially after years of increasing alienation. Either individual or group family therapy is helpful in restoring family functioning (Lovern and Zohn, 1982; Waldo and Guerney, 1983).

THE CRISIS OF DEATH AND GRIEF

Varying Circumstances of Death

Death, especially of a spouse, child, or other close relative, is among life's most stressful events. It creates considerable physical, mental, and emotional stress and tension, which may take a long period of time to subside.

Medical crises can severely test a family's ability to adjust. An initial reaction can be one of disbelief or refusal to accept the situation and may be followed by a stage of disorganization lasting for days or weeks.

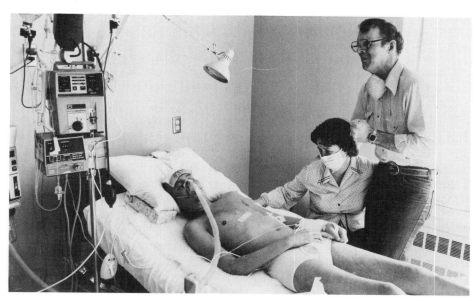

There are various circumstances of death. These include:

1. *Uncertain death.*
2. *Certain death*, either at a known or unknown time.
3. *Untimely death.* This may include *premature death*, *unexpected death*, and *calamitous death* (Pattison, 1977; Weisman, 1973).

Each of these will be discussed.

Uncertain Death

Everyone will die, but the exact time is uncertain for most people. As a consequence, most mentally healthy people do not often think about their death and are not afraid of it. Studies of groups of adults reveal variations in attitudes toward death among different age groups. One study of adults of different races, socioeconomic status, sex, and ages revealed little variation in attitudes toward death with respect to race, socioeconomic status, or sex, but substantial differences according to age (Bengtson, Cuellar, and Ragan, 1977). *Middle-aged respondents, 45 to 54, expressed the greatest fears of death; the elderly, 65 to 74, reflected the least.* The middle-aged adults were more frightened of death because they experienced a middle-age crisis and became aware of the finitude of their lives. The elderly had resolved their death fears.

> I know I'm going to die; it's something that we all have to go through. When it happens, it happens, and there's nothing I can do. I'll cross that bridge when I come to it. (Bengtson et al., 1977)

Surveys among institutionalized and noninstitutionalized persons aged from 61 to 97 years of age revealed that 51 percent said they were absolutely unafraid of death and 40 percent were indifferent to it. Only 1 percent said they had a strong fear of death. The one fear expressed was that death would be painful (Myska and Pasewark, 1978).

The circumstance of uncertain death can be very stressful, however, if people have been badly injured and are in critical condition, or if they have had radical surgery with the result uncertain. During such times, the patient and family members must live through a continuing period of acute crisis.

> Harvey is lying in a hospital bed in the intensive care unit. He has just suffered a major heart attack. He is hooked up to a machine that beeps and registers a blip on a television screen every time his heart beats. His wife is beside him, holding his hand. He is receiving oxygen. He is scared. His wife is scared. They both know the days ahead are crucial.

The most difficult part about such uncertainty is the waiting: dreading something adverse; hoping for improvement; waiting anxiously for other family members to arrive. The patient needs to avoid panic, to relax, and let healing take place. The wife and family need relief from the continued anxiety and worry; they need sleep and reassurance that their loved one will be all right.

The question of whether the patient will live or die is resolved eventually: "The next 48 hours will tell us whether she is going to make it or not." At other times, there are long-term uncertainties, such as in cases of cancer that may or may not be arrested. Ambiguity may remain for years: "If there is no return in five years, the outlook is very positive." Long years of waiting can be difficult. However, some people learn not to worry about what might happen and go about being as happy and optimistic as possible.

Certain Death

Certain death requires a different adjustment. The approximate time of death may be known or unknown or can only be surmised. Such might be the case in a deadly disease such as cancer of the pancreas. Whether the approximate time of death is known or not, the adjustments to terminal illness are difficult.

One of the best descriptions of the process of dying was given by Kubler-Ross (1969, 1974), a psychiatrist at the University of Chicago, who spent considerable time talking with 200 dying patients to try to understand and describe their reactions to terminal illness. She found considerable resistance among medical personnel to the idea of talking with patients about dying; but she also found that the patients were relieved to share their concerns.

Kubler-Ross identified five stages of dying that did not necessarily occur in a regular sequence. In fact, she said, "Most of my patients have exhibited two or three stages simultaneously and these do not always occur in the same order" (Kubler-Ross, 1974). The five identified stages were *denial, anger, bargaining, depression,* and *acceptance.*

The *denial response* of patients is, "No, not me. It can't be true." Some accuse their doctor of incompetence, and some think a mistake was made in the lab or in diagnosis. Others seek out other physicians, faith healers, or miracle cures. Some simply deny the reality of impending death and proceed as if nothing was wrong. Only a few patients maintain denial to the very end; most accept reality gradually.

As they acknowledge reality, their next reaction is one of *anger.* "Why me? It's not fair it should be happening to me." Patients in this stage become very hostile, resentful, and highly irritable, often quarreling with doctors, nurses, and loved ones.

As terminally ill patients begin to realize that death may be coming, they try *bargaining* to win a reprieve. The patient propositions God, the staff, and family, sometimes just to live a while longer to attend a wedding or complete a task. The patient says to God, "If you'll give me six more months, I'll leave most of my money to the church." If the person lives beyond the bargain period, however, the agreement is usually broken.

Once patients lose hope that life is possible and accept death as inevitable, *depression* may set in. Depression may be caused by regret at leaving behind everything and everybody that one loves. It may be caused by guilt over one's life. It may result from shame over bodily disfigurement or because of the inability to die with dignity. Some patients need to express their sorrow in order to overcome it. Others need cheering up and support to improve their morale and to regain their self-esteem.

The final stage of the dying process is *acceptance.* The patients have worked through denial, anger, depression, and fear of death; they are now exhausted and weak. This is the time for friends or family members to sit quietly holding the patient's hands, to show that death is not such a frightening experience (Rice, 1986).

Pattison (1977) presents the dying process in a little different way. He says that all of us project a **trajectory of our life** during which we anticipate a

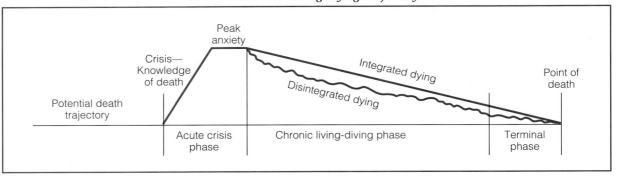

FIGURE 22.18 The Living-Dying Trajectory.

Adapted from Pattison, E. M. (1977). The experience of dying. In E. M. Pattison (Ed.), *The experience of dying*. Englewood Cliffs, NJ: Prentice-Hall, 43–60. Used by permission of the publisher.

certain life span within which we arrange our activities and our lives (see Figure 22.18). And then we are abruptly confronted with a crisis — the crisis of *knowledge of death*. Our potential trajectory is suddenly changed. We shall die in days, weeks, months, or several years. Our life has been foreshortened. Our activities must be rearranged. We cannot plan for the potential; we must deal with the actual. The period between the "crisis and knowledge of death" and the "point of death" is the **living-dying interval**. This interval is divided into three phases: (1) the *acute crisis phase*, (2) the *chronic living-dying phase*, and (3) the *terminal phase*. Family members can help the person respond to the acute crisis so that it does not result in a chaotic disintegration of the person's life during the chronic living-dying phase. The following is an example of *disintegrated dying* during the living-dying phase.

> Martha was told she had an incurable cancer. She shut herself up in her house, refused to talk to her family and friends or to see them. She never went out. Her husband couldn't stand to see her upset, so he went out most of the time. She spent most of her days depressed and crying. Finally, one afternoon her husband came home from work early and found that she had slashed her wrists in an effort to kill herself. Emergency treatment saved her life.

The following is an example of *integrated dying*, following psychiatric treatment that Martha received.

> Martha alternated between feeling terrible (when she was given chemotherapy) and feeling fairly well at other times. Her husband began to stay home more and to provide moral support and companionship. Martha and her husband started to go out to dinner occasionally. She began to call family members and friends and let them come visit. She finally decided that she was going to make the best of her life during the time she had.

The last task of family members is to give the person comfort and support as the person moves ineluctably into the *terminal phase* (Pattison, 1977).

Premature Death

The psychological reactions to death are more extreme when death occurs in childhood or at a comparatively young age. People have trouble accepting a child's death or understanding it. It seems so unfair. The child has not had a chance at life. It is difficult to reconcile what *is* with what *might have been*.

Sudden infant death syndrome or **crib death** is one of these unexpected deaths that shocks and disorganizes the family system. Survivors experience grief somatophysically and as intense subjective mental pain. Parents experience despondency, concentration difficulties, time confusion, loss of appetite, or inability to sleep. They may dread being alone and fear the responsibilities of caring for other children. They feel helpless, angry, guilty (Aadalen, 1980). Parents often blame themselves.

Research is being conducted on the best way to help families cope with the death of a child (Joyce, 1984). John Spinetta, professor of psychology at San Diego State University, has followed the course of bereavement in 120 families in which children have died of cancer, trying to distinguish the families that bounce back quickly from those that languish in grief. He asks whether the family can talk about or see reminders of the child without shedding tears, whether they have returned to normal activities like jobs, clubs, hobbies. Are they still filled with questions about why it happened? It is hoped that some guidelines for the best ways to help grieved parents will be provided (Joyce, 1984).

Unexpected Death

Unexpected death refers to the sudden death of a normal and healthy person (Weisman, 1973). The emotional impact upon survivors is gauged by how vital, alive, and distinctive the person is at the time of death. The more vital and alive the person, the harder it is to imagine that person dead. When a young adult dies, relatives react with frustration, disappointment, and anger. Career, marriage, children, and home were yet to come. Unexpected death of a middle-ager can also be tragic, but for different reasons. The middle-ager has assumed responsibilities for a family, job, and home, as well as in the community. Financial obligations are at a peak. There is extensive involvement with spouse, children, relatives, business associates, and friends. Death leaves the survivor with continuing obligations and no one to assume the responsibilities. Coping with dying involves coping with obligations already assumed.

Calamitous Death

Calamitous death is not only unpredictable, but can be violent, destructive, demeaning, and even degrading as well. It includes *accidents, involuntary manslaughter, homicide,* and *suicide*. Accidents are the leading cause of death in the United States among people 15–34 years of age (U.S. Bureau of the Census, 1987b). Most accidents have identifiable causes and are preventable, so family members are left with the knowledge that it need not have happened. The revelation of death comes as a shock, causing an extended period of disorganization before relatives can reorganize their lives to living without their loved one.

Involuntary Manslaughter

Involuntary manslaughter is the unintentional killing of another human being, most often while driving a car, less often in situations like hunting accidents.

The emotional impact of an unexpected death, such as that of a young father, is gauged by how alive and distinctive the person is at the time of death. Responsibilities often shift suddenly and heavily onto surviving family members.

Mrs. A was driving her car at night while very drunk. She swerved over the yellow center line into an oncoming car, killing the woman driver. She was convicted of involuntary manslaughter and sentenced to two years in prison. During this period of time, her husband came for counseling as preparation for the time when his wife would be released from prison. After discharge from prison, the couple both came for therapy to try to put their lives back together. (Author's counseling notes)

In this case, several other factors were significant:

1. In the beginning, the husband gave his wife no moral support. During the six months' trial, the couple never talked about what had happened. The husband didn't want to. The husband slept on the couch; the wife described her pain as terrible. She wanted to reach out to her spouse, but he was not there when she needed him. The wife said she wanted a divorce. The husband finally broke down and cried and said he didn't want one. After the wife's imprisonment, the husband came for therapy.

2. The husband was very lonesome during the period of separation and used periodic therapy as a means of support. He also mentioned that he was brought up by an abusive alcoholic father, and so he had a number of factors in his background that he was willing to deal with in therapy during the time of separation from his wife. He also admitted that there were many issues in their marriage that were never dealt with, and he was anxious to do something about them. He was able to gain a lot of insight into their problems as a couple.

3. Some of the more important marital problems included a lack of communication, different goals in life, little companionship (the husband was a TV addict), and differences in sexual appetite. The wife wanted more love and affection in their relationship.

4. The major problem in the mariage was the wife's chronic alcoholism. The wife agreed to enter a treatment and educational program for her alcoholism while she was in prison. She was successful in recovering from her disease.

5. Following release from prison, the wife was ecstatic for two weeks, going through a psychedelic high. Following the high, she suffered a **post-traumatic stress disorder**. She cried daily, lay in bed, and couldn't force herself to go to work. The simplest task — like going shopping at a grocery store — overwhelmed her. Through therapy she was able to relive some of her experiences and overcome them. Jail had been a nightmare for her. There were 25 other tough, rough women who never said hello, who were never nice to her, who were always planning drug deals. In the beginning, she was petrified and scared, then disgusted. It took her six months to accept the fact that she was doing time.

6. Three months after discharge from prison, the husband-wife communication had improved. The husband had become more loving and attentive. The wife was off antidepressants and entered an educational program for Certified Nurses' Aides. The lives of the two people were slowly coming together. (Author's counseling notes)

The preceding case history illustrates the process of disorganization and reorganization that often takes place after a severe crisis such as involuntary manslaughter. Such a happening is devastating to the whole family. Incidentally, Mr. and Mrs. A. now have a child and are doing fine in their marriage.

Homicide

Most of the stereotypes about murders and murderers have no foundation in fact. The following facts help to clear up the myths (Kastenbaum and Aisenberg, 1976).

- Most murderers are not mysterious strangers. In at least two-thirds of the cases of willful homicide and violent assault, the perpetrator and the victim are at least acquainted. A sizeable minority of homicides are committed by relatives of the victim.

- Family members or acquaintances behave more violently toward their victims than do total strangers.

- Senseless assaults by complete strangers are rare.

- Policemen are more likely to be killed while investigating domestic disturbances than in any other type of duty.

- The incidence of violent crime decreases with increases in neighborhood income.

- In most cases of violence, the perpetrator and the victims are of the same race.

What these facts suggest is that homicide is most often an outgrowth of quarrels and violence among family members or friends. The quarrels get out of hand, resulting in people slaying one another in the privacy of their own homes. Policemen who are summoned to quell domestic disturbances are sometimes killed themselves. (See Chapter 17 for further discussion of family violence).

Suicide is one of the most upsetting of family crises because it leaves family members feeling so remorseful, so guilty, so confused and hurt. Survivors inevitably ask:

Why did he or she do it?

Why didn't I sense that something was wrong?

Why didn't I do something to prevent it?

Survivors who are left with dependent children, large financial responsibilities, and other obligations are also justifiably resentful.

How could he do such a thing?

I hate him for doing this and leaving me all the responsibility of caring for the children.

If family members blame themselves for letting suicide happen, or for not preventing it from happening, or for causing it to happen, it may take considerble therapy to get over the self-incrimination.

Grief

No matter how long the death of a loved one has been anticipated, it still comes as a shock. In fact, people who have watched loved ones suffer through chronic illness and die are sometimes affected as much as or more than those whose loved ones died after a short illness (Gerber et al., 1975).

There are usually three stages of grief (Hiltz, 1978). The *first* is a short period of shock during which the surviving family members are stunned and immobilized with grief and disbelief. The *second stage* is a period of intense suffering during which individuals show physical and emotional symptoms of great disturbance. *Third,* there is a gradual reawakening of interest in life. Physical upsets during the second stage may include disturbed sleep; stomach upset and loss of appetite; weight loss; emptiness in the stomach; loss of energy and muscular strength; and shortness of breath, sighing, or tightness in the chest. Emotional reactions may include anger, guilt, depression, anxiety, and preoccupation with thoughts of the deceased. During intense grief, people need to talk with friends or family about their loss. But since grief and death are uncomfortable subjects, this opportunity is often denied, and recovery from the loss is more difficult and prolonged.

One common reaction to bereavement is to purify the memory of the deceased by mentally diminishing that person's negative characteristics. One woman who hated her husband remarked, "My husband was an unusually good man." If this idealization continues, it can prevent the formation of new intimate friendships. Extended bereavement can result in a sentimentalized, nostalgic, and morose style of life.

Men and women may respond differently to bereavement. Men find it more difficult to express grief, but they can accept the reality of death more quickly. Women are more able to continue work during bereavement than are men. Men are more apt to describe their loss as the loss of part of themselves. Women respond in terms of being deserted, abandoned, and left to fend for themselves (Glick, Weiss, and Parkes, 1974).

1. In what ways do modern funeral practices and customs help relatives to deal with grief, and in what ways do they hinder adjustment?
2. Do modern funeral practices and customs hide the reality of death? How? How not?
3. If you have experienced the grief and sorrow of losing a loved one, what helped you the most in dealing with your upset, and what was most difficult for you?
4. Why do some people have wakes before the funeral itself? How do you feel about them?
5. Should funerals be conducted in a church or synagogue, in a funeral parlor, in a private home? Explain your feelings.
6. Should children be allowed to attend funerals? Why? Why not? How can children be confronted with the reality that a loved one has died — without frightening them?

The negative impact of bereavement and the loss of a loved one cannot be minimized. Damage to the self accompanies widowhood, for example, if the spouse was a significant other (was important in the life of the partner). The degree and duration of this damage depend on the intensity of the involvement with the departed and the availability of significant others (Schneiderman, 1983).

SUMMARY

1. A crisis may be defined as a drastic change in the course of events; it is a turning point during which the trend of future events is affected.

2. There are three definable stages in family adjustment to crises: (1) onset of the crisis, (2) period of disorganization, and (3) reorganization. After reorganization the new level of family organization may be lower, at the same level, or at a higher level than before the crisis.

3. Infidelity is a crisis in many marriages because Americans enter marriage expecting and committed to sexual fidelity.

4. There are a number of reasons why people get involved in extramarital affairs.

5. Extramarital affairs are often a crisis for the single woman who is obliged to keep the affair secret, who loses control of the situation because the married man spends time with his wife and children, and who becomes hurt and disappointed when the married man doesn't divorce his wife.

6. Extramarital affairs have varying effects on married people: some marriages are never the same afterward; some are broken by divorce; some couples are stimulated to solve the problems of their own marriage; and some marriages where the emotional bonds are already broken are not affected very much by the affair.

7. In some situations, a wife discovers that her husband is unfaithful and chooses not to confront him with his actions.

8. The affairs that are most threatening to marriage are ongoing affairs that include emotional involvement as well as sexual relations.

9. There are a number of things that couples can do to prevent infidelity.

10. Alcohol abuse is a generic term that includes both alcoholism (addiction to alcohol characterized by compulsive drinking) and problem drinking (functional disability as a result of alcohol consumption).

11. Alcoholism develops in four stages. Phases one and two are discovering and learning phases during which people learn that alcohol will give them a warm good feeling and during which they begin to seek mood swings.

12. During phase three, people become harmfully and chemically dependent; drinking becomes more and more excessive; and alcoholics begin to rationalize their behavior, to project their own feelings and actions onto others, to repress their guilt, shame, and remorse, and to suffer blackouts, which are periods of amnesia. The loss of memory keeps alcoholics from recognizing what they have done and how sick they are.

13. During the acute phase, people drink just to feel normal again.

14. Two obstacles prevent alcoholics from getting the attention they need: people don't understand their helpless condition and treat them judgmentally; and rigid behavior patterns, distorted memory patterns, and impaired judgment, as well as chemical dependency, keep them locked into the self-destructive pattern.

15. Alcoholism is a progressive illness and is always fatal unless arrested.

16. Treatment consists of several aspects: (1) confronting the alcoholic with his or her condition through a program of intervention, (2) phased detoxification, (3) education about the disease, (4) individual and group psychotherapy, and (5) rehabilitation.

17. Alcoholism is a family crisis because the disease affects the whole family. In the initial stages family members are constantly adapting and readapting—first to an intoxicated family member, then to a sober one.

18. The first efforts of the wife are usually to try to get her husband to cut down, because she believes he has control of his drinking.

19. The most important role that the wife of an alcoholic husband can play is to get professional help for herself and to discover the type of treatment that her husband might be motivated to accept.

20. Death is among life's most stressful events. There are various circumstances of death: uncertain death; certain death (at either a known or unknown time); and untimely death, which includes premature death, unexpected death, and calamitous death.

21. Middle-aged persons are more fearful of death than the elderly. The most difficult part about uncertain death is the waiting, not knowing what is going to happen.

22. In certain death the time may be known or unknown. Kubler-Ross has identified five stages of adjustment in certain death: denial, anger, bargaining, depression, and acceptance.

23. Pattison presents the dying process as part of a trajectory of our life, divided into three phases: the crisis of the knowledge of death and the acute crisis that follows, the chronic living-dying phase, and the terminal phase.

24. The psychological reactions are more extreme when death occurs in childhood or at a comparatively young age.

25. Unexpected death refers to the sudden death of a normal and healthy person. This requires a wide variety of adjustments in the families of the deceased.

26. Calamitous death is unpredictable, violent, destructive, demeaning, and even degrading. It includes accidents, involuntary manslaughter, homicide, and suicide. Homicide is most often an outgrowth of quarrels and violence among family members or friends. Suicide is one of the most upsetting of family crises because it leaves family members feeling remorseful, guilty, confused, and hurt.

27. The three stages of grief include: a first period of shock, a second stage of intense suffering, and finally a gradual reawakening of interest in life.

SUGGESTED READINGS

Al-anon. (1973). *Alateen: Hope for the Children of Alcoholics.* New York: Al-Anon. A book for adolescents and older.

Figley, C. R., and McCubbin, H. T. (Eds.). (1983). *Stress and the Family: Vol. II: Coping with Catastrophe.* New York: Brunner-Mazel. Part of a two-volume book on stress. This volume discusses crises of various sorts that only some families experience.

Johnson, V. E. (1973). *I'll Quit Tomorrow.* New York: Harper and Row. One of the best available books on the development of alcoholism, its consequences and treatment.

Kastenbaum, R., and Aisenberg, R. (1976). *The Psychology of Death.* New York: Springer. A broad, integrative book on the topic.

Kubler-Ross, E. (1969). *On Death and Dying.* New York: Macmillan. Death as a social and psychological experience. Classic work on the stages of adjustment to death.

Pattison, E. M. (1977). *The Experience of Dying.* Englewood Cliffs, NJ: Prentice-Hall. The purpose of this book is to provide a broader, in-depth portrait of the dying process at different stages of the life cycle: early childhood through old age.

Sargent, M. (1980). *Caring About Kids: Talking to Children About Death.* NIMH, DHHS Pub. No. (ADM) 80–838. Washington, DC: U.S. Government Printing Office. Helpful guidance for adults in talking to children.

Schwartz, J. (1982). *Letting Go of Stress.* New York: Pinnacle Books. A practical guide.

Selye, H. (1976). *The Stress of Life.* New York: McGraw-Hill. Various stresses that people face in life.

23

THE TROUBLED FAMILY AND DIVORCE

KEY TERMS

conciliation counseling
structured separation
adversary approach
doctrine of comparative rectitude
no-fault divorce
custody
joint legal custody

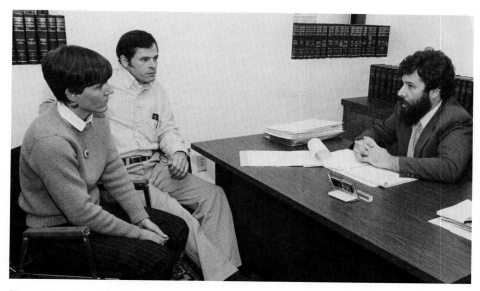

Divorce is a stressful and troubling experience for everyone involved. What factors indicate statistical probabilities as to who will divorce?

The United States has one of the highest divorce rates of any country in the world. Numerous and conflicting explanations have been given as to why this is so. Whatever the causes, the increasing numbers of divorced people have stimulated numerous new books on the subject — books that describe everything from do-it-yourself divorce to making divorce a creative experience. With the books has come increasing interest in examining divorce laws, which in their old forms created much suffering for millions of couples and their children. Most state legislatures have now changed their laws and encourage reconciliation counseling, divorce mediation, and no-fault divorce.

All of the statistics, laws, court cases, and individuals' efforts involve human beings: husbands, wives, and children who are trying to make the best of difficult situations, each in his or her own way. We need, therefore, to take a careful look at this picture — at the facts of divorce and some of the reasons; at our divorce laws old and new; and at the involvement of children in divorce, their reaction to it, and its effects on them. We also need a more sympathetic understanding of what couples go through and the difficult adjustments they face after a divorce has been granted.

INDIVIDUAL PROBABILITY OF DIVORCE: SOCIAL AND DEMOGRAPHIC FACTORS

In looking at divorce rates, let us examine first those social and demographic factors that increase or decrease the probability of divorce (Breault and Kposowa, 1987). Divorce rates vary from group to group and relate to such factors as age at marriage, religion, occupation, income, education, race, geographic area of the country in which one resides, and parental divorce (Glenn and Shelton, 1983). These factors will not pinpoint which individuals are going to get divorced, but they do indicate statistical probabilities for different groups (Fergusson, Horwood, and Shannon, 1984). Let's look at some of the more important social and demographic correlates of divorce and separation in the United States (Glenn and Supancic, 1984).

Age

Age at first marriage is one of the most important factors in marital success (Hanson and Tuch, 1984). Persons who marry quite young are more likely to divorce than those who wait until they are older (Booth and Edwards, 1985). Figure 23.1 shows the relationship between age at first marriage and the percent of white persons who had ever been divorced or legally separated, according to combined data from seven U.S. national surveys conducted from 1973 to 1980 (Glenn and Supancic, 1984). As the figure shows, the percentage

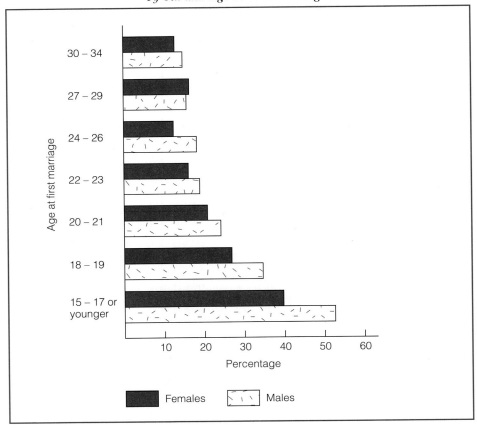

FIGURE 23.1 *Percentage of Ever-Married White Persons Who Had Ever Been Divorced or Legally Separated, by Sex and Age at First Marriage.*

Adapted from Glenn, N. D., and Supancic, M. (1984). The social and demographic correlates of divorce and separation in the United States: An update and reconsideration. *Journal of Marriage and the Family, 46,* 563–575. Copyright © 1984 by the National Council on Family Relations. Reprinted by permission.

of those divorced or legally separated who were 15–17 years of age or younger at the time of first marriage was about three times the percentage divorced or legally separated who were 24–26 years of age at the time of first marriage. Except for ages 27–29, the percentage of males who divorced was higher than the percentage of females (Glenn and Supancic, 1984).

Religion

Frequency of attendance at religious services is correlated strongly and negatively with divorce or separation. (Those who attend church regularly are less likely to divorce or separate.) There are also differences in divorce rates according to religious preference (Heaton, Albrecht, and Martin, 1985). Jews have the lowest divorce rate (Brodbar-Nemzer, 1986), Catholics the next, and Protestants are higher than these two groups. The highest rates are for persons with no religion. There are, however, considerable differences among Protestant denominations. Contrary to what one might expect, the most conservative denominations (such as Nazarene, Pentecostal, and Baptist) have relatively high dissolution rates in spite of the strong disapproval of divorce. This may partially reflect the lower average socioeconomic status of persons in these denominations. Divorce rates are lower among Presbyterians and Episcopalians, who are generally of higher socioeconomic status than those of some other denominations (Glenn and Supancic, 1984). There also seems to be some tendency for divorce rates to be higher in interfaith marriages than in those where both spouses have the same religious preference.

Socioeconomic Status

This category includes education, income, and occupation. Earlier studies have shown that rates of divorce or separation have been higher at lower socioeconomic levels. Newer studies only partially confirm this finding (Rank, 1987). Both men and women who start high school or college and then drop out are more likely to divorce than are those who graduate from either high school or college. One explanation is that those who lack persistence in completing a unit of education are also more likely to lack persistence in working out the problems of marriage. Overall, however, male and female college graduates are less likely to divorce than male or female high school graduates (Glenn and Supancic, 1984). Figure 23.2 shows the relationships.

Men who earn $25,000 a year or more are less likely to divorce than men earning lesser amounts. However, women who earn $10,000–$15,000 a year are more likely to divorce than those earning less or more than that. Those earning less may not be able to afford getting a divorce (Booth and White, 1980). When women do divorce, they may be motivated to earn more money, so increased income may be the result of divorce, not the cause of it. Women who earn much more, like men who earn much more, are more likely to possess the qualities to make marriage work.

Overall, socioeconomic variables do not explain as much variance in the possibility of divorce as do age at first marriage and frequency of attendance at religious services (Glenn and Supancic, 1984).

FIGURE 23.2 *Adjusted Percentage of Ever-Married*
White Persons Who Had Ever Been Divorced or Legally Separated,
by Sex and Years of School Completed:
Combined Data from Seven U.S. National
Surveys Conducted from 1973 to 1980.

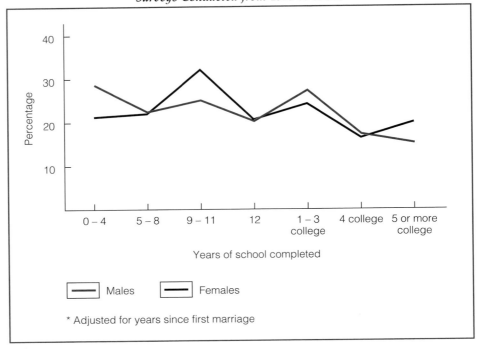

Adapted from Glenn, N. D., and Supancic, M. (1984). The social and demographic correlates of divorce and separation in the United States: An update and reconsideration. *Journal of Marriage and the Family, 46*, 563–575. Copyright © 1984 by the National Council on Family Relations. Reprinted by permission.

Race

Blacks have a higher divorce rate than whites at all income and educational levels. Similarly, in every age-at-marriage category, black divorce rates are significantly higher than those of whites (Norton and Moorman, 1987). Two out of three black marriages will eventually dissolve.

Geographic Area

Divorce rates vary across different regions of the country. In general, rates by states increase from east to west and from north to south (Glenn and Shelton, 1985). Thus, divorce rates are highest in the south and next highest in the west. Figure 23.3 shows the differences.

Parental Divorce

Persons whose parents are divorced are more susceptible to divorce themselves, partly because they have more permissive attitudes toward divorce as an alternative to unhappy marriage (Greenberg and Nay, 1982).

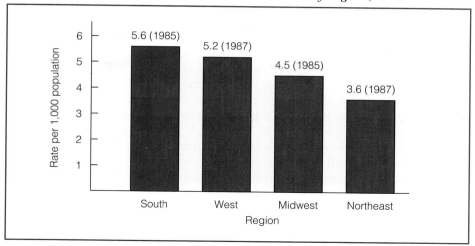

FIGURE 23.3 *Divorce and Annulment Rates by Regions, 1983.*

Statistics from U.S. Bureau of the Census. (1989). *Statistical abstract of the United States, 1989.* Washington, DC: U.S. Government Printing Office, 88.

CAUSES OF MARITAL BREAKUP

Social and demographic factors indicate the probability of divorce, but they don't reveal the precise causes of marital breakup. Causes may be determined by studying groups of those who are divorcing to find out their perceptions of the reasons why their marriages have failed.

Studies of Perception of Causes of Marital Breakup

We will analyze three studies that surveyed husband-wife perception of the causes of marital breakup.

The first study was of 275 males and 336 females in Wisconsin who had petitioned for divorce (Cleek and Pearson, 1985). Under Wisconsin law, petitioners are required to attend a divorce counseling session. During this session, single-page surveys were distributed to participants with questions about 18 possible causes of divorce. The causes were ranked according to the percentage of respondents indicating each cause. The mean age of respondents was the early thirties; they had been married on the average about 11.5 years. The average educational level was slightly more than 12 years of schooling.

The second study was of a divorcing sample of 568 black and white men and women from seven Cleveland, Ohio, suburbs (Kitson and Sussman, 1982). Seventy-three percent were white, 26 percent black, and 1 percent Oriental. Respondents ranged in age from 17 to 65, with half being 29 or older. The median length of marriage was 4.3 years. About one-fifth had been married previously. Subjects were asked: What caused your marriage to break up? Replies were coded and ranked according to the percentage indicating each complaint. Because this was an open-ended questionnaire, a greater variety of causes was indicated than in the Cleek, Pearson study.

The third study comprised 335 divorced and separated men and women from Sydney, Australia (Burns, 1984). They ranged in age from 21 to 60 with the largest single group being aged 31–40. In 70 percent of the cases, the divorce or separation was of less than three years' standing. Subjects were to check relevant items on a checklist of 18 reasons and were also asked to write in reasons on an open-response questionnaire.

The results of these studies have been summarized in Tables 23.1 and 23.2. Table 23.1 summarizes the wives' perception of the causes of divorce and Table 23.2 summarizes the husbands' perception of the causes, according to the three studies. Only the top 20 causes are listed here. Since the study populations were different, and the instruments varied in design, there were some differences as well as some similarities in results from the three studies. A composite picture has been obtained by averaging together the percent of

TABLE 23.1 *Wives' Perception of Causes of Marital Breakup*

		PERCENT MENTIONING PROBLEM			
Rank	Cause	Average	Cleek, Pearson Study	Kitson, Sussman Study	Burns' Study
1	Basic unhappiness	59.9	59.9	—	—
2	Emotional abuse	55.5	55.5	—	—
3	Communication problems	47.3	69.7	32.0	40.0
4	Incompatibility, different backgrounds	36.7	56.4	17.0	—
5	Sexual problems	36.0	32.0	—	40.0
6	No sense of family, husband's lack of time at home	30.5	—	15.0	46.0
7	Husband's alcohol abuse	29.0	30.0	21.0	36.0
8	Financial, employment problems	28.0	32.9	15.0	36.0
9	Husband's infidelity	27.7	25.2	21.0	37.0
10	Wife's lack of interest	26.0	—	—	26.0
11	Untrustworthiness, immaturity	21.0	—	21.0	—
12	Husband out with boys	20.0	—	20.0	—
13	Interests, values changed	19.0	—	19.0	—
14	Disagreements over children	14.0	8.9	—	19.0
15	Gender role conflict; women's liberation movement	13.5	3.0	24.0	—
16	Inadequate housing	13.0	—	—	13.0
17	In-laws, relatives	12.9	10.7	7.0	21.0
18	Husband's lack of interest	12.0	—	—	12.0
18	Emotional, personal problems, instability	12.0	—	12.0	—
18	Stubbornness	12.0	—	12.0	—
18	Not enough social life	12.0	—	12.0	—
18	Too young at time of marriage	12.0	—	12.0	—
18	Argue, don't agree	12.0	—	12.0	—
19	Physical, psychological abuse, cruelty	11.9	21.7	10.0	4.0
20	Wife's infidelity	8.0	3.9	—	12.0

Statistics from Cleek, M. B., and Pearson, T. A. (1985). Perceived causes of divorce: An analysis of interrelationships. *Journal of Marriage and the Family*, 47, 179–183. Kitson, G. C., and Sussman, M. B. (1982). Marital complaints, demographic characteristics, symptoms of mental distress in divorce. *Journal of Marriage and the Family*, 46, 87–101. Burns, A. (1984). Perceived causes of marriage breakdown and the conditions of life. *Journal of Marriage and the Family*, 46, 551–562.

respondents from each study who indicated each cause. The result at least gives a composite picture of causes in the three population groups studied. The results show remarkable consistency in the perceptions of husbands and wives.

The 10 most important causes of marital breakup according to the wives' perception (listed in rank order from most to least frequently mentioned) were basic unhappiness, emotional abuse, communication problems, incompatibility and different backgrounds, sexual problems, the husband's lack of sense of family and lack of time at home, the husband's alcohol abuse, financial or employment problems, the husband's infidelity, and the wives' lack of interest in the marriage. Only one of these causes — the husband's alcohol abuse — was not listed among the first 10 most important causes by the husbands. Apparently, many husbands denied the problem.

The husbands listed the following 10 most important causes of marriage breakup (listed in rank order from most important to least important): basic

TABLE 23.2 *Husbands' Perception of Causes of Marital Breakup*

		PERCENT MENTIONING PROBLEM			
Rank	Cause	Average	Cleek, Pearson Study	Kitson, Sussman Study	Burns' Study
1	Basic unhappiness	46.9	46.9	—	—
2	Sexual problems	43.1	30.2	—	56.0
3	Communication	42.1	59.3	26.0	41.0
4	Incompatibility, different backgrounds	31.4	44.7	18.0	—
5	Wife's lack of interest	25.0	—	—	25.0
6	Emotional abuse	24.7	24.7	—	—
7	Wife's infidelity	22.8	10.5	—	35.0
8	No sense of family, husband's lack of time at home	20.5	—	13.0	28.0
9	Physical abuse, cruelty	20.3	3.6	—	37.0
10	Financial problems	20.2	28.7	8.0	24.0
11	In-laws, relatives	18.2	11.6	14.0	29.0
12	Not sure what happened	18.0	—	18.0	—
13	Gender role conflict	17.8	14.5	21.0	—
14	Interests and values changed	17.0	—	17.0	—
15	Husband's lack of interest	15.0	—	—	15.0
16	Husband's alcohol abuse	13.2	9.4	—	17.0
16	Differences over children	13.2	4.4	—	22.0
17	Too young at time of marriage	13.0	—	13.0	—
17	Overcommitment to work	13.0	—	13.0	—
17	Wife's ill health	13.0	—	—	13.0
17	Not enough social life	13.0	—	13.0	13.0
18	Husband's infidelity	11.6	6.2	—	17.0
19	Jealousy	11.0	—	11.0	—
20	Untrustworthiness, immaturity	10.0	—	10.0	—

Statistics from Cleek, M. B., and Pearson, T. A. (1985). Perceived causes of divorce: An analysis of interrelationships. *Journal of Marriage and the Family, 47,* 179–183. Kitson, G. C., and Sussman, M. B. (1982). Marital complaints, demographic characteristics, symptoms of mental distress in divorce. *Journal of Marriage and the Family, 46,* 87–101. Burns, A. (1984). Perceived causes of marriage breakdown and the conditions of life. *Journal of Marriage and the Family, 46,* 551–562.

unhappiness, sexual problems, communication, incompatibility and different backgrounds, wife's lack of interest in the marriage, emotional abuse, the wife's infidelity, husbands lack of sense of family and lack of time at home, physical abuse and cruelty, and financial problems. Surprisingly, the husbands listed their physical abuse and cruelty as one of the 10 most important causes. This cause was listed in nineteenth place by the wives.

Therapists' Choices of Areas Most Damaging to Marital Relationships

The perceptions listed in Tables 23.1 and 23.2 were those of husbands and wives themselves. What do professionals perceive as the most damaging problems to marital relationships? A survey among 116 members of the *American Association of Marriage and Family Therapists* rates the frequency, severity, and treatment difficulty of 29 problems commonly experienced by distressed couples. The therapists were asked to choose and give the rank order of only the top five areas most damaging to the marital relationship and the five most difficult to treat successfully (Geiss and O'Leary, 1981). A value of 5 was assigned to an item for each first-place ranking it received, a value of 4 was given for each second-place ranking, and so on. These values were summed for each item. The 10 areas rated by respondents as having the most damaging effect on marital relationships were (Geiss and O'Leary, 1981, p. 516):

1. Communication (361)
2. Unrealistic expectations of marriage or spouse (197)
3. Power struggles (135)
4. Serious individual problems (126)
5. Role conflict (95)
6. Lack of loving feelings (92)
7. Demonstration of affection (90)
8. Alcoholism (81)
9. Extramarital affairs (80)
10. Sex (79)

Based upon these responses from marital therapists, lack of communication was ranked as having the most damaging effect. In a further analysis of data from the study, communication problems were also rated as the most frequently occurring problems in distressed marriages. These responses suggest the vital role that communication plays in well-functioning marriages.

Therapists' Choices of Areas Most Difficult To Treat Successfully

These therapists were also asked to rank the areas they had found the most difficult to deal with or treat successfully. The following areas were indicated as being the most difficult (Geiss and O'Leary, 1981, p. 517):

1. Alcoholism (275)
2. Lack of loving feelings (178)

ASSESSMENT
Marital Instability Index

The following questions will help you to evaluate the relative instability of your marriage — that is, the possibility of divorce. Answer "yes" or "no" to each of the following questions. The more questions answered "yes," the more unstable your marriage and the greater the possibility of divorce.

1. Have you or your husband/wife ever seriously suggested the idea of divorce within the last three years?

2. Have you discussed divorce or separation with a close friend?

3. Even people who get along quite well with their spouse sometimes wonder whether their marriage is working out. Have you ever thought your marriage might be in trouble?

4. Did you talk about consulting an attorney?

5. Has the thought of getting a divorce or separation crossed your mind the past three years?

Adapted from Booth, A., Johnson, D., and Edwards, J. N. (1983). Measuring marital instability. *Journal of Marriage and the Family*, *45*, 387–393.

 3. Serious individual problems (144)

 4. Power struggles (129)

 5. Addicted behavior other than alcoholism (104)

 6. Value conflicts (92)

 7. Physical abuse (90)

 8. Unrealistic expectations of marriage or spouse (84)

 9. Extramarital affairs (78)

10. Incest (62)

The first-ranked item, alcoholism, was rated substantially higher than any other item, receiving a sum of ranked responses 54 percent higher than the second-ranked item. Because it is so prevalent and difficult to treat, alcoholism has long been a major contributing factor in divorce.

THE DIVORCE DECISION

Difficulty

The decision to divorce is a difficult one for most people. Few couples are able to make such a decision easily and quickly (Melicher and Chiriboga, 1985). Couples usually agonize for months or years before finally deciding. Even then, they may change their minds a number of times. Couples may repeatedly separate, then move back together. Many couples petition for divorce, only to withdraw it. Others even go to court and then change their minds at the last minute. The reason for the uncertainty is that making such a decision is a very hard thing to do.

From a counselor's point of view, it's hard to predict who will or will not get divorced. Some couples have relatively minor problems, but give up easily.

It seems that other couples will never be able to make their marriage work, but through a high degree of intense effort and motivation overcome all obstacles and end up with a good marriage. The outcome depends partially on the motivation and commitment of the couple.

There are, of course, some couples who never divorce, but not because they really love one another or are compatible.

> Mr. and Mrs. P. have been married 43 years. He's 79 and she's 76. They absolutely hate one another. They say and do horrible things to one another. They constantly criticize one another and are in chronic conflict. They have no companionship, never share any social activities together. He's gay, has male lovers on the side, and never has intercourse with her. He's intellectual, verbal, and artistic. She's none of these things. He's a dreamer; she's practical. The only reason they give for living together is to have two social security checks instead of one. (Author's counseling notes)

Financial reasons are an important consideration in the decision to divorce. We will also discuss a number of other considerations.

Factors To Consider in Deciding

Levinger (1965, 1979) proposed a three-factor theory of marital cohesion. He said there are three basic considerations in deciding whether to remain married or not.

1. *Satisfaction or attractions of the marriage.* These are the forces that strengthen the marriage bond. They may include sexual fulfillment, emotional bonding, care, concern, need (even neurotic need) that the partners have for one another. Attractions may also include socioeconomic rewards: a better income, an improved standard of living, superior social status, being able to live in a nice house, having more economic security, or the need for the physical services that a spouse can provide.

2. *Barriers to getting out of the marriage.* These are those forces that prevent marriage breakdown. These may include religious teachings against divorce, felt obligations to the spouse and family, presence of dependent children, social or familial pressure to stay married, or job considerations. Some couples stay married because it seems easier than getting a divorce. Others are afraid of what their spouse will say or do. Others simply can't afford getting divorced. Still others stay together only because of the children. If parents believe that divorce will damage children's well-being, then the presence of children constitutes a barrier force. If, however, parents believe that a divorce will promote children's well-being by giving them a more stable, happy environment, then the existence of children will not act as a barrier force. Parents must ask, "Are the negative effects of divorce greater than those of continued conflict in the home?" (Kanoy and Miller, 1980). Sometimes, the number and presence of children delays, but does not ultimately prevent, divorce.

3. *The attractiveness of alternatives to the marriage.* These include an evaluation of personal assets: sexual attractiveness, appearance, and age factors that influence the possibilities of obtaining another spouse, if desired. Individuals with high socioeconomic status marry spouses of the same status

These days it seems like a lot of marriages are breaking up. It may not be likely, but just suppose your mate were to leave you this year. How likely do you imagine each of the following would be? Decide whether you think each item would be impossible, possible but unlikely, probable, or certain. Check the appropriate box below.

How Likely Is It That:	Impossible	Possible But Unlikely	Probable	Certain
1. You could get another mate better than he/she is?	1	2	3	4
2. You could get another mate as good as he/she is?	1	2	3	4
3. You would be quite satisfied without a mate?	1	2	3	4
4. You would be sad, but would get over it quickly?	1	2	3	4
5. You would be able to live as well as you do now?	1	2	3	4
6. You would be able to take care of yourself?	1	2	3	4
7. You would be better off economically?	1	2	3	4
8. There are many other people you could be happy with?	1	2	3	4
9. You could support yourself at the present level?	1	2	3	4

Score: Add up the total score for the nine questions. Possible scores range from 9 to 36. Then divide your total by 9. The higher your score (from 1 to 4), the more likely you could get along well without your present mate.

Adapted from Udry, J. R. (1981). Marital alternatives and marital disruption. *Journal of Marriage and the Family*, 43, 889–897. Copyright © 1981 by the National Council on Family Relations. Reprinted by permission.

(Mueller and Pope, 1980). Attractive men and men with high socioeconomic status marry women who are the most attractive. Spouses with good education, high income, and intelligence realize that if they are cut off from their spouse's earning power, they are capable of still living the good life. Udry (1981) found that couples in which both spouses are high in marital alternatives have several times the marital disruption rate of couples in which both spouses are low in marital alternatives.

A powerful motivating factor in divorce is the desire to leave one's spouse to marry another person. A person who is involved in an ongoing, emotional and sexual relationship outside of marriage is often not as hesitant about getting a divorce as a person who has no one else on the side. While an extramarital affair is often a result of an unhappy marriage, it also may be the added incentive to terminate the marriage.

There is a fourth factor that affects the decision to stay married or get divorced. The factor was not discussed by Levinger, but is an important one. *It is the intensity of the emotional pain generated by the unhappy marriage.* Some people don't really believe in divorce, but they can't tolerate the unhappiness of the marriage any longer. One man explained:

> I've remained in the marriage for 28 years because I didn't believe in divorce and because I didn't want to desert my children. But I can't take it any longer. My wife hates me and takes every occasion to let me know she does. She tells me she hopes I'll die so she can collect my life insurance. There is no love, companionship, or anything positive left in our relationship. (Author's counseling notes)

A woman commented:

> You can't imagine what it was like being married to my alcoholic husband. He was completely irresponsible. I did literally everything around the house, yard, and in raising our five children. Yet, he wouldn't admit that he had an alcohol problem. (Author's counseling notes)

In these situations, there was no question in the minds of the individuals that divorce was the only choice they could make.

ALTERNATIVES TO DIVORCE

Marriage Counseling

Some couples need to consider that there may be alternatives to divorce (Temes, 1981). One most important alternative is to get marriage counseling (Lazrus, 1981). Couples cannot be expected to live together unhappily, but breaking up the marriage may not always be the best or only answer to a problem. Divorce often substitutes one set of problems for another. An alternative answer is to see if, with professional help, the unhappy marriage can become a satisfying one. Couples are often skeptical about the outcome of counseling — especially if they have never been to a counselor before, or if they have had previous and unhappy experiences with therapists. Not all therapists are equally competent. However, some states *require* **conciliation counseling** before a divorce may be granted. Even in such situations, the counseling may help. One study in Iowa compared 12 court-ordered couples with 12 other couples who had gone voluntarily to counseling (Sampel and Seymour, 1980). Five (42 percent) of the 12 couples in court-ordered conciliation counseling decided against marital dissolution and agreed to work on their marriages. This compared to nine (75 percent) of the 12 couples in the voluntary counseling group who decided against marital dissolution. It appears that conciliation counseling did have some of the effect intended by the Iowa legislature when it added this component to its dissolution laws. This finding is similar to other research on conciliation counseling that shows that it increases the percentage of marital reconciliations (Sprenkle and Storm, 1983). The most important thing is for couples "to give their marriage their best shot."

Some states require conciliatory counseling before a divorce may be granted. Can voluntary counseling be more effective?

Separation

A trial separation is also another alternative before divorce. Couples ask: "Do you think if we separated for a while that it would help us to decide what we should do?" Separation can be an effective treatment method in some instances, especially if the separation is carefully structured and if marital therapy continues during the separation (Granvold, 1983). **Structured separation** may be defined as a time-limited approach in which the couple terminates cohabitation, commits to regularly scheduled therapy with a therapist, and agrees to regular interpersonal contact, with a moratorium on a final decision either to reunite or divorce (Granvold and Tarrant, 1983). The objective of separation is change; it is designed to interrupt old interactional patterns through the creation of an environment conducive to change. It is characterized by ambivalent feelings between the spouses and toward the marriage. The anticipated result is that spouses will move closer together or farther apart.

Separation is not to be taken lightly. It is a time of emotional upheaval and extreme stress. It is also a time of stress and upset for children. It has both potential benefits and risks. It is, however, one alternative that may be considered.

A number of types of situations may support the decision to consider structured marital separation as a treatment method (Granvold and Tarrant, 1983).

1. *Extreme conflict.* The frequency, intensity, and duration of conflict is so punishing that the couple cannot tolerate it. Physical or emotional abuse and verbal aggressiveness may be so debilitating that no positive change can take place in the relationship.

I, (Tom/Jan) Smith, agree to a marital separation from my spouse for six weeks during which time I will not make any final decisions to either divorce or remain married. I agree to the following stipulations:

Therapy — I will attend weekly conjoint marital therapy sessions for the duration of this contract. I will initiate individual therapy as I prefer and in consideration of Dr. _____'s recommendations.

Contact with Spouse — I will spend time with my partner on two occasions per week. I will have telephone contact with my spouse only to arrange our "dates" and in the case of an emergency. I will make no effort to see my spouse more frequently than the designated rate.

Sexual Contact with my Spouse — I understand that my partner and I may continue having sexual contact with one another and that either of us has the right to initiate sexual activity.

Dating — I understand that neither of us is eligible to date others.

Sexual Contact with Others — I understand that neither of us is eligible to have sexual relations with others during the contracted separation period.

Privacy — I will make no effort to oversee the activities of my spouse, "drop-in," or telephone except as specified as above.

Contact with Children (Tom) — I agree to spend individual time with my children at least weekly. I will arrange to take my children overnight unless travel with my work prevents me from doing so.

Financial Support — It is agreed that Tom will pay the house and car payments and $350.00 monthly to cover utilities, child-related expenses, etc.

Homework — I will make every effort to carry out the homework assignments to which I have agreed during therapy sessions. I understand that my marital relationship is to have priority during this separation period. I will use only positive methods to encourage my spouse to participate in doing homework.

Renegotiation — I will participate in renegotiating the separation contract at the end of this contract period should my spouse and I, in collaboration with our therapist, prefer to sustain the separation period. Furthermore, should either my partner or I wish to alter any part of this contract at any time, it is to be discussed and renegotiated during a therapy session with Dr. _____ .

Signed _____

Date _____

Adapted from Granvold, D. K. (1983). Structured separation for marital treatment and decision-making. *Journal of Marital and Family Therapy*, 9, 403–412. Copyright © 1983 American Association for Marriage and Family Therapy. Reprinted by permission.

*The therapist is not responsible for the specific terms identified in this contract but has served as a mediator/counselor in developing the contract.

2. *Absence of spouse reinforcement.* There is little or no reward, pleasure, or satisfaction from the marital relationship, and separation may help to raise the level of mutual positive exchange.

3. *Feeling constricted or smothered.* One or both partners need more space in their togetherness, relief from punishing spousal control and jealousy, and opportunity for personal growth and individual freedom while they restructure their relationship.

4. *A situational or midlife crisis.* Situation crises may include loss of a loved one, a job change, moving to a new community, or children leaving home.

A midlife crisis is characterized by disillusionment, depression, a sense of stagnation, self-doubt, directionlessness, and emotional upheaval. Respite from the marital relationship may allow the individuals to deal with the crisis before they are confronted with an intense effort to change the marriage.

5. *Indecision regarding divorce.* If couples can't decide, a structured marital separation may effect a break in the decision-making dilemma.

Some couples want a separation to pursue other sexual relationships. One man explained, "I have to be free to find out if my love for Sarah (the other woman) is genuine and will last." In this situation, the wife was understandably upset: "You want to see if it's going to work out, then if it doesn't, you're coming home to me. I'm not going to be anybody's second choice."

Few spouses will agree to a separation to free the other to pursue extramarital affairs. If the couple is really serious about straightening out the marriage, it is most helpful to first give up the affair while working on the marriage. If they give up the marriage while pursuing the affair, there usually isn't any marriage left to come back to.

WRONG AND RIGHT WAYS TO GET DIVORCED

Adversary Approach

Once a decision is made to get divorced, there is a wrong way and a right to go about it. *The wrong way is the* **adversary approach** *whereby one party brings charges against the other*, proving that the other is guilty of cruelty, desertion, nonsupport, habitual drunkenness, or some other fault. One of the spouses must be proven guilty, while the other must be blameless. If the accused proves his or her innocence, or if the court finds that both spouses are guilty, the divorce may not be granted. In some states, no matter how incompatible the partners are, no matter how miserable they are living together, if both spouses are at fault, the divorce can be denied. Some states, recognizing the folly of not granting a divorce when both parties are guilty, introduced the **doctrine of comparative rectitude**, which recognizes that the court may grant a divorce to the party least at fault (Rice, 1983).

The worst part about the adversary approach is that it forces spouses to become combatants, to attack one another like gladiators, with each trying to win over the other. This creates tremendous hostility and anger, even when couples are trying to settle amicably.

One of the results of the adversary approach is that pressure is applied against one party to grant concessions in exchange for not delaying a divorce or for not contesting it. The consequence is bargaining. The divorce itself becomes an object of trade in exchange for alimony, child custody, visitation rights, or the allocation of property.

Property and Finances

Nowhere is the injustice of adversary divorce laws more evident than in the matters relating to property and money. A minority of states have "community property" laws that entitle a wife, upon divorce, to an equal share of family income and property. In other states, the husband and the wife may fight bitterly over the distribution of family assets and money. If one spouse is at all vindictive or if the divorce drags out for months or years, the couple may be deeply in debt by the time the divorce is granted. As a result of vindictiveness, some husbands try to shut off all charge accounts to protect themselves. Husbands also can be vindictive, especially if their wives have money. One actress announced that she paid her husband a large sum of money as part of her divorce settlement in exchange for her freedom (Rice, 1983).

Alimony and Child Support

Alimony and child support, referred to as "the high cost of leaving" are usually expensive. Costs vary depending upon the family's standard of living, whether or not the wife is able to work, the value of her independent assets, the number and ages of the children, and the overall financial status of the husband versus that of the wife. Some women now reject alimony as demeaning and as a symbol of feminine dependency. Others try to sue their husbands for as much as they can. In some states, a wealthy woman may be ordered to pay alimony to her husband, particularly if he is not able to work. Today alimony payments are declining and, when granted, are usually awarded only for a limited period of time or until the former spouse remarries (Welch and Price-Bonham, 1983). Child support payments are made until children are of legal age.

Legal Fees

Most husbands are surprised to learn that they may be responsible for the legal fees of both lawyers, at least if the wife has no separate income. Fees vary according to income bracket and the amount of time and work a case demands. Whatever their financial situation, a divorce is one of the most costly economic ventures a couple can undertake — with expenses that few to-be-divorced couples weigh in advance.

Children as Pawns

In the most tragic cases, children become pawns in the battle. Children are treated as negotiable debris from the marriage, not much different from the stereo or the family car. Couples may fight over custody, each trying to win the children. In one case, the wife agreed to let her husband have the children in exchange for a $50,000 payment. In another, the wife wouldn't agree to a divorce unless the husband promised to give her the custody of the children and to move at least 1,000 miles away. Since judges often consider the wishes of older children in deciding what parent the child will live with, each parent may try to get the children to side with him or her or to turn the children against the other. One husband relates:

My wife has done everything she can to turn my son against me. She told him so many lies, which he believed, that whenever anyone comes to the door of the house where my wife and son are living, my boy answers the door with a shotgun in his hands, just in case it's me at the door. (Author's counseling notes)

Much of the upset and turmoil that children experience because of divorce arises because parents are upset or because the children are forced to take sides. The children love both parents; which one are they to believe or to defend? If they weren't upset before, they become so if couples continue to fight one another. If parents are embittered, these hostilities become deeply disturbing. The whole adversary bargaining process is wrong because it prevents justice. It destroys whatever semblance of friendly feelings might still exist between couples, and it often works great harm on children (Rice, 1983).

No-Fault Divorce

In 1960, the National Conference of Commissioners on Uniform State Laws promulgated the new Uniform Marriage and Divorce Act (Kargman, 1973). This act is not a law; it is a model for state legislatures to accept or deny in part or completely. It rejects fault grounds as a precondition for access to courts and recommends instead the right of the individual who petitions for divorce on the grounds of "irretrievable breakdown" of the marriage.

Some states now have only **no-fault** grounds for divorce. Other states recognize irreconcilable differences in addition to incurable insanity or mental incompetence. Other states merely add no-fault grounds (Freed and Foster, 1981). In these states, one spouse can still threaten to sue for divorce on grounds other than the no-fault ground if his or her demands are not met. As long as this is possible, divorce can still be a bitter contest between two partners who are each out to hurt or to win from the other.

The possibility for vengeance is removed when no-fault divorce is the only alternative offered. The law removes all fault (the question of who is to blame) and reduces the grounds to irreconcilable differences, or an irremedial breakdown of the marriage.

There are those who feel that this approach makes divorce too easy; but as it is, divorce is extremely easy to get if it is not contested. It may require only a superficial hearing in court that takes 10 to 30 minutes. Nevertheless, it is in the process of trying to work out the agreement that the harm comes. Couples fight bitterly. The interests of the children and the lives of people are traded in the negotiation. Eliminate the possibility of contest and you eliminate much of the fighting (Rice, 1983).

Mediation

One of the most helpful solutions to property, alimony, custody, child support, and other issues is to employ a mediator to help resolve differences (Grebe, 1986). Both private mediators and public or court-appointed mediators provide services throughout the United States (Pearson, Thoennes, and Milne, 1982). One

Disputes over custody may need to be solved by employing a mediator. Child custody and visitation rights resolved in mediation seem to be more successful than court imposed determinations.

advantage of using mediators is that they can objectively represent the interests of both partners and the children. Their role is to:

1. Gain a commitment to mediation and establish ground rules for the discussion.
2. Define the issues, elicit facts and all pertinent information, including the needs, desires, and feelings of the partners.
3. Process the issues by employing solutions and maintaining positive momentum, managing emotions, encouraging empathy and narrowing differences.
4. Help the couple reach a settlement and assure its implementation. The decisions that are made can be drawn up by a lawyer in the form of a legal agreement, signed by all parties, and presented to the court as the basis for settlement. (Vanderkooi and Pearson, 1983)

Mediators of property and money settlements can ask for complete financial disclosure, get a property appraisal if needed, and even hire the help of an accountant if many assets are involved. Any settlements that are agree on do not become final until approved by the court. *One advantage of a mediated settlement is that the partners are more likely to comply with decisions that are made jointly than with financial judgments that are ordered by the court against the will of the couple.* Disputes regarding child custody and visitation rights and responsibilities are settled on the basis of the best interests of the child (Scheiner, Musetto, and Cordier, 1982).

Studies of mediation as a means of resolving disputes have shown (1) considerably higher rates of pre-trial stipulations or agreements than found in control groups, (2) a significantly higher level of satisfaction with mediated agreements than with those imposed by the courts, (3) a dramatic reduction in litigation following final order, (4) an increase in joint custody arrangements, and (5) a decrease in public expenses such as custody studies and court costs (Sprenkle and Storm, 1983)

Some Effects of No-Fault Divorce

The process of no-fault divorce requires less extensive litigation (many couples file without benefit of attorneys), reduces legal expenses, and makes a "friendly divorce" easier than under the old adversary system. It has partially removed from the legal process the punitive element of moral condemnation that pervaded divorce for centuries. Some observers predicted a flood of divorce once restrictive laws were removed. This has not happened.

Some other changes bring up further questions. One of the changes has been an increase in the percentage of husbands who have filed the petition once they no longer had to make public accusations against their wives (Dixon and Weitzman, 1980). At the same time, with the threat of reprisals removed, alimony has been awarded less frequently, for shorter periods of time, and for smaller amounts. Also, household property and furniture is less likely to be awarded exclusively to the wife, and attorney's fees are more likely to be paid by both spouses. There has been a slight decrease in the percent of wives awarded full custody, and a corresponding increase in joint custody arrangements. The effect on child support payments to the custodial parent has been variable (Welch and Price-Bonham, 1983). Overall, the loss of bargaining power by the wife has resulted in a less-favorable financial settlement to many wives. Those who do not have significant earning power of their own are affected greatly, many having to reduce their standard of living significantly because of inadequate support from their ex-spouses (Dixon and Weitzman, 1980). So while no-fault divorce has many advantages, it has also created some inequalities.

ADULT ADJUSTMENTS AFTER DIVORCE

The problems of adjustment after divorce may be grouped into a number of categories (Rice, 1983):

- Getting over the emotional trauma of divorce
- Dealing with the attitudes of society
- Loneliness and the problem of social readjustment
- Finances
- Realignment of responsibilities and work roles
- Sexual readjustments
- Contacts with ex-spouse
- Kinship interaction

Under the best of circumstances, divorce is an emotionally disturbing experience (Plummer and Koch-Hattem, 1986; Thompson and Spanier, 1983). Under the worse conditions, it may result in a high degree of shock and disorientation. Krantzler (1974) refers to divorce as an emotional crisis triggered by a sudden loss. He speaks of the emotional turmoil before and during the divorce, the shock and crisis of separation, a time of mourning as the relationship is laid to rest, and a period of disruption as one attempts to regain balance. Sometimes the emotional trauma of divorce comes primarily from a drawn-out and bitter legal battle. In these cases, the actual divorce decree comes as a welcome relief from this long period of pain.

The trauma is greater when one spouse wants the divorce and the other doesn't (Huber, 1983), when the idea comes unexpectedly, when one continues to be emotionally attached to the other after the divorce, or when friends and family disapprove of the whole idea.

For most couples, the decision to divorce is viewed as an "end of the rope" decision, which is reached, on the average, over a period of about two years. One study revealed that the spouse who initiated the divorce suffered more trauma than the noninitiator (Buehler, 1987). Initiators experienced considerable stress, anxiety, fear, and guilt in making the decision to leave. Other studies reveal that during the preseparation period women report poorer psychological adjustment than men. This may be due to women's greater dissatisfaction with the marital relationship. In contrast, during the early postseparation period, men report poorer adjustment than women (Bloom and Caldwell, 1981). Men may be just beginning to come to grips with the loss of their spouse and the personal cost that loss entails (White and Bloom, 1981).

The time of greatest trauma for men is usually at the time of final separation. After that comes a long period of realization that the relationship is over emotionally as well as legally (Bloom and Caldwell, 1981). The fact that the suicide rate is much greater for divorced men and women than for married people indicates that getting divorced is no emotional picnic (Stack, 1980; Trovato, 1986, 1987; Wasserman, 1984).

Attitudes of Society

Part of the trauma of divorce is experienced because of the attitudes of society toward divorce and divorced persons. In the eyes of some, divorce represents moral failure or evidence of personal inadequacy. It takes a lot of courage to let it be known publicly that one has failed. "Friends," one woman remarked bitterly, "they drop you like a hot potato." Negative attitudes are lessening as divorce becomes more common, but such feelings still exist (Jorgensen and Johnson, 1980).

Loneliness and Social Readjustment

Even if two married people did not get along, they kept one another company. At least they knew that someone else was in the house. After divorce, they begin to realize what it is like to live alone. This adjustment is especially hard

Loneliness is one of the major problems that people face after divorce.

on those without children or whose children are living with the other spouse. Holidays are especially hard on those who are lonely. Krantzler (1974) relates:

> I celebrated Christmas one day late with my daughter. As on Thanksgiving, I was alone on Christmas and wept without shame over my solitary state and for the past I would never know again. (p. 24)

Numerous authorities suggest that *the friendship and companionship of other people is one of the most essential ingredients for a successful readjustment after divorce*, so getting involved with others is important (Leslie and Grady, 1985).

There seems to be some difference in social readjustment of divorced people according to their age at the time of divorce. Older women in particular have a hard time readjusting. Few women over 40 at the time of divorce remarry. Many have inadequate income. Many are moderately or severely lonely and depressed. Loneliness among women who do not remarry represents one of the grave consequences of divorce (Fischman, 1986).

Finances

In spite of some advances, women still receive only 62 percent of the income of males, assuming both have the same occupation, education, working experience, and hours (Rice, 1987). Furthermore, the mother still ends up with

Many women who are
divorced and do not remarry
experience a 50 percent
decline in family income.

custody of the children in 9 out of 10 cases (Jencks, 1982). Some mothers get only a little or irregular support from their ex-husbands. As a result of these factors, most divorced mothers have to work, but do so at inadequate wages. Wives who have never worked or who have no special education or skills, and have custody of one or more children, find themselves completely impoverished (Crossman and Edmondson, 1985). As a consequence, many mothers need welfare assistance (Weiss, 1984). In one study of divorcees, 71 percent said that financial difficulties were their major problem (Amato and Partridge, 1987).

It is estimated that women who get divorced and do not remarry experience a 50 percent decline in family income (Jencks, 1982). The irony is that whereas divorce lowers the living standard of both mothers and children, it typically raises that of fathers (Pett and Vaughn-Cole, 1986). According to a 1979 Census Bureau survey, only half of all divorced mothers received any money whatever from their children's father the previous year. Those who got something averaged only $1,000 per year per child (Jencks, 1982). As a result, the typical father had more money to support himself than his former wife had to support both herself and the children.

Realignment of Responsibilities and Work Roles

The divorced woman with children is faced with the prospect of an overload of work. Now she must perform all family functions, which were formerly shared by two persons (Berman and Turk, 1981). If she works outside the home, she is faced with a 16-hour day, 7 days a week, and 365 days a year. She also has to readjust her parenthood role to include taking over functions formerly fulfilled by her husband. As a consequence, she has less time to devote to the children, they listen to her less, and so she has more problems controlling and guiding them.

The roles of the divorced man also change, especially if he is a traditional male who was used to depending upon his wife for household care and

Research suggests that most divorced persons are sexually active. How might this pattern change as the AIDS crisis becomes more acute?

personal maintenance. In addition, if a father also has custody of his children, his responsibilities are total. So *whether male or female, the solo parent has to fulfill all family functions and has no relief from his or her burden.*

Sexual Readjustments

Research reveals that *most divorced persons are sexually active.* Hunt (1973) found only 9 percent of divorced women who were not sexually active. Those who were active had a median of 3.5 sexual partners per year. Divorced males had a median of 8 different sexual partners per year. Apparently, the complaint of sexual frustration that was common among divorced people a decade ago has been partially eliminated. In addition, formerly married men and women make frequent use of masturbation as a way of releasing sexual tensions when other sexual outlets are not available (Masters and Johnson, 1970).

This does not mean, however, that all of these sexual contacts are emotionally satisfying. Some divorced persons speak of meaningless sex, using sex to find companionship, to prove sexual attractiveness, or as an escape from problems. Divorced women complain frequently that they are often the targets of sexually aggressive males who believe that because divorcees are sexually experienced that they are likely to be promiscuous.

Contacts with Ex-Spouse

The more upsetting the divorce has been and the more vindictive the spouse, the less the other person wants to have any postdivorce contact. This is particularly true in cases of remarriage. Most second wives or husbands object to contacts with former spouses, because this usually leads to resentment and conflicts, especially if a bitter ex-spouse tries to cause trouble for the new couple.

TABLE 23.3 Frequency Distribution of Attachment Scores of Divorcing Spouses

Degree of Attachment	Percent	N
No attachment	15.8	28
Low attachment	41.8	74
Moderate attachment	17.5	31
High attachment	24.9	44
	100.0	177

From Kitson, G. C. (1982). Attachment to the spouse in divorce: A scale and its application. *Journal of Marriage and the Family, 44,* 379–393. Copyright © 1982 by the National Council on Family Relations. Reprinted by permission.

When contacts are maintained, it is usually in relation to the children and/or support money (Bloom and Kindle, 1985). When the children have problems, both parents become concerned and sometimes correspond or talk to one another about these problems. In this case, an amicable relationship helps them to work things out and it is easier on the children. Sometimes couples have to turn to the courts to settle disputes after the divorce.

Most of the postdivorce disputes are in relation to visitation rights, child support, or alimony. Some cities have "Fathers' Day" in court, when fathers are taken to task for not making payments on time. Other disputes may occur if a former husband seeks to reduce alimony payments or a wife to increase them. In contrast to these situations, some couples remain friends. One woman commented:

> My former husband and I get along better now than when we were married. He came over for dinner the other night; I cooked, and we had a pleasant evening. It's strange, but when we were married, we fought all the time. Now we are really good friends. (Author's counseling notes)

Some spouses have difficulty in breaking emotional attachments following divorce (McCollum, 1985). This increases the subjective stress experienced (Kitson, 1982). Table 23.3 shows the frequency of attachment of 177 divorcing spouses from seven Cleveland, Ohio, suburbs (Kitson, 1982). About half had obtained their divorce and the other half were awaiting their decrees. About three-fourths had separated from their spouse within the year prior to the interview. The greater the attachment, the more difficulty spouses had in adjusting to divorce.

Kinship Interaction

Divorce is a multigenerational process that affects grandparents and other kin as well as the divorcing couple and their children (Ferreiro, Warren, and Konanc, 1986). Positive support from grandparents can have an important effect on the divorcing child's adjustment (Spanier and Hanson, 1982). Helpful behavior includes:

Emotional support — listening, showing empathy, affirming love and affection.

Child care — usually occasional babysitting or taking grandchildren for weekends.

Good rational advice — being able to talk over decisions with parents.

Respect for autonomy with regression — divorcing children have contrasting needs. Some want autonomy in decision making; others want to regress to dependency for a while (Lesser and Comet, 1987).

Not all grandparents are helpful. Some punish their child through verbal and hostile acts. Others completely intrude into their child's life. Some grandparents refuse to accept the divorce. Others try to influence their child's spouse to stay married; yet others sever all ties with their child's spouse. Some grandparents show overconcern for the grandchildren, neglecting the needs of their own divorcing child (Ahrons and Bowman, 1982; Matthews and Sprey, 1984). Some grandparents become upset, personalizing the divorce — "Look what you're doing to me" — which increases the pressure on the divorcing child.

CHILDREN AND DIVORCE

Child Custody

The term **custody** refers to both legal custody (decision-making rights) and physical custody (where the children will live). In sole legal custody, the noncustodial parent forfeits the right to make decisions about the children's health, education, or religious training; in effect the custodial parent is given control over child rearing. In **joint legal custody**, custody is shared between the two parents with parental rights and obligations left as they were during the marriage (Ferreiro, Warren, and Konanc, 1986).

Traditionally, sole custody of the children has been granted to the mother, unless it can be established that she is unfit (Spanier and Glick, 1981). In some cases, the mother may not be competent or she may have a poor relationship with her children (Lowery, 1985). The children may be closer to the father; he may be the one who can better afford them and who can better care for them (Fischer, 1983). Most wives and husbands have to work after the divorce, as does the husband. More and more, therefore, *the overriding consideration is what the court considers the best interests of the children*. The U.S. Supreme Court has declared that even in cases where two parents are of different races, private prejudices are not permissible considerations if they might inflict injury by removing a child from a competent parent (Myricks and Ferullo, 1986).

In cases of custody dispute, a mediator may be employed or a child-development expert appointed to investigate the family situation and to recommend custody arrangements to the court (Everett and Volgy, 1983). The wishes of older children are usually taken into consideration in considering with whom they reside (Watson, 1981). One study has suggested that, when parents are divorced, boys who live with their fathers and girls who live with their mothers seem to be warmer, less demanding, more mature, sociable, independent, and to have higher self-esteem than do children living with a parent of the opposite sex. Such children do not become emotional substitutes for a spouse, and they have adult models of the same sex with whom they can identify (Hirsch, 1980; Santrock and Warshak, 1979).

1. Are any of you divorced and do you have a joint custody arrangement with your ex-spouse, or do any of you have friends who are divorced and have a joint custody arrangement? How does it work out? What are the actual benefits to the children? What are the major problems that are experienced?

2. Have any of you been reared in homes where your parents were divorced? How did the divorce affect you? What upset you the most? How might the situation have been better for you and any brothers and sisters? Which parent had custody of you? Did you see your noncustodial parent very often? Why? Why not? Would joint custody have helped the situation for you?

3. Is it disruptive for a child to have two homes rather than one? Under joint custody, will a child be bounced back and forth from home to home, and will his or her loyalties be divided?

4. Under what circumstances can you see that joint custody would not be advisable?

In some cases, joint custody is awarded with both parents responsible. The children usually reside with one parent and visit the other often. Since children need two loving parents (Franklin and Hibbs, 1980), the need is for children to have access to both parents and for both to be responsible for the welfare of the children. Important decisions are made jointly. Joint custody fathers are more likely to be actively involved in parenting than are noncustodial fathers (Bowman and Ahrons, 1985). Joint custody also takes the pressure off one parent to assume the total responsiblity (Melli, 1986).

Such arrangements require great maturity and the forbearance of both parents; otherwise numerous squabbles create continual tension (Lowery and Settle, 1985). Bringing together two people who want to be apart and who don't get along can perpetuate all of the squabbles of the unhappy marriage. Some parents also experience great stress when they interact with social institutions, family, and friends (Ahrons, 1980). For example, the desire of both parents to receive school announcements, report cards, or results of doctor's examinations commonly meets with resistance. Friends and family members may view friendly relationships as deviant and pressure couples not to have anything to do with one another. There is general agreement, however, that *joint custody, if desired by both parents, and if both are able to get along together, is a good solution to a difficult problem* (Melli, 1986).

Visitation Rights

Ordinarily, visitation rights are given to the parent not given custody. Those rights may be unlimited — to visit the children at any time — or they may be restrictive — limiting visitation only to specific times. A vindictive spouse can make life miserable by managing to "be away" with the children when it's time for the other parent to visit, by "poisoning" the children's minds against the other parent, by refusing to allow the children to phone or write, or by using visitation rights as a club to wield over the other person's head.

According to the provisions of the *Uniform Marriage and Divorce Act* of 1979:

(A) A parent not granted custody of the child is entitled to reasonable visitation rights unless the court finds, after a hearing, that visitation would endanger the child's physical health or significantly impair his emotional development.

(B) The court may modify an order granting or denying visitation rights whenever modification would serve the best interests of the child; but the court shall not restrict a parent's visitation rights unless it finds that the visitation would endanger the child's physical health or significantly impair his emotional development (Franklin and Hibbs, 1980, p. 289).

One study (Koch, 1982) indicates that *while increased visitation is associated with a good noncustodial parent-child relationship, the association is mediated by the quality of the postdivorce parental relationship.* Thus, the characteristics of the relationship between the two adults continue to be related to children's postdivorce adjustment (Lowery and Settle, 1985).

Reactions of Children

A growing number of clinicians emphasize that children perceive divorce as a major, negative event that stimulates painful emotions, confusion, and uncertainty (Jellinger and Slovik, 1981; Kalter, 1983). Some clinicians feel that the majority of children regain psychological equilibrium in a year or so and resume a normal curve of growth and development (Hetherington, Cox, and Cox, 1979). Others feel that for a substantial portion of children, the upheaval in their lives will result in interferences in wholesome, social-emotional growth (Wallerstein and Kelly, 1980). Overall, the long-term impact on social, emotional, and cognitive growth is not clear and continues to be studied and debated (Kalter, 1983).

Short-term reactions, however, have been fairly well described. Children may go through a period of *mourning and grief*, and the mood and feeling may be one of *sadness and dejection*. One seven-year-old described divorce as "when people go away" (Rice, 1979b). Other common reactions are a *heightened sense of insecurity.* Children feel that "if you really loved me, you wouldn't go away and leave me." Some become very afraid that their other parent will leave, and the child may become very possessive with that parent (Kalter, 1983). One mother remarked: "Since the divorce, Tommy has been very upset when I go to work or when he goes to school. I think he's afraid that he'll come home and not find me there" (Rice, 1979b, p. 304).

Another common reaction is to *blame themselves*. If one major source of couple conflict is over the children, the children feel they are responsible (Wallerstein and Kelly, 1980). Some children feel that the departing parent is abandoning them because they haven't been "good boys or girls." Another common reaction of children is to *try to bring their parents together*. They "wish that everyone could live together and be happy." The longing for a reunited family may go on for a long time, until children fully understand the realities of the situation and the reason for the separation.

After children get over the initial upset of divorce, one common reaction is *anger and resentment*, especially against the parent they blame for the divorce. Sometimes this is directed against the father — especially if they feel he has deserted the family. The child feels: "I hate you because you have gone off

Children often perceive divorce as a major negative event that stimulates painful emotions, confusion, and uncertainty.

and left me." When the father comes to visit, he may be surprised to find that his children remain cold and aloof. They have been hurt, and so they have erected defenses, have shut off their emotions, and have tried to remain unfeeling (Rice, 1979b).

The resentment or hostility may also be directed at the mother, especially if the children blame her for the divorce. One five-year-old blamed her mother for her father's absence: "I hate you, because you sent my daddy away." (Actually, the mother hadn't wanted the divorce.) An older girl, age 12, asked her mother, "Why did you leave my father all alone?" It was obvious that the girl did not understand the reason for the divorce (Rice, 1979b, p. 305).

Children have other adjustments to make. They have to adjust to the absence of one parent, often one on whom they have depended deeply for affection and for help. One teenage girl remarked, "The hardest thing for me was to get used to living without my father. I never really realized how much I needed him until he left." (Author's counseling notes)

Older children may also be required to assume much more responsibility for family functioning: cooking, housekeeping, even earning money to support the family. This is usually a maturing experience for them, but it's an adjustment. Some children, used to having everything, have a hard time realizing that money is short and that they can't buy the clothes and other things they used to.

Special adjustments are necessary, of course, when the parent caring for the children begins to date again and to get emotionally involved with another person. Now the children must share their parent with another adult. If the parent remarries, as the majority do, the children are confronted with a total readjustment to a stepparent (Rice, 1978b).

1. A number of factors determine probability of divorce: age at first marriage, frequency of attendance at religious services, socioeconomic status, race, geographic area of the United States in which one resides, and whether one's parents have been divorced or not.

2. Studies of the perception of husbands and wives of the causes of marital breakup reveal the ten most important causes of breakup according to the wives were: basic unhappiness, emotional abuse, communication problems, incompatibility and different backgrounds, sexual problems, the husband's lack of sense of family and lack of time at home, the husband's alcohol abuse, financial or employment problems, the husband's infidelity, and the wives' lack of interest in the marriage. The husbands listed 9 of the 10 causes that the wives had listed (although not in the same order). The husbands did not list their alcohol abuse among the first 10, but listed their physical abuse and cruelty toward their wives instead.

3. When therapists were asked to choose the areas of difficulty that were most damaging to the marital relationship, they listed the following 10: communication, unrealistic expectations, power struggles, serious individual problems, role conflict, lack of loving feelings, demonstration of affection, alcoholism, extramarital affairs, and sex.

4. When therapists were asked to choose the areas of difficulty that were most difficult to treat successfully, they chose the following 10 (in decreasing order of difficulty): alcoholism, lack of loving feelings, serious individual problems, power struggles, addicted behavior other than alcoholism, value conflicts, physical abuse, unrealistic expectations, extramarital affairs, and incest.

5. Making a decision to divorce is difficult. There are four basic considerations in deciding whether to remain married or not: satisfaction or attractions of the marriage, barriers to getting out of the marriage, the attractiveness of alternatives to the marriage, and the intensity of the emotional pain generated by the unhappy marriage.

6. There are two major alternatives to divorce: marriage counseling, and structured separation during which couples try to straighten out their problems.

7. Five types of situations may support the decision to consider structured marital separation: extreme conflict, absence of spouse reinforcement, feeling constricted or smothered, a situational or midlife crisis, and indecision regarding divorce.

8. There are right and wrong ways to get divorced. The wrong way is the adversary approach in which one spouse brings charges against the other, proving that the other is guilty of some offense.

9. The right way to get divorced is through no-fault divorce in which the spouses petition on the basis of irretrievable breakdown of the marriage or irreconcilable differences.

10. One of the most helpful solutions to property, alimony, custody, child support, and other issues is to employ a mediator to help resolve differences.

11. Many of the effects of no-fault divorce have been helpful: less extensive and expensive litigation, making friendly divorce easier, and partially removing the punitive element of moral condemnation that pervaded divorce for centuries.

12. Some effects of no-fault divorce have not always been helpful. More husbands are filing once the threat of recrimination has been removed. While this may be of some advantage to the husbands, the wives have been placed at a disadvantage in winning fair financial and property settlements. Overall, the husbands may be better off financially after the divorce; many wives and their children are forced to live in poverty.

13. The major adjustment problems of adults after divorce are: getting over the emotional trauma, dealing with the negative attitudes of society, loneliness and the problem of social readjustment, finances, realignment of responsibilities and work roles, sexual readjustments, contacts with ex-spouse, and kinship interaction.

14. The term *custody* refers to both legal and physical custody. In the past, the mother traditionally got sole custody of the children. Today, the court's overriding consideration is the best interests of the children.

15. Joint legal custody is when the responsibility for parenting is given to both parents. They have parental rights and responsibilities for child rearing as they did during the marriage. Joint custody requires the active cooperation and responsibility of both parents, and the necessity for the two parents to be able to get along with one another.

16. Ordinarily, visitation rights are given to the parent not given custody. While increased visitation is associated with good noncustodial parent-child relationships and is good for the child, the association is mediated by the quality of the postdivorce parental relationship.

17. Children perceive divorce as a major, negative event that stimulates painful emotions, confusion and uncertainty.

SUGGESTED READINGS

Alvarez, A. (1982). *Life After Marriage: People in Divorce*. New York: Simon and Schuster. A popular approach.

Gardner, R. (1981). *The Boys' and Girls' Books About Divorce*. New York: Bantam. A classic work for children.

Krantzler, M. (1974). *Creative Divorce: A New Opportunity for Personal Growth*. New York: New American Library. A personal, helpful account of one man's experience and how others can profit from the experience.

Luepnitz, D. A. (1982). *Child Custody*. Lexington, MA: D. C. Heath. Research on child custody arrangements and effects on children.

Napolitane, C., with Victoria Pellegrino. (1977). *Living and Loving After Divorce*. New York: Rawson, Wade. Guide for women.

Ricci, I. (1980). *Mom's House, Dad's House*. New York: Collier. Advice for parents.

Salk, L. (1978). *What Every Child Would Like Parents to Know About Divorce*. New York: Harper and Row. Guidelines for parents from a famous child psychologist.

Spanier, G. B., and Thompson, L. (1984). *Parting: The Aftermath of Separation and Divorce*. Beverly Hills, CA: Sage. Research findings.

Wallerstein, J., and Kelly, J. B. (1980). *Surviving the Breakup: How Children Actually Cope with Divorce*. New York: Basic Books. Longitudinal study of childrens' adjustments.

Ware, C. (1984). *Sharing Parenthood After Divorce*. New York: Bantam. Coparenting.

24

COMING TOGETHER: REMARRIAGE AND STEPPARENTING

KEY TERMS

binuclear family
sibling rivalry

Important changes have taken place in American families over the last 25 years. The most noted has been the tremendous increase in the divorce rate. A less publicized change has been an increased number of divorced parents who attempt to restore stability to their lives through remarriage. Approximately 83 percent of divorced men and 76 percent of divorced women remarry (Fine, 1986). Today, one out of every three marriages involves an adult who has been married before (Kargman, 1983). Although estimates vary, approximately 30 million American adults and 10 million children live in stepfamilies (Cherlin and McCarthy, 1985). This means that 16 percent of all American children live in stepfamilies.

Vital questions are: To what extent are remarriages successful? How might couples increase the chances of success? And what are the special problems remarrieds face?

Also, how do primary families differ from stepfamilies? How may stepmother and stepfather roles be defined? What are the problems stepmothers and stepfathers face? What are the reactions and problems of different stepchildren? What do we need to know about stepsibling relationships? What is it like growing up in a stepfamily?

REMARRIAGE

Types of Remarried Families

Remarried families (sometimes called **binuclear** families) may be grouped into categories according to family configuration.

Couples with one remarried spouse. This would include families with:

No children

Children-in-common only

Her children (stepfather families)

His children (stepmother families)

Children-in-common plus her children (natural parent plus stepfather)

Children-in-common plus his children (natural parent plus stepmother)

Both have children (two stepparents — either the husband or the wife had a child out of wedlock)

Couples with two remarried spouses. This would include families with:

No children

Children-in-common only

Her children (stepfather families)

His children (stepmother families)

Children-in-common plus her children (natural parent plus stepfather)

Children-in-common plus his children (natural parent plus stepmother)

Both of their children (two stepparents)

Children-in-common plus their children (natural parents plus two stepparents)

Family relationships can become quite involved in remarriages when one or both spouses bring children from a previous marriage and then have children of the new marriage.

Custodial children of mother plus relationships with father's children on a noncustodial basis

Custodial children of father plus relationships with mother's children on a noncustodial basis

Family relationships can become quite involved in remarriages when one or both spouses bring children from a previous marriage. Children may have natural parents, plus stepparents, both natural siblings and stepsiblings, both natural grandparents and stepgrandparents, natural aunts and uncles plus stepaunts and stepuncles, not to mention cousins and others. Adult spouses relate to one another, to their own natural parents and grandparents, to their new parents-in-law and grandparents-in-law, to their new brothers- and sisters-in-law; and they may continue to relate to their former parents- and grandparents-in-law, to their former brothers- and sisters-in-law, and other family members. It is no wonder that family integration is sometimes difficult (Ihinger-Tallman and Pasley, 1986).

Divorce and Success in Remarriage

The majority of survey studies have revealed that *the probability of divorce is slightly greater in remarriages than in first marriages* (Aguirre and Parr, 1982; Cherlin, 1981). However, both divorce rates and redivorce rates have started to decline, and the data suggest that in the future the incidence of redivorce may be quite similar to the incidence of first divorce (Norton and Moorman, 1987). The reasons for redivorce may be slightly different than for first divorce.

Remarrieds are older, more mature and experienced, and often highly motivated to make their marriages work (Goldberg, 1982). They ought to be able to make a better go of marriage the second time around. In fact, Furstenberg and Spanier (1984) concluded that *successful remarrieds stated that their new marriage was better than their first marriage.* They felt they had married the right person: "someone who allows you to be yourself" (p. 83). They felt they had learned to communicate and that they handled problems maturely. Better communication also led to better decision making. Both partners tended to feel they were more equal in remarriage and that the division of labor was more equitable.

These comments came from those who had successful remarriages. For others, *remarriage introduces some complications that were not present in first marriage. The biggest complication is children* (Bridgwater, 1982a). Children from prior marriages increase the likelihood of divorce among remarried couples (Fine, 1986). When remarrieds divorce it is often because they want to get rid of the stepchildren, not the spouse (Meer, 1986). In a majority of cases, at least one partner already has children when the remarriage begins (Cherlin and McCarthy, 1985). Since mothers most often get custody, their children are living with her and her new husband, who becomes a stepfather. The husband's children are usually living with his ex-wife, creating family ties with her household, with the potential for conflict and resentment. The wife's ex-spouse as noncustodial father usually sees his children, so he has contact with both his ex-wife and her new husband, also allowing the possibility of conflict and problems. Being a stepparent is a far more difficult task than being a natural parent, because children have difficulty accepting a substitute parental figure. The wife must adjust to his children as a noncustodial stepmother and try to develop a friendly relationship from infrequent visits — a difficult task at best (Ambert, 1986). All of the adults are co-parenting with three or four parent figures as opposed to two. The children are continually reacting to and dealing with growing up in two households, three or four adult figures, and two or more models of relationship patterns with the opposite sex (Whiteside, 1982). Both adults and children must contend with the attitudes and influences of other family members.

Stepsibling relationships also become important. There is often competition between the new spouse's and the partner's children. They each may become jealous of the time and attention their own parent shows the stepchildren. A divorced mother and her children become a "closed system" of social interaction, and it becomes difficult for a new stepfather to enter that system. Single, previously unmarried women also have trouble in finding their place in father-children relationships. His children may resent her efforts at becoming their stepmother (Aguirre and Parr, 1982). She may have given up a good job and a good deal of freedom and independence to marry, only to find she is treated like an outsider in a closed family system.

Courtship and Mate Selection in Remarriage

There are a number of ways that courtship and mate selection in remarriage are different from that of first marriage (Rogers and Conrad, 1986). *For one thing, the two people are older.* The median age at remarriage is 36 for men and 33 for women. Overall, they are likely to be more emotionally mature and more experienced and wiser than when they married the first time around. For another thing, *the majority have children.* The median age of two children at the time of remarriage is six and eight years old. This means that a custodial parent has the added responsibility of evaluating a potential mate in terms of his or her potential as a stepparent (Walker and Messinger, 1979).

Sometimes, ex-spouses and families become involved in the courtship of the couple. If the ex-spouse is vindictive, he or she may try to break up the relationship, turn the children against the new partner, exert negative influence on family members so they won't accept the newcomer, and create jealousy and tension between the new partners. If family members liked the first spouse and sympathize with him or her, they may have a very difficult time accepting the newcomer. Potential mates of formerly married persons are often introduced to other family members only after there is some assurance of commitment between the courters (Weiss, 1979). The announcement of the new involvement may come as a surprise, with family members not having much time or exposure to get used to the new relationship. New partners enter a family system with an established history (Keshet, 1980), and there are no guidelines for how they should fit in. Consequently, there may be several false starts in attempting to build relationships with the family, the children, and possibly with the ex-spouse.

There are sometimes differences also between the courtships of the never-marrieds and the divorced in relation to the speed at which courtship progresses toward marriage. The median number of years between divorce and remarriage is only four years for men and three for women. These are relatively short periods of time to get over a divorce, reestablish one's social life and date, meet and get acquainted with potential mates, select a partner, and marry again. During the period of emotional turmoil before and after a divorce, people are very vulnerable to the attention of others who are nice to them. Sexual intimacy usually commences early in a relationship, which usually intensifies the emotional involvement and the feeling of being in love.

> Mr. and Mrs. F. came to a marriage clinic in the second month of their marriage. It was a third marriage for Mrs. F., but a majority of her time in the last few years was spent in a tight, one-parent unit with her son. Mr. F. was one year out of his first marriage of sixteen years. He had custody of his daughter. Mr. and Mrs. F. had a whirlwind courtship of three months with little time spent with his and her children together. Romantically, they were remarried on Valentine's day, then moved in together. Mr. and Mrs. F. continued to hold down full-time jobs, leaving her son and his daughter to cope with unsupervised time together. Needless to say, they were thrown totally off balance by the degree of conflict which erupted and had developed few ties between them strong enough to weather the storm. The marriage lasted barely six months (Whiteside, 1982, p. 65).

There may also be subtle psychological influences at work in the mate selection process. *Some people want to marry persons whom they believe are like a spouse to whom they were married before.* When people are divorced by a spouse against their will, to whom they remain emotionally attached, or when a former spouse has died, they may seek another mate who reminds them of their former one. Actually, of course, no two people are alike, so trouble arises in the remarriage when two people discover their new mate is *not* like their former spouse or when they try to pressure their new mate to be like the former one.

Even if people don't like some characteristics of a former spouse, they may seek out a new mate with similar traits, because the reasons they married that type of person still exist. For example:

> Joe was brought up by a very domineering mother whom he rebelled against. His first wife Joan reminded him of his mother. He and his wife fought frequently; the conflict became so upsetting that Joe divorced her. He vowed never to have anything to do with that kind of woman again. But a year later, he was remarried to the same kind of woman all over again. Even though he rebelled against that kind of woman, it was the only type of relationship he knew. It brought him a sense of security. It was the one norm that he patterned his subsequent relationships after. (Author's counseling notes)

When there are large age discrepancies between mates, there may be other motivations at work (Davidson, 1983). Men who marry women considerably younger than themselves may be trying to recapture their lost youth, solve their middle-age crisis, or fulfill ego needs that have become depleted through the aging process. Many such marriages are quite successful. In fact, overall, there are no significant differences in marital quality among couples from various age-dissimilar categories (Vera, Berardo, and Berardo, 1985). The exception is when the woman is too young and immature to be married in the first place. Women who marry older men for security or because they want a father figure may be quite content if their marriage fulfills their expectations and needs. Some become quite unhappy once these needs are no longer present, and their husbands cannot fulfill new expectations. Of course, a young wife married to an older man is likely to be widowed at an early age.

Other psychological influences may lead people to marry others who have been married several times before. They may have a pervasive sense of low self-esteem that causes them to seek a relationship that substantiates an impaired concept of self (Rebal, 1984). They may expect to be no more than one of a series of spouses passing through the person's life. They may be happy to find ego

Many different motivations may be involved when there are large age discrepancies between mates, and many of these marriages are quite successful. In fact, overall, there are no significant differences in marital quality among couples from various age groups.

satisfaction from being better spouses than the previous ones. Some people prefer to marry those who have problems, who are misfits, whom they can protect and help. Marriages based on self-pity or on the need to change another person are often problematic.

Carrying Expectations from One Marriage to Another

Remarried couples face many of the same expectations as first-married couples. But in addition to these expectations, remarried couples usually have others unique to their situation as persons who have been married more than once. *One expectation is that being married to a second spouse is going to be similar in some ways to being married to the first one.* These expectations may be false and completely unfair to the second spouse. Best (1982) writes:

> If an individual responds to the second mate in the same way he or she responded to the first because of a perceived sameness or likeness, the remarried mate may not have reconciled the problems which were encountered in the first marriage or may not have resolved the sense of loss or completed the mourning. (p. 26)

One result is that spouses replicate the mistakes of their first marriage in remarriage, because they expect the situation will be the same anyhow (Furstenberg, 1982; Hyatt, 1977; Kalmuss and Seltzer, 1986).

One problem arises because of pain experienced in the previous marriage. Persons who were married before remember all too well the problem behavior of a former spouse, the excessive drinking, the affairs outside of marriage, belittling comments, the violent temper and outbursts of anger, arguments, irresponsibility, selfishness and unwillingness to think of others, the lack of love and affection. *As a result, these persons enter second marriage with real apprehension and fear that the problems and hurts that they experienced before will happen again. This fear makes them oversensitive* to anything their new mate does or says that reminds them of the difficulties they had before. One husband explained his feelings:

> My first wife hated sex and rejected me most of the time over the many years of our marriage. As a result, I'm very sensitive to anything that my second wife does which seems to be rejection. If she's tired or sick and doesn't feel like intercourse, I'm hurt by her lack of desire, even though she really doesn't mean to reject me. Actually, she's very affectionate, and loves to make love. I even had trouble accepting that. I couldn't believe that she really liked it. Gradually, though, I accepted the fact that she really wanted me, so that now I'm not upset by those rare occasions when she is not willing. (Author's counseling notes)

Sensitivity develops to many forms of behavior. One wife became very sensitive to criticism because her first husband frequently berated her, especially in relation to her role as a mother. She became upset whenever her second husband made suggestions for changing some of her methods of handling the children. The last thing she wanted was similar treatment from her second husband.

Many other examples could be given. In each case the reaction of the remarried person is quite understandable, but can create problems if it is so extreme that it interferes with the new husband-wife relationship. How can the husband who is faithful ever convince his suspicious wife that he is not having an affair with another woman? (Moore, 1984). Or, how can the wife persuade her husband that she really admires and loves him, when he is convinced that no one has ever found him admirable or lovable? When a person has lived for years with rejection and criticism, it is difficult to accept any compliment as sincere.

What can be done about oversensitivity and fear of rejection? The most obvious answer is to avoid subjects or behavior about which the other has become so sensitive. When husbands and wives become aware of what the other considers a "sore subject," consideration requires them not to bring up those topics unless really necessary and, if they are raised, to introduce them cautiously and with tact, so the problems can be discussed without the other spouse feeling picked on.

Over a period of time, oversensitivity will slowly decline if one's mate is considerate and does not do or say things that aggravate the issues. One wife remarked:

> I used to be very sensitive about my appearance because my first husband never told me I was beautiful or even that he liked the way I looked. Now my husband compliments me all the time. As a result, I have gotten over most of my inferiority feelings and have developed much more self-confidence. Now when I walk in a store to buy some clothes, I feel and act like I'm attractive and an important person. As a result, the salesgirls fall all over themselves trying to be nice to me. At last, I feel like I'm somebody. (Author's counseling notes)

If oversensitivity is extreme and continues in spite of the best efforts of the couple to deal with it, counseling may help.

Another problem in remarriage arises because of confusion that may occur over role expectations. This confusion is brought about because of the difficulty in sorting out what one's second spouse expects from what one's first mate required.

Let us suppose, for example, that a man was first married to a wife who expected him to help her with housework and with the cooking. For years he learned to help her out in performing tasks. Then his wife dies, and several years later he remarries, but this time to a woman with more traditional ideas of marital roles. His second wife likes housework and cooking and hates to have her husband underfoot when she is doing "her work." A misunderstanding is likely to arise: the husband is confused because his second wife doesn't want him to help her as his first wife did. Unless he is keen enough to sense the simple fact that no two wives are alike, he may interpret her actions as disapproval of him.

It is true that both men and women in remarriages tend to base some of their ideas and expectations of husband-wife roles on the role performance of former spouses, even though a first marriage was quite unhappy. This is rather unfair to one's present spouse, who may not be at all like a former mate. The answer is to relate to one's spouse as a unique individual, not as a person whom one expects to be like someone else.

A problem may arise based on a desire that a new mate play a role completely different from that played by one's former spouse. In this case, a person has developed an intense dislike of things a former spouse has done and, consequently, expects that a second spouse will behave in a completely different manner. This can lead to some interesting behavior. Here is one such example.

> Ann was first married to a husband who expected her to wait on him hand and foot. To keep the peace, she did so for 25 years, even though she became more

and more resentful of having to do so. Finally she could stand it no longer and got a divorce. She vowed that she never wanted anything to do with that type of man again.

Hank was first married to a wife who never assumed any responsibility for the house, the children, or for earning income. He did virtually everything for the whole family, because he couldn't stand a dirty house, unkempt children, and living in poverty. After 25 years he grew to resent it and divorced his wife. He vowed he would never marry that type of woman again.

Ann and Hank met and fell in love. Ann was very impressed that Hank was the kind of man who had always done everything at home. At last, she would be married to the kind of husband she had always wanted. Hank was delighted when he found out that Ann had waited on her husband for all those years. At last, he would have a wife who would do things for him for a change.

But in the beginning, both Ann and Hank were very much disappointed. Hank became resentful because Ann asked him to do the same things he had resented doing for his first wife. Ann was disillusioned because she found out that Hank expected her to serve him just as she had done for her first husband. It took some time before they each understood the feelings and needs of the other and before they learned to compromise in meeting those needs. (Author's counseling notes)

It can be quite unfair to expect that one's spouse fulfill those needs that had not been met in a first marriage. However, it is comprehensible that one would want important needs met that were not fulfilled before. The important emphasis is on *mutual* fulfillment, not on one person's doing all the giving and the other's doing all the receiving.

Generally speaking, widows or widowers who were happily married before are more inclined to compare a second mate unfavorably with a first mate than are divorced persons. The latter are more likely to speak of their first mate critically, and their second mate favorably. The widowed, however, are more likely to idealize the first partner, and so it becomes difficult for the second spouse to compete with the fond image that is held of the person.

Finances

Financial problems are particularly bothersome (Bachrach, 1983). A divorced father who remarries usually has to pay child support and sometimes alimony to his ex-wife, a fact that his new wife very much resents. If, in addition, he is helping to support his new wife's children, he has a double financial burden. If her ex-husband does not keep up with child support payments, the second husband doesn't get any financial help with her children while he's still supporting his own (Albrecht, 1979).

As far as the law is concerned, most states do not require stepparents to support stepchildren (Kargman, 1983; Ramsey and Masson, 1985). Only 14 states have statutes that directly obligate stepparents to support stepchildren, and then the stepparent is usually not liable unless the child is living with him or her or unless the child will become a public charge. In only one state, New Hampshire, is a stepparent's obligation to support stepchildren equated with the natural parents' obligation to support biological children. This raises the difficult question of how support is to be apportioned and the continued obligations of the natural parent (Ramsey, 1986).

Fishman (1983) describes the economic patterns that stepfamilies adopt. "Common pot" families pool all their resources for household expenses, and "two pot" couples safeguard individual resources for personal use or for their biological children. Fishman found that a "common pot" system lends itself to unifying the stepfamily while the "two pot" economy encourages biological loyalites and personal autonomy. The common pot approach is illustrated in Figure 24.1. In the Becker/Robinson (a fictional name) family, Mike and Fran live together in a stepfamily with his two boys and her three children (two daughters and a son). Fran works full-time. Mike owns a shoe store. They bought a house in both their names. All earnings are pooled together in a joint account. Fran receives sporadic child support from her first husband, which she throws into the common pot. Resources of time, services, goods and cash are distributed according to an individual family member's needs, not according to biological relationship. This is not always simple to do. Sacrifices are necessary, and tensions arise. For example, Fran's daughter Ann

FIGURE 24.1 The Common Pot.

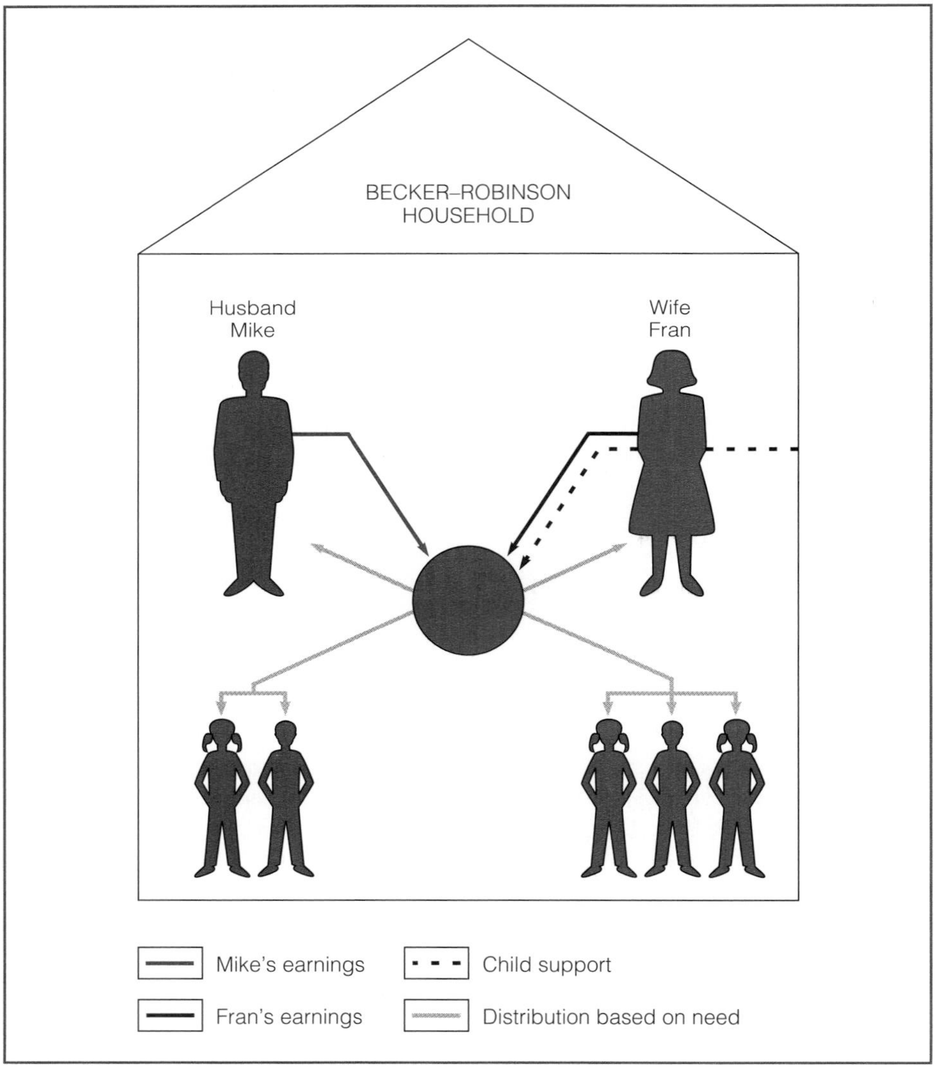

From Fishman, B. (1983). The economic behavior of stepfamilies. *Family Relations, 32,* 359–366. Copyright © 1983 by the National Council on Family Relations. Reprinted by permission.

is going to college and her expenses come from the common pot. This means that the money is not available for other things. Mike revealed a statement of Ann's: "Ann told me that when she walks down the aisle at her wedding, her real dad will be holding her arm, but I'll be footing the bill" (Fishman, 1983, p. 363).

In the two pot approach, each marital partner contributes a specific amount to the ongoing maintenance of the household, but children are supported by their biological parents. This approach is illustrated in Figure 24.2. The Marshal/Linton household consists of Harry and his wife Sheila. Sheila has three sons living with them. She receives $200 a week child support. Harry's oldest daughter Greta is away at college; Ginny (16 years) lives with her mother and new stepfather. Ginny visits regularly; Greta's visits are sporadic. Harry gives Sheila $50 per week for his share of food and small expenses. The house is in Harry's name and he pays the fixed expenses — mortgage, gas, and electric. He also sends his ex-wife a monthly stipend for Ginny's support and pays

FIGURE 24.2 Two Pot Approach.

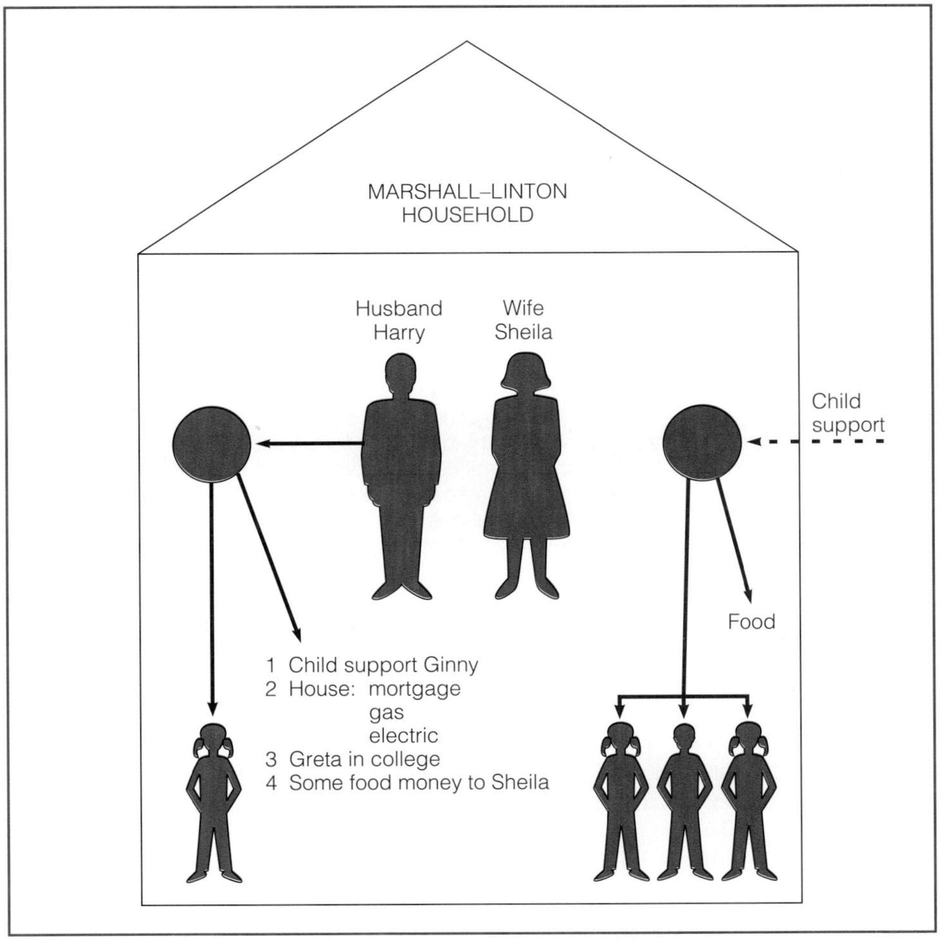

MARSHALL–LINTON HOUSEHOLD

Husband Harry

Wife Sheila

Child support

Food

1 Child support Ginny
2 House: mortgage
         gas
         electric
3 Greta in college
4 Some food money to Sheila

How are happily remarried couples able to succeed? Many factors enter in, of course, but couples who succeed seem to have a number of things in common. Most of these factors can be grouped into five categories.

The first factor is that they have given themselves time to know one another well. Like any marriage, remarriages are more complete if the couple really knows one another well beforehand.

There is another secret to remarriage that goes along with the time factor, and it is this: Happily married couples resist the many pressures to remarry before they are ready. These pressures stem from society itself and from other people, from friends and relatives who can't tolerate others being unmarried for very long, and who fix them up with dates. And then there are the pressures of loneliness and the need for love and companionship.

Remarriage is also sometimes used as a reparative measure — to try to make up to the children for the hurts and anguish caused by the death or divorce of the other parent. Such motivations may backfire — instead of helping the children, a troubled marriage or a difficult stepparent relationship may worsen the situation.

Not all reasons for marriage are desirable. Some divorced persons remarry on the rebound as a way of hurting their former spouse, to show that they are still desirable. Remarriage can also become a reenacting of an earlier, neurotic relationship, which, although unhealthy, nevertheless supplied certain needs. Couples must sort out what they most seek in their relationship and be certain that they are not pressured into marriage for the wrong reasons or before they are ready.

This brings us to the third factor in a happy remarriage: couples are able to discuss every aspect of their relationship before marriage. If they haven't before, then they do afterwards.

The fourth secret of success of couples who are happily remarried is the fact that they have learned from past mistakes. Before remarriage, they need to ask themselves: Do I understand what went wrong the first time? What were the deep underlying causes of my marital problems? Have I gained insight into my shortcomings, and am I able to overcome them (Hyatt, 1977)?

The fifth secret of those who remarry happily is that they put their marriage first. These couples have learned that the basis for sound parent-child relationships is a sound marriage. The couple's primary loyalty is to one another, second to their children.

There will be numerous forces inside and outside their homes that will be trying to pull couples apart. Unless their bond is secure, the marriage can be broken. Immature children and stepchildren may try to weaken their bond. Former spouses attempt to weaken the couple: peddling stories, half-truths, spiteful words and actions. Even other family members who resent the divorce, or the remarriage, may try to sow seeds of distrust or suspicion between the couple.

The happier the remarriage, the more secure and loving will be the environment in which children are reared (Ganong and Coleman, 1984; Rice, 1978b).

for Greta's college expenses. Sheila adds the $200 a week she gets for child support to the $50 Harry gives her. She deposits the money to her personal account. Out of this, she runs the house, and pays for clothes and incidentals for her boys and herself. The couple have no joint checking or savings account. It is obvious in this two-pot system that the financial arrangement indicates a tenuous bond in the marriage. Harry's first wife was a social butterfly, always buying more and more; she left him and sued for alimony and divorce. He is fearful to trust another woman again. Sheila tries to be a good wife. She is a homebody who does not spend much on herself. Harry still criticizes when she does buy, and she disapproves of Harry's focus on personal pleasure. The bond between them is weak.

These examples illustrate that a financial commitment to a new wife or husband comes slowly; and still more slowly, if at all, comes financial commitment to stepchildren. *The task for each stepfamily is to build the interpersonal bonds and group commitment and an economic system that meets both their family and individual needs and reflects family members' commitment to one another* (Fishman, 1983).

Jealousy Toward Ex-Spouse

One of the most persistent problems is jealousy of the new spouse in relation to the former spouse, especially if child visitation or other matters necessitate contacts. The problem is made considerably worse if one of two situations exist: (1) if the divorced man and woman still have affectionate feelings for one another, or if the second spouse believes they do (Bridgwater, 1982a), or (2) if the former spouse tries to cause trouble between the new couple. In reality, however, divorced persons seldom have affectionate feelings toward a former spouse. Usually, they have a long list of complaints. Couples in remarriages usually feel more insecure about one another in the beginning of marriage than they do after a while.

PRIMARY FAMILIES VERSUS STEPFAMILIES

Many couples enter into stepfamily relations expecting relationships similar to those of primary families (Mills, 1984). They are soon disappointed, surprised, and bewildered when they find few similarities (Skeen, Covi, and Robinson, 1985).

One reason for disappointment is that *stepparents have unrealistically high expectations of themselves and what to expect* (Turnbull and Turnbull, 1983). After all, they have been married before and have been parents before. They expect they will be able to fit into the stepparent role very nicely. They are shocked when they discover their stepchildren don't take to them the way they do to biological parents. This creates anxiety, anger, guilt, and low self-esteem. They either blame the children or begin to feel there is something wrong with themselves (Visher and Visher, 1979). They need to realize it may take several years before satisfactory relationships are worked out. Over a period of time, love and affection may develop.

Parents and stepparents enter into their new family with a great deal of guilt and regret over their failed marriage and divorce. They feel sorry for their children, whom they have put through an upsetting experience. This has several effects. Usually, parents tend to be overindulgent, not as strict as they might otherwise be, and have more trouble guiding and controlling the children's behavior (Amato, 1987). Often, they try to buy the children's affection and cooperation. One stepfather reported:

> I would get angry at something my stepdaughter did, and feel guilty afterward, so I'd take her to the store and buy her a present. One day after a similar episode, she asked; "What are you going to buy me today?" I realized she had caught on very quickly and had learned how to use my guilt to her own advantage. (Author's counseling notes)

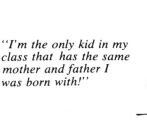

"I'm the only kid in my class that has the same mother and father I was born with!"

© Rothco Original

Stepparents' roles are ill-defined. Stepparents are neither parents nor just friends. Efforts to try to be parents may be rejected by older children. Stepparents can't be just friends; they feel responsible as adults to make a contribution to the lives of these children. They are required to assume many of the responsibilities of parents, such as financial support, physical care, providing recreational opportunities and companionship, going to PTAs or baseball games. Yet they have none of the privileges and satisfactions of parenthood. In the beginning, being a stepparent seems all give and no receive. It's frustrating.

Stepparents confront the necessity of attempting to deal with children who have already been socialized by another set of parents (Kompara, 1980). Stepparents may not agree with the way that their stepchildren were brought up. But their suddenly stepping in and trying to change things is deeply resented. Stepparents have to learn to cool it for a while and only gradually introduce changes if such are needed.

Stepparents expect gratitude and thanks for what they do, but often get rejection and criticism instead. They were expected to support and care for their own biological children, but feel they are being very generous and helpful by offering the same to stepchildren. Yet, stepchildren seem to take help for granted and ask for more, offering little thanks or appreciation for what is done for them. One stepfather complained, "I don't expect the world, but it would help to have a little thanks once in a while."

Stepparents must deal with a network of complex kinship relationships: with their own biological family members, with their stepchildren, with their former spouse's family members, and with their new spouse's family members. Instead of two major family groups, they have four family groups to contend with. This adds a more difficult dimension to their family involvements (Berstein and Collins, 1985).

Stepparents are faced with unresolved emotional issues from the prior marriage and divorce. Starting over the second time is rarely a fresh start. Stepparents are still tied to the past through their children, memories, and feelings. They need to resolve some of the hostilities that were created through the process of separation and divorce.

Stepparents must cope with stepsibling feelings and relationships. Stepchildren are rarely helpful to each other in coping with the strains of the divorce period. Instead there may be stepsibling rivalry and competition for the attention of parents (Amato, 1987).

Family cohesion tends to be lower in stepfamilies than in intact families. Life in divorced and reconstituted families tends to be chaotic and stressful during the years following remarriage (Wallerstein and Kelly, 1980). Even if life in reconstituted families settles down over time, it still remains less cohesive than in intact families as far as children are concerned.

STEPPARENT-STEPCHILDREN RELATIONSHIPS

Defining Stepmother, Stepfather Roles

Part of the problem of living in stepfamilies is that the positive roles of stepparents are not clearly defined by social custom (Pink and Wampler, 1985). Instead, negative stereotypes of stepparents have been developed that further increase the difficulty of functioning in a positive manner (Bryan, Coleman, Ganong,

Part of the problem of living in stepfamilies is that positive roles of stepparents are not clearly defined by social custom.

and Bryan, 1986; Fine, 1986; Nelson and Nelson, 1982; and Wald, 1981). Fairy tales and folklore have developed the stereotype of the cruel stepmother, a myth that is hard to overcome (Radomski, 1981). Most studies indicate that the stepmother role is more difficult than that of stepfather, primarily because the mother has more responsibilities for direct care of the children (Brand and Clingempeel, 1987; Clingempeel, Brand, and Ievoli, 1984). Stepfathers are sometimes portrayed as physically or sexually abusive, without loving feelings and concern for their stepchildren (Giles-Sims and Finkelhor, 1984). But stepparents are as different as any other parents. The following include some of the variations in types (Rice, 1978b).

1. *The "I don't like them" stepparents.* This category includes two types of stepparents: those who dislike or resent their stepchildren because of what the children say or do, or those who would rather not have any stepchildren in the house regardless of how well-behaved the children might be. Because these latter stepparents are hostile toward their stepchildren, they have trouble relating to them in positive, accepting, and understanding ways. To avoid open conflict, they may try to keep away from their step-children as much as possible. Some of these stepparents ask: "Can't they go live with their father (mother)?" or suggest: "Let's send them to summer camp and boarding school."

   Those in the first category feel they could like their stepchildren, even love them, if the children would change some of their habits, or try to be more cooperative or pleasant. A disturbed stepmother complained: "For the 15 months of my marriage, I've knocked myself out trying to be a mother to Agnes — her own mother died quite a while before I met Riley — but I never get to first base. Agnes defies my orders, ignores my requests, sneers, even if I coax or plead with her." (Author's counseling notes)

2. *The "Two more won't make any difference" stepparents.* This category includes those who like children and enjoy taking care of them. These stepparents are the opposite of those in the first category. They want to become good friends with children and love to play with them. Persons in this class naively believe, however, that bringing up stepchildren won't make any difference, either because they leave it up to their mate to take over the major responsibility for care, or because they don't recognize that raising stepchildren is not the same as caring for one's own children.

3. *The "I'll make you mind me" stepparents.* These take a rigid, authoritarian approach to childrearing, feel that the chief task of a parent is to teach children to mind, and feel that children should be seen and not heard and obey without question. Stepparents in this category may be uncertain of themselves and their own abilities and seek to hide their insecurities and to build their own egos by establishing a rule by fear and punishment. As a consequence, they can be harsh, even cruel or unfeeling in their rela-tionships with their stepchildren. Children of these stepparents don't love them; rather, they are very much afraid of them. If old enough, they have frequent arguments, often threaten to run away, or to go home to their other parent, if possible. Teenagers brought up in this atmosphere can't wait to leave home to work or to get married (Lutz, 1983).

PERSPECTIVE
Problems of Stepfathers

A summary of studies indicate that the most frequently cited problems of stepfathers include the following (Robinson, 1984; Stern, 1982):

1. Uncertainty about the degree of authority they have in the role of stepfather.

2. The amount of affection to give stepchildren and ways to show it. Stepfathers report feeling uncomfortable kissing their stepchildren.

3. The discipline of stepchildren and enforcement of rules.

4. Money conflicts.

5. Guilt over leaving children from a previous family.

6. Loyalty conflicts — how much time children spend with natural parents versus with stepparents.

7. Sexual conflict — the incest taboo is not as strong in stepfather families as it is in biological families.

8. Conflict over surnames — different names of stepfathers and stepchildren may lead to problems, but some stepchildren and stepfathers don't want the same names (Robinson, 1984, p. 382).

4. *The "Why don't you like me?" stepparents*. In this category are those whose chief desire is to be liked and/or loved by their stepchildren. Many of the parents in this category have a sincere, unselfish, and true desire to be loved by their stepchildren and are understandably hurt if the stepchildren don't respond.

There are those in this category, however, who have a deep-seated fear of rejection, who have a neurotic need for approval and acceptance themselves. Their love is narcissistic, self-centered rather than child-centered. Because of their own intense need for approval and because of their fear that their stepchildren won't like them, they may strive to win love in ways that are not beneficial to the children themselves: through overindulgence, by buying affection with too much money or privileges. Children soon learn to take advantage of these stepparents.

5. *The "No one appreciates me" stepparents*. These spouses are conscientious about being good stepparents, but are resentful because it is a difficult, thankless job.

6. *The "It's a challenge" stepparents*. In this category are conscientious, self-confident, wives, mothers, husbands, or fathers who work hard, do everything they can to build a happy home life for themselves and their stepchildren, and expect their children will work for these goals also. They often have great energy, are good organizers, and efficient parents and home managers. They are able to gain both respect and cooperation by a combination of positive expectations, attitudes, and efficiency.

7. *The "It's fun" stepparents*. These are characterized by happy, cheerful dispositions, positive, accepting attitudes toward their stepchildren; they are able to establish a warm, loving environment within their homes. Their house is not always in perfect order; they aren't organizers like stepparents

in category 6, and so aren't usually as able to teach their children responsibility, but they are able to meet their children's emotional needs and to help them to grow up as secure people.

Each stepparent, in examining the various categories, may find one in which he or she best fits. The important goal is to identify one's feelings about stepchildren and one's role in the relationship. As stepparents gain insight, they can be more objective about themselves and about their stepparent role, and they can learn to channel both their reactions and their energies in a beneficial manner. If they can't work things out themselves, they may need therapeutic help (Rice, 1978b).

Getting Acquainted and Initial Adjustments

Meeting prospective stepchildren for the first time is both exciting and an anxious experience. One prospective stepmother commented:

> I'm more nervous about meeting John's two children than I have ever been in my life. What if they don't like me? What if I don't get along? I certainly hope they'll like me. I'll do everything I can to see that they do, but I'm not sure. (Author's counseling notes)

Such feelings are understandable. Stepparents would be less than human if they didn't want to start off on the right foot with their future stepchildren. Most realize that their future happiness as a family depends partially upon being able to build harmonious relationships with all concerned. In some cases, the marital future of the couple depends upon the relationships that evolve between stepparent and stepchildren.

The first meeting ought to take place long before marriage. If a person is thinking of marrying another with dependent children, but doesn't know whether he or she wants the responsibility of caring for them, it's better to find out ahead of time. Or, if a son or daughter is very much opposed to remarriage, it's better to discover this early. Children's feelings can't be *the* deciding factor, but they need to be considered in the adjustment process.

By meeting one another's children while still courting, couples give themselves and their children a chance to get used to one another. Children usually aren't threatened as much by meeting daddy's or mama's "friend" as they are about meeting "your other daddy" or a "new mommy." Never introduce a new stepparent as the child's daddy or mommy. Even if two people know they are going to get married, it's better to say simply, "I want you to meet Jane."

In the early days of courtship, couples need to include children in many joint activities. If children are of school age, learning about their interests and hobbies and devoting time and attention to talking about these will give them and parents something in common to do together.

If both people have children, especially if they will be living together, it is helpful to give them ample opportunities to get to know one another too. If the children will be asked to share part of their existing room or living spaces with new children, there should be fair warning. Thus the following can be avoided:

> My friend and her husband didn't tell the children of their plans until a few days before their marriage . . . The bride's son faced a new school, new brothers, and another father. Her husband's boy was forced to share his bedroom with an almost total stranger, and both his children were suddenly expected to accept

a new mother they hardly knew. Who could blame these youngsters for being — and acting — upset? (Stark, 1971, p. 80)

When the decision to marry has been made more deliberately, and visiting back and forth over a period of time has allowed the children to get to know one another and their stepparents beforehand, such problems can be minimized.

One of the mistakes of new stepparents is to expect "instant love." Children can't turn on their feelings suddenly, spilling forth affection for a person they may only know slightly. Stepparents feel: "I love your mother (father); but I want to love you; I want you to love me too." But any affection that develops usually arises only gradually. Neither you nor your stepchildren can love someone you don't know. It will take time, usually months, perhaps several years. One stepfather commented, "After several years of rejection, I couldn't believe it when one day my stepdaughter came up to me, put her arms around me and said, "I love you." (Author's counseling notes)

All stepparents agree that it takes time for close relationships to develop. Some stepparents and stepchildren do establish warm, affectionate relationships. One mother spoke of her husband's relationship with her children: "He never made any issue of her being a stepchild. There are times when I think she is closer to him than she is to me" (Duberman, 1973, p. 285).

One mistake of new stepparents is to assume that because they are married to the children's mother or father that this automatically makes them the children's parent as well. It doesn't, at least in the eyes of the children. A child's basic instinct is to reject the stepparent as an intruder, an interloper, especially if the stepparent makes the mistake of trying to compete with the child's natural parent for the child's loyalty or to replace the child's absent parent. If they try, the stepchildren will shatter their hopes very quickly.

"You're not my real daddy."

"My real mother isn't mean like you."

Stepchildren compare stepparents with their over-idealized and absentee real parent, with the result that the stepparent comes out second best. Stepparents who insist that stepchildren call them "Dad" or "Mom" only succeed in adding fuel to the fires of resentment.

Whether or not children ever accept their stepparents as parents depends upon the total situation. Is the real parent alive and in contact with and showing interest in the child? If so, the child will not consciously want a new parent and will usually reject any attempts to replace the parent. In such cases, it is usually better if the stepparent attempts to be only an adult friend and guardian.

However, *if the real parent is dead and the child has accepted this fact and the period of mourning is over, he or she may be at the point where the stepparent can "step" in as a parent and be fully accepted.* Most young children want a "mommy" or "daddy." It is only that they become quite confused at adult efforts to present them with more than one such person at once.

Understanding Different Stepchildren

Since each stepchild reacts in a different way to a stepparent and the individual situation, stepparents need to relate to each child as a unique person.

Psychologically, if a natural parent is alive and showing interest in a child, the child will not consciously want a new parent and will resent any attempts to replace the parent.

Stepchildren can't all be treated alike any more than they treat all stepparents alike.

Stepchildren may be grouped into seven different categories. Each category highlights a reaction pattern and emotional needs. The seven categories are (Rice, 1978b):

1. *The "I hate you" children* — those who react to divorce, death, remarriage or stepparents with anger, hostility, or resentment, which they do not hesitate to express in word and actions. They blame the stepparent or parent for the divorce. They are often hard to love or even to like because of their hostility. Their principal need is to work through their feelings so as to be able to react in less destructive, more positive, friendlier ways.

2. *The "Do you love me?" children* — those who are very dependent, possessive, and insecure, whose principal need is for affection, love, and approval. They want to be with stepparents as much as possible, may bend over backward trying to please them or to win their acceptance of them. They are attracted to very maternal or paternal people and are supersensitive to adults who try to reject them and push them away. Their emotional needs sometimes seem insatiable, so they thrive best in relationships with very giving persons who like close emotional contact.

3. *The "Leave me alone" children* — those who feel hurt, resentment, and rejection and react by striving to become fiercely independent and self-sufficient, who want little to do with stepparents. They seek to keep them at arm's length, are fearful of any close emotional involvement or dependency. Stepparents can get along with them as long as they don't try to

boss them or make any requests of them. They will let stepparents be friends, but only up to a point.

4. *The "I don't care" children* — those who are sad, lonely, dejected, depressed, and quiet, who are hard to reach because they are withdrawn. These are the children who are still grieving, who feel abandoned and deserted because of the loss of a parent through death or divorce. Their overall mood is one of sadness. They need to work through their grief, to establish new relationships and find a renewed interest in living; but they are often hard to reach, at least for a while.

5. *The "What did you buy me?" children* — those who are jealous and competitive, who relate to a stepparent and stepsiblings as rivals, who feel insecure and want approval, but who strive to obtain it by playing one parent against the other, getting brothers and sisters in trouble, or by trying to manipulate stepparents to win approval and favors. Their need is for security and an improved self-concept and self-esteem, so that they will be willing and able to share with others and to realize that there is enough love to go around.

6. *The "Let's go fishing" children* — those who are dependent on adults for friendship, who have difficulty in making friends with those of their own age. Some of these children are shy and introverted and have never learned how to reach out to others. Because of their need for friendship, they make demands on adult time.

7. *The "Hi Bob" children* — older adolescents or young adults who seek to relate to the stepparents as another adult on an equal basis. They are usually not hostile and are able to accept the stepparent and the fact that he or she married their parent.

It is quite obvious that the children in each category are different and have individual needs, and so require their own approach. The important thing is for stepparents to deal with different stepchildren as individuals, realizing that different ones have different needs (Coleman and Ganong, 1987).

STEPSIBLING RELATIONSHIPS

The term **sibling rivalry** is a favorite expression in psychological textbooks. *It refers to the competition of brothers and sisters for the attention, approval, and affection of parents.* The problem arises because of the envy and fear that one brother or sister is receiving more physical or emotional care and benefits from parents than the other.

This situation is often exaggerated in the stepfamily. Instead of obtaining one new brother or sister, a child may get several all at once. And the stepsiblings may not be helpless infants, but children of similar or older ages who can be very demanding of the child's own parent. From the children's point of view, a tendency to be jealous is quite understandable. The children may have become quite adjusted to living with one parent and to seeking out that parent for help, comfort, and advice. Then suddenly they are confronted with the situation of their parent's turning his or her attention to a new mate and stepchildren. Because their parent is anxious to please the stepchildren, he or she may bend over backward to be accepted, granting privileges that the

In a stepfamily, instead of obtaining one new brother or sister at a time, a child may get several at once. The child may also be confronted with situations in which the parent turns attention to the stepchildren. Why might a parent grant attention and privileges to a stepchild not extended to natural children?

natural children may not enjoy, and bestowing goods and services that were formerly given to them.

Now they are forced to share living quarters, perhaps their own room, as well as all other spaces such as bathrooms and playrooms. They may find their toys broken, their cosmetics messed up, their clothes borrowed.

Sibling rivalry in the stepfamily is more complex than in the biological family because both parents and stepparents have difficulty in behaving rationally and impartially. Natural parents have a tendency to show preferential treatment. They may overindulge their own children, and require their stepchildren to do more chores or to receive less because they are loved less. They may hold up their own children as models of behavior: "My children are better behaved than yours; they have fewer problems; they are more considerate than yours." At the same time they use their stepchildren as weapons or targets, becoming more critical of them and being stricter with them than with their own children. As a result, the children are often caught in a crosscurrent of overindulgence versus exploitation and grow to hate one another because of the manner in which they are treated.

Sometimes, of course, the natural parent, in trying to show impartiality, is harder on his or her own children than on the stepchildren. In this case, the stepchildren get away with murder, while the biological children are punished for the very same things (Roosevelt and Lofas, 1977).

Parents can be encouraged by the fact that the initial reactions of stepsiblings or future stepsiblings to one another are not always indicative of the degree of problems in the future. Children who seem suspicious and distant from one another at first can grow into loyal and trusting friends. One woman remarked:

At the beginning, you would find my husband's four children playing in one corner and my two playing in another corner. But now they don't do that. There's no open hostility, and we handle it by trying very hard to be fair. Time

CLASSROOM FORUM
Growing Up in a Stepfamily

1. Did any of you grow up in a stepfamily?

2. How did you get along with your stepparent? Did you have a stepmother or a stepfather? What kind of person was he or she? What did you like about your stepparent? What did you not like?

3. How did you feel about your parent's remarrying? What upset you the most? What did you like the most?

4. Did you live with stepsiblings? Were they older, younger? How did you get along with them?

5. What kind of a relationship did you have with your noncustodial parent after your parents divorced? How did your stepparent feel about your noncustodial parent?

6. What do you feel are the biggest adjustments in learning to live in step? What suggestions do you have for others that might help them?

7. How did living in step affect you? Do you feel that you are a better or worse person because of the experience? Explain.

and adjustment have brought an improvement in the relationships among them. (Duberman, 1973, p. 286)

Stepsiblings have been known to become very proud of one another. Younger children often idolize older stepsiblings with whom they identify. Older children may become very protective of younger stepsiblings. Learning to share with one another, learning to live with others who have not been part of one's immediate family, is a broadening, enriching experience and helps children who otherwise tend to be egocentric and selfish to share and to be tolerant of others.

Duberman (1973) found in her study of reconstituted families that 24 percent of the families rated the relationship between their stepsiblings as "excellent," 38 percent rated the relationships "good," and 38 percent rated them "poor." These figures certainly indicate that some problems exist, but also that achieving excellent relationships is not impossible. Duberman found that it was easier to build positive relationships when both the children and father were young than when they were older. Generally, the younger child was more trusting and accepting than the older child and more flexible in making adjustments. Apparently, younger fathers were also better able to work out problems than were older ones. For some reason, the same did not hold true of young mothers (Duberman, 1973). Also, families with harmonious relationships between the husband and wife showed less sibling rivalry than did families where the marriage was troubled, indicating the effect of the total marriage on the children in the family.

Couples who are able to have children of their own report that having a baby improves their stepsiblings' relationships (Duberman, 1975). The new baby can serve as a bond between two groups of children. It gives them something in common, something to care for besides themselves, and can unite them around a mutual interest. One stepmother put it this way:

My children and my stepchildren like each other more since we had the baby. They all adore the baby! I don't think the older children are really pals, but at least they have the baby in common. (Duberman, 1973, p. 288)

1. Because of the high divorce rate and because the majority of divorced persons remarry, marriage more than once has become quite common. The majority of divorced persons also have children; when they remarry, new stepfamilies are created.

2. Remarried families may have one or two remarried spouses, each with or without children. Family relationships and integration become quite complicated and difficult in reconstituted families.

3. The probablility of divorce is slightly greater in remarriages than in first marriages, but successful remarrieds state that their new marriage is better than their first marriage.

4. Remarriage introduces some complications that were not present in first marriage. The biggest complication is children. Relationships with ex-spouses and stepsiblings also become important.

5. Courtship and mate selection in remarriage are different from those of first marriage. The couple is older. The majority of remarrieds have children. Ex-spouses and family members become involved in the courtship of the couple. The courtship usually progresses at a faster pace in remarriage. Some people want to marry someone like a spouse to whom they were married before, or they try to pressure their new mate to be like the former one. At times, there are large age discrepancies between mates. Also, subtle psychological influences may lead people to marry others who have been married several times before.

6. Couples carry expectations from one marriage to another. One expectation is that being married to a second spouse is going to be similar in some ways to marriage to the first one. One result is that spouses replicate the mistakes of their first marriage in remarriage, or they have real apprehension that the problems and hurts that they experienced before will happen again. This fear makes them oversensitive and reminds them of the difficulties they had before.

7. Another problem may arise because of confusion over role expectations and enactment. A person may desire a spouse to play a role similar to or completely different from the one played by a former spouse.

8. Generally speaking, widows or widowers who were happily married before are more inclined to compare a second mate unfavorably with a first mate than are divorced persons.

9. Financial problems are particularly bothersome in remarriage because of the necessity of supporting the new family and the children (and perhaps the spouse) from the old family.

10. Some remarrieds pool all of their resources in a "common pot," distributing according to each individual family member's needs. Other remarrieds use a "two-pot" system in which each partner contributes a specific amount to the ongoing maintenance of the household, with the children supported by their biological parents.

11. One of the most persistent problems is jealousy of the new spouse in relation to the former spouse.

12. In successful remarriages, couples give themselves time to know one another well; they resist the many pressures to remarry before they are

ready; they are able to discuss every aspect of their relationship before marriage; they have learned from past mistakes; and they put their marriage first.

13. Many couples enter into stepfamily relationships expecting relationships similar to those of primary families. Many are disappointed, because stepfamily and primary family relationships are not the same.

14. Part of the problem of living in step is that positive roles of stepparents are not clearly defined by social custom. Stepparents may be divided into seven basic types.

15. Problems of stepfathers include the following: authority, affection, discipline, money, guilt, loyalty, sex, and conflict over surnames.

16. Stepparents need to meet one another's children while the parents are still courting to give themselves and their children a chance to get used to one another. It is also helpful to give prospective stepsiblings a chance to get to know one another.

17. One of the mistakes of new stepparents is to expect instant love. It takes time for close relationships to develop. Another mistake on the part of the stepparents is to assume that marriage to a child's mother or father automatically makes them the stepchildren's parent. Only if the real parent is dead, or not an active part of a child's life, may the child turn to the stepparent as a substitute parent. Although most young children want a mommy or daddy, they become quite confused at adult efforts to present them with more then one such person at once.

18. Stepchildren are all individuals also. They can't be treated all alike any more than they can treat all stepparents alike. Stepchildren may be divided into seven basic categories.

19. Stepsibling rivalry refers to the competition of stepsiblings for the attention, approval, and affection of parents. The situation is often aggravated in the stepfamily.

20. Couples can be encouraged by the fact that the initial reactions of stepsiblings or future stepsiblings to one another are not always indicative of the degree of problems in the future. Many become very close and loyal friends. Couples report that having a baby of their own improves stepsibling relationships.

SUGGESTED READINGS

Berman, C. (1980). *Making It as a Stepparent: New Roles, New Rules.* Garden City, NY: Doubleday. A guide for adults.

Duberman, L. (1975). *The Reconstituted Family: A Study of Remarried Couples and Their Children.* Chicago: Nelson-Hall. An original study of 88 Cleveland, Ohio, families.

Einstein, E. (1982). *The Stepfamily: Living, Loving, and Learning.* New York: Macmillan. A helpful guide.

Hyatt, I. R. (1977). *Before You Marry Again.* New York: Random House. To keep people from repeating the mistakes of their first marriage.

Rice, F. P. (1978). *Stepparenting.* New York: Condor. A complete guide for different types of stepparents in dealing with different types of stepchildren.

Roosevelt, R., and Lofas, J. (1976). *Living in Step.* New York: Stein and Day. A popular approach.

Visher, E. B., and Visher, J. S. (1982). *Stepfamilies: A Guide to Working with Stepparents and Stepchildren.* New York: Brunner/Mazel. For professionals.

Wald, E. (1981). *The Remarried Family: Challenge and Promise.* New York: Family Service Association of America. A thoughtful presentation.

The Following Books are for Children or Adolescents

Berman, C. (1982). *What Am I Doing in a Stepfamily?* Secaucus, NJ: Lyle Stuart.

Bradley, B. (1982). *Where Do I Belong? A Kid's Guide to Stepfamilies.* Reading, MA: Addison-Wesley.

Burt, M., and Burt, B. (1983). *What's Special About Our Stepfamily?* New York: Doubleday.

Craven, L. (1982). *Stepfamilies: New Patterns of Harmony.* New York: Messner.

Gardner, R. A. (1982). *The Boys and Girls Book About Stepfamilies.* New York: Bantam.

Getzoff, A., and McClenahan, C. (1984). *Stepkids: A Survival Guide for Teenagers in Stepfamilies and for Stepparents Doubtful of Their Own Survival.* New York: Walker.

Hyde, M. (1981). *My Friend Has Four Parents.* New York: McGraw-Hill.

Lewis, H. C. (1980). *All About Families the Second Time Around.* Atlanta: Peachtree.

Phillips, C. (1981). *Our Family Got a Stepparent.* Ventura, CA: Regal.

Stenson, J. S. (1979). *Now I Have a Stepparent and It's Kind of Confusing.* New York: Avon.

GLOSSARY

abortion   The expulsion of the fetus. Can be either spontaneous or induced.

affective sensitivity   Empathy or the ability to identify with the feelings, thoughts, and attitudes of another person.

affinity   A relationship formed by marriage without ties of blood.

agape   Term used by Lee to describe unselfish, altruistic love.

AIDS   Acquired immune deficiency syndrome; a sexually transmitted disease caused by a virus and characterized by irreversible damage to the body's immune system and, eventually, death.

alcohol abuse   A general term that includes both alcoholism and problem drinking.

alcoholism   Addiction to alcohol characterized by compulsive drinking.

altruistic love   Unselfish concern for the welfare of another.

androgyny   A blending of male and female characteristics and roles, especially a lack of sex-typing with respect to roles.

Apgar score   A widely used system of scoring to evaluate the physical condition of the newborn, named after the originator, Virginia Apgar.

B-love   Term used by Maslow to describe being love, which is love for the very being and uniqueness of another person.

bag of water (amniotic sac)   Sac containing the fluid in which the fetus is suspended.

bargaining   The process by which two parties decide what each shall give and receive in arriving at a decision.

barrios   Residential ghettos in urban areas in which some Mexican Americans live.

bilateral descent   Inheritance and descent are passed through both the male and female line.

binuclear families   New families formed by the remarriage of two persons, at least one of whom has been married before.

birth order theory   A theory that says people tend to select a mate that enables them to fulfill the roles they learned in their family of origin.

blackouts   Periods of amnesia suffered by the alcoholic after which there is no remembrance of what happened during these periods.

blended or reconstituted family   Family formed when a widowed or divorced person, with or without children, remarries another person who may or may not have been married before, and who may or may not have children.

body language   Posture, facial expression, still or tense muscles, blushing, movement, panting breath, tears, sweating, shivering, or quivering, and increased pulse rate or a thumping heart or other bodily reactions that convey feelings and reactions.

bonding   Development of emotional attachment between the mother and newborn during the early hours after birth.

breech birth   Situation where the buttocks or feet are the first part of the baby to pass through the opening of the vagina.

bundling   A practice in colonial America where a courting couple was allowed to climb into bed under the covers with only outer garments removed; the couple could talk late into the night without burning precious fuel or candles.

castration   Removal of the testicles in males.

catharsis   Venting emotions to rid oneself of them, hopefully so they can be replaced by more positive ones.

cesarean section   Removal of the fetus by incising the abdominal and uterine wall.

child abuse   May include not only physical assault

of a child but also malnourishment, abandonment, neglect, emotional abuse, and sexual abuse.

chlamydial infections A family of infections caused by a bacterium causing nongonococcal urethritis and epididymitis in men and cervical infections and pelvic inflammatory disease (PID) in women.

clitoral orgasm Orgasm said to be brought on by stimulation of the clitoris.

coercive power Use of physical force or other type of punishment to force compliance.

cognition Means literally the act of knowing, the act of becoming acquainted with the world and objects, people, and conditions in it.

cohabitation According to the U.S. government definition, it is two unrelated adults of the opposite sex sharing the same living quarters in which there is no other adult present. In actual situations, there may be other adults living with the couple.

cohabiting family Two people of the opposite sex living together, sharing sexual expression, who are committed to their relationship without formal legal marriage.

cohort A group of people born during the same period of time.

coitus interruptus Withdrawal, used as an attempt at birth control.

comarital sex Extramarital sex about which the other partner knows and consents to prior to the involvement.

combination pills Oral contraceptives containing estrogen and progestogen.

common-law marriage A marriage by mutual consent, without a license, recognized as legal under certain conditions by some states.

communal family Family groups of people sharing various aspects of their life.

communication Between human beings, may be defined as a message one person sends and another receives.

compadres Mexican American godparents.

companionate love A low-keyed emotion with feelings of friendly affection and deep attachment.

compatibility The capability of living together in harmony.

complementary needs theory A theory that says people tend to select mates whose needs are opposite and complementary to their own, enabling them to mutually fulfill one another's needs.

conciliation counseling Marriage counseling ordered by a court in which couples try to decide whether they want to dissolve their marriage or agree to try to solve their problems.

condom A rubber sheath worn over the penis to prevent sperm from being ejaculated into the vagina, also prevents venereal disease.

condominium A house or apartment that is a part of a cluster of units that is individually owned but part of a larger association that cares for outside maintenance and maintenance of communal spaces. Each owner has to pay a fee to the association.

conjoint therapy Therapy with a couple together.

consanguinity The state of being related by blood, having descent from a common ancestor.

conscious love Rational, reasoning love.

constructive arguments Arguments that stick with the issues, that attack the problem, not the other person, that employ rational methods, and that result in greater understanding, consensus, compromise, and closeness between two people.

consummate love A term originated by Sternberg to describe love as a combination of intimacy, passion, and commitment.

contraceptive foam, suppositories, cream, jellies Chemical substances containing spermicides used to kill and/or immobilize sperm so they can't enter the uterus; used to prevent fertilization.

crises overload A series of one crisis after another until they become more than a person can handle.

crisis A drastic change in the course of events; a turning point that affects the trend of future events.

custody A term that refers to both legal custody (the parent's right to make decisions regarding the welfare of the child) and physical custody (the parent's right to have the child living with him or her).

D-love Term used by Maslow to describe dependent love that develops when another person meets one's needs.

date rape Forcing involuntary sexual compliance on a person while on a date.

dating The practice of a couple's arranging a time and place to meet so they can get to know one another better and participate in activities together.

dependent love Love that develops for someone who fulfills one's needs.

desire stage First stage of the human response cycle according to Kaplan.

destructive arguments Those that attack the ego of the other person rather than the problem; that increase resentment and hostility, undermine trust, friendship, and affectionate feelings; that result in greater alienation and do not solve the problem.

developmental tasks The skills, knowledge, functions, attitudes, and relationships individuals need to acquire at different times in their lives.

diaphragm A thick rubber latex dome-shaped cap that is stretched over a collapsible metal ring, designed to cover the cervical opening to prevent sperm from entering the uterus.

digital foreplay Stimulation of the sexual organs with the fingers.

discipline A process of learning or education, a means by which socialization takes place, the process of instruction in proper conduct or action.

doctrine of comparative rectitude A legal provision

whereby a court may grant a divorce to the party least at fault.

dopamine A neurotransmitter that functions in parts of the brain that control emotions.

double-bind communication Conflicting messages sent when verbal messages and body language don't agree.

douching Squirting liquid, containing vinegar or another substance, into the vagina; ineffective when used to wash out sperm after intercourse.

dual-career family A subtype of the dual-earner family where there are two career-committed spouses, both of whom are trying to continue to fulfill professional roles, which require a continuous developmental life.

dual-earner family A family where both spouses are involved in the paid labor force.

dyspareunia Painful intercourse.

ejaculatory inhibition Inability of the male to reach a climax.

endogamy The practice of marrying within one's own group.

endorphin Chemical neurotransmitter that has a sedative effect on the body.

equity theory Theory that mates are chosen on the basis of a fair exchange of benefits.

erectile dysfunction Inability of the male to maintain an erection so that coitus can take place.

erection Swelling and firming of the sexual organs when they are aroused and stimulated.

erogenous zones Sexually sensitive regions of the body.

eros Term used by Lee to describe romantic, sexual love.

erotic love Sexual, sensuous love.

exchange theory Theory which says that the basis for continuing or choosing a relationship is that each believes he or she will get as much or more from the relationship as it will cost. In choosing a mate, people tend to look for those who will maximize their chances of a rewarding marriage.

excitement phase Initial phase in the human sexual response cycle according to Masters and Johnson and the second phase according to Kaplan.

exogamy Choosing a mate across social lines, outside of one's own group.

expert power Power that is given because a person is acknowledged as generally superior in intelligence and knowledge.

expressive role of the family The role of the family in meeting the emotional and social needs of family members.

extended family You, a possible mate, any children you might have, and other relatives who might live with you in your household.

extradyadic sexual activity Engaging in sexual activity outside the dyadic or couple relationship.

familism Emphasis on the needs of the family above that of the individual.

family life cycle The family experiences divided into phases or stages over the life span; a concept that seeks to describe the changes in family structure and composition and the challenges, tasks, and problems that people face as well as the satisfactions derived during each stage.

family of origin The family into which you are born and in which you are raised.

family of procreation The family you establish when you have children of your own.

family planning Having children by choice and not by chance, having the number wanted at the time planned.

family violence Any rough and illegitimate use of physical force or aggression or of verbal abuse of one family member in relation to another.

feedback Response to the message another has sent and disclosure of one's own feelings and ideas.

femininity Personality and behavioral characteristics of a female according to culturally defined standards of femaleness.

filtering process A process by which mates are sorted by filtering out ineligibles according to various standards.

flexitime A company policy that allows employees to choose the right hours during the day when they will work, selected from hours designated by the employer.

friendship love A love based upon those who have common concerns and interests, who share companionship and have respect for the personality and character of one another.

gaslighting The process by which one person destroys the self-confidence, perception, and sense of reality of the other.

gender Includes not only one's biological sex, but also those psychosocial components that characterize one as a male or female.

gender identity A person's personal, internal sense of maleness or femaleness, which is expressed in personality and behavior.

gender role One's sex role as the outward manifestation and expression of maleness or femaleness in a social setting.

gender-role congruence A situation in which the gender-role expectations of one's spouse are in agreement with the role beliefs and performance of one's self.

gender stereotypes Assumed differences, norms, attitudes, and expectations about men and women.

genderic congruency Needs most typical of men are most correlated with needs most typical of women and vice versa.

general anesthesia Drugs used to depress the sensation of pain throughout the body, often used to put the patient to sleep.

general sexual dysfunction A woman's lack of desire for and lack of pleasure in sexual relations.

generational transmission The process by which one generation passes knowledge, values, attitudes, roles, and habits to the next generation.

genital identity A person's biological sex based upon genital examination.

genital warts A sexually transmitted disease caused by a virus that causes warts to appear.

gonorrhea Sexually transmitted disease caused by the gonococcus bacterium.

group marriage Marriage of at least four people, two female and two male, in which each partner is married to all partners of the opposite sex.

HCG (human chorionic gonadotropin) A hormone produced by the placenta, which — if present in the mother's urine — is an indication of pregnancy.

hepatitis B An infectious disease of the liver.

hermaphroditism Condition in which the individual has gonads of both sexes.

herpes simplex A sexually transmitted disease, commonly called herpes, caused by a virus.

heterogamy Choosing a mate who is different from oneself.

homogamy The tendency to choose a partner similar to oneself.

homosexual family Members of the same sex, living together, sharing sexual expression and commitment.

hypergamous union Wife marries upward on the social ladder.

hypogamous union Wife marries beneath herself on the social ladder.

ideal mate theory A theory that says people tend to marry someone who fulfills their fantasy of what an ideal mate should be like, based upon early childhood experiences.

imaging Pretense, or playacting, to present oneself in the best possible manner.

implementation power Power that sets decisions in motion.

informational power Power acquired because of knowledge of a specific area.

inhibited sexual desire Low sexual libido.

instrumental needs theory People seek relationships with those who provide maximum need gratification and minimum need punification.

instrumental role of the family The role of the family in meeting the needs of society or the physical needs of family members.

interpsychic sources of conflict Those tensions that occur in the relationships between people.

intrapsychic sources of conflict Those that originate within the individual when inner drives, instincts, and values pull against each other.

intrasomatic sources of conflict Inner tensions having a physical origin. Bodily conditions that influence behavior.

involuntary manslaughter The unintentional killing of another human being such as while driving an automobile.

involuntary stable (permanent) singles Never-marrieds and former marrieds who wanted to marry, who have not found a mate, and who have more or less accepted being single.

involuntary temporary singles Those who have actively been seeking mates but have not found them.

IUD Intrauterine device that is inserted into the uterus and worn there as a means of preventing pregnancy.

joint companionship A couple shares interests and activities.

joint legal custody Custody shared between two parents, both of whom are responsible for child rearing and for making decisions regarding the child.

labor Rhythmic muscular contractions of the uterus that expel the baby.

laparoscopy Procedure whereby a tubular instrument is passed through the abdominal wall and the fallopian tubes severed and/or closed as a sterilization technique.

latchkey children Unsupervised children who care for themselves before or after school, on weekends, or during holidays while their parents work. They commonly carry keys to let themselves in the house.

legitimate power Power that is bestowed by society on husbands and wives as their right according to social prescription.

limerence A term originated by Tennov that describes the intense, wildly emotional highs and lows of feeling when in love.

living-dying interval Period of time between the knowledge of the crisis of death and death itself.

local, regional anesthesia Injecting a drug in a localized area or region to block pain sensation only in that vicinity.

low socioeconomic status Low social class, including cultural deprivation, and low income.

lubrication Inner secretions from the vaginal walls in the female and from the Cowper's glands in the male.

ludus Term used by Lee to describe game-playing, playful love.

machismo Spanish for manhood or masculinity.

mania Term used by Lee to describe possessive, jealous, stressful, irrational love beyond emotional control.

marital adjustment The process of modifying, adapting, and altering individual and couple patterns of behavior and interaction to achieve maximum satisfaction in the relationship.

marital adjustment tasks Areas of concern in marriage in which adjustments need to be made.

masculinity Personality and behavioral characteristics of a male according to culturally defined standards of maleness.

matriarchal family Family in which the mother is head of the household with authority over other family members.

matrilineal Inheritance or descent is passed through the female line.

matrilocal A residential pattern in which newlyweds reside with or near the wife's family.

minipill An oral contraceptive containing progestogen only.

misogynist A person who hates women.

morning-after-pill Large doses of oral contraceptives taken postcoitally.

multilateral family Three or more partners, each of whom considers himself/herself to be married (or committed in a functionally analogous way) to more than one of the other partners.

myotonia Involuntary contractions of muscles

Naegele's formula A method of calculating the expected date of birth by subtracting three months from the first day of the last period and adding seven days.

narcissistic love Love of self; selfish, self-centered love.

negative identification The effort on the part of the child not to be like the parent.

neolocal A residential pattern in which newlyweds leave their parents' home and reside in a new location of their choice rather than with either family.

nepotism Patronage or favoritism showed on the basis of family relationship, commonly involving hiring another person from the same family.

no-fault divorce A legal approach that rejects fault grounds as a precondition for access to courts and recognizes the right of the individual to petition for divorce on the grounds of irretrievable breakdown of the marriage or irreconcilable differences.

nocturnal emissions Male ejaculation during sleep.

noncontingent reinforcement Unconditional approval.

norepinephrine A hormone secreted by the adrenal glands that has a stimulating effect on blood pressure.

nuclear family A father, mother, and their children.

observational modeling The process by which children observe, imitate, and model the behavior of others around them.

once-a-month pill A monthly injection of estrogen and progestogen that is rapidly absorbed into body tissues and then slowly into the bloodstream.

oral contraceptives Contraceptive pills taken orally.

orchestration power Power to make the overall important decisions that determine family life-styles.

orgasm The sudden discharge of neuromuscular tension at the peak of sexual arousal.

orgasm dysfunction Inability of the woman to reach a climax.

orgasm phase According to Masters and Johnson, the third phase in the human sexual response cycle in which there is a sudden discharge of neuromuscular tension.

parallel companionship A couple does things in the company of one another; they engage in parallel activities.

parent image theory A theory of mate selection which says that a person is likely to marry someone resembling his or her parent of the opposite sex.

parental identification and modeling The process by which the child adopts and internalizes parental values.

passionate love A wildly emotional state associated with tender feelings, elation and pain, anxiety and relief.

patriarchal family Family in which the father is head of the household with authority over other family members.

patrilineal Inheritance or descent is passed through the male line.

patrilocal A residential pattern in which newlyweds reside with or near the husband's family.

personal role redefinition Reduction of the standards of role performance as a means of reducing conflict.

pheromones Hormonal secretions of the body with an odor that is supposed to be sexually arousing.

placebo A pill having no pharmacological effect.

placenta previa The premature separation of the placenta from the uterine wall before the baby is born.

plateau phase According to Masters and Johnson, the second phase in the human sexual response cycle, characterized by a high degree of sexual excitement and by a leveling off of sexual tension.

points Each point represents 1 percent of the mortgage amount and is charged as a loan cost by the lending institution.

polyandrous family A woman married to more than one husband.

polygamous family A single family unit based on the marriage of one person to two or more mates.

polygynous family A man married to more than one wife.

positive identification The attachment of the child to positive images of desired loving behavior.

positive signs Signs of pregnancy detected by the physician that indicate positively that the woman is pregnant.

POSSLQ Abbreviation for persons of the opposite sex sharing living quarters.

post-traumatic stress disorder Severe stress reactions that occur after a person has suffered a trauma.

postparental years The years after the last child leaves home and until the husband's and wife's retirement.

power The ability of an individual within a social relationship to carry out his or her will, even in the face of resistance by others.

power processes The way that power is applied.

pragma Term used by Lee to describe logical, sensible, rational, practical love.

premature ejaculation A man's inability to delay ejaculation long enough for intercourse to take place, or for his partner to have an orgasm 50 percent of the time.

presumptive signs Signs by which the mother presumes she is pregnant.

primary erectile dysfunction Inability to have an erection where the condition has always existed.

probable signs Signs detected by the examining physician that make pregnancy probable.

problem drinking Functional disability as a result of alcohol consumption.

progestogen capsule A capsule containing progestogen that is implanted under the skin and that can remain in place for several years to prevent pregnancy.

progestogen injection An injection of progestogen four times a year to prevent pregnancy.

projection A psychological defense mechanism whereby a person explains or gives excuses for actions.

propinquity In mate selection the tendency to choose a mate who is geographically near.

prostaglandin tampons Tampons containing the chemical prostaglandin, which causes spontaneous labor and abortion.

pseudohermaphroditism Condition in either a male or female who has incompletely developed organs of his or her own sex and some characteristics of the opposite sex.

psychosocial task The skills, knowledge, functions, and attitudes individuals need to acquire at different periods in their lives.

pubic lice A parasitic insect occupying hairy regions of the body that suck blood from their human hosts, causing itching.

pushes and pulls The terms are used in reference to influences to remain single or to stay married — or to get married or to leave marriage. Pushes are negative influences. Pulls are positive attractions. For the single person, pushes are influences to marry, pulls are attractions to remain single. For the married person, pushes are influences to leave the situation; pulls are influences to remain married.

rationalization A psychological defense mechanism whereby a person explains or gives excuses for actions.

reciprocal parent-child interaction The influence of the parent on the child and the child on the parent so that each modifies the behavior of the other.

repression A psychological defense mechanism whereby one deals with unpleasant feelings or thoughts by pushing them down into the unconscious.

resolution phase Master's and Johnson's final phase in the human sexual response cycle — characterized by a gradual return of the body to its unaroused state.

resonates Experiences the emotions of another person.

Rh incompatibility Condition in which the mother has Rh negative and the fetus has Rh positive blood that causes antibodies to build up in the mother's blood and destroy red blood cells in the baby's blood, causing anemia, mental retardation, death.

rhythm method A method of birth control whereby the couple have intercourse only during those times of the menstrual cycle when the woman is least likely to get pregnant.

rites of passage Ceremonies by which people pass from one social status to another.

romantic love A profoundly tender or passionate affection for a person of the opposite sex, characterized by intense feeling and emotion.

rooming in Method of postpartum care in which the mother and father care for their newborn themselves in an area in the hospital assigned to them.

salpingectomy, tubal ligation Female sterilization by severing and/or closing the fallopian tubes so the ovum cannot pass down the tube.

scabies A parasitic infection of mites that burrow into the skin, lay eggs, and cause itching.

scapegoating Blaming someone else for every bad thing that happens.

secondary erectile dysfunction Inability to have an erection that develops under certain circumstances or situations but has not always existed.

segregated companionship A couple participates primarily in activities outside the dyadic relationship

selfism A personal value system that emphasizes that the way to find happiness is through self-gratification and narcissism.

serotonin A chemical neurotransmitter that has a stimulating effect on the body.

sex One's biological identity, whether male or female.

sex flush Appearance of reddish, spotty, rashlike color on the skin during sexual excitement.

sex role A person's outward expression of maleness or femaleness in a social setting.

sexual dysfunction A malfunction of the human sexual response system.

sexually transmitted diseases Diseases transmitted through sexual contact.

show Blood-tinged mucus that is passed when the mucus plug is expelled.

sibling rivalry The competition of brothers and sisters for the attention, approval, and affection of parents.

single-parent family Family consisting of a parent, who may or may not have been married, and one or more children.

socialization The process by which persons learn the ways of a given society or social groups so that they can function within it or with them.

steady dating Dating exclusively with one person.

stepfamily A remarried husband and/or wife plus children from a former marriage.

sterilization The process of rendering the person infertile, either by performing a vasectomy in the male or tubal ligation in the female.

stimulus-value-role theory Murstein's theory, which says that people pass through three filters: stimulus (attraction), value (exploration of interests and values), and role exploration in sorting out a mate.

storge Term used by Lee to describe best-friends, companionate, comfortable type of love.

strain-based conflicts Conflicts that arise when strain in one role affects participation in the family role or vice versa.

structural role redefinition Attempts to lessen conflict by mutual agreement on a new set of role expectations.

structure-function view of the family A view of the family that emphasizes the function of the family as a social institution in meeting the needs of society.

structured separation A time-limited approach in which couples terminate cohabitation, commit themselves to regularly scheduled therapy with a therapist, and agree to regular interpersonal contact — with a moratorium on a final decision either to reunite or to divorce.

sudden infant death syndrome or **crib death** The sudden, unexpected death of an infant while in the crib, the exact cause of which is uncertain.

syphilis A sexually transmitted disease caused by a bacterium called a spirochete.

theory of primary interest and presumed competence The person who is most interested, qualified, and involved with a particular choice will be more likely to make the decision.

time-based conflicts Conflicts that arise when time pressures from one role make it physically impossible to meet expectations arising from another.

toxemia A serious disease of pregnancy.

trajectory of our life Projection of a certain life span and the activities we are going to experience during it.

transsexual A person who has the genitals of one gender, but the gender identity of another.

transverse birth Birth in which the shoulder and arm of the baby are the first parts seen at the opening of the vagina.

tubal or **ectopic pregnancy** Attachment of the blastocyst and growth of the embryo in any location other than inside uterus.

unconditional positive regard Acceptance of another person as he or she is.

underclass Nonworking poor, a low-low lower class group.

vaginal orgasm Orgasm said to be brought on by stimulation of the vagina.

vaginal ring A contraceptive inserted in the vagina that releases progestogen to prevent pregnancy.

vaginal sponge A soft polyurethane sponge that is saturated with a spermicide; it is placed in the back of the vagina, covering the cervix, to prevent the sperm from entering the uterus.

vaginismus Involuntary contraction and spasm of the muscles of the vagina.

variable mortgage interest rates Mortgage loans with an interest rate that varies according to preestablished criteria. The rates vary according to changes in rates in the marketplace.

vasectomy Male sterilization whereby the vas deferens are cut and tied to prevent the sperm from being ejaculated out of the penis.

vasocongestion Engorgement of the sexual body parts, with blood causing erection.

ventilation Draining off negative emotions and feelings by expressing them.

void marriage A marriage never considered valid in the first place because it was illegal.

voidable marriage A marriage that can be set aside by annulment under certain prescribed legal circumstances.

voluntarily childless family A family whose members decide voluntarily not to have children.

voluntary stable (permanent) singles All those (never-marrieds and former-marrieds) who choose to be single.

voluntary temporary singles Never-marrieds and previously-marrieds who are not opposed to the idea of marriage but are not currently seeking mates.

wet dreams Erotic dreams while the man sleeps, leading to ejaculation.

wife abuse May include not only battering, but sexual abuse, rape, and verbal abuse as well.

BIBLIOGRAPHY

Aadelen, S. (1980). Coping with sudden infant death syndrome: Intervention strategies and a case study. *Family Relations, 29*, 584–590.

Abbott, D. A., and Brody, G. H. (1985). The relation of child age, gender, and number of children to the marital adjustment of wives. *Journal of Marriage and the Family, 47*, 77–84.

Abel, G. G., et al. (1979). Women's vaginal responses during REM sleep. *Journal of Sex and Marital Therapy, 5*, 5–14.

Abernathy, T. J. (1981). Adolescent cohabitation: A form of courtship or marriage? *Adolescence, 17*, 791–797.

Abortion doesn't impair the ability of women to become pregnant. (1985). *Family Planning Perspectives, 17*, 39, 40.

About new report on the pill. (1975). *U.S. News and World Report*, December 29.

Abramson, P. R. (1983). Woman attracted to man she couldn't be happy with. *Medical Aspects of Human Sexuality, 17*, 141.

Abramson, P. R. (1986). A spouse excessively attached to her own family. *Medical Aspects of Human Sexuality, 20*, 18.

Ackerman, R. J. (1983). *Children of Alcoholics* (2nd ed.). New York: Simon and Schuster.

Acock, A. C., Barker, D., and Bengston, V. L. (1982). Mother's employment and parent-youth similarity. *Journal of Marriage and the Family, 44*, 441–455.

Adamek, R. J. (1974). Abortion, personal freedom, and public policy. *The Family Coordinator, 23*, 411–419.

Adams, G. R. (1980). Social psychology of beauty: Effects of age, height, and weight on self-reported personality traits and social behavior. *Journal of Social Psychology, 112*, 287–293.

Adams, N. N., and Cromwell, R. E. (1978). Morning and night people in the family: A preliminary statement. *The Family Coordinator, 27*, 5–13.

Adams, R. G. (1985). People would talk: Normative barriers to cross-sex friendships for elderly women. *The Gerontologist, 25*, 605–611.

After a conviction — Second thoughts about abortions. (1974). *U.S. News and World Report*, March 3, 78.

Aguirre, B. E., and Parr, W. C. (1982). Husband's marriage order and the stability of first and second marriages of white and black women. *Journal of Marriage and the Family, 44*, 605–620.

Ahrons, C. R. (1980). Divorce: A crisis of family transition and change. *Family Relations, 29*, 533–540.

Ahrons, C. R., and Bowman, M. E. (1982). Changes in family relationships following divorce of adult child: Grandmothers' perceptions. *Journal of Divorce, 5*, 49–68.

Ahrons, C., and Rodgers, R. (1987). *Divorced Families: A Multidisciplinary View.* New York: Norton.

Alan Guttmacher Institute. (1981). *Teenage Pregnancy.* New York: Alan Guttmacher Institute.

Albrecht, R. (1972). A study of dates that failed. In R. E. Albrecht and E. W. Bock (Eds.), *Encounter: Love, Marriage, and Family* (pp. 57–63). Boston: Holbrook.

Albrecht, S. L. (1979). Correlates of marital happiness among the remarried. *Journal of Marriage and the Family, 41*, 857–867.

Albrecht, S. L., Bahr, H. M., and Chadwick, B. A. (1977). Public stereotyping of sex roles, personality characteristics and occupations. *Sociology and Social Research 61*, 223–240.

Aldous, J. (1987). New views on the family life of the elderly and near-elderly. *Journal of Marriage and the Family, 49*, 227–234.

Alexander, J. F. (1973). Defensive and supportive communications in normal and deviant families. *Journal of Consulting and Clinical Psychiatry. 40*, 223–231.

Allan, G. (1985). *Family Life.* Oxford: Basil Blackwell.

Allen, A., and Thompson, T. (1984). Agreement,

understanding, realization, and feeling understood as predictors of communicative satisfaction in marital dyads. *Journal of Marriage and the Family, 46,* 915–921.

Allen, C. M. (1984). On the validity of relative validity studies of "final-say" measures of marital power. *Journal of Marriage and the Family, 46,* 619–629.

Allen, K. R., and Pickett, R. S. (1987). Forgotten streams in the family life course: Utilization of qualitative retrospective interviews in the analysis of lifelong single women's family careers. *Journal of Marriage and the Family, 49,* 517–526.

Allen, S. M., and Kalish, R. A. (1984). Professional women and marriage. *Journal of Marriage and the Family, 46,* 375–382.

Allgeier, A. (1981). The influence of androgynous identification on heterosexual relations. *Sex Roles, 7,* 321–330.

Allgeier, A. R., Allgeier, E. R., and Rywick, T. (1981). Orientations toward abortion: Guilt or knowledge? *Adolescence, 16,* 273–280.

Altman, I., and Taylor, D. A. (1973). *Social Penetration: The Development of Interpersonal Relationships.* New York: Henry Holt.

Alton, J. P., McIntosh, W. A., and Wright, L. M. (1976). Extent of interfaith marriage among white Americans. *Sociological Analysis, 37,* 261–264.

Alwin, D. F., Converse, P. E., and Martin, S. S. (1985). Living arrangements and social integration. *Journal of Marriage and the Family, 47,* 319–334.

Amato, P. R. (1987). Family process in one-parent, stepparent, and intact families: The child's point of view. *Journal of Marriage and the Family, 49,* 327–337.

Amato, P. R., and Ochiltree, G. (1986). Family resources and the development of child competence. *Journal of Marriage and the Family, 48,* 47–56.

Amato, P. R., and Partridge, S. (1987). Woman and divorce with dependent children: Material, personal, family, and social well-being. *Family Relations, 36,* 316–320.

Ambert, A. (1986). Being a stepparent: Live-in and visiting stepchildren. *Journal of Marriage and the Family, 48,* 795–804.

Amirikia, H., Zarewych, B., and Evans, T. (1980). Cesarian section: A fifteen year review of changing incidence, indications, and risks. *American Journal of Obstetrics and Gynecology, 140,* 81–90.

Ammons, P., and Stinnet, N. (1980). The vital marriage: A closer look. *Family Relations, 29,* 37–42 .

Ammons, P., Nelson, J., and Wodarski, J. (1982). Surviving corporate moves: Sources of stress and adaptation among corporate executive families. *Family Relations, 31,* 207–212.

Anderson, R. N. (1980). Rural plant closures: The coping behavior of Filipinos in Hawaii. *Family Relations, 29,* 511–516.

Anderson, S. A. (1986). Cohesion, adaptability, and communication: A test of an Olson circumplex model hypothesis. *Family Relations, 35,* 289–293.

Anderson, S. A., Russell, C. S., and Schumm, W. R. (1983). Perceived marital quality and family-life cycle categories: A further analysis. *Journal of Marriage and the Family, 45,* 227–139.

Andrews, W. (1983). Herpes during pregnancy. *Medical Aspects of Human Sexuality, 17,* 39.

Annual ectopic totals rose steadily in 1970s but mortality rates fell. (1983). *Family Planning Perspectives, 15,* 85, 86.

Appleton, W. S. (1982). Decision making in marriage. *Medical Aspects of Human Sexuality 16,* 70H–70Q.

Appleton, W. S. (1983). Women at middle age: Effects on marital relationships. *Medical Aspects of Human Sexuality, 17,* 188–194.

Araji, S. K. (1977). Husbands' and wives' attitude-behavior congruence on family roles. *Journal of Marriage and the Family 39,* 309–320.

Archbold, P. B. (1983). Impact of parent-caring on women. *Family Relations, 32,* 39–45.

Argyle, M., and Furnham, A. (1983). Sources of satisfaction and conflict in long-term relationships. *Journal of Marriage and the Family, 45,* 481–493.

Arling, G. (1976). The elderly widow and her family, neighbors, and friends. *Journal of Marriage and the Family, 38,* 757–768.

Atkinson, A. M. (1987) . Fathers' participation and evaluation of family day care. *Family Relations, 38,* 146–151.

Atkinson, M. P., and Boles, J. (1984). WASP (Wives as senior partners). *Journal of Marriage and the Family, 46,* 861–870.

Atkinson, M. P., and Glass, B. L. (1985). Marital age heterogamy and homogamy, 1900 to 1980. *Journal of Marriage and the Family, 47,* 685–691.

Avery, A. W. (1982). Escaping loneliness in adolescence: The case for androgyny. *Journal of Youth and Adolescence, 11,* 451–459.

Bach, G. R. (1973). *Therapeutic Aggression.* (Set of ten cassettes). Chicago: Human Development Institute.

Bach, G. R., and Wyden, P. (1970). *The Intimate Enemy: How to Fight Fair in Love and Marriage.* New York: Avon.

Bach, G. R., and Wyden, P. (1975). The art of family fighting. In K. C. W. Kammeyer (Ed.), *Confronting the Issues* (pp. 314–320). Boston: Allyn and Bacon.

Bachrach, C. A. (1983). Children in families: Characteristics of biological, step-, and adopted children. *Journal of Marriage and the Family, 45,* 171–179.

Bachrach, C. A. (1984). Contraceptive practice among American women, 1973–1982. *Family Planning Perspectives, 16,* 255–259.

Backup, R. (1979). Implementing quality care for the

American Indian patient. *Washington State Journal of Nursing, Special Supplement,* 20–24.

Bagarozzi, J. I., and Bagarozzi, D. A. (1980). Financial counseling: A self-control model for the family. *Family Relations, 29,* 396–403.

Bahr, S. J., Chappell, C. B., and Leigh, G. K. (1983). Age at marriage, role enactment, role consensus, and marital satisfaction. *Journal of Marriage and the Family, 45,* 795–803.

Baldwin, W., and Nord, C. (1984). Delayed childbearing in the U.S.: Fact or fiction? *Population Bulletin, 39,* 4–43.

Balkwell, C. (1985). An attitudinal correlate of the timing of a major life event: The case of morale in widowhood. *Family Relations, 34,* 577–581.

Balkwell, C., and Balswick, J. (1981). Subsistence economy, family structure, and status of the elderly. *Journal of Marriage and the Family 43,* 423–429.

Balkwell, C., and Halverson, C. F., Jr. (1980). The hyperactive child as a source of stress in the family: Consequences of suggestions for intervention. *Family Relations, 29,* 550–557.

Ball, R. E. (1983). Marital status, household structure, and life satisfaction of black women. *Social Problems, 30,* 400–409.

Ball, R. E., and Robbins, L. (1986a). Marital status and life satisfaction among Black Americans. *Journal of Marriage and the Family, 48,* 389–394.

Ball, R. E., and Robbins, L. (1986b). Black husbands' satisfaction with their family life. *Journal of Marriage and the Family, 48,* 849–855.

Ballenski, C. B., and Cook, A. S. (1982). Mothers' perceptions of their competence in managing selected parenting tasks. *Family Relations, 31,* 489–494.

Balswick, J., and Avertt, C. P. (1977). Differences in expressiveness: Gender, interpersonal orientation and perceived parental expressiveness as contributing factors. *Journal of Marriage and the Family, 39,* 121–127.

Bandura, A. (1976). *Social Learning Theory.* Englewood Cliffs, NJ: Prentice-Hall.

Bankoff, E. A. (1983). Social support and adaptation to widowhood. *Journal of Marriage and the Family, 45,* 827–839.

Baranowski, M. D. (1982). Grandparent-adolescent relations: Beyond the nuclear family. *Adolescence, 17,* 575–584.

Baranowski, M. D. (1983). Strengthening the grandparent-grandchild relationship. *Medical Aspects of Human Sexuality, 17,* 106–126.

Barber, B. K., and Thomas, D. L. (1986). Dimensions of fathers' and mothers' supportive behavior: The case for physical affection. *Journal of Marriage and the Family, 48,* 783–794.

Barnett, R. C., and Baruch, G. K. (1987). Determinants of fathers' participation in family work. *Journal of Marriage and the Family, 49,* 29–40.

Barranti, C. C. R. (1985). The grandparent-grandchild relationship: Family resource in an era of voluntary bonds. *Family Relations, 34,* 343–352.

Barrett-Lennard, G. T. (1981). The empathy cycle: Refinement of a nuclear concept. *Journal of Counseling Psychology, 28,* 91–100.

Barrow, J. C., and Moore, C. A. (1983). Group interventions with perfectionistic thinking. *The Personnel and Guidance Journal, 61,* 612–615.

Barry, A. (1979). A research project on successful single parent families. *American Journal of Family Therapy, 7,* 65–73.

Bartolome, F., and Evans, P. A. L. (1980). Must success cost so much? *Harvard Business Review, 58,* 137–148.

Baruch, G., Barnett, R., and Rivers, C. (1983). *Lifeprints: New Patterns of Love and Work for Today's Women.* New York: McGraw-Hill.

Bassoff, E. S. (1984). Relationships of sex-role characteristics and psychological adjustment in new mothers. *Journal of Marriage and the Family, 46,* 449–454.

Baur, P. A., and Okun, M. A. (1983). Stability of life satisfaction in late life. *The Gerontologist, 23,* 261–265.

Bean, C. (1974). *Methods of Childbirth.* New York: Dolphin.

Bean, F. D., Clark, M. P., Swicegood, G., and Williams, D. (1983). Husband-wife communication, wife's employment, and the decision for male or female sterilization. *Journal of Marriage and the Family, 45,* 395–403.

Beckman, L. J., and Houser, B. B. (1982). The consequences of childlessness on the social-psychological well-being of older women. *Journal of Gerontology, 37,* 243–250.

Beckman-Brindley, S., and Tavormina, J. (1978). Power relationships in families: A social exchange perspective. *Family Process, 17,* 423–436.

Bell, C. S., Johnson, J. E., McGillicuddy-Delishi, A. V., and Sigel, I. E. (1980). Normative stress and young families: Adaptation and development. *Family Relations, 29,* 453–458.

Bell, R. A., Daly, J. A., and Gonzalez, M. C. (1987). Affinity-maintenance in marriage and its relationship to women's marital satisfaction. *Journal of Marriage and the Family, 49,* 445–454.

Bell, R. R. (1971). Female sexual satisfaction as related to levels of education. *Sexual Behavior,* November, 8–14.

Bell, R. R. (1972). Some emerging social expectations among women. In R. R. Bell and M. Gordon (Eds.), *The Social Dimension of Human Sexuality* (pp. 158–165). Boston: Little, Brown.

Bell, R. R. (1975). *Marriage and Family Interaction* (4th ed.). Homewood, IL: Dorsey.

Bell, R. R., and Coughey, K. (1980). Premarital sexual experience among college females, 1958, 1968, and 1978. *Family Relations, 29,* 353–357.

Bem, S. (1975). Sex role adaptability: One consequence of psychological androgyny. *Journal of Personality and Social Psychology, 31,* 634–643.

Bem, S. (1979). Theory and measurement of androgyny: A reply to the Pedhazer-Tetenbaum and Locksley-Colton critiques. *Journal of Personality and Social Psychology, 37,* 1047–1054.

Bem, S., and Lenney, E. (1976). Sex typing and the avoidance of cross-sex behavior. *Journal of Personality and Social Psychology, 33,* 48–54.

Bem, S., Martyna, W., and Watson, C. (1976). Sex-typing and androgyny: Further explorations of the expressive domain. *Journal of Personality and Social Psychology 34,* 1016–1023.

Bengtson, V. L., Cuellar, J. B., and Ragan, P. K. (1977). Stratum contrasts and similarities in attitudes toward death. *Journal of Gerontology, 32,* 76–88.

Bengtson, V. L., Cutler, N. E., Mangen, D. J., and Marshall, V. W. (1985). Generations, cohorts and relations between age groups. In R. H. Binstock and E. Shanas (Eds.), *Handbook of Aging and Social Sciences* (pp. 304–338). New York: Van Nostrand Reinhold.

Benin, M. H., and Nienstedt, B. C. (1985). Happiness in single- and dual-earner families: The effect of marital happiness, job satisfaction, and life cycle. *Journal of Marriage and the Family, 47,* 975–984.

Berardo, D. H., Shehan, C. L., and Leslie, G. R. (1987). A residue of tradition: Jobs, careers, and spouses' time in housework. *Journal of Marriage and the Family, 49,* 381–390.

Berardo, F. M., and Vera, H. (1981). The groomal shower: A variation of the American bridal shower. *Family Relations, 30,* 395–401.

Berk, R. A., Newton, P. J., and Berk, S. F. (1986). What a difference a day makes: An empirical study of the impact of shelters for battered women. *Journal of Marriage and the Family, 48,* 481–490.

Berkowitz, A. D., and Perkins, H. W. (1984). Stress among farm women: Work and family as interacting systems. *Journal of Marriage and the Family, 46,* 161–166.

Berkowitz, L. (1973). The case for bottling up rage. *Psychology Today 7,* 24–31.

Berman, W. H., and Turk, D. C. (1981). Adaptation to divorce: Problems and coping strategies. *Journal of Marriage and the Family, 43,* 179–189.

Bernard, J. (1975). *Women, Wives, Mothers.* Chicago: Aldine.

Bernard, J. (1982). *The Future of Marriage* (2nd ed.). New Haven: Yale University Press.

Bernard, J. L., and Bernard, M. L. (1984). The abusive male seeking treatment: Jekyll and Hyde. *Family Relations, 33,* 543–547.

Bernard, J. L., Bernard, S. L., and Bernard, M. L. (1985). Courtship violence and sex-typing. *Family Relations, 24,* 573–576.

Bernard, M. L., and Bernard, J. L. (1983). Violent intimacy: The family as a model for love relationships. *Family Relations, 32,* 283–286.

Berne, E. (1964). *Games People Play: The Psychology of Human Relationships.* New York. Grove.

Berry, R. E., and Williams, F. L. (1987). Assessing the relationship between quality of life and marital income satisfaction: A path analytic approach. *Journal of Marriage and the Family, 49,* 107–116.

Berscheid, E., and Walster, E. (1974). Physical attractiveness. *Experimental Social Psychology, 7,* 157–215.

Berstein, B. E., and Collins, S. K. (1985). Remarriage counseling: Lawyer and therapists' help with the second time around. *Family Relations, 34,* 387–391.

Best, G. A. (1982). First wife vs. second wife. *Medical Aspects of Human Sexuality, 16,* 16–26.

Beutell, N. J., and Greenhaus, J. H. (1980). Some sources and consequences of interrole conflict among married women. *Proceedings of the Annual Meeting of the Easter Academy of Management, 17,* 2–6.

Biller, H. B. (1971). *Father, Child, and Sex-role: Paternal Determinants of Personality Development.* Lexington, MA: Heath.

Biller, H. B., and Bahm, R. M. (1971). Father absence, perceived maternal behavior and masculinity of self-concept among junior high school boys. *Development Psychology, 4,* 178–181.

Billingham, R. E. (1987). Courtship violence: The patterns of conflict resolution across seven levels of emotional commitment. *Family Relations, 36,* 283–294.

Billings, A. (1979). Conflict resolution in distressed and nondistressed married couples. *Journal of Consulting and Clinical Psychology, 47,* 368–376.

Billingsley, A. (1968). *Black Families in America.* Englewood Cliffs, NJ: Prentice-Hall.

Bird, G. A., and Bird, G. W. (1985). Determinants of mobility in two-earner families: Does the wife's income count? *Journal of Marriage and the Family, 47,* 753–758.

Bird, G. W., and Bird, G. A. (1987) . In pursuit of academic careers: Observations and reflections of a dual-career couple. *Family Relations, 36,* 97–100.

Bird, G. W., Bird, G. A., and Scruggs, M. (1984). Determinants of family task sharing: A study of husbands and wives. *Journal of Marriage and the Family, 46,* 345–355.

Bischof, L. J. (1976). *Adult Psychology* (2nd ed.). New York: Harper.

Bishop, S. M., and Lynn, A. G. (1983). Multi-level vulnerability of adolescent marriages: An eco-system model of clinical assessment and intervention. *Journal of Marital and Family Therapy, 9,* 271–282.

Black S. L., and Biron, C. (1982). Androstenol as a human pheromone: No effect on perceived physical attractiveness. *Behavioral and Neural Biology, 34,* 326–330.

Blechman, E. A. (1982). Are children with one parent at psychological risk? A methodological review. *Journal of Marriage and the Family, 44,* 179–195.

Block, C. R., Norr, K. L., Meyering, S., Norr, J., and Charles, A. G. (1981). Husband gatekeeping in childbirth. *Family Relations, 30,* 197–204.

Blood, R. O., Jr., and Wolfe, D. M. (1960). *Husbands and Wives: The Dynamics of Married Living.* New York: The Free Press.

Bloom, B. L., and Caldwell, R. A. (1981). Sex differences in adjustment during the process of marital separation. *Journal of Marriage and the Family, 43,* 693–701.

Bloom, B. L., and Kindle, K. R. (1985). Demographic factors in the continuing relationship between former spouses. *Family Relations, 34,* 375–381.

Bloom, D. E., and Trussell, J. (1983). *What Are the Determinants of Delayed Childbearing and Voluntary Childlessness in the United States?* Cambridge, MA: National Bureau of Economic Research, Working paper no. 1140.

Blumenthal, L. (1980). Upsurge in violence, stress, blamed in eruptions. *Seattle Times,* July 25, p. Al.

Blumstein, P., and Schwartz, P. (1983). *American Couples: Money, Work, Sex.* New York: Morrow.

Boffey, P. M. (1983). Injected contraceptives: Hazard or boon? *New York Times,* January 11, p. 13.

Bohannan, P. (1984). *All the Happy Families.* New York: McGraw-Hill.

Bokemeier, J. L., and Monroe, P. A. (1983). Continued reliance on one respondent in family decision-making studies: A content analysis. *Journal of Marriage and the Family, 45,* 645–652.

Bolig, R., Stein, P. J., and McKenry, P. C. (1984). The self-advertisement approach to dating: Male-female differences. *Family Relations, 33,* 587–592.

Bolton, C. (1961). Mate selection as the development of a relationship. *Marriage and Family Living,* August, 234–240.

Booth, A., and Edwards, J. N. (1985). Age at marriage and marital instability. *Journal of Marriage and the Family, 47,* 67–75.

Booth, A., and White, L. (1980). Thinking about divorce. *Journal of Marriage and the Family, 42,* 605–616.

Booth, A., Johnson, D., and Edwards, J. N. (1983). Measuring marital instability. *Journal of Marriage and the Family, 45,* 387–393.

Boss, P. (1987). Family stress. In M. B. Sussman and S. K. Steinmetz (Eds.), *Handbook of Marriage and the Family* (pp. 695–723). New York: Plenum.

Boss, P. G. (1980). Normative family stress: Family boundary changes across the life span. *Family Relations, 29,* 459–465.

Boston Women's Health Collective. (1984). *The New Our Bodies, Ourselves.* New York: Simon and Schuster, Inc.

Bowen, G. L., and Orthner, D. K. (1983). Sex-role congruency and marital quality. *Journal of Marriage and the Family, 45,* 223–230.

Bowlby, J. (1969). *Attachment and Loss: Vol. 1. Attachment.* London: Hogarth.

Bowman, M. E., and Ahrons, C. R. (1985). Impact of legal custody status on fathers' parenting post-divorce. *Journal of Marriage and the Family, 47,* 481–488.

Boxer, L. (1970). Mate selection and emotional disorder. *The Family Coordinator, 19,* 173–179.

Boyarsky, R., and Boyarsky, S. (1983). Psychogenic factors in male infertility: A review. *Medical Aspects of Human Sexuality, 17,* 86H–86T.

Bozzi, V. (1985). Body talk. *Psychology Today, 19,* 20.

Brand, E., and Clingempeel, W. G. (1987). Interdependence of marital and stepparent-stepchild relationships and children's psychological adjustment: Research findings and clinical implications. *Family Relations, 36,* 140–145.

Branden, N. (1980). *The Psychology of Romantic Love.* Los Angeles: J. P. Tarche.

Brandt, A. (1982). Avoiding couple karate: Lessons in the marital arts. *Psychology Today, 16,* 38–43.

Brandwein, R. A., Brown, C. A., and Fox, E. M. (1974). Women and children last: The social situation of divorced mothers and their families. *Journal of Marriage and the Family, 36,* 498–514.

Braun, J. (1975). The struggle for acceptance of a new birth technique. *Parade Magazine,* November 23.

Braun, J., and Chao, H. (1978). Attitudes toward women: A comparison of Asia-born Chinese and American caucasians. *Psychology of Women Quarterly, 2,* 195–201.

Breault, K. D., and Kposowa, A. J. (1987). Explaining divorce in the United States: A study of 3,111 counties, 1980. *Journal of Marriage and the Family, 49,* 549–558.

Brehm, S. S. (1985). *Intimate Relationships.* New York: Random House.

Breiner, S. J. (1980). Sequential chronological stress in the family. *Family Therapy, 7,* 247–254.

Bridgwater, C. A. (1982). Second marriages fare better with childless husbands. *Psychology Today, 16,* 18.

Bridgwater, C. A. (1982). Throbbing makes the heart grow fonder. *Psychology Today, 16,* 26.

Bridgwater, C. A. (1985). Exercise: A love-hate affair. *Psychology Today, 19,* 12, 13.

Brill, M. L., Halpin, M., and Genne, W. H. (1973). *Write Your Own Wedding.* New York: Association Press.

Brim, O. G., Jr. (1976). Theories of the male midlife crisis. *Counseling Psychologist, 6,* 2–9.

Brodbar-Nemzer, J. Y. (1986). Divorce and group commitment: The case of Jews. *Journal of Marriage and the Family, 48,* 329-340.

Broderick, C. B. (1984). *Marriage and the Family* (2nd ed.). Englewood Cliffs, NJ: Prentice-Hall.

Brody, C. J., and Steelman, L. C. (1985). Sibling structure and parental sex-typing of children's household tasks. *Journal of Marriage and the Family, 47,* 265–273.

Brody, G. H., Stoneman, Z., and Sanders, A. K. (1980). Effects of television viewing on family interaction: An observational study. *Family Relations, 29,* 216–220.

Bronfenbrenner, U. (1975). Liberated women: How they're changing American life. Interview conducted for *U.S. News and World Report, 49.*

Bronfenbrenner, U. (1978). Who needs parent education? *Teachers College Record, 79,* 767–787.

Browning, J., and Dutton, D. (1986). Assessment of wife assault with the conflict tactics scale: Using couple data to quantify the differential reporting effect. *Journal of Marriage and the Family, 48,* 375–377.

Bryan, L. R., Coleman, M., Ganong, L., and Bryan, S. H. (1986). Person perception: Family structure as a cue for stereotyping. *Journal of Marriage and the Family, 48,* 169–174.

Bryson, R., Bryson, B., and Johnson, M. F. (1978). Family size, satisfaction, and productivity in dual-career couples. *Psychology of Women Quarterly, 8,* 67–77.

Buckner, L. P., and Salts, C. J. (1985). A premarital assessment program. *Family Relations, 34,* 513–520.

Buehler, C. (1987). Initiator status and divorce transition. *Family Relations, 36,* 82–86.

Buehler, C. J., and Well, B. L. (1981). Counseling the romantic. *Family Relations, 30,* 452–458.

Bulcroft, K., and O'Connor, M. (1986). The importance of dating relationship on quality of life for older persons. *Family Relations, 35,* 397–401.

Bumpass, L. (1984). Children and marital disruption: A replication and update. *Demography, 21,* 7–82.

Bumpass, L. L., and Sweet, J. A. (1972). Differentials in marital instability: 1970. *American Sociological Review 37,* 754–766.

Burden, D. S. (1986). Single parents and the work setting: The impact of multiple job and homelife responsibilities. *Family Relations, 35,* 37–43.

Burgess, E. W., and Wallin, P. (1953). *Engagement and Marriage.* Philadelphia: Lippincott.

Burgess, E. W., Locke H. J., and Thomas, M. M. (1971). *The Family* (4th ed.). New York: Van Nostrand and Reinhold.

Burgess, E., and Locke, H. (1953). *The Family: From Institution to Companionship.* New York: American Book.

Burke, R. J., and Weit, T. (1976). Relationship of wives' employment status to husband, wife, and pair satisfaction and performance. *Journal of Marriage and the Family, 35,* 279–287.

Burns, A. (1984). Perceived causes of marriage breakdown and the conditions of life. *Journal of Marriage and the Family, 46,* 551–562.

Burns, D. D. (1983). The spouse who is a perfectionist. *Medical Aspects of Human Sexuality, 17,* 219–230.

Burns, D. G. (1980). The perfectionist's script for self-defeat. *Psychology Today, 14,* 34–52.

Burrows, P. (1980). *Mexican Parental Roles: Differences Between Mothers' and Fathers' Behavior to Children.* Paper presented at the annual meeting of the Society for Cross-cultural Research. Philadelphia.

Buscaglia, L. (1982). *Living, Loving, and Learning.* New York: Fawcett Columbine.

Buunk, B. (1982). Strategies of jealousy: Styles of coping with extramarital involvement of the spouse. *Family Relations, 31,* 13–18.

Caldwell, M. A., and Peplau, L. A. (1982). Sex differences in same-sex friendships. *Sex Roles, 8,* 721–732.

Calhoun, L. G., and Selby, J. W. (1980). Voluntary and involuntary childlessness and having children: A study of social perceptions. *Family Relations, 29,* 181–183.

Calhoun, L., Selby, J., and King, E. (1981). The influence of pregnancy on sexuality: A review of current evidence. *Journal of Sex Research, 17,* 139–151.

Callan, V J. (1985). Perceptions of parents, the voluntary and involuntary childless: A multidimensional scaling analysis. *Journal of Marriage and the Family, 47,* 1045–1050.

Callan, V. J. (1983). Childlessness and partner selection. *Journal of Marriage and the Family, 45,* 181–186.

Campbell, F. A., Breitmayer, B., and Ramey, C. T. (1986). Disadvantaged single teenage mothers and their children: Consequences of free educational day care. *Family Relations, 35,* 63–68.

Caplan, G. (1981). Mastery of stress: Psychological aspects. *American Journal of Psychiatry, 138,* 413–420.

Caplan, P. J. (1986). Take the blame off mother. *Psychology Today, 20,* October, 70, 71.

Caplow, T., Bahr, H. M., Chadwick, A. A., Hill, R., and Williamson M. H. (1982). *Middletown Families: Fifty Years of Change and Continuity.* Minneapolis: University of Minnesota Press.

Cardell, A. S., Parke, R. D., Sawin, D. B. (1980). Father's views on fatherhood with special reference to infancy. *Family Relations, 29,* 331–338.

Cargan, L. (1981). Singles: An examination of two stereotypes. *Family Relations, 30,* 377–385.

Cargan, L., and Melko, M. (1982). *Singles: Myths and Realities.* Beverly Hills, CA: Sage.

Carter, E., and Welch, D. (1981). Parenting styles and children's behavior. *Family Relations, 30,* 191–195.

Carter, S., and Sokol, J. (1987). *Men Who Can't Love.* New York: M. Evans.

Casas, J. M., and Ponterotto, J. G. (1984). Profiling an invisible minority in higher education: The Chicana. *Personnel and Guidance Journal, 62,* 349–353.

Casparis, J. (1979). The bridal shower: An American rite of passage. *Indian Journal of Social Research, 20,* 11–21.

Cattell, R. B., and Nesselroad, J. R. (1967). Likeness and completeness theories examined by 16 personality factor measures on stable and unstable married couples. *Journal of Personality and Social Psychology, 7,* 351–361.

Centers, R. (1975). *Sexual Attraction and Love: An Instrumental Theory.* Springfield, IL: C. C. Thomas.

Centers, R., Raven, B. W., and Rodriques, A. (1971). Conjugal power structure: A reexamination. *American Sociological Review, 36,* 264–278.

Chantiny, J., Kagan, B., and Crowell, D. (1973). Day care of infants in family settings. *American Journal of Orthopsychiatry, 43,* 218–220.

Charny, I. W. (1972). *Marital Love and Hate.* New York: Macmillan.

Chavers, D. (1975). New direction in Indian education. *Indian Historian, 4,* 43–46.

Cheek, J. M., and Busch, C. M. (1981). The influence of shyness on loneliness in a new situation. *Personality and Social Psychology Bulletin, 7,* 572–577.

Cherlin, A. (1980). Postponing marriage: The influence of young women's work expectations. *Journal of Marriage and the Family, 42,* 355–365.

Cherlin, A. (1981). *Marriage, Divorce, and Remarriage: Social Trends in the United States.* Cambridge, MA: Harvard University Press.

Cherlin, A. J., and Furstenberg, F. F., Jr. (1986). *The New American Grandparent.* New York: Basic Books.

Cherlin, A., and McCarthy, J. (1985). Remarried couple households: Data from the June 1980 current population survey. *Journal of Marriage and the Family, 47,* 23–30.

Cherlin, A., and Walters, P. B. (1981). Trends in the United States men's and women's sex-role attitudes: 1972–1978. *American Sociological Review, 46,* 453–460.

Cherpas, C. C. (1985). Dual-career families: Terminology, typologies, and work and family issues. *Journal of Counseling and Development, 63,* 616–620.

Chess, T. A. (1984). The genesis and evolution of behavior disorders: From infancy to early adult life. *American Journal of Psychiatry, 141,* 1.

Chesser, B. J. (1980). Analysis of wedding rituals: An attempt to make weddings more meaningful. *Family Relations, 29,* 204–215.

Chilman, C. (1978). *Families of Today.* Paper presented at the Building Family Strengths Symposium, University of Nebraska, Lincoln, May.

Chilman, C. S. (1980). Parent satisfactions, concerns, and goals for their children. *Family Relations, 29,* 339–345.

Chira, S. (1984). Town experiment cuts TV. *New York Times,* February 11.

Chiriboga, D. A. (1982). Adaptation to marital separation in later and earlier life. *Journal of Gerontology, 37,* 109–114.

Cicirelli, V. G. (1980). A comparison of college women's feelings toward their siblings and parents. *Journal of Marriage and the Family, 42,* 111–118.

Cimbalo, R. S., Faling, V., and Mousan, P. (1976). The course of love: A cross-sectional design. *Psychological Reports 38,* 1292–1294.

Clark, H. (1980). *Cases and Problems on Domestic Relations* (3rd ed.). St. Paul, MN: West.

Clark, J. H., and Zarrow, M. X. (1971). Influence of copulation on time of ovulation in women. *American Journal of Obstetrics and Gynecology, 109,* 1083–1085.

Clark, L. (1970). Is there a difference between a clitoral and a vaginal orgasm? *Journal of Sex Research, 6,* 25–28.

Clark, P. G., Siviski, R. W., and Weiner, R. (1986). Coping strategies of widowers in the first year. *Family Relations, 35,* 425–430.

Clatworthy, N. M., and Scheid, S. (1977). *A Comparison of Married Couples: Premarital Cohabitants with Nonpremarital Cohabitants.* Unpublished manuscript, Ohio State University, Columbus. Cited in Macklin, 1983.

Cleek, M. G., and Pearson, T. A. (1985). Perceived causes of divorce: An analysis of interrelationships. *Journal of Marriage and the Family 47,* 179–183.

Clemens, A. W., and Axelson, L. J. (1985). The not-so-empty nest: The return of the fledgling adult. *Family Relations, 34,* 259–264.

Cleveland, M. (1979). Divorce in the middle years: The sexual dimension. *Journal of Divorce, 2,* 255–262.

Clingempeel, W. G., Brand, E., and Ievoli, R. (1984). Stepparent-stepchild relationships in stepmother and stepfather families: A multimethod study. *Family Relations, 33,* 465–473.

Cogle, F. L., and Tasher, G. E. (1982). Children and housework. *Family Relations, 31,* 395–399.

Cohen, J. (1987). Parents as educational models and definers. *Journal of Marriage and the Family, 49,* 339–351.

Cole, C., and Rodman, H. (1987). When school-age children care for themselves: Issues for family life educators and parents. *Family Relations, 36,* 92–96.

Coleman, M., and Ganong, L. (1987). An evaluation of the stepfamily self-help literature for children and adolescents. *Family Relations, 36,* 61–65.

Colletta, N. D. (1985). Stressful lives: The situation of divorced mothers and their children. *Journal of Divorce, 6,* 19–31.

Colp, R. (1982). Dead-end affairs with married men. *Medical Aspects of Human Sexuality 16,* 64–66.

Communicable Disease summary. (1985). *AIDS Update.* Oregon Health Division, 34, November, 1–3.

Conant, M., Spicer, C., and Smith, C. (1986). Herpes simplex virus transmission: Condom studies. *Sexually Transmitted Diseases, 11,* 94–95.

Condron, J., and Bode, J. (1982). Rashomon, working wives, and family division of labor: Middletown, 1980. *Journal of Marriage and the Family, 44,* 421–426.

Conger, R. D., Burgess, R. L., and Barrett, C. (1979). Child abuse related to life change and perceptions of illness: Some preliminary findings. *The Family Coordinator, 28,* 73–78.

Conger, R. D., McCarty, J. A., Yang, R. K., Lahey, B. B., and Burgess, R. L. (1984). Mother's age as a predictor of observed maternal behavior in three independent samples of families. *Journal of Marriage and the Family, 46,* 411–424.

Conklin, G. H. (1979). Cultural determinants of power of women within the family: A neglected aspect of the family research. *Journal of Comparative Family Studies, 10,* 35–54.

Constantine, L. L., and Constantine, J. M. (1973). *Group Marriage.* New York: Collier.

Cook, D. R., and Frantz-Cook, A. (1984). A systematic treatment approach to wife battering. *Journal of Marital and Family Therapy, 10,* 83–92.

Cook, E. P. (1985). Androgyny: A goal for counseling. *Journal of Counseling and Development, 63,* May, 567–571.

Cooney, R. S., Rogler, L. H., Hurrell, R. M., and Ortez, V. (1982). Decision making in intergenerational Puerto Rican families. *Journal of Marriage and the Family, 44,* 621–631.

Cooper, J. E., Holman, J., and Braithwaite, V. A. (1983). Self-esteem and family cohesion: The child's perspective and adjustment. *Journal of Marriage and the Family, 45,* 153–159.

Cooper, K. L., and Gutmann, D. L. (1987). Gender identity and ego mastery style in middle-aged, pre- and post-empty nest women. *The Gerontologist, 27,* 347–352.

Corman, L., and Schaefer, J. B. (1973). Population growth and family planning. *Journal of Marriage and the Family, 35,* 89–92.

Corrales, C. G. (1975). Power and satisfaction in early marriage. In R. E. Cromwell and D. H. Olson (Eds.), *Power in Families.* New York: Wiley.

Cost of childrearing at least $30,000–$80,000 according to the USDA. (1982). *Family Planning Perspectives, 14,* 151–152.

Cote, R. M., and Koval, J. E. (1983). Heterosexual relationship development: Is it really a sequential process? *Adolescence, 18,* 507–514.

Cote, R. M., Henton, J. M., Koval, J., Christopher, P. S., and Lloyd, S. (1982). Premarital abuse: A social psychological perspective. *Journal of Family Issues, 3,* 79–90.

Council for Children. (1984). *Taking Action for Latchkey Children.* Charlotte, NC: Council for Children.

Cousins, P. C., and Vincent, J. P. (1983). Supportive and adversive behavior following spousal complaints. *Journal of Marriage and the Family, 45,* 679–682.

Coverman, S., and Sheley, J. F. (1986). Change in men's housework and child-care time, 1965–1975. *Journal of Marriage and the Family, 48,* 413–422.

Cox, C. (1982). A golden rule test. *Psychology Today, 16,* 78.

Crane, W. E., and Coffer, J. H. (1964). *A Religious Attitudes Inventory.* Saluda, NC: Family Life Publications.

Creecy, R. F., Berg, W. E., and Wright, R. (1985). Loneliness among the elderly: A causal approach. *Journal of Gerontology, 40,* 487–493.

Critelli, J. W. (1977) Romantic attraction and happiness. *Psychological Reports, 41,* 721–722.

Cromwell, V., and Cromwell, R. (1978). Perceived dominance in decision making and conflict resolution among black and Chicano couples. *Journal of Marriage and the Family, 40,* 749–759.

Crosby, J. F. (1985). *Illusion and Disillusion: The Self in Love and Marriage* (3rd ed.). Belmont, CA: Wadsworth.

Crossman, S. M., and Edmondson, J. E. (1985). Personal and family resources supportive of displaced homemakers' financial adjustment. *Family Relations, 34,* 465–474.

Cuber, J. F., and Harroff, P. B. (1965). *The Significant Americans: A Study of Sexual Behavior Among the Affluent.* New York: Appleton-Century-Crofts.

Curran, D. (1983). *Traits of a Healthy Family.* New York: Ballantine.

Curran, J. W. (1980). Economic consequences of pelvic inflammatory disease in the United States. *American Journal of Obstetrics and Gynecology, 138,* 848–851.

Currant, E. F., et al. (1979). Sex-role stereotyping and assertive behavior. *Journal of Psychology, 101,* 223–228.

657

Dail, P. W., and Way, W. L. (1985). What do parents observe about parenting upon prime time television? *Family Relations, 34,* 491–499.

Daly, M., and Wilson, M. (1980). Discriminative parental solicitude: A biological perspective. *Journal of Marriage and the Family, 42,* 277–288.

Daniluk, J. C., and Herman, A. (1984). Parenthood decision-making. *Family Relations, 33,* 607–612.

Darling, C. A., and Hicks, M. W. (1982). Parental influence on adolescent sexuality: Implications for parents and educators. *Journal of Youth and Adolescence, 11,* 231–244.

Darling, L. (1976). *An Interactionist Interpretation of Bachelorhood and Late Marriage: The Process of Entering Into, Remaining In, and Leaving Careers of Singleness.* Ph.D. dissertation, University of Connecticut.

Davey, A. J., and Paolucci, B. (1980). Family interaction: A study of shared time and activities. *Family Relations, 29,* 43–49.

David, D. S., and Brannon, R., ed. (1976). *The Fortynine Percent Majority: The Male Sex Role.* Reading, MA: Addison-Wesley.

Davidson, B., Balswick, J., and Halverson, C. (1983). Affective self-disclosure and marital adjustment: A test of equity theory. *Journal of Marriage and the Family, 45,* 93–102.

Davidson, J. K. (1983). Age of one's second wife. *Medical Aspects of Human Sexuality, 17,* 22–23.

Davidson, S. (1983). Proliferating POSSLQ. *Psychology Today, 17,* 84.

Davis, J. D. (1978). When boy meets girl: Sex roles and the negotiation of intimacy in an acquaintance exercise. *Journal of Personality and Social Psychology, 36,* 684–692.

Davis, K. E. (1985). Near and dear: Friendship and love compared. *Psychology Today, 19,* 22–30.

Davis-Brown, K., Salamon, S., and Surra, C. A. (1987). Economic and social factors in mate selection: An ethnographic analysis of an agriculture community. *Journal of Marriage and the Family, 49,* 41–55.

DeCindio, L. A., Floyd, H. H., Wilcox, J. and McSeveney, D. R. (1983). Race effects in a model of parent-peer orientation. *Adolescence, 18,* 319–379.

DeJong, G. F., Faulkner, J. E., and Warland, R. H. (1976). Dimensions of religiosity reconsidered: Evidence from a cross-cultural study. *Social Forces, 54,* 866–889.

DeMaris, A., and Leslie, G. R. (1984). Cohabitation with the future spouse: Its influence upon marital satisfaction and communication. *Journal of Marriage and the Family, 46,* 77–84.

Denny, N., Field, J., and Quadagno, D. (1984). Sex differences in sexual needs and desires. *Archives of Sexual Behavior, 13,* 233–245.

deTurck, M. A., and Miller, G. R. (1986). The effect of husbands and wives social cognition on their marital adjustment, conjugal power and self-esteem. *Journal of Marriage and the Family, 48,* 715–724.

Deutscher, I. (1964). The qualities of postparental life: Definitions of the situation. *Journal of Marriage and the Family, 26,* 52–59.

Development of six new birth control methods among 1989 goals of WHO special programs. (1983). *Family Planning Perspectives, 15,* 226–228.

Dhir, K. S., and Markman, H. J. (1984). Application of social judgment theory to understanding and treating marital conflict. *Journal of Marriage and the Family, 46,* 597–610.

Diaz, S., Pavez, M., Miranda, P., Robertson, D. N., Sevin, I., and Croxatto, H. B. (1982). A five-year clinical trial of Loveonogestrel Silastic-implants (Norplant). *Contraception 25,* 447–456.

Dibble, U., and Straus, M. A. (1980). Some social structure determinants of inconsistency between attitudes and behavior: The case of family violence. *Journal of Marriage and the Family, 42,* 71–80.

Dill, D., Feld, E., Martin, J., Beukema, S., and Belle, D. (1980). The impact of the environment on the coping effects of low-income mothers. *Family Relations, 29,* 503–509.

Dillard, K. D., and Pol, L. B. (1982). The individual economic costs of teenage childbearing. *Family Relations, 31,* 249–259.

Dixon, R. B., and Weitzman, L. J. (1980). Evaluating the impact of no-fault divorce in California. *Family Relations, 29,* 297–307.

Dizmang, L. H., et al. (1974). Adolescent suicide at an Indian reservation. *American Journal of Orthopsychiatry, 44,* 43–49.

Doe v. Bolton, 410 U.S. 179 (1973).

Doherty, W. J. (1981). Locus of control differences and marital dissatisfaction. *Journal of Marriage and the Family, 43,* 369–377.

Dominick, J. (1979). The portrayal of women in prime time. *Sex Roles, 5,* 405–411.

Donovan, P. (1983). Judging teenagers: How minors fare when they seek court-authorized abortions. *Family Planning Perspectives, 15,* 259–267.

Dornbusch, S. M., Carlsmith, J. M., Bushwall, S. J., Ritter, P. L., Leidman, H., Historf, A. H., and Gross, R. T. (1985). Single parents, extended households, and the control of adolescents. *Child Development, 56,* 326–341.

Doten, D. (1938). *The Art of Bundling.* New York: Farrar.

Dowd, J. (1980). *Stratification Among the Aged.* Monterey, CA: Brooks/Cole.

Dowling, C. (1983). The relative explosion. *Psychology Today, 17,* 54–59.

Downs, W. R. (1982). Alcoholism as a developing family crisis. *Family Relations, 31,* 5–12.

Doyle, J. A. *Sex and Gender*. Dubuque, IA: Wm. C. Brown.

Draughn, P. S. (1984). Perceptions of competence in work and marriage of middle-age men. *Journal of Marriage and the Family, 46,* 403–409.

Driscoll, R., Davis, K. E., and Lipetz, M. E. (1972). Parental interference and romantic love: The Romeo and Juliet effect. *Journal of Personality and Social Psychology, 24,* 1–10.

Duberman, L. (1973). Step-kin relationships. *Journal of Marriage and the Family, 35,* 283–292.

Duberman, L. (1975). *The Reconstituted Family.* Chicago: Nelson-Hall.

Duncan, O. D. (1982). Recent cohorts lead rejection of sex typing. *Sex Roles, 8,* 127–133.

Duncan, G. J. (1984). *Years of Poverty, Years of Plenty.* Ann Arbor: University of Michigan, Survey Research Center, Institute for Social Research.

Dunn, M. S. (1979). *Marriage Role Expectation Inventory.* Saluda, NC: Family Life Publications.

Dutton, D., and Aron, A. P. (1974). Some evidence of heightened sexual attraction under conditions of high anxiety. *Journal of Personal and Social Psychology, 30,* 510–517.

Duvall, E. M. (1954). *In-laws: Pro and Con.* New York: Association Press.

Dweck, C. S., et al. (1978). Sex differences in learned helplessness: II. The contingencies of evaluation feedback in the classroom and III. An experimental analysis. *Developmental Psychology, 14,* 268–276.

Dyk, P. A. H. (1987). Graduate student management of family and academic roles. *Family Relations, 36,* 329–332.

Eberhardt, C. A., and Schill, T. (1984). Differences in sexual attitudes and likeliness of sexual behaviors of black lower-socioeconomic father-present vs. father-absent female adolescents. *Adolescence, 19,* 99–105.

Ectopic pregnancy: A potentially lethal condition of women of childbearing age. (1984). *Medical Aspects of Human Sexuality, 18,* 19.

Eidelson, R. J. (1983). Affiliation and independence issues in marriage. *Journal of Marriage and the Family, 45,* 683–688.

Eisenstock, B. Sex-role differences in children's identification with counterstereotypic television portrayals. *Sex Roles 10,* 417–430.

Ekman, P., Levenson, R. W., and Friesen, W. V. (1983). Autonomic nervous system activity distinguishes among emotions. *Science, 221,* 1208–1210.

Elbaum, P. L. (1981). The dynamics, implications and treatment of extramarital sexual relationships for the family therapist. *Journal of Marital and Family Therapy, 7,* 489–495.

Electrocautery: A highly effective, rapid male steril-ization technique, two physicians claim. (1984). *Family Planning Perspectives, 16,* July/August, 192.

Elkin, M. (1977). Premarital counseling for minors: The Los Angeles experience. *The Family Coordinator, 26,* 429–443.

Elkind, D. (1970). *Children and Adolescents: Interpretive Essays on Jean Piaget.* New York: Oxford University Press.

Elliot, F. R. (1986). *The Family: Change or Continuity?* Atlantic Highlands, NJ: Humanities Press.

Elman, M. R., and Gilbert, L. A. (1984). Coping strategies for role conflict in married professional women with children. *Family Relations, 33,* 317–327.

Epstein, G. F., and Bronzaft, A. I. (1972). Female freshmen view their roles as women. *Journal of Marriage and the Family, 34,* 671–672.

Ericksen, J. A., Yancey, W. L., and Ericksen, E. P. (1979). The division of family roles. *Journal of Marriage and the Family, 41,* 311.

Erikson, E. H. (1959). *Identity and the Life Cycle.* New York: International Universities Press.

Essex, M. J., and Nam, S. (1987). Marital status and loneliness among older women: The differential importance of close family and friends. *Journal of Marriage and the Family, 49,* 93–106.

Etaugh, C., and Malstrom, J. (1981). The effect of marital status on person perception. *Journal of Marriage and the Family, 43,* 801–805.

Evans, L., Eberdt, D. J., and Bosse, R. (1985). Proximity to retirement and anticipatory involvement: Findings from the normative aging study. *Journal of Gerontology, 40,* 368–374.

Evans, R. (1964). *Conversations with Carl Jung.* Princeton, NJ: Van Nostrand.

Everett, C. A., and Volgy, S. S. (1983). Family assessment in child custody disputes. *Journal of Marital and Family Therapy, 9,* 343–353.

Falbo, T., and Peplau, L. A. (1980). Power strategies in intimate relationships. *Journal of Personality and Social Psychology, 38,* 618–628.

Falik, L. A. (1984). Psychosexual effects of infertility. *Medical Aspects of Human Sexuality, 18,* 82–92.

Farley, F. H., and Davis, S. A. (1980). Personality and sexual satisfaction in marriage. *Journal of Sexual and Marital Therapy, 6,* 56–62.

Farris, C. E., and Farris, L. S. (1976). Indian children: The struggle for survival. *Social Work, 21,* 386–389.

Fass, P. S. (1977). *The Damned and the Beautiful.* New York: Oxford University Press.

Faux, M. (1984). *Childless by Choice.* Garden City, NY: Doubleday.

Feazell, C. S., Mayers, R. S., and Deschner, J. (1984). Services for men who batter: Implications for programs and policies. *Family Relations, 32,* 217–223.

Feingold, A. (1982). Do taller men have prettier girl-friends? *Psychological Reports, 50,* 810.

Feldman, H. (1981). A comparison of intentional parents and intentionally childless couples. *Journal of Marriage and the Family, 43,* 593–600.

Feldman, H., and Feldman, M. (1975). The family life cycle: Some suggestions for recycling. *Journal of Marriage and the Family, 37,* 277–284.

Feldman, L. B. (1982). Dysfunctional marital conflict: An integrative interpersonal-intrapsychic model. *Journal of Marital and Family Therapy, 8,* 417–426.

Felton, G., and Segelman, F. (1978). Lamaze childbirth training and changes in belief about personal control. *Birth and Family Journal, 5,* 141–150.

Fergusson, D. M., Horwood, L. J., and Shannon, F. T. (1984). A proportional hazards model of family breakdown. *Journal of Marriage and the Family, 46,* 539–549.

Ferree, M. M. (1976). Working-class jobs, housework, and paid work as sources of satisfaction. *Social Problems, 22,* 431–441.

Ferreiro, B. W., Warren, N. J., and Konanc, J. T. (1986). ADAP: A divorce assessment proposal. *Family Relations, 35,* 439–449.

Figley, C. R. (1973). Child density and the marital relationship. *Journal of Marriage and the Family, 35,* 272–282.

Filsinger, E. E., and Lamke, L. K. (1983). The lineage transmission of interpersonal competence. *Journal of Marriage and the Family, 45,* 75–80.

Filsinger, E. E., and Wilson, M. R. (1983). Social anxiety and marital adjustment. *Family Relations, 32,* 513–519.

Filsinger, E. E., and Wilson, M. R. (1984). Religiosity, socioeconomic rewards, and family development: Predictors of marital adjustment. *Journal of Marriage and the Family, 46,* 663–670.

Fine, M. A. (1986). Perceptions of stepparents: Variation in stereotypes as a function of current family structure. *Journal of Marriage and the Family, 48,* 537–543.

Fine, M., and Hovestadt, A. J. (1984). Perceptions of marriage and rationality by levels of perceived health in the family of origin. *Journal of Marriage and Family Therapy, 10,* April, 193–195.

Finkelhor, D., and Araji, S. (1986). Explanations of pedophilia: A four factor model. *The Journal of Sex Research, 22,* 145–161.

Finlay, B. A. (1981). Sex differences in correlates of abortion: Attitudes among college students. *Journal of Marriage and the Family, 43,* 571–581.

Fischer, C. S., and Phillips, S. L. (1982). Who is alone? Social characteristics of people with small networks. In L. A. Peplau and D. Perlman (Eds.), *Loneliness: A Sourcebook of Current Theory, Research, and Therapy.* New York: Wiley Interscience.

Fischer, J. L. (1983). Mothers living apart from their children. *Family Relations, 32,* 351–357.

Fischer, L. R. (1983). Mothers and mothers-in-law. *Journal of Marriage and the Family, 45,* 187–192.

Fischman, J. (1986). Women and divorce: Ten years after. *Psychology Today, 20,* 15.

Fisher, B. L., Giblin, P. R., and Hoopes, M. H. (1982). Healthy family functioning. *Journal of Marriage and Family Therapy, 8,* 273–284.

Fisher, S. (1973). *The Female Orgasm: Psychology, Physiology, Fantasy.* New York: Basic Books.

Fisher, W. A., and Byrne, D. (1978). Sex differences in response to erotica? Love vs. lust. *Journal of Personality, 36,* 117–125.

Fishman, B. (1983). The economic behavior of stepfamilies. *Family Relations, 32,* 359–366.

Fitzpatrick, M. A., Fallis, S., and Vance, L. (1982). Multifunctional coding of conflict resolution strategies in marital dyads. *Family Relations, 31,* 61–70.

Flake-Hobson, C., Skeen, P., and Robinson, B. E. (1980). Review of theories of research concerning sex-role development and androgyny with suggestions for teachers. *Family Relations, 29,* 152–162.

Fleck, J. R., Fuller, C. C., Molin, S. Z., Miller, D. H., and Acheson, K. R. (1980). Father psychological absence and heterosexual behavior, personal adjustment, and sex-typing in adolescent girls. *Adolescence, 15,* 847–860.

Fleishman, W., and Dixon, P. L. (1973). *Vasectomy, Sex and Parenthood.* Garden City, NY: Doubleday.

Flynn, C. P. (1987). Relationship violence: a model for family professionals. *Family Relations, 36,* 295–299.

For safety and efficacy, most methods of tubal sterilization are similar. (1983). *Family Planning Perspectives, 15,* May/June, 141, 142.

Ford, D. A. (1983). Wife battery and criminal justice: A study of victim decision-making. *Family Relations, 32,* 463–469.

Forer, L., with Henry Still. (1976). *The Birth Order Factors: How Your Personality is Influenced by Your Place in the Family.* New York: David McKay.

Forrest, J. D. (1986). The end of IUD marketing in the United States: What does it mean for American women? *Family Planning Perspectives, 18,* 52–57.

Forsstrom-Cohen, B., and Rosenbaum, A. (1985). The effects of parental marital violence on young adults: An exploratory investigation. *Journal of Marriage and the Family, 47,* 467–472.

Forward, S. (1986). *Men Who Hate Women: The Women Who Love Them.* New York: Bantam.

Foster, D., Klinger-Vartabedian, L., and Wispe, L. (1984). Male longevity and age differences between spouses. *Journal of Gerontology, 39,* 117–120.

Fotherby, K. G., et al. (1982). A preliminary pharmacological trial of the monthly injectable contraceptive cycloprovera. *Contraception, 25,* 261–272.

Fowers, B. J., and Olson, D. H. (1986). Predicting marital success with PREPARE: A predictive validity study. *Journal of Marital and Family Therapy, 12,* 403–413.

Fowler, C. R. (1982). How to destroy marriage. *Medical Aspects of Human Sexuality, 16,* 16–31A.

Fowler, C. R. (1983). The need for "liking" as well as "loving" in marriage. *Medical Aspects of Human Sexuality, 17,* 217–232

Fox, G. L. (1980). The mother-adolescent daughter relationship as a sexual socialization structure: A research review. *Family Relations, 29,* January, 21–28.

Franklin, R. L., and Hibbs, "B." (1980). Child custody in transition. *Journal of Marital and Family Therapy, 6,* 285–291.

Freed, D. J., and Foster, H. H., Jr. (1981). Divorce in the fifty states: An overview. *Family Law Quarterly, 14,* 229–284.

Freedman, J. (1978). *Happy People: What Happiness Is, Who Has It, and Why.* New York: Harcourt Brace Jovanovich.

Freud, S. (1953). *Three Essays on the Theory of Sexuality.* (Standard ed.). Vol. 7. London: Hogarth, 1953.

Freudiger, P. (1983). Life satisfaction among three categories of married women. *Journal of Marriage and the Family, 45,* 213–219.

Friedland, G., Saltzman, G., Rogers, M., Kahl, P., Lesser, M., Mayers, M., and Klein, R. (1986). Lack of transmission of HTLV-III/LAV infection to household contacts of patients, with AIDS OR AIDS-related complex with oral candidiases. *The New England Journal of Medicine, 314,* 344–349.

Friedman, R., Hurt, S., Arnoff, M., and Clarkin, J. (1980). Behavior and the menstrual cycle. *Signs, 5,* 719–738.

Fromm, E. (1956). *The Art of Loving.* New York: Harper.

Fruch, T., and McGhee, P. (1975). Traditional sex role development and amount of time watching television. *Developmental Psychology, 11,* 109.

Furstenberg, F. F., and Spanier, G. (1984). *Recycling the Family: Remarriage After Divorce.* Beverly Hills, CA: Sage.

Furstenberg, F. F., Herceg-Baron, R., Shea, J., and Webb, D. (1984). Family communication and teenagers' contraceptive use. *Family Planning Perspectives, 16,* 163–170.

Furstenberg, F. F., Jr. (1976) . Premarital pregnancy and marital instability. *Journal of Social Issues, 32,* 67–86.

Furstenberg, F. F., Jr. (1982). Conjugal succession: Reentering marriage after divorce. In P. B. Baltes and O. G. Brim (Eds.), *Life Span Development and Behavior,* Vol. 4. New York: Academic Press.

Furstenberg, F. F., Jr., and Nord, C. W. (1985). Parenting apart: Patterns of childrearing after marital disruption. *Journal of Marriage and the Family, 47,* 893–904.

Gabriel, A., and McAnarney, E. R. (1983). Parenthood in two subcultures: White, middle-class couples and black, low-income adolescents in Rochester, New York. *Adolescence, 18,* 595–608.

Gadpaille, W. J. (1982). Current thinking on influence of parents on marital happiness. *Medical Aspects of Human Sexuality, 16,* 89–98.

Gaesser, D. L., and Whitbourne, S. K. (1985). Work identity and marital adjustment in blue-collar men. *Journal of Marriage and the Family, 47,* 747–751.

Galambos, N. L., and Garbarino, J. (1983). Identifying the missing links in the study of latchkey children. *Children Today, 12,* 2–4, 40.

Gallup, G. H. (1979). *The Gallup Poll: Public Opinion 1978.* Wilmington, DE: Scholarly Resources.

Galvin, K. M., and Brommel, B. J. (1986). *Family Communication: Cohesion and Change* (2nd ed.). Glenview, IL: Scott, Foresman.

Gannon, M. J., and Hendrickson, D. H. (1973). Career orientations and job satisfaction among working wives. *Journal of Applied Psychology, 57,* 339–340.

Ganong, L. H., and Coleman, M. (1984). The effects of remarriage on children: A review of the empirical literature. *Family Relations, 33,* 389–406.

Ganong, L., Colman, M., and Brown, G. (1981). Effect of family structure on marital attitudes of adolescents. *Adolescence, 16,* 281–288.

Garcia, L. (1982). Sex-role orientation and stereotypes about male-female sexuality. *Sex Roles, 8,* 863–876.

Garland, D. R. (1981). Training married couples in listening skills: Effects on behavior, perceptual accuracy, and marital adjustment. *Family Relations, 30,* 297–306.

Gary, L., Beatty, L., Berry, G., and Price, M. (1983). *Stable Black Families. Final Report.* Institute for Urban Affairs and Research. Washington, DC: Howard University.

Gary, L., et al. (1986). Strong black families: Models of program development for black families. In S. Van Zandt, et al. (Eds.), *Family Strengths 7: Vital Connections* (pp. 453-468). Lincoln, NE: Center for Family Strengths.

Gaudin, J. M., and Davis, K. B. (1985). Social networks of black and white rural families: A research report. *Journal of Marriage and the Family, 47,* 1015–1021.

Gebhard, P. H. (1966). Factors in marital orgasm. *Journal of Social Issues, 22,* 88–95.

Gecas, V., and Ny, F. I. (1974). Sex and class differences in parent-child interaction: A test of Kahn's hypothesis. *Journal of Marriage and the Family, 36,* 742–749.

Geiss, S. K., and O'Leary, K. D. (1981). Therapists ratings of frequency and severity of marital problems: Implications for research. *Journal of Marital and Family Therapy, 7,* 515–520.

Gelles, R. J. (1980). Violence in the family: A review of

research in the seventies. *Journal of Marriage and the Family, 42,* 873–885.

Gelles, R. J. (1982). Applying research on family violence to clinical practice. *Journal of Marriage and the Family, 44,* 9–20.

Gelles, R. J., and Maynard, P. E. (1987). A structural family systems approach to intervention in cases of family violence. *Family Relations, 36,* 270–275.

Gellman, M. I., Hoffman, R. A., Jones, M., and Stone, M. (1984). Abused and nonabused women: MMPI profile differences. *The Personnel and Guidance Journal, 62,* 600–604.

Gerber, I., et al. (1975). Anticipatory grief and aged widows and widowers. *Journal of Gerontology, 30,* 225–229.

Gershenson, H. P. (1983). Redefining fatherhood in families with white adolescent mothers. *Journal of Marriage and the Family, 45,* 591–599.

Gigy, L. L. (1980). Self-concept of single women. *Psychology of Women Quarterly, 5,* 321–340.

Gilbert, L. A., Hanson, G. R., and Davis, B. (1982). Perceptions of parental role responsibilities: Differences between mothers and fathers. *Family Relations, 31,* 261–269.

Gilbert, L. A., Holahan, C. K., and Manning, L. (1981). Coping with conflict between professional and maternal roles. *Family Relations, 30,* 419–426.

Giles-Sims, J. (1985). A longitudinal study of battered children of battered women. *Family Relations, 34,* 205–210.

Giles-Sims, J., and Finkelhor, D. (1984). Child abuse in stepfamilies. *Family Relations, 33,* 407–413.

Gilford, R. (1984). Contrasts in marital satisfaction throughout old age: An exchange theory analysis. *Journal of Gerontology, 39,* 325–333.

Gilford, R., and Black, D. (1972). *The Grandchild- Grandparent Dyad: Ritual or Relationship?* Paper presented at the annual meeting of the Gerontological Society, San Juan, Puerto Rico.

Gilliland, N. C. (1979). The problem of geographic mobility for dual career families. *Journal of Marriage and Family Studies, 10,* 345–358.

Gladow, N. W., and Ray, M. P. (1986). The impact of informal support systems on the well-being of low income single parents. *Family Relations, 35,* 123–125.

Glass, J. C., and Grant, K. A. (1983). Counseling in later years: A growing need. *The Personnel and Guidance Journal, 62,* 210–213.

Gleason, J., and Prescott, M. R. (1977). Group techniques for pre-marital preparation. *The Family Coordinator, 26,* 277–280.

Glenn, N. D. (1975). Psychological well-being in the postparental stage: Some evidence from national survey. *Journal of Marriage and the Family, 37,* 105–110.

Glenn, N. D. (1982). Interreligious marriage in the United States: Patterns and recent trends. *Journal of Marriage and the Family, 44,* 555–566.

Glenn, N. D. (1984). A note on estimating the strength of influences for religious endogamy. *Journal of Marriage and the Family, 46,* 725–727.

Glenn, N. D., and McLanahan, S. (1981). The effects of offspring on the psychological well-being of older adults. *Journal of Marriage and the Family, 43,* 409–421.

Glenn, N. D., and McLanahan, S. (1982). Children and marital happiness: A further specification of the relationship. *Journal of Marriage and the Family, 44,* 63–72.

Glenn, N. D., and Shelton, B. A. (1983). Pre-adult background variable and divorce: A note of caution about overreliance on explained variance. *Journal of Marriage and the Family, 45,* 405–410.

Glenn, N. D., and Shelton, B. A. (1985). Regional differences in divorce in the United States. *Journal of Marriage and the Family 47,* 741–652.

Glenn, N. D., and Supancic, M. (1984). The social and demographic correlates of divorce and separation in the United States: An update and reconsideration. *Journal of Marriage and the Family, 46,* 563–575.

Glenn, N. D., and Weaver, C. N. (1981). The contribution of marital happiness to global happiness. *Journal of Marriage and the Family, 43,* 161–168.

Glenn, N., and Supancic, M. (1984). The social and-demographic correlates of divorce and separation in the United States: An update and recommendation. *Journal of Marriage and the Family, 46,* 563–575.

Glenwick, D. S., and Mowrey, J. D. (1986). When parent becomes peer: Loss of intergenerational boundaries in single parent families. *Family Relations, 35,* 57–62.

Glick, I. O., Weiss, R. S., and Parkes, C. M. (1974). *The First Year of Bereavement.* New York: Wiley.

Glick, P. C. (1984). Marriage, divorce, and living arrangements: Prospective changes. *Journal of Family Issues, 5,* 7–26.

Glick, P. C., and Lin, S. (1986). More young adults are living with their parents: Who are they? *Journal of Marriage and the Family, 48,* 107–112.

Glick, P. C., and Spanier, G. B. (1980). Married and unmarried cohabitation in the United States. *Journal of Marriage and the Family, 42,* 19–30.

Goddard, H. L., and Leviton, D. (1980). Intimacy-sexuality needs of the bereaved: An exploratory study. *Death Education, 34,* 347–358.

Goedert, J., Biggar, R., Winn, D., Greene, M., Weiss, S., Grossman, R., Strong, D., and Blattner, W. (1984). Determinants of retrivirus (HTLV-III) antibody and immunodeficiency conditions in homosexual men. *The Lancet,* September 29, 711–715.

Goff, D., Goff, L., and Lehrer, S. (1980) Sex-role portrayals of selected female television characters. *Journal of Broadcasting 24*, 467–478.

Goffman, E. (1977). Genderisms. *Psychology Today, 11*, 60–63.

Goldberg, M. (1982). Current thinking on remarriages: Commentary. *Medical Aspects of Human Sexuality, 16*, 151–158.

Goldstein, C., and Rosenbaum, A. (1985). An evaluation of the self-esteem of maritally violent man. *Family Relations, 34*, 425–428.

Goldstine, D., et al. (1977). *The Dance-away Lover.* New York: Morrow.

Goodenough, F. L. (1931). *Anger in Young Children.* Minneapolis: University of Minnesota Press.

Goodman, H. (1982). Assertiveness breeds attempt. *Psychology Today, 16*, 75.

Goodrich, W., Ryder, R. G., and Raush, H. L. (1968). Patterns of newlywed marriage. *Journal of Marriage and the Family, 30*, 383–389.

Gordon, J. S., and Haire, D. (1981). Alternatives in childbirth. In P. Ahmed (Ed.), *Pregnancy, Childbirth, and Parenthood.* New York: Elsevier.

Gordon, L., and O'Keefe, P. (1984). Incest as a form of family violence: Evidence from historical case records. *Journal of Marriage and the Family, 46*, 27–34.

Gordon, M. (1981). Was Walter ever right? The rating and dating complex reconsidered. *Journal of Marriage and the Family, 43*, 67–76.

Gottman J. M., and Porterfield, A. (1981). Communicative competence in the nonverbal behavior of married couples. *Journal of Marriage and the Family, 43*, 817–824.

Gottman, J., Markman, H., and Notarius, C. (1977) The topography of marital conflict: A sequential analysis of verbal and nonverbal behavior. *Journal of Marriage and the Family, 39*, 461–477.

Gould, R. (1979). Transformations in midlife. *New York University Education Quarterly, 10*, 2–9.

Gould, R. E. (1982). Do grandparents still play an important role in families? *Medical Aspects of Human Sexuality, 16*, 45–60.

Granvold, D. K. (1983). Structured separation for marital treatment and decision-making. *Journal of Marital and Family Therapy, 9*, 403–412.

Granvold, D. K., and Tarrant, R. (1983). Structured marital separation as a marital treatment method. *Journal of Marital and Family Therapy, 2*, 189–198.

Gravitz, H. L., and Bowden, J. D. (1985). *Guide to Recovery: A Book for Adult Children of Alcoholics.* Holman Beach, FL: Learning Publications.

Gray-Little, B. (1982). Marital quality and power processes among black couples. *Journal of Marriage and the Family, 44*, 633–646.

Grebe, S. C. (1986). Mediation in separation and divorce. *Journal of Counseling and Development, 64*, 397–382.

Green, G. (1964). *Sex and the College Girl.* New York: Dial.

Greenberg, E. F., and Nay, W. R. (1982). The intergenerational transmission of marital instability reconsidered. *Journal of Marriage and the Family, 44*, 335–347.

Greenblat, C. S. (1983). The salience of sexuality in the early years of marriage. *Journal of Marriage and the Family, 45*, 289–299.

Greenhaus, J. H., and Beutell, N. J. (1985). Sources of conflict between work and family roles. *Academy of Management Review, 10*, 76–88.

Grief, G. L. (1985). Children and housework in the single father family. *Family Relations, 34*, 353–357.

Grief, G. L. (1986). Mothers without custody and child support. *Family Relations, 35*, 87–93.

Grimes, D. A. (1984). Conception after tubal sterilization. *Medical Aspects of Human Sexuality, 18*, 95.

Gross, D. R., and Robinson, S. E. (1987). Ethics, violence, and counseling: Hear no evil, see no evil, speak no evil? *Journal of Counseling and Development, 65*, 340–344.

Gross, H. W. (1980). Dual-career couples who live apart: Two types. *Journal of Marriage and the Family, 42*, 567–576.

Gross, L., and Jeffries-Fox, X. (1978) What do you want to be when you grow up, little girl? In G. Tuckman, A. Danick, and J. Benet (Eds.), *Hearth and Home.* New York: Oxford University Press.

Grover, K. J., Russell, C. S., Schumm, W. R., and Paff-Bergen, L. A. (1985). Mate selection processes and marital satisfaction. *Family Relations, 34*, 383–386.

Grusec, J. E., and Kuczynski, L. (1980). Direction of effect of socialization: A comparison of the parents' versus the child's behavior as determinants of disciplinary techniques. *Developmental Psychology, 16*, 1–9.

Grusky, O., Bonacich, P., and Perjiot, M. (1984). Physical contact in the family. *Journal of Marriage and the Family, 46*, 715–723.

Grzech, E., and Trost, C. (1978). The success of a series. *Behavior Today, 8*, 6–7.

Gubrium, J. F. (1976). Being single in old age. In J. F. Gubrium (Ed.), *Time, Roles and Self in Old Age.* New York: Human Sciences Press.

Guinzburg, S. (1983). Mothers and married sons. *Psychology Today. 17*, 14.

Gulligan, C. (1982). Why should a woman be more like a man? *Psychology Today, 16*, 68ff.

Gully, K. J., Dengerink, H. A., Pepping, M., and Bergstrom, D. (1981). Research note: Sibling contribution to violent behavior. *Journal of Marriage and the Family 43*, 333–337.

Gutman, H. G. (1976). *The Black Family in Slavery and Freedom, 1750–1925.* New York: Pantheon Books.

663

Guttmacher, A. F. (1983). *Pregnancy, Birth, and Family Planning* (Revised and updated by I. H. Kaiser). New York: New American Library.

Gwartney-Gibbs, P. A. (1986). The institutionalization of premarital cohabitation: Estimates from marriage license applications, 1970 and 1980. *Journal of Marriage and the Family, 48,* 423–434.

Gwartney-Gibbs, P. A., Stockard, J., and Bohmer, S. (1987). Learning courtship aggression: The influence of parents, peers, and personal experiences. *Family Relations, 36,* 276–282.

Haas, L. (1980). Role-sharing couples: A study of egalitarian marriages. *Family Relations, 29,* 289–296.

Hagestad, G. O., and McDonald, M. (1979). *What Grandfather Knows Best.* Paper presented at the annual meeting of the Gerontological Society, Washington, DC.

Haggstrom, G. W., Kanouse, D. E., and Morrison, P. A. (1986). Accounting for the educational shortfalls of mothers. *Journal of Marriage and the Family, 48,* 175–186.

Haley, J. (1982). Restoring law and order in the family. *Psychology Today, 16,* 61–69.

Hall, D. T., and Gordon, F. E. (1973). Career choices of married women: Effects on conflict, role behavior, and satisfaction. *Journal of Applied Psychology, 58,* 42–48.

Hall, J. R., and Black, J. D. (1979). Assertiveness, aggressiveness, and attitudes toward feminism. *The Journal of Social Psychology, 107,* 57–62.

Haller, M. (1981). Marriage, women, and social stratification: A theoretical critique. *American Journal of Sociology, 86,* 766–795.

Halperin, S. L. (1981). Abused and non-abused children's perceptions of their mothers, fathers, and siblings: Implications for a comprehensive family treatment plan. *Family Relations, 30,* 89–96.

Hansen, D., and Hill, R. (1964). Families under stress. In H. T. Christensen (Ed.), *Handbook of Marriage and the Family.* Chicago: Rand McNally.

Hansen, G. L. (1987). Extradyadic relations during courtship. *The Journal of Sex Research, 23,* 382–390.

Hansen, G. L. (1981). Marital adjustment and conventionalization: A reexamination. *Journal of Marriage and the Family, 43,* 855–863.

Hansen, J. E., and Schuldt, J. W. (1984). Marital self-disclosure and marital satisfaction. *Journal of Marriage and the Family, 46,* 923–926.

Hanson, S. L., and Tuch, S. A. (1984). The determinants of marital instability: Some methodological issues. *Journal of Marriage and the Family, 46,* 631–642.

Hanson, S. M. H. (1986). Healthy single parent families. *Family Relations, 35,* 125–132.

Hanson, S. M. H., and Bozett, F. W. (1987). Fatherhood: A review and resources. *Family Relations, 36,* 333–340.

Hardy, G., Orzek, A., and Heistad, S. (1984). Learning to live with others: A program to prevent problems in living situations. *Journal of Counseling and Development, 63,* 110–112.

Haring-Hidore, M., Stock, W. A., Okun, M. A., Witler, R. A. (1985). Marital status and subjective well-being: A research synthesis. *Journal of Marriage and the Family, 47,* 947–953.

Harkins, E. B. (1978). Effects of empty nest transition on self-report of psychological and physical well-being. *Journal of Marriage and the Family, 40,* 549–556.

Harlow, H. F., and Suomi, S. J. (1970). Nature of love — Simplified. *American Psychologist 25,* 161–168.

Harlow, H. G. (1958). The nature of love. *The American Psychologist, 13,* 673–685.

Harnett, J., Mahoney, J., and Bernstein, A. (1977). The errant spouse: A study in person perception. *Perceptual and Motor Skills, 45,* 747–750.

Hartman, M., and Hartman, H. (1983). Sex-role attitudes of Mormons vs. non-Mormons in Utah. *Journal of Marriage and the Family, 45,* 897–902.

Hartman, W., and Fithian, M. (1984). *Any Man Can: Multiple Orgasmic Response in Males.* Paper presented at the Regional Conference of The American Association of Sex Education, Counselors, and Therapists, Las Vegas, Nevada.

Hartshorne, T. S., and Manaster, G. J. (1982). The relationship with grandparents: Contact, importance, role conceptions. *International Journal of Aging and Human Development, 15,* 233–245.

Hashell, D. (1979). The depiction of women in leading roles in prime-time television. *Journal of Broadcasting, 23,* 191–196.

Hatch, R. C., James, D. E., and Schumm, W. R. (1986). Spiritual intimacy and marital satisfaction. *Family Relations, 35,* 539–545.

Hatcher, R. A., Stewart, G. K., Guest, F., Schwartz, D. W., and Jones, S. A. (1980). *Contraceptive Technology, 1980–1981.* New York: Irvington.

Hatfield, E. (1982). Passionate love, companionate love, and intimacy. In M. Fisher and G. Stricker (Eds.), *Intimacy* (pp. 267–292). New York: Plenum Press.

Hawkes, G., and Taylor, M. (1975). Power structure in Mexican and Mexican-American farm labor families. *Journal of Marriage and the Family, 37,* 807–811.

Hawkins, J. L., Weisberg, C., and Ray, D. W. (1980). Spouse differences in communication style: Preference, perception, behavior. *Journal of Marriage and the Family, 42,* 585–593.

Hayes, M. (1981). *Family Ordinal Position of Status Offenders.* Unpublished monograph. University of California, Department of Sociology.

Health service issues AIDS guidelines. (1985). *Portland Press Herald,* November 15.

Heaton, T. B., Albrecht, S. L., and Martin, T. K. (1985). The timing of divorce. *Journal of Marriage and the Family, 47,* 631–639.

Heckman, N. A., Bryson, R., and Bryson, J. B. (1977). Problems of professional couples: A content analysis. *Journal of Marriage and the Family, 29,* 323–330.

Heer, D. M. (1974). The prevalence of black-white marriages in the United States, 1960 and 1970. *Journal of Marriage and the Family, 36,* 246–258.

Heilbrun, A. B. (1984). Identification with the father and peer intimacy of the daughter. *Family Relations, 33,* 597–605.

Heilbrun, A. B., and Loftus, M. P. (1986). The role of sadism and peer pressure in the sexual aggression of male college students. *The Journal of Sex Research, 22,* 320–332.

Heiman, J. (1980). Female sexual response patterns. *Archives of General Psychiatry, 37,* 1311–1316.

Henker, F. O. (1983). Parents and grownup children working through old misunderstandings and hurts. *Medical Aspects of Human Sexuality, 17,* August, 128–143.

Henker, F. O. (1984). Sudden disappearance of libido. *Medical Aspects of Human Sexuality, 18,* 167–172.

Hennessee, J. A. (1983). "Monkey see, monkey do" dating. *Psychology Today, 17,* May, 74.

Henninger, D., and Esposito, N. (1971). Indian schools. In D. Gottlieb and A. L. Heinsohn (Eds.), *America's Other Youth: Growing Up Poor.* Englewood Cliffs, NJ: Prentice-Hall.

Henshaw, S. K., and Wallisch, L. S. (1984). The medicaid cutoff and abortion services for the poor. *Family Planning Perspectives, 16,* 170–180.

Henson, C., Rubin, H. B., and Henson, D. E. (1979). Women's sexual arousal concurrently assessed by three genital measures. *Archives of Sexual Behavior, 8,* 459–479.

Henton, J., Cate, R., Koval, J. Lloyd, S., and Christopher, S. (1983). Romance and violence in dating relationships. *Journal of Family Issues, 4,* 467–482.

Hepworth, J., Ryder, R. G., and Dreyer, A. S. (1984). The effects of parental loss on the formation of intimate relationships. *Journal of Marital and Family Therapy, 10,* 73–82.

Herbst, A. L. (1979). Coitus and the fetus. *New England Journal of Medicine, 301,* 1235–1236.

Herman, J., and Hirschman, L. (1977). Father-daughter incest. *Journal of Women in Culture and Society, 2,* 735–756.

Hern, W. M. (1971). Pregnancy Really Normal? *Family Planning Perspectives,* 3.

Herrigan, J., and Herrigan, J. (1973). *Loving Free.* New York: Grosset and Dunlap.

Herzerberger, S. D., and Tennen, H. (1985). The effect of self-relevance on judgments of moderate and severe disciplinary encounters. *Journal of Marriage and the Family, 47,* 311–318.

Hetherington, E. M., Cox, M., and Cox, R. (1979). Play and social interaction in children following divorce. *Journal of Social Issues, 35,* 26.

Hetherington, E. M., Cox, M., and Cox, R. (1982). Effects of divorce on parents and children. In M. Lamb (Ed.), *Nontraditional Families: Parenting and Child Development.* Hillsdale, NJ: Lawrence Erlbaum.

Hicks, M. W., and Williams, J. W. (1981). Current challenges in educating for parenthood. *Family Relations, 30,* 579–584.

Hill, C., and Spector, M. (1974). Natality and mortality of American Indians compared with U.S. whites and non-whites. *Health Services and Mental Health Administration Reports,* 68.

Hill, E. A., and Dorfman, L. T. (1982). Reaction of housewives to the retirement of their husbands. *Family Relations, 31,* 195–200.

Hill, R. B. (1971). *The Strengths of Black Families.* New York: Emerson Hall.

Hill, W., and Scanzoni, J. (1982). An approach for assessing marital decision making processes. *Journal of Marriage and the Family, 44,* 927–941.

Hiller, D. V., and Philliber, W. W. (1978). The derivation of status benefits from occupational attainments of working wives. *Journal of Marriage and the Family, 40,* 63–69.

Hiller, D. V., and Philliber, W. W. (1982). Predicting marital and career success among dual-career couples. *Journal of Marriage and the Family, 44,* 53–62.

Hiltz, S. R. (1978). Widowhood: A roleless role. *Marriage and Family Review, 1,* 1–10.

Hirsch, B. (1980). The superiority of mother and daughter, father and son custody. *Psychology Today, 14,* 28, 29.

Hite, S. (1981). *The Hite Report: A Nationwide Study of Female Sexuality.* New York: Dell.

Hite, S. (1982). *The Hite Report on Male Sexuality.* New York: Ballantine.

Hobbs, D. F., and Wimbish, J. M. (1977). Transition to parenthood by black couples. *Journal of Marriage and the Family, 39,* 677–689.

Hock, E., Christman, K., and Hock, M. (1980). Career-related decisions of mothers of infants. *Family Relations, 29,* 325–330.

Hodson, D., and Skeen, P. (1987). Child sexual abuse: A review of research and theory with implications for family life educators. *Family Relations, 36,* 215–221.

Hofferth, S. L. (1985). Updating children's life course. *Journal of Marriage and the Family, 47,* 93–115.

Hofferth, S. L., and Phillips, D. A. (1987). Child care in the United States, 1970 to 1975. *Journal of Marriage and the Family, 49,* 559–571.

Hoffman, E. (1979–1980). Young adults' relations with their grandparents: An exploratory study. *International Journal of Aging and Human Development, 10,* 299–310.

Hoffman, S. R., and Levant, R. F. (1985). A comparison of childfree and child-anticipated married couples. *Family Relations, 34,* 197–203.

Hoge, D. R., Petrillo, G. H., and Smith, E. I. (1982). Transmission of religious and social values from parents to teenage children. *Journal of Marriage and the Family, 44,* 569–580.

Holahan, C. D. (1983). The relationship between information search in the childbearing decision and life satisfaction for parents and nonparents. *Family Relations, 32,* 527–535.

Hollinghead, A. B. (1949). *Elmtown's Youth.* New York: John Wiley.

Holmstrom, L. L. (1973). *The Two-career Family.* Cambridge, MA: Schenkman.

Honeycutt, J. M. (1986). A model of marital functioning based on an attraction paradigm and social-penetration dimension. *Journal of Marriage and the Family, 48,* 651–667.

Honeycutt, J. M., Wilson, C., and Parker, C. (1982). Effects of sex and degrees of happiness as perceived styles of communicating in and out of the marital relationship. *Journal of Marriage and the Family, 44,* 395–406.

Hooker, K., and Ventis, D. G. (1984). Work ethic, daily activities, and retirement satisfaction. *Journal of Gerontology, 39,* 478–484.

Hopkins, J., Marcues, M., and Campbell, S. B. (1984). Postpartum depression: A critical review. *Psychological Bulletin, 95,* 498–515.

Hopkins, N. M., and Mullis, A. K. (1985). Family perceptions of television viewing habits. *Family Relations, 34,* 177–181.

Horn, J. C. (1981). In cities, fast friends come slowly. *Psychology Today, 15,* 32, 100.

Hornung, C. A., McCullough, B. C., and Sugimoto, T. (1981). Status relationships in marriage: Risk factors in spouse abuse. *Journal of Marriage and the Family, 43,* 675–692.

Horowitz, R. (1983). *Honor and the American Dream.* New Brunswick, NJ: Rutgers University Press.

Horwitz, A. V. (1982). Sex-role expectations, power, and psychological distress. *Sex Roles, 8,* 607–624.

Houseknecht, S. K., and Macke, A. S. (1981). Combining marriage and career: The marital adjustment of professional women. *Journal of Marriage and the Family, 43,* 651–661.

Houser, B. B., and Berkman, S. L. (1984). Aging parent/mature child relationships. *Journal of Marriage and the Family, 46,* 245–299.

Hoyenga, K., and Hoyenga, K. (1979). *The Question of Sex Differences.* Boston: Little, Brown

Hoyt, D. R., Kaiser, M. A., Peters, G. R., and Babchuk, N. (1980). Life satisfaction and activity theory: A multi-dimensional approach. *Journal of Gerontology, 35,* 935–941.

Hoyt, M. F. (1986). Neuroticism and mate selection. *Medical Aspects of Human Sexuality, 20,* 11.

Huang, C., and Grachow, F. (n.d.). *The Dilemma of Health Services in Chinatown.* New York: Department of Health.

Huber, C. H. (1983). Feelings of loss in response to divorce: Assessment and intervention. *The Personnel and Guidance Journal, 61,* 357–361.

Huber, J., and Spitze, G. (1983). *Sex Stratification: Children, Housework, and Jobs.* New York: Academic Press.

Huberman, R. (1987). Marital fights about money may indicate other problems. *Medical Aspects of Human Sexuality, 21,* 47.

Hughes, H. M. (1982). Brief interventions with children in a battered women's shelter: A model preventive program. *Family Relations, 31,* 495–502.

Hunt, M. M. (1974). *Sexual Behavior in the 1970s.* Chicago: Playboy Press.

Hunt, M. M. (1973). Sexual Behavior in the 1970s. *Playboy,* October, p. 204.

Hurst, C. E., and Guldin, D. A. (1981). The effects of intra-individuals and inter-spouse status inconsistency on life satisfaction among older persons. *Journal of Gerontology, 36,* 112–121.

Huser, W. R., and Grant, C. W. (1978). A study of husbands and wives from dual-career and traditional-career families. *Psychology of Women Quarterly, 3,* 78–79.

Huston, T. L. (1983). Power. In H. H. Kelley, E. Berscheid, A. Christensen, and others (Eds.), *Close Relationships.* New York: Freeman.

Hyatt, I. R. (1977). *Before You Marry Again.* New York: Random House.

Ibrahim, F. A., and Herr, E. L. (1987). Battered women: A developmental life-career counseling perspective. *Journal of Counseling and Development, 65,* 244–248.

Ihinger-Tallman, M., and Pasley, K. (1986). Remarriage and integration within the community. *Journal of Marriage and Family Living, 48,* 395–405.

Increasing rates of ectopic pregnancies. (1984). *Medical Aspects of Human Sexuality, 18,* 14.

Ishii-Kuntz, M., and Lee, G. R. (1987). Status of the elderly: An extension of the theory. *Journal of Marriage and the Family, 49,* 413–420.

Jaco, D. E., and Shepard, J. M. (1975). Demographic homogeneity and spousal consensus: A methodological perspective. *Journal of Marriage and the Family, 37,* 161–169.

Jacobs, L., Walster, E., and Berscheid, E. (1971). Self-esteem and attraction. *Journal of Personality and Social Psychology, 17,* 84–91.

James, B. E. (1983). When wives take sexual initiative. *Medical Aspects of Human Sexuality, 17,* 250.

Jaques, E. (1965). Death and the midlife crisis. *International Journal of Psychoanalysis, 46,* 502–514.

Jedlicka, A. (1980). Formal mate selection networks in the United States. *Family Relations, 29,* 199–203.

Jedlicka, D. (1984). Indirect parental influences on mate choice: A test of the psychoanalytic theory. *Journal of Marriage and the Family, 46,* 65–70.

Jeffress, J. E. (1982). Reasons women have affairs with married men. *Medical Aspects of Human Sexuality, 16,* 164.

Jellinger, M. S., Slovik, L. S. (1981). Current concepts in psychiatry: Divorce — impact on children. *New England Journal of Medicine, 305,* 552.

Jencks, C. (1982). Divorced mothers, unite! *Psychology Today, 16,* 73–75.

Jergensen, S. R. (1986). *Marriage and the Family: Development and Change.* New York: Macmillan.

Joanning, H., Brewster, J., and Koval, J. (1984). The communication rapid assessment scale: Development of behavioral index of communication quality. *Journal of Marital and Family Therapy, 10,* 409–417.

Joe, T., and Yu, P. (1984). *The "Flip-side" of Black Families Headed by Women: The Economic Status of Black Men.* Washington, DC: The Center for the Study of Social Policy.

Johnson, B. H. (1986). Single mothers following separation and divorce: Making it on your own. *Family Relations, 35,* 189–197.

Johnson, C. L. (1975). Authority and power in Japanese-American marriage. In R. E. Cromwell and D. H. Olson (Eds.), *Power in Families.* New York: Wiley.

Johnson, J. (1984). Contraception — The morning after. *Family Planning Perspectives, 16,* 267–270.

Johnson, J. H. (1982). Tubal sterilization and hysterectomy. *Family Planning Perspectives, 14,* 28–30.

Johnson, J. H. (1983). Vasectomy — An international appraisal. *Family Planning Perspectives, 15,* 45–48.

Johnson, M. P., and Milardo, R. M. (1984). Network interference in pair relationships: A social psychological recasting of Slater's theory of social regression. *Journal of Marriage and the Family, 46,* 893–899.

Johnson, P. (1976). Women and power: Toward a theory of effectiveness. *Journal of Social Issues, 32,* 99–110.

Johnson, V. E. (1973). *I'll Quit Tomorrow.* New York: Harper and Row.

Johnston, M. W., and Eklund, S. J. (1984). Life-adjustment of the never-married: A review with implications for counseling. *Journal of Counseling and Development, 63,* 230–236.

Jones, A. P., and Butler, M. C. (1980). A role transition approach to the stresses of organizationally induced family role disruption. *Journal of Marriage and the Family, 42,* 367–376.

Jones, W. H., Freeman, J. E., and Goswick, R. A. (1981). The persistence of loneliness: Self and other determinants. *Journal of Personality, 49,* 27–48.

Jones, W. H., Hobbs, S. A., and Hackenbury, D. (1982). Loneliness and social skills deficits. *Journal of Personality and Social Psychology, 42,* 682–689.

Jones, W. H., Sansome, C., and Helm, B. (1983). Loneliness and interpersonal judgments. *Personality and Social Psychology 9,* 437–442.

Jones, W. M., and Jones, R. A. (1980). *Two Careers — One Marriage.* New York: AMACOM.

Jorgensen, S. R. (1979). Socioeconomic rewards and perceived marital quality: A re-examination. *Journal of Marriage and the Family, 41,* 825–835.

Jorgensen, S. R. (1986). *Marriage and the Family.* New York: Macmillan.

Jorgensen, S. R., and Gaudy, J. C. (1980). Self-disclosure and satisfaction in marriage: The relationship examined. *Family Relations, 29,* 281–287.

Jorgensen, S. R., and Johnson, A. C. (1980). Correlates of divorce liberality. *Journal of Marriage and the Family, 42,* 617–626.

Joyce, E. (1984). A time of grieving. *Psychology Today, 18,* 42–46.

Kacerguis, M. A., and Adams, G. R. (1979). Implications of sex-typed child rearing practices, toys, and mass media in restricting occupational choices of women. *Family Coordinator, 28,* 361–375.

Kafka, D., and Gold, R. B. (1983). Food and drug administration approves vaginal sponge. *Family Planning Perspectives, 15,* 146–148.

Kagan, N., and Schneider, J. (1987). Toward the measurement of affective sensitivity. *Journal of Counseling and Development, 65,* 459–464.

Kahn, S. S. (1983). *The Kahn Report on Sexual Preferences: What the Opposite Sex Likes and Dislikes — and Why.* New York: St. Martin's Press.

Kalisch, P., and Kalisch, B. (1984). Sex-role stereotyping of nurses and physicians on prime-time television: A dichotomy of occupational portrayals. *Sex Roles, 10,* 533–553.

Kallen, D. J., and Stephenson, J. J. (1982). Talking about sex revisited. *Journal of Youth and Adolescence, 11,* 11–23.

Kalmuss, D. (1984). The intergenerational transmission of marital aggression. *Journal of Marriage and the Family, 46,* 11–19.

Kalmuss, D. S., and Straus, M. A. (1982). Wife's marital dependency and wife abuse. *Journal of Marriage and the Family, 44,* 277–286.

Kalmuss, D., and Seltzer, J. A. (1986). Continuity of marital behavior in remarriage: The case of spouse abuse. *Journal of Marriage and the Family, 48,* 113–120.

Kalter, N. (1983). How children perceive divorce. *Medical Aspects of Human Sexuality, 17,* 18–45.

Kando, T. (1973). *Sex Change: The Achievement of Gender Identity Among Feminized Transsexuals.* Springfield, IL: Charles C. Thomas.

Kanin, E. J., and Parcell, S. R. (1977). Sexual aggression: A second look at the offended female. *Archives of Sexual Behavior, 6,* 67–76.

Kanoy, K., and Miller, B. C. (1980). Children' s impact on the parental decision to divorce. *Family Relations, 29,* 309–315.

Kaplan, H. S. (1974). *The New Sex Therapy.* New York: Brunner/Mazel.

Kaplan, H. S. (1979). *Disorders of Sexual Desire.* New York: Simon and Schuster.

Kargman, M. W. (1973). The revolution in divorce law. *The Family Coordinator, 22,* 245–248.

Kargman, M. W. (1983). Stepchild support obligations of stepparents. *Family Relations, 32,* 231–238.

Kastenbaum, R., and Aisenberg, R. (1976). *The Psychology of Death.* New York: Springer.

Katch, V., Campaigne, B., Freedson, F., Sady, S., Katch, F., and Behnke, A. (1980). Contribution of breast volume and weight to body fat distribution in females. *American Journal of Physical Anthropology, 53,* 93–100.

Katz, B. J. (1972). Cooling motherhood. *National Observer,* December 20.

Katz, M. H., and Piotrkowski, C. S. (1983). Correlates of family role strain among employed black women. *Family Relations, 32,* 331–339.

Keating, N. C., and Cole, P. (1980). What do I do with him 24 hours a day? Change in the housewife role after retirement. *The Gerontologist, 20,* 84–89.

Keith, D. V., and Whitaker, C. A. (1982). Helping patients deal with marital conflicts caused by money. *Medical Aspects of Human Sexuality, 16,* 145–159.

Keith, P. M. (1986). Isolation of the unmarried in later life. *Family Relations, 35,* 389–395.

Keith, P. M., and Schafer, R. B. (1980). Role strain and depression in two-job families. *Family Relations, 29,* 483–488.

Keith, P. M., and Schafer, R. B. (1985). Role behavior, relative deprivation, and depression among women in one- and two-job families. *Family Relations, 34,* 227–233.

Kellam, S. G., Adams, R. G., Brown, C. H., and Ensminger, M. E. (1982). The long-term evaluation of the family structure of teenage and older mothers. *Journal of Marriage and the Family, 44,* 539–554.

Keller, J. E. (1971). Drinking problem? Philadelphia: Fortress Press.

Kelley, D. (1985). Sex, guilt, and authoritarianism: Differences in responses to explicit heterosexual and masturbatory slides. *Journal of Sex Research, 21,* 68–85.

Kellogg, M. A. (1982). Could it be love at first cassette? *T.V. Guide,* July 2, 33–36.

Kelly, R. F., and Voydanoff, P. (1985). Work/family role strain among employed parents. *Family Relations, 34,* 367–374.

Kemper, T. D., and Bologh, R. W. (1980). The ideal love object: Structural and family sources. *Journal of Youth and Adolescence, 9,* February, 33–48.

Kenkel, W. F. (1985). The desire for voluntary childlessness among low-income youth. *Journal of Marriage and the Family, 47,* 509–512.

Kenkel, W. F., and Gage, B. A. (1983). The restricted and gender-typed occupational aspirations of young women: Can they be modified? *Family Relations, 32,* 129–138.

Kennedy, E. C. (1972). *The New Sexuality: Myths, Fables, and Hang-ups.* Garden City, NY: Doubleday.

Kennedy, L. W., and Stokes, D. W. (1982). Extended family support and the high cost of housing. *Journal of Marriage and the Family, 44,* 311–318.

Kerckhoff, A., and Davis, K. (1962). Value consensus and need complementarity in mate selection. *American Social Review, 27,* 295–303.

Keshet, J. K. (1980). From separation to stepfamily: A subsystem analysis. *Journal of Family Issues, 1,* 517–532.

Keshna, R. (1980). Relevancy of tribal interests and tribal diversity in determining the educational needs of American Indians. In *Conference on the Education and Occupational Needs of American Indian Work.* Washington, DC: U.S. Department of Education, National Institute of Education.

Kets deVries, M. F. R. (1978). The midcareer conundrum. *Organizational Dynamics, 7,* 45–62.

Keye, W. R. (1983). Update: Premenstrual syndrome. *Endocrine and Fertility Forum, 6,* 1–3.

Kieren, D., Henton, J., and Marotz, R. (1975). *Hers and His: A Problem Solving Approach to Marriage.* Hinsdale, IL: Dryden.

Kilpatrick, A. C. (1982). Job change in dual-career families: Danger or opportunity. *Family Relations, 31,* 363–368.

Kilpatrick, A. C. (1986). Some correlates of women's childhood sexual experiences: A retrospective study. *The Journal of Sex Research, 22,* 221–242.

Kilpatrick, A. C. (1987) Childhood sexual experiences: Problems and issues in studying long-range effects. *The Journal of Sex Research, 23,* 173–196.

Kilty, K. M., and Behling, J. H. (1985). Predicting the retirement intentions and attitudes of professional workers. *Journal of Gerontology, 40,* 219–227.

Kilty, K. M., and Behling, J. H. (1986). Retirement financial planning among professional workers. *The Gerontologist, 26,* 525–530.

Kimlicka, T., Cross, H., and Tarnai, J. (1983). A comparison of androgynous, feminine, masculine, and undifferentiated women on self-esteem body satisfaction, and sexual satisfaction. *Psychology of Women Quarterly, 1,* 291–294.

Kinsey, A. C., Pomeroy, W., and Martin, C. (1948). *Sexual Behavior in the Human Male.* Philadelphia: Saunders.

Kinsey, A. C., Pomeroy, W., Martin, C., and Gebhard, P. (1953). *Sexual Behavior in the Human Female.* Philadelphia: Saunders.

Kinston, W., Loader, P., and Miller, L. (1987). Quantifying the clinical assessment of family health. *Journal of Marriage and Family Therapy, 13,* 49–67.

Kipnis, D. (1984). The view from the top. *Psychology Today, 18,* 30–36.

Kirschner, B. F., and Walum, L. R. (1978). Two-location families: Married singles. *Alternative Lifestyles, 1,* 513–525.

Kitano, H. H., Yeung, W., Chai, L., and Hatanaka, H. (1984). Asian-American interracial marriage. *Journal of Marriage and the Family, 46,* 179–190.

Kitson, G. C. (1982). Attachment of the spouse in divorce: A scale and its application. *Journal of Marriage and the Family, 44,* 379–393.

Kitson, G. C., and Sussman, M. B. (1982). Marital complaints, demographic characteristics, and symptoms of marital stress in divorce. *Journal of Marriage and the Family, 44,* 87–101.

Kitson, G. C., and Sussman, M. B. (1982). Marital complaints, demographic characteristics, symptoms of mental distress in divorce. *Journal of Marriage and the Family, 44,* 87–101.

Kivett, V. R. (1978). Loneliness and the rural widow. *The Family Coordinator, 27,* 389–394.

Kivett, V. R. (1985). Grandfathers and grandchildren: Patterns of association, helping, and psychological closeness. *Family Relations, 34,* 565–571.

Kivett, V. R., and Learner, R. M. (1980). Perspectives on the childless rural elderly: A comparative analysis. *The Gerontologist, 20,* 708–716.

Kivnick, H. Q. (1982). Grandparenthood: An overview of meaning and mental health. *The Gerontologist, 22,* 59–66.

Klagsbrun, F. (1985). *Married People Staying Together in the Age of Divorce.* New York: Bantam.

Klaus, H. (1984). Natural family planning. *Medical Aspects of Human Sexuality, 18,* 59–70.

Klaus, M., and Kennel, J. (1982). *Parent-infant Bonding* (2nd ed.). St. Louis: Mosby.

Klein, M. M., and Shulman, S. (1981). Adolescent masculinity-femininity in relation to parental models of masculinity-femininity and marital adjustment. *Adolescence, 16,* 45–48.

Klimek, D. (1979). *Beneath Mate Selection and Marriage: The Unconscious Motives in Human Pairing.* New York: Van Nostrand Reinhold.

Knaub, P. K. (1986). Growing up in a dual-career family: The children's perception. *Family Relations, 35,* 431–437.

Knoepfler, P. T. (1983). Desire cycle in men. *Medical Aspects of Human Sexuality, 17,* 261.

Knox, D. (1975). *Marriage: Who? When? Why?* Englewood Cliffs, NJ: Prentice-Hall.

Knox, D. (1980). Trends in marriage and the family — The 1980s. *Family Relations, 29,* 145–150.

Knox, D. (1985). *Choices in Relationships: An Introduction to Marriage and the Family.* New York: West.

Knox, E., and Wilson, K. (1981). Dating behavior of university students. *Family Relations, 30,* 255–258.

Knox, E., and Wilson, K. (1983). Dating problems of university students. *College Student Journal, 17,* 225–228.

Koch, M. P. (1982). *The Visitation Experience of Divorced, Noncustodial Fathers.* Unpublished doctoral dissertation, University of Kentucky.

Komarovsky, M. (1964). *Blue Collar Marriage.* New York: Random House.

Komarovsky, M. (1967). *Blue Collar Marriage.* New York: Vintage Books.

Kompara, D. R. (1980). Difficulties in the socialization process of stepparenting. *Family Relations, 29,* 69–73.

Koop, C. E. (1986). *Surgeon General's Report on Acquired Immune Deficiency Syndrome.* Washington, DC: U.S. Department of Health and Human Services.

Korman, S. (1983a). Nontraditional dating behavior: Date-initiation and date expense-sharing among feminists and nonfeminists. *Family Relations, 32,* 575–581.

Korman, S. K. (1983b). The feminist: Familial influences on adherence to ideology and commitment to a self-perception. *Family Relations, 32,* 431–439.

Korman, S., and Leslie, G. (1982). The relationship between feminist ideology and date expense-sharing to perceptions of sexual aggression in dating. *The Journal of Sex Research, 18,* 114–129.

Kornhaber, A., and Woodward, K. L. (1981). *Grandparents/Grandchildren: The Vital Connection.* Garden City, NY: Anchor Press/Doubleday.

Kovar, M. G. (1986). Aging in the eighties: Age 65 years and over and living alone, contacts with family, friends, and neighbors. *Advance Data from Vital and Health Statistics,* no. 116 (DHHS Publication No [PHS] 86–1250). Washington, DC: National Center for Health Statistics.

Kozma, A., and Stones, M. J. (1983). Prediction of happiness. *Journal of Gerontology, 38,* 626–628.

Krane, R. J., and Siroky, M. B. (1981). Neurophysiology of erection. *Urologic Clinics of North America, 8,* 91–102.

Krantzler, M. (1974). *Creative Divorce.* New York: New American Library.

Krein, S. F. (1986). Growing up in a single parent family: The effect on education and earning of young men. *Family Relations, 35,* 161–168

Krupenski, J., Marshall, E., and Yule, V. (1970). Patterns of marital problems in marriage guidance clinics. *Journal of Marriage and the Family, 32,* 138–143.

Kubler-Ross, E. (1969). *On Death and Dying.* New York: Macmillan.

Kubler-Ross, E. (1974). *Questions and Answers on Death and Dying.* New York: Macmillan.

Labov, T., and Jacobs, J. A. (1986). Intermarriage in Hawaii, 1950–1983. *Journal of Marriage and the Family, 48,* 79–88.

Ladewig, B. H., and McGee, G. W. (1986). Occupational commitment, a supportive family environment, and marital adjustment: Development and estimation of a model. *Journal of Marriage and the Family, 48,* 821–829.

LaManna, M. A., and Riedman, A. (1985). *Marriages and Families: Making Choices Throughout the Life Cycle* (2nd ed.). Belmont, CA: Wadsworth.

Lamaze, F. (1970). *Painless childbirth.* Chicago: Regency.

Landers, A. (1985). Is affection more important than sex? *Family Circle,* June 11.

Landis, J. T., and Landis, M. G. (1977). *Building a Successful Marriage* (7th ed.). Englewood Cliffs, NJ: Prentice-Hall.

Laner, M. R., and Thompson, J. (1982). Abuse and aggression in courting couples. *Deviant Behavior, 3,* 229–244.

Langley, R., and Levy, R. C. (1977). *Wife Beating: The Silent Crisis.* New York: Dutton.

Lansky, M. R. (1983). Proposal of marriage on first date. *Medical Aspects of Human Sexuality, 17,* 9.

LaRossa, R. (1979). Sex during pregnancy: A symbolic interactionist analysis. *The Journal of Sex Research, 15,* 119–128.

Larson, J. H. (1984). The effect of husband's unemployment on marital and family relations in blue-collar families. *Family Relations, 33,* 503–511.

Larzelere, R. E., and Huston, T. L. (1980). The dyadic trust scale: Toward understanding interperson trust in close relationships. *Journal of Marriage and the Family, 42,* 595–603.

Lasswell, M. E. (1982). What should a parent tell a child who asks advice about marrying a certain person? *Medical Aspects of Human Sexuality, 16,* 113.

Lasswell, M., and Lasswell, T. (1987). *Marriage and the Family* (2nd ed.). Belmont, CA: Wadsworth.

Lasswell, M., and Lobsenz, N. (1980). *Styles of Loving.* Garden City, NY: Doubleday.

Lauer, J., and Lauer, R. (1985). Marriage made to last. *Pyschology Today, 19,* 22–26.

Laufer, R. S., and Gallops, M. S. (1985). Life course effects of Vietnam combat and abusive violence: Marital patterns. *Journal of Marriage and the Family, 47,* 839–853.

Lavee, Y., McCubbin, H. I., and Patterson, J. M. (1985). The double ABCX model of family stress and adaptation: An empirical test by analysis of structural equations with latent variables. *Journal of Marriage and the Family, 47,* 811–825.

Layde, P. M., Ory, H. W., and Schlesselman, J. J. (1982). The risk of myocardial infarction in former users of oral contraceptives. *Family Planning Perspectives, 14,* 78–80.

Lazrus, A. A. (1981). Divorce counseling or marriage therapy? A therapeutic option. *Journal of Marriage and the Family, 7,* 15–22.

Leboyer, F. (1975). *Birth Without Violence.* New York: Knopf.

Lee, G. R., and Ellithorpe, E. (1982). Intergenerational exchange and subjective well-being among the elderly. *Journal of Marriage and the Family, 44,* 217–224.

Lee, G. R., and Petersen, L. R. (1983). Conjugal power and spousal resources in patriarchal cultures. *Journal of Comparative Family Studies, 14,* 23–38.

Lee, G. R., and Stone, L. H. (1980). Male-selection systems and criteria: Variation according to family structure. *Journal of Marriage and the Family, 42,* 319–326.

Lee, J. (1973). *Colours of Love.* Toronto: New Press.

Lee, J. (1974). Styles of loving. *Psychology Today, 8,* 44–51.

Lee, J. (1976). *The Colors of Love.* Englewood Cliffs, NJ: Prentice-Hall.

Leifer, M. (1980). *Psychological Effects of Motherhood: Study of First Pregnancy.* New York: Praeger.

Leigh, G. K. (1982). Kinship interaction over the family life span. *Journal of Marriage and the Family, 44,* 197–208.

Leigh, G. K., Holman, T. B., and Burr, W. R. (1984) . An empirical test of sequence in Murstein's SVR theory of mate selection. *Family Relations, 33,* 225–231.

LeMasters, E. E. (1957). *Modern Courtship and Marriage.* New York: Macmillan.

Lentz, S., and Zeiss, A. (1984). Fantasy and sexual arousal in college women: An empirical investigation. *Imagination, Cognition, and Personality, 3,* 185–202.

Leon, J. (1985). A recursive model of economic well-being in retirement. *Journal of Gerontology, 40,* 494–505.

Leslie, G. R., and Korman, S. K. (1985). *The Family in Social Context* (6th ed.). New York: Oxford University Press.

Leslie, L. A., and Grady, K. (1985). Changes in mothers' social networks and social support following divorce. *Journal of Marriage and the Family, 47,* 663–673.

Leslie, L. A., Huston, T. L., and Johnson, M. P. (1986). Parental reactions to dating relationships: Do they make a difference? *Journal of Marriage and the Family, 48,* 57–66.

Lesser, E. K., and Comet, J. J. (1987). Help and hindrance: Parents of divorcing children. *Journal of Marital and Family Therapy, 2,* 197–202.

Lester, G. (1979). Reflection on married life. *Marriage and Family Living, 61,* 6–9.

Levant, R. F., Slattery, S. C., and Loiselle, J. E. (1987). Fathers' involvement in housework and child care with school-age daughters. *Family Relations, 36,* 152–157.

Levin, R. J., and Levin, A. (1975a). Sexual pleasure: The surprising preferences of 100,000 women. *Redbook,* September, 51–58.

Levin, R. J., and Levin, A. (1975b). The Redbook report on premarital and extramarital sex. *Redbook,* October, 38.

Levinger, G. (1965). Marital cohesiveness and dissolution: An integrative review. *Journal of Marriage and the Family, 27,* 19–28.

Levinger, G. (1979). A social psychological perspective on marital dissolution. In G. Levinger and O. C. Moles (Eds.). *Divorce and Separation* (pp. 37-60). New York: Basic Books.

Levinson, D. J. (1978). *The Seasons of a Man's Life.* New York: Ballantine.

Lewis, R. A. (1972). A developmental framework for the analysis of premarital dyadic formation. *Family Process, 11,* 17–48.

Lewis, R. A. (1973). A longitudinal test of a developmental framework for premarital dyadic formation. *Journal of Marriage and the Family, 35,* 16–25.

Lewis, R. A., Freneau, P. J., and Robert, C. L. (1979). Fathers and the postparental transition. *The Family Coordinator, 28,* 514–520.

Liang, J. (1982). Sex differences in life satisfaction among the elderly. *Journal of Gerontology, 37,* 100–108.

Liebowitz, M. R. (1983). *The Chemistry of Love.* Boston: Little, Brown.

Lincoln, R. (1984). The pill, breast, and cervical cancer, and the role of progestogens in arterial disease. *Family Planning Perspectives, 16,* 55–63.

Lipkin, M. J., and Lamb, G. S. (1982). The couvade syndrome: An epidemiologic study. *Annals of Internal Medicine, 96,* 509–511.

Lips, H. M. (1988). *Sex and Gender: An Introduction.* Mountain View, CA: Mayfield.

Littlejohn, S. (1983). *Theories of Human Communication.* Columbus, OH: Charles Merrill.

Lloyd, S. A., and Cote, R. M. (1984). Predicting premarital relationship stability: A methodological refinement. *Journal of Marriage and the Family, 46,* 71–76.

Lockhart, L. L. (1987). A reexamination of the effects of race and social class on the incidence of marital violence: A search for reliable differences. *Journal of Marriage and the Family, 49,* 603–610.

Locksley, A. (1980). On the effects of wives' employment on marital adjustment and companionship. *Journal of Marriage and the Family, 42,* 337–346.

Locksley, A. (1982). Social class and marital attitudes and behavior. *Journal of Marriage and the Family, 44,* 427–440.

Long, T. J., and Long, L. (1983). *The Handbook for Latchkey Children and Their Parents.* New York: Arbor House.

Long, T., and Long, L. (1981). *Latchkey Children: The Child's View of Self-care.* ERIC Documents. Ed. 211229.

Longino, C. F., and Lipman, A. (1981). Married and spouseless men and women in planned retirement communities: Support network differentials. *Journal of Marriage and the Family, 43,* 169–177.

Lopata, H. Z. (1971). *Occupation: Housewife.* London: Oxford University Press.

Lopata, H. Z. (1981). Widowhood and husband sanctification. *Journal of Marriage and the Family, 43,* 439–450.

LoPiccolo, J. (1985). *Advances in Diagnosis and Treatment of Sexual Dysfunction.* Paper presented at the 28th annual meeting of the Society for the Scientific Study of Sex, San Diego, September 22.

Lott, J. (1976). *Asian-American Reference Directory.* Washington, DC: U.S. Department of HEW, Office for Asian American Affairs.

Lovern, J. D., and Zohn, J. (1982). Utilization and indirect suggestion in multiple-family group therapy with alcoholics. *Journal of Marital and Family Therapy, 8,* 325–333.

Lowe, G. D., and Witt, D. D. (1984). Early marriage as a career contingency: The prediction of educational attainment. *Journal of Marriage and the Family, 46,* 689–698.

Lowen, A. (1972). The spiral of growth: Love, sex and pleasure. In H. A. Otto (Ed.), *Love Today* (pp. 17–26). New York: Association Press.

Lowenthal, M. F., Thurnher, M., Chiriboga, D., and Associates (1975). *Four Stages of Life: A Comparative Study of Women and Men Facing Transition.* San Francisco: Jossey-Bass.

Lowery, C. R. (1985). Child custody in divorce: Parents' decisions and perceptions. *Family Relations, 34,* 241–249.

Lowery, C. R., and Settle, S. A. (1985). Effects of divorce on children: Differential impact of custody and visitation patterns. *Family Relations, 34,* 455–463.

Lueptow, L. B. (1980). Social structure, social change, and parental influences in adolescent sex-role socialization: 1964–1975. *Journal of Marriage and the Family 42*, 93–100.

Lupri, E., and Frideres, J. (1981). The quality of marriage and the passage of time: Marital satisfaction over the family life cycle. *Canadian Journal of Sociology, 6*, 283–305.

Lutwak, N. (1985). Fear of intimacy among college women. *Adolescence, 77*, 15–20.

Lutz, P. (1983). The stepfamily: An adolescent perspective. *Family Relations, 32*, 367–375.

Lydon, S. (1974). Understanding orgasm. In J. H. Skolnick (Ed.), *Intimacy, Family, and Society* (pp. 157–162). Boston: Little, Brown.

Lyman, S. M. (1977). *The Asian in North America*. Santa Barbara, CA: ABC-Clio Press.

Mace, D., and Mace, V. (1980). Enriching marriages: The foundation stone of family strength. In N. Stinnett et al. (Eds.), *Family Strengths: Positive Models for Family Life*. Lincoln: University of Nebraska Press.

Mace, D. (1982). *Close Companions: The Marriage Enrichment Handbook*. New York: Continuum.

Mace, D. R. (1972a). *Abortion: The Agonizing Decision*. Nashville: Abingdon.

Mace, D. R. (1972b). Contemporary areas in marriage. In R. E. Albrecht and E. W. Bock (Eds.), *Encounter, Love, Marriage and Family* (pp. 2–12). Boston: Holbrook.

Mace, D. R. (1982). Current thinking on marriage and money. *Medical Aspects of Human Sexuality, 16*, 109–118.

Mace, D., and Mace, V. (1960). *Marriage East and West*. Garden City, NY: Doubleday.

Mace, D., and Mace, V. (1974). *We Can Have Better Marriages If We Really Want Them*. Nashville: Abingdon.

Macfarlane, A. (1977). *The Psychology of Childbirth*. Cambridge, MA: Harvard University Press.

Macklin, E. D. (1978). Nonmarital heterosexual cohabitation. *Marriage and Family Review, 1*, 2–10.

Macklin, E. D. (1980). Nontraditional family forms: A decade of research. *Journal of Marriage and the Family, 42*, 905–920.

Macklin, E. D. (1983). Nonmarital heterosexual cohabitation: An overview. In E. D. Macklin and R. H. Rubin (Eds.), *Contemporary Families and Alternate Lifestyles: Handbook on Research and Theory* (pp. 49–73). Beverly Hills: Sage.

Madden, M. E., and Janoff-Bulman, R. (1981). Blame, control, and marital satisfaction: Wives' attributions for conflict in marriage. *Journal of Marriage and the Family, 43*, 663–674.

Makepeace, J. (1981). Courtship violence among college students. *Family Relations, 30*, 97–102.

Makepeace, J. M. (1986). Gender differences in courtship violence victimization. *Family Relations, 35*, 383–388.

Makepeace, J. M. (1987). Social factor and victim-offender differences in courtship violence. *Family Relations, 36*, 87–91.

Mancini, J. A., and Orthner, D. K. (1978). Recreational sexuality preferences among middle-class husbands and wives. *Journal of Sex Research, 14*, 96–105.

Maneker, J. S., and Ranking, R. P. (1985). Education, age at marriage, and marital duration: Is there a relationship? *Journal of Marriage and the Family, 47*, 675–683.

Marcus, I. M. (1983). The need for flexibility in marriage. *Medical Aspects of Human Sexuality, 17*, 120–131.

Margolin, G. (1987). The multiple forms of aggressiveness between marital partners: How do we identify them? *Journal of Marital and Family Therapy, 13*, 77–84.

Margolin, G., Talovic, S., Fernandez, V., and Onorato, R. (1983). Sex role considerations and behavior marital therapy: Equal does not mean identical. *Journal of Marital and Family Therapy, 9*, 131–145.

Margolis, M. (1984). *Mothers and Such: Views of American Women and Why They Changed*. Berkeley: University of California Press.

Marini, M. M. (1978). The transition to adulthood: Sex differences in educational attainment and age in marriage. *American Sociological Review, 43*, 483–507.

Marini, M. M. (1981). Effects of the timing of marriage and first birth on fertility. *Journal of Marriage and the Family, 43*, 27–46.

Marion, M. (1982). Primary prevention of child abuse: The role of the family life educator. *Family Relations, 31*, 575–582.

Markides, K. S., and Vernon, S. W. (1984). Aging: sex-role orientation, and adjustment: A three-generation study of Mexican Americans. *Journal of Gerontology, 39*, 586–591.

Markides, K. S., Hoppe, S. V., Martin, H. W., and Timbers, D. M. (1983). Sample representativeness in a three-generation study of Mexican Americans. *Journal of Marriage and the Family, 45*, 911–916.

Markowski, E. M., and Johnston, M. J. (1980). Behavior, temperament and idealization of cohabiting couples who married. *International Journal of Sociology of the Family, 10*, 115–125.

Markowski, E. M., Croake, J. W., and Keiler, J. F. (1978). Sexual history and present behavior of cohabiting and married couples. *The Journal of Sex Research, 14*, 27–39.

Martin, D., and Martin, M. (1984). Selected attitudes toward marriage and family life among college students. *Family Relations, 33*, 293–300.

Martin, M. J., and Walters, J. (1982). Family correlates of selected types of child abuse and neglect. *Journal of Marriage and the Family, 44*, 267–275.

Martin, M. J., Schumm, W. R., Bugaighis, M. A., Jurich, A. P., and Bolemen, S. R. (1987). Family violence and adolescents' perceptions of outcomes of family conflict. *Journal of Marriage and the Family, 49,* 165–171.

Martinez, G. A., and Dodd, D. A. (1982). Milk feeding patterns in the U.S. during the first 12 months of life. *Pediatrics, 68,* 863–868.

Maslow, A. (1970). *Motivation and Personality* (2nd ed.). New York: Harper and Row.

Maslow, A. H. (1962). *Toward a Psychology of Being.* Princeton, NJ: Van Nostrand.

Masters, W. H., and Johnson, V. E. (1966). *Human Sexual Response.* Boston: Little, Brown.

Masters, W. H., and Johnson, V. E. (1967). *Major Questions in Human Sexual Response.* A lecture presented to the Harris County Medical Society, Houston, TX, March 1967.

Masters, W. H., and Johnson, V. E. (1970). *Human Sexual Inadequacy.* Boston: Little, Brown.

Matteo, S., and Rissman, E. (1984). Increased sexual activity during the midcycle portion of the human menstrual cycle. *Hormones and Behavior, 18,* 249–255.

Matthews, S. H., and Sprey, J. (1984). The impact of divorce on grandparenthood: An exploratory study. *Gerontologist, 24,* 41–47.

May, K. A. (1982). Factors contributing to first-time father's readiness for fatherhood: An exploratory study. *Family Relations, 31,* 353–361.

May, R. (1967). *Psychology and the Human Dilemma.* New York: Van Nostrand.

Mayes, A., and Valentine, K. (1974). Sex-role stereotyping in Saturday morning cartoon shows. *Journal of Broadcasting, 23,* 41–50.

Maynard, F. (1974). Understanding the crises in men's lives. In C. E. Williams and J. F. Crosby (Eds.), *Choice and Challenge* (pp. 135–144). Dubuque, IA: William C. Brown.

Maynard, P., Maynard, N., McCubbin, H. I., and Shao, D. (1980). Family life and the police profession: Coping patterns wives employ in managing job stress and the family environment. *Family Relations, 29,* 495–501.

Mazur, A. (1986). U.S. trends in feminine beauty and overadaptation. *The Journal of Sex Research, 22,* 281–303.

McAdoo, H. P. (1982). Stress absorbing systems in black families. *Family Relations, 31,* 479–488.

McAuley, W. J., and Nutty, C. L. (1982). Residential preferences and moving behavior: A family-life cycle analysis. *Journal of Marriage and the Family, 44,* 301–307.

McAuley, W. J., and Nutty, C. L. (1985). Residential satisfaction, community integration, and risk across the family life cycle. *Journal of Marriage and the Family, 47,* 125–130.

McCabe, M. P. (1987). Desired and experienced levels of premarital affection and sexual intercourse during dating. *The Journal of Sex Research, 23,* 23–33.

McCary, J. L., and McCary, S. P. (1982). *McCary's Human Sexuality* (4th ed.). Belmont, CA: Wadsworth.

McClelland, K. A. (1982). Self-conception and life satisfaction: Integrating aged subculture and activity theory. *Journal of Gerontology, 37,* 723–732.

McCollum, E. E. (1985). Recontacting former spouses: A further step in the divorce process. *Journal of Marital and Family Therapy, 11,* 417–420.

McCubbin, H. I., Joy, C. B., Cauble, A. E., Comeau, J. K., Patterson, J. M., and Needle, R. H. (1980). Family stress and coping: A decade review. *Journal of Marriage and the Family, 42,* 855–871.

McCullough, D. (1983). Mama's boys. *Psychology Today, 17,* 32–38.

McDonald, G. W. (1980). Family power: The assessment of a decade of theory and research, 1970–1979. *Journal of Marriage and the Family, 42,* 841–854.

McGee, T. F., and Kostrubala, T. (1964). The neurotic equilibrium in married couples applying for group psycho-therapy. *Journal of Marriage and the Family, 26,* 77–82.

McGillicuddy-De Lisi, A. V. (1980). The role of parental beliefs in the family as a system of mutual influences. *Family Relations, 29,* 317–323.

McHugh, G. (1979). *Sex Knowledge Inventory.* Saluda, NC: Family Life Publications.

McHugh, G., and McHugh, T. G. (1976). *A Sex Attitude Survey and Profile.* Saluda, NC: Family Life Publications.

McIlroy, J. H. (1984). Midlife in the 1980s: Philosophy, economy, and psychology. *The Personnel and Guidance Journal, 62,* 623–628.

McLanahan, S. (1985). Family structure and the reproduction of poverty. *American Journal of Sociology, 90,* 873–901.

McLanahan, S. S., Wedemeyer N. V., and Adelberg, T. (1981). Network structure, social support, and psychological well-being in a single-parent family. *Journal of Marriage and the Family, 43,* 601–612.

McLaughlin, S. D., and Micklin, M. (1983). The timing of the first birth and changes in personal efficacy. *Journal of Marriage and the Family, 45,* 47–55.

McLeod, B. (1986). The oriental express. *Psychology Today, 20,* 48–52.

McLeod, P. B., and Ellis, J. R. (1983). Alternative approaches to the family life cycle in the analysis of housing consumption. *Journal of Marriage and the Family, 45,* 699–708.

McMillan, E. L. (1969). Problem buildup: A description

of couples in marriage counseling. *The Family Coordinator, 18,* 260–267.

McNamara, M. L. L., and Bahr, H. M. (1980). The dimensionality of marital role satisfaction. *Journal of Marriage and the Family, 42,* 45–55.

Mead, M. (1950). *Sex and Temperament in Three Primitive Societies.* New York: Merton Books.

Mead, M. (1959). Introduction. In W. Ehrman (Ed.), *Premarital Dating Behavior.* New York: Holt.

Meeks, S., Arnkoff, D. B., Glass, C. R., and Notarius, C. I. (1986). Wives' employment status, hassles, communication and relational efficacy: Intra- versus extra-relationship factors and marital adjustment. *Family Relations, 34,* 249–255.

Meer, J. (1985a). Flexitime and sharing. *Psychology Today, 19,* 74.

Meer, J. (1985b). Loneliness. *Psychology Today, 19,* 28–33.

Meer, J. (1985c). The dating game: Ladies choice. *Psychology Today, 19,* 16.

Meer, J. (1986). Yours, mine, and divorce. *Psychology Today, 20,* 13.

Meiselman, K. C. (1978). *Incest.* San Francisco: Jossey-Bass.

Melicher, J., and Chiriboga, D. A. (1985). Timetables in the divorce process. *Journal of Marriage and the Family, 47,* 701–708.

Melli, M. S. (1986). The changing legal status of the single parent. *Family Relations, 35,* 31–35.

Mendelberg, H. E. (1984). Split and continuity in language use of Mexican-American adolescents of migrant origin. *Adolescence, 19,* 171–182.

Menning, B. (1979). Counseling infertile couples. *Contemporary OB/GYN, 13,* 101–108.

Menstrual changes after tubal ligation. (1984). *Medical Aspects of Human Sexuality, 18,* 247.

Merriam, S. (1979). Middle age: A review of the research. *New Directions for Continuing Education, 2,* 7–15.

Messer, A. A. (1983). Continuation in adult life of parent-child relationships: Effect on marriage. *Medical Aspects of Human Sexuality, 17,* 28–143.

Meyerowitz, J. H. (1970). Satisfaction during pregnancy. *Journal of Marriage and the Family, 32,* 38–42.

Michels, L. (1970). Why we don't want children. *Redbook,* January.

Miller, B. C., and Bowen, S. L. (1982). Father-to-newborn attachment behavior in relation to prenatal classes and presence at delivery. *Family Relations, 31,* 71–78.

Miller, B. C., and Sollie, D. L. (1980). Normal stresses during the transition to parenthood. *Family Relations, 29,* 459–465.

Miller, D. (1975). *American Indian Socialization to Urban Life.* San Francisco: Institute for Scientific Analysis.

Miller, D. (1980). The native American family: The urban way. In E. Corfman (Ed.), *Families Today* (pp. 441–484). Washington, DC: U.S. Government Printing Office.

Miller, J., Turner, J. G., and Kimball, E. (1981). Big Thompson flood victims: One year later. *Family Relations, 30,* 111–116.

Mills, C. J. (1981). Sex roles, personality, and intellectual abilities in adolescents. *Journal of Youth and Adolescence, 10,* 85–112.

Mills, D. M. (1984). A model for stepfamily development. *Family Relations, 33,* 365–372.

Mirowsky, J., and Ross, C. E. (1987). Belief in innate sex roles: Sex stratification versus interpersonal inference in marriage. *Journal of Marriage and the Family, 49,* 527–540.

Moeller, I., and Sherlock, J. (1981). Making it legal: A comparison of previously cohabiting and engaged newlyweds. *Journal of Sociology and Social Welfare, 8,* 97–110.

Moen, P. (1979). Family impacts of the 1975 recession: Duration of unemployment. *Journal of Marriage and the Family, 41,* 561–572.

Moen, P. (1983). Unemployment, public policy, and families: Forecasts for the 1980s. *Journal of Marriage and the Family, 45,* 751–760.

Monahan, T. (1977). Illegitimacy by race and mixture of race. *International Journal of Sociology of the Family, 7,* 45–54.

Monroe, P. A., Bokemeier, J. L., Kotchen, J. M., and McKean, H. (1985). Spousal response consistency in decision-making research. *Journal of Marriage and the Family, 47,* 733–738.

Montemayor, R., and Leigh, G. K. (1982). Parent-absent children: A demographic analysis of children and adolescents living apart from their parents. *Family Relations, 31,* 567–573.

Montgomery, B. M. (1981). The form and function of quality communication in marriage. *Family Relations, 30,* 21–30.

Montgomery, J. E. (1982). The economics of supportive services for families with disabled and aging members. *Family Relations, 31,* 19–27.

Moore, C. L. (1984). Establishing trust in a second marriage. *Medical Aspects of Human Sexuality, 18,* 103.

Moore, K.A., Peterson, J. L., and Furstenberg, F. F. (1986). Parental attitudes and the occurrence of early sexual activity. *Journal of Marriage and the Family, 48,* 777–782.

Morgan, L. A. (1981). Economic change at mid-life widowhood: A longitudinal analysis. *Journal of Marriage and the Family, 43,* 899–907.

Mornell, P. (1979). *Passive Men, Wild Women.* New York: Simon and Schuster.

Morrell, M., Dixen, J., Carter, C., and Davidson, J. (1984). The influence of age and cycling status on sexual arousability in women. *American Journal of Obstetrics and Gynecology, 148,* 66–71.

Morris, N. M., and Udry, J. R. (1978). Pheromonal influences on human sexual behavior: An experimental search. *Journal of Biosocial Science, 13.*

Morris, S., and Charney, N. (1983). Workaholism: Thank God it's Monday. *Psychology Today, 17,* 88.

Moss, N. E., and Abramowitz, S. I. (1982). Beyond deficit-filling and developmental stakes: Cross-disciplinary perspectives on parental heritage. *Journal of Marriage and the Family, 44,* 357–366.

Most women find no change in menstrual cycle following sterilization: Some cite improvement. (1984). *Family Planning Perspectives, 16,* March/April, 92–93.

Movius, M. (1976). Voluntary childlessness — The ultimate liberation. *The Family Coordinator, 25,* 57–63.

Moynihan, D. P. (l965). The Negro Family: The Case For National Action. Washington, DC: U.S. Government Printing Office.

Mueller, C. W., and Pope, H. (1980). Divorce and female marriage mobility. *Social Forces, 58,* 726–738.

Mueller, D. P., and Cooper, P. W. (1986). Children of single parent families: How they fare as young adults. *Family Relations, 35,* 169–176.

Mukhopadhyay, C. C. (1979). The function of romantic love: A re-appraisal of the Coppinger and Rosenblatt study. *Behavior Science Research, 14,* 57–63.

Murdock, G. P. (1949). *Social Structure.* New York: Macmillan.

Murstein, B. (1980). Mate selection in the 1970s. *Journal of Marriage and the Family 42,* 777–792.

Murstein, B. I. (1970). Stimulus-value-role theory: A theory of marital choice. *Journal of Marriage and the Family, 32,* 465–481.

Murstein, B. I. (1976). *Who Will Marry Whom? Theories and Research in Marital Choice.* New York: Springer Publishing Company.

Murstein, B., Cerreto, M., and McDonald, M. G. (1977). A theory and investigation of the effect of exchange orientation on marriage and friendship. *Journal of Marriage and the Family, 39,* 543–548.

Myricks, N., and Ferullo, D. L. (1986). Race and child custody disputes. *Family Relations, 35,* 325–328.

Myska, M. J., and Pasewark, R. A. (1978). Death attitudes of residential and non-residential rural aged persons. Part II. *Psychological Reports, 43,* 1235–1238.

Naffziger, C. C., and Naffziger, K. (1974). Development of sex-role stereotypes. *The Family Coordinator, 23,* 251–258.

Nahemow, N. (1983). Mate selection. *Medical Aspects of Human Sexuality, 17,* 106–123.

National Center for Education Statistics. (1983). *Participation of Black Students in Higher Education: A Statistical Profile from 1970–71 to 1980–81.* Washington, DC: U.S. Department of Education.

National Institute of Mental Health. (1973). *Suicide, Homicide, and Alcoholism among American Indians: Guidelines for Help.* Washington, DC: U.S. Government Printing Office.

Nelson, J. A. (1986). Incest: Self-report findings from a nonclinical sample. *The Journal of Sex Research, 22,* 463–477.

Nelson, M., and Nelson, G. K. (1982). Problems of equity in the reconstituted family: A social exchange analysis. *Family Relations, 31,* 223–231.

Neubeck, G. (1979). In praise of marriage. *The Family Coordinator, 28,* 115–117.

Neugarten, B. L. (1976). Adaptation and the life cycle. *Counseling Psychologist, 6,* 16–20.

Neugarten, B., and Weinstein, K. (1964). The changing American grandparents. *Journal of Marriage and the Family, 26,* 199–204.

New York Times, January 23, 1973, 1.

Newcomb, M. D., and Bentler, P. M. (1980). Cohabitation before marriage: A comparison of married couples who did and did not cohabit. *Alternative Lifestyles, 3,* 65–83.

Newcomb, P. R. (1979). Cohabitation in America: An assessment of consequences. *Journal of Marriage and the Family, 41,* 597–602.

Newcomer, S. F., and Udry, R. (1984). Mother's influence on the sexual behavior of their teenage children. *Journal of Marriage and the Family, 46,* 477–485.

Newcomer, S. F., and Udry, R. (1985). Parent-child communication and adolescent sexual behavior. *Family Planning Perspectives, 17,* 169–174.

Nichols, S., and Metzen, E. (1982). Impact of wife's employment upon husband's housework. *Journal of Family Issues, 3,* 199–216.

Nicholson, S. I., and Antill, J. K. (1981). Personal problems of adolescents and their relationship to peer acceptance and sex-role identity. *Journal of Youth and Adolescence, 10,* 309–325.

Nickols, S. A., Fournier, D. G., and Nickols, S. Y. (1986). Evaluation of a preparation for marriage workshop. *Family Relations, 35,* 563–571.

Nofz, M. P. (1984). Fantasy-testing-assessment: A proposed model for investigation of mate selection. *Family Relations, 33,* 273–289.

Norton, A. J. and Moorman, J. E. (1987). Current trends in marriage and divorce among American women. *Journal of Marriage and the Family, 49,* 3–14.

Norton, A. J., and Glick, P. G. (1986). One-parent families: A social and economic profile. *Family Relations, 35,* 9–13.

Notarius, C. I., and Johnson, J. S. (1982). Emotional expression in husbands and wives. *Journal of Marriage and the Family, 44,* 483–489.

Nutter, D., and Gontron, M. (1983). Sexual fantasy and activity patterns of females with inhibited sexual desire versus normal controls. *Journal of Sex and Marital Therapy, 9,* 276–282.

O'Connell, M., and Rogers, C. C. (1984). Out of wedlock births, premarital pregnancies and their effect on family formation and dissolution. *Family Planning Perspectives, 16,* 157–162.

O'Leary, K. D., and Curley, A. D. (1986). Assertion and family violence: Correlates of spouse abuse. *Journal of Marital and Family Therapy, 12,* 281–289.

O'Neill, N., and O'Neill, G. (1972). *Open Marriage.* New York: Avon.

Oakley, D. (1985). Premarital childbearing decision making. *Family Relations, 34,* 561–563.

Okraku, I. O. (1987). Age and attitudes toward multigenerational residence, 1973 to 1983. *Journal of Gerontology, 42,* 280–287.

Olson, D. H., Fournier, D. G., and Druckman, J. M. (1979, 1982). *PREPARE-ENRICH Counselors Manual* (rev. ed.). Available from PREPARE-ENRICH, P. O. Box 1363, Stillwater, OK, 74076.

Olson, D. H., McCubbin, H. I., and Associates. (1983). *Families: What Makes Them Work.* Beverly Hills, CA: Sage.

Olson, J. T. (1981). The impact of housework on child care in the home. *Family Relations, 31,* 75–81.

Olson, L. (1983). *Cost of Children.* Lexington, MA: Lexington Books.

Opinion roundup. (1983). *Public Opinion, 6,* 34. Washington, DC: The American Enterprise Institute for Public Policy Research.

Orlofsky, J. L. (1982). Psychological androgyny, sex typing, and sex role ideology as predictors of male-female interpersonal attraction. *Sex Roles, 8,* 1057.

Orthner, D. K. (1981). *Intimate Relationships: An Introduction to Marriage and the Family.* New York: Random House.

Ory, H. W. (1982). The noncontraceptive health benefits from oral contraceptive use. *Family Planning Perspectives, 14,* 182–184.

Osherson, S., and Dill, D. (1983). Varying work and family choices: Their impact on men's work satisfaction. *Journal of Marriage and the Family, 45,* 339–346.

Osmond, M. W. (1978). Reciprocity: A dynamic model and a method to study family power. *Journal of Marriage and the Family, 40,* 49–61.

Osmond, M. W., and Martin, P. Y. (1978). A contingency model of marital organization in low income families. *Journal of Marriage and the Family, 40,* 315–329.

Ostrov, E., and Offer, D. (1980). Loneliness and the adolescent. In J. Hartog, J. R. Audy, and T. A. Cohen (Eds.), *The Anatomy of Loneliness.* New York: International Universities Press.

Otto, M. L. (1984). Child abuse: Group treatment for parents. *The Personnel and Guidance Journal, 62,* 336–338.

Otto, M. L., and Smith, D. G. (1980). Child abuse: A cognitive behavioral intervention model. *Journal of Marital and Family Therapy, 6,* 425–429.

Papousek, H. (1973). Group rearing in day care centers and mental health: Potential advantages and risks. Research publication series, *Association for Research in Nervous and Mental Diseases, 51,* 398–411.

Parachini, A. (1987). Condoms fail government tests. *Portland Press Herald,* Portland, ME, August 19, 1987.

Parades, A. (1983). Alcoholic marriages. *Medical Aspects of Human Sexuality, 17,* 300–302.

Pare, C. M. B., and Raven, H. (1970). Follow-up of patients referred for termination of pregnancy. *Lancet, 1,* 635–638.

Parks, P. L., and Smeriglio, V. L. (1986). Relationships among parenting knowledge, quality of stimulation in the home, and infant development. *Family Relations, 35,* 411–416.

Patterson, J. M., and McCubbin, H. I. (1984). Gender roles and coping. *Journal of Marriage and the Family, 46,* 95–104.

Pattison, E. M. (1977). The experience of dying. In E. M. Pattison (Ed.), *The Experience of Dying* (pp. 43–60). Englewood Cliffs, NJ: Prentice-Hall.

Pattison, E. M. (1982). Living together: A poor substitute for marriage. *Medical Aspects of Human Sexuality, 16,* 71–91.

Peabody, E., McKenry, P., and Cordero, L. (1981). Subsequent pregnancy among adolescent mothers. *Adolescence, 16,* 563–568.

Pearlin, L. I. (1975). Status inequality and stress in marriage. *American Sociological Review, 40,* 344–357.

Pearlman, C. K. (1972). Frequency of intercourse in males at different ages. *Medical Aspects of Human Sexuality, 6,* 92–113.

Pearson, J., Thoennes, N., and Milne, A. (1982). *A Directory of Mediation Services.* Denver: The Divorce Mediation Research Project, The Association of Family Conciliation Courts.

Peck, E. (1971). *The Baby Trap.* New York: Geis.

Peek, C. W., and Brown, S. (1980). Sex prejudice among white Protestants: Like or unlike ethnic prejudice? *Social Forces, 59,* 169–185.

Peek, C. W., Fischer, J. L., and Kidwell, J. S. (1985). Teenage violence toward parents: A neglected dimension of family violence. *Journal of Marriage and the Family, 47,* 1051–1058.

Peele, S. (1983). Through a glass darkly. *Psychology Today, 17,* 38–42.

Pendleton, B. F., Poloma, M. M., and Garland, T. N. (1980). Scales for investigation of the dual-career family. *Journal of Marriage and the Family, 42,* 269–276.

Peplau, L. A., Bikson, T. K., Rook, K. S., and Good-child, J. D. (1982). Being old and living alone. In L. A. Peplau and D. Perlman (Eds.), *Loneliness: A Sourcebook of Current Theory, Research, and Therapy.* New York: Wiley Interscience.

Peplau, L. A., Miceli, M., and Morasch, B. (1982). Loneliness and self-evaluation. In L. A. Peplau and D. Perlman (Eds.), *Loneliness: A Sourcebook of Current Theory, Research, and Therapy.* New York: Wiley Interscience.

Peretti, P. O. (1980). Perceived primary group criteria in the relational network of closest friendships. *Adolescence, 15,* 555–565.

Perlman, D. and Peplau, L. A. (1981). Toward a social psychology of loneliness. In S. Duck and R. Gilmour (Eds.), *Personal Relationships. 3: Personal Relationships in Disorder.* New York: Academic Press.

Perlman, S. D., and Abramson, P. R. (1982). Sexual satisfaction among married and cohabiting individuals. *Journal of Consulting and Clinical Psychology, 50,* 458–460.

Perrucci, C. C. (1968). Mobility, marriage, and child-spacing among college graduates. *Journal of Marriage and the Family, 30,* 273–282.

Perrucci, C. C. (1974). Minority status and the pursuit of professional careers: Women in science and engineering. In C. C. Perrucci and D. B. Targ (Eds.), *Marriage and the Family* (pp. 376–397). New York: David McKay.

Pershing B. (1979). Family policies: A component of management in the home and family setting. *Journal of Marriage and the Family, 41,* 573–581.

Petersen, J. R., Kretchner, A., Nellis, B., Lever, J., and Hertz, R. (1983). The Playboy readers' survey, Parts I and II. *Playboy,* February and March.

Petersen, L. R. (1986). Interfaith marriage and religious commitment among Catholics. *Journal of Marriage and the Family, 48,* 725–735.

Petersen, L. R., Lee, G. R., and Ellis, G. J. (1982). Social structure, socialization values, and disciplinary techniques: A cross-cultural analysis. *Journal of Marriage and the Family, 44,* 131–142.

Peterson, G. W., and Rollins, B. C. (1987). Parent-child socialization. In M. B. Sussman and S. K. Steinmetz (Eds.), *Handbook of Marriage and the Family* (pp. 471–507). New York: Plenum Press.

Pett, M. A., and Vaughan-Cole, B. (1986). The impact of income issues and social status in post-divorce adjustment of custodial parents. *Family Relations, 35,* 103–111.

Philliber, S. G., and Graham, E. H. (1981). The impact of age of mother on mother-child interaction patterns. *Journal of Marriage and the Family, 43,* 109–115.

Piaget, J., and Inhelder, J. (1969). *The Psychology of the Child.* New York: Basic.

Pichitino, J. P. (1983). Profile of the single father: A thematic integration of the literature. *The Personnel and Guidance Journal, 5,* 295–299.

Pickford, J. H., Signoria, E. I., and Rempel, H. (1966). Similar or related personality traits as a factor in marital happiness. *Journal of Marriage and the Family, 28,* 190–192.

Pill does not increase risk of breast cancer, even after years of use. (1982). *Family Planning Perspectives, 14,* July/August, 216–219.

Pingree, S., et al. (1978). Anti-nepotism's ghost: Attitudes of administrators toward hiring professional couples. *Psychology of Women Quarterly, 3,* 22–29.

Pink, J. E. T., and Wampler, K. S. (1985). Problem areas in stepfamilies: Cohesion, adaptability, and the step-father-adolescent relationship. *Family Relations, 34,* 327–335.

Pinney, E. M., Gerrard, M., and Denney, N. W. (1987). The Pinney Sexual Satisfaction Inventory. *The Journal of Sex Research, 23,* 233–251.

Pinups and letdowns (1983). *Psychology Today, 17,* 83.

Pittman, J. F., Price-Bonham, S., and McKenry, P. C. (1983). Marital cohesion: A path model. *Journal of Marriage and the Family, 45,* 521–531.

Platzker, A. C., Lew, C. D., and Stewart, D. (1980). Drug "administration" via breast milk. *Hospital Practice,* September, 111–122.

Playboy readers' sex survey: Part I. (1983). *Playboy,* January, 108, 241–250.

Plummer, L. D., and Koch-Hattem, A. (1986). Family stress and adjustment to divorce. *Family Relations, 35,* 523–529.

Poffenberger, T. (1964). Three papers on going steady. *The Family Life Coordinator, 13,* 7–13.

Porter, B. R., and Chatelain, R. S. (1981). Family life education for single parent families. *Family Relations, 30,* 517–525.

Porter, N. L., and Christopher, F. S. (1984). Infertility: Toward an awareness of a need among family life practitioners. *Family Relations, 33,* 309–315.

Postcoital pills in U.K. (1984). *Outlook, 2,* 6.

Poulshock, S. W., and Deimling, G. T. (1984). Families caring for elders in residence: Issues in the measurement of burden. *Journal of Gerontology, 39,* 230–239.

Powers, W. G., and Hutchinson, K. (1979). The measurement of communication apprehension in the marriage relationship. *Journal of Marriage and the Family, 41,* 89–95.

Price-Bonham, A., and Balswick, J. O. (1980). The non-institutions: Divorce, desertion, and remarriage. *Journal of Marriage and the Family, 42,* 959–972.

Przbyla, D., and Byrne, D. (1984). The mediating role of cognitive processes in self-regulated sexual arousal. *Journal of Research in Personality, 18,* 54–63.

677

Quarm, D. (1981). Random measurement error as a source of discrepancies between the reports of wives and husbands concerning marital power and task allocation. *Journal of Marriage and the Family, 43*, 521–535.

Quinn, N. (1982). "Commitment" in American marriage: Cultural analysis. *American Ethnologist, 9*, 775–798.

Quinn, W. H. (1983). Personal and family adjustment in later life. *Journal of Marriage and the Family, 45*, 57–73.

Rachlin, V. C. (1987). Fair vs. equal role relations in dual-career and dual-earner families: Implications for family interventions. *Family Relations, 36*, 187–192.

Radlove, S. (1983). Sexual response and gender roles. In E. R. Allgeier and N. B. McCormick (Eds.), *Changing Boundaries: Gender Roles and Sexual Behavior*. Palo Alto, CA: Mayfield.

Radomiski, M. (1981). Stereotypes, stepmothers, and splitting. *American Journal of Psychoanalysis, 41*, 121–127.

Rainwater, L. (1966). Some aspects of lower-class sexual behavior. *Journal of Social Issues, 22*, 96–109.

Ramsey, S. H. (1986). Stepparent support of stepchildren: The changing legal context and the need for empirical policy research. *Family Relations, 35*, 363–369.

Ramsey, S., and Masson, J. (1985). Stepparent support of stepchildren: A comparative analysis of policies and problems in the American and English experience. *Syracuse Law Review, 36*, 659–714.

Rank, M. R. (1987). The formation and dissolution of marriages in the welfare population. *Journal of Marriage and the Family, 49*, 15–20.

Ransford, H. E., and Miller, J. (1983). Race, sex, and feminist outlook. *American Sociological Review, 48*, 46–59.

Rao, S.L.N. (1974). A comparative study of childlessness and never pregnant status. *Journal of Marriage and the Family, 36*, 149–157.

Rapoport, R. N., and Rapoport, R. (1978). Dual-career families: Progress and prospects. *Marriage and Family Review, 1*, 1–12.

Rapoport, R., and Rapoport, R. N. (1971). *Dual-Career Families*. Baltimore: Penguin.

Raschke, H. J., and Raschke, V. J. (1979). Family conflict and children's self-concepts: A comparison of intact and single-parent families. *Journal of Marriage and the Family, 41*, 367–374.

Raush, H. L., et al. (1974). *Communication, Conflict, and Marriage*. San Francisco: Jossey-Bass.

Rawlings, S. (1978). Perspectives on American husbands and wives. *Current Population Reports*, ser. p-23, no. 77. Washington, DC: U.S. Bureau of the Census.

Re: act. (1984). Viewing goes up. *Action for Children's Television Magazine, 13*, 4.

Reading, J., and Amatea, E. S. (1986). Role deviance or role diversification: Reassessing the psychosocial factors affecting the parenthood choice of career-oriented women. *Journal of Marriage and the Family, 48*, 255–260.

Rebal, R. F., Jr. (1984). Counseling the woman about to marry a man married several times before. *Medical Aspects of Human Sexuality, 18*, 155–161.

Red Horse, J. G., Lewis, R., Feit, M., and Decker, J. (1979). Family behavior of urban American Indians. *Social Casework, 59*, 67–72.

Redfield, R., Markham, P., Salahuddin, S., Wright, D., Sarngadharan, M., and Gallo, R. (1985). Heterosexually acquired HTLV-III/LAV disease, AIDS-related complex and AIDS: Epidemiologic evidence for female-to-male transmission. *The Journal of the American Medical Association, 254*, 2094–2096.

Reed, J. P. (1975). The current legal status of abortion. In J. G. Well (Ed.), *Current Issues in Marriage and the Family* (pp. 200–208). New York: Macmillan.

Reedy, M. N. (1977). *Age and Sex Differences in Personal Needs and the Nature of Love: A Study of Happily Married Young, Middle-aged, and Older Adult Couples*. Ph.D. dissertation, University of Southern California.

Register, J. C. (1981). Aging and race: A black-white comparative analysis. *The Gerontologist, 21*, 438–443.

Reik, T. A. (1944). *A Psychologist Looks at Love*. New York: Farrar and Rinehart.

Reik, T. A. (1957). *Of Love and Lust*. New York: Straus and Cudahy.

Reiner, B. S., and Edwards, R. L. (1974). Adolescent marriage: Social or therapeutic problem? *The Family Coordinator, 23*, 383–390.

Reis, H. T., Nezlek, J., and Wheeler, L. (1980). Physical attractiveness and social interaction. *Journal of Personality and Social Psychology, 38*, 604–617.

Reis, J., Barbara-Stein, L., and Bennett, S. (1986). Ecological determinants of parenting. *Family Relations, 35*, 547–554.

Reiss, I. L. (1960). Toward a sociology of the heterosexual love relationship. *Marriage and Family Living, 22*, 139–145.

Reiss, I. L. (1973). *Heterosexual Relationships: Inside and Outside of Marriage*. Morristown, NJ: General Learning Press.

Reiss, I. L. (1980). *Family Systems in America* (3rd ed.). New York: Holt, 1980.

Reiss, I. L., Anderson, R. E., and Sponaugle, G. C. (1980). A multivariate model of the determinants of extramarital sexual permissiveness. *Journal of Marriage and the Family, 42*, 395–411.

Reker, G. T., Peacock, E. J., and Wong, P. T. P. (1987). Meaning and purpose in life and well-being: A life-span perspective. *Journal of Gerontology, 42*, 44–49.

Renshaw, D. C. (1984). Touch hunger — A common marital problem. *Medical Aspects of Human Sexuality, 18,* 63–70.

Requests for reversal of tubal sterilization linked with young age at surgery and marital disruption. (1984). *Family Planning Perspectives, 16,* 139–140.

Researchers confirm induced abortion to be safer for women than childbirth; refute claims of critics. (1982). *Family Planning Perspectives, 14,* 271–272.

Resman, B. (1986). Can men "mother"? Life as a single father. *Family Relations, 35,* 95–102.

Rice, B. (1981a). Can companies kill? *Psychology Today, 15,* 78–85.

Rice, B. (1981b). How not to pick up a woman. *Psychology Today, 23,* 15–17.

Rice, D. G. (1978). *Dual-Career Marriage: Conflict and Treatment.* New York: Free Press.

Rice, F. P. (1966). *Parents, In-laws, and Grandparents in the Family.* Orono, ME: University of Maine, Cooperative Extension Service, Bulletin 521.

Rice, F. P. (1978a). *Sexual Problems in Marriage.* Philadelphia: Westminster Press.

Rice, F. P. (1978b). *Stepparenting.* New York: Condor.

Rice, F. P. (1979a). *Marriage and Parenthood.* Boston: Allyn and Bacon.

Rice, F. P. (1979b). *Working Mother's Guide to Child Development.* Englewood Cliffs, NJ: Prentice-Hall.

Rice, F. P. (1983). *Contemporary Marriage.* Boston: Allyn and Bacon.

Rice, F. P. (1986). *Adult Development and Aging.* Boston: Allyn and Bacon.

Rice, F. P. (1987). *The Adolescent: Development, Relationships, and Culture* (5th ed.). Boston: Allyn and Bacon.

Rice, F. P. (1989). *Human Sexuality.* Dubuque, IA: William C. Brown.

Richardson, L. (1986). Another world. *Psychology Today, 20,* 22–27.

Riley, M. W., and Foner, A. (1968). *Aging and Society.* Vol. 1. New York: Russell Sage Foundation.

Risman, B. J., Hill, C. T., Rubin, Z., and Peplau, L. A. (1981). Living together in college: Implications for courtship. *Journal of Marriage and the Family, 43,* 77–83.

Roacil, A. J., Frazier, L. P., and Bowden, S. R. (1981). The marital satisfaction scale: development of a measure for intervention research. *Journal of Marriage and the Family, 43,* 537–546.

Robbins, M., and Jensen, G. (1978). Multiple orgasms in males. *Journal of Sex Research, 14,* 21–26.

Roberto, K. A., and Scott, J. P. (1986). Equity considerations in the friendships of older adults. *Journal of Gerontology, 41,* 241–247.

Robertson, J. F. (1976). Significance of grandparents: Perceptions of young adult grandchildren. *The Gerontologist, 16,* 137–140.

Robinson, B. E. (1984). The contemporary American step-father. *Family Relations, 33,* 381–388.

Robinson, B. E., Rowland, B. H., and Coleman, M. (1986). Taking action for latchkey children and their families. *Family Relations, 35,* 473–478.

Robinson, I. E., and Jedlicka, D. (1982). Change in sexual attitudes and behavior of college students from 1965 to 1980: A research note. *Journal of Marriage and the Family, 44,* 237–240.

Rodgers, R. H., and Witney, G. (1981). The family cycle in twentieth century Canada. *Journal of Marriage and the Family, 43,* 727–740.

Rodman, H. (1967). Marital power in France, Greece, Yugoslavia, and the United States: A cross-national discussion. *Journal of Marriage and the Family, 29,* 320–325.

Rodman, H. (1972). Marital power and the theory of resources in cultural context. *Journal of Comparative Family Studies, 3,* 50–69.

Rodman, H., Pralto, D. J., and Nelson, R. S. (1985). Child care arrangements and children's functioning: A comparison of self-care and adult-care children. *Developmental Psychology, 21,* 413–418.

Roe v. Wade, 410 U.S. 113 (1973).

Rogel, M. J. (1978). A critical evaluation of the possibility of higher primate reproductive and sexual pheromones. *Psychological Bulletin, 85,* 810–830.

Rogers, R. H., and Conrad, L. M. (1986). Courtship for remarriage: Influences on family reorganization after divorce. *Journal of Marriage and the Family, 48,* 767–775.

Rogler, L. H., and Procidano, M. E. (1986). The effect of social networks on marital roles: A test of the Bott hypothesis in an intergenerational context. *Journal of Marriage and the Family, 48,* 693–701.

Rollins, B. C., and Cannon, K. L. (1974). Marital satisfaction over the family life cycle: A reevaluation. *Journal of Marriage and the Family, 36,* 271–282.

Roosevelt, R., and Lofas, J. (1977). *Living in Step.* New York: McGraw-Hill.

Roscoe, B., and Benaske, N. (1985). Courtship violence experienced by abused wives: Similarities in pattern of abuse. *Family Relations, 34,* 419–424.

Rosen, B. C., and Aneshansel, C. (1978). Sex differences in educational occupational expectation process. *Social Forces, 57,* 164–186.

Rosenbaum, A., and O'Leary, K. D. (1981). Marital violence: Characteristics of abusive couples. *Journal of Consulting and Clinical Psychology, 49,* 63–71.

Rosenbaum, V. (1979). Friendship in marriage. *Marriage and Family Living, 61,* September, 6–7.

Rosenblatt, P. C. (1983). How vacations affect marital relationships. *Medical Aspects of Human Sexuality, 17,* 189–193.

Rosenblatt, P. C., and Cunningham, M. R. (1976). Television watching and family tensions. *Journal of Marriage and the Family, 38,* 105–111.

Rosenblatt, P. C., and Keller, L. O. (1983). Economic vulnerability and economic stress in farm couples. *Family Relations, 32,* 567–573.

Rosenblatt, P. C., et al. (1979). Marital system differences and summer-long vacations: Togetherness — apartness and tension. *The American Journal of Family Therapy, 7,* 77–84.

Rosenthal, S. (1984). The need for friendships in marriage. *Medical Aspects of Human Sexuality, 18,* 110–120.

Rosenthal, S., and Rosenthal, P. A. (1983). Workaholics. *Medical Aspects of Human Sexuality, 17,* 9.

Rossie, A. S. (1968). Transition to parenthood. *Journal of Marriage and the Family, 30,* 26–39.

Rotter, J. B. (1980). Trust and gullibility. *Psychology Today, 14,* 35–42.

Roy, L., and Sawyers, J. K. (1986). The double bind: An empirical study of responses to inconsistent communications. *Journal of Marital and Family Therapy, 12,* 395–402.

Rubenstein, C. (1980). Vacations. *Psychology Today, 13,* 62–76.

Rubenstein, C. (1981). Money and self-esteem, relationships, secrecy, envy, and satisfaction. *Psychology Today, 15,* 29–44.

Rubenstein, C. (1982). Real men don't earn less than their wives. *Psychology Today, 16,* 36–41.

Rubenstein, C. M., and Shaver, P. (1982). *In Search of Intimacy.* New York: Delacorte.

Rubin, G. L. (1978). Ectopic pregnancy in the United States: 1970 through 1978. *Journal of the American Medical Association, 249,* 1725–1729.

Rubin, L. B. (1976). *Worlds of Pain: Life in the Working-class Family.* New York: Basic Books.

Rubin, L. G. (1979). *Women of a Certain Age: The Midlife Search for Self.* New York: Harper and Row.

Rubin, Z. (1970). Measurement of romantic love. *Journal of Personality and Social Psychology, 16,* 265–273.

Rubin, Z. (1973). *Liking and Loving: An Invitation to Social Psychology.* New York: Holt, Rinehart and Winston.

Rubin, Z., Hill, C. T., Peplau, L. A., and Dunkel-Schetter, C. (1980). Self-disclosure in dating couples: Sex roles and the ethic of openness. *Journal of Marriage and the Family, 42,* 305–317.

Rubin, Z., Peplau, L. A., and Hill, C. T. (1981). Loving and learning: Sex differences in romantic attachments. *Sex Roles, 7,* 821–835.

Ruble, D. N., and Brooks-Gunn, J. (1982). The experience of menarche. *Child Development, 53,* 1557–1566.

Rushing, W. A. (1979). Marital status and mental disorder: Evidence in favor of a behavioral model. *Social Forces, 58,* 540–556.

Russell, C. S. (1974). Transition to parenthood — Problems and gratifications. *Journal of Marriage and the Family, 36,* 294–302.

Ryff, C. D. (1982). Successful aging: A developmental approach. *The Gerontologist, 22,* 209–214.

Sabetelli, R. M., and Cecil-Pigo, E. F. (1985). Relational interdependence and commitment in marriage. *Journal of Marriage and the Family, 47,* 131–433.

Sadker, M., and Sadker, M. (1985). Sexism in the schoolroom of the 80s. *Psychology Today, 19,* 54–57.

Safilios-Rothschild, C. (1973). Patterns of family power and influence. In A. V. Kline and M. L. Medley (Eds.), *Dating and Marriage* (pp. 292–304). Boston: Holbrook.

Safilios-Rothschild, C. (1976). A macro- and micro-examination of family power and love: An exchange model. *Journal of Marriage and the Family, 37,* 355–362.

Salamon, S., and Keim, A. M. (1979). Land ownership and women's power in a midwestern family community. *Journal of Marriage and the Family, 41,* 109–119.

Salk, L. (1974). *Preparing for Parenthood.* New York: Bantam.

Sampel, D. D., and Seymour, W. R. (1980). A comparative analysis of the effectiveness of conciliation counseling on certain personality variables. *Journal of Marital and Family Therapy, 6,* 269–275.

Sanik, M. M., and Mauldin, T. (1986). Single versus two-parent families: A comparison of mothers' time. *Family Relations, 35,* 53–56.

Santrock, J. W. (1970a). Influence of onset and type of paternal absence on the first four Eriksonian developmental crises. *Developmental Psychology, 3,* 273–274.

Santrock, J. W. (1970b). Paternal absence, sex-typing and identification. *Developmental Psychology, 2,* 264–272.

Santrock, J. W., and Warshak, R. A. (1979). Father custody and social development in boys and girls. *Journal of Social Issues, 35,* 112–125.

Santrock, J. W., and Wohlford, P. (1970). Effects of father absence: Influences of, reasons for, and onset of absence. *Proceedings of the 78th Annual Convention of the American Sociological Association, 5,* 265–266.

Sarason, I. G. (1981). *The Revised Life Experiences Survey.* Unpublished manuscipt, University of Washington.

Sarvis, B., and Rodman, H. (1974). *The Abortion Controversy.* New York: Columbia University Press.

Saul, L. J. (1983). How to cope with adultery. *Medical Aspects of Human Sexuality, 17,* 90–106.

Saunders, J. M., and Edwards, J. N. (1984). Extramarital sexuality, a predictive model of permissive attitudes. *Journal of Marriage and the Family, 46,* 825–835.

Saxena, B. B. (1980). Criteria for clinically valid measurement of human chorionic gonadotropin. *Research in Reproduction, 12,* 1, 2.

Saxton, L. (1972). *The Individual, Marriage, and the Family* (2nd ed.). Belmont, CA: Wadsworth.

Saxton, L. (1977). *The Individual, Marriage, and the Family* (3rd ed.). Belmont, CA: Wadsworth.

Saxton, L. (1986). *The Individual, Marriage, and the Family* (6th ed.). Belmont, CA: Wadsworth.

Scanzoni, J. (1979). Social exchange and behavioral independence. In R. Burgess and T. Huston, *Social Exchange in Developing Relationships.* New York: Academic Press.

Scanzoni, J. (1980). Contemporary marriage types. *Journal of Family Issues, 1,* 125–140.

Scanzoni, J., and Fox, G. L. (1980). Sex roles, family, and society: The seventies and beyond. *Journal of Marriage and the Family, 42,* 743–756.

Scanzoni, J., and Polonko, K. (1980). A conceptual approach to explicit marital negotiation. *Journal of Marriage and the Family, 42,* 31–44.

Scanzoni, J., and Szinovacz, M. (1980). *Family Decision-making: A Developmental Sex Role Model.* Beverly Hills: Sage.

Scanzoni, J., and Szinovacz, M. E. (1980). *Family Decision-making: Sex Roles and Change Over the Family Life Cycle.* Beverly Hills, CA: Sage.

Schacter, S., and Singer, J. F. (1962). Cognitive, social, and physiological determinants of emotional state. *Psychological Review, 69,* 379–399.

Schaefer, M. T., and Olson, D. H. (1981). Assessing intimacy: The pair inventory. *Journal of Marital and Family Therapy, 7,* January, 47–60.

Schafer, R. B., and Keith, P. M. (1981). Equity in marital roles across the family life cycle. *Journal of Marriage and the Family, 43,* 359–367.

Schaffer, H. R., and Emerson, P. E. (1964). The development of social attachments in infancy. *Monographs of The Society for Research in Child Development, 29,* 3.

Schaninger, C. M., and Buss, W. C. (1986). A longitudinal comparison of consumption and finance handling between happily married and divorced couples. *Journal of Marriage and the Family, 48,* 129–136.

Schaper, K. K. (1982). Toward a calm baby and relaxed parents. *Family Relations, 31,* 409–414.

Scheirer, M. A. (1983). Household structure among welfare families: Correlates and consequences. *Journal of Marriage and the Family, 45,* 761–771.

Scher, M., and Stevens, M. (1987). Men and violence. *Journal of Counseling and Development, 65,* 351–355.

Schneiderman, G. (1983). How physicians can help adults cope with death of a parent. *Medical Aspects of Human Sexuality, 17,* 18–40.

Schneiner, L. C., Musetto, A. P., and Cordier, D. C. (1982). Custody and visitation counseling: A report of an innovative program. *Family Relations, 31,* 99–107.

Schram, R. W. (1979). Marital satisfaction over the family life cycle: A critique and proposal. *Journal of Marriage and the Family, 41,* 7–12.

Schumm, W. R., and Bugaighis, M. A. (1986). Marital quality over the marital career: Alternative explanations. *Journal of Marriage and the Family, 48,* 165–168.

Schumm, W. R., Barnes, H. L., Bollman, S. R., Jurich, A. P., and Bugaighis, M. A. (1986). Self-disclosure and marital satisfaction revisited. *Family Relations, 34,* 241–247.

Schwartz, M. A. (1976). *Career Strategies of the Never-married.* Paper presented at the 71st annual meeting of the American Sociological Association, New York.

Schwartz, P., and Lever, J. (1985). Fear and loathing at a college mixer. In J. M. Henslin, *Marriage and Family in a Changing Society* (2nd ed.). New York: The Free Press.

Schwartz, R., and Schwartz, L. J. (1980). *Becoming a Couple.* Englewood Cliffs, NJ: Prentice-Hall.

Schwertfeger, M. M. (1982). Interethnic marriage and divorce in Hawaii: A panel study of 1968 first marriages. *Marriage and Family Review, 5,* 49–60.

Scott, J. P., and Kivett, V. R. (1980). The widowed, black, older adult in the rural South: Implications for policy. *Family Relations, 29,* 83–90.

Seeman, M. V. (1983). Love as a delusion. *Medical Aspects of Human Sexuality, 17,* 162–170.

Seixas, J. S., and Youcha, G. (1985). *Children of Alcoholism.* New York: Harper and Row.

Semmens, J. P., and Tsai, C. C. (1984). Some gynecological causes of sexual problems. *Medical Aspects of Human Sexuality, 18,* 174–181.

Sena-Rivera, J., and Moore, E. (1979). La familia Chicana. In E. Corfman (Ed.), *Families Today.* Washington, DC: U.S. Department of HEW.

Shanas, E. (1980). Older people and their families: The new pioneers. *Journal of Marriage and the Family, 42,* 9–15.

Shaver, P., and Freedman, J. (1976). Your pursuit of happiness. *Psychology Today, 9,* 26ff.

Shaver, P., and Rubenstein, C. (1980). Healthy loners. *Psychology Today, 13,* 27, 95.

Shea, J. A., and Adams, G. R. (1984). Correlates of romantic attachment: A path analysis study. *Journal of Youth and Adolescence, 13,* 27–44.

Sherwin, R., and Corbett, S. (1985). Campus sexual norms and dating relationships: A trial analysis. *The Journal of Sex Research, 21,* 258–274.

Shonick, H. (1975). Pre-marital counseling: Three years' experience of a unique service. *The Family Coordinator, 24,* 321–324.

Shore, J. H. (1975). American Indian suicide: Fact and fantasy. *Psychiatry, 28,* 86–91.

Siegall, B. (1977). Incest: An American epidemic. *Los Angeles Times,* August 21.

Sigusch, V., et al. (1970). Psychosexual stimulation: Sex differences. *Journal of Sex Research, 6,* 10–24.

Sih, P. K. T., and Allen, L. B. (1976). *The Chinese in America.* New York: St. John's University Press.

Silber, T. (1980). Abortion in adolescence: The ethical dimension. *Adolescence, 15,* 461–474.

Simenauer, J., and Carroll, D. (1982). *Singles: The New Americans.* New York: Simon and Schuster.

Sindberg, R. M., Roberts, A. F., and McClain, D. (1972). Mate selection factors in computer matched marriages. *Journal of Marriage and the Family, 34,* 611–614.

Sinnott, J. D. (1982). Correlates of sex roles of older adults. *Journal of Gerontology, 37,* 587–594.

Skeen, P., Covi, R. B., and Robinson, B. E. (1985). Step-families: A review of the literature with suggestions for practitioners. *Journal of Counseling and Development, 64,* 121–125.

Skinner, D. A. (1980). Dual-career family stress and coping: A literature review. *Family Relations, 29,* 473–480.

Skovholt, T. M., and Thoen, G. A. (1987). Mental imagery and parenthood decision making. *Journal of Counseling and Development, 65,* 315–316.

Slater, E. J., Stewart, K. J., and Linn, M. W. (1983). The effects of family disruption on adolescent males and females. *Adolescence, 18,* 931–942.

Slesinger, D. P. (1980) . Rapid changes in household composition among low-income mothers. *Family Relations, 29,* 221–228.

Slovenko, R. (1983). Marriage contracts. *Medical Aspects of Human Sexuality, 17,* 277–281.

Small, A., Teagno, L., and Selz, K. (1980). The relationship of sex role to physical and psychological health. *Journal of Youth and Adolescence, 9,* 305–314.

Smart, M. S., and Smart, R. C. (1972). *Children: Development and Relationships* (2d ed.). New York: Macmillan.

Smilgis, M. (1987). The big chill: Fear of AIDS. *Time,* February 16, 58–59.

Smith, D. E. (1982). Dealing with family problems caused by alcohol abuse. *Medical Aspects of Human Sexuality, 16,* 127–132.

Smith, D. S. (1985). Wife employment and marital adjustment: A cumulation of results. *Family Relations, 34,* 483–490.

Smith, K. R., and Zick, C. D. (1986). The incidence of poverty among the recently widowed: Mediating factor in the life course. *Journal of Marriage and the Family, 48,* 619–630.

Smith, M. D., and Self, G. D. (1980). The congruence between mothers' and daughters' sex-role attitudes: A research note. *Journal of Marriage and the Family, 42,* 105–109.

Smith, M. J. (1980). The social consequences of single parenthood: A longitudinal perspective. *Family Relations, 29,* 75–81.

Smith, R. M., and Smith, C. W. (1981). Childrearing and single-parent fathers. *Family Relations, 30,* 411–417.

Smith, T. E. (1982). The case for parental transmission of educational goals: The importance of accurate offspring perceptions. *Journal of Marriage and the Family, 44,* 661–674.

Snow, J. H. (1971). *On Pilgrimage: Marriage in the '70's.* New York: Seabury.

Snyder, D. K. (1979). Multidimensional assessment of marital satisfaction. *Journal of Marriage and the Family, 41,* 813–823.

Snyder, M. (1982). Self-fulfilling stereotypes. *Psychology Today, 16,* 60ff.

Solano, C. H., Batten, P. G., and Parish, E. A. (1982). Loneliness and patterns of self-disclosure. *Journal of Personality and Social Psychology, 43,* 524–531.

Solberg, D. A., Butler, J., and Wagner, N. N. (1973). Sexual behavior in pregnancy. *New England Journal of Medicine, 288,* 1098–1103.

Sollie, D. I., and Scott, J. P. (1983). Teaching communication skills: A comparison of videotape feedback methods. *Family Relations, 32,* 503–511.

Solomon, K., and Minor, H. W. (1982). Need for privacy in marriage. *Medical Aspects of Human Sexuality, 16,* 104–115.

Soloway, N. M., and Smith, R. M. (1987). Antecedents of late birth: Timing decisions of men and women in dual-career marriages. *Family Relations, 36,* 258–262.

Soltz, D. F. (1978). Sex and the psychology of "playing dumb": A reevaluation. *Psychological Reports, 43,* 111–114.

Sonenblick, J. (1981). *The Legality of Love.* New York: Jove.

Spanier, B. G., and Glick, P. C. (1981). Marital instability in the United States: Some correlates and recent changes. *Family Relations, 31,* 329–338.

Spanier, G. B. (1976). Measuring dyadic adjustment: New scales for assessing the quality of marriage and similar dyads. *Journal of Marriage and the Family, 38,* 25–28.

Spanier, G. B. (1983). Married and unmarried cohabitation in the United States: 1980. *Journal of Marriage and the Family, 45,* 277–288.

Spanier, G. B., and Hanson, S. (1982). The role of extended kin in the adjustment to marital separation. *Journal of Divorce, 5,* 33–48.

682

Spanier, G. B., and Lewis, R. A. (1980). Marital quality: A review of the seventies. *Journal of Marriage and the Family, 42*, 825–839.

Spanier, G. B., Lewis, R. A., and Cole, C. L. (1975). Marital adjustment over the family life cycle: The issue of curvilinearity. *Journal of Marriage and the Family, 37*, 263–275.

Spanier, G., and Glick, P. C. (1980). Mate selection differentials between whites and blacks in the United States. *Social Forces, 58*, 707–725.

Sparks, S. (1983). *Latchkey Children.* Charlotte, NC: University of North Carolina at Charlotte. Paper submitted in partial fulfillment for a certificate of advanced study.

Speare, A., and Goldscheider, F. K. (1987). Effects of marital status change on residential mobility. *Journal of Marriage and the Family, 49*, 455–464.

Spencer, S. (1980). *Endless Love.* New York: Avon.

Spencer, S. L., and Zeiss, A. M. (1987). Sex roles and sexual dysfunction in college students. *The Journal of Sex Research, 23*, 338–347.

Spitze, G. D., and Waite, L. J. (1981). Wives' employment: The role of husbands' perceived attitudes. *Journal of Marriage and the Family, 43*, 117–124.

Sprecher, S. (1985). Sex differences in bases of power in dating relationships. *Sex Roles, 12*, 449–462.

Spreitzer, E., and Riley, L. L. (1974). Factors associated with singlehood. *Journal of Marriage and the Family, 36*, 533–542.

Sprenkle, D. H., and Storm, C. L. (1983). Divorce therapy outcome research: A substantive and methodological review. *Journal of Marital and Family Therapy, 9*, 239–258.

Sprey, J., and Matthews, S. H. (1982). Contemporary grandparenthood: a systematic transition. *Annals of the American Academy of Political and Social Sciences, 464*, 91–103.

St. John-Parson, D. (1978). Continuous dual-career families: A case study. *Psychology of Women, 3*, 30–42.

Stack, S. (1980). The effect of marital dissolution on suicide. *Journal of Marriage and the Family, 42*, 83–92.

Staples, R. (1981). *The World of Black Singles: Changing Patterns of Male–Female Relationships.* Westport, CT: Greenfield.

Staples, R. (1982). *Black Masculinity: The Black Male's Role in American Society.* San Francisco: The Black Scholar Press.

Staples, R. (1985). Changes in black family structure: The conflict between family ideology and structural conditions. *Journal of Marriage and the Family, 47*, 1005–1013.

Staples, R., and Miranda, A. (1980) Racial and cultural variations among American families: A decennial review of the literature on minority families. *Journal of Marriage and the Family, 42*, 887–903.

Stark, E. (1984). The unspeakable family secret. *Psychology Today, 18*, 38–46.

Stark, E. (1986). A grandmother at 27. *Psychology Today, 20*, 18.

Stark, G. U. (1971). Seven on a honeymoon. *Parents' Magazine, 46*, May, 445.

Starr, J. R., and Carns, D. E. (1972). Singles in the city. *Society, 9*, 43–48.

Stayton, W. R. (1983). Preventing infidelity. *Medical Aspects of Human Sexuality, 17*, 36C–36D.

Steckel, R. H. (1980). Slave marriage and the family. *Journal of Family History, 5*, 406–421.

Stein, J., (Ed.). *The Random House Dictionary of the English Language.* Unabridged. New York: Random House, 1973.

Stein, P. J. (1978). The lifestyles and life chances of the never married. *Marriage and Family Review, 1*, 3–11.

Stein, P., ed. (1981). *Single Life: Unmarried Adults in Social Context.* New York: St. Martin's Press.

Steinhoff, P. G. (1973). Background characteristics of abortion patients. In H. J. Osofsky and J. D. Osofsky (Eds.), *The Abortion Experience: Psychological and Medical Impact* (pp. 206–231). New York: Harper.

Steinman, D. L., et al. (1981). A comparison of male and female patterns of sexual arousal. *Archives of Sexual Behavior, 10*, 529–548.

Steinmetz, S. K. (1978). Violence between family members. *Marriage and Family Review, 1*, 1–16.

Steinmetz, S. K., and Straus, M. A. (1973). The family as a cradle of violence. *Society, 10*, 50.

Steinmetz, S. K., and Straus, M. A. (1974). *Violence in the Family.* New York: Dodd, Mead.

Stephen, T. D. (1985). Fixed-sequence and circular-causal models of relationship development: Divergent views on the role of communication in intimacy. *Journal of Marriage and the Family, 47*, 955–963.

Sterilizations exceeed one million in 1983; vasectomies up sharply. (1985). *Family Planning Perspectives, 17*, January/February, 43.

Stern, P. N. (1982). Affiliating in stepfather families: Teachable strategies leading to a stepfather-child friendship. *Western Journal of Nursing Research, 4*, 76-89.

Sternberg, R. (1986). A triangular theory of love. *Psychological Review, 93*, 119–135.

Stewart, A. J., and Rubin, Z. (1976). The power motive in the dating couple. *Journal of Personality and Social Psychology, 34*, 305–309.

Stewart, M., and Stewart, S. (1975). *Teaching-learning Interactions in Chinese-American and Anglo-American Families: Study in Cognitive Development and Ethnicity.* Unpublished paper.

Stichler, J. P., and Alfonso, D. D. (1980). Cesarean birth. *American Journal of Nursing, 80*, 466–468.

Stinnett, N., and DeFrain, J. (1985). *Secrets of Strong Families.* Boston: Little, Brown.

Stinnett, N., Knorr, B., DeFrain, J., and Rowe, G. (1981). How strong families cope with crises. *Family Perspective, 15,* 159–166.

Stock, W., and Geer, J. A. (1982). A study of fantasy-based sexual arousal in women. *Archives of Sexual Behavior, 11,* 33–47.

Stoller, E. P. (1985). Exchange patterns in the informal support networks of the elderly: The impact of reciprocity on morale. *Journal of Marriage and the Family, 47,* 335–342.

Strate, J. M., and Dubnoff, S. J. (1986). How much income is enough? Measuring the income adequacy of retired persons using a survey based approach. *Journal of Gerontology, 41,* 393–400.

Straus, M. A. (1974). Leveling, civility, and violence in the family. *Journal of Marriage and the Family, 36,* 13–29.

Straus, M. A. (1979). Measuring intrafamily conflict and violence: The conflict tactics (CT) scales. *Journal of Marriage and the Family, 41,* 75–88.

Straus, M. A., and Gelles, R. J. (1986). Societal change and change in family violence from 1975 to 1985 as revealed by two national surveys. *Journal of Marriage and the Family, 48,* 465–479.

Straus, M., Gelles, R., and Steinmetz, S. (1980). *Behind Closed Doors: Violence in the American Family.* New York: Van Nostrand Reinhold.

Streltzer, A. A. (1979). A grandchild's group in a home for the aged. *Health Social Work, 4,* 167–183.

Stroman, S. H., and Duff, E. (1982). The latchkey child: Whose responsibility? *Childhood Education, 59,* 76–79.

Strong, B., Wilson, S., Robbins, M., and Johns, T. (1981). *Human Sexuality* (2d ed.). New York: West.

Strouse, J. S. (1987). College bars as social settings for heterosexual contacts. *The Journal of Sex Research, 23,* 374–382.

Strube, M. J., and Barbour, L. S. (1983). The decision to leave an abusive relationship: Economic dependence and psychological commitment. *Journal of Marriage and the Family, 45,* 785–793.

Strube, M. J., and Barbour, L. S. (1984). Factors related to the decision to leave an abusive relationship. *Journal of Marriage and the Family, 46,* 837–844.

Stryker, S. (1980). *Symbolic Interactionism.* Menlo Park, CA: Benjamin/Cummings.

Stuart, R. B., and Stuart, F. (1975). *Premarital Counseling Inventory.* Champaign, IL: Research Press.

Study of some 20,000 men finds no evidence vasectomy has any adverse health consequences. (1984). *Family Planning Perspectives, 16,* January/February, 35, 36.

Substantially higher morbidity and mortality rates found among infants born to adolescent mothers. (1984). *Family Planning Perspectives, 16,* March/April, 91.

Sue, D. (1979). Erotic fantasies of college students during coitus. *Journal of Sex Research, 15,* 299–305.

Suitor, J. J. (1987). Mother-daughter relations when married daughters return to school: Effects of status similarity. *Journal of Marriage and the Family, 49,* 435–444.

Sussman, M. B. (1974). *Personal Contracts Study: General and Specific Research Issues and Questions.* Cleveland, OH: Case Western University, Institute on Family and Bureaucratic Study. Mimeographed.

Swensen, C. H. (1983). Post-parental marriages. *Medical Aspects of Human Sexuality, 17,* 171–194.

Swensen, C. H., Eskew, R. W., and Kohlhepp, K. A. (1981). Stage of family life cycle, ego development, and the marriage relationship. *Journal of Marriage and the Family, 43,* 841–851.

Szinovacz, M. E. (1983). Using couple data as a methodological tool: The case of marital violence. *Journal of Marriage and the Family, 45,* 633–644.

Szinovacz, M. E. (1987). Family power. In M. B. Sussman and S. K. Steinmetz, *Handbook of Marriage and the Family* (pp. 651–693). New York: Plenum.

Tanfer, K. (1987). Patterns of premarital cohabitation among never-married women in the United States. *Journal of Marriage and the Family, 49,* 483–497.

Tanfer, K., and Horn, M. C. (1985). Contraceptive use, pregnancy, and fertility patterns among single American women in their 20s. *Family Planning Perspectives, 17,* 10-19.

Tavris, C. (1982). Anger diffused. *Psychology Today, 16,* 25–29.

Taylor, D. A. (1968). Some apsects of the development of interpersonal relationships: Social penetration process. *Journal of Social Psychology, 75,* 79–90.

Taylor, R. J. (1985). The extended family as a source of support to elderly blacks. *The Gerontologist, 25,* 488–495.

Taylor, R. J. (1986). Receipt of support from family among black Americans: Demographic and familial differences. *Journal of Marriage and the Family, 48,* 67–77.

Temes, R. (1981). New rules for marital unhappiness? *Psychology Today, 15,* 17.

Tennov, D. (1979). *Love and Limerence: The Experience of Being in Love.* New York: Stein and Day.

Teti, D. M., Lamb, M. E., and Elster, A. B. (1987). Long-range socioeconomic and marital consequences of adolescent marriage in three cohorts of adult males. *Journal of Marriage and the Family, 49,* 499–506.

The denial of Indian civil and religious rights. (1979). *Indian Historian, 8,* 43–46.

The way singles are changing U.S. (1977). *U.S. News and World Report,* January 31, 59–60.

Thomas, L. E., McCabe, E., and Berry, J. E. (1980).

Unemployment and family stress: A reassessment. *Family Relations, 29,* 517–524.

Thomas, S., Albrecht, K., and White, P. (1984). Determinants of marital quality in dual-career couples. *Family Relations, 33,* 513–521.

Thompson, A. P. (1983). Extramarital sex: A review of the research literature. *Journal of Sex Research, 19,* 1–22.

Thompson, A. P. (1984). Emotional and sexual components of extramarital relations. *Journal of Marriage and the Family, 46,* 35–42.

Thompson, K. S. (1980). A comparison of black and white adolescents' beliefs about having children. *Journal of Marriage and the Family, 42,* 133–139.

Thompson, L., and Spanier, G. B. (1983). The end of marriage and acceptance of marital termination. *Journal of Marriage and the Family, 45,* 103–113.

Thompson, L., and Walker, A. J. (1984). Mothers and daughters: Aid patterns and attachment. *Journal of Marriage and the Family, 46,* 313–322.

Thompson, L., and Walker, A. J. (1987). Mothers as mediators between grandmothers and their young adult granddaughters. *Family Relations, 36,* 72–77.

Thompson, M. E. (1981). Sex differences: Differential access to power or sex-role socialization? *Sex Roles, 7,* 413–424.

Thornton, A., Alwin, D. F., and Camburn, D. (1983). Causes and consequences of sex-role attitudes and attitude change. *American Sociological Review, 48,* 211–227.

Thornton, A., and Freedman, D. (1982). Changing attitudes toward marriage and single life. *Family Planning Perspectives, 14,* 297–303.

Tickamyer, B. R. (1979). Women's roles and family intentions. *Pacific Sociological Review, 22,* 167–184.

Tiggle, R. B., Peters, M. D., Kelley, H. H., and Vincent, J. (1982). Correlational and discrepancy indices of understanding and their relation to marital satisfaction. *Journal of Marriage and the Family, 44,* 209–216.

Timnick, L. (1982). How you can learn to be likable, confident, socially successful for only the cost of your present education. *Psychology Today, 16,* 42–49.

Todd, J. (1982). Predicting marital success or failure. *Medical Aspects of Human Sexuality, 16,* 69–96.

Tognoli, J. (1980). Male friendships and intimacy across the life span. *Family Relations, 29,* 273–279.

Toman, W. (1969). *Family Constellation: Its Effect on Personality and Social Behavior.* New York: Springer.

Tomeh, A. K. (1978). Sex-role orientation: An analysis of structural and attitudinal predictors. *Journal of Marriage and the Family, 40,* 341–354.

Tooth, G. (1985). Why children's TV turns off so many parents. *U.S. News and World Report,* February 18, 65.

Traupman, J., Eckels, E., and Hatfield, E. (1982). Intimacy in older women's lives. *The Gerontologist, 22,* 493–498.

Trotter, R. J. (1986). The three faces of love. *Psychology Today, 20,* 46–54.

Trovato, F. (1986). The relationship between marital dissolution and suicide: The Canadian case. *Journal of Marriage and the Family, 48,* 341–348.

Trovato, F. (1987). A longitudinal analysis of divorce and suicide in Canada. *Journal of Marriage and the Family, 49,* 193–203.

Tsai, M., and Wagner, N. N. (1978). Therapy groups for women sexually molested as children. *Archives of Sexual Behavior, 7,* 417–427.

Turnbull, S. K., and Turnbull, J. M. (1983). To dream the impossible dream: An agenda for discussion with stepparents. *Family Relations, 32,* 227–230.

Turner, P. H., and Smith, R. M. (1983). Single parents and day care. *Family Relations, 32,* 215–226.

Tyrer, L. B. (1984). Precautions in diaphragm use. *Medical Aspects of Human Sexuality, 18,* 243, 247.

U.S. Bureau of the Census. (1975). *Historical Statistics of the United States, Colonial Times to 1970: Parts I and II.* Bicentennial Edition. Washington, DC: U.S. Government Printing Office.

U.S. Bureau of the Census. (1979). Divorce, child custody, and child support. *Current Population Reports,* ser. p-23, no. 84. Washington, DC: U.S. Government Printing Office.

U.S. Bureau of the Census. (1980). American families and living arrangements. *Current Population Reports,* ser. p-23, no. 104. Washington, DC: U.S. Government Printing Office.

U.S. Bureau of the Census. (1983). Fertility of American women: June 1982 (Advance report). *Current Population Reports,* ser. p-20, no. 379. Washington, DC: U.S. Government Printing Office.

U.S. Bureau of the Census. (1985). Households, families, marital status, and living arrangements: March 1985. *Current Population Reports,* ser. p-20, no. 402. Washington, DC: U.S. Government Printing Office.

U.S. Bureau of the Census. (1986a). Household and family characteristics, March 1985. *Current Population Reports,* ser. p-20, no. 411. Washington, DC: U.S. Government Printing Office.

U.S. Bureau of the Census. (1986b). Marital status and living arrangements: March 1985. *Current Population Reports,* ser. p-20, no. 410. Washington, DC: U.S. Government Printing Office.

U.S. Bureau of the Census. (1986c). Women in the American economy, by C. M. Taeuber and V. Valdisera. *Current Population Reports,* ser. p-23, no. 146. Washington, DC: U.S. Government Printing Office.

U.S. Bureau of the Census. (1987a). Households, families, marital status, and living arrangements: March

1987. *Current Population Reports,* ser. p-20, no. 417. Washington, DC: U.S. Government Printing Office.

U.S. Bureau of the Census. (1987b). *Statistical Abstract of the United States,* March 1987 (107th ed.). Washington, DC: U.S. Government Printing Office.

U.S. Commission on Civil Rights. (1977). *Window Dressing on the Set: Women and Minorities in Television.* Washington, DC: U.S. Government Printing Office.

U.S. Department of Health and Human Services. (1980). Births, marriages, divorces, and deaths for May 1980. *Monthly Vital Statistics Report, 29,* no. 5. Washington, DC: U.S. Department of HHS.

U.S. Department of Health and Human Services. (1987). Births, marriages, divorces, and deaths for November 1986. *Monthly Vital Statistics Report, 35.* Hyattsville, Md: National Center for Health Statistics.

U.S. Department of HEW, Public Health Service. (1980a). *The Alcohol, Drug Abuse, and Mental Health National Data Book.* Rockville, MD: Alcohol, Drug Abuse, and Mental Health Administration.

U.S. Department of HEW, Public Health Service. (1980b). *7th Annual Report.* Rockville, MD: National Institute of Alcohol Abuse and Alcoholism.

U.S. Department of the Interior. (1965). *Indians of Oklahoma.* Washington, DC: Bureau of Indian Affairs.

Udry, J. R. (1981). Marital alternatives and marital disruption. *Journal of Marriage and the Family, 43,* 889–893.

Ulbrich, P., and Huber, J. (1981). Observing parental violence: Distribution and effects. *Journal of Marriage and the Family, 43,* 623–631.

Unger, S. (1977). *The Destruction of American Families.* New York: Association on American Indian Affairs.

Updegraff, S. C. (1968). Changing role of the grandmother. *Journal of Home Economics, 60,* 177–180.

Usui, W. M., Keil, T. J., and Durig, K. R. (1985). Socioeconomic comparisons and life satisfaction of elderly adults. *Journal of Gerontology, 40,* 110–114.

Vaillant, G. E. (1977a). *Adaptation of Life.* Boston: Little, Brown.

Vaillant, G. E. (1977b). The climb to maturity: How the best and brightest come of age. *Psychology Today, 11,* 34ff.

Valentine, D. P. (1982). The experience of pregnancy: A developmental process. *Family Relations, 31,* April, 243–248.

Van Meter, M. J. S., and Agronow, S. J. (1982). The stress of multiple roles: The case for role strain among married college women. *Family Relations, 31,* 131–138.

Vander Mey, B. J., and Neff, R. L. (1984). Adult-child incest: A sample of substantiated cases. *Family Relations, 33,* 549–557.

Vander Mey, B. J., and Rosher, J. H. (1981). *Marriage Contracting: Sex Role Liberation?* Paper presented to the Southern Sociological Society, April 1981.

Vanderkooi, L., and Pearson, J. (1983). Mediating divorce disputes: Mediator behavior, styles, and roles. *Family Relations, 32,* 557–566.

Veevers, J. E. (1973a). Voluntary childlessness: A neglected area of family study. *The Family Coordinator, 22,* 199–205.

Veevers, J. E. (1974a). The life style of voluntarily childless couples. In L. Larson (Ed.). *The Canadian Family in Comparative Perspective.* Toronto: Prentice-Hall.

Veevers, J. E. (1974b). Voluntary childlessness and social policy: An alternative view. *The Family, 23,* 397–406.

Veevers, J. E. (1980). *Childless by Choice.* Scarborough, Ontario: Butterworth.

Veevers, J. E. (l973b). Voluntary childless wives. *Sociology and Social Research, 57,* 356–366.

Vera, H., Berardo, D. H., and Berardo, F. M. (1985). Age heterogamy in marriage. *Journal of Marriage and the Family, 47,* 553–569.

Verbrugge, L. (1979a). Marital status and health. *Journal of Marriage and the Family, 41,* 267–285.

Verbrugge, L. M. (1979b). Multiplicity in adult friendships. *Social Forces, 57,* 1286–1309.

Veroff J., and Veroff, J. B. (1972). Reconsideration of a measure of power motivation. *Psychological Bulletin, 78,* 279–291.

Veroff, J., Kulka, R. A., and Douvan, E. (1981). *The Inner American: A Self-Portrait from 1957 to 1976.* New York: Basic Books.

Visher, E., and Visher, J. (1979). *Stepfamilies: A Guide to Working with Stepparents and Stepchildren.* New York: Brunner/Mazel.

Vitousek, B. M. (1979). Mixed marriages are a mixed bag. *Family Advocate, 1,* 16ff.

Voth, H. M., Perry, J. A., McCranie, J. E., and Rogers, R. R. (1982). How can extramarital affairs be prevented? *Medical Aspects of Human Sexuality, 16,* 62–74.

Voydanoff, P. (1980). Work roles as stressors in corporate families. *Family Relations, 29,* 489–494.

Voydanoff, P., and Kelly, R. F. (1984). Determinants of work-related family problems among employed parents. *Journal of Marriage and the Family, 46,* 881–892.

Vreeland, R. S. (1972). Is it true what they say about Harvard boys? *Psychology Today, 5,* 65–68.

Vuchinich, S. (1987). Starting and stopping spontaneous family conflicts. *Journal of Marriage and the Family, 49,* 591–601.

Vukelich, C., and Kliman, D. S. (1985). Mature and teenage mothers' infant growth expectations and use of child development information sources. *Family Relations, 34,* 189–196.

686

Wachowiai, D., and Bragg, H. (1980). Open marriage and marital adjustment. *Journal of Marriage and the Family, 42,* 57–62.

Walbroehl, G. (1984). Sexuality during pregnancy. *American Family Physician, 29,* 273–275.

Wald, E. (1981). *The Remarried Family: Challenge and Promise.* New York: Family Service Assocation of America.

Waldo, M., and Guerney, B. G. (1983). Marital relationship enhancement therapy in the treatment of alcoholism. *Journal of Marital and Family Therapy, 9,* 321–323.

Waletzky, L. (1981). Emotional illness in the postpartum period. In P. Ahmed (Ed.), *Pregnancy, Childbirth, and Parenthood.* New York: Elsevier.

Walfish, S., and Myerson, M. (1980). Sexual identity and attitudes toward sexuality. *Archives of Sexual Behavior, 9,* 199–203.

Walker, A. J. (1985). Reconceptualizing family stress. *Journal of Marriage and the Family, 47,* 827–837.

Walker, K. N., and Messinger, L. (1979). Remarriage after divorce: Dissolution and reconstruction of family boundaries. *Family Process, 18,* 185–192.

Walker, L. E. (1979). *The Battered Woman.* New York: Harper and Row.

Waller, W. (1937). The rating and dating complex. *American Sociological Review, 2,* 727–734.

Wallerstein, J. S., and Kelly, J. B. (1980). *Surviving the Breakup: How Children and Parents Cope with Divorce.* London: Grant McIntyre.

Wallis, C. (1987). You haven't heard anything yet. *Time,* February 17.

Wallston, B. S., Foster, M. A., and Berger, M. (1978). I will follow him: Myth, reality, or forced choice — Job-seeking experiences of dual-career couples. *Psychology of Women Quarterly, 3,* 9–21.

Walstedt, J. (1977). The altruistic other orientation: An exploration of female powerlessness. *Psychology of Women Quarterly, 2,* 162–196.

Walster, E. G., Walster, W., and Berscheid, E. (1978). *Equity Theory and Research.* Boston: Allyn and Bacon.

Walster, E., and Walster, G. W. (1978). *A New Look at Love.* Reading, MA: Addison-Wesley.

Walster, E., Walster, G. W., and Traupmann, J. (1978). Equity and premarital sex. *Journal of Personality and Social Psychology, 36,* 82–92.

Walters, C. M., and McKenry, P. C. (1985). Predictors of life satisfaction among rural and urban employed mothers: A research note. *Journal of Marriage and the Family, 47,* 1067–1071.

Walters, J., and Walters, L. H. (1980). Parent-child relationships: A review of 1970–1979. *Journal of Marriage and the Family, 42,* 807–822.

Walters, L. H. (1982). How habits strain marriage. *Medical Aspects of Human Sexuality, 16,* 48K–48CC.

Waltner, R. (1986). Genital identity: A core component of sexual- and self-identity. *The Journal of Sex Research, 22,* 399–408.

Wampler, K. S., and Powell, G. S. (1982). The Barrett-Lennard Relationship Inventory as a measure of marital satisfaction. *Family Relations, 35,* 539–545.

Warlick, J. L. (1985). Why is poverty after 65 a woman's problem? *Journal of Gerontology, 40,* 75–757.

Warner, R. L., Lee, G. R., and Lee, J. (1986). Social organization, spousal resources, and marital power: A cross-cultural study. *Journal of Marriage and the Family, 48,* 121–128.

Wasserman, I. M. (1984). A longitudinal analysis of the linkage between suicide, unemployment, and marital dissolution. *Journal of Marriage and the Family, 46,* 853–859.

Waterlow, J. C., and Thompson, A. M. (1979). Observations on the adequacy of breast feeding. *Lancet, 2,* 238–242.

Watkins, H. D., and Bradbard, M. R. (1982). Child maltreatment: An overview with suggestions for intervention and research. *Family Relations, 31,* 323–333.

Watson, M. A. (1981). Custody alternatives: Defining the best interests of the children. *Family Relations, 30,* 474–479.

Watson, R. E. L. (1983). Premarital cohabitation vs. traditional courtship: Their effects on subsequent marital adjustment. *Family Relations, 32,* 139–147.

Watson, R. E. L., and DeMeo, P. W. (1987). Premarital cohabitation vs. traditional courtship and subsequent marital adjustment: A replication and follow-up. *Family Relations, 36,* 193–196.

Weigel, R. R., Weigel, D. J., and Blundall, J. (1987). Stress, coping, and satisfaction: Generational differences in farm families. *Family Relations, 36,* 45–48.

Weis, D. L., and Slosnerick, M. (1981). Attitudes toward sexual and nonsexual extramarital involvements among a sample of college students. *Journal of Marriage and the Family, 43,* 349–358.

Weis, D. L., Slosnerick, M., Cote, R., and Sollie, D. L. (1986). A survey instrument for assessing the cognitive association of sex, love, and marriage. *The Journal of Sex Research, 22,* 206–220.

Weisman, A. D. (1973). Coping with untimely death. *Psychiatry, 36,* 366–378.

Weiss, R. S. (1979). *Going It Alone.* New York: Basic Books.

Weiss, R. S. (1984). The impact of marital dissolution on income and consumption in single-parent households. *Journal of Marriage and the Family, 46,* 115–127.

Weitzman, L. J. (1981). *The Marriage Contract: Spouses, Lovers, and the Law.* New York: The Free Press.

Welch, C. E., and Price-Bonham, S. (1983). A decade of no-fault divorce revisited: California, Georgia, and Washington. *Journal of Marriage and the Family, 45*, 411–418.

Welch, R., et al. (1979). Subtle sex-role cues in children's commercials. *Journal of Communication, 29*, 202–209.

Wells, B. (1983). Nocturnal orgasms: Females' perceptions of a "normal" sexual experience. *Journal of Sex Education and Therapy, 9*, 32–38.

Wells, J. G. (1976). A critical look at personal marriage contracts. *Family Coordinator, 25*, 33–38.

Wells, K. (1980). Gender-role identity and psychological adjustment in adolescence. *Journal of Youth and Adolescence, 9*, 59–73.

Wernick, M., and Manaster, G. J. (1984). Age and the perception of age and attractiveness. *The Gerontologist, 24*, 408–414.

Westoff, C. F., and Parke, R., Jr. (Eds.). (1972). *Demographic and Social Aspects of Population Growth: Vol. I.* Washington, DC: U.S. Commission on Population Growth and the American Future.

Westoff, L. A., and Westoff, C. (1971). *From Now to Zero* Boston: Little, Brown.

Wetzel, L., and Ross, M. A. (1983). Psychological and social ramifications of battering: Observations leading to a counseling methodology for victims of domestic violence. *The Personnel and Guidance Journal, 61*, 423–428.

Whelan, E. (1980). *A Baby? . . . Maybe.* New York: Bobbs-Merrill.

Whipple, C. M., and Whittle, D. (1976). *The Compatibility Test.* Englewood Cliffs, NJ: Prentice-Hall.

White, D. (1981). Pursuit of the ultimate aphrodisiac. *Psychology Today, 15*, 9–11.

White, J. M. (1987). Premarital cohabitation and marital stability in Canada. *Journal of Marriage and the Family, 49*, 641–647.

White, K. M. (1980). Problems and characteristics of college students. *Adolescence, 15*, 23–41.

White, L. K. (1983). Determinants of spousal interaction: Marital structure or marital happiness. *Journal of Marriage and the Family, 45*, 511–519.

White, L. K., and Brinkerhoff, D. B. (1981). Children's work in the family: Its significance and meaning. *Journal of Marriage and the Family, 43*, 789–798.

White, L., Brinkerhoff, D. B., and Booth, A. (1985). The effects of marital disruption on child's attachments to parents. *Journal of Family Issues, 6*, 5–22.

White, M. J., and Tsui, A. O. (1986). A panel study of family-level structural change. *Journal of Marriage and the Family, 48*, 435–446.

White, S. W., and Bloom, B. L. (1981). Factors related to the adjustment of divorcing men. *Family Relations, 30*, 349–360.

Whitehouse, J. (1981). The role of the initial attracting quality in marriage: Virtues and vices. *Journal of Marital and Family Therapy, 7*, 61–67.

Whiteside, M. F. (1982). Remarriage: A family developmental process. *Journal of Marital and Family Therapy, 8*, 59–68.

Wiest, W. (1977). Semantic differential profiles of orgasm and other experiences among men and women. *Sex Roles, 3*, 399–403.

Wilcoxon, S. A. (1985). Healthy family functioning: The other side of family pathology. *Journal of Counseling and Development, 63*, 495–499.

Wilcoxon, S. A. (1987). Grandparents and grandchildren. *Journal of Counseling and Development, 65*, 289–290.

Wilcoxon, S. A., and Hovestadt, A. J. (1983). Perceived health and similarity of family of origin experiences as predictors of dyadic adjustment for married couples. *Journal of Marital and Family Therapy, 9*, 431–434.

Wilkening, E. A., and Bharadwaj, L. K. (1967). Dimensions of aspirations, work roles, and decision-making of farm husbands and wives in Wisconsin. *Journal of Marriage and the Family, 29*, 703–711.

Wilkie, J. R. (1981). The trend toward delayed parenthood. *Journal of Marriage and the Family, 43*, 583–591.

Wilkinson, M. L. (1978). Romantic love and sexual expression. *The Family Coordinator, 27*, April, 141–148.

Williams, C. E. (1974). Conflict: Modeling or taking flight. In C. E. Williams and J. F. Crosby (Eds.), *Choice and Challenge* (pp. 218–223). Dubuque, IA: William C. Brown.

Willie, C. U. (1981). *A New Look at Black Families* (2nd ed.). Bayside, NY: General Hall.

Willie, C. V., and Greenblatt, S. L. (1978). Four "classic" studies of power relationships in black families: A review and look to the future. *Journal of Marriage and the Family, 40*, 691–696.

Wilson, J., Carrington, E., and Ledger, W. (1983). *Obstetrics and Gynecology.* St. Louis, MO: Mosby.

Winch, R. (1971). *The Modern Family.* New York: Holt.

Winch, R. F. (1958). *Mate Selection: A Study of Complementary Needs.* New York: Harper and Row.

Winch, R. F. (1967). Another look at the theory of complementary needs in mate selection. *Journal of Marriage and the Family, 29*, 756–762.

Winter, D. G., Stewart, A. J., and McClelland, D. C. (1977). Husband's motives and wife's career level. *Journal of Personality and Social Psychology, 35*, 159–166.

Wiseman, J. P. (1980). The "home treatment": The first steps in trying to cope with an alcoholic husband. *Family Relations, 29*, 541–549.

Witkin, S. L., Edleson, J. L., Rose, S. D., and Hall, J. A. (1983). Group training in marital communication: A comparative study. *Journal of Marriage and the Family, 45*, 661–669.

Woititz, J. G. (1983). *Adult Children of Alcoholics.* Pompano Beach, FL: Health Communications.

Wolfe, L. (1981). *The Cosmo Report*. New York: Arbor House.

Women who never used pill are twice as likely as users to develop endometrial or ovarian cancer. (1982). *Family Planning Perspectives, 14*, 195.

Wright, J. D. (1978). Are working women really more satisfied? Evidence from several national surveys. *Journal of Marriage and the Family, 40*, 301–313.

Wright, P. H. (1982). Men's friendships, women's friendships, and the alleged inferiority of the latter. *Sex Roles, 8*, 1–20.

Wyly, M. V., and Hulicka, I. M. (1977). Problems and compensations in widowhood. In I. M. Hulicka (Ed.), *Empirical Studies in the Psychology and Sociology of Aging*. New York: Crowell.

Ybarra, L. (1977). *Conjugal Role Relationships in the Chicano Family*. Unpublished doctoral dissertation. University of California.

Yeung, W., Chai, L., Hatanaka, H., and Kitano, H.H.L. (1984). Asian-American interracial marriage. *Journal of Marriage and the Family, 46*, 179–190.

Yllo, K., and Straus, M. A. (1981). Interpersonal violence among married and cohabiting couples. *Family Relations, 30*, 339–347.

Yogev, S., and Brett, J. (1985). Perceptions of division of housework and child care and marital satisfaction. *Journal of Marriage and the Family, 47*, 609–618.

Young American women delaying motherhood: 25 percent may remain permanently childless. (1983). *Family Planning Perspectives, 15*, 224, 225.

Young, N. F. (1972). Socialization of patterns among the Chinese in Hawaii. *Amerasia Journal, 1*, 31–51.

Zabin, L. S. (1981). The impact of early use of prescription contraceptives on reducing premarital teenage pregnancies. *Family Planning Perspectives, 13*, 72ff.

Zelkowitz, P. (1987). Social support and aggressive behavior in young children. *Family Relations, 36*, 129–134.

Zelnik, M., and Shah, F. K. (1983). First intercourse among young Americans. *Family Planning Perspectives, 15*, 64–70.

Zelnik, M., and Kantner, J. P. (1974). The resolution of teenage first pregnancies. *Family Planning Perspectives, 6*, 74–80.

Zelnik, M., and Kantner, J. P. (1980). Sexual activity, contraceptive use and pregnancy among metropolitan-area teenagers: 1971–1973. *Family Planning Perspectives, 12*, 230.

Zelnik, S., and Kantner, J. S. (1978). Contraceptive patterns and premarital pregnancy among women aged 15–19 in 1976. *Family Planning Perspectives, 10*, 135–142.

Zimmerman, D. H., and West, C. (1975). Sex roles, interruptions and silences in conversations. In B. Thorne and N. Henley (Eds.), *Language and Sex: Differences and Dominance*. Rowley, MA: Newbury House.

Zollar, A. C., and Williams, J. S. (1987). The contribution of marriage to the life satisfaction of black adults *Journal of Marriage and the Family, 49*, 87–92.

Zube, M. (1982). Changing behavior and outlook of aging men and women: Implications for marriage in the middle and later years. *Family Relations, 31*, 147–156.

NAME INDEX

694

INDEX

Boldface numbers indicate pages on which key terms are defined.

Cancer, and oral contraceptives, 463–464, 465
Career. *See* Dual-career family; Work; Working women
Cars, 368–371
Castration, **470**
Catharsis, **435**–436
Catholics
    divorce among, 589
    interfaith marriages of, 189–191
    See also Religion
Cervical cancer, 464
Cervical mucus method of birth control, 471–472
Cesarean section, **499**
Chicanos. *See* Mexican Americans
Child abuse, **441**–444, 455
Childbirth, 495–499
    anesthesia during, 498
    breech, **496**
    calculating date of, 486–487
    Cesarean section, 499
    father's role in, 496–497
    home vs. hospital delivery, 496, 497
    knowledge of, 504
    labor and delivery, 495–499
    Lamaze method of, 494–495
    Leboyer method of, 499–500
    postpartum period, 499–503
    prepared, 494–495
    sexual activity after, 493
Child care
    female-headed families and, 522, 523
    infants and, 515
    need for, 18
Child custody, **611**–613
Childless family, **5**, 452–453, 454–456
Child-rearing, 507–529
    abusiveness and, 62–66
    alcoholism and, 66–69
    in Chinese American families, 40–41
    cognitive development and, 517–519
    cohabitation and, 255
    discipline and, 519–521
    in dual-career families, 340–341
    emotional needs and, 513–517
    as family function, 8
    gender roles in, 314–316
    low socioeconomic status and, 31
    in Mexican American families, 39
    in Native American families, 45–46

parental roles in, 510–513
philosophies of, 508–509
in single-parent families, 5, 19–20, 360–361, 522–527
socialization and, 519–521
working women and, 17–18
See also Parenthood; Parents
Children
    adult, 287, 291–293, 532–544
    autonomy of, 516–517
    cognitive development of, 517–519
    cost of, 349–350
    differences in, 509
    discipline of, 519–521
    divorce and, 602–603, 611–614
    effects of single-parent families on, 525–527
    emotional needs of, 513–517
    grandparents and, 544–551
    housework and, 316–317, 521
    latchkey, **511**–513
    meeting needs of, 510–511
    roles in household tasks, 316–317, 521
    socialization of, 519–521
    as source of power, 409
    spoiling, 515–516
    stepchildren, 631–639
    stepsiblings, 620, 636, 637, 639
    See also Child-rearing; Parenthood; Parents
Child support, 602
Chinese Americans, 40–43
    child-rearing among, 40–41
    education of, 42
    health of, 42
    housing of, 42
    immigration of, 40
    interracial marriages of, 187–188
    prejudice and, 42
    sex roles among, 43
Chlamydial infections, 225
Chores, of children, 316–317, 521
Class
    differences among blacks, 35–36
    mate selection and, 184
    underclass, 36
    See also Socioeconomic status
Clitoral orgasm, **207**
Clitoris, 204, 207
Coercive power, **408**
Cognition, **517**
Cognitive development, 517–519
Cohabitation, nonmarital, 246–255
    as alternative to marriage, 250–251
    children and, 255

dating and, 253–254
effects on marriage, 254–255
marriage vs., 252–253
patterns of relationships, 249–251
as prelude to marriage, 250
reactions to, 251–253
reasons for increase in, 247–249
statistics on, 246–247
Cohabiters
    characteristics of, 248
    communication between, 251
    intimacy of, 251
Cohabiting family, **7**, 100–101
Cohort, 15
Coitus interruptus, **472**–473
College bars, 129–130
College mixers, 130
Comarital sex, **562**–563
Combination (contraceptive) pills, **461**
Commitment
    marital success and, 75–79
    premature, in dating, 144
Common-law marriage, **238**
Communal family, **6**
Communication, 60–62, **421**–428
    barriers to, 423–425
    clarity of, 426–427
    cohabitation and, 251
    date rape and, 139
    dating problems and, 143
    double-bind, **423**
    improving skills in, 425–428
    marital success and, 77, 85, 421–422
    nonverbal, 422–423
    sexuality and, 216
    as source of power, 407
Compadres, **38**
Companionate love, **155**
Companionship, 374–393
    family and, 374–381
    outside family, 387–391
    importance of, 113
    joint, **376**
    in leisure, 382–387
    loneliness and, 377–380, 381
        (*see also* Loneliness)
    marital success and, 77, 88
    as motive for marriage, 374
    parallel, **376**
    segregated, **376**–377
    singlehood and, 113
    styles of, 376–377
    See also Friendship
Comparative rectitude, doctrine of, **601**
Compartmentalization, 328
Compatibility, **180**, 192–193

706

family relationships and,
237–238
fear of, 102
fulfillment of needs in, 74–75
group, **6**
happiness and, 106–108, 112,
116–117, 268–269
honeymoons and, 261
hypergamous, **185**
hypogamous, **185**
ideals in, 73–74
infidelity and, 560–566
interfaith, 189–191
interracial, 186–188
law and, 236–239
low socioeconomic status and,
30–31
mistakes in mate selection
and, 198–199
motives for, 232–233, 374
as personal contract, 239–241
preparing for, 241–246
readiness for, 230–236
remarriage, 22–23
satisfaction in (*see* Marital
satisfaction)
success in (*see* Marital success)
timing of, 232
trial, 250
void, **239**
voidable, **239**
wedding and, 259–261
See also Divorce, Remarriage
Marriage counseling, 225, 598,
599
Marriage partners
dating partners vs., 128–129,
145
selection of, 127 (*see also*
Dating; Mate selection)
Marriage rates, 13
*Marriage Role Expectation
Inventory*, 246
Married Women's Property Act,
12
Masculinity, **303**–310, 312–313
See also Gender role(s); Sex
role(s)
Masturbation, 215
Mate selection, 127, 174–200
age differentials and, 193–194
attitudes and, 195–196
attraction and, 179
compatibility and, 179, 192–193
faith and, 189–191
family background and, 182–
186
filtering process of, 180–182
parents and, 182–183, 537–540
personal habits and, 197
personality and, 191–194

propinquity and, 179
race and, 186–188
remarriage and, 620–623
sex roles and, 196–197
values and, 195–196
wrong choices in, 198–199
See also Dating
Mate selection theories, 174–182
birth order, **175**–176
complementary needs, **176**
developmental process, 179–
182
equity, **178**
exchange, **178**–179
ideal mate, **174**–175
instrumental needs, **176**–178
needs, 176–178
parent image, **174**
psychodynamic, 174–176
stimulus-value-role, **178**–179
Matriarchal family, **6**
Matrilineal descent, **10**
Matrilocal residence, **10**
Mediation, 603–605
Men
abuse of women by, 62–66
in dual-career marriages, 336–
337
emotional reactions to
pregnancy, 489
friendships of, 388–390
as head of single-parent
family, 524–525
loneliness and, 113–114
money and, 352–353
provider role of, 325–326
role in childbirth, 496–497
sexual dysfunction in, 221–222
sexual response in, 204–207,
208
unmarried, 563–564
widowhood of, 296–297
workaholic, 326–329
See also Gender role(s); Sex
role(s)
Mental deficiency, 238
Mental health, during
pregnancy, 493–494
Mental stimulation, and sexual
response, 214–215
Mexican Americans, 37–39
birthrates of, 38
child-rearing among, 39
divorce among, 37, 38
education of, 39
familism among, 37–38
power and, 404
sex roles among, 38–39
Middle adulthood, adjustments
during, 280–284
Midlife crisis, 284

Minipill (contraceptive), **462**–463
Minority groups, demographics
of, 32–33
See also Blacks; Ethnic groups;
Race
Miscarriage, 490
Misogynists, **62**–65
Modeling
observational, **50**, 51
parents and, 50, 51, 60
Modern Courtship and Marriage
(LeMasters), 125
Money management, 355–358
analyzing expenditures and,
358
budgeting and, 357
goals in, 357
record keeping and, 358, 359
systems of, 355–357
See also Finances
Morning-after pill, **461**–462
Mortality, awareness of, 280–281
Mortgage interest rates, 365–366
variable, **366**
Mother-daughter relationships,
535–537
See also Parenthood; Parents
Mothers-in-law, 540–541
Moving, in dual-career families,
338–339
Multilateral family, **6**
Multiple orgasms, 208–209
Murder, 581
Myotonia, **204**–205

Naegele's formula, **487**
Narcissistic love, **155**
Native Americans, 43–46
child-rearing among, 45–46
cultural conflict among, 46
education of, 44–45
family life of, 45
population of, 43
relocation of, 43
statistics on, 44
Needs
of children, 510–511, 513–517
extramarital affairs, 561
fulfillment of, in marriage, 74–
75
hierarchy of, 160
love and, 160–161, 162
Needs theories, of mate
selection, 176–178
Negative identification, **534**
Negotiation, 411
*Negro Family: The Case for National
Action* (Moynihan), 33
Neolocal residence, **12**
Nepotism, **338**

709

Newborn
  care of, 500
  feeding of, 502
  Leboyer method for, 499–500
  parental contact with, 500–501
  See also Infants
Nineteenth Amendment, 12
Nocturnal emissions, **215**
No-fault divorce, **603**, 605
Noncontingent reinforcement, **86**
Nonverbal communication, 422–423
Norepinephrine, **157**
Norms
  cultural, 403–404
  gender, 405
  as sources of power, 403–405
Nuclear family, **5**, 6

Observational modeling, **50**, 51
Oedipus complex, 174
Olfactory stimulation, and sexual response, 214
Once-a-month (contraceptive) pill, **462**
One-parent family. *See* Single-parent family
Oral contraceptives, **461**–465
  advantages of, 461, 464–465
  effectiveness of, 461
  health risks of, 463–464
  mistakes made with, 475
  types of, 461–463
Oral-genital stimulation, and sexual response, 210–212
Orchestration power, **409**
Orgasm, **205**–207
  clitoral, **207**
  frequency of, 219
  marital happiness and, 203
  multiple, 208–209
  vaginal, **207**
Orgasm dysfunction, **223**
Orgasm phase of sexual response cycle, **204**, 205, 206, 207
Orientation, family of, **5**
Over-dependency, 534–535
Overprotectiveness, 412
Ovulation method of birth control, 471–472

Parallel companionship, **376**
Parent adult-child relationships, 532–544
  elderly parents in, 287, 291–293
  in-laws, 540–544
  mate selection and, 537–540
  mothers and daughters, 535–537

over-dependency in, 534–535
  parental identification and, 533–534
  parental rejection and, 532–533
Parental identification and modeling, **305**–306
Parent-child interaction, reciprocal, **50**
Parenthood
  adjustments to, 278–280
  decision about, 452–458
  delayed, 453–454
  family size and, 15–17
  role modeling and, 50, 51, 60
  singlehood and, 103–104
  single-parent families, 5, 19–20
  stepparenting, 23
  unmarried, 25–26
  working mothers and, 17–18
  See also Child-rearing; Children; Parents
Parent image theory, **174**
Parents, 507–529
  bonding with newborns, 500–501
  child-rearing philosophies of, 508–509
  consent to marriage, 237
  dating and, 133–134
  discipline and, 519–521
  emotional emancipation from, 234–235
  identification with, 533–534
  mate selection and, 182–183, 537–540
  rejection by, 532–533
  roles of, 510–513
  sharing responsibilities, 511
  single (*see* Single-parent family)
Parents Without Partners, 524
Passionate love, **155**
Patriarchal family, **5**, 10–12
Patrilineal descent, **10**
Patrilocal residence, **10**
Pelvic inflammatory disease (PID), 465
Penis, 204, 208, 210
Personal advertisements, 131–132
Personality
  attractiveness and, 152–153
  dating and, 127, 142
  family violence and, 443
  love and, 156
  marriage and, 103
  mate selection and, 191–194
  as source of power, 406
Personal role redefinition, **328**
Persuasion, 410
Pheromones, **214**
Physical abuse. *See* Violence

Physical attractiveness, 149–152, 159, 180
Placebo, **461**
Placenta previa, **490**
Plateau phase of sexual response cycle, **204**, 205, 206, 207
Points, **366**
Polyandrynous family, **5**
Polygamous family, **5**
Polygynous family, **5**
Positive Couple Agreement (PCA) score, 245–246
Positive identification, **533**–534
Positive regard, unconditional, **86**
Positive signs of pregnancy, **485**
Possessiveness, 377, 378
POSSLQ, **246**
Postparental years, **282**–284
Post-traumatic stress disorder, **581**
Poverty, 350–351
Power, 395–419
  coercive, **408**
  decision making and, 398–402
  expert, **406**
  family, 395–396
  implementation, **409**
  informational, **406**
  legitimate, **397**
  marital satisfaction and, 416
  meaning of, 395–396
  orchestration, **409**
  reasons for wanting, 396–398
  socioeconomic status and, 30
  struggles for, 414–417
Power neutralization strategies, 415
Power processes, **409**–414
Power sources, 402–409
  children, 409
  circumstances, 409
  communication ability, 407
  cultural norms, 403–404
  economic, 405
  education, 406
  emotional, 407–408
  gender norms, 405
  legal, 403
  personality, 406
  physical, 408
Pragma, **167**
Pregnancy, 484–506
  abortion and, 474–480
  developmental tasks of, 489
  ectopic, 465, **491**
  emotional reactions to, 488–489
  infertility, 503–505
  labor and delivery, 495–499
  major complications of, 490–491